THE POLICE
AND CRIMINAL EVIDENCE
ACT 1984

AUSTRALIA
The Law Book Company
Brisbane ● Sydney ● Melbourne ● Perth

CANADA
Carswell
Ottawa ● Toronto ● Calgary ● Montreal ● Vancouver

Agents
Steimatzky's Agency Ltd, Tel Aviv;
N.M. Tripathi (Private) Ltd, Bombay;
Eastern Law House (Private) Ltd, Calcutta;
M.P.P. House, Bangalore;
Universal Book Traders, Delhi;
Aditya Books, Delhi;
Macmillan Shuppan KK, Tokyo;
Pakistan Law House, Karachi, Lahore.

THE POLICE AND CRIMINAL EVIDENCE ACT 1984

(Third Edition)

BY

MICHAEL ZANDER

Professor of Law, London School of Economics

LONDON
SWEET & MAXWELL
1995

Published in 1995 by
Sweet & Maxwell Limited of
100 Avenue Road, Swiss Cottage,
London NW3 3PF
http://www.smlawpub.co.uk
Typeset by Mendip Communications Ltd,
Frome, Somerset
Printed and bound in Great Britain by
Butler & Tanner Ltd, Frome and London

Second Edition 1990
Third Edition 1995
Reprinted 1997
Reprinted 1999

No natural forests were destroyed to make this product:
only farmed timber was used and replanted

ISBN 0 421 52040 X

**A catalogue record for this book is available from
the British Library**

Cover copyright P.A. Ltd. Reproduced with their permission.

All rights reserved. No part of this publication may be reproduced or
transmitted in any form or by any means, electronic, mechanical,
photocopying, recording or otherwise, or stored in any retrieval system of
any nature, without the written permission of the copyright holder and
the publisher, application for which shall be made to the publisher.

©
Michael Zander
1995

FOREWORD TO THE FIRST EDITION

The Police and Criminal Evidence Act effects a long overdue reform and modernisation of the law governing the investigation of crime. The Government's aim has throughout been to ensure that the police have the powers they need to bring offenders to justice, but at the same time to balance those powers with new safeguards to ensure that these powers are used properly, and only where and to the extent that they are necessary.

The Act therefore forms a means of securing our general aim to equip the police to work in a way which commands public confidence: confidence that the law will be enforced effectively and confidence that it will be enforced fairly, responsibly and with proper regard to the rights of the individual who may be suspected of crime. It is for this reason that the Act does not deal with police powers alone. It also effects important reforms of the law of criminal evidence and of the police complaints and discipline procedures. And it provides for consultation between the police and the local community about policing matters.

Although, as Professor Zander rightly points out, we have in this legislation departed in various specific respects from the recommendations of the Royal Commission on Criminal Procedure, the Act is firmly based on the Commission's proposals. The underlying concept of the balance to be struck between powers and safeguards is that proposed by the Commission; and the three tests against which its provisions should be judged are those developed by the Commissions. Are they fair? Are they open? Are they workable?

The Act is therefore a wide-ranging measure; and its success will in large part depend on the extent to which its provisions are generally understood by the public and to which its underlying philosophy is reflected in the actions of the individual police officer.

I therefore very much welcome Professor Zander's book as a contribution towards making the legislation more generally accessible and understood. He is not only a distinguished academic lawyer; he has also taken a close interest in the progress of the Act through Parliament over the past two years and has himself made a number of valuable suggestions for its improvement. He is therefore well qualified to provide this guide to its provisions, and I hope that it will promote understanding of matters which are of concern to everyone in a free society.

October 31, 1984

LEON BRITTAN
HOME SECRETARY

FOREWORD TO THE FIRST EDITION

PREFACE TO THE THIRD EDITION

The purpose of this book remains what it was for the first edition, namely to provide a work on the Police and Criminal Evidence Act 1984 which is equally useful to judges, legal practitioners, police officers, academic lawyers and law students. It is not a book that offers the author's reflections as to the merits or otherwise of the law. It attempts only to unravel the complexities of the Act.

The third edition is somewhat longer than the two earlier editions to reflect the considerable growth of relevant material affecting the Police and Criminal Evidence Act.

There have first been some statutory amendments to the 1994 Act. By far the most important is the change made by the Criminal Justice and Public Order Act 1994 (CJPOA) in regard to the right to silence. This is dealt with in a new and separate chapter. There is secondly a mass of new case law. The number of cases on PACE listed in the Table of Cases has increased by over two hundred. A very high proportion are decisions of the Court of Appeal. The text also reflects the relevant recommendations of the Runciman Royal Commission on Criminal Justice which reported in June 1993. Fourthly, there has been a great increase in the amount of empirical research on aspects of PACE.

A new feature of the book is a substantial PACE bibliography (see pp. 543–45 below) with details of the most important writings in this area. (This bibliography is to a great extent based on a major research report conducted by David Brown of the Home Office Research and Planning Unit—*Research on PACE: A Review of the Literature*, forthcoming 1995.) References to publications listed in this bibliography are given simply as *e.g.* Bottomley *et al.* (1989), Brown (1993), etc.

The book proceeds basically in the same way as the first edition—with a commentary with full references on the sections of the Act in chronological order, and their corresponding provisions in the Codes of Practice, followed at the end of each chapter by a Question and Answer section with few references. The unusually full index is intended to provide maximum assistance to the user—including references in different printing styles for the author's text, the Act and the Codes. It also includes all terms defined anywhere in the Act.

With the permission of the Controller of Her Majesty's Stationery Office the book reprints the statute itself, as amended. It reprints the five Codes of Practice, which are also Crown copyright. The Codes have now been amended twice, once in 1991 and again in 1995. The latest revision affects some 275 paragraphs of the five Codes. (Fortunately, the Home Office decided that the new edition of the Codes should preserve the numbering scheme of the 1991 edition. Where additional paragraphs have been inserted they were, therefore, sub-numbered.) The revised Codes became effective as from April 10, 1995. In the book the codes are printed with a vertical line against text that is new in 1995. The position in regard to Northern Ireland was unfortunately not quite resolved by the time the book went to press. In regard both to the 1989 Northern Ireland PACE Order and to the Northern Ireland PACE Codes changes were in hand but had not yet been completed.

In regard to the 1989 Police and Criminal Evidence (Northern Ireland) Order, the Northern Ireland Office produced a draft amending Order at the end of April 1995—the Police (Amendment) (Northern Ireland) Order 1995. The purpose of the Order was to effect changes to bring Northern Ireland into line with Great Britain in three areas—police powers, police discipline and police complaints. For police powers the changes were mainly based on the provisions of the Criminal Justice and Public Order Act 1994. For police discipline the changes were mainly based on the provisions of the Police and Magistrates' Courts Act 1994. The proposed amendments are referred to here in the form in which they appeared in the draft Order. The effect of the changes was explained by the Northern Ireland Office in an Explanatory Document published together with the draft Order. The text of this document appears in Appendix 4. The Order was laid before Parliament on July 14, 1995. It was to be debated in October and was expected to come into force on January 31, 1996.

The Northern Ireland Codes are broadly the same as those in England and Wales.[1] However, the changes made in the PACE Codes in England and Wales as from April 1991 were not introduced at the time in the province. But those changes, and the further changes made in England and Wales as from April 1995, are being introduced in Northern Ireland in a single composite reform to come into effect in the province, it was hoped together with the Order on January 31, 1996. The exception is Code E regarding tape-recording which is still not to be brought into force. Otherwise, the Northern Ireland changes will broadly be the same as those introduced in 1991 and 1995 for England and Wales. Until the changes are made, the Codes in Northern Ireland remain those introduced originally in January 1990. As in the last edition, the Index to the Act (pp. 327–331 below) has the numbers of the equivalent provisions, if any in the Order. The differences between the Act and the Order are indicated in the author's text.

I would acknowledge with grateful thanks all those who helped in the preparation of this new edition—and especially Mr Nick Sanderson at the Home Office and Mr David Finegan at the Northern Ireland Office who responded to my questions with unfailing patience and courtesy. My publishers dealt with a difficult manuscript with their customary efficiency.

The text has been brought up to date to July 1, 1995.

London   M.Z.
July 1995

---

[1] The Police and Criminal Evidence (Northern Ireland) Order 1989 was the subject of a whole issue in the *Northern Ireland Quarterly*—vol. 40, No. 4, Winter 1989.

THE BACKGROUND

The Police and Criminal Evidence Act was the result of more than 10 years' travail. Official dissatisfaction with the rules of the criminal process goes back in fact even further to the mid 1960s when the Home Office asked the Criminal Law Revision Committee to inquire into the rules of evidence in criminal cases. Their eight year study culminated in 1972 with the publication of the ill-fated 11th Report of that prestigious Committee. Their report[1] was received with a barrage of criticism most of which was actually directed at one only of the Committee's many recommendations, that the right of silence in the police station should be abolished. This proposal led to such a storm of abuse that the report was effectively still-born. No Government could implement even the uncontroversial recommendations of a report so widely regarded as fatally flawed.[2]

For some years the Home Office shelved the whole topic. But in June 1977, the Labour Government announced that it was setting up a Royal Commission on Criminal Procedure whose terms of reference were to consider the investigation of offences in the light of police powers and duties as well as the rights and duties of suspects. The Philips Commission was asked to examine the issues, "having regard both to the interests of the community in bringing offenders to justice and to the rights and liberties of persons suspected or accused of crime, and taking into account also the need for the efficient and economical use of resources." (The Philips Commission was also asked to look into the problem of the responsibility for the prosecution process, but that part of the Commission's report is not dealt with in this book since the topic was treated separately in the Prosecution of Offences Act 1985.)

The Philips Royal Commission's remit was to attempt to reach an agreed solution to a series of highly contentious issues. Its members included representatives of many of the interested groups—a judge, two police officers, a Queen's Counsel, a stipendiary magistrate who had formerly been a justices' clerk, a defence lawyer, and several lay magistrates. The lay members included the chairman, Sir Cyril Philips a Professor of History and former Vice-Chancellor of London University. Under his unassuming but effective leadership the Commission achieved the almost impossible task of obtaining unanimity or near unanimity on all the topics in their report. On many issues there were one or two (unidentified) dissenters. But virtually all the recommendations in the report were endorsed by the overwhelming majority of the 15 members.

The report was well received by the police and tolerably well received by the legal profession. It was condemned as too prosecution minded by the political Left including organisations like the National Council for Civil

---

[1] *Evidence (General)*, Cmnd. 4991, 1972.
[2] M. Zander, "The CLRC report—a survey of reactions" *Law Soc. Gaz.* October 2, 1974, p. 954.

Liberties and the Legal Action Group, as well as the official Labour Opposition.

The Home Office showed every sign of wanting to legislate to implement the report. It set up internal working parties to consider the proposals and issued a long list of examination type specific questions for comment by interested groups and persons. In November 1982, only 20 or so months after the Royal Commission had reported, the then Home Secretary Mr. William Whitelaw introduced the first version of the Police and Criminal Evidence Bill. Broadly, it was based on the report of the Philips Royal Commission, though in many respects the Government had exercised its political right to discriminate as to what it would and would not accept of the Royal Commission's proposals. To some extent therefore the carefully constructed package of proposals hammered out over three years around the Royal Commission's table became unstitched. The Government had put together its own somewhat different package.

The Bill proved to be highly controversial and during its passage through the House of Commons in the winter of 1982–1983 it was subject to fierce criticism. The debate on the right to silence which sunk the 11th Report of the Criminal Law Revision Committee was barely mentioned. The Royal Commission had decided that the right to silence in the police station should stay—because it was too important to abolish and moreover so few people were actually silent that it would achieve little to abolish it. (As will be seen, the right to silence question was however re-opened dramatically in July 1987 and in the Criminal Justice and Public Order Act 1994 the so called right to silence was abolished.[3])

In 1982–1983 the furious debate over the Bill was mainly about whether the police should have the right to ask to see a doctor's files or the priest's notes of what transpired in the confessional or the records of a citizen's advice bureau. The number of times per year that the police would want to exercise such powers must be rather small, but the heat of the debate suggested that the Government were proposing a serious invasion of fundamental principles. Even the bishops got involved. Eventually the Government retreated and, in addition, amended the Bill on many other less highly publicised issues.

The first Bill failed to pass however because the Prime Minister called a General Election in May, 1983 when it was just completing its Report stage in the House of Commons. At that point a very large number of government amendments had been incorporated in the Bill but a large number of other Government amendments which were already tabled had not been reached.

The new Home Secretary Mr. Leon Brittan then spent the summer months considering the Bill. In October, 1983 when he unveiled his Bill Mark II it was found to have included not only all the Government amendments that had already been tabled but a considerable number of further amendments which in some respects departed from policies of his predecessor in office. Thereafter the process of argument and debate continued with interest groups such as the National Council for Civil Liberties assisting the Labour Opposition to mount a sustained campaign against the Bill.

The Committee stage in the House of Commons broke the record for the

---

[3] See below pp. 303–323.

highest number of sittings. But in spite of all the sound and fury in both Houses and in spite of the fact that the Government moved hundreds of amendments to its own Bill, on the whole they were of relatively minor import. The Act as it finally emerged at the end of October 1984 was very recognisable as the Bill which was first unveiled a year previously in October, 1983.

There can be no denying that the whole exercise was an example of the democratic system working. The subject was taken off the shelf by the Labour Government when it set up the Royal Commission in 1977. The Commission had its first meeting in early 1978 and three years later, after taking vast quantities of evidence, it had produced a report together with a substantial series of research volumes. There was extensive debate about the proposals before the Conservative Government introduced first one and then a second Bill. Both Bills were massively amended by the Government itself. In a few instances the amendments were made because the Government was swept off course by political tides that were too strong to resist. This was true in particular of the changes made to the first Bill in regard to the search for confidential material and the change in the second Bill giving police officers appealing from serious disciplinary proceedings the right to legal representation (on which the Police Federation formed an unholy alliance with the Law Society and the National Council for Civil Liberties!). But the vast majority of the amendments were moved by the Government because Ministers and officials were persuaded that they represented genuine improvements in the proposed legislation. The Home Office throughout showed itself willing to listen and to respond constructively to suggestions from a wide variety of bodies and individuals.

Now, after the Act has been in force for some years it is possible to get a sense of its impact—partly from the case law, partly from empirical research and partly from the views about the Act's operation expressed by a variety of commentators and concerned organisations.

In 1991 the Government established the Runciman Royal Commission on Criminal Justice.[4] Its very wide terms of reference were to "examine the effectiveness of the criminal justice system in England and Wales in securing the conviction of those guilty of criminal offences and the acquittal of those who are innocent, having regard to the efficient use of resources". The Commission, of which the writer was a member, received mountains of evidence. None of that evidence called into question the basic structure created by PACE. It has clearly been accepted by all as a piece of legislation that, subject no doubt to occasional amendment, will be with us into the indefinite future.

---

[4] The Royal Commission's Report was published in July 1993—Cm 2263, HMSO.

CONTENTS

Contents

THE POLICE AND CRIMINAL EVIDENCE ACT 1984

CODES OF PRACTICE

APPENDICES

TABLE OF CASES

Table of Cases

xvi

Table of Cases

Table of Cases

Table of Cases

Table of Cases

Table of Cases

Table of Cases

Table of Cases

Table of Cases

TABLE OF STATUTES

COMMENTARY ON THE ACT

POWERS TO STOP AND SEARCH

Definition of powers of stop and search: section 1[1]

The Philips Royal Commission's Report

The Philips Royal Commission identified two main defects in the existing law. First, police powers to stop and search varied from one part of the country to another. In London for instance the police could use the powers under section 66 of the Metropolitan Police Act 1839 to stop and search for stolen goods and similar local powers existed in Birmingham, Manchester, Liverpool and Rochdale,[2] but equivalent powers did not exist in most other parts of the country. Secondly, existing powers were either inadequate or at best uncertain and required clarification or redefinition. There were some 16 statutes that gave the police powers to stop and search but in other situations the police lacked powers they needed. The police said, "they frequently have to lay themselves open to the risk of civil action by stopping and searching in circumstances where they have no power to do so but where equally they will be criticised for failing to act. One example cited is the carrying of offensive weapons by football supporters."[3]

The Philips Commission proposed first that the police should be given a uniform power of stop and search throughout England and Wales and, secondly, that this should replace all existing powers. Its content would cover searches in a public place of anyone reasonably suspected of conveying stolen goods or of being in possession of anything whose possession in a public place is of itself a criminal offence—for example prohibited drugs, firearms or housebreaking implements.[4] The main innovation, the Philips Commission said, would be in relation to offensive weapons, though the Prevention of Crimes Act 1953 already gave the police some powers in this regard. That Act makes it an offence to carry offensive weapons in a public place without lawful authority or reasonable excuse but the police power of arrest in this connection arises only if the suspect's name and address cannot be ascertained or to prevent an offence in which an offensive weapon might be used. The proposed new power permitted search simply on the basis that

---

[1] In the Police and Criminal Evidence (Northern Ireland) Order 1989 the equivalent numbered article is Art. 3. (The Order will be referred to throughout the book as the "N.I. PACE Order".)
[2] For a full list see Philips Royal Commission on Criminal Procedure, *Law and Procedure Volume* (Cmnd. 8092–1 (1981)). (The Royal Commission's Report is referred to throughout in the notes simply as "Philips Report".)
[3] Philips Report, para. 3.15.
[4] Philips Report, para. 3.20.

someone is reasonably suspected of being in possession of offensive weapons.

This topic led to the biggest row in the deliberations of the Philips Royal Commission with two members (Mr Jack Jones, former General Secretary of the Transport and General Workers Union, and Canon Wilfrid Wood, a black magistrate) dissenting. In fact Mr Jones and Canon Wood both signed the report but, somewhat unconventionally, Mr Jones sent a letter to the press just before publication of the report attacking the Commission's proposals especially on this issue and Canon Wood, seemingly a little reluctantly, associated himself with Mr Jones' critique.

Mr Jack Jones and Canon Wood were concerned that this proposal created a danger of random and discriminatory searches "which could further worsen the relationship between the police and young people, particularly black youth".[5]

The majority of the Philips Royal Commission thought, however, that safeguards could be introduced to reduce the danger of random and discriminatory searches. They took the view that "if Parliament has made it an offence to be in possession of a particular article in a public place, the police should be able to stop and search persons suspected on reasonable grounds of committing that offence".[6]

Pre-PACE empirical data

The danger that stops and searches under this proposed general power might be virtually random was illustrated by the statistics regarding the use of then existing powers of this kind. The Royal Commission's *Law and Procedure Volume*[7] showed the results of stops and searches nationally for drugs under the Misuse of Drugs Act 1971 and in London for stolen goods under the 1839 Act. The figures for drugs indicated that between 1972 and 1978 in England and Wales, apart from the Metropolitan area, the proportion of persons searched who were found to be in illegal possession of drugs fell from 30 per cent in 1972 to 22 per cent in 1978. The figures for the Metropolitan area showed that in 1977, 34 per cent of stops under the 1971 Act led to arrests and in 1978 the percentage was 39 per cent. But it is not known how many of the arrests were for illegal possession of drugs. In relation to stolen goods, out of 40,477 stops under the 1839 Act in July 1978, 13 per cent led to arrests and in January 1979 the figure was 12 per cent out of 35,298 stops. The difference in the percentage indicated that it was twice as likely that the police would successfully detect a person carrying illegal drugs as stolen goods but even in the case of drugs, between seven and eight stops out of 10 proved unsuccessful.

Later evidence about the success rate in stop and search in London emerged in the study by the Policy Studies Institute (P.S.I.) published in November 1983. This included a study based on interviews with 2,420 Londoners. It showed that only 3 per cent of those stopped were arrested and charged with an offence, 5 per cent had an offence reported and in 1 per cent of cases the person was arrested but not in fact charged.[8]

---

[5] Philips Report, para. 3.21.
[6] *ibid.*
[7] Cmnd. 8092–1 (1981), Apps. 2 and 3.
[8] David J. Smith, *Police and People in London: A Survey of Londoners* (1983), p. 115.

On the other hand, there was evidence that a high proportion of arrests resulted from the exercise of stop and search powers. The P.S.I. survey of police officers showed that no less than 23 per cent of arrests in the previous six weeks had resulted from a stop.[9] Also the *number* of arrests following on from stops pre-PACE was high. In the Metropolitan Police Area for instance there were an estimated 1½ million stops per year, about 100,000 (7 per cent) of which resulted in offences being discovered.[10] The P.S.I. study suggested that as many as half of all stops were not recorded.[11] (For post-PACE statistics see pp. 17–18 below.)

The Act

The Government accepted the Royal Commission's recommendation that stop and search powers should extend to offensive weapons. It also accepted that stop and search powers should be uniform throughout the country. But it did not agree with the Commission's recommendation that one single new statutory provision should replace all existing statutory powers of stop and search.

The Act gives the police the power to search "any person or vehicle" and "anything which is in or on a vehicle, for stolen or prohibited articles" and to detain a person or vehicle for the purpose of such a search (s.1(2)). A constable may not, however, search a person or vehicle under section 1 "unless he has reasonable grounds for suspecting that he will find stolen or prohibited articles" (s.1(3)). Any stolen or prohibited article found in the course of such a search may be seized (s.1(6)). The section does not deal with anything else found in the course of such a search.

It is not clear whether "stolen articles" includes not only articles acquired contrary to sections 1–7 Theft Act 1968, but also those obtained or acquired contrary to section 15 which covers obtaining by criminal deception and section 22 which covers handling stolen goods. It seems that the wider definition is probably the correct one.

An article is "prohibited" for the purpose of the statute if it is either an offensive weapon or it is "made or adapted for use" in the course of or in connection with burglary, theft, taking a motor vehicle without authority or obtaining property by deception or is intended by the person having it with him for such use by him or by some other person (s.1(7)). An offensive weapon is defined as meaning "any article made or adapted for use for causing injury to persons or intended by the person having it with him for such use by him or by some other person" (s.1(9)). This definition is taken from the Prevention of Crime Act 1953, section 1. It has two categories— items that are offensive weapons *per se* and items that are not offensive weapons but that are intended to be used as such. If the item is in the former category, the prosecution need only prove that the defendant had it with him to put the onus onto the accused to show that he had a lawful excuse. (There has been a considerable case law as to what counts as an offensive weapon

---

[9] *ibid.*
[10] *ibid.* pp. 311 and 346.
[11] *ibid.* p. 114. See to like effect Carole Willis, *The Use, Effectiveness and Impact of Police Stop and Search Powers*, Home Office Research and Planning Unit, Paper 15 (1983), p. 10.

per se.[12]) If it is in the second category, the prosecution has to prove also that the accused intended it to be used to cause injury by himself or someone else.

The Criminal Justice Act 1988, s.139 expanded the concept of offensive weapons. The object was to make unlawful *per se* mere possession, in a public place without lawful authority or reasonable excuse, of most knives. The onus is therefore on the carrier to show that he had a reasonable excuse (s.139). It applies to any article which has a blade or is sharply pointed—with the exception of folding pocket knives with a blade of less than three inches. Subsection (5) states that, without prejudice to the generality of the defence of good reason or lawful authority in subsection (4), it would be a valid defence to have such a knife for use at work or for religious reasons or as part of any national costume. There is no specific exception for items carried in connection with sports such as javelins, darts or fishing tackle.

The case law on the 1953 Act[13] makes it clear that the courts will not countenance the carrying of offensive weapons for generalised self-defence unless there is some immediate and identifiable threat. Women are therefore acting unlawfully if they carry knives or other offensive weapons to deal with the possibility of attack in the street.

Section 140 of the Criminal Justice Act 1988 added the items covered by section 139 to the list of those for which a stop and search could be made under PACE, s.1.

"Reasonable suspicion"

The Act (s.1(3)) requires that stops and searches be based on reasonable grounds and the requirement of reasonable grounds and reasonable suspicion are critical to the operation of this power.[14] As will be seen, the Criminal Justice and Public Order Act 1994 gave the police a significant and wholly unprecedented power to stop and search without any ground to suspect the individual, providing a superintendent reasonably believes that incidents involving serious violence may occur in the locality. (See p. 9 below.) The matter is given detailed treatment in Code A, the Code of Practice on Stop and Search. (On the Codes of Practice in general see pp. 168–173 below.) The objective plainly was to try to stop a practice of stop and searching based on some form of stereotyping. The P.S.I. study of policing in London showed that in a great proportion of cases stop and search powers were based on no better reason than that the individual concerned belonged to a particular group or type or that the stop was made in a particular neighbourhood.[15] Annex B of the original version of Code A stated categorically that "Reasonable suspicion, in contrast to mere suspicion, must be founded on fact. There must be some concrete basis for the officer's belief, related to the individual person concerned, which can be considered and evaluated by an objective third person."

Mere suspicion, in contrast, was "a hunch or instinct which cannot be

---

[12] For a discussion of the issue see G. Broadbent, "Offensive Weapons and the Criminal Justice Act." Law Soc. Gaz. July 12, 1989, p. 23.

[13] *ibid.* p. 24.

[14] Note that suspicion can be of innocent possession—Code A, para. 1.7A. See further Willis, *op. cit.*, note 11. See also Bottomley *et al.* and S.H. Bailey and D.J. Birch, "Recent Developments in the Law of Police Powers" [1982] Crim.L.R. 475–476.

[15] n.8 above, pp. 232–234.

explained or justified to an objective observer". An officer who has such a hunch or instinct might well be justified in keeping the person under observation, but additional grounds were needed to bring suspicion up to the level of "reasonable suspicion".

Such additional grounds could not come from the fact that the person concerned was black even if it was the case that blacks committed more of a particular category of offence than others. Nor was the fact that the person was dressed in a particular way or had a certain hairstyle nor that he had previous convictions for possession of an unlawful article.

The Code put the point even more strongly: "The degree or level of suspicion required to establish the reasonable grounds justifying the exercise of powers of stop and search is not less than the degree or level of suspicion required to effect an arrest" (*ibid.*).

The notes for guidance accompanying the Code warned officers that it was important "to ensure that the powers are used responsibly and sparingly". Over-use of the powers was "as likely to be harmful to police support in the long term as misuse; both can lead to mistrust of the police among sections of the public" (para. 1A).

The 1991 revised Code of Practice eliminated Annex B and substituted paragraphs 1.6 and 1.7 but, with two exceptions (see below), the broad effect is very similar and amounts to a tidying up and redraft rather than a change in the rules. Thus paragraph 1.6 still requires an objective basis and still requires the officer to consider all the circumstances, including the time and the place and the person's behaviour. Paragraph 1.6 adds that covert or wary actions or attempts to hide something, or the carrying of an item at an unusual time or in an area where burglaries or thefts have occurred recently, could all be grounds for reasonable suspicion. But personal factors such as colour, age, hairstyle, manner of dress, prior convictions—whether alone or together—still cannot be the sole basis for a stop and search. Nor can such suspicion be based on stereotyped images of persons or groups. Officers are still warned in a note for guidance (1A) that stop and search powers should be exercised "responsibly"—not only because mis-use may worsen police–public relations, but because the use of the power may have to be justified to superior officers. The note still says that it is particularly important to ensure that the person searched is "treated courteously and considerately". The 1995 revision of Note 1A of Code A adds for good measure that officers "should be careful to ensure that the selection and treatment of those questioned or searched is based upon objective factors and not upon personal prejudice".

Note 1B spells out more clearly even than before that there is no intention to affect the ability of officers to speak to or question a person in the absence of reasonable suspicion without detaining him or exercising any element of compulsion.

There were three significant changes in the 1991 revised Code A, one favourable to the police, the other two designed to strengthen the position of the citizen. The first was that it was no longer stated as in the former Annex B that the level of suspicion to justify stop and search is the same as for an arrest. This mystified police officers and has now simply been removed. Initially nothing was put in its place. But in the 1995 revision of the Codes a new provision was added (para. 1.7A) stating where an officer has reasonable grounds to suspect that someone is in innocent possession of an item for which he is empowered to search he may stop and search him even though there would be no power of arrest. But every effort should be made to secure the person's co-operation before resorting to the use of force.

"Voluntary searches"

The second significant change was in note 1Db. which concerns voluntary searches. Under the original Code this was not dealt with specifically at all. Previous note 4A said the routine searching of persons entering sports grounds or other premises with their consent or as a condition of entry was outside the scheme of the Act. (This is preserved in 1Da.) The police worked on the basis that "voluntary" searches were also outside the control of the Act. This was obviously a difficult area since a cynically broad interpretation of the concept of voluntary searches would drive the proverbial "coach and four" through the provisions on stop and search.

The Home Office Circular on PACE issued to the police and the courts in December 1985 (No. 88/1985) said on this subject (para. 1): "In any situation where a constable exercises a power of search under this Act, the co-operation of the citizen should not be taken as implying consent, and the exercise of the power should be noted in the appropriate record. Whilst it is legitimate to invite co-operation from the public in circumstances where there is no power to require it, the subject of a voluntary search must properly understand the position and not be left with the impression that a power is being exercised. Voluntary search must not be used as a device for circumventing the safeguards established in Part I of the Act." It would be surprising if all forces and all personnel concerned had taken this approach to heart. It seems that there are too many situations where the concept of consensual search has been used as a way of avoiding the main thrust of the safeguards. This was addressed in the overt requirement in the 1991 note for guidance 1Db. that "in these circumstances, an officer should always make it clear that he is seeking the co-operation of the person concerned", and a 1995 amendment to paragraph 1Db. requires the officer to say that the person need not consent *and that without his consent he will not be searched!* (emphasis supplied). This new requirement is obviously intended to reduce the number of stop and searches that are not genuinely voluntary.

The third significant change in 1991 was guidance note 1E which states: "If an officer acts in an improper manner this will invalidate a voluntary search. Juveniles, people suffering from a mental handicap or mental disorder and others who appear not to be capable of giving an informed consent should not be subject to a voluntary search." This goes much further than the previous Code in restricting the scope of voluntary searches.

Note that paragraph 3.2 of Code A says that "The co-operation of the person to be searched should be sought in every case, even if he initially objects to the search". A forcible search may only be made if it has first been established that the person is unwilling to co-operate (*e.g.* by opening a bag) or resists.

**Note: New stop and search powers *without* reasonable suspicion—
anticipated local violence and prevention of terrorism**

The Criminal Justice and Public Order Act 1994, section 60 gave a police
officer in uniform a new power to stop and search pedestrians, vehicles,[16] and
their drivers and passengers for offensive weapons or "dangerous instruments"[17] "whether or not he has any grounds for suspecting that the person
or vehicle is carrying weapons or articles of that kind" (subs. (4)(5)). The
pre-conditions for the valid exercise of this power are that:

(1) an officer of the rank of superintendent[18] or above reasonably
believes that "incidents involving serious violence may take place in
any locality in his area" and that it is expedient to authorise such
powers to stop their occurrence (subs. (1) and Code A, para. 1.8);
(2) such authority is given in regard to any place in that locality for a
period up to 24 hours (*ibid.*);
(3) the period authorised should be no longer than appears reasonably
necessary to prevent incidents of serious violence[19] (Code A, para.
1.8);
(4) the authority is given in written form specifying the locality and the
period covered (subs. (9)).

The power does not apply retrospectively to incidents that have already
occurred. It applies only prospectively to incidents that it is thought will
occur. However incidents that have occurred may provide a basis for a
concern that they will occur again. Situations involving racial violence would
be an obvious example.

It is for the authorising officer to determine what may reasonably
constitute a locality. The Code says that in deciding this the officer:

"may wish to take into account factors such as the nature and venue of the
anticipated incident, the numbers of people who may be in the immediate
area of any possible incident, their access to surrounding areas and the
anticipated level of violence" (Code A, note 1G).

He should not set a wider area than he believes necessary for the purpose of
preventing the anticipated violence (*ibid.*).

The power can be extended for up to six hours if it appears to the officer
who gave the authority or to a superintendent that it is expedient to do so
"having regard to offences which have, or are reasonably suspected to have,
been committed in connection with any incident falling within the authorisation" (subs. (3)). Such a direction must also be in writing (subs. (10)).
Where written authority in advance is not practicable it must be recorded in
writing as soon as practicable (*ibid.*).

[16] The section extends also to ships, aircraft and hovercraft (s.60(7)).
[17] "Dangerous instruments" are defined as "instruments which have a blade or are sharply pointed"
(s.60(11)).
[18] The power may however be exercised by a chief inspector or inspector if he reasonably believes that
incidents involving serious violence are imminent and no superintendent is available.
[19] The period should be the minimum considered necessary to deal with the risk (Code A, Note 1F).

A similar power to stop and search persons and vehicles without reasonable grounds to suspect exists in regard to prevention of terrorism. It exists at ports and airports under the provisions of the Prevention of Terrorism (Temporary Provisions) Act 1989, Schedule 5, paragraph 4(2). By virtue of an amendment to the 1989 Act in the Criminal Justice and Public Order Act 1994 it now exists also in regard to stops and searches in the street where a locality has been earmarked by an officer of the rank of assistant chief constable (or in London, commander). (See p. 16 below.)

Action before a search is carried out

The power conferred by section 1 is a power to stop and search—not a power to stop and question. But in *Daniel v. Morrison*[20] the Divisional Court held that the power under section 66 of the 1839 Metropolitan Police Act to stop, search and detain anyone suspected of having stolen goods included the power to question him as well, though only briefly. See to the same effect *Green*[21] in relation to stop and search for prohibited drugs under the Misuse of Drugs Act 1971. The Code of Practice states that a person can only be detained against his will if there are grounds for suspicion beforehand. ("There is no power to stop or detain a person against his will in order to find grounds for a search." (Para. 2.1).) Before carrying out a search the officer could question the person and if a satisfactory explanation of anything suspicious emerged, no search should take place. Section 2(1) of the Act makes the same point when it says that a constable need not conduct a search of someone whom he has detained if it appears to him subsequently that no search is required. The police are therefore not legally at fault if they stop, and do not search but the legality of the stop depends on whether there were or were not grounds for reasonable suspicion before the stop was made.

The power of stop and search can be exercised: "(a) in any place to which at the time, the public or any section of the public has access, on payment or otherwise, as of right or by virtue of express or implied permission; or (b) in any other place to which people have ready access ... but which is not a dwelling" (s.1(1)). Subsection (a) would cover places such as parks, streets, roads and car parks and, while open to the public, shops, pubs and sports grounds. Subsection (b) would cover places such as school yards or gardens that are readily accessible from the street. So the police can stop and search someone who has aroused reasonable suspicion who is lurking in a garden next to the road.

However, the section makes it clear that if a person is in a garden or yard or other land attached to a dwelling-house, the officer cannot search him unless he has reason to believe that he does not live there and that he does not have the express or implied permission of the person who lives there to be on the premises (s.1(4)). Similar provisions apply equally to a search of a vehicle (s.1(5)). In other words, people and their cars are not to be searched on their own private land.

[20] (1979) 70 Cr.App.R. 142.
[21] [1982] Crim.L.R. 604.

Safeguards regarding stop and search powers: section 2[22] and Code A, section 3

Section 2 sets out the procedural safeguards relating to stop and search powers, both under the Act *and under any other statutory provisions*. These procedural safeguards apply therefore not only to the police exercising their powers under PACE but also to all the various other statutory powers of stop and search and to similar powers enjoyed by other forces such as the British Transport Police and the Port of London Police. They do not apply however to police at airports, ports and similar places ("statutory undertakers") where vehicles come in and out constantly and routine checks are a regular feature of the movements of such vehicles (s.2(2)(b) and s.6). They do not apply to stop and search under the Aviation Act 1982, section 27(2).

They also do not apply to searches carried out in Northern Ireland under sections 19, 20 or 26 of the Northern Ireland (Emergency Provisions) Act 1991.[23]

The Code as amended in 1995 says that the Code applies to stops and searches requiring reasonable grounds for suspicion that articles unlawfully obtained or possessed are being carried. But it then says that it also applies[24] to three kinds of stop and search power where there is no requirement of reasonable suspicion of the individual. These are:

(1) the new power under the Criminal Justice and Public Order Act, section 60 (reasonable suspicion that a violent incident may occur in the locality, see p. 9 above);
(2) the similar new power under section 13A of the Prevention of Terrorism (Temporary Provisions) Act 1989[25] (stopping persons and vehicles to prevent acts of terrorism in a locality, see p. 16 below); and
(3) stops and searches under the terrorism legislation at ports and airports.[26]

The provisions of section 2 and Code A broadly followed the recommendations of the Philips Royal Commission. The first is that before searching a person or vehicle or detaining a person or vehicle for the purpose of such a search, the officer must take reasonable steps to bring to the person's attention his name (in terrorism cases or in Northern Ireland his number[27]), the name of the police station to which he is attached, the object of the search and his grounds of authorisation for making it (s.2(3); Code A, para. 2.4). In *Fennelley*[28] the prosecution was unable to establish that the defendant had been told why he was stopped, searched and arrested in the street. The evidence of the search which produced some jewellery was excluded at the trial. The evidence of two packets of heroin found in his underpants during a strip search at the police station was also excluded for

---

[22] See N.I. PACE Order, Art. 4.
[23] Formerly ss.15, 16 and 20 of the Northern Ireland (Emergency Provisions) Act 1928.
[24] The word "applies" is stronger than in the 1991 version of the Code which said (Note 1C) that the provisions of the Code should be applied in such cases "so far as practicable".
[25] As amended by the Criminal Justice and Public Order Act 1994, s.80.
[26] Prevention of Terrorism (Temporary Provisions) Act 1989, Sched. 5, para. 4(2).
[27] See N.I. PACE Order, Art. 4(4)(a).
[28] [1989] Crim.L.R. 142.

the same reason. If the officer is not in uniform he must produce documentary evidence that he is a police officer (para. 2.5). The officer must also inform the person being searched that he is entitled to a record of the search—see section 2(3)(d)—and to which police station he should apply to get the record (Code A, para. 2.6). However, this duty need not be performed if it appears to the officer that it is not practicable to make a record—for instance because of the size of the group involved (s.2(4)). If the person to be searched, or in charge of the vehicle to be searched, does not understand what is being said, the officer must take "reasonable steps" to bring the information to his attention (Code A, para. 2.7).

If the search is of unattended vehicles, the officer must leave a notice stating that he has searched the vehicle, giving the name of his police station, stating that an application for compensation for any damage done should be made to that station and that the owner can request a copy of the record of the search (s.2(6)).

The procedural safeguards apply only to searches. They therefore need not be complied with if the stop does not lead to a search. This is based on the Philips Royal Commission's view that it would not be desirable, practicable or necessary to require the police to record each occasion on which they stop a member of the public, possibly for an informal conversation. "It is a search following upon a stop and based upon reasonable suspicion that is the main intrusion upon the person and it is that and the reason for it which should be recorded."[29]

The time for which someone may be detained is limited to such time as is reasonably necessary to permit the search to be carried out there or nearby (subs. 8). Code A states that where the power of stop and search requires reasonable suspicion the thoroughness of the search depends on what is suspected of being carried. If it relates to an article which is seen to be slipped into a pocket the search should be limited to that pocket, unless there are other grounds of suspicion. In the case of a small article, such as drugs, capable of being easily concealed, a more extensive search may be necessary. Where the search does not require reasonable suspicion the officer "may make any reasonable search to find what he is empowered to search for" (Code A, para. 3.3).

It is specifically stated (s.2(9)(a)) that no power to stop and search short of arrest authorises a police officer to *require* a person to remove any of his clothing in public other than an outer coat, jacket or gloves (and in Northern Ireland, headgear).[30] Any such search would therefore have to take place at least out of public view, for instance in a police van. So if there is no suitable place for a more extensive search to be conducted nearby it cannot be done save at a police station. But the Code does state that a person can be asked to take off more than the statutory minimum voluntarily (Code A, note 3A). A search involving removal of more than outer coat, jacket, gloves, headgear or footwear can only be conducted by an officer of the same sex and may not even be made in the presence of the opposite sex unless this is specifically requested (Code A, para. 3.5).

The police are now permitted to search an arrested person's mouth in public (by virtue of an amendment to s.32 of PACE in the Criminal Justice and Public Order Act 1994, s.59(2)). It would seem that this cannot however

[29] Philips Report, para. 3.26.
[30] See N.I. PACE Order, Art. 4(10)(a).

be construed so as to apply also to stop and search. By ordinary canons of interpretation, the fact that the legislature specifically considered the point in regard to search after arrest implies that it intended not to extend search in public where the stop and search powers are being used. If a search of the mouth is indicated by the situation—for instance the suspect is seen to put a package in his mouth—the officer would have two choices. One would be swiftly to take the suspect somewhere that is not "in public". The second would be to arrest him on suspicion of possession and then search him under the new section 32 power.

Where a pedestrian is stopped under the new power for stops and searches without reasonable suspicion under section 13A of the Prevention of Terrorism (Temporary Provisions) Act (p. 16 below), a search can only be made of a bag, case or other thing carried by him. The pedestrian himself must not be searched under this power unless in the course of the baggage search the officer formed reasonable grounds for suspicion justifying a further search. (See PTA, s.13A(3)(c) and Code A, para. 3.5A.)

Subsection 9 also makes it clear that only a police officer in uniform can lawfully require a person driving a vehicle to stop for the purpose of any exercise of a power of stop and search (s.2(9)(b)). The power to require a driver to stop now under section 163 of the Road Traffic Act 1988 (formerly s.159 of the 1972 Act) is not affected by section 1 and stopping a vehicle under that provision therefore still does not require the test of reasonable suspicion to be satisfied.

Subsection (10) extends the power of stop and search to vessels, aircraft and hovercraft.

Duty to make records concerning searches: section 3[31] and Code A, section 4

The Philips Royal Commission recommended that as a further control against arbitrary and discriminatory searches police officers should be under a duty to make records of what transpires.[32] Also the individual, it thought, should have a right to a copy of such a record. The Government accepted both recommendations. An officer who has searched someone under statutory powers of stop and search (other than a search by a statutory undertaker—for which see s.6 below), must make a written record of the search, unless this is not practicable, for instance because of the numbers involved or in situations of disorder (s.3(1); Code A, 4.1). If he is under a duty to make a record but it is not practicable to make such a record at the time, it must be done "as soon as is practicable after the completion of the search" (s.3(2)).

The record must include the classification of the person's ethnic origin,[33] the object of the search, the grounds for making it, the date, and time when, and the place where, it was made, its result, details of any injury or damage to property caused and the identity of the constable (s.3(6) or in terrorism cases the warrant number—Code A, para. 4.5(x)). It should also identify the name of the person searched, if known—but he may not be detained for the purpose of discovering his name (s.3(3)). If no name is known, the officer is

---

[31] See N.I. PACE Order, Art. 5.
[32] Philips Report, para. 3.26.
[33] Code A, para. 4.5(ii).

supposed at least to record some description of the person (s.3(4)). The record of a search of a vehicle should describe it (subs. (5)). Where the search does not require reasonable grounds to suspect (see above), the record must also state the authority provided to carry out such a search (Code A, para. 4.7).

Anyone who, or whose vehicle has been searched under stop and search powers is entitled to ask for a copy of the record made (if any has been made) providing he asks for it within 12 months (s.3(7), (8), and (9)). (If both the person and his vehicle are searched the police should make separate records.) The power to get a copy of the authorisation also applies to pedestrians stopped and to the new powers of stop and search without reasonable grounds to suspect—p. 9 above (Code A, para. 4.7A and note 4C).

The Philips Royal Commission recommended that supervising police officers should scrutinise figures of searches and their results. They should watch for signs "that searches are being carried out at random, arbitrarily or in a discriminatory way".[34] Moreover H.M. Inspectors of Constabulary should give attention to this matter on their annual inspection of each force. Not surprisingly, nothing of this appears in the Act. It is obviously more appropriate to deal with such matters by internal police regulation, and training. Numbers of stop and searches must be contained in the chief constable's annual report so as to make the application of the powers subject to scrutiny by the police authority as will be seen in section 5 of the Act. (See further p. 16 below.)

The Commission proposed that failure to provide reasons for a search should make the search unlawful which would entitle the person concerned to resist and also to sue for assault. This recommendation was not reflected in the Act.

Road checks: section 4[35]

The pre-PACE police power to set up road blocks derived from section 159[36] of the Road Traffic Act 1972 which required drivers to stop when required to do so by a constable in uniform. There was no mention in the section as to the purpose for which the power may be used. The police did use it not only to set up road blocks for road traffic or vehicle excise purposes but also where they believed it to be necessary in connection with a serious crime or when they were hunting an escaped prisoner. Section 159 did not give any power to search a vehicle. The 1972 Act has been repealed and the powers contained in section 159 are now to be found in section 163 of the Road Traffic Act 1988.

Road blocks are inevitably random in their effect and the Philips Royal Commission said that in general such powers should not be used in connection with crime. "Infringement of a person's liberty to go about his business should be allowed only on suspicion of his involvement in an offence."[37]

But an exception should be made, it thought, for special emergencies. An

---

[34] Philips Report, para. 3.26.
[35] See N.I. PACE Order, Art. 6.
[36] Now s.163 of the Road Traffic Act 1988.
[37] Philips Report, para. 3.30.

officer of the rank of assistant chief constable or above should have the power to authorise in writing road checks in two kinds of situation. One would be when a person wanted in connection with a grave offence was thought to be in the area. Second was where it was reasonably thought that a grave offence might be committed in a defined area during a specified period. But the power to establish road blocks should not give the police any right to search vehicles. "That would have to be justified in each case by reference to a suspicion on reasonable grounds that there was evidential material in the vehicle."[38]

The Government departed from the Philips Royal Commission's approach in two main particulars. First, the Act allows authorisation by an officer of the rank of superintendent, or in a case of urgency by an officer of *any* rank providing it is subsequently reported to a superintendent or above as soon as practicable (s.4(3), (5), (6) and (7)).

Secondly, the Act substitutes the concept of a "serious arrestable offence" for the Philips Royal Commission's concept of a "grave offence". This has relevance at various points in a comparison between the Act and Commission's report. (For discussion of "serious arrestable offences" see p. 296 below. For definition see s.116 and Sched. 5.)

The provisions of PACE apply whenever a road check is made to stop all vehicles or vehicles selected by any criterion such as, for example, all blue Cortinas (s.4(2)).

The Act divides road checks under section 163 of the Road Traffic Act 1988 into those involving serious arrestable offences for which the special rules of section 4 are applicable and any other checks. The section 4 road check is permitted to see if a vehicle is carrying someone who has committed a serious arrestable offence, or is a witness to such an offence or someone intending to commit such an offence, or an escaped prisoner (s.4(1)). An officer may only authorise a road check under section 4 where it is reasonably suspected that a person reasonably suspected of having committed a serious arrestable offence or who is unlawfully at large is, or is about to be in the locality; or where the search is for someone intending to commit a serious arrestable offence, that he is or is about to be in the locality (s.4(4)(c)(ii)). When the road check is for potential witnesses it is only necessary for the superintendent to have reasonable grounds for believing that the offence is a serious arrestable one. Authorisation can only be given for seven days at a time but this can be renewed in writing from time to time for a further such period (subss. (11), (12)).

It is doubtful whether the provisions of section 4 legitimised the kind of road blocks set up in the City of London in November/December 1992 to combat an IRA bombing campaign—unless it could be supposed that the police had information that wanted terrorists were or were about to be in the area. The reality probably was rather that the police had no knowledge of any actual immediate planned bombings but hoped that the road blocks would act as a general deterrent and that conceivably, by good luck, they might even catch some terrorists.[39] Such objectives could hardly be brought within the very restricted terms of section 4.

But the position has now been regularised by section 81 of the Criminal

---

[38] Philips Report, para. 3.32.

[39] For a description of other exceptional measures taken to protect the City see O. Kelly, "By all means necessary", *Police Review*, April 15, 1994. Mr Kelly was the former Commissioner of the City Police.

Justice and Public Order Act 1994 which added a new section 13A to the
Prevention of Terrorism (Temporary Provisions) Act 1989. In order to
prevent acts of terrorism,[40] a senior officer[41] may authorise stops and
searches of persons and vehicles in a specified locality for a period of up to 28
days[42] without any need to have reasonable grounds to suspect. Such stops
and searches can be carried out by any constable in uniform. The power does
not however cover a search of pedestrians—as opposed to what they are
carrying, such as briefcases or bags. But it does cover a search of the driver
and any passenger in a vehicle as well as the vehicle itself (s.13A(3)). It is
made a summary only offence to fail to stop or wilfully to obstruct a
constable in the exercise of these powers (s.13A(7)). The new provisions in
Code A regarding the identification of the locality by the authorising officer
(described p. 9 above) apply here too. Both the driver and the pedestrian
who has been stopped under these powers can ask for a written statement
about the search, provided it is asked for within 12 months (s.13A(9)).

   There seems little doubt that the section 4 road check is intended to apply
where a serious arrestable offence is involved. But it is arguable that (due
perhaps to legislative oversight) such a road check could be set up by an
officer of a rank below that of superintendent for *any* offence. As has been
seen, subsection (3) requires the authority of a superintendent save where an
officer of a lower rank sets up a road block as a matter of urgency under
subsection (5). This can be done for one of the purposes specified in
subsection (1)—which makes no reference to serious arrestable offences. If
a court had to consider the matter however, this interpretation might be held
to be wrong as contrary to the purpose and thrust of the system of controls
established by the section.

   Every authorisation of a road check must specify the ground, the period
covered, the locality to which it relates and the name of the officer
authorising it. It must also mention the serious arrestable offence in question
(s.4(10), (13) and (14)). Where a vehicle is stopped the person in charge of it
is entitled to a written statement of the reason for the road check if he asks
for it within 12 months (s.4(15)). But there is no requirement that he be told
of this right. Road checks which are not under section 4 continue to be
legitimate under section 163 of the Road Traffic Act 1988 (see *Lodwick v.
Saunders* [1985] 1 W.L.R. 382).

Reports of recorded searches and road checks: section 5[43]

   The chief officer's annual report must contain information about the use
made by his force of powers of stop and search and of road checks set up for
purposes other than those of road traffic and vehicle excise duties. As the
Philips Royal Commission said, this would make the exercise of such powers
subject to the independent scrutiny of the police authority and of H.M.
Inspectors. Information about searches does not give details of individual

---

[40] Other than terrorism connected solely with the affairs of the U.K. or any part of the U.K. other than
Northern Ireland (s.13A(2)).
[41] In the metropolitan area and the City of London of the rank of commander or above; elsewhere of the rank
of assistant chief constable or above (s.13A(1)).
[42] It can be extended by further periods of not more than 28 days at a time (s.13A(8)).
[43] See N.I. PACE Order, Art. 7.

cases but it includes the total number of searches in each month for stolen articles and offensive weapons and for other prohibited articles and the total numbers arrested in each month in respect of each such category (s.5(2)). The information about road blocks must include the reasons for and the result of each road check (s.5(3)).

Empirical Data

(1) Stop and search

The Home Office produces an annual *Statistical Bulletin* giving the data required by the Act. At the time of writing, the latest of these, giving the figures for 1993 was published in June 1994.

There are two problems with these figures. The first is that it is certain that the police record only a proportion (and probably a small proportion) of the stops and searches they are required to record.[44] Secondly, they are required by PACE section 5 to record only stops and searches—not stops which do not lead to searches. The Home Office research study (*op. cit.* n. 11 above), which was carried out pre-PACE, suggested (p. 22) that only a quarter of stops led to searches being carried out.

Subject to these two caveats, it is worth noting that the statistics show a consistent annual increase in the numbers of recorded stops and searches— from 109,800 in 1986 to 442,800 in 1993.[45] The figures also show that the reasons for stops and searches have remained remarkably stable. By far the most common reason is stolen property and "going equipped" (59 per cent in 1993), followed by drugs (31 per cent). All the other categories account in aggregate for around 10 per cent. Offensive weapons, which provoked such great controversy at the time of the Philips Royal Commission's Report, accounts for a mere 5 per cent.

The overall "success-rate" namely, the proportion of stops and searches leading to an arrest, has fluctuated slightly from year to year. In the period 1986 to 1990 it was 16 to 18 per cent. Since then it has steadily declined: 1991, 15 per cent, 1992, 14 per cent, 1993 13 per cent. (Note however that this figure does not include proceedings by way of summons or caution.)

The Home Office *Statistical Bulletin* for 1993 (p. 4) showed seemingly wide variations in the policy of different forces in regard to stop and search (or at least the recording of stop and search) as judged by the number per 100,000 of the population. In some force areas[46] there were over 1,000 stops and searches per 100,000 population. In some[47] there were 601 to 1,000. In 18 there were 301 to 600, in a few[48] there were 201 to 300 and in the remaining forces[49] there were from 1 to 200.

---

[44] Dixon *et al.* (1990) report that officers said they might carry out up to four or five stop/searches in one shift. Yet the national figures for stops and searches show only two or three per officer *per year*.

[45] There is no way of knowing whether this reflects more stops and searches or only more recording of stops and searches—or both. As to the level of stop and search see also the periodic British Crime Survey; the two surveys conducted in Islington (Crawford *et al.* 1990); the survey conducted in Hammersmith and Fulham (Painter *et al.* 1989); and the study by Professor Keith Bottomley and colleagues (Bottomley *et al.*, 1989).

[46] City of London, Dyfed Powys, Leicestershire, Manchester Merseyside, the Metropolitan area, South Wales, Surrey.

[47] Cumbria, Norfolk, Warwickshire, West Mercia.

[48] Avon and Somerset, Dorset, Durham, Kent, Thames Valley.

[49] Cheshire, Devon and Cornwall, Hampshire, Humberside, Nottinghamshire, Staffordshire, West Yorkshire.

As to the general effectiveness and impact of the PACE provisions on stop and search see especially Bottomley *et al.*, (1991a).[50] The overall verdict to be deduced from the research seems to be that:

(1) the PACE rules seem to have had little impact on decision-making by officers on the beat;
(2) stop and search records and statistics are wholly unreliable[51];
(3) there is little supervision of beat-officer decisions.

On the question whether stop and search powers are exercised in a discriminatory way as between whites and non-whites, the empirical evidence is equivocal. The British Crime Survey ("BCS") Skogan,[52] and the Second Islington Survey (Crawford *et al.*, 1990) show that Afro-Carribeans are more likely to be stopped than white people. But the Hammersmith survey (Painter *et al.*, 1989) showed little difference. Moreover in both the BCS and the Islington survey, when variables were controlled much of the difference disappeared. Thus, young Afro-Carribean males were only slightly more likely to be stopped and searched than their white counterparts. The BCS does not show significant differences between whites and Afro-Carribeans in regard to the frequency of occasion when they are stopped and searched.[53]

(2) Road checks

The number of road checks fluctuated for the first six years. The lowest number was 222 in 1991, the highest was 445 in 1992. But in 1993 the number jumped to 3,560—due to over 3,200 being conducted in the City of London following increased IRA terrorism activity in London. The number of arrests resulting from the reason for the road checks was however small—no more than 20 to 50 per year. Even in 1993 it was only 50—two fewer than in 1998. In the six years from 1986 to 1992 there were also a few arrests for other reasons. But in 1993 there were 902 arrests for such "other reasons" resulting from road checks.[54]

Special provisions for statutory undertakers: section 6[55]

Constables employed by a railway, canal, dock or harbour undertaking are given a power under the Act to stop, search and detain for the purpose of searching any vehicle before it leaves parts of the undertaker's premises used for the storage and handling of goods. The special feature of the power is that there is no requirement that the constable have any reasonable suspicion that the vehicle is carrying stolen or prohibited goods. Also it extends the power beyond public places.

Its object is to make it possible for statutory undertakings to check

---

[50] See also Dixon *et al.* (1986b) and Dixon *et al.* (1990).

[51] Not least because of the variable way in which forces and officers within forces deal with stops and searches "by consent".

[52] W. Skogan, *The Police and Public in England and Wales* 1990 (Home Office Research Study No. 117).

[53] The pre-PACE PSI study (p. 8 above) and the Hammersmith survey, Painter *et al.* (1989) *do* show such significant differences.

[54] Home Office *Statistical Bulletin*, Issue 15/94, June 1994, p. 5.

[55] See N.I. PACE Order, Art. 8.

outgoing loaded lorries on a random or routine basis as a means of reducing the practice of pilfering. The power is not one that would be likely to affect ordinary members of the public. The power was not entirely new. It was based on similar provisions in section 27 of the Aviation Security Act 1982 in regard to airports. Statutory undertakings for the purposes of this section are defined in section 7(3). The section does not however confer any power to search the person. This therefore requires reasonable suspicion.

Subsection (3) extends the power to the United Kingdom Atomic Energy Authority's constables in relation to property owned or controlled by British Nuclear Fuels Ltd and subsection (4) extends the application of subsection (3) to Northern Ireland.

Repeals of existing stop and search powers: section 7[56]

Section 7 repeals six statutory provisions giving constables stop and search powers which are now superseded by section 1. The best known is section 66 of the Metropolitan Police Act 1839. The section also repeals stop and search powers under Acts promoted by local authorities. Other stop and search powers in public general Acts are preserved (s.7(2)(a)(i)). Stop and search powers conferred on statutory undertakings are preserved and need not any longer be renewed periodically (s.7(2)(a)(ii) and (b)).

Subsection 7(3) defines "statutory undertakers".

QUESTIONS AND ANSWERS

1. STOP AND SEARCH

1. Who can exercise the power of stop and search under PACE?

Any police officer whether in uniform or not.

2. Where can the power be exercised?

(1) Any place to which the public have access whether for payment or not (street, park or football ground, but not a private club, school or university); and

(2) any other place which is not a dwelling to which people have ready access (*e.g.* a garden next to the street). But a person cannot be searched in a garden or a yard attached to a dwelling unless it appears that he is not the owner and that he does not have the owner's permission to be there.

3. What does the power consist of?

To stop someone and to speak briefly to him before deciding whether or not to search him. If the decision is to search him he can only be searched superficially. He cannot be required to take off any garments other than his outer coat, his jacket and his gloves (and in Northern Ireland, his headgear).

---

[56] See N.I. PACE Order, Art. 9.

He can be asked to remove other items of clothing but if he refuses he cannot be compelled to do so. The stop and search power is clearly intended to be restricted in public to a superficial search in the form of a "patting down". If the police want to conduct a more extensive search it must be done "not in public". Code A (para. 3.5) says that where on reasonable grounds it is considered necessary to conduct a more thorough search ("*e.g.* by requiring a person to take off a T-shirt or headgear") this should be done out of public view, for instance in a police van or police station. This would apply also to the new power to search a person's mouth without consent where he has not been arrested. But it is unlikely that the courts would in any circumstances permit the stop and search power to be used for an extensive search of the person, let alone a strip search.

4. On what grounds can a person be stopped in order to be searched?

Before stopping the person concerned, the police officer must normally have reasonable grounds for suspecting that he will find either stolen goods or "prohibited articles" on him or his vehicle. But there are now also some circumstances in which the police have power to stop and search persons randomly, without having reasonable grounds of suspicion. Such powers are restricted to particular localities identified by the police for a limited period in connection either with prevention of terrorism or where outbreaks of violence are anticipated.

5. What amounts to reasonable grounds to suspect?

The concept of reasonable grounds to suspect is inevitably somewhat imprecise. But it means basically that there must be some grounds for suspecting that particular individual himself. It is not enough to feel that he is one of a group of a particular type who might be prone to commit that sort of offence—skinheads, young blacks, yobbos or any other category. There must be something about that individual which sparks off suspicion. The concept of "reasonable" suspicion means fairly strong suspicion with a concrete basis that could be evaluated by an objective third person.

6. Can reasonable suspicion be based on the knowledge that the person concerned has committed offences before?

The short answer is No. There must be something about his conduct, manner, appearance, way of moving or other surrounding circumstances which suggest that he has done something recently or is about to do something.

7. What are "prohibited articles"?

The Act established two categories of prohibited items. One is something made or adapted for use in connection with burglary, theft, taking a motor vehicle without authority or obtaining property by deception. The other is "offensive weapons". The Criminal Justice Act 1988 added an article with a blade or point other than a short bladed folding penknife. But many other statutes give the police power to stop and search, *e.g.* for drugs, for explosives, for firearms, etc.

8. What is meant by an offensive weapon?

An offensive weapon is either something made or adapted for use for causing injury (such as a flick-knife, cosh or knuckle-duster) or something which in itself is innocent but which is intended by the person having it to be used by him or others to cause someone injury.

9. What must the officer do before carrying out a search?

It is an absolute rule that before searching anyone the officer must do his best to inform the person concerned by telling him:

(1) his own name (in Northern Ireland his number) and that of his police station;
(2) the object of the proposed search;
(3) the officer's grounds or reasons for wanting to make it;
(4) that the person searched has the right to ask for a copy of the record of the search at the police station within 12 months.

If the officer is in plain clothes he must also first produce evidence that he is in fact a police officer.

10. What happens if the person concerned does not understand English. Is any search therefore unlawful?

No. The duty is not to inform the person but to "take reasonable steps to bring the information to his attention". If everything has been done that could reasonably be done to get him to understand the relevant information, the officer can proceed to carry out a search.

11. What if the officer wants to search a number of persons in a short space of time which would make it difficult to conform to the duty to give each of them the requisite information?

He must nevertheless do his best to inform them of his name and the name of his station, the object of the search and the reason why he wants to make it. But he is not under a duty to mention the person's right to get a record of the search if the circumstances are such as to make it impracticable to make a record.

12. For how long can a person be detained under the stop and search power?

No longer than is reasonably necessary to carry out the search. (The notes for guidance in Code A (3B) only states that "such searches should be completed as soon as possible".)

13. When must a record be made of a stop and search?

A record must be made unless it is not practicable to do so, *e.g.* because considerable numbers have been stopped and searched for instance outside a football ground. But the officer is not exonerated from the duty to make a record where he can in practice make a record later, only if he cannot make one at all. If it is not practicable to make the record on the spot but it is feasible to make it later, the duty is to make it "as soon as practicable".

14. Must a record be made if there is no search?

No. The duty to make a record only arises if there is a search.

15. What is the record supposed to include?

The name of the person searched, if known, and, if not, some description of him including details of his race; the object of the search; the grounds for making it; the date and time; the place; whether anything and, if so, what was found; and the identity of the officer who made the search.

16. Do the powers to stop and search a person apply to stopping and searching a vehicle?

They do apply in much the same way. But there are some differences. One is that a police officer in uniform has the power to stop any vehicle under section 163 of the Road Traffic Act 1988. That Act does not require the police officer to be suspicious of anything in particular. But a stop under the Road Traffic Act does not entitle the officer to search the vehicle. A search under the 1984 Act requires reasonable grounds to suspect that the vehicle is carrying stolen goods or prohibited articles.

Another difference is that the Act makes special provision for the search of an unattended vehicle where reasonable grounds for suspicion exist. In that case the officer must leave a notice in or on the vehicle stating that he has searched it, giving the name of his police station and stating that the owner can get a copy of the record of the search if he applies within 12 months. The record of a search of a vehicle should describe it.

17. Are there any stop and search powers apart from the 1984 Act?

Yes. There are many statutes which give the police stop and search powers, most of which continue to exist. But the 1984 Act has repealed some of these powers such as the power of the Metropolitan Police dating from 1839 to stop and search persons on reasonable suspicion that they are carrying stolen goods.

18. Can a person be stopped and searched by consent?

Yes, but the Code (note 1E) states that "juveniles, persons suffering from a mental handicap or mental disorder and others who appear not to be capable of giving an informed consent should not be subject to a voluntary search". When it is a voluntary search the various safeguards of the new Act do not apply. The difficulty is in knowing whether a stop is by consent. This is notoriously a grey area. The Code of Practice states that the Code provisions do not affect "the routine searching of persons entering sports grounds or other premises with their consent or as a condition of entry" (note 1Da.). Code A also states that when a police officer is searching someone on the street on a voluntary basis he should always make this clear to the person concerned (note 1D(b)).

2. ROAD CHECKS

19. The police had an unlimited right to stop any vehicle under the Road Traffic Act. How was that right affected by PACE?

The 1984 Act set up a procedure for establishing a road check when the purpose is to discover whether a vehicle is carrying someone who has committed a serious criminal offence or someone who is a witness to such an offence or someone intending to commit such an offence or an escaped prisoner.

20. What is the procedure?

The road check must normally be authorised in advance and in writing by an officer of the rank of superintendent or above. The authorisation must specify the period for which it is to operate (up to a maximum of one week at a time) and the locality in which it is to operate. It must also state the name of the officer giving it; the purpose of the road check; and the nature of the offence in question.

In an emergency, where no superintendent is available, an officer of any rank can authorise a road check but he must then as soon as is practicable notify a superintendent and make a record of the time at which he granted authority for the road block. The superintendent can then authorise the continuation of the check or can order that it is discontinued.

The person in charge of any vehicle that is stopped in the course of such a check has the right to a written statement as to the grounds for the road check providing he applies for it within 12 months.

21. What grounds justify the setting up of a road block?

There are five possible grounds:

(1) That there are reasonable grounds for believing that someone who has committed a "serious arrestable offence" (for discussion see p. 296 below) is or is about to be in the area.

(2) That the police are looking for a witness to a "serious arrestable offence". In this category there is no requirement that they *expect* to find a witness in the area. They can therefore try their luck without any commitment.

(3) That they are looking for a person who intends to commit a "serious arrestable offence" and that there are reasonable grounds for suspecting that the person is or is about to be in the locality.

(4) That there are reasonable grounds to believe that an escaped prisoner is in the area.

(5) That it is a road block set up under new powers to prevent acts of terrorism in a specified locality authorised by a very senior officer for periods of up to 28 days at a time. (See p. 16 above.)

22. Does the power of setting up road blocks include a power of search?

Section 4 of the Act speaks only of stopping vehicles and says nothing of a power of search. The power to search must therefore arise under section 1 (on reasonable suspicion that the vehicle is carrying stolen or prohibited articles) or section 17 (on reasonable suspicion that there is in the vehicle a person who has committed an arrestable offence).

PART II

POWERS OF ENTRY, SEARCH AND SEIZURE

The provisions in the Act regarding entry, search and seizure are partly based on the recommendations of the Philips Royal Commission. But in some important respects they differ from what the Commission proposed. This part of the Act proved to be the one which was most buffeted in the Committee stage on the first version of the Bill and it was here that the Government made the most significant changes to its original Bill.

The Philips Royal Commission's Report

The Philips Royal Commission recommended[1] that existing powers of entry and search under warrant needed to be supplemented. The existing powers were somewhat haphazard and, there were surprising omissions. There was no power for instance to get a search warrant to search the scene of a murder or a kidnap, apart from the power to search premises after an arrest. In the Commission's view a new compulsory power of search for evidence should be available, though it should be a limited power and one subject to stringent safeguards. ("A compulsory power of search for evidence should be available only as a last report. It should be granted only in exceptional circumstances and in respect only of grave offences."[2])

Under the then existing law the police had authority to enter to search premises under different levels of supervision. In most cases the supervising authority was a magistrate but in some circumstances authority for a search could be given by a senior police officer and in others there had to be the permission of a judge. In the view of the Commission in general the appropriate supervision could continue to be provided by the magistracy. But in cases of great urgency in searching for prohibited goods, a police officer not below the rank of superintendent should be able to authorise a search.

When it came to searches for evidence, however, supervision should be by a judge. The procedure should have two stages. The police should first have to apply for a court order similar to a witness summons in a criminal case or an order for discovery in a civil case. Such an order would require the person to whom it was directed to allow the police to look at the items covered by the order. There should be a right of appeal to the court against the order. If the person refused to comply with the order, the police should have the right to get a warrant. They should also have a right to ask for a warrant forthwith

[1] Philips Report, para. 3.42.
[2] *ibid.*

25

"where there is reason to believe that the evidence will disappear, or be disposed of if the person concerned is alerted to the police interest in it".[3]

An order should be made by a judge only if he was satisfied that other methods of investigation had failed, that the nature of the items was specified with some precision, that there were reasonable grounds for thinking that the items would be found at those premises and that the evidence would be of substantial value to identify those responsible for the crime or to determine the particulars of offences.[4]

The PACE Bills and the Act

The Government gave only partial effect to these proposals. It did not accept the Royal Commission's recommendation that a senior officer should in an emergency be permitted to authorise a search for prohibited goods. But on the other hand, the Government did not agree with the Commission that searches for *evidence* should always require the authority of a judge subject to a two stage process of an order and a warrant. It decided that a judge's authority would have to be obtained however if the evidence was held on a confidential basis. In other circumstances it would be enough to get a magistrate's permission. The Home Office made the point that there were already some 40 statutes which gave magistrates powers to authorise searches of premises, including in some instances searches for evidence.[5]

When the first PACE Bill was published it gave the police the right to seek a search warrant from a justice of the peace to look for evidence of a serious arrestable offence. The only qualification was that the application to the magistrate had to indicate how the evidence in question related to the inquiry.

Where however the evidence was held on a confidential basis the first Bill provided a special procedure by way of application to a circuit judge. This was in two stages. In the first instance, the police would normally have to ask for an order to produce. If this had already proved abortive or if the order was bound to fail the police could ask for a search warrant.

These provisions were subjected to fierce criticism especially by the medical profession, the clergy, lawyers, journalists, Citizens' Advice Bureaux and other advisory agencies. All were concerned that the powers as they stood would have permitted a judge to authorise a search of *any* records held in confidence. As a result of the pressure placed upon it the Government made a series of concessions the most important of which were:

   (1) to provide that the hearing before the judge would normally have to be *inter partes* (*i.e.* with both sides present), though not if the police could satisfy the judge that there was reason to believe that the person holding the material in question was in some way implicated in the crime;
   (2) that certain categories of material could be generally exempt from any police scrutiny—notably the records of doctors, clergymen and advisory agencies; and

---

[3] *ibid.*
[4] Philips Report, para. 3.43.
[5] The list was set out in the Commission's *Law and Procedure Volume* (Cmnd. 8092–1 (1981), App. 5).

(3) that enforcement of a judicial order to produce confidential material which is not exempt would be by proceedings for contempt and not by a search warrant.

The categories of material exempted were those subject to legal professional privilege, and what is called "excluded material"—namely confidential personal records of doctors and caring professions and advisory agencies, and material held in confidence by journalists. Material held in confidence that is not exempt is called "special procedure" material, access to which has to be sought from a circuit judge[6] rather than from a magistrate.

Applications to justices of the peace for search warrants: section 8[7]

Section 8 provides for the issue by magistrates of warrants to enter and search premises for evidence of serious arrestable offences.

The section gives a justice of the peace, on written application from a constable, power to issue a search warrant where he is satisfied that there are reasonable grounds for believing that a serious arrestable offence (as defined in s.116 and Sched. 5; see pp. 296–298 below) has been committed. He must also be satisfied:

(1) that there is material on the premises likely to be of substantial value to the investigation (s.8(1)(b));

(2) that it is likely to be "relevant evidence" (*i.e.* admissible in evidence—ss.8(1)(c) and 8(4));

(3) that it is not and does not include "excluded material" (see s.11), or "special procedure material" (see s.14); or material subject to legal privilege (s.10); and

(4) that any of the conditions in subsection (3) applies.

The conditions in subsection (3) are basically that it is not practicable to gain entry to the premises in question without a search warrant. Thus examples are where entry has been refused or no one with authority to grant access can be reached or the purpose of the search may be frustrated unless an officer can gain immediate entry.

In *R. v. Guildhall Magistrates' Court, ex p. Primlaks Holdings Co. (Panama) Inc.*[8] it was held that if in doubt whether material is covered by legal privilege or is special procedure material the magistrates should refuse the application under section 8 and leave the applicant to proceed under section 9. The magistrates had granted search warrants authorising the search of two solicitors' firms. In support of the application for search warrants it had been said that although the material sought might be covered by legal professional privilege, such privilege was void in that the documents were held in furtherance of a criminal enterprise (for which see below p. 37). The searches were carried out and documents were seized. An application for judicial review was granted by the Divisional Court on the ground that there was no material on which the magistrate could properly have been satisfied that there were reasonable grounds for believing that the corre-

[6] In Northern Ireland a county court judge.
[7] See N.I. PACE Order, Art. 10.
[8] [1989] 2 W.L.R. 841.

spondence sought did not include items within the definition of section 10(1), or, if it did, that it was not privileged under subsection (2) or was not special procedure material. It was impossible to believe that Parliament could have intended that a magistrate should be able on an *ex parte* application to authorise a search for and seizure of documents, when it had created a procedure in which any question of privilege being lost could be dealt with by a circuit judge.

The Divisional Court said that section 8 conferred a draconian power and it must be clearly understood that it was for the magistrate to satisfy himself that there were reasonable grounds for believing the matters set out. The fact that a police officer stated that there were reasonable grounds was not enough. The magistrate had to be satisfied himself. In this case the magistrate could not have been satisfied that there were reasonable grounds for believing that the conditions specified in section 8(3) applied. There was no substance in the allegation that no one in the two firms could be contacted or, in the case of one of the firms, that the material would have been disposed of.

The decision is a helpful reminder to magistrates (and their clerks) that when deciding whether to grant a police application for a search warrant, magistrates must not allow themselves to act as rubber stamps for the police. All too often, it seems, this is what happens in practice. In contrast to applications under section 9 (see below), it is not however necessary for the magistrates to be persuaded that other methods of obtaining the sought material have been tried without success.[9]

Subsection (5) makes it clear that the power to issue a search warrant under subsection (1) is in addition to any existing power to issue warrants. Existing provisions for the issue of search warrants (which were listed in Appendix 5 to the Philips Royal Commission's *Law and Procedure Volume*), include powers to search for evidence of various offences.

Access to "excluded" and "special procedure" material: section 9 and Schedule 1[10]

Section 9 deals with the question of police access to material held on a confidential basis. It also applies the procedures envisaged under the Act to searches for such material under the authority of other legislation. (Access to such material in terrorism cases is dealt with in the Prevention of Terrorism (Temporary Provisions) Act 1989, Sched. 7.)

Subsection (1) states that the police may only seek access to excluded or special procedure material (as defined in ss.11 and 14 respectively) by applying to a circuit judge under Schedule 1 to the Act. (Recorders have no jurisdiction to hear special procedure applications.[11]) Application must also be made to the judge where the material sought is partly excluded or special procedure and partly other material (Schedule 1, para. 2(1)(ii) and 3(1)). The judge may order the material to be produced or, in exceptional

[9] *R. v. Billericay Justices and Dobbyn, ex p. Frank Harris (Coaches) Ltd* [1991] Crim.L.R. 472 (Div.Ct.); cp. s.9 applications *R. v. Crown Court at Leeds, ex p. Hill* (1990) 93 Cr.App.R. 60 (Div.Ct.).
[10] See N.I. PACE Order, Art. 11 and Sched. 1.
[11] *R. v. Central Criminal Court, ex p. Francis & Francis* [1989] A.C. 346 (H.L.), *per* Lord Bridge, p. 368 and Lord Griffiths, p. 382.

circumstances, may issue a search warrant. But the police can only gain access to "excluded material" if a search warrant could have been obtained under the previous law for such material (*e.g.* stolen medical records for which a search warrant could have been issued under the Theft Act 1981, s.26(1)). (For a full list of all then existing police powers to enter and search premises under warrant or other written authority see Philips Royal Commission, *Law and Procedure Volume*, Appendix 5.)

Subsection (2) repealed all existing enactments in so far as they empowered judges or magistrates to authorise searches for excluded or special procedure material consisting of documents or records. All applications for searches for such material, whether in connection with a serious arrestable offence (defined in s.116 and Sched. 5) or not, must now therefore be made under subsection (1) and Schedule 1.

Schedule 1 contains the detailed provisions for the making of orders by circuit judges.

The judge must be satisfied that one or other of the two sets of access conditions are satisfied. *The first set of access conditions* set out in paragraph 2 of the Schedule relate only to special procedure material. (Nearly all the applications made have been under the first set of access conditions.) The conditions are: (a) that there are reasonable grounds for believing that the material is likely to constitute relevant evidence of a serious arrestable offence or that the material is likely to be of substantial value to the investigation; (b) that other methods of getting the material have been tried and failed or have not been tried because it appeared that they would be bound to fail; and (c) that the public interest would be served by an order requiring access to the material. In weighing the public interest the judge is required to balance the benefit to the investigation of gaining access to the material and "the circumstances under which the person in possession of the material holds it" (para. 2(c)).

In a case arising out of riots in St Pauls, Bristol, the Divisional Court ruled that the police were entitled to an order for the production of press photographs of the riot. The public interest in the impartiality of the press would not be undermined since the production would be in response to a court order, nor would it create special additional risks for press photographers.[12] In *R. v. Central Criminal Court, ex p. Carr, The Independent*, March 5, 1987 Glidewell L.J. took the view that once it is shown that the documents are on the premises and that they are likely to be of substantial value to the investigation and relevant evidence, it followed that it was in the public interest that they be produced. See to the same effect *R. v. Crown Court at Northampton, ex p. D.P.P.*[13] Even if this is too broad a view it will be difficult to establish that it would not be in the public interest for the material to be produced to the police.

The *second set of access conditions* (para. 3) applies to both excluded and special procedure material. The effect of this paragraph in Schedule 1 and section 9 is that a judge can order the production of the material (rather than issue a warrant) if a warrant could have been issued pre-PACE to search for it and the issue of such a warrant would have been appropriate. The material need not relate to a serious arrestable offence.

---

[12] *R. v. Bristol Crown Court, ex p. Bristol Press and Picture Agency* (1987) 85 Cr.App.R. 190 (Div.Ct.). See also *R. v. Central Criminal Court, ex p. Ellis Carr* (Div.Ct.) *The Independent*, March 5, 1987, and Lexis.
[13] (1991) 93 Cr.App.R. 376 (Div.Ct.).

Paragraph 4 states that an order made by the judge is an order to produce the material to the police or to give the police access to it within seven days or such other time as it specifies.

Paragraph 5 parallels provisions in section 19(4) (below) regarding access to information in a computer and paragraph 6 applies provisions of sections 21 and 22 regarding access and copying and retention of articles seized to items seized under Schedule 1.

When the first Bill was published it provided for such applications to be made *ex parte* (*i.e.* with only the police represented)—as recommended by the Philips Royal Commission. The judge may in his discretion sit in open court.[14] Paragraph 7, however, provides that an application for such an order must be made *inter partes*. As has been seen this represented a major concession by the Government—though the application is often not in fact contested.

Paragraphs 8 to 10 deal with the service of notice of the application on the person concerned.[15] Paragraph 11 provides that a person served with such a notice must not "conceal, destroy, alter or dispose of the material", save with the leave of a judge or the written consent of a police officer until the application is either dismissed or abandoned or the order under paragraph 4 is complied with.

Paragraph 12 of the Schedule provides for the issue of a search warrant by the judge instead of an order to produce under paragraph 4. An application for a warrant would be made *ex parte* by virtue of section 15(3) of the Act.

Before issuing a search warrant the judge must be satisfied first that one or other of the two sets of access conditions is satisfied and further that any of the conditions in paragraph 14 (See below) are fulfilled. He may also issue a warrant if an order for production has been disobeyed, but only if the order related to material for which a warrant could have been issued under the previous law.

If an order for the production of special procedure material issued under the first set of access conditions is disobeyed no search warrant can be issued. Such an order can only be enforced by proceedings for contempt (paras. 12(b) and 15). This again was an important concession by the Government which originally proposed that disobedience of any order for production by the circuit judge should be followed by an application for a search warrant.

The conditions set out in paragraph 14 are:

(a) that it is not practicable to communicate with anyone able to authorise entry to the premises; or
(b) to give access to the material in question; or
(c) that it is excluded material subject to a restriction or obligation of secrecy under any enactment as mentioned in section 11(2)(b) and that the material is likely to be disclosed in breach of such restriction if a warrant is not issued; or
(d) that service of a notice of an application for an order of production might seriously prejudice the investigation—or in Northern Ireland also "other investigations"[16] introduced to give additional protection for sensitive information.

---

[14] *R. v. The Independent Newspaper, ex p. D.P.P.* (Div.Ct.), March 30, 1988, Lexis.
[15] The equivalent in Northern Ireland is in the Interpretation Act (Northern Ireland) Act 1954.
[16] See N.I. PACE Order, Sched. 1, para. 11(d).

Terrorism cases

Where the police enquiries are being made under the Prevention of Terrorism (Temporary Provisions) Act 1989, Sched. 7, paragraph 3 of that Act permits an application to a circuit judge (or in Northern Ireland a county court judge) *even for access to excluded material.* Only material covered by legal professional privilege is protected. Under subparagraph (5) the judge needs only to be satisfied (a) that a terrorist investigation (as defined in the Act) is being carried out and that there are reasonable grounds for believing that the material is likely to be of substantial value to the investigation; and (b) that there are reasonable grounds for believing that it is in the public interest that the material should be produced.[17] If the material is not in the person's possession the judge may order that person to state to the best of his knowledge and belief where it is (sub-para. (2)). An order may relate to material to come into existence or become available to the person concerned at any time within 28 days of the order (sub-para. (3)).

Under paragraph 5 of Schedule 7 an application for a search warrant can be made to a judge where an order under paragraph 3 to produce the material has not been complied with. The more "gentlemanly" contempt of court procedure which, as has been seen, normally applies to non-compliance with production orders, does not apply therefore to terrorism cases.

A search warrant can of course also be applied for in the same situations as normally under PACE—both from magistrates (para. 2) and from a judge (para. 5(2) and (3)).

There are three further exceptional provisions in Schedule 7. One is the possibility of asking the judge to order anyone to provide an explanation of any material seized or produced (para. 6). However, legal professional privilege cannot be invaded by such a requirement, except that a lawyer can be required to reveal the name of his client (para. 6(2)). Moreover, any answers cannot be used in evidence against the maker of the statement—save in proceedings for refusal to answer such questions or to show that evidence is inconsistent with the statement. (This provision is similar to that in the Criminal Justice Act 1987, s.2 for dealing with serious fraud inquiries.)

In urgent cases of great emergency where immediate action is needed "in the interests of the State" a police officer of the rank of at least superintendent may, by written order, authorise a search which would normally require a search warrant (para. 7(1)).

There is a remarkable further provision by which the Secretary of State can replace the magistrates' court or the judge and himself give orders or issue search warrants equivalent to those available under paragraphs 2, 3 and 5 of Schedule 7. The power exists only in relation to investigations under Part III of the 1989 Act (which deals with financial assistance for terrorism connected with the affairs of Northern Ireland). He must first be satisfied of the same matters of which the magistrates or the judge must be satisfied and secondly, that disclosure of the information required by the application to a court would prejudice the capability of the Royal Ulster Constabulary or the safety of the State (para. 8).

---

[17] See *R. v. Middlesex Guildhall Crown Court, ex p. Salinger* (1993) 2 All E.R. 310 and *D.P.P. v. Channel 4 Television Co. Ltd* New Law J., October 16, 1992, p. 1412, and comments at p. 1417.

The special procedure under Schedule 1

Schedule 1 does not specify what must be the contents of a notice of intention to make an application for access to special procedure material. It is not surprising therefore that a number of reported cases have concerned the requirement of notice.

It has been held that the notice must be given to the person holding the material not to the person under investigation.[18] Lord Justice Watkins said; "It seems to me to be beyond doubt that . . . the only parties referred to in the 1984 Act and the Schedule are the police who make the application and the person or institution in whose custody the special procedure material is thought to be."[19] An application did not require that there be a suspect, let alone someone charged. Where the material was held by someone other than the person under investigation, there was no question of giving that person a right to have notice of the application. Moreover, there is nothing wrong with the police indicating in strong terms that they do not wish the persons under suspicion to be informed of the fact of the application.[20]

In a later case[21] the Court of Appeal held that a bank is not under a duty to inform its customer when it receives notice under section 9 of and Schedule 1 to the Act that the police are applying for access to special procedure material. Its relationship of confidentiality with the customer gives rise to no implied contractual obligation that it will either oppose the police application or inform the customer. Lord Donaldson M.R. said that the normal duty of confidence owed to the customer could be displaced in four situations: (a) under compulsion of law; (b) where there was a public duty to disclose; (c) where the interests of the bank required it; and (d) where it was done with the express or implied consent of the customer. Here the exception was compulsion of law. The case did not deal quite so clearly with the converse question of whether banks are under a duty *not* to inform their clients of the fact of police attempts to gain access to special procedure material. Lord Donaldson thought[22] that banks "were no doubt free to ignore a request [by the police] that [the client] not be informed of the application". But he went on to say that he would have been "surprised and disappointed if they had done so in the context of a criminal investigation unless they were under a legal duty to do so".

In terrorist cases banks would be affected by section 17(2) of the Prevention of Terrorism (Temporary Provisions) Act 1989 which makes it an offence to make any disclosure likely to prejudice the investigation, knowing or having reasonable cause to suspect that a warrant or order has been issued, made or applied for under Schedule 7 to the Act.

In *ex p. Adegbesan*, the police wished to examine documents of an accountant connected with the Youth Association on the Broadwater Farm Estate. It was held that the notice must set out a description of all the material sought—even if that would create a risk that it might be destroyed.[23]

---

[18] *R. v. Crown Court at Leicester, ex p. D.P.P.* (Div.Ct.) [1988] 86 Cr.App.R. 254; [1987] 3 All E.R. 654.
[19] *ibid.* p. 656.
[20] *R. v. Manchester Crown Court, ex p. Taylor* (Div.Ct.) (1988) 87 Cr.App.R. 358; [1988] 1 W.L.R. 705 at 716.
[21] *Barclay's Bank plc (trading as Barclaycard) v. Taylor and another; Trustee Savings Bank of Wales and Border Counties and another v. Taylor and another* [1989] 1 W.L.R. 1066; [1989] 3 All E.R. 563, C.A.
[22] p. 1074, *ibid. ibid.* p. 569.
[23] *R. v. Central Criminal Court at Manchester, ex p. Adegbesan* (Div.Ct.) (1987) 84 Cr.App.R. 219; [1986] 1 W.L.R. 1292.

(If the application would seriously prejudice the investigation, the police should apply for a search warrant under paragraph 14(d).) The notice initially only said that an application would be made for an order under Schedule 1. On being asked for further information, the police supplemented the original notice by stating that the application would be "on the first set of access conditions". As Lord Justice Watkins said, "That told the applicants very little more than they already knew".[24] The police had in fact prepared a detailed information to be used on the hearing of the application setting out what they wanted. Counsel for the applicants argued that his clients should have been served with this detailed information. The Divisional Court rejected this argument. But it accepted that they should be supplied with some information as to what was sought. Where the information is sensitive the amount of information supplied to the recipient of the order may however be restricted.[25]

In *ex p. Baines & Baines*,[26] the Divisional Court held that the police were not required to provide in advance the evidence they intended to rely on at the hearing. But anything given to the judge should be given, at the latest on the day of the hearing, also to the party against whom the order was sought. If the police chose not to give that party copies of the evidence they intended to rely on prior to the date of the hearing, the judge should be prepared to grant an adjournment if evidence was given which could not be responded to adequately there and then. The court quashed the order made because neither the solicitors against whom the order was sought, nor counsel acting for them had been given a copy of the police proof of evidence. The court also spoke very unfavourably of the way the evidence had been presented to the judge by the police. The evidence should not contain, as it did in that case, inadmissible and prejudicial material. ("It has, of course, to be recognised that in an application such as this, compliance with strict rules of evidence is not to be expected but statements which have no substance to the prejudice of the party who is the subject of the order sought are impermissible. They ought not to be made and if made should be ruled out by the judge."[27]) Disclosure must give the court the material it needs to make the decision, including anything that might weigh against making such an order.[28] This is especially so since many of these applications are effectively made *ex parte* because the bank or other party holding the material usually does not contest the application and indeed is not even there at the hearing.[29]

The police must state what material they seek. If this were not done how could the person concerned know what material he had to preserve? Failure to preserve the material was after all subject to penalties. Because this had not been done the Divisional Court quashed the order made by the judge.

The court also touched on the question of whether an unincorporated body was a "person" to whom a special procedure notice could be sent. It left the question open for future decision and advised the police to avoid the

---

[24] *ibid.* p. 1297.
[25] *R. v. Middlesex Guildhall Crown Court, ex p. Salinger* [1993] 2 All E.R. 310 (Div.Ct.) involving material regarding the Lockerbie bombing sought from ABC News International. The application was made under Sched. 7 of the Prevention of Terrorism (Temporary Provisions) Act 1989 the terms of which are similar to the equivalent provisions of PACE.
[26] *R. v. Inner London Sessions Crown Court, ex p. Baines & Baines* [1988] 1 Q.B. 579 (Div.Ct.).
[27] *ibid.* p. 584, *per* Watkins L.J.
[28] *R. v. Lewes Crown Court, ex p. Hill* (1990) 93 Cr.App.R. 60, [1991] Crim.L.R. 376 (Div.Ct.).
[29] *ibid.*

problem by always naming as the person against whom they were moving for an order an officer of the body, such as, for example, the chairman or the secretary.

In a further case arising out of the same fact situation, the Divisional Court said that the notice must also specify the nature of the offence but that it is sufficient if it indicates this in general terms ("theft", "fraud", "blackmail", etc.).[30] It must also show the address where the material is supposedly held.[31] The judge should state his reasons for finding that the access conditions were satisfied. But failure to do so was not fatal if the person concerned was not prejudiced by the failure. The reasons need not be very full.[32]

In exceptional circumstances the detailed information about the material sought can be communicated orally rather than in writing. The case which established this point concerned an inquiry by the Manchester Police into the affairs of a prominent local businessman Mr Kevin Taylor.[33] The police had sought an order from the Cooperative Bank requiring them to produce material relating to the affairs of Mr Taylor in connection with a fraud on the bank. The order made was challenged by way of judicial review, by Mr Taylor. (Since the court rejected the challenge it did not have to decide whether Mr Taylor had the necessary standing to bring such proceedings.)

The ground of challenge was that the notice given had been defective. The evidence showed that the police suspected that employees of the bank were implicated in the offence. The officer therefore told the assistant bank manager what material he was looking for and in regard to what offence, but said that in the written notice he would not identify the account holders in question or the offences of which they were suspected. The Divisional Court held that in the circumstances of the case the bank had had sufficient notice. What was vital, Lord Justice Glidewell said, was that "the party against whom the order is made should know before the order is made what it is he has to produce or allow access to, and in my judgment, he should know the nature of the offence that is being investigated".[34] In most cases it would be best to put this information into the notice or accompanying documents. But where it was proved that the information had been communicated orally previously and the recipient of the notice was specifically told the name of the person to whom the information had been given orally, that was sufficient.

Search warrants should not be granted easily by the judge. In *ex p. Waitt*[35] the Divisional Court said that an *ex parte* application under paragraph 12 should never become a matter of common form. Satisfaction as to fulfilment of the conditions set out in the paragraph was an important matter of substance. The applicant was a solicitor. The police had obtained a search warrant and had searched his offices in connection with an investigation into frauds on building societies. The applicant thought that many, if not all, of the documents seized by the police were subject to legal privilege. He sought judicial review of the issue of the warrant and succeeded. The Divisional Court quashed the warrant and ordered that the seized documents be

---

[30] *R. v. Central Criminal Court, ex p. Ellis Carr, The Independent*, March 5, 1987, and on Lexis.
[31] *ibid.*
[32] *ibid.*
[33] *R. v. Manchester Crown Court, ex p. Taylor* (Div.Ct.) [1988] 1 W.L.R. 705.
[34] *ibid.* p. 717.
[35] *R. v. Maidstone Crown Court, ex p. Waitt* [1988] Crim.L.R. 384 (Div.Ct.).

returned. It appeared that the first reason why the judge had issued a search warrant was that it was not practicable to communicate with the person entitled to grant entry to the premises (para. 14(a) (b)).[36] That was a bad reason since it was possible to communicate with the senior partner. Nor were the conditions in paragraph 14(c) satisfied in regard to material subject to a restriction or obligation under section 11(2)(b) of the Act.

The court said that the special procedure was a serious inroad upon the liberty of the subject. The responsibility for ensuring that the procedure was not abused lay with the circuit judges. It was of cardinal importance that they should be scrupulous in discharging that responsibility. The responsibility was greatest when the police were seeking a search warrant. It was always preferable that applications for special procedure material should be made *inter partes*.

Even if the application had been for a production order made by the police *inter partes* it is not certain that it would have succeeded because of the two conditions set out in paragraph 2(b) of Schedule 1: (i) that other ways of obtaining the information had been tried and had failed or (ii) that they would be bound to fail. No apparent effort had been made by the police to satisfy the first.[37] The onus was therefore on the police to satisfy the second. Macpherson J., *obiter*, thought that it should not be assumed that the solicitor would necessarily decline a request to produce the matter in question.

An order made by a judge under Schedule 1 to produce or give access to special procedure material is an order made in a "criminal cause or matter" within section 18(1)(a) of the Supreme Court Act 1981, even though criminal proceedings have not yet been instituted. It follows that the Court of Appeal has no jurisdiction in the matter. Challenge by way of an application for judicial review must go from the Divisional Court direct to the House of Lords.[38] If the police lose a judicial review case, it does not prevent them starting afresh in seeking an order for production or search warrant under the Schedule.

One commentator has suggested[39] that the fact that challenges to the special procedure have so far come in the form of judicial review may explain why the courts seem generally to have been more willing to quash orders on procedural grounds than on grounds of substance. ("The courts are prepared to quash orders where, *e.g.* inadequate notice has been given, and to set out guidelines for what notice should be given in future. They are much more reluctant to get involved with interfering with a judge's decision on whether the access conditions have been satisfied."[40]) He suggested that a possible alternative approach might be to challenge the order by way of case stated (which had been proposed by Glidewell L.J. in *R. v. Central Criminal Court, ex p. Carr*[41]). This would enable the Divisional Court to take a more

---

[36] See, by contrast, *R. v. Leeds Crown Court, ex p. Switalski* [1992] Crim.L.R. 559 (Div.Ct.) where the firm itself was under suspicion and the Divisional Court refused to set aside the warrant for search of a solicitors' office even though para. 14(a) not 14(d) was relied on.

[37] In *R. v. Lewes Crown Court, ex p. Hill* (1991) 93 Cr.App.R. 60; [1991] Crim.L.R. 376 the Divisional Court quashed a special procedure order because there was no sufficient basis for the judge to have been satisfied that the application was substantially the last resort. An application could and should first have been made under the Bankers' Books Evidence Act 1879.

[38] *Carr v. Atkins* [1987] 1 Q.B. 963, C.A.

[39] R.T.H. Stone, "PACE: Special Procedures and Legal Privilege", [1988] Crim.L.R. 498 at 506.

[40] *ibid.*

[41] *The Independent*, March 5, 1987.

active role in deciding whether an order should have been granted and in developing legal rules governing the use of Schedule 1 powers.[42]

Meaning of "items subject to legal privilege": section 10[43]

Material covered by legal professional privilege can neither be searched for nor seized by the police. In the first Bill as first published legal privilege was confined to communications between a professional legal adviser and his client made in connection with the giving of legal advice to the client. This was then extended by amendment in Committee to include also communications between a professional legal adviser and his client or between such an adviser or his client and any other person made in connection with or in contemplation of legal proceedings and for the purpose of such proceedings.

Subsequently by further amendment the Government changed the definition again. The final version which was adopted in the second Bill and which became law in section 10(1) described the categories covered as (a) communications made in connection with the giving of legal advice between the professional legal adviser and his client "or any person representing his client"; and (b) communications made[44] in connection with or in contemplation of legal proceedings and for the purposes of such proceedings made between the professional legal adviser and his client or any person representing his client or between such a legal adviser or his client or any such representative and any other person.

Documents or other items mentioned or enclosed with such communications are also covered by legal privilege if the communication is made[45] in connection either with the giving of legal advice or in connection with or contemplation of legal proceedings and for the purpose of such proceedings and if they are in the possession of someone entitled to possession of them (s.10(1)(c)). But documents or articles held with the intention of furthering a criminal purpose are stated not to be items subject to legal privilege (see below).

In *R. v. Inner London Sessions Crown Court, ex p. Baines & Baines*[46] the police were seeking information concerning the purchase of various properties following the £26 million Brink's-Mat Ltd robbery at Heathrow Airport. A judge granted the police a production order against a firm of solicitors, requiring them to make available for inspection "all client account records including ledgers, day books, cash books, account books and other records used in the ordinary business of the [firm]" in whatever form, in connection with the purchase of a named property. As has been seen above (p. 33) the Divisional Court quashed the order on the ground that the formalities had not been properly observed. The court also briefly considered the argument for the solicitors that the material sought was covered

---

[42] *op. cit.* note 38 above, pp. 506–507.
[43] See N.I. PACE Order, Art. 12. The same definition of legally privileged material is incorporated in the Drug Trafficking Offences Act 1986, s.27 and the Prevention of Terrorism (Temporary Provisions) Act 1989, Sched. 7, para. 1.
[44] *R. v. Leeds Magistrates' Court ex p. Dumbleton* (April 27, 1993, unreported, Div.Ct.) No. CO/2129/92—"made" means lawfully made and does not extend to forged documents. See further *ex p. Francis and Francis* below.
[45] "Made" here means brought into existence—see *R., The Times*, February 2, 1994 C.A., where it was held that a DNA test obtained by the defence was protected by legal professional privilege and the prosecution were not entitled to ask for its production or for the production of a scientist's opinion based on the test.
[46] [1988] 1 Q.B. 579, C.A.

by legal professional privilege. It held that an item was covered by legal privilege if it was a communication made in connection with the giving of advice. Records of conveyancing transactions were not privileged since they were not connected with advice. But correspondence between the client and his solicitor seeking or giving advice would be privileged. Correspondence regarding financial transactions might therefore be privileged because it could contain advice.

It was held in *R. v. Guildhall Magistrates' Court, ex p. Primlaks Holdings Co. (Panama) Inc.*[47] however that documents of clients sent to solicitors together with correspondence for the purpose of obtaining legal advice are not covered by legal professional privilege if they are pre-existing documents, unless they were made in connection with the giving of legal advice or in connection with or in contemplation of legal proceedings and for the purpose of such proceedings.

The head of the Law Society's Legal Practice Directorate, legal adviser's branch, commenting on the decision in *ex p. Baines & Baines*, recommended[48] that a practitioner faced with a production order should go through his relevant files and make lists of any communications falling within section 10(1)(a). "He should also make a note of each document or other item which was enclosed with or referred to in any such communication if it is at least arguable that it was made in connection with the giving of legal advice."[49] The list should be served on the police with a copy to the judge. The solicitor should also of course seek instructions from the client since the privilege is that of the client. Also, opposing a production order may be a costly business and the solicitor will require his client's approval to incur the necessary expense.

In *R. v. Snaresbrook Crown Court, ex p. D.P.P.*[50] the D.P.P. was seeking access to a legal aid application in connection with a possible charge of attempting to pervert the course of justice. The form was held by the Law Society which claimed that legal privilege applied even though the application may have been made in furtherance of a criminal purpose. The Divisional Court ruled that since the Law Society did not hold the form in furtherance of any criminal purpose, section 10(2) did not apply and it could not be made to deliver up the document. It was covered by privilege.

To the considerable disquiet of solicitors, this decision was wholly or at least largely overruled in November 1988 by the House of Lords in *R. v. Central Criminal Court, ex p. Francis & Francis.*[51] The police sought an order under the Drug Trafficking Offences Act 1986, section 27 for access to correspondence and attendance notes held by a firm of solicitors concerning property transactions entered into by a client. (Sections 27 to 32 of the 1986 Act sets out a scheme regarding access to special procedure and excluded material which is similar to that in PACE and the phrase "legal privilege" is given the same definition.[52]) The police suspected that the client had innocently been put in funds by a relative who was thought to be involved in drug trafficking. The police obtained a production order from a judge

---

[47] [1989] 2 W.L.R. 841, (H.L.).
[48] Eric Hiley, "Production orders under the Police and Criminal Evidence Act; two important cases", L.S.Gaz., October 28, 1987, p. 3088.
[49] *ibid.* p. 3090.
[50] [1988] Q.B. 532; [1987] Crim.L.R. 824.
[51] [1989] A.C. 346.
[52] See s.29(2).

requiring the solicitors to produce all their files relating to a particular transaction. A judge gave leave to have the order quashed in so far as it concerned some privileged documents but on the substantive hearing the Divisional Court refused the application for judicial review on the ground that the documents were held with the intention of furthering a criminal purpose within section 10(2).[53] The criminal intention was not that of either the solicitor or his client but of a third party. The House of Lords (Lord Bridge and Oliver dissenting) upheld the Divisional Court. Since the documents held by the solicitors were intended by the third person to further the purpose of laundering the proceeds of drug trafficking, section 10(2) deprived the documents of privilege. The fact that the solicitor and even the client were innocent of any such intention was irrelevant.

In his dissenting speech Lord Oliver said that " 'Items held with the intention of furthering a criminal purpose' cannot, as a matter of plain, ordinary English, refer to items in relation to which the holder has no such intention but which figure in the intentions of some quite different person who is not the holder."[54]

But Lord Brandon, for the majority, derived his interpretation of section 10 from the fact that since crooked solicitors were rare, the contrary view would not advance the purpose of the statutory provision and would protect the perpetrators of serious crime. By contrast, the broader construction he favoured "would materially assist in achieving the purpose of Part II of the Act and would prevent the principle of legal privilege being used to protect the perpetrators of serious crimes".[55]

Lord Goff said that the broader construction reflected the common law position under *Cox and Railton*.[56] (This is challenged by the commentary on the case in the *Criminal Law Review*.[57]) He also agreed with the view of Lord Brandon that the broader interpretation must be assumed to have been what Parliament intended.

Moreover it seems that the "criminal purpose" does not have to be a specific one of committing a particular crime. It is enough if the purpose is simply to "salt away" the proceeds of crime through the purchase of property (*per* Lord Goff[58]).

On the question as to what point in time must the criminal purpose arise or exist, Lord Goff said the critical moment is when the communication is made: did the client or some third person have a criminal purpose at the moment when the communication in question came into the solicitor's possession? That is the point in time at which legal privilege would be negatived under section 10(2).

Lord Goff said, *obiter*,[59] that although the decision in the case undermined part of the reasoning in *R. v. Snaresbrook Crown Court, ex p. D.P.P.* (above), it did not necessarily undermine the actual decision. He was inclined to think that the common law principle of legal professional privilege could not be excluded on the grounds of a criminal purpose where a communication was made by a client regarding the conduct of his case in

[53] [1988] 1 All E.R. 677.
[54] *op. cit.* note 51 above, p. 387.
[55] *op. cit.* note 51 above, p. 381.
[56] (1884) 14 Q.B.D. 153.
[57] [1989] Crim.L.R. 444 at 447.
[58] *op. cit.* note 51 above, pp. 393–394.
[59] *ibid.* p. 397.

criminal or civil proceedings merely because it is untrue and would, if acted upon, lead to perjury.

Not surprisingly, the House of Lords' decision has caused much concern to the professions generally and to the solicitors' branch of the legal profession in particular. Its impact affects barristers and accountants, as well as solicitors.[60]

The Law Society's view expressed in the *Gazette* by a senior member of the Legal Practice Directorate, is that *ex p. Francis and Francis* does not go so far as to say that the criminal intention of a third party will, in all cases, deprive an innocent client of privilege. Examination of the speeches of Lords Brandon and Goff suggested that the client's privilege would only be lost if the third party was using the client as an intermediary or innocent tool.[61] But even if this is correct it does not solve the practical problem that where the police allege a criminal intention on the part of a third person it will be difficult for a solicitor to establish the nature of the relationship between his client and the third party.[62] Material obtained by the police under Part II of PACE which is subject to legal professional privilege cannot be passed by the police to private individuals for the purposes of civil litigation.[63]

Meaning of "excluded material": section 11[64]

Section 11 defines "excluded material". Anything which is in this category is totally exempt from any order or warrant under Schedule 1 unless the police could have obtained a search warrant to look for it pre-PACE, *e.g.* because it is a stolen or forged article for which a search warrant could have been obtained under pre-PACE legislation such as the Theft Act 1968 (or cases under the Prevention of Terrorism (Temporary Provisions) Act 1989. (But it should be noted that the fact that something is excluded material does not prevent the person holding it from handing it over voluntarily to the police.[65])

Subsection (1) provides that "excluded material" consists of three categories of material held on a confidential basis: (a) personal records (defined in s.12); (b) samples of human tissue or tissue fluid taken for the purpose of diagnosis or medical treatment and which are held in confidence; and (c) journalistic material (defined in s.13) consisting of documents or records if held in confidence (defined in subs. (3)).

Subsections (2) and (3) define what is meant by the concept of "held in confidence" for excluded material other than journalistic material and for journalistic material respectively.

Excluded material other than journalistic material is held in confidence if

---

[60] For a severely critical assessment of the House of Lords' decision see L. Newbold, "The Crime/Fraud Exception to Legal Professional Privilege", 53 Mod.L.Rev., 1990, pp. 472–484.

[61] Peter Stevenson, "Privilege: *Francis & Francis* and other recent cases", Law Soc.Gaz., February 1, 1989, p. 26.

[62] See also L. Alt, "Raids: against the law?" 135 Sol.J., November 15, 1991, p. 1248.

[63] *Marcel v. Metropolitan Police Comr.* [1992] 1 All E.R. 72 (C.A. Civil Division) rejecting an appeal on that point from a decision by the Vice-Chancellor [1991] 1 W.L.R. 1118, [1991] 1 All E.R. 845.

[64] See N.I. PACE Order, Art. 13.

[65] *Singleton* [1995] Crim.L.R. 236 C.A. Dentist voluntarily handed over to the police dental records of a patient. The record was part of the prosecution's case. The patient was convicted. He failed to persuade the Court of Appeal to quash the conviction. The confidentiality was that of the dentist not that of the defendant and it could therefore be waived without reference to the suspect.

it is held subject to an express or implied undertaking to hold it in confidence or it is held subject to a restriction on disclosure or obligation of secrecy contained in any statute. Journalistic material is held in confidence if held subject to such an undertaking, restriction or obligation and it has been continuously so held, whether by one or more than one person, since it was first acquired or created for the purposes of journalism. This last requirement does not apply to other categories of excluded material, apparently because of a sense that they are intrinsically more sensitive.

Meaning of "personal records": section 12[66]

"Personal records" for this purpose are defined to mean documents and other records concerning an individual (whether living or dead) who can be identified from them which relate: (a) to his physical or mental health[67]; or (b) to spiritual counselling or assistance given or to be given to him; or (c) to counselling or assistance given or to be given to him for the purposes of his personal welfare and involving counselling given or to be given to him by any voluntary organisation or by any individual who by reason of his office or occupation has responsibility for his personal welfare or by reason of a court order has responsibility for his supervision.

The exemption of personal records, as defined, from any access by the police is absolute. This was in response to the fierce campaign waged in particular by the British Medical Association, the bishops and Citizens' Advice Bureaux. The definition is very wide. It would cover not simply the records of probation officers, social workers and advisory agencies but school and university personal files and records. It does not however cover "things" such as the bullet taken from a wound, or bloodstained clothing. The contents of a stomach pumped out by the doctors would probably be excluded material as human tissue or tissue fluids. So too would be any form of medical record. But the records of accountants or other professional advisers do not qualify—save in so far as they gained exemption through legal privilege. An accountant is not an individual who through his office or occupation has responsibility for the client's "personal welfare" within the meaning of the phrase. There is no definition of this phrase in the Act, but the section is plainly intended to cover the caring professions and their voluntary counterparts.

Meaning of "journalistic material": section 13[68]

Mr William Whitelaw on the first Bill was persuaded to grant an exemption from police action also to the journalists' lobby. Subsequently some journalists and newspaper editors expressed disquiet about the desirability of this special status but Mr Leon Brittan on the second Bill

---

[66] See N.I. PACE Order, Art. 14.

[67] An attempt to get access to hospital out-patient records failed where the record sought was that of a man suspected of murder who had been injured during the killing. The argument that the records were "administrative" rather than "personal" was rejected by the circuit judge (K. W. Lidstone, "Powers of Entry, Search and Seizure," N.I.L.Q. 1989, 333, n. 18, p. 338). See also *R. v. Cardiff Crown Court, ex p. Kellam (1993)*, *The Times*, May 3, 1993 (Div.Ct.).

[68] See N.I. PACE Order, Art. 15.

decided not to respond to their fears. He maintained the concession agreed by his predecessor. (Note however that if the police can gain access to the material under other legislation—such as the Theft Act or the Official Secrets Act 1911 (now replaced by the Official Secrets Act 1989)—the "excluded material" category does not give protection. Nor is it protected if the material in question is sought in connection with an inquiry into terrorist offences within Schedule 7 of the Prevention of Terrorism (Temporary Provisions) Act 1989.)

As has been seen, excluded material is defined (in s.11(1)(c)) to include journalistic material which consists of documents or other records, held in confidence. Journalistic material is only deemed to be held in confidence in this context if it is both held subject to an undertaking, restriction or obligation to hold it in confidence and if it has been continuously held by one or more persons subject to such an undertaking, restriction or obligation since it was first acquired or created for the purposes of journalism (s.11(2) and (3)). Most material sent to journalists is sent for the purposes of publication and is therefore unlikely to qualify as excluded material, though it could still qualify as special procedure material. The fact that the person who passes the information does not wish to be identified as the source does not in itself make the information excluded material.

Journalistic material is defined as material "acquired or created for the purposes of journalism" (s.13(1)). Journalism is not defined but it includes any form of publication. It is not confined to publication for reward nor to full-time or even professional journalists. Material is only journalistic material however if it is in the possession of someone who either acquired or created it for the purposes of journalism (s.13(2)). This would protect material passed by a journalist to his superiors or to the organisation for which he worked. But it would not cover material that was held by someone not involved in journalism. The Act states that a person who receives unsolicited material from someone who intends that he should use it for the purposes of journalism is taken to have acquired it for that purpose (s.13(3)). Journalistic material that does not qualify as "excluded material" could still be "special procedure material".

Meaning of "special procedure material": section 14[69]

Section 14 defines "special procedure material" for the purposes of section 9 of the Act. In essence it comprises material held on a confidential basis which does not qualify as excluded material or material subject to legal privilege.

Subsection (2) states that material is special procedure material if (not being excluded material or subject to legal privilege) it is held subject to an express or implied undertaking of confidentiality or a statutory restriction on disclosure or obligation of secrecy (for instance under the Official Secrets Act) by someone who acquired it or created it in the course of a trade, business, profession or other occupation or for the purpose of any office whether paid or unpaid. This would include, say, company accounts or stock records held on behalf of a client by a bank, solicitor or accountant. The question of whether there is an implied confidential relationship will be

[69] See N.I. PACE Order, Art. 16.

determined by the nature of the relationship, the kind of information imparted together with any relevant custom, usage or understanding.[70]

Subsection (3) provides that material acquired by employees from their employer or by a company from an associated company is only special procedure material if it was such material immediately before it was acquired. This means that company records cannot be special procedure material simply by virtue of an instruction by an employer to an employee that they should be held in confidence. The special procedure is intended primarily for material held in confidence by a third party. But if it is special procedure material it remains special procedure material even though it may be passed by an employer to an employee—say in an accountants' firm or a bank.

Subsections (4) and (5) make similar provision for special procedure material created by an employee in the course of employment or by a company on behalf of an associated company.

The police have used the power to seek access to special procedure material very extensively. Ken Lidstone in 1989 reported over 2,000 such applications.[71] The police have found the procedure especially useful in investigation of mortgage frauds in relation to records held by banks, building societies, estate agents and solicitors.

Safeguards for obtaining search warrants: sections 15 and 16, Code B, section 2[72]

The Philips Royal Commission recommended that new safeguards should be laid down to apply to the issue of all search warrants[73] and these proposals were incorporated in section 15.

An application for a search warrant must state the grounds for making the application, the statutory authority covering the claim, and in as much detail as possible, the object of the warrant and the premises concerned. The survey by Ken Lidstone showed a tendency in informations and warrants to use[74] generic terms such as "electrical goods", which he suggested was not good enough. The application, which is invariably made *ex parte* (*i.e.* without the person affected being present), must be supported by an information in writing (s.15(3)). The constable must answer on oath any questions put by the justice of the peace (s.15(4)). (Ken Lidstone's study of warrants before PACE showed a reliance on the formula "As a result of information received from a previously reliable source" and a total lack of questioning as to such reliability by magistrates. A post-PACE study suggested that this formula continued to be used, though somewhat less frequently, and that magistrates were no more questioning than they were before the Act![75]) Each warrant can authorise entry on only one occasion (s.15(5)). If nothing is found, the police therefore cannot return to have another attempt, unless they can get a second warrant. The warrant must specify the name of the

---

[70] See *Gilbert v. Star Newspapers Ltd* (1984) 11 T.L.R. 4; *Talbot v. General Television Corpn. Pty Ltd* [1981] R.P.C. 1; *Fraser v. Thames Television Ltd* [1984] Q.B. 44; *Coco v. A. N. Clark (Engineers) Ltd* [1969] R.P.C. 41 at 47.
[71] Ken Lidstone, "Entry, Search and Seizure," N.I.L.Q. 1989, p. 333 at p. 342.
[72] See N.I. PACE Order, Arts. 17 and 18.
[73] Philips Report, paras. 3.46 and 3.47.
[74] See Lidstone, *op. cit.* note 71 above, p. 351, n.54.
[75] *ibid.* n.55.

person applying for it; the date of issue; the statutory power under which it is issued; the premises to be searched; and, so far as possible, the articles or persons sought and when the search is to take place (s.15(6)). In *ex p. AJD Holdings* the Divisional Court held that before applying for a search warrant the police should consider very carefully what material they hoped the search would reveal. In complex special procedure applications it might be appropriate to ask in the first instance for discovery of documents appearing to relate to the matter under investigation. Also on such applications a note should be taken of what was said by the police and the judge. There should be careful briefing of the officers who executed the warrant and both the extent and the limits of the search should be fully understood. Also the articles identified must be those in the information.[76] Two copies must be made: (s.15(7)), and certified as copies (s.15(8)) by the court itself, though both functions can be delegated to the court staff.[77] The warrant of which copies must be made includes any schedule setting out the particulars of documents and other material sought.[78] One copy is for the occupier of the premises to keep (see s.16(5)) and one is to be retained by the police. The original goes back to the issuing court (see s.16(10)). The judge or magistrate who issues the warrant should sign the authorisation and ideally should also initial all other pages attached to it.[79]

There is one ambiguity in section 15. Subsection (1) states that "an entry on or search of premises under a warrant is unlawful unless it complies with this section and section 16 below". The ambiguity relates to the word "it". Must the warrant comply or the whole entry and search? In *Longman*[80] Lord Lane C.J. said, *obiter*, "With some hesitation we are inclined to think it probably refers to the warrant, but the real probability is that the intention of the framers of the Act was to provide that the warrant should comply with the terms of section 15 and the entry and search should comply with section 16. But, that is not what it says. So we leave that problem unresolved."[81] In *R. v. Chief Constable of Lancashire, ex p. Parker and Magrath* the Divisional Court said it read "it" as referring to the entire process so that in order for the process to be lawful the application for and issue of the warrant has to be in compliance with section 15 and its execution has to comply with section 16.[82] This seems the better view.

Execution of warrants: section 16 and Code B for the searching of premises and the seizure of property[83]

Section 16 contains provisions to ensure that warrants are executed in a proper and reasonable manner. The provisions are supplemented by Code B for the searching of premises promulgated under the authority of section 66. The section applies to all warrants executed by the police. In so far as other statutes lay down different conditions they are repealed (s.15(1)). The courts have held that a search is a draconian though necessary power and there

---

[76] *R. v. Central Criminal Court, ex p. AJD Holdings* [1992] Crim.L.R. 669 (Div.Ct.).
[77] *R. v. Chief Constable of Lancashire, ex p. Parker and Magrath* [1993] 2 All E.R. 56, 61 (Div.Ct.).
[78] *ibid.* at p. 59.
[79] *ibid.* at p. 63.
[80] (1988) 88 Cr.App.R. 148; [1988] 1 W.L.R. 619; [1988] Crim.L.R. 534 C.A.
[81] *ibid.* p. 623.
[82] *op. cit.* n.77 above, at pp. 60–61.
[83] See N.I. PACE Order, Art. 18.

should be a careful briefing of the officers who are to execute it so as to ensure that they understand the extent and limits of the search and seizure operation.[84]

Subsection (1) provides that any constable may execute any warrant. This overrides provisions in a number of statutes which specify that only the constable named in the warrant may execute it. Subsection (2) states that a warrant may authorise persons to accompany the officer executing it, such as a witness.

The section provides that entry and search under a warrant must be within one month from the date of its issue (subs. (3)). It must be at a "reasonable hour" unless "it appears to the constable executing it that the purpose of a search may be frustrated on an entry at a reasonable hour" (subs. (4)). The test is subjective—qualified only by the condition that his belief must be honest. Where the occupier of the premises is present, the constable must produce a copy of the warrant and must give a copy to him (subs. (5)). Failure to do so has been held to be ground for making the search and seizure unlawful which required return by the police of everything seized.[85] If he is not present, a copy must be left there in a prominent place on the premises (subs. (7)). An officer executing a warrant must identify himself and if he is not in uniform he must produce documentary evidence that he is a constable even without being asked (subs. 5). If the occupier is not there but someone else is who appears to be in charge, the police should treat him as the occupier for the purposes of this section (subs. (6)).

In *R. v. Longman*[86] the police came to the premises with a search warrant for drugs. But in order to gain entry without alerting the occupants to their impending arrival a plain clothes officer posed as a delivery girl from Interflora. When the door was opened a number of officers burst in. They therefore had not identified themselves as required by section 16(5), nor had they shown the householder their search warrant as required by Code B on the Entry of Premises, para. 5.5 (see below). The Court of Appeal held that force or subterfuge could legitimately be used for the purposes of gaining entry with a search warrant. The warrant was "produced" within the meaning of section 16(5)(a) and (b) when the occupier was given a chance of inspecting it. It was not enough simply to show him the warrant. But in this particular case the occupier had not tried to look at it. Instead he had shouted a warning to others in the building and had then attacked the officers with a knife. In those circumstances the strict terms of section 16(5) and Code B, para. 5.5 did not have to be complied with. Moreover the court made it clear that it would be prepared to overlook failure to comply with sections 15 and 16 as regards producing the warrant whenever the circumstances made it wholly inappropriate, such as, for example, a search for drugs or in a terrorism case.[87]

The warrant must be executed by the police. Even if they have civilian aides they must be effectively in charge. This was shown dramatically in *R. v. Reading Justices, ex p. South West Meat Ltd.*[88] The warrant was for search of

---

[84] *R. v. Central Criminal Court, ex p. AJD Holdings*, n.76 above.
[85] *ibid.*
[86] *op. cit.* n.80 above. For comment see Robert Stevens, "Search Warrants—Entering Uninvited and Unintroduced", *Justice of the Peace*, August 27, 1988, p. 551.
[87] For commentary on the decision see J. Kodowo Bentil, "Power of Police Officers to Enter Premises to Search for Drugs", *Justice of the Peace*, August 26, 1989, p. 542.
[88] [1992] Crim.L.R. 672 (Div.Ct.).

a food company's premises. The police conducted the search in conjunction with officials from the Board of Agricultural Produce, who decided what documents should be seized and where they should be taken. The Divisional Court held that the police had gone too far in delegating their functions. It quashed the warrant, declared that its issue was a nullity and that the search and seizure were unlawful. The court awarded general damages of £3,000 and exemplary damages of £22,000 against the chief constable and the Board jointly.

A search under a warrant "may only be a search to the extent required for the purpose for which the warrant was issued" (subs. (8)). In other words, if the search is for large items it would not be legitimate to tear up the floor boards, whereas if it were for prohibited drugs such a search might be lawful. This is an important provision.

Note that a warrant authorising a search of premises does not in itself entitle the police to search persons on the premises. As the Home Office Circular on PACE (p. 8 above) stated: "Such persons may only be searched if arrested or if there is a specific power to search in the warrant (*e.g.* warrants issued under section 23 of the Misuse of Drugs Act 1971 and section 46 of the Firearms Act 1968)."

Subsection (9) requires the police to endorse a warrant stating whether the articles or persons sought were found and whether any other articles were seized. This is intended to enable the courts to monitor the success or otherwise of search warrants.

Under subsection (10) the police are subject to a duty to return an executed warrant or one which has expired to the court which issued it. This is intended to give the court basic information as to how the powers are used by the police, though there is no evidence that magistrates have been kept informed by their clerks of the results.

Under subsection (11) warrants must then be retained by the courts for 12 months. The occupier has the right to inspect the endorsed warrant at any time within the 12 months.

Subsection (12) gives the householder the right to inspect the warrant at any time during the 12 months period during which it has to be retained under subsection (11). But the Home Office Circular on PACE (p. 8 above) stated that, in the opinion of the Secretary of State, such a request "should relate to a specific warrant of which the occupier is aware, issued in respect of his premises. There is no requirement under the sub-section to respond to non-specific enquiries about warrants which the occupier claims may have been issued" (para. 7).

The form of a search warrant is prescribed in the Schedule to the Magistrates' Courts (Forms) (Amendment) Rules 1985, which amended the Magistrates' Courts (Forms) Rules 1981.

Code B on Entry, Search and Seizure

Further requirements concerning the obtaining and execution of search warrants are laid down in Code B for the searching of premises and the seizure of property. Code B does not apply however to routine scenes of crime searches nor to searches following the activation of fire or burglar alarms or calls to a fire or a burglary made by the occupier or bomb threat calls. (Code B, para. 1.3.) It also does not apply to searches under a statutory power to enter and search premises without any requirement of reasonable grounds to suspect that an offence has been committed (Code B, para. 1.3B). It does however apply to searches under sections 17, 18 and 32 of PACE—see below—and to searches under warrant under section 1 and Schedule 1 of PACE or section 15 or Schedule 7 of the Prevention of Terrorism (Temporary Provisions) Act 1989.

Inspector's authority

The code requires first that police officers check their information carefully before applying for a search warrant to ensure that the information is accurate, recent and has not been provided maliciously or irresponsibly. The identity of the informer need not be revealed but an application may not be made on the basis of information from an anonymous source where corroboration has not been sought. Save in an emergency, no request for a warrant should be made without the authority at least of an inspector or, in the case of a production order under Schedule 1 (see p. 28 above and p. 414 below) or under the Prevention of Terrorism legislation, a superintendent (Code B, paras. 2.1–2.4). The Notice of Powers and Rights (see below) provides for the indication of authority for the search on the Notice. If that is not practicable, it should be indicated elsewhere. Thus if the search is of an arrested person's premises under section 18 it could be indicated on the custody record form.[89] The details of the authorisation should however be given *verbally* to the officer in charge of the search and a proper record be made of the fact.[90] If there is reason to believe that a search "might have an adverse effect on relations between the police and the community", the local police community liaison officer should be consulted, save in urgent cases where he ought to be informed as soon as practicable (Code B, para. 2.5). In such cases, the local police/community consultative group (where it exists) or its equivalent, should equally be informed after a search (Code B, note 2B). If the application is refused, no further applications may be made for a warrant to search those premises unless there are fresh grounds (para. 2.8).

Superintendent's authority for a search of premises

It should be noted that the Act, Schedule 7 repealed section 26(2) of the Theft Act 1968 which gave a superintendent the power to grant written authority for a search for stolen goods. But the power of a superintendent to issue written orders of search under section 73 of the Explosives Act 1875 (to search for explosives in cases of emergency) and under section 9(2) of the Official Secrets Act 1911 (to search for evidence of breaches of s.1 of the Act in cases of great emergency that in the interests of the State make immediate action necessary) were not affected and therefore remain.

Occupier's consent

Where it is proposed to search with the consent of the owner or occupier of the premises in question (there being no search warrant or arrest) the

---

[89] Home Office Circular 15/1991, para. 7.
[90] *ibid.* para. 8.

police are required if it is practicable to get consent in writing on a Notice of Powers and Rights (see below) before the search takes place. The officer must satisfy himself that the person who gives consent has power to do so (Code B, paras. 4.1). An important addition to Code B in the 1991 revision was that an officer does not have a power to search premises "with consent" if the consent has been given under duress or "is subsequently withdrawn before the search is completed" (para. 4.3). Consent, in other words, can be first granted and later validly withdrawn.

The person who is the occupier need not have entire control over the premises. He could for instance be a statutory tenant,[91] a student in a university hall,[92] or even possibly someone who had no right to be on the premises at all, such as a squatter.[93] But in the case of a lodging house or similar accommodation a search should not be made on the basis solely of the landlord's consent unless the tenant, lodger or occupier is unavailable and the matter is urgent (note 4A).

Before getting written consent the police officer has to explain the purpose of the proposed search and inform the person concerned that he is not obliged to consent and that anything seized may be produced in evidence. If the person is not suspected of an offence, the officer should say so (para. 4.2). The notes for guidance accompanying this rule state, "In the case of a lodging house or similar accommodation a search should not be made on the basis solely of the landlord's consent unless the tenant, lodger or occupier is unavailable and the matter is urgent" (note 4A).

There is no necessity to seek consent however where to do so would "cause disproportionate inconvenience to the person concerned" (para. 4.4). This is intended to apply to situations where innocent occupiers would agree and indeed expect the police to act—for instance to make a quick check of gardens in the pursuit of a thief at night to see whether he is hiding there or has discarded stolen articles as he ran away (note 4C).

Notice of Powers and Rights

A new provision in 1991 was for a notice to be given to the occupier *whenever a search is to be made under Code B*. The notice is in a standard format (Code B, 5.7). It (i) specifies whether the search is made under warrant or with consent or under sections 17, 18 or 32 of the Act; (ii) summarises the powers of search and seizure in the Act; (iii) explains the rights of the occupier and of anyone whose property is taken as a result of search; (iv) explains that compensation may be payable in appropriate cases for damage caused in entering and searching premises and giving the address to which an application for compensation should be sent; and (v) states that a copy of Code B can be consulted at any police station.

The notice is not itself an authority to search, nor does it replace the search warrant where one is required.

If the occupier is present, the notice together with the warrant if the search is under warrant, should be given to him before the search, unless the officer in charge reasonably believes that to do so would frustrate the object of the

[91] *Brown v. Minister of Housing and Local Government* [1953] 1 W.L.R. 1370.
[92] *R. v. Tao* [1976] 3 W.L.R. 25.
[93] *R. v. Josephs and Christie* (1977) 65 Cr.App.R. 253.

search or endanger police officers. If the occupier is not there, the notice and a copy of the warrant should be left in a prominent place on the premises (Code B, 5.8).

Conduct of searches

Paragraph 5.9 of Code B states the general proposition already referred to that premises may be searched only to the extent necessary to achieve the object of the search "having regard to the size and nature of whatever is sought". A search under warrant may not continue under the authority of the warrant once the items specified in the warrant have been found (*ibid.*).

Where premises are entered by force, no more than the reasonably necessary degree of force should be used (Code B, 5.10). Searches must be conducted "with due consideration for the property and privacy of the occupier searched and with no more disturbance than necessary" (*ibid.*). If the occupier wishes to have a friend to witness the search he should be allowed to do so unless the officer in charge reasonably believes that this would seriously hinder the investigation or endanger the officers or other people (para. 5.11).

If premises have been entered by force the officer in charge is required to satisfy himself before leaving them that they are secure (para. 5.12).

If the wrong premises are searched by mistake "everything possible should be done at the earliest opportunity to allay any sense of grievance". In appropriate cases assistance should be given to obtain compensation (note 5C).

Special procedure material

A search under warrant for "special procedure" material (*i.e.* one for confidential material authorised by a circuit judge after an application under Sched. 1 to the Act[94]), must be under the authority of an inspector or above who must be there at the time. The officer would be responsible to ensure "that the search is conducted with discretion and in such a manner as to cause the least possible disruption to any business or other activities carried on in the premises" (para. 5.13).

The officer should ask the person in charge of the premises to produce the special procedure material in question. He may also ask to see any index to files and may inspect any files which according to the index appear to contain any of the material sought. But a more extensive search of the premises can only be made if access to the material sought is refused or if it appears that the index is inaccurate or incomplete, or if "for any other reason the officer in charge has reasonable grounds to believe that such a search is necessary in order to find the material sought" (para. 5.14).

Record

Full records must be made of the details of the search and of what is taken (Code B, para. 7.1). If a search is under warrant it must be returned to the

---

[94] The same applies to searches for excluded or special procedure material authorised under Schedule 7 to the Prevention of Terrorism (Temporary Provisions) Act 1989.

court that issued it, endorsed to show whether any of the articles specified in the warrant were found, whether any other articles were seized, the date, duration and time of execution and the names of the officers who executed it (paras. 7.2 and 7.3). Under the Northern Ireland PACE Order, Art. 18(9) the return must be made to the clerk of the petty sessions for the district in which the *premises* are situated).

Entry for purpose of arrest, etc.: section 17[95]

Section 17 makes comprehensive provision for the circumstances in which the police may enter premises in order to effect an arrest (premises for these purposes include vehicles). It does not however affect statutory provisions giving the police the power to enter premises without a warrant other than to make an arrest.[96]

Subsection (1) gives the police the power to enter and to search for any of the following purposes:

(a) (i) To execute a warrant of arrest in connection with or arising out of criminal proceedings. This follows the existing common law. The Home Office Circular on PACE said of this subsection that it was "deliberately widely drawn". It would for instance enable entry to be made to search for someone wanted under a warrant for non-payment of a fine (p. 8 above, para. 8).

(ii) To execute a warrant committing a fine defaulter to prison when magistrates have issued a warrant under section 76 of the Magistrates' Court Act 1980. This removes the doubt as to whether an entry was lawful to execute a warrant of commitment for failure to pay a fine or maintenance order.

(b) To arrest a person for an arrestable offence. The category of arrestable offence (defined in s.24(1) and (2); see p. 66 below) is slightly wider than under the previous law.

(c) To arrest for some offences under the Public Order Act 1936 or the Criminal Law Act 1977. These powers follow the provisions of section 26(2) (which with Sched. 2 *inter alia* preserves an unqualified power of arrest without warrant of anyone reasonably suspected of being in the act of committing an offence under ss.1, 4 or 5 of the Public Order Act 1986), and section 11 of the Criminal Law Act 1977. The Criminal Law Act powers (which relate to the offences of entering or remaining on property) can only be exercised by a constable in uniform (subs. 3). The power of arrest now extends also to a person who fails to comply with an interim possession order made against squatters under the Criminal Justice and Public Order Act 1994— "CJPOA" Schedule 10, para. 53(a).

(d) To recapture someone unlawfully at large whom he is pursuing. This reproduces the common law power. It includes those who have escaped from a prison, or a court or the police and those who have

---

[95] See N.I. PACE Order, Art. 19.
[96] *e.g.* under the Gaming Act 1968, s.43(2) or the Misuse of Drugs Act 1971, s.23(1), which are set out in Tables 5.2 and 6 in Apps. 5 and 6 of the *Law and Procedure Volume* of the Royal Commission's Report.

absconded from detention in mental hospitals or other institutions of compulsory detention. But the power only applies to cases of "hot" or at least "warm" pursuit.[97] Otherwise, unless the occupier consents or (b) above applies, the police would have to get a warrant of arrest. (In the equivalent provision in the Northern Ireland Order, the definition of "unlawfully at large" was to be extended in 1996 to include someone who has escaped from a prison or other listed institution— see Appendix 4, p. 532 below [Art. 4].

(e) To save life or limb or prevent serious damage to property. This restates the common law in relation to the premises entered. Strictly construed, the subsection would seem to permit entry of premises because of risks to persons or property on *other* premises or elsewhere not on premises at all but this interpretation is probably not sound.

Subsection (2) states that, save when the entry is under (e) above, a constable can only exercise these powers if he has reasonable grounds for believing that the person sought is on those premises.[98] In the case of a block of flats the power to enter and search only applies to the actual flat in which he is suspected to be, and any common parts. There would be no power without a warrant to search all the flats or a number of them.

Subsection (4) states that the search must be consistent with the purpose of the entry to make an arrest. A general search of the premises would therefore be unlawful. But once an arrest has been made, a search under sections 18 or 32 for evidence of the offence for which the person was arrested would presumably be lawful.

The only common law power of entry without a warrant that remains now is that to deal with or to prevent a breach of the peace. But before exercising the power the police must have a genuine belief that there was a real and imminent risk of a breach of the peace occurring and must act with great care and discretion.[99] (There is no requirement that the breach of the peace be serious. All the rest are abolished (subss. (5) and (6)).

Entry and search after arrest: section 18[1]

For some time prior to PACE it had been assumed that the police had power to search the home of an arrested person at least for evidence connected with the crime for which he was arrested; see especially dicta in *Jeffrey v. Black*.[2] But in *McLorie v. Oxford*,[3] the Divisional Court held, somewhat surprisingly, that the police had no right to enter the premises of a

---

[97] *D'Souza v. D.P.P.* [1992] 1 W.L.R. 1073 (H.L.), which concerned entry of premises to recapture someone who had discharged herself from a mental hospital where she had been taken under a warrant issued under s.135 of the Mental Health Act 1983. Held forcible entry to recapture her was not lawful even though she was "unlawfully at large" because there was no evidence that she was someone who was being pursued. It may be however that an escaped prisoner *is* by definition being pursued within the meaning of the concept whether or not officers are actually out looking for him.

[98] For cases on what is meant by reasonable grounds for suspicion see *Kynaston v. D.P.P.*; *Heron (Joseph) v. D.P.P.*; *Heron (Tracey) v. D.P.P.* (1988) 87 Cr.App.R. 200; *Castorina v. Chief Constable of Surrey*, The Times, June 15, 1988.

[99] *McLeod v. Commissioner of Police of the Metropolis* [1994] 4 All E.R. 553 C.A.

[1] See N.I. PACE Order, Art. 20.

[2] [1978] 1 Q.B. 490 (Div.Ct.).

[3] [1982] Q.B. 1290.

person arrested for attempted murder to search for the motorcar which it was alleged had been the weapon used. (The decision was especially striking since the accused had actually been arrested on those same premises, but the police had taken him away and then later wanted to come back to pursue their inquiries.)

The 1929 Royal Commission on the police said that the police commonly searched the home of an arrested person and that the position should be regularised by law. The Philips Royal Commission took the same view, subject to the proviso that a search of the arrested person's premises (or vehicle) should only be permitted where there were reasonable grounds for suspicion that relevant evidence might be found there. Search of any other premises should require a warrant. Also, in order to reduce the risk of "fishing expeditions" the decision to search and the reasons should be recorded prior to the search.[4]

This broadly was the scheme adopted in PACE. It gives a police officer power to enter and search "any premises occupied or controlled by a person who is under arrest for an arrestable offence, if he has reasonable grounds for suspecting that there is on the premises evidence (other than items subject to legal privilege) that relates (a) to that offence; or (b) to some other arrestable offence which is connected with or similar to that offence" (subs. (1)). This reversed the decision in *McLorie v. Oxford.*

If the police suspect that evidence of other unconnected offences may be found on the premises, their only recourse is to get a search warrant or to get the householder's consent to a search. This would apply equally if the arrest was not for an arrestable offence (as defined in section 24).

A search of a person's home after an arrest normally requires the written authority of an inspector or above (subs. (4)). In *Badham*[5] it was held that this meant that the inspector must create an independent document setting out his authorisation. The crown court quashed a conviction by magistrates because the inspector had merely written down a confirmation of his oral authorisation. This was not sufficient.

It has been suggested[6] that the authorisation should state: (1) the name of the arrested person; (2) the nature of the offence for which he was arrested; (3) the grounds for suspecting that the evidence is on the premises; (4) the nature of the offence to which the evidence is thought to relate; (5) the address of the premises; (6) the fact that the premises are occupied or controlled by the arrested person, and (7) the name and rank of the authorising officer. Unless it is not practicable the authorisation should be given on the Notice of Power and Rights (p. 47 above)—Code B, para. 3.3.

Subsection (5) makes an exception to the requirement when the arrested person is taken straight to his home rather than to the police station (see s.30 below); in which case there might not be any way of getting prior written authority. If this is not obtained in advance, a report must be made after the event to an officer of that rank (subs. (6)). In either case the inspector must make a written record of the grounds for the search and the nature of the evidence sought (subss. (7)–(8)). Again, a search must not go beyond what is reasonably required to discover the evidence in question. No general search is permitted (subs. (3)).

---

[4] Philips Report, para. 3.12.
[5] [1987] Crim.L.R. 202 (Cr.Ct.).
[6] D.J. Feldman, *The Law Relating to Entry, Search and Seizure* 1986, Butterworths, p. 18.

As will be seen below (p. 79) section 32 gives the police a power to enter premises after an arrest but that power is only available more or less at the time of arrest. In *Badham* the entry was made three hours later. It was held that section 32 could not apply. It seems that the police use section 18 far more frequently than section 32.[7]

Seizure of articles: section 19[8]; Code B, section 6

One of the most troublesome problems regarding police powers is the extent of the power to seize articles found in the course of a search. At common law, prior to PACE, where the search was under warrant the police could seize anything they found which was or which they reasonably believed to be covered by the warrant.[9] If the search was not under warrant the common law had developed to the point of permitting seizure of evidence where:

(i) it implicated the owner or occupier of the premises searched in the offence for which the search was conducted[10];
(ii) it implicated the owner or occupier in some other offence[11];
(iii) it implicated third persons in the same offence for which the search was conducted[12]; or
(iv) it was taken from someone innocent of involvement in the crime where his refusal to hand it over was wholly unreasonable.[13]

The Philips Royal Commission said that "it defies common sense to expect the police not to seize items incidentally found during the course of a search".[14] At the same time "the risk that premises may be ransacked as soon as a warrant is granted for any offence must be minimised".[15] The old law was "uncertain and of little help in this respect".[16]

The Commission said it wished to avoid legitimising general searches. So the police should only be permitted to seize items found incidentally if they were evidence of a grave offence and then only if the search was carried out lawfully—in accordance with the terms of the warrant and in a manner appropriate to the items being searched for. Items seized otherwise could not be used in evidence.

The Act however defined the power of seizure very much more broadly. It provides that where a constable is searching premises under statutory

---

[7] Ken Lidstone, *op. cit.* n.71 above, p. 355, n.67 reported that in a survey of two city forces s.18 accounted for some 75 per cent, compared with 2 per cent under s.32 and 6 per cent under s.17. Another study, carried out by Professor Keith Bottomley and colleagues found that searches after arrest under s.18 constituted about two thirds of all recorded searches and that they had increased significantly since PACE. In fact s.18 searches had become almost routine in certain types of cases. Only 15 per cent of recorded searches were with consent. Searches under warrant were one in eight of those recorded. See Bottomley *et al.* (1991).
[8] See N.I. PACE Order, Art. 21.
[9] *Chic Fashions (West Wales) Ltd v. Jones* [1968] 2 Q.B. 299 C.A.
[10] *Ghani v. Jones* [1968] 2 Q.B. 299 C.A.; *Garfinkel v. Metropolitan Police Commissioner* [1972] Crim.L.R. 44; *Frank Truman Export Ltd v. Metropolitan Police Commissioner* [1977] Q.B. 952.
[11] *ibid.*
[12] *Ghani v. Jones* [1968] 2 Q.B. 299 C.A.
[13] *ibid.*
[14] Philips Report, para. 3.48.
[15] *ibid.*
[16] *ibid.*

powers or by consent he may seize anything on the premises (other than something exempted from seizure) if he reasonably believes that it is evidence in relation to an offence which he is investigating *or any other offence* and that it is necessary to seize it in order to prevent it being concealed, lost, altered or destroyed (s.19(3)(b)) or that it has been obtained in consequence of the commission of an offence; in which case the reasons for seizure also include the possible damage of the material seized. (This difference between s.19(2)(b) and (3)(b) looks like a drafting oversight.) Items exempted from seizure are those reasonably believed to be subject to legal professional privilege (subs. (6)). Excluded material could therefore be seized even though it is usually exempt from a search warrant.

When seizable material is stored in a computer the police officer may require it to be produced in a form in which it is visible and legible (subs. (4)).

The section differs from the recommendation of the Philips Royal Commission in not being limited to grave offences. Indeed it is not even limited to serious arrestable offences.

As will be seen below, the Act also did not give effect to the Philips Royal Commission's view that evidence seized in the course of an unlawfully conducted search should be inadmissible. On the other hand, the section went beyond what the Commission recommended in permitting seizure only if the evidence would otherwise be concealed, lost or destroyed—though this is not likely to prove much of a safeguard since presumably the police would almost always be able to claim that this condition was fulfilled. This condition does not apply, however, if the item to be seized is the very one for which a search under warrant was authorised. Sections 8(2), 18(2), 32(8) and Schedule 1, para. 13 give the police an unqualified right to seize anything for which a search was authorised. The condition in section 19 as to what can be seized only applies to *other* items found in the course of the search.

The section extends the common law by permitting seizure of the fruits of crime and the evidence of crime regardless of the crime and of who is implicated. It applies to seizure from suspects and non-suspects alike.

Because of the broad scope of the seizure power it appears that the power of search has also been broadened.[17] The insistence since *Entick v. Carrington*[18] in 1765 that general warrants are unlawful must therefore be qualified by the knowledge that once the police have entered premises lawfully it is difficult to hold them to a search restricted to the specific purpose of the search. The only serious restraint is the requirement in section 16(8) that a search under warrant must be carried out in a manner consistent with the items being looked for and in Code B, paragraph 5.9 which states that "premises may be searched only to the extent necessary to achieve the object of the search having regard to the size and nature of whatever is sought". This appears to apply to searches of all premises.

Where an officer decides not to seize an item because of an appropriate explanation given by the person holding it (but he has reasonable grounds for believing that it has been obtained in consequence of the commission of an offence by someone) he should inform the holder of his suspicions and explain that if he disposes of the property he may be liable to civil or criminal proceedings (Code B, para. 6.3).

---

[17] On the former common law see for instance *Chic Fashions (West Wales) Ltd v. Jones* [1968] 2 Q.B. 299 C.A.; *Ghani v. Jones* [1970] 1 Q.B. 693 C.A.
[18] (1765) 19 St. Tr. 1030.

Extension of powers of seizure to computerised information: section 20[19]; Code B, paragraph 6.5

Section 20 simply extends the powers of seizure available in any act (including any passed after the 1984 Act) to enable the police to require that information contained in a computer be produced in a form in which it can be taken away and in which it is visible and legible. The police in other words can legitimately object if they are simply handed a floppy disc. In some situations it might be appropriate to secure the computer in order to make sure that a print-out is produced before it can be destroyed or tampered with.

Seized articles: access and copying: section 21[20]; Code B, section 6

Section 21 makes provision for access to property held by the police. There were no previous statutory rules on the subject. The provisions of section 21 apply not only to property seized under section 19 but also to that seized under all other provisions in the Act or any other Act.

Subsection (1) states that a person who can show that he was the occupier of premises from which items have been seized by the police or that he had custody or control immediately before the seizure may request that he be given a record of what was taken and such a request shall be complied with. The record must be supplied within a reasonable time (subs. (2) and Code B, 6.8).

Subject to subsection (8), if requested to do so, the investigating officer shall grant that person or someone acting on his behalf, access to such items under the supervision of a police officer (subs. (3) and Code B, 6.9). Similarly and again subject to subsection (8), the investigating officer should either allow that person or someone acting on his behalf access under supervision for the purpose of photographing or copying the items or should have the items photographed or copied for him (subs. (4)).

Photographs or copies made under subsection (4) should then be supplied to the person who made the request within a reasonable time (subss. (6) and (7)). The caveat in subsection (8) is that there is no duty to grant access to the material or to allow its copying where the officer in charge of the investigation has reasonable grounds for believing that to do so would prejudice the investigation of that offence or of other offences or any criminal proceedings.

A challenge against an allegedly wrongful refusal of access under these provisions should be by way of judicial review.[21] The same is the case where the applicant seeks to correct an error by the Crown Court judge.[22]

---

[19] See N.I. PACE Order, Art. 22.
[20] See N.I. PACE Order, Art. 23. See also Drug Trafficking Offences Act 1986, s.29.
[21] *Allen and others v. Chief Constable of Cheshire, The Times*, July 16, 1988 C.A.
[22] *R. v. Liverpool Crown Court, ex p. Wimpey plc* [1991] Crim.L.R. 635 (Div.Ct.).

Retention of seized articles: section 22[23]; Code B, section 6.6

At common law the police could retain items seized for such time as is reasonable in all the circumstances. The Act provides the same power with somewhat more detail.

Subject to subsection (4), anything which has been seized by a police officer in a lawful search and seizure (see below) may be retained[24] so long as is necessary in all the circumstances. In particular anything seized for the purposes of a criminal investigation may be held by the police for use as evidence at the trial or for forensic examination or for investigation in connection with any offence (subs. (2)(a)). It may also be retained in order to establish its true owner where there are reasonable grounds for believing that it has been obtained as the result of the commission of a criminal offence (subs. (2)(b)).

If, however, the police seize something on the ground that it may be used to cause physical injury or damage to property or to interfere with evidence, or to assist an escape, it cannot be kept by the police once the person from whom it was taken has been released from custody (subs. (3)).

No article may be retained by the police if a photograph or a copy would suffice for their purposes (subs. (4)). Subsection (5) preserves the provisions of section 1 of the Police (Property) Act 1897. If someone from whom the police have seized something thinks that it has been retained too long he may make an application to the courts under the 1897 Act, which empowers a magistrates' court to "... make an order for the delivery of the property [held by the police] to the person appearing to the magistrate or court to be the owner thereof". Such applications can be made "by an officer of police or by a claimant of the property". If the search or seizure was unlawful the documents or other material seized must be returned—*R. v. Chief Constable of Lancashire, ex p. Parker and Magrath.*[25]

Note that section 22(5) does not apply to the customs and excise. Most of the 1984 Act was applied to the customs by the Police and Criminal Evidence Act 1984 (Application to Customs and Excise) Order 1985 (S.I. 1985/1800) (For text of which see Appendix 2 below) but section 22(5) was one of the exceptions.

Nor can someone whose property has been seized by the customs use for aid section 1 of the Police (Property) Act 1897, since that Act only applies to property in the possession of the police.

Section 48 of the Magistrates' Courts Act 1980 relates to the return of property taken from an accused person on his arrest, or after an arrest warrant or summons has been issued. It requires the police to report to the court what property has been seized. The court is then given a discretion as to whether the property, or any part of it, should be returned to the accused. But again this does not apply to seizures by the customs and excise.

In *R. v. Southampton Magistrates' Court, ex p. Newman*[26] the Divisional

---

[23] See N.I. PACE Order, Art. 24. See also Drug Trafficking Offences Act 1986, s.29.

[24] The word "retained" permits a customs officer to retain material as long as is permitted by the Drug Trafficking Act 1986. The material can also be made available to foreign law enforcement agencies by copying, but the seized material itself must be retained by the officer. (*R. v. Southwark Crown Court, ex p. Customs and Excise Comrs., R. v. Same, ex p. Bank of Credit and Commerce International SA* [1990] 1 Q.B. 650 (Div.Ct.).)

[25] [1993] 2 All E.R. 56 (Div.Ct.).

[26] (1988) 152 J.P. 664.

Court, said that this was an anomaly which should be "speedily disposed of" by the legislature. There was so much activity these days by customs and excise in the investigation of drugs offences that a magistrates' court should have power to deal effectively at any time with applications for restoration of seized property. (In that case the customs were still retaining eight address books.)

The only recourse in this situation, the Divisional Court said, was the inherent jurisdiction of the magistrates who could to some extent control their own procedure. So, if an accused person could not prepare his defence without access to certain documents the court could adjourn or refuse to go ahead unless the police or customs handed over the material. Alternatively, a civil action could be brought.

Interpretation: section 23[27]

Section 23 defines "premises", a definition which is very broad. It includes "any place" and, in particular, any vehicle, vessel, aircraft or hovercraft, any offshore installation and any tent or movable structure. The Home Office Circular on PACE (p. 8 above) stated however that although theoretically "any place" could mean any open air site, it ought to be restricted to something that is capable of being premises in the ordinary sense of the word ("That is, it should be a distinct piece of land in single occupation or ownership" (para. 10)).

Note however that the meaning of the word "premises" as used in the Codes of Practice is determined not by section 23 but by section 66 which requires that the Home Secretary issue Codes of Practice in regard to "(c) searches of premises by police officers; and (d) the seizure of property found by police officers on persons or premises." The word "premises" there is seemingly governed by section 23, but the word "premises" as used in the codes is technically not so tied.

The Home Office Circular (p. 8 above, para. 53) suggested that the word "premises" in Code C should be given a meaning which "conforms to common usage". But the 1991 revised Code B stated that "premises" for the purposes of the Code is defined in section 23 of PACE and "includes any place" (para. 1.3).

QUESTIONS AND ANSWERS

ENTRY AND SEARCH OF PREMISES, SEIZURE OF PROPERTY

1. In what circumstances can police enter upon premises without a search warrant?

Normally a search warrant is needed for the police to get into private premises. But there are some exceptions, namely:

(1) Where the occupier consents to entry. This justification of entry was in

---

[27] See N.I. PACE Order, Art. 25.

fact a very common one,[28] but the reality of the consent must sometimes be a matter of some doubt. The Code of Practice on the searching of premises and the seizure of property laid down new rules in regard to the obtaining of consent which are directed to this precise point. There is no current information as to the use made by the police of search of premises by consent post-PACE.

The Code states that consent must be in writing and the occupier must be told that he is not obliged to consent and that anything seized may be used in evidence. If the person in question is not himself suspected of any complicity in the alleged crime he must be told so.

(2) To prevent or to stop a breach of the peace which is imminent or taking place, or to save life or limb or to prevent serious damage to property.

(3) To effect an arrest of someone for whom a warrant of arrest has been issued. The police do not need a separate search warrant.

(4) To arrest someone for an arrestable offence.

(5) Where the police enter to search premises of someone who has been arrested for an arrestable offence, where they have reasonable grounds for believing that they will find evidence of that offence or of some similar or connected offence.

(6) To search the premises in which an arrested person was immediately before his arrest, for evidence relating to that offence but only if the officer has reasonable grounds for believing that such evidence is there.

(7) To recapture an escaped prisoner.

2. In what circumstances can an officer get a search warrant?

There are a variety of statutes, including the Police and Criminal Evidence Act, which allow an application to be made to the justices for a search warrant. A magistrate can, under the Act, grant a search warrant if he is satisfied that there are reasonable grounds to believe that:

(1) a "serious arrestable offence" (p. 296) has been committed;
(2) what is sought is likely to be relevant admissible evidence; and
(3) any one of the following conditions applies:
    (i) that there is no practicable way of contacting someone able to grant entry or to grant access to the evidence; or
    (ii) that entry will only be granted if a warrant is produced; or
    (iii) that the purpose of the search may be frustrated or seriously prejudiced if the officers arrive and are then unable to get in immediately (the occupiers would be alerted and could take steps to make the evidence unavailable).

But there are two exceptional categories where no search warrant can normally be obtained:

---

[28] The first study to produce empirical data about police use of powers of entry and search was published by the Royal Commission on Criminal Procedure in its *Law and Procedure Volume* (Cmnd. 8092–1 (1981)). Ten police forces kept figures for a four-week period in September 1979. The study was not statistically random but the figures based on a total of 341 searches are nevertheless of some interest.

The largest group of all the searches (43 per cent) were after arrest without a warrant. Thirty five per cent were based on a magistrate's warrant, and 13 per cent were made prior to arrest with the consent (explicit or otherwise) of the householder. (See Appendix 7, pp. 126–129.)

1. Items subject to legal professional privilege or

2. Material given special immunity under the 1984 Act—"excluded material"

There is also a category created by the 1984 Act where the material is not immune but where because of its sensitivity a special procedure is required to get a search warrant—*"special procedure material"* (As will be seen below, to complicate matters, in some circumstances "excluded material" does not qualify for full immunity but does have the status of "special procedure material" (see pp. 59–60 below).

3. What is meant by legal professional privilege?

Legal professional privilege covers:
(1) Communications between a professional legal adviser and his client (or anyone representing the client) in connection with the giving of legal advice. This need not be in connection with any pending legal proceedings.
(2) Communications between the lawyer and his client (or anyone representing the client) or between the lawyer or the client or the representative and anyone else in connection with actual or pending legal proceedings.
When legal proceedings are in contemplation or are actually in being, the privilege is therefore broader since it then includes communications to third parties. So documents sent to an accountant, a handwriting expert or even just to a witness would be covered by the privilege if the communication was made "in connection with or in contemplation of legal proceedings and for the purposes of such proceedings".
(3) Anything enclosed with communications under (1) above for the purposes of getting advice or with communications under (2) above in connection with actual or pending legal proceedings is also privileged if it is in the hands of someone entitled to possession.

4. Whose privilege is it?

The privilege is that of the client not the lawyer. This means that if the material is not privileged it cannot become privileged by the simple expedient of being sent to the lawyer. On the other hand, the client can release the privilege even if the lawyer does not agree.

5. Does the privilege apply if the documents are evidence of a crime?

The law does not prevent the police from getting a search warrant to seek evidence of a conspiracy between lawyer and client. The 1984 Act states that "items held with the intention of furthering a criminal purpose are not items subject to legal privilege". Nor would there be any privilege if the client, or a third person who is "using" the client, has a criminal purpose in seeking advice unbeknown to the solicitor.

6. What about if the client has a criminal purpose of which the lawyer knows nothing?

The privilege is lost by virtue of the fact that the client has sent the documents to the lawyer in order to further a criminal purpose.

7. What is included in the category of "excluded material"?

There are three types of "excluded material":

(1) personal records;
(2) journalistic material;
(3) human tissues or tissue fluid taken for the purpose of diagnosis or medical treatment.

8. What do they cover?

(1) *"Personal records"*: are those acquired in the course of a trade, business, profession or other occupation and held in confidence. They must be documents or records that make it possible to identify individuals and which relate to their physical or mental health (*e.g.* medical or psychiatric records); or spiritual counselling or help (*e.g.* the files of priests or clergymen); or counselling or help given for the purposes of the individual's personal welfare by any voluntary agency or by an individual who has responsibility for the person's personal welfare (such as a university or school careers adviser, social worker, or volunteer advisory agency such as a Citizens' Advice Bureau).

(2) *"Journalistic material"* covers anything which comes into existence or is acquired for the purposes of journalism providing it is in the hands of a person who either acquired or created it for that purpose. This would cover for instance the contents of the journalist's notebook, or documents sent to a journalist with a view to their being considered for publication. Once it passes out of the possession of someone who acquired it or created it for the purposes of journalism it ceases to be "excluded material" though, as will be seen, it can still be "special procedure material".

There is no need for the journalism to be of any very exalted kind to attract the total immunity. The Act does not define what is meant by journalism but it covers any form of the activity however humble, paid or unpaid. It is not clear to what extent it would be held to cover the writers of books.

(3) *"Human tissue or tissue fluid"* are not further defined and seem to be reasonably unproblematic.

9. In what circumstances must access to material be sought from a judge rather than from a magistrate?

The 1984 Act establishes two basic types of "special procedure material", access to which can only be sought from a judge. If and in so far as the previous law already permitted the police to get a search warrant for anything that is now defined as "excluded material", it becomes "special procedure material" and application for access must be made to a circuit judge. In other words the term "excluded material" covers two different categories of material. One is material covered by any of the definitions of excluded material for which the police could search prior to 1984 say, under the Theft Act or the Official Secrets Act. The Act does not give such material immunity but it does require the special procedure of an application to the judge. However, anything covered by the definition of excluded material for which the police had no legal right to seek access prior to the 1984 Act now gains complete immunity from a production order (unless it is sought as part of an enquiry into a terrorism offence). Secondly, the Act requires an application to a circuit judge for material held on a confidential basis, for instance by a bank. It is special procedure material if it is held in confidence by someone who acquired or created it in the course of a trade, business, profession or other occupation or for the purpose of any paid or unpaid office.

10. What form does the application to the judge take?

An application to the judge is made under Schedule I to the Act. The person against whom the order is sought must be given advance notice of the hearing and is entitled to attend—though often he does not do so. But this does not apply where advance notice of the application might "seriously prejudice the investigation". Another exception to the principle is where it proves impossible to find anyone to grant access to the premises or to the material sought.

The normal application under Schedule I is for an order requiring the person concerned to produce the material in question to the police within seven days so that they can take it away or to give them access to it. It is not an application for a search warrant.

But a search warrant can be obtained in two situations. One is where the material could have been the subject of a search warrant before the 1984 Act and an order to give the police access to the material has been disobeyed. The other is where the application by the police was for a search warrant in the first place because advance notice of the hearing would have seriously prejudiced the investigation. This would be the case where the police were able to satisfy the judge that there was good reason to suspect that the person who had the material was himself implicated in the crime.

When the material could have been the subject of a search warrant under the previous law the judge must grant the application for an "order to produce", providing he is satisfied that the issue of the warrant under the old law would have been appropriate. It does not appear what tests the judges should apply to determine this question.

But such cases will be very rare since there were hardly any statutes that authorised search warrants for what is now termed "excluded material". If the police want access to "excluded material" it will almost always come under the new rules which require the judge to be satisfied that there are reasonable grounds for believing that:

(1) a serious arrestable offence (see p. 296) has been committed;
(2) material of the kind sought is on the premises;
(3) it would be likely to be of substantial value to the investigation of the offence in question and would be likely to be relevant admissible evidence;

(4) other means of getting the material have failed or were not tried because it seemed they were bound to fail;

(5) it is in the public interest that the material should be produced having regard both to its value to the investigation and to the circumstances in which it is held.

If a person fails to comply with an order to produce the material or to make it available to the police, the sanction is for the police to return to the judge to ask him to punish the person concerned for contempt. As has been seen, they can only get a search warrant as a remedy for disobedience in the rare case where such a warrant could have been sought before the 1984 Act.

11. What happens if the police want material from premises, some of which requires a warrant from the magistrates and some of which requires an order or a warrant from a judge?

The application must be made to the judge who will then deal with it as a whole.

12. Were the rules in regard to search warrants changed by PACE?

The 1984 Act established a uniform procedure for applying for and executing a search warrant under any past or future act.

(1) This requires a written application stating the grounds on which it is made; the Act under which the warrant would issue; details of the premises in question; and identification "so far as is practicable" of the articles or persons sought.

(2) The application is heard "*ex parte*", *i.e.* with only the police present.

(3) Answers to questions put by the justice of the peace must be given on oath.

(4) The warrant can only be used once. If the police wish to return to the premises they must get another warrant, unless the occupier is prepared to give consent.

(5) There must be two copies of the warrant, one for the person whose premises are to be searched.

(6) The warrant must be executed within a month. If it is not, and the police wish to try again, another warrant must be obtained.

(7) Entry and search under a warrant should be at a reasonable hour unless it appears to the constable executing it that the purpose of a search may be frustrated on an entry at a reasonable hour. (This seems to leave sufficient scope for the dawn raid in cases where it is thought to be necessary. It is left to the judgment of the officer concerned. Providing he reaches his decision honestly it could not be unlawful even if it was unreasonable.)

The Code of Practice on the searching of premises and the seizure of property (Code B) lays down further rules in regard to the obtaining of a search warrant.

The code requires an officer, before applying for a search warrant, to check his information carefully. No such application should be made (save in an emergency) without the approval of an inspector or above. If there is any risk of the search having adverse effects on community relations, contact should be made, if there is time, with the police community liaison officer.

13. What rules govern the process of getting into the premises to be searched?

The rules derive partly from the Act and partly from Code B.

The 1984 Act states that if the person whose premises are to be searched under warrant is there, the officer must identify himself. If he is not in uniform he must produce documentary evidence that he is a police officer. He must produce the search warrant and give the occupier a copy. If the person named is not there but someone else who appears to be in charge is present, then he should be told instead. (If entry is gained by force or subterfuge, the officer must identify himself and show the occupier his warrant as soon as practicably possible.) If there is no one there at all, the search may be carried out but a copy of the warrant must be left in a prominent place on the premises.

Code B requires the police to give the occupier a notice of Powers and Rights explaining what powers have been exercised and why. This is in addition to showing him the warrant. The officer must explain the purpose of the search and that the person concerned need not consent.

If the search is one to which the Code applies the police must supply the occupier with a notice specifying whether the search is made under warrant or with consent or in the exercise of other statutory powers. The notice must summarise the powers of search and seizure under the Act, must explain the rights of the occupier and of the owner of property seized and it must state that a copy of the Code is available to be consulted at any police station.

14. Can the occupier's consent be withdrawn after it has been given?

Yes. Consent can be withdrawn at any time. Code B (para. 4.3) states that an officer does not have a power to search premises with consent if the consent is given under duress or "is withdrawn before the search is completed".

15. Once in the premises, what can the police search for?

If the search is under warrant, they must stick to the terms of the warrant and search only for what it authorises. This means that the manner of the search must be determined by what is being sought. A search for large items will obviously be restricted in a way that a search for something very small is not.

If the entry is without a warrant (see pp. 56–57 above for a list of the situations in which that is possible) the search will normally be for a person and must be limited to what is reasonable in such a search. Where the search is of the premises after an arrest, as has been seen, it can only be for evidence of the offence or a similar or connected offence.

Code B states that a search may not continue after the police have found what they came to find. It must also cease when it is clear that the items for which the police are looking are not there.

16. How should a search be made?

The Code states "Searches must be conducted with due consideration for the property and privacy of the occupier of the premises searched and with no more disturbance than is necessary. Reasonable force may only be used where this is necessary" (para. 5.9). If the occupier wishes to have a friend with him to witness the search this should be allowed unless the officer in charge has reasonable grounds for believing that this would seriously hinder the search. But a search need not be delayed for the purpose.

At the end of the search the premises should be left secure.

Where the search is under Schedule 1 for special procedure material the police are required to exercise particular circumspection (see Code B, paras. 5.13–5.14, below). An officer of the rank of inspector should take over the search and be present. He is responsible for seeing that the search is carried out with discretion. He should ask for the documents which he is seeking. He can also ask for the index to files held on the premises. A more extensive search is only permitted if the person responsible for the premises refuses to produce the material sought or to allow access to the index of files, or if for some other reason the officer in charge has reasonable grounds for believing that such a search is necessary to find the material sought.

17. To what kinds of searches does Code B apply?

The Code applies to the following searches:

(1) any search of premises for the purpose of an investigation of an alleged offence, with the occupier's consent, other than routine searches at the scene of the crime or searches following the activation of fire or burglar alarms;
(2) searches of premises under the power conferred by sections 17, 18 and 32 of PACE;
(3) searches of premises under a search warrant granted under section 15 of or Schedule 1 to PACE. Section 15 applies to search warrants under any legislation.

The Code of Practice also applies to searches of premises under a search warrant issued under section 15 or Schedule 7 to the Prevention of Terrorism (Temporary Provisions) Act 1989.

18. What can be seized during a search?

The police can seize anything (including "excluded" material and "special procedure" material) they come across in the course of a lawful search which is covered by any warrant or which they have reasonable grounds for believing is either evidence of any offence or has been obtained in consequence of the commission of an offence (such as the proceeds of a robbery). The only exception is anything covered by legal professional privilege, which is wholly immune from seizure.

19. What access must be given to the person from whom the material has been seized?

The person from whom the material has been taken should, if he asks for it, be given a record of what has been seized within a reasonable time. If he requests access to the material or permission to copy or photograph it, this should be allowed (or he should be given police-made copies or photographs) unless the officer in charge of the case reasonably considers that it would prejudice the investigation of any offence or any criminal proceedings.

20. How long can material seized in a search be held?

Items may be held by the police as long as is necessary—for instance for forensic examination or for use as evidence at a trial or for return to the true owner.

21. Must the police make any reports or returns about the success or otherwise of a search of premises?

The Act requires that where a search is conducted under a warrant the officer to whom it was issued must endorse on it a statement as to whether it was executed within the one month time limit and, if so, whether the articles sought or any other articles were found. The warrant must then be returned to the court which issued it.

Note—empirical evidence about entry and search powers

For empirical post-PACE evidence on the subject of this chapter see Lidstone (1987), Bottomley *et al.* (1991a), Brown (1991).

PART III

ARREST

The Philips Royal Commission, dealing with arrest, said "there is a lack of clarity and an uneasy and confused mixture of common law and statutory powers of arrest, the latter having grown piecemeal and without any consistent rationale".[1] The Royal Commission said it had two main objectives in its proposals:

> "to restrict the circumstances in which the police can exercise the power to deprive a person of his liberty to those in which it is genuinely necessary ... and to simplify, clarify and rationalise the existing statutory powers of arrest".[2]

The Philips Commission recommended that there should be a statutory definition of the criteria justifying an arrest ("the necessity principle"[3]). It proposed that the definition of arrestable offences should be expanded, in particular to include all offences carrying any sentence of imprisonment.[4] It also recommended that there be a new power given to the police where an officer saw someone committing a non-arrestable offence and he did not know that person's name and address. He should be able to arrest and detain him whilst he discovered his identity.[5] The Commission also favoured a new power to detain temporarily anyone found at the scene of a grave incident such as a murder so as to prevent possible suspects or witnesses from leaving. The power would allow persons to be held while names and addresses were obtained, a suspect was identified or the matter was otherwise resolved.[6]

The Government did not, however, accept all the Royal Commission's recommendations. In particular, the Government thought the definition of arrestable offences proposed by the Philips Commission was to wide but that the definition of the power to arrest for non-arrestable offences was too narrow.

[1] Philips Report, para. 3.68.
[2] *ibid.* para. 3.75.
[3] *ibid.* para. 3.76.
[4] *ibid.* para. 3.83.
[5] *ibid.* para. 3.86.
[6] *ibid.*

Arrest without warrant for arrestable and other offences: section 24[7]

Section 24 starts by providing that the power of arrest for arrestable offences applies (a) to offences for which the penalty is fixed by law (*e.g.* murder and treason); (b) to offences carrying a penalty of five or more years of imprisonment; and (c) to offences in subsection (2).

The result is to extend the concept of arrestable offences to two categories not previously covered. One is common law offences carrying five or more years imprisonment. These were not covered by the definition of arrestable offences in the Criminal Law Act 1967, s.2(1), because that section stated that the penalty had to arise under an enactment.

Some common law offences in question are quite serious. They include kidnapping, attempting to pervert the course of justice, conspiring to defraud and false imprisonment. There was no power of arrest in relation to these offences. The Act made them arrestable. Subsection (2) made into arrestable offences various statutory offences which were not previously "arrestable" (though some did already carry powers of arrest). They include some offences under the Official Secrets Acts (including any provision of the 1989 Act), offences of indecent assault on a woman under section 14 of the Sexual Offences Act 1956 and taking a motor vehicle without authority and going equipped for stealing. The former was already deemed to be an arrestable offence by section 12(3) of the Theft Act 1968 and the latter also carried a power of arrest. Now it became a full arrestable offence carrying the other investigative powers available for arrestable and serious arrestable offences (see below).

The Criminal Justice and Public Order Act 1994 (CJPOA), section 85 added two new arrestable offences: publishing or possessing for publishing for gain obscene matter contrary to section 2 of the Obscene Publications Act 1959[8]; and taking, distributing or showing, possessing with a view to distribution or advertising indecent photographs of children under the age of 16, contrary to section 1 of the Protection of Children Act 1978.[9] Both offences also became serious arrestable offences. The new provisions apply also to Northern Ireland.[10] The CJPOA, section 155 added publishing or distributing written material intended or likely to stir up racial hatred.[11] The CJPOA, section 166(4) added sale of tickets by ticket touts.[12] The CJPOA, section 167(7) added touting for taxi or car hire services.[13]

The power of summary arrest for arrestable offences includes also conspiracy to commit, attempting to commit or inciting, aiding, abetting or procuring any such offence (subs. (3)). Section 24(4)–(7) goes on to reproduce section 2(2)–(5) of the Criminal Law Act 1967, on the circumstances in which arrest without a warrant may be effected on reasonable suspicion that an arrestable offence has been committed, is being committed or is about to be committed.

Powers of arrest are divided into two categories: those which anyone

---

[7] See N.I. PACE Order, Art. 26.
[8] CJPOA, s.85(2).
[9] *ibid.*
[10] CJPOA, s.85(4)(5)(6).
[11] This is now PACE, s.24(2)(i).
[12] This is now PACE, s.24(2)(h).
[13] This is now PACE, s.24(2)(j).

(including a constable) may exercise and those that can be used only by a constable.

Anyone may arrest without a warrant (a) a person who is in the act of committing an arrestable offence; or (b) anyone whom he has reasonable grounds for suspecting to be committing such an offence (s.24(4)).

Where an arrestable offence has been committed, any person may arrest without a warrant:

(a) anyone guilty of the offence; or
(b) anyone whom he has reasonable grounds for suspecting of having committed the offence (s.24(5)).

Note however that this power operates only if an arrestable offence has been committed. In *R. v. Self*[14] D ran away after being accused of shoplifting by a store detective. After a chase he was arrested by a passer-by. He was charged with theft and assault with intent to resist arrest. The jury acquitted him of theft. The Court of Appeal held that he therefore could not be found guilty of assault with intent to resist arrest because the precondition for the application of section 24(5) was not fulfilled.

Where a constable has reasonable grounds for suspecting that an arrestable offence has been committed, he may arrest without a warrant anyone whom he has reasonable grounds for suspecting to be guilty of the offence (s.24(6)). A police officer may also arrest without warrant:

(a) anyone who is about to commit an arrestable offence;
(b) anyone whom he has reasonable grounds for suspecting to be about to commit an arrestable offence (s.24(7)).

The Criminal Law Act 1967, section 2 used the formula "may arrest without a warrant anyone whom he with reasonable cause suspects ..." Here, there was a requirement of actual suspicion.[15] Now in section 24 there is only a requirement that reasonable grounds exist, which raises the question whether the person making the arrest must himself have such suspicion. He may for instance not have directed his mind to the issue of whether an arrestable offence has been committed.

In *Siddiqui v. Swain*[16] the Divisional Court held that the words "has reasonable grounds to suspect" in section 8(5) of the Road Traffic Act 1972 (now s.7 of the Road Traffic Act 1988) "import the further requirement that the constable in fact suspects".[17]

In *Chapman v. D.P.P.*[18] the Divisional Court adopted the same approach without argument. It quashed a conviction for assaulting a police officer in the execution of his duty on the ground that the justices had not found as a fact that the officer reasonably suspected that an arrestable offence had occurred. Lord Justice Bingham said that reasonable suspicion was "the source from which all a police constable's powers of arrest flow". This was so

---

[14] (1992) 95 Cr.App.R. 42, C.A.
[15] The House of Lords held in 1984 that where a police officer reasonably suspects an individual of having committed an arrestable offence, he may arrest that person with a view to questioning her in a police station; *Holgate-Mohammed v. Duke* [1984] A.C. 437.
[16] [1979] R.T.R. 454.
[17] *ibid.* 457.
[18] (1988) 89 Cr.App.R. 190, C.A. [1988] Crim.L.R. 843.

not least because otherwise how could the officer inform the suspect of the offence in question (previously required at common law by *Christie v. Leachinsky* (below) and now codified in section 28).

But since in section 24(4)(a), (5)(a) and (7)(a) there is no requirement of reasonable grounds it appears that under those subsections the arrester need have no reasonable grounds for his belief providing that an arrestable offence is being or was being or is about to be committed.

But what are "reasonable grounds"? In *Castorina v. Chief Constable of Surrey*[19] the Court of Appeal had to decide what inquiries the police should make before effecting an arrest. A burglary at the plaintiff's former workplace appeared to have been an "inside job". The managing director told the police that the plaintiff had recently been sacked and might have a grudge. The police went to the plaintiff's home, having ascertained that she was of previous good character, and without further inquiry arrested her. She was held for three and three quarter hours. The trial judge awarded her damages of £4,500 on the ground that the police lacked reasonable cause for the arrest. He took the definition of "reasonable cause" to be an "honest belief founded on a reasonable suspicion leading an ordinary cautious man to the conclusion that the person arrested was guilty of the offence". He took the view that an ordinary man would have sought more information from the suspect before arresting her. (He relied on dicta of Scott L.J. in *Dumbell v. Roberts*[20] that the principle that every man was presumed innocent until proved guilty applied also to the arrest situation.)

On appeal the Court of Appeal (Purchas and Woolf L.JJ. and Sir Frederick Lawton) held that the judge had applied too severe a test in asking whether the officers had an honest belief as opposed to a suspicion or conjecture. Purchas L.J. said that "reasonable cause" was an objective issue and had nothing to do with the officer's subjective state of mind. The judge had therefore misdirected himself in making honest belief the test. Also the fact that the officer might have made further inquiries did not mean that the arrest was unlawful. The question was whether the officer had had reasonable grounds to suspect her of the offence. In the circumstances of this case the officer had had sufficient reason to suspect the woman.

Woolf L.J. suggested that when it is alleged that an arrest is unlawful there are three questions to be considered:

(a) Did the arresting officer suspect that the person who was arrested was guilty of the offence? This depended on the finding of fact as to the officer's subjective state of mind.

(b) Assuming the officer had the necessary suspicion, was there reasonable proof of that suspicion? This was an objective requirement to be determined by the judge.

(c) If the answer to both these questions was affirmative then the officer had a discretion to arrest. In *Holgate-Mohammed v. Duke*[21] the House of Lords said that discretion to arrest was justified in order to prevent a suspect or to dispel or confirm reasonable suspicion by questioning him or seeking further evidence. The question then was whether a reasonable police officer would have thought it reasonable to make an

---

[19] [1979] R.T.R. 454 [1988] New L.J. 180, C.A.
[20] [1944] 1 All E.R. 326 at 329.
[21] See n.15 above.

arrest in those circumstances. This is the test of so-called "*Wednes-bury* unreasonableness".[22]

Sir Frederick Lawton said that the facts upon which a reasonable cause was said to have been founded did not have to be such as to lead an ordinary cautious man to conclude that the person arrested was guilty of the offence. It was enough if they could lead a reasonable person to suspect that he was guilty.

This is not a very exacting standard. Moreover, as the House of Lords' decision in *Holgate-Mohammed*[23] makes clear, once the police officer objectively has reasonable cause to make an arrest the decision can only be challenged successfully if he acted improperly within the *Wednesbury* principle by taking something irrelevant into account. (In that case the police arrested a former lodger for theft of jewellery from the house where she had lived in order to question her at the police station. The trial judge awarded her damages of £1,000 for false imprisonment. The Court of Appeal set the award aside and the decision was upheld by the House of Lords.)

But it has been powerfully argued by two barrister authors, Richard Clayton and Hugh Tomlinson, that sometimes a failure to make inquiries before making an arrest could show that there were insufficient grounds.[24] In *Hussein v. Chong Fook Kam*[25] it was accepted that a failure to ask relevant questions could mean that the officer did not have reasonable grounds to suspect. As Lord Devlin said: "It was ... a premature arrest rather than one which was unjustified from first to last. The police made the mistake of arresting before questioning; if they had questioned first and arrested afterwards, there would have been no case against them." But Lord Devlin also said that in formulating reasonable suspicion, the police can take account of evidence which could not be put in evidence in court. "Suspicion in its ordinary meaning is a state of conjecture or surmise where proof is lacking: 'I suspect but I cannot prove.' Suspicion arises at or near the starting point of an investigation of which the obtaining of prima facie proof is the end."[26]

There is no doubt that reasonable cause will only be present if a reasonable man in the position of the officer at the time of the arrest would have thought that the plaintiff was probably guilty of the offence.[27] The police officer need not prove every possible explanation or follow up every lead but it would be surprising if the law were such as not to require that he make at least obvious inquiries before making an arrest.

Purchas L.J. in *Castorina* suggested that if they had enough to go on it was irrelevant to consider what further inquiries the police might have made. They had been told that it was an "inside job" and the plaintiff seemed to be the only person with the relevant inside knowledge. But it would be remarkable if this were right. As Clayton and Tomlinson have said: "If the police are justified in arresting a middle aged woman of good character on

---

[22] Laid down by Greene M.R. in *Associated Provincial Picture Houses Ltd v. Wednesbury Corpn.* [1948] 1 K.B. 223.
[23] Note 15 above.
[24] "Arrest and reasonable grounds for suspicion", *Law Soc. Gaz.*, September 7, 1988, p. 22. The writer is indebted to the authors of the article for several of the points made here. They are co-authors also of *Civil Actions Against the Police* (1992, Sweet & Maxwell).
[25] [1970] A.C. 942 (H.L.).
[26] At p. 948.
[27] *Dallison v. Caffery* [1965] 1 Q.B. 348, 371; *Wiltshire v. Barrett* [1966] 1 Q.B. 312, 322.

such flimsy grounds, without even questioning her as to her alibi or possible motives, the law provides very scant protection for those suspected of crime."[28] The officers should have inquired into what she said. "Any other approach would mean that the law would be encouraging an arrest-first, ask-questions-later policy which would be both sloppy police work and a serious interference with civil liberties."[29] (See also *Ward v. Chief Constable of Avon & Somerset Constabulary*[30] and *Kynaston v. D.P.P.; Heron (Joseph) v. D.P.P.; Heron (Tracey) v. D.P.P.*[31])

Powers of arrest for cross-border enforcement

New powers of arrest for cross-border enforcement have been conferred on the police in England and Wales, Scotland and Northern Ireland by the Criminal Justice and Public Order Act 1994 (CJPOA).

Until now police officers in one country had no power or authority in the others. Likewise the courts had no jurisdiction over offences committed in the other country. The CJPOA has now addressed the problem of a lack of police powers. The new arrangements came into effect in February 1995 supported by a protocol agreed by chief officers in all United Kingdom countries under which officers can work in each others' countries. The basic concept is that investigators take with them their own law and powers in regard to arrest and detention of suspects and that those rules take precedence over the local rules.

Under the protocol agreed by chief officers, cross-border actions should not be undertaken unless the commander of the local area concerned has been informed of the circumstances and what is planned and guidance or even directions from the local force have been sought. Subject to that, the investigating team are supposed, so far as possible, to be self-sufficient in terms of staff, vehicles, documentation and equipment to preserve evidence, to manage an arrest and detention and to take the suspect back to their own country.

Section 137 provides that if an officer in England and Wales has reasonable grounds for suspecting that someone has committed an arrestable offence in England or Wales and that that person is in Scotland or Northern Ireland he can arrest him in Scotland and Northern Ireland. The same power of arrest applies equally to the circumstances permitting arrest under section 25 below, and to arrest warrants. Equivalent reciprocal powers are given to the police in Scotland and Northern Ireland.[32]

When arrested, the person should then be taken as soon as practicable to the nearest convenient police station in the jurisdiction where the offence is being investigated.[33] The Act makes appropriate supplementary provisions for power to search the arrested person (for evidence of an offence) and the premises where he was when or immediately before he was arrested (for evidence relating to the offence for which he was arrested).[34] Anything found in the course of such a search that appears to be evidence of an offence

[28] Clayton and Tomlinson, *op. cit.* p. 26.
[29] *ibid.*
[30] *The Times*, June 26, 1986.
[31] (1988) 87 Cr.App.R. 200, C.A.
[32] CJPOA, ss.136, 137(1)–(6) and 138.
[33] CJPOA, s.137(7).
[34] CJPOA, s.139.

may be seized.[35] A police officer in one jurisdiction in the United Kingdom who is in another part of the United Kingdom may use the powers of arrest applicable to the jurisdiction where he is.[36]

General arrest conditions: section 25[37]

Section 25 gives the police a new general power of arrest far beyond what the Philips Commission recommended. Not that such offences becomes arrestable. The Act at various points gives the police special powers that relate to arrestable offences, or serious arrestable offences. The only offences which are arrestable offences are those defined in section 24. For offences in that category the power of arrest is unqualified.

All other offences now carry a limited power of arrest under section 25 if a constable has reasonable grounds for suspecting that any offence has been committed or attempted or is being committed or attempted and it appears to him that service of a summons is impracticable or inappropriate because "any of the general arrest conditions is satisfied".

The thinking behind the section is that the police should be able to make an arrest for an offence normally not arrestable where either he does not know the person's name or address or it is necessary to prevent or stop one of a list of particular social evils.

The first general arrest condition is that the officer does not know and cannot readily ascertain the name and address of the suspect or he reasonably believes that the name and address he has been given are false, or he doubts whether the suspect has given a satisfactory address for service of a summons, either because he has given no address at all or because it is doubtful whether he will be there long enough to accept service and there is no one else who can do so (subs. (3)(a)(b)(c)). This is obviously much wider than the power proposed by the Philips Royal Commission which was confined to cases where the officer actually saw the offence being committed.

It is sufficient if the officer asks for the name and address of someone suspected of having committed a non-arrestable offence who refuses to give it. He need not specifically explain that he wants the name and address in order to be able to serve a summons.[38] But the ground for the arrest given by the police must be a valid ground. It is not valid, for instance, where he says "You're nicked for obstruction" after trying unsuccessfully to get the person to spit out something suspected of being cannabis which he had seen the suspect put into his mouth. The offence under section 23(4)(a) of the Misuse of Drugs Act 1971 *was* obstruction but the power of arrest for the offence had been repealed by section 26 of PACE. There was therefore no right to arrest for obstruction and section 25 could not apply because the ground was invalid.[39] (The officer should have said "You're nicked for suspected possession of cannabis".)

---

[35] CJPOA, s.10.
[36] CJPOA, s.140.
[37] See N.I. PACE Order, Art. 26.
[38] *Nicholas v. D.P.P.* [1987] R.T.R. 199; [1987] Crim.L.R. 474 (Div.Ct.).
[39] *Edwards v. D.P.P.* (1993) 97 Cr.App.R. 301 (Div.Ct.). See also *G. v. D.P.P.* [1989] Crim.L.R. 150 (Div.Ct.). But see Professor D. J. Birch's comments on this case, following the report, and A. Lawson [1993] Crim.L.R. 568–569.

The second condition (in subs. (3)(d)) is that there are reasonable grounds for believing that the arrest is necessary to prevent the suspect causing: (i) physical harm to himself or to someone else; (ii) loss of or damage to property; (iii) an unlawful obstruction of the highway (this replaces s.137(2) of the Highways Act 1980); or (iv) an offence against public decency in circumstances "where members of the public going about their normal business cannot readily avoid the person to be arrested" (subs. 5). (This last category is seemingly intended to deal for instance with the case of a "flasher"). It is also permissible to arrest someone to protect a child or other vulnerable person from the person to be arrested (subs. (3)(e)). This broad power was not recommended by the Philips Royal Commission at all.

The Bill originally included a power for an officer to detain anyone while he verified the name and address given to him, exercisable if it appeared that verification could be carried out quickly. This in essence is the power given to the police in Scotland by section 2(2) of the Criminal Justice (Scotland) Act 1980. However, the power was deleted by the Government on the Report stage in the House of Commons. No such power exists therefore. Another change made in the course of the Bill's passage was the elimination of the definition of "physical harm" as including serious disease.

Note that there is legislation which gives the police the power to arrest for summary only offences. Examples are: the Sporting Event (Control of Alcohol etc.) Act 1985, giving a power of arrest for possession of intoxicating liquor in connection with a designated sporting event; the Public Order Act 1986 which created various new powers of arrest for summary offences[40]; and the Criminal Justice and Public Order Act 1994 which likewise gives the police new powers of arrest for non-arrestable offences—for being a squatter[41]; for being involved in a rave,[42] for aggravated trespass[43] and for organising or taking part in a trespassory assembly.[44]

Repeal of statutory powers of arrest without warrant: section 26[45]

The section provides for the repeal of virtually all statutory powers of arrest by constables without a warrant. With the enactment of the general power of arrest in section 25 these are no longer needed. The Act did not however repeal all other statutory powers of arrest. Those preserved are listed in Schedule 2 (p. 416 below). They include for instance powers of arrest in connection with drink driving offences and terrorism legislation. Also Schedule 6, para. 21(b) specifically preserves the power to arrest a person for disorderly behaviour while drunk—under s.91(1) of the Criminal Justice Act 1967.[46] The repeal does not affect powers of arrest at common law to prevent or deal with a breach of the peace[47] nor those dependent on a warrant or order of a court nor those available to persons other than constables (*e.g.* to game keepers under s.2 of the Poaching Act 1828).

[40] See s.5 (conduct likely to cause harassment, alarm or distress), ss.12–14 (offences relating to processions or assembles) and s.39(2) (failing to comply with a police direction to a trespasser).
[41] ss.61(5) and 73 creating new s.7(6) of the Criminal Law Act 1977.
[42] ss.63(8), 65(5).
[43] s.68(4).
[44] ss.70 and 71 creating new ss.14B(4) and 14C(4) of the Public Order Act 1986.
[45] See N.I. PACE Order, Art. 28.
[46] See *D.P.P. v. Kitching* [1990] Crim.L.R. 394 (Div.Ct.).
[47] For discussion by the Court of Appeal of the scope of this power see *D.P.P. v. Orum* [1989] 1 W.L.R. 88. See also F. Sampson, "Breach of the Peace—a Breach in PACE?", J.P., May 4, 1991, p. 281.

There are some powers of arrest given by statute to "any person".[48] These powers were not repealed by section 26 but can they still be exercised by constables on the ground that they come within the concept of "any person", even though statutory powers of arrest for constables were generally abolished by section 26? The better view seems to be that these powers of arrest remain.[49] The Home Office Circular on PACE suggested that to avoid uncertainty and accusations of arbitrariness, police forces may consider it prudent to use these powers only where the general arrest condition in section 25 are also met.[50]

Arrest without warrant for fingerprinting: section 27[51]

Until 1984 the compulsory taking of fingerprints in the investigation stage of crime was only possible in certain limited circumstances and on the authority of a magistrate. PACE changed the rules by putting the power essentially in the hands of the police. As will be seen, the main provision is in section 61 which is principally concerned with the investigation stage. But subsection (6) gives the police power to take a person's fingerprints without his consent if he has been convicted of a recordable offence (s.117 and Code D, para. 3.2 legitimise the use of reasonable force for the taking of such fingerprints).

Where a person has been convicted of a recordable offence but he has never been in police detention the question of fingerprinting is dealt with by section 27. This section is therefore limited to the situation of someone who has been convicted of a recordable offence but has been neither finger-printed nor detained by the police.

Within one month of the conviction (providing at least seven days notice is given) a constable may require such a person to attend a police station at a specified time in order to obtain his fingerprints. The power is backed not only by the power to use reasonable force but also by a power of arrest if the person concerned has failed to comply with a request to attend within seven days at a police station (s.27(3)). There is no equivalent power of arrest under section 61.

Section 27 grants the Home Secretary power to make regulations by statutory instrument specifying the offences constituting recordable offences, and making provision for such offences to be recorded in national police records (subss. (4)–(5)).

A statutory instrument providing a general description of recordable offences was made in 1985. It specified as recordable offences (and therefore fingerprintable without consent) all offences punishable with imprisonment and a few other miscellaneous Acts.[52]

---

[48] See, *e.g.* Prevention of Offences Act 1851, s.11; Vagrancy Act 1824, s.6 (as amended by Criminal Justice Act 1948, s.68); Sexual Offences Act 1956, ss.32, 41; Licensing Act 1872, s.12; Criminal Justice Act 1967, s.91; Licensing Act 1902, s.1; Sexual Offences Act 1967, s.5(3); Theft Act 1978, s.3(4).

[49] See for instance Home Office Circular (No. 88/1985) on the 1984 Act, para. 11; D.J. Birch, "Powers of Arrest and Detention" [1985] Crim.L.R. 545, 550.

[50] *ibid.*

[51] See N.I. PACE Order, Art. 29.

[52] National Police Records (Recordable Offences) Regulations 1985, S.I. 1985 No. 1941 as amended by S.I. 1989 No. 694. The miscellaneous additional provisions are the Street Offences Act 1959, s.1 (loitering or soliciting); the Telecommunications Act 1984, s.43 (improper use of public facilities); Road Traffic Act 1972, s.29 (now Road Traffic Act 1988, s.25) (tampering with motor vehicles); Malicious Communications Act 1988, s.1 (sending letters with intent to cause anxiety); and Criminal Justice Act 1988, s.139(1) (having an article with a blade or point in public).

Those offences which have to be reported to the National Identification Bureau were listed in Appendix F to the Home Office Circular on PACE (p. 8 above).

Information to be given on arrest: section 28[53]

The Philips Royal Commission recommended[54] that the common law rule requiring an arrested person to be told that he is under arrest and the grounds of his arrest should be put into statutory form. This section implements that proposal and adds for good measure that when the arrest is by a police officer (but not otherwise) the requirement to inform the suspect that he is under arrest and the grounds applies regardless of whether the fact of the arrest or the ground for it is obvious. It does not apply however, if he escapes before the information can be communicated to him (subs. (5))! Subsection (3) makes the lawfulness of the arrest dependent on the arrested person having been informed at the time of arrest, or as soon as practicable thereafter, of the fact of and the grounds of arrest[55] (The Northern Ireland PACE Order, Art. 30(3) exempts from this requirement arrests made under the Northern Ireland (Emergency Provisions) Act 1991, s.18(2).[56]

In *Hawkins*[57] the Divisional Court held that there is an exception where the defendant makes it impossible (for instance by his violent conduct) for the officer to communicate the reasons to him. In that situation the arrest is lawful and remains lawful until such time as the reasons should have been given. The fact that the reasons were not then given does not retrospectively invalidate the original arrest and does not therefore mean that the officer was not acting in the execution of his office when assaulted. Similarly, where the arrest was initially unlawful, when it becomes lawful by the officer conveying the grounds, that does not alter the original unlawfulness of the arrest.[58] *Brosch*,[59] decided by the Court of Appeal, confirms that it is not necessary for the arrest to be accompanied by words such as "I arrest you" for it to be valid.

This was further confirmed by the Court of Appeal's decision in *Abbassey and Others v. Newman and Others*.[60] A sued the police for false imprisonment after he had been arrested by the police over the ownership of the car he was driving. At the trial Leonard J. held that the explanation given by the WPC for the arrest ("unlawful possession") was insufficient as a matter of law and that the arrest had accordingly been unlawful. The Court of Appeal allowed an appeal by the police and ordered a retrial. Woolf L.J. said that the most helpful guidance as to the extent of the explanation that has to be given on arrest was still that given in *Christie v. Leachinsky*[61] in 1947. Lord Simon

---

[53] See N.I. PACE Order, Art. 30.
[54] Philips Report, para. 3.87.
[55] On "at the time of … arrest" see *Nicholas v. D.P.P.* (or *Parsonage*) [1987] R.T.R. 199, [1987] Crim.L.R. 474 (Div.Ct.). The case stands also for the proposition that when the arrest is under section 25 there should be mention of the offence as well as of the ground.
[56] Formerly Northern Ireland (Emergency Provisions) Act 1978, s.14(2).
[57] *Hawkins* [1988] 1 W.L.R. 1166.
[58] *Lewis v. Chief Constable of South Wales Constabulary* [1991] 1 All E.R. 206, C.A. applying the principle established pre-PACE in *Kulynycz* [1970] 3 All E.R. 881.
[59] *Brosch* [1988] Crim.L.R. 743. See also *Nicholas v. Parsonage* [1987] R.T.R. 199.
[60] *The Independent*, August 15, 1989; *The Times*, August 18, 1989; *The Guardian*, October 3, 1989; *Justice of the Peace*, September 23, 1989, p. 601.
[61] [1947] A.C. 573.

had said that there was no need for technical or precise language, provided that the person knew why he had been arrested. Woolf L.J. said that this was a question of fact which ought to be answered normally by the jury. No reference need be made as to the power of arrest nor to whether the arrest was under statute or common law. The reason given must be the correct reason. If an incorrect reason is given, the arrest is unlawful and so is the arrest of someone else who intervenes to prevent it—even if there could in fact have been some other valid basis for the arrest.[62]

For consideration of whether in different sections of PACE the word arrest means "lawful arrest" see J. Marston, "The Reasons for an Arrest", J.P., March 2, 1991, p. 131.

Voluntary attendance at police station: section 29[63]

The police frequently find it convenient to blur the line between freedom and arrest. The newspaper phrase "a man is helping the police with their inquiries" has become a polite euphemism to describe this shadowy area. But in law the position is not in doubt. A person is either under arrest or he is not. If he is not technically under arrest, he is free to go.

The Philips Royal Commission recommended that this be made clear in the statute[64] and section 29 represents a partial attempt by the Home Office to spell out the details. It specifies first that where a person attends voluntarily at a police station or anywhere else "for the purpose of assisting with an investigation", "he shall be entitled to leave at will unless he is placed under arrest" and "he shall be informed at once that he is under arrest if a decision is taken by a constable to prevent him from leaving at will".

The object of this section no doubt is to ensure that the suspect should always know that if he has not been told that he is under arrest he is free to go. But in practice, the suspect will often wrongly assume that he is under arrest and will therefore fail to take advantage of his right to leave. By the time he is told that he is under arrest, it will of course be too late. He will then be unable to depart.

The only way to avoid this dilemma would be to give a suspect who is asked whether he would mind coming down to the police station to answer a few questions a warning that this does not mean that he is under arrest and that he is free to come or not to come as he pleases. This would logically complement the later warning that the suspect need not say anything if he does not want to do so.

The Philips Royal Commission's Report did not discuss this issue and made no recommendation that such a warning should be given and there is nothing about it in the Act. The undoubted value of section 29 is therefore considerably qualified by the fact that the information about his status will usually be communicated to the suspect only at the moment of being cautioned or arrested.

The point was in fact considered expressly in the House of Lords. Lord Hutchinson moved an amendment which would have had the effect of requiring that a person on arrival voluntarily at the police station be

[62] *Edwards v. D.P.P.* (1993) 97 Cr.App.R. 301 (Div.Ct.).
[63] See N.I. PACE Order, Art. 31.
[64] Philips Report, para. 3.97.

informed both orally and in writing that he was free to leave at any time, that he was under no obligation to answer questions, that he was entitled to have someone told that he was at the police station and to consult a solicitor privately.

Lord Denning said that he supported the amendment. If an interview was wholly voluntary, he said, it should be conducted at the person's home—

> "But to say to him, 'Are you willing to come along to the police station?' or 'Will you come along to the police station?' is half way to making an arrest. When he has got to the police station, the ordinary person can half feel he is under arrest, even though the police are said to be making inquiries. Then is the time to make clear to him that he is there voluntarily and that he can leave at that moment if he likes. This virtually means in many cases that he is under suspicion. In those circumstances he ought to be told, 'Well you can have a solicitor, if you like; you need not say anything' and so forth. In other words, give him all the protection which should surround a man who is under suspicion, because that is why he is there. A clause like that ... will ensure the protection of the individual."[65]

In reply the Home Office Minister, Lord Elton, said that Lord Hutchinson's amendment would impose "an enormous administrative burden on the police".[66]

> "A great many people attend police stations voluntarily for all sorts of reasons. They include, for example, victims of burglary attending to identify property and victims of assault attending to identify a suspect or to provide a statement ... If these amendments are accepted, the first thing that must happen would be that a policeman would inform them orally and in writing that they were entitled to leave at will unless placed under arrest. Is that the way to treat a shaken victim or a hesitating and irresolute witness? Such people need encouragement to come to the police, and particularly in the case of victims of rape and sexual assault ... Similarly, the large volume of paper that would be produced by the voluntary attendance forms would be entirely disproportionate to any good it would achieve."[67]

Lord Elton thought that the problem was met adequately by the requirement that a person be cautioned as soon as there were any grounds to believe that he had committed an offence. At that point he must be told of his right to silence, his right to have someone informed of his whereabouts, and his right to legal advice. He went on to assert that "the person must also be told ... that he is free to leave the police station if he wishes ... The right to leave is a most fundamental right."[68] But this only arises after the detainee has been cautioned (Code C, para. 10.2). If he is cautioned away from the police station and is not then under arrest the same paragraph of the Code requires that he be told so. This would then presumably inform him that he is not under any compulsion to come with the police officer. The problem of

[65] House of Lords, *Hansard*, July 5, 1984, Col. 502.
[66] *ibid.*
[67] *ibid.* Col. 503.
[68] *ibid.*

proper accountability for those attending voluntarily at the police station arises not only in regard to those who are genuinely volunteers but also to those defined as volunteers by the police who might reasonably be regarded as there under some degree of compulsion. Research has shown that some forces use the category of voluntary attendance much more than others, indicating a radically different approach.[69] This is less than satisfactory.

Arrest elsewhere than at police station: section 30[70]

The Philips Royal Commission recommended that persons who have been arrested should normally be taken straight to a police station so that their detention could become subject to the general supervisory measures which the Philips Commission proposed for detained persons.[71] Both the Act and Code C contain various rights for suspects and duties for the police which start to operate from the time of arrival at a police station. It is therefore important that these controls and safeguards take effect from the earliest practicable time. In particular, the time-limit clock only starts to run on arrival at the police station. (There is in any event some value in discouraging the police from "taking the scenic route to the police station" as a way of providing additional time and opportunity for questioning away from the scrutiny of station colleagues.)

The Act implements the Philips Royal Commission's proposal by stating that where a person is arrested away from a police station he shall be taken to a police station "as soon as practicable" (subs. (1)). However, the effect of this provision is somewhat weakened by subsection (10) which allows the police to delay taking him to a police station if the presence of that person elsewhere is necessary to carry out investigations of an offence. But that does not give the police *carte blanche* to undertake an interrogation of the suspect which ought to be carried out in the police station.[72] Save in exceptional circumstances,[73] interviews of suspects have to be carried out at the police station or other authorised place of detention (Code C, para. 11.1, see p. 470 below).

If there is such delay the reasons for it must be recorded on first arrival at the police station (subs. (11)).

The section does not however affect the special powers of the police to hold persons elsewhere than in a police station in immigration and terrorism cases nor the right of the police under the Criminal Justice Act 1972, section 34 to take a drunk to a detoxification centre (subs. (11) and (12)). Normally, according to section 30(1), a person who has been arrested must be taken to a "designated police station" (defined in s.35). But he may be taken to a non-designated station if any of three alternative conditions is satisfied. The first is where the officer is working in the area of a non-designated police

---

[69] McKenzie *et al.* (1990) 23, 27–33.
[70] See N.I. PACE Order, Art. 32.
[71] Philips Report, para. 3.102.
[72] *R. v. Khan* [1993] Crim.L.R. 54, C.A.
[73] For an example of such circumstances see *R. v. Kerawalla* [1991] Crim.L.R. 451, C.A. The C.A. approved a fair and properly tape-recorded interview of the suspect in a hotel room. There was a reasonable basis for the view that the investigation might be prejudiced if others saw the suspect leave the hotel. See also *R. v. Keane* [1992] Crim.L.R. 306, C.A. where the breach of s.30(10) was disregarded because of the suspect's "admitted, indeed almost boastful experience of being arrested".

station—unless it appears that the suspect will have to be held for longer than six hours (subss. (3) and (4)). If he is being held in a non-designated station he must be moved to a designated station if he is to be held more than six hours (subs. (6)). The second (s.30(5)(a)) is where the person is arrested by a police officer acting on his own, no other officer is available to help him and it appears to the arresting officer that he will not be able to take him to a designated station without the detained person injuring someone (himself, the officer or another person). (In Northern Ireland he may be taken to any police station if there is any physical danger: N.I. PACE Order, Art. 32(6), (7) and (8).) The third situation in which he may be taken to a non-designated station (s.30(5)(ii)) is where the officer has taken the person into custody from someone other than a police officer (*e.g.* after a citizen's arrest) and again there is no other officer to help him, and taking him to a designated station creates a risk of the suspect causing someone injury.

If the officer is satisfied before the arrested person has reached a police station that there are no grounds for keeping him under arrest, he must release him (subs. (7)). He need not take him to the police station in order to book him before allowing him to go. Obviously this creates the possibility of attempts to corrupt the officer as a way of securing immediate release. The Police Federation spokesman in the House of Commons took this sufficiently seriously to argue strenuously during the Committee stage that there ought to be a duty for the arresting officer always to take the suspect to the station. But the Government rejected this view, preferring to trust officers and to give the citizen the advantage of immediate release if preliminary inquiries show that no arrest is necessary.[74] The safeguard, for what it is worth, is that, where someone is released in this way a record of the fact must be made (subs. (8)). Obviously, if a bribe or other improper inducement has been offered it is hardly likely that a record would be made!

Arrest for further offence: section 31[75]

Section 31 addresses the situation of someone at a police station in connection with several offences, and provides that he must be told afresh if there are grounds to arrest him for any second or later offence. Each time that he is notionally arrested again he must be so informed.

The Court of Appeal has suggested that the reason for this rule is to prevent the release and immediate re-arrest of an alleged offender.[76] But, it said, the section does not impose any duty on the police officer to arrest immediately. ("We see nothing in the section which would prevent the constable delaying arresting him until the time (if it ever arrived) when his release was imminent.")

If he is under arrest for one offence but there is not enough evidence to arrest him in regard to another offence he can nevertheless be questioned about the second offence providing he is cautioned and advised about his right to have a solicitor present.[77] The time limits on detention in the police station under the Act are not affected. Regardless of how many offences are being investigated whilst he is in custody the police have the same amount of

[74] See House of Commons, *Hansard*, Standing Committee E, February 2, 1984, Cols. 912–928.
[75] See N.I. PACE Order, Art. 33.
[76] *R. v. Samuel* [1988] Q.B. 615, p. 622.
[77] *R. v. Mason and Stephens* C.A. (Unreported) Case no. 90/398/Y4.

time before they have to bring him before a magistrate under section 43. Unless he is released on bail, the time limits are normally measured as from his first arrest (s.41(2) and (3); see below).

Search upon arrest: section 32[78]

Section 32 deals with search after an arrest somewhere other than at a police station and gives the police a power to search that is somewhat broader than that previously enjoyed at common law. The common law allowed the police to search an arrested person for a weapon or for evidence material to the offence for which he was arrested.[79] The Philips Royal Commission said it had not received any proposals for alteration of these rules and it recommended that they be confirmed in statute.[80]

Subsection (1) allows the police to search someone arrested where there are grounds for believing that he may present a danger to himself or to others. The right to search for a weapon is unqualified.

Subsection (2) permits a search of the arrested person for anything that might be used to effect an escape or which might be evidence relating to any offence. In addition, subsection (2)(b) gives the police the power to enter and search the premises in which he was when arrested, or immediately before he was arrested, for evidence relating to the offence for which he was arrested.[81] Unlike the power to search under section 18, it is not limited to arrestable offences. Nor need the premises be occupied or controlled by him. But the power of search under subsection (2)(b) only exists if there are reasonable grounds for believing that the search might prove productive of something for which a search is permitted (subss. (5) and (6)). Random or automatic searching is therefore not lawful, as was already determined by the courts.[82] Also, a person searched in public cannot be required to take off anything other than his coat, jacket or gloves (subs. (4)).[83] Since 1995 his mouth can also be searched.[84] But he could be required to take off more elsewhere than in public provided reasonable grounds for a more extensive search exist. Also a person could offer to remove other items even in public if he did so voluntarily, but of such consent must be genuine.

Where the person is arrested in a block of flats or other premises consisting of two or more separate dwellings, only the premises in which he was when arrested or immediately beforehand and any common parts (such as landings, stairways, yards, etc.) shared with other occupiers may be searched (subs. (7)).

It will be noticed that the power under this section to search the premises where an arrest takes place is narrower than that under section 18 to enter and search premises of an arrested person. Under section 18 the police may

---

[78] See N.I. PACE Order, Art. 34.
[79] *Dillon v. O'Brien and David* (1887) 16 Cox C.C. 245.
[80] Philips Report, para. 115.
[81] The question whether the police genuinely entered for that reason is one for the jury—*Beckford* (1991) 94 Cr.App.R. 43; [1991] Crim.L.R. 918.
[82] *Lindley v. Rutter* [1981] Q.B. 128 and *Brazil v. Chief Constable of Surrey* (1984) 148 J.P. 22. See also *Mann-Cairns v. Ministry of Defence, Legal Action*, September 1988, 21; this resulted in damages of £2,001 being awarded to a Greenham Common demonstrator. Evidence by a policewoman in a previous trial was to the effect that she had searched some 750 women from the camp.
[83] The N.I. PACE Order, Art. 34(4) also added headgear.
[84] A new provision expressly added by the CJPOA, s.59(2) and in Northern Ireland, see Appendix 4, p. 532, [Art. 5] below.

come in and look for evidence relating to the offence for which he was arrested or "to some other offence which is connected with or similar to that offence". Under this section they may look only for evidence relating to the actual offence for which the arrest was made. On the other hand, under section 32 they can search the arrested person himself for evidence of *any* offence which enlarges the common law power and goes beyond what the Philips Royal Commission recommended.

In *Badham*,[85] as has been seen, it was held that section 32 only applies to a search made at the time of the arrest. It does not apply to permit the police to return to the premises several hours after the arrest (in that case three hours later).

In *R. v. Churchill*,[86] C was arrested on suspicion of burglary and placed in a police car. The police asked him for the car keys—to lock the car and so prevent vandalism or theft and to preserve it for a later search at the police station. C refused to hand over the keys and during a struggle he hit a police officer. C was convicted of assault. On appeal he argued that the police had had no power to take the keys since they were not evidence of any crime. The Court of Appeal allowed the appeal and quashed his conviction. The Court said that the case could have been dealt with on the basis of the officer's duty to preserve property. But this was not how it had been argued.

Section 32 confers a power to search, either for evidence or a weapon, not only the arrested person but also any premises he was in at the time or immediately before his arrest. This would have included the car since the definition of "premises" in section 23(a) specifically covers any vehicle. But, as the comment in the *Criminal Law Review* argues, the seizing of the car was not for the purposes of a search, because the car was unlocked.

Execution of warrant not in possession of constable: section 33[87]

The common law was that the constable had to have the warrant with him when he came to execute it. This rule was changed for warrants of arrest by the Magistrates' Courts Act 1980, s.125(3). Section 33 extends the same rule to the various kinds of warrants referred to in the section, including even a warrant to arrest a person for breach of community service order.[88]

But note *D.P.P. v. Peacock*[89] where it was held that the officer was not acting in the execution of his duty because he did not have the non-payment of fine means inquiry warrant with him when making the arrest. Most warrants for non-payment of fine are issued under section 83 of the Magistrates' Courts Act 1980, namely for the purpose of enabling inquiry to be made under section 82 which provides that a magistrates' court must not issue a warrant of commitment until inquiry has been made into the person's ability to pay. Section 83 is not included in section 125 of the Act, though section 76 (enforcement of sums adjudged to be paid) is. So the officer must have the warrant with him when executing it. A means inquiry warrant

---

[85] [1987] Crim.L.R. 202 (Cr.Ct.).
[86] [1989] Crim.L.R. 226, C.A.
[87] No equivalent in N.I. PACE Order because this became the law there under Art. 156 of the Magistrates' Courts (Northern Ireland) Order.
[88] See *Jones v. Kelsey* (1987) 151 J.P. 429 (Div.Ct.).
[89] [1989] Crim.L.R. 373 (Div.Ct.).

under section 83 is not a warrant to arrest in connection with an offence so it is necessary to check whether the warrant is to arrest for non-payment of a fine (in which case the warrant need not be in his possession), or to arrest in order to inquire into a person's ability to pay (in which case it must be in his possession).

Note—empirical evidence regarding arrest

The annual *Criminal Statistics* show the proportion of persons proceeded against in magistrates' courts who have been arrested or summonsed. In 1993, 2.1m persons were proceeded against. Of these 960,000 were dealt with for motoring offences. These are excluded from the figures that follow.

Five hundred and eighty-seven thousand were dealt with for indictable offences, of whom 78 per cent were arrested and bailed from the police station, 12 per cent were arrested and held in custody by the police and 10 per cent were summonsed.[90] Eighty-seven thousand were committed for trial.

Five hundred and sixty-five thousand were dealt with for summary offences, of whom 76 per cent were summonsed, 21 per cent were arrested and bailed by the police and 3 per cent were arrested and held in custody.[91]

The Home Office produce an occasional Statistical Bulletin entitled *Cautions, court proceedings and sentencing, England and Wales.*

There are no regularly published statistics on how many persons are arrested but not proceeded against or arrested and then proceeded against by summons. Brown *et al.* (1992) had figures on this derived from large 1990 and 1991 samples.[92] This showed (at p. 108) that 41 per cent of those arrested were charged, 12 per cent were cautioned, 10 per cent were summonsed, 10 per cent were bailed to return, 16 per cent were released and 11 per cent were dealt with by a variety of other means or the information was not available—based on 10,167 custody record forms.

On arrest, see also: Gemmill and Morgan-Giles, 1980, a study conducted for the Philips Royal Commission, showing variations in arrest/summons policy as between forces; Bottomley *et al.* (1991); Irving and McKenzie (1989); Dixon *et al.* (1989a), McConville *et al.* (1991) a study of 1,000 non-Road Traffic arrests and summonses in three forces which found that almost all had been arrested; and Brown (1991), a study of household burglary cases.

---

[90] The Report of the Philips Royal Commission (para. 3.72) indicated huge variations as between forces in the percentage of persons dealt with for indictable offences who were arrested and summonsed. In Cambridgeshire, Cleveland and the Metropolitan District only 1 per cent of adults accused of indictable offences were brought to court by way of summons, compared with over 40 per cent in Thames Valley, West Yorkshire, Wiltshire and North Wales.

[91] *Criminal Statistics*, 1993, Cm. 2680, (HMSO) Table 8.2, p. 191.

[92] For details of the different samples in this study see p. 138 below.

QUESTIONS AND ANSWERS

ARREST

1. What is the difference between "helping the police with their inquiries" and being under arrest?

Being under arrest means being subject to restraint as to one's movements. One is either under arrest or one is not; there is no half-way stage. A person who is "helping the police with their inquiries" is therefore free to go if he pleases.

2. Are the police obliged to inform someone being questioned that he is not under arrest?

In general the answer is No. When the police ask someone to come down to the police station to answer a few questions, they are not obliged to caution him that he is under no compulsion to do so. Nor are they obliged to advise him on arrival at the police station of his rights including his right to legal advice, the right to have someone informed of where he is and the right to leave. If he happens to know of these rights he is free to exercise them.

The first point at which the police must inform him of these rights is when he is cautioned, whether or not in the police station. They must also tell him at the moment when he is under arrest, but by then it is obviously too late for him to leave.

3. What procedures follow when someone is arrested?

The only strict rule on arrest is that the person concerned must as soon as practicable be told that he is under arrest and why he has been arrested, even, the Act says, if it is obvious. (However, this does not apply if he is struggling or running away.) In principle he should then be taken to a police station as soon as possible, though an exception is allowed where his presence is needed elsewhere in the interests of the investigation.

4. To what police station should someone who is arrested be taken?

If it is clear that the suspect will have to be detained for longer than several hours, he should be taken to one of the police stations in the area named by the chief constable as "designated stations" for the receipt of persons in custody. If the police station to which he is taken is not a designated one the suspect cannot be held there for longer than six hours. At that point he must be transferred to a designated police station.

5. On what grounds can someone be arrested?

There are two main categories of situations where someone can be arrested. One is broadly the same as under the previous law—on reasonable suspicion of having committed, being about to commit or committing an arrestable offence. The second is where the officer believes that an arrest is necessary for a non-arrestable offence because of the particular circumstances of the case. One ground is that the culprit refuses to supply his name and address or gives a Mickey Mouse name and address. But the broader ground is that the arrest is thought to be necessary to prevent the person concerned from causing physical injury to himself or others; or suffering physical injury; or causing loss of or damage to property; or committing an offence against public decency; or causing an unlawful obstruction of the highway. There also remains the common law power to arrest someone for a breach of the peace.

If someone has been arrested for one offence and it seems to an officer that, if released, he would be liable to be arrested for other offences he should be arrested for those other offences.

6. Can a person who has been arrested be searched and if so, for what reason?

A person who has been arrested can be searched if there are reasonable grounds to think:

(1) that he may present a danger to himself or others; or
(2) that he might have on him evidence of a crime or something which he could use to escape.

The police may also enter and search any premises in which he was when arrested or immediately before he was arrested but only to look for evidence of that offence.

The Code states that on arrival at a police station the custody officer (see below) is under a duty to itemise what property he has (unless he is to be held only very briefly) and to that end he may search him for that purpose if it is necessary. Searches may not however take place on a routine basis, without regard to the circumstances.

See further p. 15 and see also pp. 149–153 below on intimate searches and the taking of body samples.

PART IV

DETENTION

The section on detention runs to no less than 19 sections. It establishes a new framework for the regime of detention and, in particular, in relation to time limits, supervision by a custody officer and record keeping.

Limitations on police detention: section 34[1]

Section 34 provides in essence that detention in a police station must be in conformity with the provisions of the Act.

Subsection (2) states that the custody officer (see s.36 below) must order the release of anyone whose continued detention by the police cannot be justified under the Act. Subsection (5) requires that release in such a case be unconditional unless further investigation in the matter is needed or future proceedings may be taken against the detained person, in either of which cases the release may be subject to bail. A new subsection (7) added by the Criminal Justice and Public Order Act section 29(3) states that someone who returns to the police station to answer to bail or is arrested under new subsection 46A (for failure to answer to police bail, p. 104 below) is treated as arrested for an offence, and the offence in connection with which he was granted bail is deemed to be that offence. (For the equivalent change in Northern Ireland see Appendix 4, p. 532 below [Art. 7].)

"Police detention" is defined in section 118(2) as where someone has been taken to a police station after being arrested or is arrested at a police station after attending there voluntarily. But a person at court after being charged is no longer in police detention for these purposes.

Strictly, the concept of police detention only applies to those in detention in connection with an offence. But paragraph 1.10 of Code C states: "Subject to paragraph 1.12, this Code applies to people who are in custody at police stations in England and Wales *whether or not they have been arrested for an offence* [emphasis supplied] and to those who have been removed to a police station as a place of safety under sections 135 and 136 of the Mental Health Act 1982." (Reviews and extensions of detention apply however only to persons under police detention.)

Paragraph 1.12 specifies those who are not covered by Code C. They are people arrested by Scottish police exercising their powers of detention under the Criminal Justice and Public Order Act 1994, section 137(2) (cross border power of arrest); people arrested under the Asylum and Immigration Act 1993, section 3(5) for the purpose of having their fingerprints taken; people

[1] See N.I. PACE Order, Art. 35.

who have been served a notice of detention under the Immigration Act 1971; and convicted or remanded prisoners held in police cells on behalf of the Prison Service under the Imprisonment (Temporary Provisions) Act 1980. But the provisions on conditions and treatment of prisoners in sections 8 and 9 of Code C "must be considered as the minimum standards of treatment for such detainees" (*ibid.*). The Home Office Circular on PACE (p. 8 above) stated that accordingly "the Code of Practice on detention etc. will apply so far as in common sense it is applicable including, possibly the opening of a custody record as an administrative convenience" (para. 33). The Circular stated that similar considerations apply to persons in police custody in connection with extradition proceedings. The role of the police in such proceedings is not investigative. Interviews of suspects take place not in order to obtain evidence to justify holding the prisoner, but to try to find information which could help the authorities in the requesting state. But although the objectives are therefore somewhat different from ordinary police detention, paragraph 1.10 of the Code makes the provision of the Codes applicable. The Home Office Circular (para. 36) states that although Part IV of the Act does not apply, "a fugitive offender should be properly treated as far as practicable" and that he should "continue to be treated in many respects like any other person suspected of a serious offence".

Code C, note 1A adds that those who are at a police station voluntarily "should be treated with no less consideration (*e.g.* offered refreshments at appropriate times)", as well as enjoying an absolute right to obtain legal advice or communicate with anyone outside the police station.

Designated police stations: section 35[2]

Until a late stage the Bill drew no distinction between busy police stations with large numbers of officers available and small rural stations with slight manpower resources. When the Bill was before the House of Lords however the Government introduced amendments to take account of these differences in terms of the functions and duties of the custody officer.

The scheme devised by the Government was to make the full range of custody officer duties and functions available from "designated police stations", whilst other stations would be restricted as to the time for which they could hold suspects. As has already been seen, section 30 provides that a person may not be held in a non-designated police station for longer than six hours. The distinction between designated and non-designated police stations is spelled out in sections 35 and 36.

The chief officer in each area must designate which "are to be the stations in that area to be used for the purpose of detaining arrested persons" (s.35(1)). If a police force maintained by a statutory undertaker (such as the British Transport Police) wants one of its stations to be "designated" it must still be done by the chief officer of the police force in that area. Enough must be designated to meet the needs of that area (subs. (2)). Each designated police station must have one or more custody officers appointed (s.36(1)). A station cannot be designated for parts of a day, though it can be designated for brief periods of one day, one week or one month.

[2] See N.I. PACE Order, Art. 36.

Custody officers at police station: section 36[3]

Section 36(1) states that "One or more custody officers shall be appointed
for each designated police station."[4] In non-designated police stations there
must simply be someone able to take on the job if the need arises. In *Vince v.
Chief Constable of Dorset Police*[5] the Court of Appeal reversed the ruling by
Mr Justice Pain that there had to be enough appointed custody officers at
designated stations to ensure that there was always one on duty. It held that
the chief constable's duty under section 36(1) was to appoint one custody
officer for each designated police station and that he had a discretion to
appoint more than one. That discretion had to be exercised reasonably—but
the courts have repeatedly held that they will not lightly interfere with the
daily operation of a police force. The effect of the ruling is that there is no
requirement to have an appointed custody officer on duty at all times. The
appointment of the custody officer must either be by the chief constable
himself or by someone acting under delegated powers from the chief
constable (s.36(2)). Section 36(3) states that no one may be appointed as a
custody officer unless he is of the rank of sergeant but subsection (4) allows
an officer who is not a sergeant to perform the functions of a custody officer
at a designated station "if a custody officer is not readily available to perform
them". In *Vince* the Court of Appeal held that an officer who was not a
sergeant could only perform the duties of custody officer if an appointed
custody officer was not at the station and could not, without much difficulty,
be brought there.

There is nothing in the Act to require that a custody officer perform his
functions over any particular period of time. In some forces officers are
detailed to be custody officer over a period of weeks or months so that they
are playing that role every day. In others, an officer may not know until he
comes on duty on the day whether he is performing the function of custody
officer.

Section 36(5) makes it plain that at designated police stations the
investigative and custodial functions should be basically distinct. Subject to
the provisions of section 39(2) (p. 358 below), "none of the functions of a
custody officer ... shall be performed by an officer who at the time when the
functions falls to be performed is involved in the investigation of an offence
for which that person is in police detention at that time". But the prohibition
on the custody officer undertaking investigative functions is not total. So the
custody officer can do anything authorised by the Act or the Codes—such as
searching a suspect or his clothing. He can undertake duties in connection
with the identification of the suspect or his clothing. He can undertake duties
in connection with the identification of the suspect such as taking fingerprints and he can do anything required by section 7 of the Road Traffic Act
1988 (driving with excess alcohol), such as administering a breath test (subs.
(6)). Equally, a person who has previously been the arresting or investigating
officer could, in the absence of anyone else appropriate, act later as custody
officer. Obviously, the intention and expectation is that the roles should be
kept wholly apart. But if this is not possible, subsection (5) prevents one
person playing both roles at the same time.

---

[3] See N.I. PACE Order, Art. 37.
[4] This gave effect to the Philips Royal Commission's recommendation, para. 3.112.
[5] [1993] 1 W.L.R. 415; [1993] 2 All E.R. 321, C.A.

What if the suspect is taken to a non-designated police station? In that case section 36(7)(a) states that the functions which would be those of the custody officer in a designated police station must be carried out by someone not involved in the investigation, "if such officer is readily available". This clearly leaves scope for the police to plead that no such officer was readily available. In that case the functions may be carried out by the officer who took the person concerned to the station "or any other officer" (s.36(7)(b)). When this occurs such an "acting custody officer" must as soon as practicable notify an officer of the rank of inspector or above at a designated police station that this is the case (subss. (9) and (10)). There is no requirement that the notification has to be in writing and normally it will be by telephone or radio. The fact that the notification must be as soon as practicable shows that it is intended to operate before any action is taken, so that the inspector at the larger station can consider whether to have the suspect brought there instead.

Subsection (6), as amended, provides that a person arrested on suspicion of driving with excess alcohol under section 6(5) of the Road Traffic Act 1988 is arrested for an offence for the purposes of subsection (1). This settles the doubt about the matter raised by *R. v. Mackenzie.*[6]

Duties of custody officer before charge: section 37[7]

As will be seen, custody officers have many duties in regard to prisoners. The chief purpose of section 37 is to ensure that a person brought to the police station is charged if there is enough evidence to charge him, but that if there is not sufficient evidence he should be released unless the custody officer has reasonable grounds for believing that his detention is needed to preserve or obtain evidence of the offence for which he was arrested.

Subsection (1) states that where someone is arrested without a warrant or on a warrant not endorsed for bail[8] the custody officer at any police station to which he is taken must first consider whether there is sufficient evidence to justify a charge for the offence for which he was arrested.

The duty laid on the custody officer by subsection (1) to consider whether there is enough evidence to justify a charge must be carried out as soon as practicable after the suspect's arrival at the police station or, where he was arrested at the police station, after the arrest (subs. (10)).

Under subsection (2) of section 37, if the custody officer determines that he does not have enough evidence to charge the person detained, he must be released on bail or unconditionally, unless he "has reasonable grounds for believing that his detention without being charged is necessary to secure or preserve evidence relating to an offence for which he is under arrest or to obtain such evidence by questioning him". If so, further detention may be authorised (subs. (3)).[9] In other words, detention is permitted primarily for the purpose of questioning. However, as Mr Douglas Hurd, the then Home Office Minister, emphasised in the House of Commons, the phrase is that

---

[6] [1971] 1 All E.R. 729.
[7] See N.I. PACE Order, Art. 38.
[8] This now includes someone who returns to the police station to answer to bail—by virtue of the Criminal Justice and Public Order Act, s.29(3) which adds a new subsection (7) to s.34 of PACE, to the effect that such a person is treated as arrested for an offence.
[9] Research suggests that it is extremely rare for the custody officer not to authorise initial detention; see I. McKenzie *et al.* (1990) 23–24.

"This detention was necessary—not desirable, convenient or a good idea but necessary.[10]

Subsection (4) requires that as soon as practicable, the custody officer make a written record of the grounds of detention and under subsection (5) this should normally be done in the presence of the suspect who must be told the grounds by the custody officer. This would not be required however if he is not in a fit state to be told (subs. (6)). Under paragraph 1.8 of Code C the explanation must then be given as soon as practicable.

If there is enough evidence to charge him he must either be charged (in which case the provisions of section 38 apply) or released with or without bail (subss. (7) and (8)). The 1991 revised Code C amplified this provision in a new paragraph 16.1 which states that:

"When an officer considers that there is sufficient evidence to prosecute a detained person, and that there is sufficient evidence for a prosecution to succeed, and that the person has said all that he wishes to say about the offence, he should without delay ... bring him before the custody officer who shall then be responsible for considering whether or not he should be charged."

Paragraph 16.1 had a further new provision which is more problematic—that "When a person is detained in respect of more than one offence it is permissible to delay bringing him before the custody officer until [the police are ready to charge the suspect] in respect of all the offences." It is not easy to see that this can be reconciled with the plain words of section 37(7) and it may be *ultra vires*. The Code cannot amend the statute. If valid it has consequences, for instance in terms of permitting further delay in access to a solicitor.[11]

If no decision has been made as to whether he will be prosecuted he should be so informed (subs. (8)). If he is not in a fit state to be charged he may be detained until he is in a fit state (subs. (9)). Such detention cannot however be for more than 24 hours and must cease when he is in a fit state if that is earlier. This follows from the general prohibition on detention for more than 24 hours in section 41, subject to exceptions which do not apply in such a case.

Subsections (11) to (14) dealt with arrested juveniles. They were not brought into effect and were repealed by the Criminal Justice Act 1991, section 72.

Subsection (15) defines "arrested juvenile" and "endorsed for bail".

It has been held that the duties performed by custody officers under section 37 (and s.38) cannot be performed on behalf of a private prosecutor, even when it is intended that the prosecution be carried forward by the private prosecutor. In *R. v. Ealing Justices, ex p. Dixon* the Divisional Court held that under the Prosecution of Offences Act 1985, section 3 all prosecutions had to be taken over by the D.P.P. or the Crown Prosecution Service. If charges were preferred by the police they could not be conducted by a private prosecutor.[12]

---

[10] House of Commons, *Hansard*. Standing Committee E, February 16, 1984, Col. 1229.
[11] The Court of Appeal held in *Samuel* [1988] Q.B. 615, that when a suspect had been charged with one offence he could no longer be denied access to a solicitor under Annex B of Code C, even though he was still being questioned in connection with other offences.
[12] *R. v. Ealing Justices, ex p. Dixon* [1989] 3 W.L.R. 1098; [1989] 2 All E.R. 1050 (Div.Ct.).

But in *R. v. Stafford Justices, ex p. Commissioners of Customs and Excise*[13] this decision was rejected by the Divisional Court itself at least as concerns offences conducted by Customs and Excise. A customs officer investigating an offence had all relevant powers except that of charging an arrested person. He therefore had to take the arrested person to the police for charging. But, the court said, it should not be thought that this meant that the Customs and Excise surrendered the prosecution of the offence to the D.P.P. Section 6 of the 1985 Act envisaged that persons other than the D.P.P. might institute proceedings and prosecute. The right under section 6 of other persons to conduct a prosecution would be nugatory if the prosecution had to be taken over by the police from the moment of charging. It followed, Lord Justice Watkins said, that *ex p. Dixon* was wrongly decided.

Duties of custody officer after charge: section 38[14]

Section 38 establishes the principles on which the custody officer must decide whether to keep someone in custody after he has been charged. Note however that the Criminal Justice and Public Order Act 1994, section 25 circumscribed the custody's officer's discretion by laying down rules as to certain offences where bail cannot be granted. Thus a person cannot be granted bail if having been previously convicted anywhere in the United Kingdom or murder, attempted murder, manslaughter,[15] rape or attempted rape he is again charged with such an offence. Subject to those new provisions, the custody officer must decide whether the accused person is a good risk for bail with or without conditions. The power to grant bail subject to conditions is new—it was granted by the CJPOA 1994, section 27. Note however that this new power only applies to persons who have been charged. It therefore does not apply to someone who has been released on bail to return to a police station at a later date.

Bail from the police station

Subsection (1) sets out the detention conditions after charge. Where someone who has been arrested without warrant or under a warrant not endorsed for bail is charged, the custody officer must release him with or without bail unless one or more of a number of detention conditions apply:

(1) If it appears that he has not provided a satisfactory address for service of a summons.

(2) If there are reasonable grounds for believing he will fail to appear at court to answer to bail.[16]

(3) Where someone is arrested for an imprisonable offence, if there are reasonable grounds for believing that detention is necessary to prevent him from committing an offence.

---

[13] [1991] 2 Q.B. 339 (Div.Ct.).

[14] See N.I. PACE Order, Art. 39.

[15] Provided that he was sentenced to a term of imprisonment—CJPOA, s.25(3).

[16] In that case a surety or sureties can be required and if he is likely to go abroad a security can be required in the form of a promise to pay (recognisance) or of actual cash. And other conditions can be imposed to ensure that he attends court.

(4) Where someone is arrested for an offence that is not imprisonable, if there are reasonable grounds for believing that detention is necessary to prevent him from causing physical injury to anyone (*e.g.* assault) or from causing loss of or damage to property (*e.g.* theft or criminal damage).

(5) If there are reasonable grounds for believing that detention is necessary to prevent him from interfering with the administration of justice or with the investigation of offences or

(6) If there are reasonable grounds for thinking that detention is needed for his own protection.[17]

In taking these decisions (except for those referred to in (1) and (6)) the custody officer is supposed to have in mind the same considerations that the magistrates are required to bear in mind when considering whether to grant bail to persons arrested for or convicted of imprisonable offences.[18] They are:

(a) the nature and seriousness of the offence and the probable penalty;
(b) the defendant's character, antecedents, associations and community ties;
(c) his record in regard to any previous grant of bail; and
(d) the strength of the evidence; together with any other relevant consideration.

Home Office Circular 111/92 gave guidance on the matters that custody officers should take into account. These would include:

(1) the suspect's intentions as expressed for instance in any threats;
(2) his disposition as expressed in violent behaviour; and
(3) his prior record.

A criminal record would not in itself justify detention but the custody officer must consider that further detention is *necessary* to prevent injury, loss or damage. It would be legitimate to conclude that such injury, loss or damage exists where there is evidence of persistent and repetitive offending. The grounds for detention would be significantly strengthened if the suspect had previously offended whilst on bail. However the police should have in mind the nature of the breach of bail. An arrest for burglary in breach of bail for burglary was more of an indication for detention than where he was on bail for some unrelated offence. Each case must be considered on its individual merits.

The government estimated that giving the police the power to grant bail subject to conditions could reduce the numbers held overnight in police custody pending production in court by up to 40,000 out of a current total of around 100,000.

The procedure for releasing a person on bail from the police station is dealt with in Schedule 3 of the 1994 Act. If bail is given subject to conditions, the reasons must be stated by the custody officer on the custody record. The accused can ask the custody officer or another custody officer to vary the

---

[17] The above circumstances set out in s.38(1) are stated as amended by the Criminal Justice and Public Order Act 1994, s.28(2).
[18] The Criminal Justice and Public Order Act 1994, s.28(3) states that they are as set out in the Bail Act 1976, Schedule 1, Part I, paragraph 9.

conditions of bail. Such a request could result in more, as well as less, onerous conditions being imposed. When the matter reaches the magistrates they are free to impose whatever conditions seem right to them. The magistrates can deal with the matter not simply when the matter reaches the court in the ordinary way. Schedule 3 of the 1994 Act gives the accused the right to go to the magistrates simply for the purpose of seeking a variation of the conditions imposed by the police (new section 43B of the Magistrates' Courts Act 1980). See also section 47 below. (Bail after arrest.)

Detention of juveniles

The release of juveniles on bail is covered by exactly the same rules as apply to adults, except that a juvenile may also be denied bail if it is in his own interests.[19] An example of this might be the youngster picked up for an offence after he has run away from home. If it is not in practice possible to send him home on overnight bail he could be held in custody "in his own interests".

There are special rules in regard to juveniles who are not released on bail. The basic rule is that juveniles under the age of 17 must be transferred to local authority accommodation. There are however two exceptions. The first is where the custody officer certifies that it is impracticable to make the transfer to local authority accommodation.[20] These circumstances must be specified in the certificate. The Home Office Circular to the police issued in August 1992 (78/1992) stated (para. 9):

> "The construction of the statutory provision makes it clear that the type of accommodation in which the local authority propose to place the juvenile is *not* a factor which the custody officer may take into account in considering whether the transfer is impracticable. In particular, the unavailability of local authority secure accommodation does not make the transfer impracticable. The circumstances in which a transfer would be impracticable are those, and only those, in which it is physically impossible to place the juvenile in local authority accommodation. These might include extreme weather conditions (*e.g.* floods or blizzards) or the impossibility, despite repeated efforts, of contacting the local authority."

The Circular drew attention to the fact that Code C, Note 16B specifically states that neither a juvenile's behaviour nor the nature of the offence with which he is charged provides grounds for the custody officer to hold him in police custody on the ground of impracticability.

Some police forces have interpreted the word "impracticable" to cover cases where they considered the juvenile needed to be kept in secure accommodation which the local authority could not or would not provide. This interpretation was in effect approved by the Divisional Court in *R. v. Chief Constable of the Cambridgeshire Constabulary, ex p. Michel.*[21] The

---

[19] PACE, s.38(1)(b)(ii).

[20] This exception was originally in s.38(6) of PACE. The Criminal Justice Act 1991, s.59 replaced subsection (6) by a new (6) and (6A). The test of whether it is "impracticable" was however not altered. For the background see R. Leng, "Children in police cells—no change", *Solicitors' Journal*, December 6, 1991, p. 1312.

[21] (1990) 91 Cr.App.R. 325; [1991] 2 All E.R. 777 (Div.Ct.).

police had certified that it was impracticable to transfer a boy of 16 to local authority care because they feared he might commit further offences or interfere with the course of justice. The Divisional Court held that the police could legitimately hold the boy in police cells if the custody officer believed that the local authority's accommodation would be insufficient to prevent the very consequences which led to the original decision to refuse bail. As has been seen, a juvenile arrested for an imprisonable offence, like an adult, can for instance be refused bail to prevent him committing other offences. Paragraph 9 of the Home Office Circular quoted above as to the meaning of "impracticability" has to be read in light of the Divisional Court's decision.

The second exception to the general rule of transfer of juveniles to local authority accommodation originally affected 15 and 16 year olds. The Criminal Justice Act 1991, section 59 provided that the custody officer did not have to transfer to the local authority a juvenile aged 15 or over where no secure accommodation is available and keeping him in other accommodation would "not be adequate to protect the public from serious harm". But the Criminal Justice and Public Order Act 1994 lowered the age of 15 to 12 (s.24). This means that any juvenile between the ages 12 and 17 can now be held in police cells if the custody officer thinks it necessary to protect the public from serious harm. "Serious harm" is defined in the statute in relation to charges of sexual or violent offences quite narrowly as referring to "death or serious personal injury, whether physical or psychological, occasioned by further such offences".[22] "Serious harm" is not defined in relation to other offences but the Home Office Circular was presumably correct in suggesting that the statutory definition for sexual and violence offences indicated the gravity of risk of harm before the test would be satisfied.

Could children also be held in police cells because of the absence of secure accommodation even if there is no reason to fear serious harm to the public? There is obviously an argument that by making specific provision for detention of children in police cells where the police fear that the public would otherwise suffer serious harm, Parliament intended to indicate that detention for less reason would be illegitimate. But given the Divisional Court's broad interpretation of the word "impracticable" in *ex p. Michel*, this view cannot be advanced with complete confidence. The matter remains to be decided.

Responsibilities in relation to detained persons: section 39[23]

Section 39 concerns the responsibility of the custody officer for the proper treatment of detained persons as recommended by the Philips Royal Commission.[24] Subsection (1) requires the custody officer to ensure that anyone detained at his police station is treated in accordance with the requirements of the Act of any Code of Practice made under it. It states that the duties of the custody officer include responsibility also for seeing that everything required to be recorded in the custody record is in fact recorded. Code C spells this duty out further by the provision that the custody officer is "responsible for the accuracy and completeness of the custody record" (para. 2.3).

---

[22] New subsection (6A) in s.38 of PACE.
[23] See N.I. PACE Order, Art. 40.
[24] Philips Report, para. 3.112.

If the custody officer transfers custody of the suspect to the investigating officer, his duties in this regard are taken over by the person who has custody of the suspect (subs. (2)).[25] When he returns the suspect to the custody officer's custody the officer is supposed to report "as to the manner in which this section and the Codes of Practice have been complied with" (subs. (3)). If an arrested juvenile is handed over to the local authority under section 38(7) the custody officer's responsibility ceases (subs. (4)).

The Philips Royal Commission recommended[26] that even where the investigating officer outranks the custody officer it should be the latter not the former who has the decisive responsibility. Subsection (6) gives effect to this view, by requiring that if there is any conflict between the two the custody officer must refer the issue at once to a superintendent or more senior officer in charge of the police station. This makes it clear that the custody officer is directly responsible to the divisional or sub-divisional commander.

Evidence from the police to the Runciman Royal Commission expressed concern that the Code did not acknowledge the difficulty that, for reasons beyond their control, custody officers sometimes faced in complying strictly with the Code's rules. The Runciman Royal Commission supported the police concern.[27] A new provision in the 1995 revised Code now deals with the point. It states (Code C, para. 1.1A.) that a custody officer shall not be in breach of the Code for delay in processing a suspect "provided that the delay is justifiable and that every reasonable step is taken to prevent unnecessary delay". (*ibid.*) The custody record should indicate where such delay has occurred and why. Note for Guidance 1H states that excusable delay may occur for instance where a large number of suspects are brought into the police station simultaneously or the interview rooms are all being used or where difficulties are experienced in contacting an appropriate adult or solicitor.

Reviews of police detention: section 40[28]

The Philips Royal Commission recommended[29] that the need for detention should be reviewed periodically: on arrival at the police station, after six hours and then after 24 hours. The section adopts this approach but makes the requirement somewhat more onerous by specifying that it must be carried out within the first six hours and then at not more than nine hour intervals from the previous review. Time is measured from the time that detention was first authorised, *not*, as is the case for detention limits, from first arrival at the police station (subs. (3)(a)). Where the person concerned has already been charged the review would be by the custody officer; if not, it would be by an officer not involved in the investigation of the rank of inspector or above. The person performing the function is known as the review officer. His review is separate from and in addition to the first assessment by the custody officer on the suspect's arrival at the police station under section 37(2) and (3). These reviews must take place even though continued detention under section 42 has been authorised or a warrant of

---

[25] See for instance *R. v. Ismail* [1990] Crim.L.R. 109, C.A.
[26] Philips Report, para. 3.112.
[27] Recommendation 48, based on para. 34, Report, pp. 33–34.
[28] See N.I. PACE Order, Art. 41.
[29] Philips Report, para. 3.105.

further detention under section 43 has been issued. The purpose of the reviews is to ensure that the detainee is being properly treated and that he is released as soon as possible. Any conflict between the review officer and a more senior officer involved in the case must be referred at once by the review officer to a superintendent or above (subs. (11)).

A review may be postponed if, having regard to the circumstances, "it is not practicable" to have it at the specified time, or the suspect is actually being questioned at the time and the review officer is satisfied that interruption would prejudice the investigation or if no review officer is readily available (subs. (4)). It must however be conducted as soon as practicable. When the delay is because the suspect is being questioned, the review would take place normally in the next break in questioning. The grounds of any delay must be recorded in the custody record. Moreover, when there has been delay the next review must take place within the time limit as measured from the time when the prior review should have taken place not when it did in fact take place. Otherwise the suspect would be penalised by the fact of the delay (subs. (6)).

The grounds for keeping the suspect in detention must be given to the detainee in his presence if practicable. If not the information must be given as soon as practicable and in any case before he is first questioned (Code C para. 3.4). The grounds must be recorded in the custody record. But before authorising continued detention the review officer must give the suspect (unless he is asleep at the time) or any solicitor representing him who is available at the time, the opportunity of making representations (subs. (12)). The review officer can refuse to hear oral representations by the suspect himself "if he considers that he is unfit to make such representations by reason of his condition or behaviour" (subs. (14)). In that case he cannot however refuse to hear representations from a solicitor. In the custody officer's discretion, "other persons having an interest in the person's welfare" may also be allowed to make representations on his behalf (Code C para. 15.1 below). If the detainee is likely to be asleep at the time when the review needs to take place it should be brought forward so that he can make representations without being woken up (note 15A).

In the case of terrorism suspects the review of the need for initial and subsequent detention arises under Schedule 3 to the Prevention of Terrorism (Temporary Provisions) Act 1989. This provides that the first review must be as soon as practicable after the beginning of the detention and thereafter at intervals of not more than 12 hours (para. 3). The review officer in the first 24 hours should be an inspector and thereafter should be a superintendent. But no further review need be made after an application has been made to the Home Secretary for authority to detain the suspect beyond 48 hours.[30] The same persons as can make representations under section 40 may do so equally in regard to further detention under section 42 below (see Code C, paras. 15.1–15.2).

If in the circumstances the only practicable way of conducting a review is over the telephone then this is permissible. Reviews conducted over the telephone are by no means uncommon. But the review of the need for continued detention beyond 24 hours must always be conducted in person rather than over the telephone (Code C, note 15C).

[30] Under s.14(5) of or Sched. 5, para. 6(3) to the 1989 Act.

A new provision in the 1995 revision of Code C states that the officer conducting the review should not ask the suspect any questions about his involvement in any offence—any such questions would turn the review into an interview (para. 15.2A).

Time limits on detention without charge: section 41[31]

Under the pre-PACE law the time limit on police detention depended on whether the officer was regarded by the police as "serious". Section 43 of the Magistrates' Court Act 1980 required that where the offence was not serious and the suspect could not be brought before a magistrates' court within 24 hours he had to be released on bail. But where the offence was serious (and there was no definition in the Act) he simply had to be brought before a court "as soon as practicable" (s.43(4)).

The police tended to interpret the phrase "as soon as practicable" to mean "as soon as we have decided whether to charge him", rather than "as soon as a court can be found that is sitting". The result was that some suspects were held for long periods without charges. The only safeguard against this was the rare intervention of an application for habeas corpus which usually had the effect of forcing the police either to charge or release the suspect.[32]

The Philips Royal Commission took the view that this problem required drastic change and recommended that a proper system of time limits be imposed. The police, they recommended,[33] should not be permitted to hold a suspect without charges for more than 24 hours unless they had sought and obtained permission from a magistrates' court at a full hearing held in private at which the suspect would be entitled to be both present and legally represented. Moreover there should be no power to hold anyone for more than 24 hours unless he was suspected of having committed a grave offence.

Under the Philips Royal Commission's proposed scheme the magistrates' court would have been able to authorise further detention for periods of not more than 24 hours at a time—with no overall limit. After 48 hours however there would have been a right of appeal to a judge.

When the first Bill was first published it showed that the Government had made certain important modifications in the Philips Royal Commission's proposed scheme.

Its basic provision was that holding a suspect without charges for more than 24 hours would require a magistrate's permission. In the first instance an application would be made *ex parte* to a single magistrate. The hearing could be in the magistrate's own home. The suspect would only have had the right to appear before the magistrates after 48 hours. On the other hand, the magistrates could not authorise more than a total of 96 hours detention without charges. The provisions for holding a suspect beyond 24 hours only applied to serious arrestable offences.

These provisions were criticised from different vantage points. Some argued that it was wrong to delay the suspect's right to a full hearing to review further detention as long as 48 hours. Others contended that the

---

[31] See N.I. PACE Order, Art. 42.
[32] See generally C. Munro, "Detention after arrest" [1981] Crim.L.R. 802, and D. Wolchover, "The Police Bill and the scope of existing powers of detention for questioning" (1983) 80 L.S.Gaz. 2978. The most important cases were: *Houghton and Franciosy* (1978) 68 Cr.App.R. 197; *Hudson* (1980) 72 Cr.App.R. 163; *Sherman and Apps* (1981) 72 Cr.App.R. 266 and *Nycander, The Times*, December 9, 1982.
[33] Philips Report, para. 3.106.

application after 24 hours to a single magistrate possibly in his home and without requiring him to be attended by his clerk would tempt the police to shop around for a compliant magistrate. Also it was undesirable to have matters of such moment determined by a magistrate at his home.

The Government eventually decided to amend the scheme by abolishing the *ex parte* application to the magistrates and by advancing the time of the full hearing before the magistrates' court from the 48 hour point to the 36 hour stage. It resisted the argument that it should be brought forward even further to the 24 hour point mainly on the ground of the burden this would throw on all concerned.[34] Lengthy detention in a police station is relatively rare. The Philips Royal Commission said that about three-quarters of suspects were dealt with within six hours and about 95 per cent within 24 hours. The number of persons held for more than 24 hours was some 22,000 compared with only a few hundred held for over 36 hours. A survey done for the Philips Commission by the Metropolitan Police for three months in 1979 showed that only 0.4 per cent of 48,343 persons had been held for over 72 hours before being charged or released without charges.[35] (For more recent figures see p. 107 below.) The Philips Commission recommended that for the first 24 hours therefore authority for detention would be for the review officer. At the end of 24 hours it would have to be authorised by an officer of the rank of superintendent or above and from 36 hours onwards it could only be authorised by a magistrates' court after a full hearing at which the suspect could be present and legally represented. This scheme is that adopted in the Act.

The PACE provisions

Subsection (1) of section 41 provides that, subject to later provisions of the section and to sections 42 and 43, a person may not be detained without charge in police custody for more than 24 hours. This is the basic rule. Unless his further detention is authorised, he must be released with or without bail and cannot be re-arrested for the same offence unless new evidence comes to light (subss. (7) and (9)). As will be seen, detention can be authorised in some cases for up to an overall maximum of 96 hours, but after 36 hours it requires the permission of magistrates. The exception is terrorism cases where the initial period of detention without charges on the authority of the police themselves is a maximum of 48 hours and thereafter detention can be authorised by the Home Secretary for up to an overall maximum of seven days.[36] Detention under the PTA is separate from detention under PACE and very occasionally it happens that a suspect is held consecutively under the two regimes for a total in excess of seven days.[37]

Subsection (2) defines the time from which the period of detention is to be calculated (the "relevant time"). The normal case in paragraph (d) is where the arrest takes place locally for an offence committed in the same area. In

[34] House of Commons, *Hansard*, Standing Committee E, February 16, 1984, Col. 1218.

[35] Philips Report, para. 3.96.

[36] See Prevention of Terrorism (Temporary Provisions) Act 1989, s.14(5) and Sched. 5, para. 6(3).

[37] In Brown (1993), out of 253 terrorism detainees there were 10 who had previously been held for non-terrorist offences under PACE. In seven of these cases the period of PACE detention was under six hours. In two, PACE detention was for over 30 hours and in one it was over 40 hours. There were four cases in which overall detention was for more than seven days. The longest in the sample was eight days and three hours. (p. 53)

such a case time starts to run from the moment that the arrested person first arrives at the first police station after his arrest. This applies even if he has to be taken to another, possibly quite distant, police station in the same force area for questioning.

Where the person is arrested outside England and Wales, the time starts to run from the moment that he arrives at the first police station to which he is taken in the area in which the offence for which he was arrested is being investigated, or 24 hours after his arrival in England and Wales, whichever is the earlier. If therefore he has not arrived at his destination within 24 hours of entering England and Wales, time starts to run at that point (s.41(2)(b)).

If at any stage of being in police detention the detainee is taken to a hospital for medical treatment, time involved in travel there or back or at the hospital counts if he is actually being questioned about any offence but not otherwise (subs. (6)). Code C (para. 14.2) states that a person in police detention in hospital "may not be questioned without the agreement of a responsible doctor".

In the case of somebody already under arrest who is then arrested for further offences under section 31, time runs from the first offence for which he was brought into custody (subs. (4)). Otherwise time could be extended by the simple expedient of adding more and more arrests. For someone who comes to the police station voluntarily, time starts to run from the moment of his arrest (subs. 2(c)).

But what if the arrested person is actually wanted by police in some other area.[38] According to paragraph (a) of subsection (2), if the arrested person is arrested in one police area in England and Wales but is wanted in another, time starts to run when he comes into the custody of the second police force or 24 hours, whichever is the earlier.[39]

This is stated to be on the assumption that the force which have first arrested him make no inquiries into the alleged offence. If they in fact do start to question him after he has been arrested about the offence for which they arrested him, then time starts to run under paragraph (c) from the time that he first comes to a police station in the first area (subs. (3)(c)).

Code C states however that if a person has been arrested by one police force on behalf of another and lawful detention under section 37 has not yet commenced, he may not be questioned whilst in transit except to clarify a voluntary statement (para. 14.1).

If the suspect is wanted for questioning both where he is and in another area, there would in effect be two relevant times. In relation to the second area the relevant time would be 24 hours after leaving the first area or the moment of arriving at any police station in the second area, whichever was the earlier (subs. (5)).

Authorisation of continued detention: section 42[40]

Section 42 permits an officer of the rank of superintendent or above to authorise the detention of a person without charge beyond 24 hours and up

---

[38] This problem does not occur in Northern Ireland since the whole province is one police force area.

[39] It seems that the numbers transferred from one force to another are very low. In a sample of 5,500 prisoners in 10 force areas 1.5 per cent had been transferred from custody in one area to another: D. Brown (1989), p. 16, n.13.

[40] See N.I. PACE Order, Art. 43.

to 36 hours if this is necessary for the effective investigation of a serious arrestable offence (defined in s.116). No one may be detained beyond 24 hours without such authorisation.

The preconditions are that the senior officer must be satisfied that the investigation is being conducted diligently and expeditiously and that the detention of the suspect is still *necessary* to secure or preserve evidence relating to the offence or to obtain such evidence by questioning him (subs. (1)). The review, as has been seen, must be conducted on the spot rather than on the telephone (Code C, note 15C).

Such an authorisation may not be given more than 24 hours after time has started to run in regard to detention nor before the second review of detention under section 40 has taken place (subs. (4)). The purpose of the latter limitation is to ensure that continued detention is not authorised prematurely. If detention is authorised for less than the full 36 hours it may later be extended up to the 36 hours providing the conditions set out in subsection (1) still apply (subs. (2)).

When authorisation for continued detention has been given, the suspect must be told the grounds of the decision and they must be recorded in the custody record (subs. (5)).

The section also requires the police again to give the suspect (or his solicitor or, in the discretion of the custody officer, other persons interested in his welfare) an opportunity to make oral or written representations (subs. (6)). The requirement to allow representations to be made is mandatory. Failure to comply with it can be fatal to any application by the police to magistrates for extra time to question the suspect. This was the result in a case in 1987 in which the magistrate held that he had no jurisdiction to grant a warrant of further detention where the police had failed to allow the suspect's solicitor to make representations as required by section 42(6).[41]

The right of the suspect himself to make oral representations can be withheld if the police officer concerned considers that he is unfit by reason of his condition or behaviour (subs. (8)). If the suspect has not yet exercised his rights under sections 56 or 58 (to have someone informed of his whereabouts and to have legal advice) the officer must remind him of those rights (including the fact that legal advice is free—para. 15.3) and decide whether he should be allowed to exercise them. His decision must be recorded in the custody record, as must the reasons if he is refused permission (subs. (9)).

A person who has not been charged must be released within 36 hours after the detention clock has started to run unless further detention has been authorised by magistrates under section 43 (s.42(10)). If he has been charged, section 46 applies (see pp. 103, 365 below).

A person who has been released may not be re-arrested for the same offence unless new evidence justifying a further arrest has come to light since his release (subs. (11)). (But he can be re-arrested for failing to answer to police bail.[42])

Note that section 42 has nothing to do with the question of the moment in time that a suspect has to be charged. In *Samuel* the superintendent delayed charging a suspect in the belief that she was exercising a power granted by

---

[41] "In the matter of an application for a warrant of further detention" [1988] Crim.L.R. 296; also reported *sub nom. Police v. Mudd and McDonough*, Legal Action, Nov. 1987, p. 19.
[42] Amendment to subs. (11) of s.42 made by CJPOA s.29(4)(b). On the new power of the police to arrest for failure to answer bail see p. 104 below.

section 42. The Court of Appeal held that this was mistaken. ("We cannot accept this argument. In our judgment s.42 is dealing, and dealing only, with authorisation of continued detention and does not give the police any power to delay charging someone where the police have sufficient evidence to charge."[43])

Warrants of further detention: section 43[44]

Section 43 deals with the hearing before a magistrates' court to decide whether the police can hold the suspect for a longer period without any charge after the initial 36 hours. If so, the magistrates grant a warrant of "further detention" (and later perhaps an extension of the warrant: see s.44 below). By contrast, the authority of a superintendent to continue holding a suspect for longer than 24 hours in the police station is called, as has been seen, authorisation of "continued detention".

An application for permission to hold the suspect beyond 36 hours must be made on oath and *inter partes* to a magistrates' court. It must be supported by an information from the police officer, a copy of which must have been supplied in advance to the detainee. The court cannot start the hearing unless he has a copy and he is physically present (subs. (2)). If he does not have a lawyer and wishes to have one, the hearing has to be adjourned. He can be kept in police custody during such an adjournment (subs. (3)). If satisfied that there are sufficient grounds, the court may issue a warrant of further detention (subs. (1)). The tests for the magistrates are exactly the same as those for the superintendent considering further detention under section 42(1)[45]: that detention is necessary to secure or preserve evidence relating to a serious arrestable offence for which he is under arrest or to obtain such evidence by questioning him and that the investigation is being conducted diligently and expeditiously.

The court would clearly be entitled to take into account the suspect's response to police questioning. If therefore the evidence was that he had refused to answer all or most questions and if the court took the view that the real purpose of prolonging his detention was to break down his silence it would presumably refuse to grant the police application for further time. (This should still be so even now that the so called right to silence has been abolished—see pp. 303–323 below.)

The Opposition tried at the Committee stage in the House of Commons to persuade the Government to accept an amendment which would have required the magistrates, when considering an application for a warrant of further detention, to have regard specifically to whether he was answering questions willingly. The Government refused to accept the amendment. But the then Home Office Minister, Mr Douglas Hurd, made it clear that the principle was accepted:

"I do not doubt that in practice when interpreting the Bill the court would ask questions and want to hear evidence on how fruitful interviews had been if the application for further detention were based on this ground. That would clearly be an important consideration, and evidence on this

---

[43] [1988] Q.B. 615, 623, C.A.
[44] See N.I. PACE Order, Art. 44.
[45] See p. 98 above, p. 361 below.

subject—because we are talking of an *inter partes* hearing—would be given by the detained person who would be present and would be legally represented."[46]

Mr Hurd then referred to the fact (already mentioned above) that the phrase in the Act was that detention for questioning must be "*necessary* to secure or preserve evidence relating to an offence ... or to obtain such evidence by questioning him" (italics supplied) not that such questioning would be, "desirable, convenient or a good idea".[47] He also drew the attention of the Opposition spokesman to the provision in the Bill (now section 43(14)) which laid down what the police officer had to specify in the way of information in support of an application. Subparagraph (d) said the police must give "the reasons for believing the continued detention of that person to be necessary"—"again not convenient, desirable or a good idea but necessary" for the purposes of such further inquiries. A court he said would need to be satisfied on those points.[48]

Timing of applications

An application for a warrant of further detention may be made at any time before the detention clock has run for 36 hours, or if it is not practicable for a court to sit when the 36 hours expires but it can sit within six hours of that time, up to six hours after the expiry of the 36 hours (subs. (5)). In other words, the police can exceed the 36 hour limit by up to six hours where the 36 hour limit would expire, say, at 8 a.m. If the suspect is held in police custody for more than 36 hours, the fact and the reason must be recorded in the custody record (subs. (6)).

But this extra time has to be regarded as available only in special circumstances. If the court thinks that the police could and should have brought the application within the 36 hour period, they *must* dismiss the application—and as a result the suspect would have to be released (subs. (7)).

In *R. v. Slough JJ., ex p. Stirling*[49] the application was made two hours after the expiry of the 36 hour period. The 36 hours expired at 12.53 p.m. The clerk of the magistrates asked them to hear it a few minutes before 12.53. At that time the court was sitting but it postponed hearing the application until after lunch and actually heard the case at 2.45 p.m. They granted the police extra time. The Divisional Court allowed an application for judicial review on the ground that the police could have made their application for extra time between 10.30 a.m. and 11.30 a.m.

The commentary in the *Criminal Law Review* suggests that the decision "throws the whole system into unpredictable chaos" by saying that a court can legitimately postpone the hearing into the six hour period of extra time beyond the 36 hour period and then to have to refuse it because it could have been made earlier. The simple solution it was suggested would be to regard the application as made when the officer asks the court to consider it. But this is not the position under section 43. This was made clear by *R. v.*

---

[46] House of Commons, *Hansard*, Standing Committee E, February 16, 198, Cols. 1228–1229.
[47] *ibid.* Col. 1229.
[48] *ibid.*
[49] [1987] Crim.L.R. 576 (Div.Ct.).

Sedgefield Justices and another, ex p. Milne.[50] In that case the police contacted the court for a hearing at around 9 a.m. The 36 hour period was due to expire at 10.48 a.m. The court sat at noon but the hearing only took place at 12.54 p.m. The court thought it was legitimately within the extra six hour period. The Divisional Court said that the application was made when the police actually gave evidence. In this instance the police had acted reasonably but the court criticised the magistrates for not hearing the application sooner ("magistrates should perhaps be more open than the magistrates were on this occasion to the possibility of dealing with an application such as this at the first available opportunity"). The Police and Criminal Evidence Act 1984 laid down a precise timescale. The court had received the information about the need for a hearing at around 9 a.m. There was a court due to sit at 10 a.m. There was no sufficient reason to postpone the hearing until the end of the morning. There is therefore considerable pressure on the courts to have the hearing as soon as possible.

These hearings may require the court to sit at unsociable hours. But the note for guidance in Code C states that applications for a warrant of further detention (or its extension) should be made between 10 a.m. and 9 p.m. and if possible during court hours (note 15B below).

The court's decision

Under subsection (8), if the court is not satisfied that the further detention of the suspect is justified, it must either dismiss the application and thereby require the release of the suspect or, if time permits, adjourn the hearing until some later stage in the 36 hour period. (Obviously the latter would only be possible if the application has been made well prior to the expiry of the 36 hour period.)

The warrant of further detention must state the time at which it is issued and shall authorise the further detention of the suspect for whatever period the magistrates think—up to a maximum of 36 hours (subss. (10), (11) and (12)).

The court can take into account the fact that the police intend to move the suspect to a different police area (subs. (13)).

An information for the purpose of this section must be on oath in writing and must state the nature of the offence, the general nature of the evidence on which he was arrested, what inquiries have already and are still to be made, and the reasons why further detention is necessary for the purpose of such further inquiries (subs. (14)).

When an application is refused, the suspect must then immediately be either charged or released, on bail or unconditionally, unless subsection (16) applies (subs. (15)).

Subsection (16) permits the police to continue to hold the suspect for the full initial 36 hour period notwithstanding that permission to hold him longer than 36 hours from the relevant time has not been granted by the magistrates. This would obviously only apply where application had been made to the magistrate well before the expiry of the 36 hours and where a superintendent had authorised continued detention from the 24 hour to the 36 hour point. The right to hold him for the whole of the 36 hour period is so

[50] Lexis (November 5, 1987, Unreported) (Div.Ct.).

that the police are not penalised for making an early application. The court is asked whether he can be held beyond 36 hours from the relevant time. A refusal does not mean that detention up to 36 hours is improper.

A form of warrant of further detention and the endorsement to be used where a magistrates' court extends a warrant further are provided in the Schedule to the Magistrates' Courts (Forms) (Amendment) Rules 1985 which amended the Magistrates' Courts (Forms) Rules 1981.

The provisions for legal representation at such hearings is dealt with below.

It is important for a solicitor acting in an application for a warrant of further detention to insist that he be given reasonable time to take instructions and to prepare his argument. It seems that in some cases there has been a tendency to expect the solicitor to be ready within minutes of seeing his client.[51] The solicitor should ask to have a sight of the custody record form. (The notice given to suspects on arrival at the police station states that the custody record form will be available if the suspect is taken before a court.)

There is no valid reason why the magistrates on such a hearing should be informed of the suspect's previous convictions. His record is not relevant to the issue before the court: namely, whether further detention is still necessary to secure or preserve evidence relating to an offence for which he is under arrest or to obtain such evidence by questioning him; whether the offence is a serious arrestable offence; and whether the inquiry is being conducted diligently and expeditiously.[52]

Obviously, the solicitor acting for the suspect will need to check the custody record form to see that the requirements of the Code have been strictly adhered to. If he cannot persuade the court to refuse the application, he may at least succeed in getting a warrant that extends the period of detention by something less than the maximum of 36 hours.

The right to continue to hold the suspect is of course subject to the overriding principles stated in section 34(2) that the suspect must always be released if there do not appear to be any sufficient grounds to hold him any longer and in section 40 that the need for further detention must be reviewed periodically.

Where an application has been refused by the court, the police cannot make a further application unless further evidence has come to light (subs. (17)).

If a warrant of further detention is issued, the person concerned must be released on or before its expiry unless he has previously been charged (in which case ss.38, 40 and 46 apply) or an extension has been obtained. Someone who has been released on the expiry of a warrant of further detention cannot be re-arrested without a warrant for the same offence unless new evidence has come to light (subs. (19) paralleling s.41(9)).

Extension of warrants of further detention: section 44[53]

The police can apply to the magistrates for one or more further extensions of the time period up to the limit of 96 hours. The length of any such

---

[51] John Clegg, "Warrants of further detention", 132, Sol.J., March 4, 1988, p. 278 at p. 280.
[52] *ibid.*
[53] See N.I. PACE Order, Art. 45.

extension is in the discretion of the magistrates, save that no single extension can be for more than 36 hours. Such an application must again be made at an *inter partes* hearing and the suspect is entitled to be legally represented. There must again be an information under oath. Subsections (2), (3) and (14) of section 43 apply to such a hearing. If the application is refused the suspect must be either charged or released (subs. (7)), save that he can be held for the full period allowed by the previous application to the court (subs. (8)).

Detention before charge supplementary: section 45[54]

This section makes it clear that a magistrates' court for the purposes of this Part of the Act means a court sitting with two or more justices in private.

It also states that references to periods of time or times of day shall be treated as approximate only. Police officers therefore do not have to worry if they slightly exceed any specified time limit. It is for the courts to determine what degree of slippage will be regarded as venial. The Home Office Minister assured the House of Commons that there was no suggestion that this would be abused:

"The Hon. Lady ... will accept that in some matters that we have discussed where time limits are contained in the Bill, it is difficult to operate by a stopwatch. It should not be a matter of seconds or minutes either way. There will be circumstances when it would not be entirely reasonable to expect absolute and complete exactitude. That is why the word 'approximate' is in the clause. I do not believe that a court will give much leeway because of that word. ... We do not intend that the word should be used to undermine the important safeguards in the Bill. Equally, I hope that she will accept that some policing matters cannot be conducted with an exact regard for seconds or a few minutes."[55]

Detention after charge: section 46[56]

This section clarifies the law as to when a person must be brought before a court after he has been charged. Broadly, it provides that he must be brought before a court within 36 hours.

The basic provision is subsection (2) which states that he must be brought before a court "as soon as is practicable" but this hallowed phrase is amplified by the additional provision "and in any event not later than the first sitting after he is charged with the offence".

If there is no sitting arranged for the day when he is charged or the next day the custody officer must inform the clerk to the justices so that a special sitting can be arranged (subs. (3)).

If the suspect is to appear at a court in a different part of the country, he must be taken there as soon as is practicable and must similarly be brought before a court there as soon as is practicable—and in any event not later than the first sitting in that area after his arrival (subs. (4)). Subsection (5) requires the police to inform the justices' clerk if there is no sitting scheduled for that day or the next day.

[54] See N.I. PACE Order, Art. 46.
[55] House of Commons, *Hansard*, Standing Committee E, February 21, 1984, Col. 1260–1261.
[56] See N.I. PACE Order, Art. 47.

When the clerk to the justices has received information under subsection (3) or (5), he is under a duty to arrange a special sitting of the court for the day after the charge (or in the case of the person brought from a different part of the country, the day after his arrival in the area where he is to come before the court).[57] Sundays, Good Friday and Christmas Day can be ignored in this context (subss. (6), (7) and (8)). A person in hospital need not be brought to court if he is not well enough (subs. (9)).

Bail after arrest: section 47[58]

Release on bail by the police under this Part of the Act is stated to be under the ordinary provisions of the Bail Act 1976 (subs. 1).

Hitherto the police had no power to release someone on bail subject to conditions. As has been seen above, the Criminal Justice and Public Order Act 1994, section 27 gave the police that power for persons who have been charged.[59] Bail can now be granted by a custody officer subject to conditions similar to the conditions that can be imposed by a court under the Bail Act 1976.[60] (But the police cannot require a person to reside at a bail hostel nor to attend anywhere for the preparation of psychiatric or other reports.[61]) Conditions should not be imposed unless it is necessary to secure:

   (i) that the person surrenders to custody;
  (ii) that he does not commit an offence while on bail; or
 (iii) that he does not interfere with witnesses or otherwise obstruct the course of justice.[62]

Examples of normal conditions imposed would be to report to the police station, surrender of passport, a requirement to reside at a particular address, compliance with curfew requirements, not to go to a particular place or to see particular people, such as the apparent victim. If it is believed that the person will abscond, a surety or sureties can be required and if he is likely to leave the country, financial security can be required. The security can be in the form of cash or whatever else is considered appropriate. But in juvenile cases, the parent or guardian who must consent to be a surety, cannot be bound for a sum greater than £50—see Bail Act 1976, section 3(7).

The conditions can be varied by the same or a different custody officer—as well as by a court. But the variation may consist in imposing more as well as less onerous conditions.[63]

Arrest for failure to answer police bail: The Criminal Justice and Public Order Act section 29(2) gives the police a power they previously did not have, namely to arrest a person who fails to answer police bail.[64] For the

---

[57] For administrative problems created by the provisions see *R. v. Avon Magistrates' Courts Committee, ex p. Bath Law Society* [1988] Q.B. 409 (Div.Ct.); *R. v. Avon Magistrates' Courts Committee, ex p. Broome* [1988] 1 W.L.R. 1246 (Div.Ct.).
[58] See N.I. PACE Order, Art. 48.
[59] CJPOA, s.27(1) which added a new subsection 1A to s.47 of PACE giving the "normal powers to impose conditions of bail" where the custody officer releases a person under s.38 (*i.e.* after charge). The normal powers are those given by s.3(6) of the Bail Act 1976.
[60] The change was proposed by the Runciman Royal Commission—see Report p. 73, para. 33.
[61] Criminal Justice and Public Order Act 1994, s.27(3).
[62] Bail Act 1976, s.3A(5) added by CJPOA s.27(3).
[63] Bail Act 1976, s.3A(4) added by CJPOA s.27(3).
[64] New s.46A added to PACE by s.29(2) of the CJPOA.

purposes of sections 30 and 31 of PACE such an arrest is to be treated as an arrest for an offence. The arrested person should be taken as soon as practicable to the police station appointed as the place where he was supposed to surrender to custody.[65]

For the purposes of the provisions in Part IV of PACE regarding police detention, a person arrested for failing to answer police bail is to be treated as arrested for the offence in connection with which he was granted bail.[66]

A person released on bail subject to a duty to attend at a police station can also be re-arrested without a warrant if new evidence justifying a further arrest comes to light after his release (subs. (2)). Where someone has been granted bail subject to a condition of attending at a police station the custody officer has the power to cancel this requirement by notice in writing (subs. (4)). A person who comes back to the police station to answer to bail or is arrested there is "detained at a police station".

Subsection (8)(a) of section 47 substitutes a new section for section 43 of the Magistrates' Courts Act 1980. This deals with the court fixing a later date for a bail hearing and the enforcement of a recognisance of sureties.

Subsection (8)(b) slightly amends the procedure where someone is arrested on a warrant of commitment for fine default under section 117(2)(b) of the 1980 Act. Instead of his having to be taken to a police station to have his recognisance taken, it can be taken on the spot and he can then be released on bail. The purpose is to save the journey to the police station where this is unnecessary.

The person who takes the recognisance and gives the release must be qualified to do so. Outside the police station that means the police officer (or civilian enforcement officer) executing the warrant. If the case is dealt with at a police station it would be the custody officer.

Remands to police custody: section 48[67]

Under section 128(7) of the Magistrates' Courts Act 1980, the magistrates have power to remand a person who has been charged with offences to police custody for up to three days. This has to be for the purpose of allowing questioning about other offences. The section provides that in relation to such detention the "necessity principle" applies and when there is no longer any need to detain the suspect to question him about other offences he must be brought back to the magistrates' court. Whilst detained, the custody officer is responsible for him and the ordinary rules about periodic reviews under section 40(1) apply. Contrary to the view expressed in previous editions of this book, it now seems to this writer that these should be conducted by an officer of the rank of inspector, rather than by the custody officer. There are arguments to support either view. The view of the Home Office is that it should be an inspector.[68] The reason is that police detention after charge ordered by the magistrates (commonly referred to as a "three

---

[65] New ss.46A(1) and (2) of PACE added by CJPOA s.29(2). For the equivalent change in Northern Ireland see Appendix 4, p. 532 [Art. 7(1)].

[66] New s.34(7) of PACE added by CJPOA, s.29(3). For the equivalent change in Northern Ireland see Appendix 4, p. 532 below [Art. 7(2)].

[67] There is no equivalent in the N.I. PACE Order. The R.U.C. said they did not want the power.

[68] See opinion dated August 7, 1991, quoted in *Police Review*, October 18, 1991, p. 2109. The view is shared by Ken Sloan, Legal Editor of *Police Review*—see P.R. December 27, 1991, p. 2637.

day lie-down") is specifically stated to be solely for the purpose of inquiry into other offences[69] for which, by definition, the suspect has not yet been charged. On this view, it is, therefore, right that the reviews should be conducted in the manner appropriate to the situation where the suspect has not been charged (s.40(b)) rather than where he has been charged (s.40(1)(a))—even though he has been charged with different offence(s). The writer is persuaded that this is the better view.

Police detention to count towards custodial sentence: section 49[70]

Section 49 amends section 67 of the Criminal Justice Act 1967 so as to provide that any period spent in police detention (defined in s.118(2)) or under the terrorism legislation shall count towards any subsequent custodial penalty. But this only applies if the custody was in respect of the same offence.[71]

In order to ensure that the prison service has the necessary information to enable it to make the computations, the police are supposed to pass to the prosecution the details of times and dates of any police custody in connection with the offence. The prosecution should then hand the information to the clerk so that it can be linked to the warrant of commitment and passed on to the prison. In the instance of cases dealt with summarily the police should endorse the warrant of commitment themselves with the details, including the name of the police station where he was held and the name of the prison to which he is sent.

Records of detention: section 50[72]

The section requires each police force to keep records of the numbers of cases where persons are detained for longer than 24 hours and then released without charges, the numbers of applications for warrants of further detention, and the results of such applications and the periods of further detention authorised by the courts and the periods actually spent in custody in such cases. The record must also show whether persons detained under such warrants were eventually released without charges. Every annual report of a chief constable and of the Metropolitan Police Commissioner must likewise include such information.

Unfortunately, the records resulting from the provisions of section 50 published in the Home Office *Statistical Bulletin* have proved unsatisfactory. Part of the problem has been different methods of collecting the data used by different forces. Another has been confusion in the way the categories are defined. But the main problem is that the data the police have been asked to collect is not very informative. The figures show the numbers released without charges after being detained for more than 24 and 36 hours and

---

[69] "He shall not be kept in such detention unless there is a need for him to be so detained for the purposes of inquiries into other offences" (new s.128(8)(a) of the Magistrates' Courts Act 1980 added by s.48 of PACE).
[70] See N.I. PACE Order, Art. 49.
[71] *R. v. Towers* (1988) 86 Cr.App.R. 335, C.A.; *R. v. Secretary of State for Home Affairs, ex p. Read* (1987) 9 Cr.App.R.(S.) 206.
[72] See N.I. PACE Order, Art. 50.

under a warrant of further detention. It also shows the number of warrants of further detention, how many were granted and extended and the periods of time under such warrants. (Thus in 1993, warrants of further detention without charge beyond 36 hours were applied for in 310 cases, of which 301 (97 per cent) were granted. Of these 244 or 81 per cent were eventually charged.[73])

But even if these figures were produced in a clear and consistent way, they would tell us little of interest without figures as to the overall numbers arrested and the periods for which they are held prior to application for further time to the magistrates. The Runciman Royal Commission recommended that section 50 be amended so as to require the collection of figures that would show the numbers arrested, the numbers arrested subsequently charged and the numbers charged and not charged held for varying periods of time—under six hours, 6–12 hours, 12–24 hours, 24–36 hours, 36–72 hours and over 72 hours.[74]

A sounder basis for evaluation of the detention provisions in the Act is David Brown's Home Office study (Brown, 1989) based on police custody records of 5,500 prisoners held in March 1987 in 10 force areas.

The study provides a wealth of important facts. The salient facts relating to detention that emerge from this study are the following:

- Detention without charge for more than 24 hours occurred in less than 1 per cent of the sample (p. 61);
- Warrants for further detention (beyond 36 hours) were issued in only 11 out of 5,519 cases (0.2 per cent) (pp. 50–51);
- Just over half of those detained (56 per cent) were charged (p. 56);
- Only 12 per cent of those detained were released unconditionally— half with charges refused and half with no further action taken (p. 56);
- The mean period of detention for the sample, irrespective of outcome, was five hours and 10 minutes (the report states "this figure may seem high but ... this was because a minority of prisoners were held for much longer periods: 11 per cent were held for more than 12 hours" (p. 61)). The median length of detention was three hours and 19 minutes. By the six-hour mark, just over three quarters (76 per cent) of detainees had been dealt with. By the 12 hour point, 89 per cent had been dealt with and by 24 hours, as has already been seen, 99 per cent (see Table 6.5, p. 62). These figures suggested that overall, suspects were being processed somewhat more quickly than pre-PACE (pp. 62–63)[75];
- Excluding those detained very briefly after charges (for instance to check an address), 18 per cent of those charged were held in custody prior to court appearance, usually on the ground that they were likely to default on bail or that it was necessary to protect property, the prisoner or others (pp. 65–66);
- The mean length of detention after charge was nearly 16 hours (p. 67).

A later study by David Brown and colleagues, based on similarly large

---

[73] Home Office, *Statistical Bulletin*, June 1994, pp. 6–7.
[74] Recommendation 42 based on para. 21, Report, p. 30.
[75] See also the before and after research carried out in the Brighton police station by B. Irving and I. McKenzie (1989), pp. 81–84, 151–155.

samples drawn in 1990 and 1991, showed that the length of detention had not changed. The mean period of detention in the 1990 sample was five hours one minute, and in 1991, five hours 18 minutes. The median period in 1990 was three hours 13 minutes and in 1991 was three hours 20 minutes. (See Brown *et al.* (1992), pp. 104–105.)

In terrorism cases periods of detention are distinctly longer. Brown (1993) a study of 253 persons detained in 1989–1990 under the PTA showed an average period of detention of nearly 29 hours with a median of 16 hours 24 minutes. Just under 40 per cent of detainees had been released within 12 hours and nearly two-thirds within 24 hours (p. 50).

On the phenomenon of longer detention than pre-PACE for less serious offences see Irving and MacKenzie (1989) and Bottomley *et al.* (1991).

Savings: section 51[76]

Section 51 makes an exception from the provisions of Part IV of the Act for immigration officers in relation to controls of entry, police officers in relation to arrest and detention under the Prevention of Terrorism (Temporary Provisions) Act 1989[77] or police officers detaining military deserters, absentees or persons under escort.

Paragraph (d) of the section also preserves the right of persons detained by the police to apply for a writ of habeas corpus or any other prerogative remedy.

Children: section 52[78]

Section 52 dealt with the detention of children under 10 in community or other suitable places. It was repealed by the Children Act 1991, Schedule 15.

Note—further empirical evidence regarding detention

On decision-making by custody officers, see Bottomley *et al.* (1991a) and McKenzie *et al.* (1990) both of which showed that the initial decision to authorise detention and to approve continued detention were largely routinised rubber-stamping.

On custody officers generally see also Maguire (1988); Brown (1989); Sanders *et al.* (1989); Irving and McKenzie (1989); Bottomley *et al.* (1991a); Dixon *et al.* (1989a).

---

[76] See N.I. PACE Order, Art. 51.
[77] As amended.
[78] See N.I. PACE Order, Art. 52.

QUESTIONS AND ANSWERS

DETENTION

1. Who is responsible for the well-being of persons in custody?

The custody officer is required to ensure that persons in custody are treated in accordance with the Act and the Codes of Practice. Custody officers of the rank of sergeant or above must be appointed for all designated police stations. But an officer of any rank can perform the functions of the custody officer if none is readily available. At non-designated police stations the role of custody officer should always be played if possible by someone other than the investigation officer, but this is not an absolute requirement.

2. What happens if the custody officer and the investigating officer disagree as to how the suspect should be treated?

The custody officer is supposed to be separate from the investigating officer. It is the custody officer who is basically in charge. If the investigating officer is senior in rank and there is some disagreement between them as to the handling of the detainee, the custody officer is required to refer the matter at once to an officer of the rank of superintendent or above responsible for that police station. (The same applies to review officers, see below.)

3. What are the custody officer's duties before charge?

He must oversee all aspects of the detainee's treatment. He must ensure that the custody record form is properly maintained with all details of what transpires during the period of the suspect's detention. It is the custody officer's duty, *inter alia*, to decide initially whether the detention of the suspect is warranted.

4. On what grounds can someone be detained without charges?

There is only one ground of police detention prior to a charge—namely, that the custody officer reasonably thinks that such detention is "necessary to secure or preserve evidence relating to an offence for which he is under arrest or to obtain such evidence by questioning him" (s.37(2)).

When the suspect first arrives at the police station, it is the custody officer's duty to decide whether there is sufficient evidence to justify charging him. As soon as there is enough evidence he must be charged. If not, the question arises as to whether he should be detained. The question of the suspect's detention must then be kept under periodic review.

5. How often must there be reviews of the need for further detention?

The need for further detention has to be reviewed periodically after the initial consideration of the question by the custody officer. In the case of someone who has not been charged the review should be by a "review officer" of at least the rank of inspector who has not been directly involved in the investigation. The first review is supposed to be not more than six hours after the initial authorisation of detention by the custody officer. Thereafter the review should be at nine hour intervals.

Before deciding whether to authorise continued detention the review officer must give the person concerned or any solicitor representing him who is available at that time the chance to make representations either orally or in writing.

6. What happens if the time limits cannot be adhered to because the suspect is asleep or ill, is being questioned or for some other reason?

The Act allows for the review to be postponed "if ... it is not practicable to carry out the review at that time" (s.40(4)(a)).

7. How long can a suspect be held in the police station without charges?

The basic rule is that if the police wish to hold the suspect for more than 24 hours such extended detention must be authorised by a superintendent or above after inviting representations from the suspect or his solicitor. If the police wish to hold the suspect beyond the 36 hour point approval must be obtained from a magistrates' court. The magistrates cannot authorise detention for longer than a total of 96 hours. There are successive stages:

(1) Initial review of detention by the custody officer as soon as possible after arrival at the police station.
(2) Review of the necessity for further detention after the first six hours by an inspector (the review officer) and then at nine hour intervals.
(3) Review of the necessity for further detention after 24 hours by a superintendent; approval can be given for further detention up to the 36 hour point.
(4) Review of the necessity for further detention after 36 hours by a magistrates' court—the court is permitted to authorise detention for a maximum of 36 hours at one hearing. There must therefore be at least two hearings if the suspect is to be held for the full 96 hours.

8. Must these time limits be strictly adhered to?

The answer is both yes and no. There is a provision in the Act that "Any reference ... to a period of time or a time of day is to be treated as approximate only" (s.45(2)). This reflects the view that officers are not expected to walk around with stop watches. Also, the actual rules in the Act and Code make some allowance for the variety of problems that may come up. Thus, as has been seen, the review within the police station may be postponed if it is not practicable to conduct it at the right time. Though when this happens the next review is to be held at the time it should have been held if the first review had been at the correct time.

The hearing in the magistrates' court can be at any stage up to the 36 hour point. But the Act goes further and gives another six hours leeway, thus making a total of 42 hours. So if the 36 hour period would expire say at 6 a.m., the police have a further six hours and can lawfully bring the suspect to the court during the ordinary morning hearing. But if the court takes the view that the application for approval of further detention could and should have been brought within the 36 hours period it must dismiss the application.

Although there is therefore some flexibility in the time limits they are certainly not to be treated lightly.

9. From when is time counted?

In the ordinary case time starts to run from the moment that the suspect arrives at the first police station to which he is taken. But there are some special cases where the rules are different.

If he is arrested in one police force area but is wanted elsewhere, time starts to run from the time that he arrives at the first police station to which he is taken in the area where he is wanted for questioning—or 24 hours, whichever is the shorter. This is on the assumption however that he is not questioned in the area where he was arrested nor on the way to the second area. If he is in fact questioned time starts to run from that time.

If he is wanted in two areas, time starts to run in the second area 24 hours after leaving the first area or the moment when he reaches any police station in the second area—whichever is the earlier.

If he is arrested outside England and Wales, the detention clock starts from the time that he comes to a police station in the area where the case against him is being investigated or 24 hours, whichever is the shorter.

If at any stage he is taken to hospital whilst in police detention, time during which he is actually being questioned, whether en route or at the hospital counts but the rest of the time involved does not count.

10. What is the time limit if the suspect is arrested for other offences?

The time limit is unaffected. The time from which detention is measured is on the basis of the offence for which he was first arrested.

11. What sort of hearing is there before the magistrates?

The application must be heard by a magistrates' court with at least two magistrates and a court clerk sitting in private. The hearing cannot start unless the suspect is present and unless he has received a copy of the police application for the warrant of further detention. The suspect is entitled to be legally represented and if he has no lawyer and wishes to have one, the case must be adjourned while a lawyer is found. The costs of such representation are to be borne by the legal aid fund. There will be no means-test and no contribution from the suspect.

The police will make their application usually through the C.P.S. and the suspect or his lawyer, or both, will reply. The onus or burden of proof is on the prosecution to show why his further detention is necessary.

12. On what grounds can the police and the magistrates approve further detention?

The grounds on which further detention can be approved by the court are the same as those already applied by the superintendent at the 24 hour point:

(1) whether detention is necessary "to secure or preserve evidence relating to an offence for which he is under arrest or to obtain such evidence by questioning him";
(2) that the offence is a serious arrestable one; and
(3) that the investigation is being conducted diligently and expeditiously.

13. If the suspect has not been answering police questions can the court grant a warrant for further detention in the hope that that will enable the police to break him down by further questioning?

The answer to this question may in the end require a decision by the courts. But it would seem that the better view is that if that were indeed the reason for granting a warrant of further detention it would be unlawful. If the police have failed to get the suspect to co-operate with them after 36 hours their only hope of changing his attitude would be through conduct that would run the risk of being oppressive.

The justification for the 96 hour period of detention given time and time again by Home Office Ministers was that it would be necessary in a few very complex and important cases. There was never any suggestion that it was needed in order to "crack" the hard cases. On the contrary, this was repeatedly denied.

14. On what grounds can the suspect be held after he has been charged?

Once a person has been charged, the grounds for further detention change. In principle at that point he should not be questioned further; though the Code does now allow slightly more scope for questioning after charge than the old Judges' Rules (See Code, para. 16.5).

The sole permitted grounds for detention after charge (under s.38(1)) are:

(1) that his name or address have not been satisfactorily established;
(2) that the custody officer has reasonable grounds for believing that detention is necessary—
"for his own protection"; or
"to prevent him from causing physical injury to any other person"; or
"from causing loss of or damage to property"; or
"that he will fail to appear in court to answer to bail"; or
"that his detention is necessary to prevent him from interfering with the administration of justice or with the investigation of offences or a particular offence."

If he is an arrested juvenile there is an additional ground—

"that he ought to be detained in his own interests".

15. How long can the suspect who has been charged be held in custody without being brought before a court?

The old law was that he had to be brought before a court "as soon as practicable". This formula is also that adopted in the 1984 Act (s.46(2)). But it is strengthened by further provisions in the same section. These state that if there is no sitting of a local magistrates' court on the day on which he is charged or the next day (not counting Sundays, Christmas Day or Good Friday), the custody officer must inform the clerk to the justices that there is a person in custody for whom a special hearing will have to be held.

The Act then lays upon the clerk to the justices the duty of arranging a hearing not later than the day after he has been charged (or in the case of someone brought from another police district, the day after he arrives in the area).

16. Can the police impose conditions on a person granted bail from the police station?

Yes—under the provisions of the Criminal Justice and Public Order Act 1994. The police can now impose many of the same sort of conditions as can be imposed by the courts—to hand in a passport, to report to the police, not to go to a particular place or to talk to particular individuals, to reside at a particular address and the like. They cannot however make residence at a bail hostel a condition of getting bail. Failure to comply with the conditions gives the police the right to arrest the person concerned.

17. Can the police demand sureties as a condition of granting bail?

Yes.

18. If a person objects to the conditions imposed by the police, where can he go to have them changed?

He or his representatives can return to the police station to see whether the custody officer, (or a different custody officer) is willing to alter the conditions. Alternatively, he can ask the local magistrates' court.

Part V

QUESTIONING AND TREATMENT OF PERSONS BY POLICE

Abolition of certain powers of constables to search persons: section 53[1]

Section 53 abolished all common law and statutory powers to search persons at a police station including intimate searches. The present powers to carry out such searches are now to be found in sections 54 and 55 of PACE.

Searches of detained persons: section 54[2] and Code C, section 4

Prior to PACE there was no statutory basis for searching someone who had been arrested. The common law recognised the right of the police to do what was necessary to prevent the arrested person escaping, injuring himself or others or destroying evidence and the Philips Royal Commission recommended[3] that the power should be put on to a proper statutory basis and that it should include the power of making a full inventory. On the other hand, it said the process could be "humiliating and disturbing" and it should not be done routinely and, save in exceptional circumstances, a suspect should not be deprived of his watch.[4]

Section 54 and Code C, para. 4.1 requires the custody officer to take charge of this process. He must make or cause to be made a record of all the suspect's property unless the suspect is to be detained for only a short period and is not to be put in a cell, in which case in the officer's discretion it would be enough to make an abbreviated list—listing a handbag, for instance, without itemising the contents separately (note 4A). The duty to itemise the suspect's property applies when someone is brought to the police station under arrest or after being committed to police custody by order or sentence of a court or when someone is arrested after coming voluntarily to the station. In the case of an arrested person the record becomes part of their custody record. He should be allowed to check and sign the record of property as correct (para. 4.4). However he may be searched only if the custody officer considers it necessary in order to make a complete list of all his property and only to the extent that the custody officer considers it necessary for that purpose (subs. (6)). There is no right therefore to search

---

[1] See N.I. PACE Order, Art. 54.
[2] See N.I. PACE Order, Art. 55 and Code C, s.4.
[3] Philips Report, para. 3.116.
[4] *ibid.*, para. 3.117.

all suspects as a matter of course or routine.[5] But this is a broader power than under the previous law since it places the power to search on the need to make an inventory of the detainee's effects. Also it only requires the custody officer's honest belief that a search is necessary for it to be lawful. In fact searches are very common; virtually routine. Also, by virtue of an amendment to section 54 made by section 147 of the Criminal Justice Act 1988, the police can search anyone in police custody whether at a police station or elsewhere to ascertain whether he has with him anything which he could use to cause physical injury, damage property, interfere with evidence or assist him to escape (subs. (6A)). This amendment was designed to deal with items passed to the suspect by fellow detainees or visitors and also with searches outside the police station.

A search must be carried out by a constable and only by one who is the same sex as the person being searched (subss. (8) and (9)).

The 1995 revision of Code C deals with strip searches in a new section B of Annex A. A strip search is defined as a search "involving the removal of more than outer clothing". (For details of the rules for strip searches see p. 479 below.)

The custody officer may in his discretion retain anything which the arrested person has (subs. (3)), except for things subject to legal professional privilege and clothes and personal effects.

According to subsection (4), the custody officer may only retain clothes and personal effects if the custody officer believes that they might be used by the arrested person to cause physical injury to himself or anyone else, to damage property, to interfere with evidence or to assist him to escape. He may also retain such items if he has reasonable grounds for believing that they may be evidence relating to an offence. Note the difference between the two halves of this provision. The seizure of items that might be used to do harm does not have to be based on reasonable grounds, on the ground that police officers cannot be expected to anticipate what exactly the suspect might do. Seizure of evidence does, however, need to be on reasonable grounds. There is no mention in either the Act or the Code of the Royal Commission's recommendation that a suspect should always be allowed to keep his watch.

Where property is seized, the person from whom it is taken must (under subs. (5)) be told the reason (unless he is or is likely to become violent or is incapable of understanding what is said to him) and the reason must be recorded (Code C, para. 4.5). Section 22(2)(a) provides for the retention by the police of items seized.

Intimate searches and strip searches: section 55 and Code C, Annex A[6]

The subject of intimate searches of body orifices is dealt with separately in section 55. The Philips Royal Commission recommended[7] that if the search was of intimate parts of the body it should be carried out only by a doctor and only where the offence in question was a grave one. It should require the authorisation of a sub-divisional commander.

---

[5] *Lindley v. Rutter* [1981] Q.B. 128 (Div.Ct.) and *Brazil v. Chief Constable of Surrey* [1983] 3 All E.R. 537 (Div.Ct.). But see also *Middlewick v. Chief Constable of Merseyside, The Times,* August 1, 1986.
[6] See N.I. PACE Order, Art. 56 and Code C, Annex A.
[7] Philips Report, para. 3.118.

The Government did not agree with the Royal Commission's safeguards. When the first Bill was published, an intimate search required the approval only of a superintendent. Such authorisation could be given if the offence in question was a serious arrestable one and there were reasonable grounds for believing that such a search would produce relevant evidence or that such a search was necessary to establish that the detainee had nothing that could be used to injure himself or others. The second Bill at first qualified this by limiting the ground for an intimate search to a search for something that could be used as a weapon or to injure oneself or others. Searches for evidence (or drugs offences for instance) were not permitted. The decision was largely based on the view of the doctors who, according to the former Home Office Minister, Lord Elton, said that they would not be willing to conduct searches without consent to obtain evidence of crime but would do so to protect life.[8] Needless to say the police regarded this alteration as thoroughly unhelpful. Also they criticised the logic of denying the police the right to conduct intimate searches for evidence but retaining the power for Customs and Excise officers at airports and ports. The then Home Office Minister Mr Douglas Hurd conceded that the powers available to the Customs and Excise under the Customs and Excise Management Act 1979, s.164 were "valuable" and should be retained. For reasons that he did not explain, that, however, was a different issue.[9]

But during the summer recess, between the Report stage and the Third Reading in the House of Lords, the Government changed its mind again on this controversial issue. It introduced an amendment to the Bill designed after all to permit an intimate search for drugs. The rules for searches for weapons and searches for drugs are, however, different in certain important respects.

The rules apply to an "intimate search" which is defined in section 65[10] as "a search which consists of the physical examination of a person's body orifices other than the mouth". This would mean anus, vagina, nostrils and probably ears. The Home Office Circular on PACE (p. 8 above, paras. 43–44) said that a physical insertion into a body orifice would constitute an intimate search as would "any application of force to a body orifice or its immediate surroundings". The circular also suggested that even a mere visual inspection of intimate parts of a body should be regarded as an intimate search "even though physical contact may be absent". But in *Hughes*[11] the Court of Appeal held that making a suspect spit out something (in that case a plastic wrapper containing cannabis) he had just put into his mouth was not an intimate search. It was not a search so much as action taken to prevent destruction of evidence. A search required some physical intrusion into a body orifice, some physical examination rather than mere visual examination or an attempt to get the person to extrude what was contained in a body orifice.

All intimate searches are subject to the following rules: (1) the search must be authorised by an officer of the rank of superintendent or above on the basis of reasonable belief that the arrested person in police detention has

---

[8] House of Lords, *Hansard*, July 19, 1984, Col. 710.
[9] House of Commons, *Hansard*, Standing Committee E, February 23, 1984, Col. 3059.
[10] Intimate searches were previously defined in s.118 of PACE. The Criminal Justice and Public Order Act 1994, s.59 moved the definition to s.65 and excluded searches of the mouth.
[11] *The Times*, November 12, 1993, C.A.

concealed on him anything which could be used to cause physical injury to himself or to others and that he might so use it or a class A drug (subs. (1)); (2) authorisation may be oral or written, but if oral it must be confirmed in writing (subs. (3)); (3) authorisation may not be given unless there are reasonable grounds for believing that the item in question cannot be found without such a search (subs. (2)). If therefore it could be expected to pass through the natural bodily functions and there is time to wait for this to happen, this should be preferred; (4) the suspect must be told the reasons for the intimate search (Annex A(a) para. 1).

The rules diverge however in regard to who may carry out such a search. Searches for weapons can in the last analysis be carried out by police officers. The former Home Office Minister Mr Douglas Hurd said on this issue that all were agreed that if possible intimate searches should be carried out by a doctor both because it was safer and because "it provides a degree of human dignity and reassurance". But it might be that no doctor could be found who could carry out the search within a reasonable time or the doctor might not be willing to carry out such a search.[12] Swift action might be necessary. The British Medical Association, he said, accepted that in exceptional circumstances there might be a need for an intimate search to be carried out without the person's consent to remove an object which was of immediate danger to the life of the suspect and those in his proximity. Guidance would be made available to doctors by the B.M.A. to that effect. But there was no way of guaranteeing that the particular doctor approached would agree to carry out such a search without the consent of the suspect. It was therefore necessary to have the reserve power that permitted such a search to be conducted by a police officer.[13]

Such a search must be made by a "suitably qualified person" unless an officer of at least the rank of superintendent considers that this is not practicable (subs. (5)). The use of the word practicable in this context is not entirely clear. Presumably it is intended to cover the situation where a doctor is asked but refuses to carry out the search without the consent of the suspect. But does it also cover the rather different case where no effort is made to contact a doctor because the police believe there is none likely to be available at that hour of the day or night, or because the police know that any doctor asked would be likely to refuse? A "suitably qualified person" is either a doctor or a registered nurse (subs. (17)). There is no stated requirement on the police to make any attempt to get such a person to carry out the search, nor even to ask the suspect whether he wishes the search to be carried out by a qualified person, though this duty was in an earlier version of the Code.

Where such a search is not carried out by a doctor or nurse it must be carried out by a police officer of the same sex as the suspect. Code C (Annex A, Pt. A, para. 6) states that when the intimate parts of the body are searched, no one of the opposite sex who is not a doctor or nurse may be present (unless the person is a juvenile or mentally handicapped or disordered and specifically requests the presence of a particular adult of the opposite sex (Annex A, Pt. A, para. 5)). The custody record must show as soon as practicable which parts of the body were searched and why (subss.

---

[12] *op. cit.* n.8 above, Col. 3039.
[13] *ibid.* Col. 3040.

(10) and (11)). The Code (Annex A, s.A, paras. 7 and 8) requires that the record must also show who carried out the search, who was present, the reason for the search and the result. Intimate searches (like strip searches, see below) should be conducted "with proper regard to the sensitivity and vulnerability of the suspect this circumstance" (Annex A, paras. 6, 11(d)).

If the search is for drugs, it can only be carried out by a doctor or registered nurse and it cannot be carried out in a police station (subss. (4) and (9)). Intimate searches for drugs are limited to those for hard drugs defined as Class A drugs in Schedule 2 to the Misuse of Drugs Act 1971 (There are over 80 drugs listed in the Schedule. They do not include cannabis.) But the superintendent who authorises the intimate search must reasonably believe not only that the suspect has such drugs concealed in a body orifice but that he was in possession of them at the time of his arrest with intent either to supply or export them (subss. (1)(b)(ii) and (17)). Someone suspected merely of being a user could therefore not be subjected to an intimate search.

Anything found in the course of an intimate search may be seized by the police if it could be used to cause physical injury, or damage to property, interfere with evidence or to assist an escape or if there are reasonable grounds for thinking that it could be evidence relating to an offence (subs. (12)). The power of seizure is therefore broader (in covering evidence) than the power of intimate search.

The chief constable's annual report must include information about the total number of intimate searches, the number carried out by doctors or nurses, the number carried out by someone else in the presence of such a person, and the result of the searches (subss. (14), (15) and (16)).

The Home Office gives annual figures for the number of intimate searches. The highest number recorded (in 1986) was 104; the lowest (in 1993) was 41. Almost all these searches are made by "suitably qualified persons".[14]

Strip searches

Code C, Annex A, as revised in April 1995, separates for the first time the regime for intimate searches[15] from that for strip searches.[16] A strip search may take place only "if it is considered necessary to remove an article which a person would not be allowed to keep, and the officer reasonably considers that the person might have concealed such an article" (Annex A, Pt. B, para. 10). Hitherto authorisation of a strip search had to be by the custody officer. Under the 1995 revised Code this requirement has been dropped. The regime for strip searches (Annex A, Pt. B) provides:

(a) that the officer should be of the same sex (para. 11(a));
(b) that the search should take place where it cannot be observed by persons who do not need to be present nor a person of the opposite

---

[14] "Operation of Certain Police Powers Under PACE", Home Office Statistical Bulletin, June 1993. In Brown *et al.*, (1989), intimate searches were found in only seven out of 5,519 cases, 0.1 per cent (p. 53).
[15] "An intimate search is a search which consists of the physical examination of a person's body orifices other than the mouth" (Annex A, Pt. A, para. 1).
[16] "A strip search is a search involving the removal of more than outer clothing" (Annex A, Pt. B, para. 9).

sex save for an appropriate adult with the agreement of the suspect (para. 11(b));

(c) that wherever possible two but not more than two persons other than the suspect should be present (para. 11(c));

(d) suspects should not be required to remove all their clothes at the same time (para. 11(d)); and

(e) that a person may be required to hold his or her arms in the air or to stand with legs apart and to bend forward so as to permit examination of the genital and anal areas—provided that no physical contact is made with any body orifice (para. 11(e)). Removal of any article from a body orifice constitutes an intimate search.

Code C (Annex A, Pt. B, para. 12) requires that a record of a strip search be made on the custody record including the reason why it was considered necessary, those present and any result. Even if authority is not given by the custody officer, he should if possible always be consulted in advance, failing which, informed after the event.

The right to have someone informed when arrested: section 56 and Code C, section 5 and Annex B[17]

Section 56 states that a suspect has a right to have someone informed of the fact of his arrest. It replaced section 62 of the Criminal Law Act 1967. The power can only be delayed on the authority of a superintendent and only if the offence is a serious arrestable one. (It is to be distinguished from the quite separate right created by Code C, paragraph 5.6 to make a telephone call "for a reasonable time to one person". This cannot only be delayed it can be denied altogether. A decision to delay or deny can be taken by an inspector and it can be made if the offence is merely an arrestable one. (See p. 120 below).)

The Philips Royal Commission recommended[18] that this right be retained but that the details be spelled out even more fully. This recommendation was reflected in the Act and Code C.

Section 56 states that when a suspect is under arrest and is being held in custody in a police station or elsewhere he is entitled, if he so requests, to have "one friend or relative or other person who is known to him or who is likely to take an interest in his welfare", to be told at public expense as soon as practicable that he is under arrest and his whereabouts (subs. (1) and Code C, 5.1). Terrorism suspects in Northern Ireland have similar rights under section 14 of the Northern Ireland (Emergency Provisions) Act 1987. The Prevention of Terrorism (Temporary Provisions) Act 1989, Sched. 3, para. 7(1) says that if a terrorism suspect in England and Wales has not exercised his right under section 56 by the time the need for further detention is reviewed by an inspector (within 24 hours) or a superintendent (thereafter) he should be informed of the right. If its exercise is being delayed he should be so informed. The right to have someone informed as to one's whereabouts is not specifically applied to persons attending a police station as volunteers though they can, of course, ask for this to be done.

If such a person cannot be contacted, Code C says that two alternates may

---

[17] See N.I. PACE Order, Art. 57; Code C, s.5 and Annex B.
[18] Philips Report, para. 4.80.

be nominated. If they too cannot be contacted, the custody officer has a discretion to allow further alternates until the information has been conveyed (para. 5.1). If the suspect knows no one to contact, the custody officer should consider contacting any local agency that might be able to help him (note 5C).

Delay is only permissible in the case of serious arrestable offences[19] and only if authorised by an officer of the rank at least of superintendent (subs. (2)). There is no requirement however that the superintendent be independent of the investigation. An attempt to persuade the Government to accept this requirement failed.[20] Equally it is not required that the serious arrestable offence necessarily be the one for which the suspect was arrested.[21] Under Code C (paras. 3.1–2) this right is one of which the suspect must be told both orally and in writing "when a person is brought to a police station under arrest or is arrested at the police station having attended there voluntarily". A person who is still voluntarily at the police station is not covered by this requirement since he is deemed to be free to go if he pleases. But there is no doubt that he has a right to have someone informed of his whereabouts and this right is not subject to the provisions for delay.

The grounds for delaying are set out in Annex B which is dealt with more fully at page 131 below. Broadly, they are that there are reasonable grounds for believing that telling the named person of the arrest will lead to interference with or harm to evidence or witnesses or the alerting of others involved in such an offence; or the recovery of any property (subs. (5) and Code, Annex B). These are the identical grounds for delaying access to legal advice under section 58 below. As will be seen (pp. 131–135) the courts have interpreted this power to delay very strictly against the police. Presumably the same approach applies to this power. The courts have held that section 56 is quite separate and independent of section 58—as is indeed specifically stated to be the case by Code C.[22] Delay under section 56 therefore has to be separately approved.[23]

If delay is authorised, the suspect must be told of the fact and of the reasons for it and the reasons must be noted on his custody sheet (subs. (6)). When the grounds for delay cease to apply the suspect must be permitted to exercise his right to have someone informed of his whereabouts (subs. (9)). If the suspect is moved from one police station to another, the right to have someone informed of his whereabouts arises again (subs. (8)).

Brown (1989) found that 18 per cent of the 5,500 or so suspects in the sample requested that someone interested in their welfare be told of their detention (p. 34).

The take-up varied considerably between police stations. Some of the variation was explicable but some was not. The author suggested that variations both in this regard and in regard to take-up of legal advice (see below) could have been affected "by the way in which custody officers outline detainees' rights to them and levels of awareness among the criminal community of their rights" (p. 35).

---

[19] See s.116, and Sched. 5.
[20] House of Commons, *Hansard*, Standing Committee E, February 23, 1984, Col. 1385.
[21] *ibid.* Col. 1387.
[22] "The fact that the grounds for delaying notification of arrest under paragraph 1 above may be satisfied does not automatically mean that the grounds for delaying access to legal advice will also be satisfied." (Code C, Annex B, Note B5.)
[23] *R. v. Parris* (1989) Cr.App.R. 68, C.A.; *Lifely, The Times*, July 16, 1990 C.A.

It appeared from the custody record that the police managed to contact the designated person in two-thirds of cases where notification was sought. Usually, this was a parent or other relative (65 per cent of cases) but in a minority of cases either a friend (16 per cent) or a social worker (4 per cent).

Contact was generally made quickly. In half the cases it was done within 15 minutes, in 60 per cent within half an hour and in 75 per cent within one hour (p. 35).

Authority to delay notification was given by a superintendent in 53 cases (just under 1 per cent, p. 35).

Brown *et al.* (1992) found that delays were being imposed even less frequently—in only 0.1 per cent of cases (p. 68). Bottomley *et al.* (1991a) found that sometimes the police resort to informal means to achieve delay, for instance by carrying out the duty to inform only when they come to search the suspect's home. This obviously does not comply with the duty to carry out intimation "as soon as practicable" as required by PACE section 56(1).

Where an inquiry as to the whereabouts of a detained person is made by his friends or relatives, or a person with an interest in his welfare, they should be told where he is, unless the exceptions permitting delay in Annex B apply or unless the suspect himself does not consent to this (Code C, para. 5.5). Action taken under this paragraph must be recorded on the custody record. No one may be prevented from notifying the outside world of the fact of his arrest under section 56 for more than 36 hours (subs. (3)) from "the relevant time" as defined in section 41. The time limit applies even to terrorism cases (subs. (11)).[24] However, in regard to terrorism cases there are additional grounds on which delay of exercise of the right up to a total of 48 hours can be approved as was recommended by Lord Jellicoe's report[25]: namely where notifying someone would be likely to lead to interference with the gathering of information about acts of terrorism or make it more difficult to prevent an act of terrorism or to secure the arrest, prosecution or conviction of anyone in connection with terrorism charges (subs. (11)).

Brown (1993) found that far higher proportions of those detained under the terrorism provisions request that someone be informed of their detention. One reason may be that they can be detained longer. Another may be that they are often arrested at ports and airports and would want to notify those expecting them. Of those detained over an 18 month period, 43 per cent asked to exercise this right. The power to delay was used extensively—in over 70 per cent of cases where requests were made (p. 25). In about half (48 per cent) the delay had not been lifted by the time the detention ended (p. 27).

The permitted telephone call Code C, paragraph 5.6 provides that, subject to some conditions, the suspect should be supplied with writing materials on request and should be allowed to speak on the telephone for a reasonable time to one person. This is specifically stated (in note 5E) to be separate from the right to have someone informed about the fact of his arrest under paragraph 5.1 and the right to seek legal advice in person or on the telephone under paragraph 6.1.

---

[24] The N.I. PACE Order, Art. 57(10) disapplies subs. (11). The relevant provision for Northern Ireland is in the Northern Ireland (Emergency Provisions) Act 1987, s.14.

[25] *Review of the Operation of the Prevention of Terrorism (Temporary Provisions) Act*, Cmnd. 8803 (1983), para. 112.

Whether the call is at public expense is in the discretion of the custody officer. Any officer may listen to what is being said, unless the call is to a solicitor, and may terminate the call if it is being abused (para. 5.7).

The detainee must be cautioned that what he says in any letter, call or message (other than in communication to his solicitor) may be read or listened to and may be given in evidence (para. 5.7).

There is no obligation to inform the suspect of the right to make a telephone call—though the Notice of Entitlements does contain the information. Few suspects request to make a telephone call. Brown (1989, pp. 35–36) found that only 6 per cent did so. Brown *et al.* (1992, p. 58) found requests by 12 per cent of the sample drawn after the 1991 revision of the Codes.

Also, as has been seen, whereas if it is a serious arrestable offence the rights under paragraphs 5.1 and 6.1 can be delayed only on the authority of a superintendent, *these* rights can be delayed *or denied*[26] on the authority of an inspector if paragraph 1, 2 or 8 of Annex B apply[27] and the suspect is in detention in connection with an arrestable or serious arrestable offence. But, according to police records, they are in practice very rarely either delayed or denied. Brown (1989) found 4 per cent of requests delayed; Brown *et al.* (1992) found 2 per cent delayed or denied (p. 58). The latter study does suggest however that there is under-recording both of requests and of the outcome of the request. Their observational data suggested that 12 per cent of suspects request telephone calls and their interviews with suspects suggested that up to a quarter of requests are delayed or refused (p. 58). Also the decision was sometimes taken without reference to the inspector as required by the Code.

In terrorism cases, Brown (1993) found a higher level of requests for telephone calls (49 out of 253 or 19 per cent) and a higher level of delays (17 out of 49 or 35 per cent). Nevertheless, calls were eventually made in 12 out of the 17 cases (or 71 per cent) in which delay was authorised. In two of these cases the call was however only made after the suspect had been charged (pp. 27–28).

Foreigners

The previous somewhat muddling rules relating to foreigners and Commonwealth citizens in Code C, section 7 were simplified in the 1991 revision of the Code. Instead of making distinctions between categories of overseas persons they are now all treated alike. Paragraph 7.1 states that a citizen of an independent Commonwealth country or a foreign national, including one from Eire, "may communicate at any time with his High Commission, Embassy or Consulate". He must be informed of this right as soon as practicable (Code C, para. 3.3). He must also be told as soon as practicable of his right to have the High Commission, Embassy or Consulate told of his whereabouts and the grounds for his detention. In the case of Commonwealth citizens or foreigners from a country with which a consular Convention is in force,[28] his High Commission, embassy or consulate must be informed as soon as practicable (para. 7.2) unless he is a political refugee

---

[26] This power was added by the April 1991 revision of Code C.
[27] Broadly, these provisions cover interference with the investigation—see pp. 481–482 below.
[28] A list of such countries as at January 1, 1995 appears in Annex F (see p. 486 below).

(para. 7.4). It is therefore surprising that at least in terrorism cases the rules seem quite often to be flouted. Brown (1993) found 70 terrorism cases in which the suspect came from a country with which there was no consular convention in force. Most, (64) were from the Irish Republic. Embassies were informed in only 17 of the 70 cases. All 17 were Irish cases. In a further 15 cases the suspect was told of his right to inform his Embassy but declined to exercise it (pp. 37–38).

Consular officials are stated to be free to visit one of their nationals "to talk to him and if required to arrange for legal advice" (para. 7.3). Such visits "shall take place out of the hearing of a police officer" (*ibid.*).

The rights of Commonwealth citizens and foreign nationals to inform someone of their whereabouts after arrest cannot be interfered with even when it is a case covered by Annex B (Code C, note 7A).

Juveniles

As will be seen (p. 186 below), the custody officer must inform the parents of those under 17 or another "appropriate adult" of his detention. This is a duty laid upon the custody officer which the juvenile cannot veto. It is technically distinct from the right of notification under section 56. A juvenile could therefore request that someone in addition to the appropriate adult be informed.

Visitors

Suspects have no absolute right to visitors while in custody but they are entitled to receive visitors at the custody officer's discretion (Code C, para. 5.4, and note 5B). This is referred to in the Notice or Rights and Entitlements but it is very rarely exercised. Brown (1989, p. 36) found that only 5 per cent of suspects had a visitor, usually a parent or other relative (50 per cent) or friend (24 per cent). In terrorism cases Brown (1993, p. 28) found 8 per cent of suspects had visitors.

Additional rights of children and young persons: section 57[29]

Section 57 replaced section 34(2) of the Children and Young Persons Act 1933 which provided that where a child or young person has been arrested, reasonable steps must be taken to inform his parent or guardian. The Philips Royal Commission recommended[30] that this provision should be reaffirmed and section 57 gave effect to the recommendation. It requires that when a child or young person is in police detention such steps as are practicable must be taken to ascertain the identity of a person "who has, for the time being, assumed responsibility for his welfare" (Code C, para. 3.7). That person should, if possible, be informed as soon as practicable that the child or young person has been arrested, why and where he is being held (subss. (3) and

[29] See also text of the Act, p. 374 below.
[30] Philips Report, para. 4.80.

(4)). This rule applies even if the child or young person is held in connection with a terrorism investigation (subs. (10)).

The person responsible for his welfare, in addition to the parent or guardian, is "any other person who has for the time being assumed responsibility for his welfare" (subs. 5). For a child in care this means the local authority or voluntary organisation which has him in care. For someone in respect of whom there is a supervision order it means the person responsible for his supervision. In case no one else can be located the social services of the local authority or any other responsible adult should be notified.

Code C, as will be seen (pp. 160, 185–189 below), has various provisions regarding the interviewing of juveniles. The relevant one regarding notification of the fact of arrest is paragraph 3.9 which requires that if the arrested person is a juvenile the custody officer must as soon as practicable inform the "appropriate adult" (see pp. 186–189 below) of the grounds for his detention and his whereabouts and ask the adult to come to the police station to see the juvenile.

The custody officer's duty to inform an appropriate adult of the juvenile's arrest and to get him to the police station is quite separate from the juvenile's right to have someone informed of his arrest under section 56 (subs. (9)). Section 57 is headed "Additional rights of children and young persons" but it deals in fact with *duties* of the police.

Access to legal advice: section 58; Code C, section 6[31]

The pre-PACE law regarding access to legal advice for suspects in the police station was to be found in the Preamble to the Judges' Rules and in the dicta of judges in a number of cases.[32] It was generally agreed that few suspects asked to see a solicitor and that, of those who did, the majority were refused such access.[33]

The Philips Royal Commission[34] thought that a suspect should be informed that generally he had a right to see a solicitor privately. The right to see a solicitor should be withheld only in exceptional circumstances which it listed and which should be confined, it thought, to grave offences.[35] Refusal of access to a solicitor it said[36] should require the authority of a sub-divisional commander and the grounds should be specified on the custody sheet. If for any reason a suspect could not be brought before a magistrate within 24 hours, he should be seen by a solicitor whose duty it would be to ensure that he was being properly cared for.[37]

The Act 1984 broadly adopted the Philips Royal Commission's approach.

---

[31] See N.I. PACE Order, Art. 59 and Code C, s.6.
[32] See especially *Allen* [1977] Crim.L.R. 163; *Lemsatef* [1977] 2 All E.R. 835; *Elliott* [1977] Crim.L.R. 551; *Reid* [1982] Crim.L.R. 514.
[33] See, for instance, M. Zander, "Access to a Solicitor in the Police Station" [1972] Crim.L.R. 342; J. Baldwin and M. McConville, "Police Interrogation and the Right to See a Solicitor" [1979] Crim.L.R. 145; P. Softley, "An Observation Study in Four Police Stations" *Royal Commission on Criminal Procedure*, Research Study 4 (1981), p. 68.
[34] Philips Report, para. 4.87.
[35] Philips Report, para. 4.91.
[36] *ibid.*
[37] Philips Report, para. 3.107.

Granting the suspect an absolute right to legal advice (s.58(1)) subject to a strictly defined power to delay such advice in exceptional circumstances (s.58(8)) see below p. 131).

The right to legal advice

The basic provision is section 58(1) which states that "A person arrested and held in custody in a police station[38] or other premises shall be entitled, if he so requests, to consult a solicitor *privately* at any time" (emphasis added). Code C, paragraph 6.1 (as revised in April 1995) states:

> "Subject to the provisos in Annex B all people in police detention must be informed that they may at any time consult and communicate privately, whether in person, in writing or by telephone with a solicitor, and that independent legal advice is available free of charge from the duty solicitor."

The only kind of suspect who does not have this right to consult privately with a solicitor is one held under the terrorism legislation. Such a suspect does now have the right to legal advice[39] but an officer of the rank of inspector can, in certain circumstances, direct that the consultation be in the sight and hearing of a uniformed officer.[40] The situations are the same as those for which the police can delay access to a solicitor (under subs. (8) and Annex B—see below) plus, in addition, the reasonable belief that otherwise there would be interference with the gathering of information about acts of terrorism or that by alerting anyone it might make it more difficult to prevent an act of terrorism or to apprehend other terrorism suspects (s.58(12), (14) and (15)).

A person who is at a police station voluntarily has the same right to legal advice as a person who is there under arrest (Code C, note 1A) but he need not be specifically so informed unless he asks.

Where the suspect being detained by the police is a juvenile or someone who is mentally handicapped or disordered either the detainee or the appropriate adult (see p. 186) may exercise the right to ask for legal advice (Code C, para. 3.13). Note 3G of the 1995 revised Code C says that if the juvenile, mentally disordered or mentally handicapped person wishes to exercise the right to legal advice, action should be taken straightaway and not delayed until the appropriate adult arrives.

Where a suspect has been permitted to consult a solicitor and the solicitor is available, he must be allowed to have the lawyer present during the interview (Code C, para. 6.8).

The consultation can be either in person, on the telephone, or in writing

---

[38] A person on remand in custody at a magistrates' court is technically not within this phrase but it was held that such a person has a common law right to consult a solicitor "as soon as practicable". The police were therefore not justified in having a rule refusing a person in custody at court access to a solicitor if the request was made after 10 a.m. See *R. v. Chief Constable of South Wales, ex p. Merrick* [1994] Crim.L.R. 852; New L.J., March 25, 1994, p. 423 (Div.Ct.).

[39] Introduced following the Report of Lord Jellicoe, *Review of the Operation of the Prevention of Terrorism (Temporary Provisions) Act*, Cmnd. 8803 (1983), paras. 108–110. The provision of legal advice for terrorist suspects in Northern Ireland is in the Northern Ireland (Emergency Provisions) Act 1987, Art. 15.

[40] Research has shown that this power is used very rarely. Out of 384 police station consultations between suspects held under the P.T.A. there were only nine directions, involving two cases, that consultations should take place within the sight and hearing of a police officer. (Brown (1993), p. 16.)

(Code C, para. 6.1). Requests to see a solicitor must be recorded on the custody record (subs. (2)). (This requirement does not apply however if the request is made "at a time while he is at court after being charged with an offence" (subs. (3)). The Government's reasoning was that he would then be in the custody of the court rather than of the police.)[41] Normally the request must be allowed as soon as practicable (subs. (4)) and in any event it must be allowed within 36 hours (subs. (5)) or in terrorism cases, 48 hours—from the time of arrest, not the time of arrival at the police station (subs. (13)(a)).

Code C (para. 3.5) requires that when the custody officer authorises a person's detention in the police station (see below) he must be asked to sign on the custody record to signify whether he wants legal advice at that point. The 1991 revised Code emphasised the point by adding a new sentence that the custody officer is responsible to make sure that he signs in the correct place.

Informing the suspect of his right to free legal advice

Under the U.S. Supreme Court's famous ruling in *Miranda v. Arizona*[42] the American police are required to inform a suspect of his right to legal advice at the point of arrest. The basic English approach, by contrast, is that the suspect should be told of his right to have a lawyer on arrival at the police station. Section 58 itself does not deal with the point directly but it states that a person is entitled to *exercise* the right if he has been arrested and *is held in a police station*. Code C deals with the point in the same way by requiring that all persons *in police detention* must be informed about the right to consult a solicitor. The English rule is based on the theory that, since the suspect must be taken to the police station as soon as practicable (s.30), and interviewing should only be conducted at the police station (Code C, para. 11.1[43]), there is no need to inform him of his right to consult a solicitor prior to arrival at the police station. Whether that view is sensible is debatable. But what if he is *in fact* interviewed elsewhere? There is conflicting Court of Appeal authority as to whether in those circumstances he must be informed of his right to have legal advice.[44] It is submitted that the better view is that if the suspect is in fact interviewed at a place other than a police station he must be informed of this important right[45]—whether or not it is practicable to make the necessary arrangements for the solicitor to arrive before the interview takes place. Otherwise the right to be told about the availability of legal advice may come too late to be of any use.[46]

---

[41] But see *ex p. Merrick*, n.38 above.

[42] 384 U.S. 436 (1966).

[43] "Following a decision to arrest a suspect he must not be interviewed about the relevant offence except at a police station" unless delay would cause certain unacceptable consequences set out in para. 11.1.

[44] See *Kerawalla* [1991] Crim.L.R. 451, C.A.—interview of drugs suspect by customs officers in a hotel; cp. *Sanusi* [1992] Crim.L.R. 43, C.A.—interview of drugs suspect by customs officers in customs area at Gatwick. In the former case the court held there was no duty to inform the suspect of his right of access to legal advice. In the latter, the court, which included Lord Taylor C.J., took the contrary view.

[45] The Court of Appeal in *Samuel* said: "Perhaps the most important right given (or rather renewed) to a person detained by the police is his right to obtain legal advice." ((1988) 87 Cr.App.R. 232 at p. 241, *per* Hodgson J.) A person who has been arrested is plainly a person detained by the police.

[46] In *Sanusi*, above, the suspect made admissions when first interviewed. At a later point he was told he could have a solicitor. From then on he declined to answer questions until the solicitor arrived. The Court of Appeal drew attention to this fact when holding that the first interview should have been excluded.

A person must be told of his right to consult privately with a solicitor "when a person is brought to a police station under arrest" or is arrested there after coming voluntarily (Code C, para. 6.1). That means forthwith.

The April 1995 revision of the Code added new provisions designed to strengthen access to legal advice.[47] The custody officer must act on a request for legal advice "without delay" (para. 6.5). If the detainee declines legal advice, the custody officer must now point out that the right to legal advice includes the right to speak with a solicitor on the telephone and ask whether he wants to do so (*ibid.*). If the detainee still declines legal advice, the custody officer should ask his reasons and record them (*ibid.*).[48] There are also provisions requiring that the detainee be reminded of the right to legal advice at different stages. Where someone chooses to speak to a solicitor on the telephone "he should be allowed to do so in private unless this is impractical because of the design and layout of the custody area or the location of the telephones" (note 6J).

Legal advice in the police station is free

Legal advice given to a suspect in the police station is free of charge regardless of the suspect's means and regardless of whether he chooses to have his own solicitor or a duty solicitor. The suspect must be informed of this fact when he is first brought to a police station under arrest or is arrested there. (Code C, para. 3.1(ii)). It is one of the items of information he must also be given in written form. (Code C, para. 3.2.)

The Code also lays down that police stations advertise the right to legal advice in posters "prominently displayed in the charging area of every police station" (para. 6.3). When that would be helpful and it is practicable, the poster should have translations into the main relevant ethnic minority languages and the principal European Community languages (Note 6H).

The Code lays down precise rules as to the point in time at which someone in a police station must be informed of his right to legal advice and whether such notification should be oral, written or both:

(1) As has been seen, a person who comes to the station under arrest must be told immediately both orally and in writing (Code C, paras. 3.1 and 3.2).

(2) A person who comes to the police station voluntarily, if he asks about legal advice, must be given a written notice about legal advice (Code C, para. 3.16). (But there is no duty to inform him if he does not ask!)

(3) A person who comes to the station voluntarily and is arrested there must then be told of his right to legal advice both orally and in writing (Code C, paras. 3.1 and 3.2).

(4) A person who comes to the station voluntarily and is then cautioned must then be given verbal notice of the right to legal advice (Code C, para. 3.15), and he should be given a copy of the notice explaining the arrangements for getting free legal advice (para. 3.16). He should be told that free legal advice includes a right to speak with a solicitor on the telephone and asked whether he wants to do so (para. 3.15).

Code C (note 6B) says that a person who asks for legal advice should be

---

[47] Along lines proposed by the Runciman Royal Commission, Recommendation 59, based on Report, para. 49, p. 36.

[48] "Once it is clear that a person neither wishes to speak to a solicitor in person or by telephone he should cease to be asked his reasons" (para. 6.5).

given an opportunity to consult a specific solicitor (for example his own solicitor or one known to him or someone else from that firm), or the duty solicitor (see below). Failing this he should be given an opportunity of choosing a solicitor from a list of those willing to provide legal advice. If this solicitor is unavailable, he can choose up to two alternatives. If these attempts to secure legal advice are unsuccessful, the custody officer has discretion to allow further attempts until a solicitor has been contacted who agrees to provide legal advice. But the police officer is not to advise the suspect about any particular firm of solicitors (*ibid.*).

Revised Code C has a new provision that no police officer shall at any time do or say anything with the intention of dissuading a person in detention from obtaining legal advice (para. 6.4); and that reminders of the right to legal advice must be given in accordance with paragraph 11.2 (commencement or re-commencement of interviews), paragraphs 15.3 (reviews of further detention), 16.4 (inviting comment on someone else's statement after charge), 16.5 (questions after charge and Code D, paragraphs 2.15(ii) (before identity procedure) and 5.2 (request to take an intimate sample).

If a solicitor arrives at the police station to see someone, that person must be informed that the solicitor is there and asked whether he wishes to see him—even if he has already declined legal advice (para. 6.15).[49] This will apply especially when the solicitor has been sent by a family member or friend without the suspect's knowledge. (See to like effect Annex B, para. 3 after access to a solicitor has been delayed.)

Duty solicitor schemes were originally provided for by section 59 of the Act which enabled the Law Society to establish such schemes. (To encourage participation by solicitors, section 59 included a provision making it possible to require those doing duty solicitor work in magistrates' courts also to undertake duty solicitor work in police stations.)

Duty solicitor schemes run by local committees were set up all over the country under the Legal Aid (Duty Solicitor) Scheme 1985[50] and directions and guidance issued by the Law Society's Legal Aid Committee.[51] The scheme was modified slightly in 1988. But in 1989 it was taken over with the rest of the legal aid system by the Legal Aid Board established by the Legal Aid Act 1988. The 1988 Act repealed section 59. The Act does not actually require the Legal Aid Board to provide duty solicitor services, but it provides enabling provisions in Part III relating to advice and assistance. In April 1989 the Duty Solicitor Arrangements 1989 replaced the Legal Aid (Duty Solicitor) Scheme 1988. The latest version is the 1994 Arrangement.

There is no statutory duty solicitor scheme in Northern Ireland and therefore nothing about it in the Northern Ireland PACE Order. There are voluntary schemes at Belfast and Craigavon but it seems that the demand and the interest to date is low. It is anticipated that some such scheme as in England may eventually be set up.

Duty solicitors

The Duty Solicitor Arrangements provides that duty solicitors must be persons vetted and approved by the local committee on the basis that they

---

[49] See *Franklin, The Times*, June 16, 1994, C.A.
[50] For text see *Law Soc.Gaz.*, November 20, 1985, pp. 3319–3330.
[51] *ibid.* pp. 3313–3319.

are qualified solicitors with practising certificates who "regularly practise in criminal defence work" and have "comprehensive experience of criminal defence work including advocacy in magistrates' courts throughout the previous eighteen months. ..."[52] (There are slightly different requirements for those who have been in full-time employment in the prosecution system.)

Sending a representative

Advice in the police station is frequently given by non-solicitor representatives. Such a representative sent by a duty solicitor must be a person authorised to do such work.

The Arrangements provide for the local committee to approve a request that the work of the duty solicitor be done by a "representative". The committee must be satisfied that such a person is in full or part-time employment and "has had experience of providing advice at a police station on behalf of the duty solicitor" on the basis of experience depending on his status. (Those who are solicitors are supposed to have had four months experience of criminal cases as a solicitor or articled clerk; a solicitor's clerk should have had at least three year's experience of criminal defence work; a trainee solicitor should have had at least six months experience including four months in criminal cases.)[53] The committee must also be satisfied that the person in question "is competent to act as a duty solicitor's representative".

The Duty Solicitor Arrangements (1994, para. 53(3)) state however that a duty solicitor can only arrange for a representative to give advice after he has first himself given the suspect initial advice (usually on the telephone)—as to which see below p. 130. The representative must also now be "accredited" under the new training arrangements.[54]

Training arrangements for representatives

Under a new scheme taking effect from February 1995 the Legal Aid Board will only pay for police station work done by "own solicitor" representatives if they are on the accreditation list.[55] It was announced in January 1995 that duty solicitor representatives and trainee solicitors were also being brought into the accreditation scheme but that this would be staggered to give practitioners time to plan for the change.[56]

---

[52] Legal Aid Board Duty Solicitor Arrangements, 1994, para. 32(f).
[53] *ibid.* para. 45.
[54] For the background and an assessment of the new scheme see L. Bridges and J. Hodgson, "Improving Custodial Advice" [1995] Crim.L.R. 101–113.
[55] An accredited representative must be certified by a supervising solicitor as of suitable character to give police station advice. Would-be advisers not accredited by February 1, 1995 must register for a probationary period on a provisional basis for up to six months before doing the test. During that time they can only advise in non-indictable cases.

Before becoming accredited they must present a portfolio of nine cases. In at least two they must have (a) observed a solicitor giving advice; (b) have been observed by a solicitor when giving advice; and (c) have given advice when unaccompanied.

The portfolio presented must include details of the training and study undertaken by the representative. There is a two-hour written test on criminal law and procedure. Finally there is a "critical incidents test" the purpose of which is to assess effectiveness in simulated situations in the police station. Tapes are played and responses to the situation have to be given on tape.

Those who fail the test cannot register again on a provisional basis for a year and can only do so a total of three times. The Law Society has produced a massive training pack. For further details see *Law Soc.Gaz.*, June 22, 1994, p. 34 and January 11, 1995, p. 29.
[56] *Law Soc.Gaz.*, January 11, 1995, p. 29.

Guides

The Law Society has put out an impressive—and costly—comprehensive training pack—*Police Station Skills for Legal Advisers* (London, The Law Society, 1994). (It consists of *Advising a Suspect in the Police Station*; *Putting Skills into Practice—A Workbook*; *A Pocket Reference*; *Becoming Skilled—A Resource Book*; *A Supervisor's Guide*; and a two-cassette audio tape.)

See also especially Ed Cape, *Defending Suspects at Police Station* (Legal Action Group, 1993).

The telephone service

The duty solicitor is contacted through a special telephone service covering the whole of England and Wales. From January 1992 it has been run by the Automobile Association. When a suspect asks for the duty solicitor a call is made to the service (it does not handle calls to a named solicitor or a solicitor chosen from a list. They are contacted by the police). The service then contacts either the rota duty solicitor or duty solicitors on the panel until one is found who is willing to assist the suspect.

In rota schemes an identifiable solicitor is on duty; in panel schemes the service calls the solicitors on the panel in the order in which they appear on the list, starting with the next one after the last one used.

A duty solicitor on a rota is under an obligation to accept a referral unless already engaged with another suspect.[57] A panel duty solicitor is not under such a duty. The advantage of a rota is that the service only has to contact one solicitor and that he is in principle guaranteed to be available—subject obviously to the duty solicitor work he already has in hand. The disadvantage is that a solicitor has to hold himself available to go to a police station. Among the advantages of the panel arrangements are that it allows the duty solicitors on the panel to carry on with their normal occupations, but it may lead to delay in actually finding a solicitor.

Advice on the telephone or attendance in person

The Duty Solicitor Arrangements (para. 53(2)) provide that the duty solicitor is required to give initial advice by speaking directly to the suspect on the telephone unless he is so close to the police station as to be able to provide advice in person "immediately".

In certain circumstances the duty solicitor *must* advise the suspect. These are where:

(1) the suspect has been arrested in connection with an arrestable offence and the police intend to interview him;
(2) the police intend to resolve an identification issue by parade, group, film, video or confrontation; or
(3) the suspect complains of serious maltreatment by the police.[58]

If any of these circumstances apply and the suspect requests attendance at

---

[57] Duty Solicitors Arrangements, 1994, para. 53(1).
[58] *ibid.* para. 54.

the police station, the duty solicitor must attend either in person or by an authorised representative unless there are exceptional circumstances justifying non-attendance. If the police postpone an interview until after the duty solicitor goes off duty he must make arrangements for someone else to be there.

In other circumstances the duty solicitor has a discretion whether to attend the police station in person. One of the matters to be taken into account is whether in practice advice can be given on the telephone with sufficient confidentiality. Where the suspect is a juvenile or a person otherwise at risk the duty solicitor must work on the basis of a presumption that he should attend in person.[59]

Delaying access to legal advice

Unless the suspect is being questioned about a serious arrestable offence[60] there is no legal right to delay access to legal advice. On the contrary Code C, paragraph 6.5 states: "Whenever legal advice is requested (and unless Annex B applies) the custody officer must act without delay to secure the provision of such advice to the person concerned." If however the suspect is being held in police detention[61] in connection with a serious arrestable offence, access to legal advice may be delayed if the case comes within the terms of section 58(8) and Annex B (see below).

If delay is authorised, the detained person must be told the reason for it and the reason must be recorded in the custody record (subs. (9)). There can be no more delay once the reason for authorising delay no longer applies (subs. (11)). If the grounds for delay cease to apply the person must, as soon as practicable, be asked if he wishes to exercise the right, the custody record must be noted accordingly, and action must be taken (Annex B, para. 4 and 9).

The maximum period of delay is normally 36 hours (Annex B, para. 4). At that stage the suspect is entitled as of right to have legal advice in connection with the hearing which must take place to determine whether the police can hold him further. In the case of those held under the Prevention of Terrorism (Temporary Provisions) Act such delay can continue for up to 48 hours (Annex B, para. 8).

Grounds for delay: section 58(8); Code C, section 6, Annex B

Delay has to be authorised by an officer of the rank of superintendent. It can only be authorised where he has reasonable grounds for believing that the exercise of the right:

(a) will lead to interference with or harm to evidence connected with a serious arrestable offence or interference with or physical injury to other persons; or
(b) will lead to the alerting of other persons suspected of having committed such an offence but not yet arrested for it; or

---

[59] *ibid.* para. 55.
[60] Defined in s.116 and Sched. 5—see p. 296 below.
[61] Defined in s.118(2).

(c) will hinder the recovery of any property obtained as a result of such an offence.

Annex B of Code C specifies two additional grounds for delaying access to legal advice for terrorism suspects—namely where there are reasonable grounds for believing that it will lead to "interference with the gathering of information about the commission, preparation or instigation of acts of terrorism; or by alerting any person, will make it more difficult to prevent an act of terrorism" or to secure the apprehension or conviction of someone for a terrorist offence (*ibid.* para. 8).

Delay can also be authorised where the offence involves drug trafficking and the officer has reasonable grounds for believing that the suspect has benefited from such trafficking and that the recovery of the value of the proceeds will be hindered (Code C, Annex B, para. 2).[62]

During the Parliamentary debates on the Bill the Home Secretary Mr Douglas Hurd put the following gloss on the words of section 58(8): "The only reason under the Bill for delaying access to a legal adviser relates to the risk that he would either intentionally or inadvertently convey information to confederates still at large that would undercut an investigation in progress. What a suspect's legal adviser says to him can never be a ground for delaying a consultation between them, nor can anxiety about what the legal adviser might say to the suspect. Delay can be authorised only on the basis of what the legal adviser may do once the consultation has been completed."[63] The Code specifically states that access to a solicitor may not be delayed or denied on the ground that he may advise the person not to answer questions nor on the ground that someone else instructed the solicitor to attend— provided that the detained person then wishes to see the solicitor (Annex B, para. 3).

The attitude of the courts toward section 58

The courts have frequently held that breach of the main thrust of section 58 is a serious matter—in the jargon used by the courts a significant and/or substantial breach of the Act and the Code. Sometimes this has led to the court penalising such breaches by excluding evidence or, on appeal, quashing the conviction. Sometimes the courts have declared there to have been a breach but have upheld the conviction by "applying the proviso".[64] Sometimes, the courts have in effect condoned the breach, usually on the ground that the suspect knew his rights and legal advice would have made no difference to him.

The leading case is *Samuel*.[65] The Court of Appeal quashed a 10 year prison sentence because the police had refused the suspect access to a solicitor under section 58(8). A superintendent had denied the request on the ground that there was a risk that giving the suspect access to a solicitor would result in accomplices being alerted. The Court of Appeal said that

---

[62] This does not apply however in Northern Ireland since there is no equivalent drug trafficking legislation.
[63] House of Commons, *Hansard*, Standing Committee E, February 2, 1984, Col. 1417.
[64] The proviso to s.2 of the Criminal Appeal Act 1968 allows the court to uphold a conviction even when it accepts that the appellant had a valid point of appeal, on the ground that no substantial miscarriage of justice has occurred. But see now Criminal Appeal Act 1994.
[65] [1988] Q.B. 615, [1988] 2 W.L.R. 920, [1988] 2 All E.R. 135, C.A. See to like effect *inter alia, Absolam* (1989) 88 Cr.App.R. 332, C.A. and *Walsh* (1989) 91 Cr.App.R. 161, C.A.

access to a solicitor was "a fundamental right of a citizen". It was not enough for the police to believe that giving access to a solicitor *might* lead to the alerting of other suspects. They had to believe that it very probably would and that the solicitor either would commit the criminal offence of alerting other suspects or would do so inadvertently or unwillingly. Either belief could only rarely be genuinely held by the police officer. Solicitors are intelligent professional people. The expectation that they would alert accomplices "seems to contemplate ... a naivety and lack of common sense in solicitors, which we doubt often occurs. When and if it does, we think it would have to have reference to the specific person detained. The archetype would, we imagine, be the sophisticated criminal who is known or suspected of being a member of a gang of criminals." The first question was whether the police officer subjectively held the belief. The second question was whether the belief was objectively reasonable. The difficulty of establishing the grounds for delaying access to a solicitor existed would be especially great where the suspect wanted to consult a duty solicitor. "Duty solicitors will be well known to the police, and we think it will therefore be very difficult to justify consultation with the duty solicitor being delayed." The police suspicion had to relate to the actual adviser who was being called.[66] The decision in *Samuel* made the power to delay given by section 58(8) virtually unusable in relation to solicitors.[67]

Matters that the court have emphasised have included the following:

- Would the solicitor have advised silence—*Samuel*,[68] *Parris*,[69] *Silcott*,[70] *Anderson*.[71]
- Was the defendant able to cope—was he of low mental capacity or otherwise unable to look after his own interests—was he knowledgeable about the police station and his rights—*Hughes*,[72] *Chahal*,[73] *Alladice*,[74] *McGovern*,[75] *Gokan and Hassan*.[76]

---

[66] This is now reflected in Code C, Annex B, Note B4: "The officer may authorise delaying access to a specific solicitor only if he has reasonable grounds to believe that specific solicitor will, inadvertently or otherwise, pass on a message from the detained person or act in some other way which will lead to any of the three results [alerting of accomplices, etc., set out in s.58(8) and Annex B, para. 1] coming about. In these circumstances the officer should offer the detained person access to a solicitor (who is not the specific solicitor referred to above) on the Duty Solicitor Scheme."

[67] For a rare case where delay was justified by the delicate nature of the investigation see *R. v. Governor of Pentonville Prison, ex p. Walters* [1987] Crim.L.R. 577 (Div.Ct.).

Note also Code C, paras. 6.12–6.13 and note 6F regarding denial of access to unqualified representatives on which see further p. 137 below.

[68] n.65 above. The solicitor gave evidence that he would probably have advised silence.

[69] (1989) 89 Cr.App.R. 68; [1989] Crim.L.R. 214, C.A. Conviction for armed robbery quashed. The suspect was deprived of the solicitor both as adviser and as "umpire" to see that evidence was not fabricated.

[70] *The Times*, December 9, 1991, C.A.

[71] [1993] Crim.L.R. 447, C.A.

[72] [1988] Crim.L.R. 519, C.A. No breach of s.58. H was an educational psychologist.

[73] [1992] Crim.L.R. 124, C.A. No breach of s.58. C, a mature businessman twice said he did not want a solicitor. *Cf. Franklin, The Times*, June 16, 1994, C.A. F, young, unemployed, no experience of police stations, interviews wrongly admitted.

[74] (1988) 87 Cr.App.R. 380, C.A. A, who was 18, was arrested for robbery. Asked for a solicitor but request denied. Held there was breach of section 58 but appeal dismissed because A said he was well able to cope and a solicitor would not have added to his knowledge of his rights. See to same effect *Dunford* (1990) 91 Cr.App.R. 150, C.A.

[75] (1991) 92 Cr.App.R. 228; (1991) Crim.L.R. 124, C.A. Manslaughter. M had I.Q. of 73. Wrongfully denied access to solicitor. Conviction quashed even though the confession was true.

[76] *Sub nom. Beycan* [1990] Crim.L.R. 185, C.A. D who was a foreigner was asked: "Are you happy to be interviewed in the normal way we conduct these interviews, without a solicitor, friend or representative?" He said yes. Conviction quashed. For a similar case involving a foreigner see *Sanusi* [1992] Crim.L.R. 43, C.A. See also *Silcott*, n.70, above.

- Was the defendant likely to confess anyway—*Oliphant*,[77] *Anderson*.[78]

The presence or absence of good faith on the part of the police officers is sometimes referred to as being a significant matter. Thus where the police show bad faith it is much more likely that the court will hold the search to be substantial and significant—see for instance *Canale*.[79] Where there is good faith the court has sometimes referred to that as a factor to be taken into account when deciding that the breach was insufficient to justify excluding the evidence or quashing the conviction.[80] But the fact that the officers acted in good faith does not mean that the court will necessarily overlook or condone the breach. In *Walsh*[81] the Court of Appeal said that although bad faith may make substantial or significant that which might not otherwise have been so, the contrary did not follow. "Breaches which are in themselves significant and substantial are not rendered otherwise by the good faith of the officers." The Court quashed the conviction even though the police had acted in good faith. The trial judge had said that even if the defendant had had a solicitor it would not have made any difference. But he had not heard the defendant and when the defendant eventually saw a solicitor he exercised his right to silence. At most it could be said that it was perhaps uncertain whether the presence of a solicitor would have made a difference.

The "abolition of the right to silence" as from April 1995 (on which see pp. 303–323 below) will introduce a new consideration. There is no way of knowing whether the change will lead to solicitors advising silence more or less frequently than before. The Law Society has issued solicitors with guidance regarding the many circumstances where advice to a client not to answer police questions will still be appropriate or at least legitimate. (See pp. 315–316 below.) Commenting on the new law, the Law Society's guidance states: "You should not be panicked into thinking that these changes mean that you have to adopt a completely different approach to formulating your advice to a client. In practical terms, the changes make little difference to the actual advice you give." In view of this guidance it would be wrong for courts to assume that because of the change in the law any "self-respecting" or "upright" solicitor would probably now advise silence.

But what will be the attitude of the courts under the new regime when the police have wrongfully denied the suspect access to legal advice. Hitherto, the defendant has been able to say that had he had legal advice he would have been silent and therefore not have made admissions. This argument will still lie but the defence will now have to contend with the prosecution argument that, since silence could give rise to adverse inferences, the solicitor would have been less likely to advise silence. The outcome may be much affected by the evidence given by the legal adviser as to what he would have advised. On the other hand, when the defendant has made admissions, it may be possible to argue that had he had legal advice he would have been advised to make a statement rather than being silent[82]—and that therefore

---

[77] [1992] Crim.L.R. 40, C.A. He knew his rights. A solicitor would have made no difference.
[78] n.71 above.
[79] [1990] 2 All E.R. 187, C.A. (A "flagrant, deliberate and cynical" breach of the Act and the Code by experienced police officers. Conviction quashed.
[80] See for instance *Kerawalla* [1991] Crim.L.R. 451, C.A.
[81] (1989) 91 Cr.App.R. 161, [1989] Crim.L.R. 822, C.A.
[82] In the study by McConville and Hodgson (1993) 78 per cent of police station advisers counselled the client to co-operate with the police.

adverse inferences should not be drawn. The issue bristles with conundrums to vex the courts.[83]

Interviewing before the solicitor arrives

In addition to the power of the police to delay access to a solicitor in cases involving serious arrestable offences, there is also a right to start questioning suspects in other cases where a solicitor has not yet arrived if the situation is an emergency or the solicitor is likely not to arrive for a considerable period. This power is dealt with in Code C, para. 6.6.

There are three situations mentioned which are exceptions to the general rule that a person who asks for legal advice may not be interviewed or continue to be interviewed until he has received it. One is where Annex B applies (*e.g.* the urgent cases mentioned above affecting only serious arrestable offences). The second is where an officer of the rank of superintendent or above has reasonable grounds to believe that delay will involve "an immediate risk of harm to persons or serious loss of or damage to property", or that awaiting the arrival of a solicitor "would cause unreasonable delay to the process of investigation". In such cases questioning can commence even though the suspect has exercised his legal right to ask for a solicitor and even though the police are not entitled to postpone calling him. In considering whether this exception applies the police should bear in mind the time the solicitor is likely to take in coming to the station, the time for which detention is permitted, the time of day, whether a rest period is imminent and the requirements of other investigations in progress (Code C, note 6A, p. 464 below). If the solicitor says that he is on his way it will not normally be appropriate to begin an interview before he arrives (*ibid.*).

The third exception is where the solicitor cannot be contacted or declines to attend and the suspect, having been told about the duty solicitor scheme, declines to ask for the duty solicitor (or the duty solicitor is unavailable). In that case the interview can begin if an inspector agrees. Also if the suspect, having first asked for legal advice, changes his mind, the interview can start provided an officer of the rank of inspector or above, having inquired into the reasons for the suspect's change of mind,[84] agrees and the suspect's change of mind is recorded on tape or in writing (Code C, para. 6.6). The authorisation can be over the telephone if the inspector is able to satisfy himself as to the suspect's change of mind and that it is proper to continue the interview (Code C, note 6I). The name of the authorising officer and the reason for the suspect's change of mind should be recorded and repeated on tape at the beginning or re-commencement of interview.[85] It seems that about 4–5 per cent of all interviews in police stations follow such change of mind by the suspect.[86] Refusal of consent by the inspector is virtually unheard of.[87]

In *R. v. Vernon*,[88] it was held that the defendant's consent to being

---

[83] See generally H. Fenwick, "Curtailing the right to silence, access to legal advice and section 78" [1995] Crim.L.R. 132–136.

[84] This requirement was added by the April 1995 revision of the Code.

[85] *ibid.* This sentence was added by the April 1995 revision of the Code.

[86] Brown *et al.* (1992) at p. 88. The figure is based on a sample of nearly 7,000 interviews.

[87] "Observers witnessed many instances in which such authorities were sought, and consent was almost always a formality. No case was observed in which an inspector declined to give this permission." (*ibid.* at p. 89.)

[88] [1988] Crim.L.R. 445 (Cr.Ct.).

interviewed was vitiated by the fact that she had not been informed of the duty solicitor scheme or of the fact that a solicitor was actually on his way. But see also *R. v. Hughes*[89] in which consent was held to be valid even though it was based on an error of fact.

The police do not have to delay taking a breath, blood or urine sample from a motorist until a solicitor arrives at a police station.[90]

Conduct and misconduct by solicitors

Code C (para. 6.8) specifies that a person who is permitted to consult a solicitor may have his solicitor present while he is being interviewed and a solicitor may only be required to leave the interview if his conduct is such as to prevent the proper putting of questions to the suspect (para. 6.9). This would seem to give the police only the narrowest of grounds for refusing a suspect permission to have his solicitor present during questioning. Moreover, note 6D says affirmatively: "A detained person has a right to free legal advice and to be represented by a solicitor. *The solicitor's only role in the police station is to protect and advance the legal rights of his client"* (Emphasis supplied[91]) Note 6D says that the solicitor may seek to challenge an improper question to his client or the manner in which it is put, or advise his client not to reply to particular questions, or if he wishes to give his client further legal advice.[92] He should not be asked to leave unless his approach or conduct "prevents or unreasonably obstructs proper questions being put to the suspect or his response being recorded" (*ibid.*).

A new addition to note 6D reminds police officers that "It is the duty of a solicitor to look after the interests of his client and to advise him without obstructing the interview." Examples of misconduct, it suggests, might include answering questions on the client's behalf, or providing written replies for the client to quote. *Advising a client not to reply to questions does not count as misconduct* (note 6D and see also Annex B, para. 3).

If the investigating officer thinks the solicitor is acting in such a way as to justify his removal he must stop the interview and inform an officer of at least the rank of superintendent, failing which an inspector who is unconnected with the investigation. If that officer decides to confirm the decision to ask the solicitor to leave, the suspect must be given a chance to get another solicitor before the interview continues (para. 6.10).

The removal of a solicitor is a serious step and an officer of the rank of superintendent should consider whether the matter ought to be reported to the Law Society (para. 6.11). Where the solicitor is a Duty Solicitor, the report should also be to the Legal Aid Board (*ibid.*).

---

[89] [1988] Crim.L.R. 519, C.A.

[90] *D.P.P. v. Billington* [1988] 1 W.L.R. 535 (Div.Ct.).

[91] The Runciman Royal Commission recommended that there should be a more positive reference to the solicitor's role—Recommendation 64, based on Report, para. 53, p. 36. The Commission also suggested that police training should include formal instruction in the role that solicitors are properly expected to play in the criminal justice system. (Report, para. 54, pp. 36–37.)

[92] It seems in fact to be rare for solicitors to play much of a role in police interviews. The Home Office study Brown *et al.* (1992, p. 89) stated that suspects were asked if they had been given any advice during police interviews. Suspects could recall such interruption in only 8 per cent of interviews. In less than half was it likely to impede the flow of questioning: "remain silent", "don't be rushed (or bullied) into answering questions", etc. In a quarter it was more likely to help the police : "tell the truth", "admit the offence", etc.

Refusing access to a solicitor's clerk

Prior to April 1995, Code C distinguished access to the police station for qualified solicitors from access to solicitors' clerks. Whereas solicitors could only be excluded in the context of a particular interview if they behaved in such a way as to make continuation of the interview impossible (Code C, para. 6.9 above), a clerk could be excluded if a police officer considered that that clerk's visit to the police station would hinder the investigation of crime (Code C, [para. 6.12]). As from April 1995 this has been changed. A "solicitor" for these purposes means a solicitor who holds a practising certificate but in addition is now deemed to include also "a trainee solicitor, a duty solicitor representative or an accredited representative included on the register of representatives maintained by the Legal Aid Board" (*ibid.*). (Note that in Northern Ireland, the Code there [para. 6.12] specifies that "a solicitor means a solicitor qualified to practice". There is no custom there, yet, of sending unqualified clerks.) From April 1995 therefore the police will be able to exercise their discretion to exclude clerks only if they are "non-accredited (see p. 129 above) or probationary representatives" of solicitors' firms. Such non-accredited or probationary representatives should be admitted, unless an officer of the rank of inspector or above considers that such a visit will hinder the investigation of crime and directs otherwise (Code C, para. 6.12). In *ex parte Robinson*[93] the Divisional Court held that this discretion can be based on the subjective judgment of the police officer based on his knowledge of the clerk concerned.[94] The police were entitled to refuse access to a clerk who was not a genuine clerk or whose visit the police knew or believed from his criminal record or associations would hinder the investigation of crime or who the police knew or believed was not capable of providing legal advice.

Guidelines issued by the Law Society after the *Robinson* case recommended that the clerk should carry a letter signed by a partner confirming his status and giving him authority to attend police stations. The clerk should identify himself and confirm his status at the same time to the client, giving the name of the partner responsible for his actions. Solicitors were also reminded that their clerks must behave politely and properly at all times and that they are responsible for the clerk's conduct.

If a clerk is refused admission under paragraph 6.12, the solicitor is advised to ask for written reasons and if the solicitor thinks these are wrong in fact or law or otherwise he should inform the Law Society's Legal Adviser's branch. A copy of the guidelines was sent to all chief constables and the gist was published in *Police Review*.

Code C, revised after *Robinson*, has a new provision (para. 6.13) giving police officers guidance as to what they should take into account when exercising their discretion under paragraph 6.12. This advises that they should take into account whether the identity and status of the non-accredited or probationary representative had been satisfactorily established; whether he is of suitable character to provide legal advice (a person with a criminal record was unlikely to be suitable unless the conviction was

---

[93] *R. v. Chief Constable of the Avon and Somerset Constabulary, ex p. Robinson* [1989] 1 W.L.R. 793 (Div.Ct.).
[94] For a worrying instance of the exercise of this subjective judgment see Sean Webster, "Judgment increases danger of miscarriages of justice, say lawyers", Sol.J. December 10, 1993, p. 1227, commenting on the Divisional Court's decision in *R. v. Chief Constable of Leicester, ex p. Menning*.

for a minor offence and was not of recent date); and any other matters in a written letter of authorisation provided by the solicitor. Note 6F states that if an officer of the rank of inspector thinks that a particular firm of solicitors is persistently sending as clerks or legal executives persons who are unsuited to provide legal advice, he should inform an officer of at least the rank of superintendent, who might wish to take the matter up with the Law Society.

The problems regarding solicitors' clerks are aggravated by the fact that solicitors use all sorts of persons to help out, including some who have had little training or experience in the work. In *Re B*[95] it was held that a person could be regarded as a solicitor's clerk for the purposes of disciplinary proceedings against the solicitor, even though the clerk worked as an independent contractor as an inquiry agent. In that case the clerk was a former police officer with convictions. There was no master-servant relationship. He had worked for the firm only some three times. But this was held to be enough to make the solicitor liable for employing him.

Legal advice: official figures and empirical research

(1) *Official figures*

In 1995, only 8 out of 1,836 police stations (0·4 per cent) did not have a police station duty solicitor scheme.[96] 666,000 suspects received advice under the scheme at a cost of £68.3m. Two-thirds of the advice under the scheme was given by "own solicitors" and one third by duty solicitors. Seventy-seven per cent of the advice was given at the police station, the rest was given over the telephone.[97]

(2) *Studies*

There have been various studies of access of legal advice in the police station. The biggest are the two studies carried out by David Brown of the Home Office in 1989 and 1993 respectively. The first, Brown (1989) was based on a sample of over 5,000 cases.[98] The second, Brown *et al.* (1992) was based on samples of around 5,000 taken in 1990 before (Phase 1) and 5,000 taken after (Phase 2) the April 1991 revision of the Code.[99] David Brown also carried out a study of access to legal advice for suspects in terrorism cases (Brown (1993)) based on a study of custody record forms in regard to 253 PTA detainees held in England and Wales between March 1989 and November 1990. The great majority (85 per cent) were held in connection with Northern Irish terrorism.

---

[95] *The Times*, May 12, 1989.
[96] Legal Aid Board's Annual Report for 1994–95, p. 77.
[97] *ibid.* p. 80.
[98] D. Brown, "*Detention at the Police Station under the Police and Criminal Evidence Act 1984*", Home Office Research Study No. 104, 1989, p. 20.
[99] D. Brown, T. Ellis and K. Larcombe, *Changing the Code: Police Detention under the Revised PACE Codes of Practice*, Home Office Research Study, 1992. (The study was summarised in Home Office Research and Statistics Department, Research Findings No. 5, March 1993.) It was based on a sample of 10,167 custody record forms from 12 police stations in six force areas, 980 cases that were observed by researchers at six of those police stations and interviews with 810 arresting officers and 543 detained persons in the observed cases.

There are also other studies—See especially Maguire (1988), Sanders *et al.* (1989), Dixon *et al.* (1989a) and McConville and Hodgson (1993).

The results reported here are drawn principally from the Home Office studies by Brown.

(a) Asking for a solicitor Brown (1989, p. 20) showed that 18 per cent of suspects asked for a solicitor initially and another 6 per cent first declined the offer but later changed their minds. In Brown *et al.* (1992, p. 47), according to the custody record sample, the proportion of suspects who asked for a solicitor in Phase 1, before the 1991 revised Codes came into effect, was again 24 per cent. In Phase 2, conducted after the revised Codes had been introduced,[1] the proportion had risen to 32 per cent. The rise for juveniles was comparable—from 19 per cent to 26 per cent, but the variation as between police stations in regard to juveniles was even greater than for adults.[2] Some of the variation was due to the attitude of the social workers regarding the value of legal advice for juveniles.

The great majority of suspects were told about their right to legal advice. In Phase 1, no less than 97 per cent of suspects said they had been told about their right to legal advice.[3] In Phase 2, this increased to 99 per cent. Whether the suspect did or did not have any prior experience of being arrested made no difference. In Phase 1, 88 per cent of suspects signed to indicate that they had received the written notice (though the observational study suggested that 3 per cent of these were not given the notice). In Phase 2, 91 per cent signed to the same effect (though 4 per cent were observed not to have received it). The proportion who were told orally that legal advice was free went up significantly between Phase 1 and Phase 2—from 5 per cent to 73 per cent![4] This was probably a critical factor in explaining the increase in the proportion requesting legal advice.

The rise between Phase 1 and Phase 2 in the proportion requesting legal advice was not related to any increase in the percentage of suspects who had experience of the criminal justice system, nor to any increase of the presentation of rights by the police in a neutral way.[5] Nor was there any indication that the introduction of reminders of the right to legal advice at specified points during custody led to more requests for solicitors.[6] But asking for a solicitor was associated statistically with the gravity of the case. Where the offence was "Very serious", around half asked for legal advice both in Phase 1 and Phase 2 (53 per cent and 51 per cent). Where it was "Moderately serious", 27 per cent requested legal advice in Phase 1 compared with 36 per cent in Phase 2. Where it was "Less serious" 18 per cent asked for legal advice in Phase 1 compared with 24 per cent in Phase 2.[7]

In terrorism cases the proportion asking for a solicitor is higher than in

---

[1] The crucial changes introduced by the April 1991 revision of the code were a requirement that (1) the suspect be told that the entitlement to independent legal advice is free of charge regardless of means and is a continuing right, (2) that a poster about the right to free and independent legal advice be displayed in police stations, and (3) that the code has a new provision expressly warning police officers not to dissuade the suspect from opting for legal advice.
[2] The biggest variation was between 4 per cent asking for a solicitor at one police station compared with 42 per cent at another. (Brown *et al.*, 1992, p. 76.)
[3] Brown *et al.* (1992), Table 3.1, p. 40.
[4] Brown *et al.* (1992), Tables 2.3 and 2.4, pp. 24, 26.
[5] Brown *et al.* (1992), pp. 51, 52.
[6] *cf.* Sanders *et al.* (1989).
[7] Brown *et al.* (1992), Table 3.5, p. 49.

other cases. Brown (1993) showed that 125 out of 253 (49 per cent) asked for legal advice at some stage (p. 9).

(b) Reasons for not asking for a solicitor According to interviews with suspects in Brown *et al.* (1992) the two most common reasons given for declining legal advice were "Would not assist" (57 per cent in Phase 1 and 63 per cent in Phase 2); and "Would delay release" from the police station (9 per cent in Phase 1 and 12 per cent in Phase 2).[8]

In Brown *et al.* (1992), those who did not request legal advice on arrival at the police station were asked if they would have done so if a solicitor had been available at that stage (p. 53). Nearly half said they would have done so. This suggests that between one half and two-thirds of suspects would wish to have solicitors if they were readily available.

In the study by Sanders *et al.* (1989), the researchers found that a major factor in suspects not asking for, or not getting access to solicitors was a variety of "ploys" by the police. (On this see Brown *et al.* (1992), pp. 48–49.)

(c) Making contact with the solicitor In Brown *et al.* (1992), the police managed to contact a solicitor in 80 per cent of the custody record sample in Phase 1 and 87 per cent in Phase 2 (pp. 58–59). (These figures include a considerable number of cases where the suspect first asked for legal advice and later changed his mind.) The average time between the request for a solicitor and contact made was a little over one hour both in the Phase 1 and the Phase 2 samples. In a little over half the cases contact was made within half an hour. The median figures were 25 minutes and 30 minutes (p. 61). The report said that the increase in time taken to make contact was "almost certainly accounted for by the rise in requests for legal advice" (p. 63).

(d) Actual consultation with legal advisers Brown (1989, p. 26) suggested that some 7 per cent of contacts, for one of a variety of reasons, did not lead to any legal consultation. Brown *et al.* (1992) broadly found much the same. In Phase 1, consultation took place in 90 per cent and in Phase 2, 91 per cent of cases where a request had been made.[9] In aggregate therefore, 72 per cent of those who requested legal advice in Phase 1 and 79 per cent of those who requested it in Phase 2 received it (p. 64). Whereas in Phase 1 some 18 per cent of all suspects in the custody record sample actually consulted a solicitor, this had risen to 25 per cent in Phase 2 (p. 64).

(e) Solicitor or clerk? Sanders *et al.* (1989) found that over 40 per cent of advice given at the police station was given by non-solicitor representatives. McConville and Hodgson (1993, p. 17) found that three-quarters of all police station attendances were by non-solicitors. Brown *et al.* (1992) found that it was much less—14 per cent in Phase 1 and 9 per cent in Phase 2.[10] But Brown admitted that accurate information about the status of the adviser was not

---

[8] *ibid.* Table 3.6, p. 51. In the study by Sanders *et al.* (1989) the most common reason was that seeking legal advice would cause delay.

[9] This figure does not include the 1 per cent of suspects who come to the police station with their solicitor.

[10] Brown *et al.* (1992), pp. 65–66.

always available and that the figure may well be higher. McConville and Hodgson suggest that probably between two-fifths and one half of all attendances at the police station are by persons other than qualified solicitors.

(f) Quality of legal advice in police station McConville and Hodgson (1993) severely criticised the quality of work done by advisers in police stations. Thus they stated that few advisers sought significant details of the case from custody officers. In 86 per cent of cases no inquiries were made of the custody officer. A request to see the custody record form was made in only 10 per cent of cases. In half the cases in the sample the adviser spent less than 10 minutes in private conversation with the client. Baldwin in a study of 182 audio or video tapes found that in two-thirds of interviews the adviser said nothing during the police interview.[11]

(g) Advice at the police station or only on the telephone? Sanders *et al.* (1989) found that 26 per cent of all advice was by telephone. Brown *et al.* (1992) found in the custody record sample that it was even higher—in Phase 1 (36 per cent), reducing to 30 per cent in Phase 2 (Table 4.3). On these figures, 17 per cent of all suspects now see a solicitor (compared with 11 per cent at the time of Phase 1). But the overall figures concealed huge differences as between different police stations—the proportion of tele-phone only advice ranged from 81 per cent at one station to 6 per cent at another (Table 4.3, p. 67).

Brown *et al.* (1992) also showed that although between 1990 and 1991 there had been a significant increase in the number of suspects receiving legal advice prior to interview, and an increase in personal attendance at the police station by advisers, there had been a significant decline in the proportion of interviews attended by advisers—from 84 per cent of interviews attended after advice in person in Phase 1 to 57 per cent in Phase 2. (Table 6.6, p. 87). The conclusion drawn was that whilst the economics of solicitors' firms might permit more attendance in police stations "the profession can only cope with a finite amount of additional demand" and that "This may have led to reluctance to prolong attendance at the police station by staying for interviews." (pp. 88–89).

(h) Time to first consultation Brown *et al.* (1992) found that during the day the average wait for a solicitor to arrive at the police station was around two hours with a median of one hour. At night, the average was three and a half hours, with a median of around 1 hour 40 minutes.[12]

(i) Delaying access to legal advice in serious arrestable offence cases Brown (1989, p. 48) showed that serious arrestable offence are some 2 per cent of the total and that in about half of these cases, the police delay access to legal advice (p. 49). In Brown *et al.* (1992), serious arrestable offences constituted between 1 and 2 per cent of all arrests. But only one case was found (in

[11] J. Baldwin (1992a) p. 49. See also n.92 above.
[12] *op. cit.*, n.99, p. 68.

Phase 2) of legal advice being delayed (p. 69). The difficulty of satisfying the test established by section 58 of PACE as interpreted by the Court of Appeal and the provisions of Code C, Annex B, note B4 was manifest "in the almost total non-use of the delaying power".

In terrorism cases, not surprisingly, the power to delay is used much more extensively. Delay of access was authorised in 26 per cent of cases (66 out of 253).[13] (In 11 cases the senior officer called on to authorise delay refused the request.[14] In three cases the custody record stated that access would be granted to the duty solicitor but not to the solicitor nominated by the suspect.)[15] Around a third of delays (33 per cent) were for periods of less than six hours, but over a quarter (28 per cent) were for more than a day.[16] Most of the suspects who asked for legal advice where the police delayed eventually found a solicitor (21 or 58 per cent of 36).[17]

Tape recording of interviews: section 60[18]

The background

Section 60 places upon the Home Secretary a duty to issue a Code of Practice for the tape recording of police interviews with suspects. A statutory instrument had to be laid before Parliament subject to annulment by resolution in either House.

The Code was approved by Parliament in July 1988.[19] The Police and Criminal Evidence Act 1984 (Code of Practice) Order 1988 (S.I. 1988/1200) appointed July 29, 1988 the date for operation of the Code of Practice on Tape Recording (Code E).

The Philips Royal Commission had proposed a very limited experiment with tape-recording only of the final stages of interviews. Starting in 1984, the Government undertook a much broader experiment which, to the surprise of many (especially the police) proved a great success. This led to the gradual introduction of tape-recording until in 1992 it became compulsory by virtue of Police and Criminal Evidence Act (Tape-recording of Interviews) No. 1 Order 1991, S.I. 91/2687. This came into force on January 1, 1992. Guidance to the police was issued by the Home Office in Circulars Nos. 76/1988, 39/1991 and 21/1992.

What interviews have to be tape-recorded?

Since January 1, 1992 it has been compulsory for all interviews (for the meaning of an interview see p. 184 below) with persons who have been cautioned in respect of offences triable on indictment (including either way

---

[13] Brown (1993), p. 16. However, in the event, legal advice was not requested in 30 of these 66 cases; the ban was introduced as a precautionary measure only (p. 19).

[14] *ibid.* p. 16.

[15] *ibid.* p. 17.

[16] *ibid.* Table 2.5, p. 19.

[17] *ibid.*

[18] See N.I. PACE Order, Art. 60.

[19] House of Commons, *Hansard*, Vol. 138, July 27, 1988, Cols. 444–463; House of Lords, *Hansard*, Vol. 500, July 28, 1988, Cols. 443–453.

offences) to be tape-recorded. (Code E, para. 3.1(a).) The requirement of tape-recording applies equally to the putting of further questions put to such a person and when a written statement is brought to the notice of a person charged with or informed that he may be prosecuted for such an offence.

Tape recording is not required for offences triable summarily only. Nor does it apply to interviews with terrorism suspects but from 1992–95 there was an experiment with the taping of interviews with terrorism suspects.[20] No report is to be published but it is understood that such taping is likely to continue. When someone comes to the police station voluntarily, tape-recording of any interview only has to be started when he should be cautioned as a suspect. (Code E, para. 3.4.)

The custody officer can authorise the interviewing officer not to record the interview if the equipment is not working, or no suitable room is available and the interview should not be delayed. He can also authorise non-recording if it is clear from the outset that no prosecution will result (para. 3.3).

The rules require that the whole interview be recorded, including the taking and reading back of any statement (para. 3.5).

There are elaborate rules that have to be followed to ensure that the process is not open to contamination by tampering. Thus, for instance, a master tape has to be unwrapped, placed in the tape-recorder and at the end sealed, all in the suspect's presence.

The suspect must be cautioned—now in terms of the new caution which warns him as to the possible adverse effects of silence. (See p. 179 below.)

The officer must remind the suspect of his right to free and independent legal advice and that he can speak to a solicitor on the telephone. (Code E, para. 4.3A.)

The officer should then put to the suspect any previous significant statement or silence ("*i.e.* failure or refusal to answer a question or to answer it satisfactorily") which occurred before the start of the tape-recorded interview and should ask "whether he confirms or denies that earlier statement or silence or whether he wishes to add anything" (Code E, paras. 4.3B).[21]

After the interview is over, if proceedings are to follow, a written record of the interview must be made. The preparation by the police of summaries of tape-recorded interviews has been a very vexed issue of considerable practical importance not least because of the immense amount of time they take to prepare. The Runciman Royal Commission recommended that the Home Office undertake further study of the matter.[22] Instead of the previous detailed rules in Code E,[23] the April 1955 revised Code now simply states: "Any written record of a tape recorded interview shall be made in accordance with national guidelines approved by the Secretary of State" (Code E, note 5A). These guidelines are now to be found in Home Office Circular 26/1995.[24] This states that where proceedings are to follow, a written

---

[20] House of Commons, *Hansard*, Vol. 168, March 1, 1990, Col. 273.
[21] The Runciman Royal Commission recommended this procedure in regard to statements—not silence. (See Recommendation 87 based on Report para. 50, pp. 60–61.)
[22] For discussion of the problem by the Runciman Royal Commission see Report, pp. 41–42.
[23] See previous Code E, paras. 5.3 and 5.4 and Notes 5A to 5C.
[24] The Circular replaces Home Office Circular 21/1992. It was published in full in 159 *Justice of the Peace*, May 6, 1995, p. 303.

record of the interview must be made by or on behalf of the interviewing officer. It can be done by a civilian employee but the interviewing officer is responsible for the accuracy of the written record which he should sign. It is stated that the main purpose of the record of interview is to provide "a balanced, accurate and reliable summary of what has been said which contains sufficient information to enable the Crown Prosecutor to decide whether a criminal prosecution should proceed, whether the proposed charges are appropriate, what lines of defence to anticipate and what mode of trial is appropriate".

Annex A of the Home Office Circular on tape-recording lays down the requirements as regards records of interviews. It distinguishes between straightforward cases and complex cases. In straightforward cases it is deemed to be sufficient to write the summary largely in indirect speech—though any admission or confession and the questions leading to them should be in direct speech. Generally the record of interview in such cases would not take more than one side of paper.

Complex cases are defined to include: indictable only cases; either way cases likely to be tried in the Crown Court; cases where the defendant is likely to deny the charges (including all cases where he has not admitted the offence and its commission was not witnessed by an officer); cases where the defendant has been charged with assault; and cases where the suspect is under 14 and the prosecution must rebut the presumption that the youth did not appreciate that what he was doing was "seriously wrong". In complex cases, not only all admissions but all the important points of the interview should be in direct speech. This includes questioning of or statements by the suspect regarding intent, possible defences, the granting of bail, or discussions about alternative charges or pleas. It also includes any questions or answers by the new law on the right to silence under section 34–37 of the Criminal Justice and Public Order Act 1994 (see pp. 307–323 below). In exceptionally difficult or important cases the police should supply the Crown Prosecution Service (C.P.S.) with a transcript of the entire interview—with or without a record of interview.

Where the police believe that the material is "sensitive", as defined by the Attorney-General's Guidelines for the disclosure of unused material to the defence, or that it contains prejudicial or inadmissible material, the police should draw the fact to the attention of the C.P.S. Any editing of the tapes is supposed to be done under the direction of the crown prosecutor.

A police officer has no authority to break the seal on the master tape. If it needs to be done, it should be done in the presence of a representative of the C.P.S. and, if they wish to attend, the defence (Code E, para. 6.2).

A suspect retains his right to make a *written* statement under caution. Such statements should be taken whilst the tape is running.

The prosecutor normally expects to rely on the written record of the interview, so keeping to a minimum the occasions when the C.P.S. have to listen to a tape or read a transcript.

Experience shows that transcripts are only rarely necessary, save in complex cases. If the police needs a transcript they provide it to the C.P.S. who make it available to the defence.

If the defence wish to have a transcript of a tape which is still in the possession of the police, the police should provide them with a copy of the tape so that they can make their own arrangements for the transcript to be made. The solicitor whose client is legally aided should apply to the Legal Aid Board in advance for approval of the cost of having a transcript prepared.

In order to save costs and time, each side is supposed to hand any transcript it may have had made to the other. Any disagreements as to the accuracy of the tape which cannot be resolved pre-trial are normally settled by playing the tape at the trial.

The Home Office Circular 76/1988 stated (para. 38) that "It is in the spirit of the tape recording arrangements that the content of the record of the taped interview should be agreed between the prosecution and the defence before the case comes to court."

The tapes are physically kept by the police. If the defence want access to a tape, they should either be given copies or allowed to listen to them at the police station. The Home Office 1988 Circular stated (*ibid.* para. 40): "Unadmitted employees of defence solicitors should normally be given the same right of access but should have the prior authority of an admitted solicitor."

If the suspect is not legally represented, he should be allowed access to the tapes, either in the prison where he is held, or in police cells or, if he is on bail, at a police station or at home. But applications for the defence to have access to the tapes should be made normally to the C.P.S.

If the defence requires an officer to come to court to prove the tape according to the guidelines laid down by the Court of Appeal in *Rampling*,[25] this should be brought to the attention of the crown prosecutor.

Court guidelines

In *Rampling* the court laid down the following guidelines:

(1) The tape can be produced and proved by the interviewing officer or any other officer present when it was taken. There is no need to call the audio-typist.

(2) The officer should have listened to the tape before the trial so that he can deal with any objections to authenticity that may be made.

(3) As regards authenticity, he can prove who spoke on the tape.

(4) On accuracy, he can deal with any challenge as, for instance, that the tape has been falsified by alteration.

(5) The transcript can be produced by the interviewing officer who should have checked it previously for accuracy. The tape is the evidence. The transcript is like a schedule and available for convenience.

(6) The use made of the tape is an administrative matter for the discretion of the judge. In many cases the defendant will agree for the transcript to be used with no need to play the tape. The transcript can then be read by the officer who produces it, like a contemporaneous note. But the defendant can have the tape played if he wishes.

(7) If the tape is played, it is for the judge to decide whether the jury should have the transcript whilst the tape is being played.

(8) The defendant's consent is not necessary. The court said that "in the collective experience of this court, a transcript is usually of very

[25] [1987] Crim.L.R. 823, C.A.

considerable value to the jury to follow the evidence and to take to the jury room when they retire".

The mechanics for dealing with tape recordings in court were the subject of a Practice Direction issued in May 1989.[26]

Tape-recording: the empirical evidence

For early research on tape-recording see C. Willis *et al.*, "The Tape-recording of Police Interviews with Suspects", 2nd Interim Report (Home Office Research Study No. 97) 1988. Broadly, this showed that the experiment was a success in that interviews tended to be shorter, the rate of confessions and suspects' talk about others involved in crime did not go down, the rate of guilty pleas went up and there were fewer disputes at court as to what was said in the police station.

For research identifying problems associated with tape-recording and making summaries of tapes see especially Baldwin (1991) and Baldwin (1992a).

When should the defence solicitor listen to the tape?

The Law Society has laid down guidelines as to the situations in which solicitors acting for the defence should listen to the tape recording of the interview in the police station.[27] Each case must be judged on its merits. The written police record of interview was intended to be a balanced account of the interview but solicitors "should use their own experience of recent written records in deciding to what extent reliance should be placed on them".

If the solicitor doubts the reliability of the written record he should listen to the tape in three situations:

(1) When the client instructs him to do so, or when the client cannot confirm the accuracy of the record of interview.
(2) If the client intends to plead not guilty or is unsure how to plead,
    (a) where there is a material dispute about the content of the written record;
    (b) where the client complains that the conduct of the police was such as to make his confession unreliable,
    (c) where the client tells the solicitor that the "tone", "timing" or "intonation" of the interview are significant;
    (d) where the C.P.S. and/or prosecuting counsel have listened to the tape.

---

[26] *Practice Direction (Crime: Tape Recording of Police Interviews)* (1989) 1 W.L.R. 631. For consideration of the special problems of taping interviews with interpreters see G. Brown, "Tape Recording Interviews with Foreigners", [1989] Crim.L.R. 643. For detailed guidance as to the needs of defence solicitors and operation of the system see David Snook, "Getting your clients taped", 133 Sol.J. 1366.
[27] *Law Soc.Gaz.*, April 20, 1994, p. 29.

(3) In the case of a guilty plea where the solicitor has reason to believe that there may be mitigatory factors on the tape which do not appear on the written summary.

Video recording: common parts of the police station

The Runciman Royal Commission recommended that police stations be fitted for continuous 24-hour a day video recording of all public parts in the custody area where suspects are likely to be. Suspects, it thought, should be informed of the fact that cameras in custody suites are switched on, but should not have the right to require them to be switched off.[28] The April 1995 revised Code C, paragraph 3.5A implements this proposal.

"If video cameras are installed in the custody area, notices which indicate that cameras are in use shall be prominently displayed. Any request by a detained person or other person to have video cameras switched off shall be refused."

Video-recording of interviews

Video recording of interviews is just beginning and is likely to develop. The Home Office issued a circular on the subject in February 1993 (6/1993). This referred to the considerable cost of video recording[29] for which there was no current provision. Chief officers were "strongly discouraged from moving too quickly to the wholesale introduction of video recording interviews". For the immediate future, it was suggested that such recording should be confined to the most serious cases in which there were specified, justifiable reasons for requiring a visual record. These might include serious violence including serious sexual assaults. The decision in individual cases should be made at inspector level or above. Chief officers who decided to use video recording on a wider basis were asked to recognise that this would "cause them and all agencies in the criminal justice system to divert resources from other work".

The procedural guidance in the circular (Annex B) stated that if the suspect objects to being video-recorded the interviewing officer should turn off the recording equipment. The discretion to continue recording despite objections which exists where audio recording is concerned (under para. 4.5 of Code E) did not apply to video-recording. The procedural steps and safeguards for video tapes are basically the same as for audio tapes.

Fingerprinting: section 61 and Identification Code D, section 3[30]

The pre-PACE law on fingerprinting in section 49 of the Magistrates' Courts Act 1980 provided that fingerprints could be taken compulsorily only on the order of a magistrates' court, if the person was 14 years old and if proceedings against him had already begun. The Philips Royal Commission

---

[28] Recommendation 51, based on Report paras. 36–38, pp. 33–34.
[29] Estimated to be £10m capital cost and £25–28m annual running cost for the police and the C.P.S. combined if all interviews currently taped were recorded by video. In addition there would be an estimated £59m cost for the L.C.D., mainly in legal aid fees for lawyers' viewing time.
[30] See N.I. PACE Order, Art. 61 and Code D, s.3. See also Prevention of Terrorism (Temporary Provisions) Act 1989, s.15(10).

recommended[31] that the minimum age should be reduced to 10 years and that it should be possible to take fingerprints, where it was necessary for purposes of the investigation, before proceedings were started. It also proposed[32] that supervision or control should be transferred from the magistrates to the police on the ground that in an operational matter of this nature the magistrates could not in practice exercise any real supervision. Section 61 gave effect to those proposals.

It states that, except as provided, no one's fingerprints may be taken without consent, as defined in section 65. Under section 65, consent of a person over 17 must be his own and in the case of someone under 14 the consent must be that of a parent or guardian. For someone between 14 and 17 consent must be his own *and* that of his parent or guardian.

Consent in a police station (though not elsewhere it seems) must be given in writing (s.61(2); Code D, para. 3.1). This therefore does not affect the practice of fingerprinting the victims of burglaries in their homes in order to distinguish their prints from any others found there. However, fingerprints may be taken without consent if an officer at least of the rank of superintendent authorises it, and he has reasonable grounds for suspecting the involvement of the person in a criminal offence and that his fingerprints "will tend to confirm or disprove his involvement" (subs. (3)(a) and (4) and Code D, para. 3.2(a)). The compulsory taking of fingerprints for investigative purposes therefore requires the authority of a superintendent.

But fingerprints can also be taken compulsorily without such authority if the person affected is in police detention and he has been charged with or convicted of an offence recordable in national police records (a "recordable offence"), or he has been told that he will be reported for such an offence (subss. (3)(b) and (6) and Code D, para. 3.2(b)(c)). It seems that in some police areas this provision is interpreted to refer also to cases of reporting a juvenile to the Juvenile Bureau or to the situation when the suspect is bailed pending consideration of the case by the C.P.S.

Note that although fingerprints can in some circumstances be taken from a juvenile without either his consent or that of his parent or guardian, Code D, paragraph 1.14[33] would seem to require the presence of an appropriate adult for fingerprinting of a juvenile which precedes the decision whether to charge, to caution or to take no further action.

Reporting takes place either to consider the issue of a summons or where the institution of proceedings requires the consent of the Attorney-General or the Director of Public Prosecutions.

National police records of convictions are kept by the National Identification Bureau at New Scotland Yard (N.I.B.). Only serious offences are recorded by N.I.B.—broadly those punishable by imprisonment. N.I.B. records consist of convictions and the national fingerprint collection.

Under section 27(3), as has been seen,[34] police officers are given a power to request someone to come to the police station to be fingerprinted and a power of arrest for the purposes of taking fingerprints for recordable

---

[31] Philips Report, paras. 3.128–3.132.
[32] Philips Report, para. 3.131.
[33] "Any procedure in this code involving the participation of a person (whether as a suspect or a witness) who is ... a juvenile must take place in the presence of the appropriate adult."
[34] See p. 73 above.

offences and the section also requires the Home Secretary to incorporate the list of recordable offences in a statutory instrument (see the National Police Records (Recordable Offences) Regulations 1985 (S.I. 1985/1941)).

But the power under section 27 only applies if the person convicted has not at any time been in police detention. Moreover, there is no power of arrest associated with the section 61 power. This seems to mean that if the defendant has received a non-custodial penalty and declines a request to come in to have his fingerprints taken, there is no power to compel him to do so. It is therefore important to ensure that anyone who has been charged with a recordable offence, or told that he will be reported for such an offence, has been fingerprinted before he leaves the police station.

Where a person's fingerprints are taken without his consent, he must be told the reason beforehand and this must be recorded. If he is detained at a police station at the time, the reason must be put into the custody record (subss. (7) and (8)).

The Criminal Justice and Public Order Act 1994 added a requirement of a new caution for anyone whose fingerprints are taken, with or without consent, telling them that they may be the subject of a "speculative search" against other records, and the fact that they have been told this must be recorded as soon as practicable after the fingerprints have been taken.[35]

There are no official statistics about the use of the compulsory fingerprint power. But Brown (1989) stated that there were only five such cases in the sample of 5,519 cases (0.09 per cent) (p. 54).

Subsection (9) preserves the power of compulsory fingerprinting contained in immigration and terrorism legislation. The Prevention of Terrorism (Temporary Provisions) Act 1989 gives the police power to fingerprint a suspect to see whether he has been concerned in an act of terrorism or whether he is subject to an exclusion order (subs. 15(10) and Sched. 5, para. 7(6)). The same now also applies in terrorism cases to body samples (whether intimate or non-intimate, see below). This is by virtue of an amendment to the 1989 Act made by the Criminal Justice and Public Order Act 1994, Schedule 10—and Code D, para. 1.16, as revised from April 1995. The effect is to allow samples to be taken in terrorist cases to help determine whether a person is or has been involved in terrorism. But the duty to destroy fingerprints or body samples does not apply in terrorism cases (Code D, para. 1.16).

Intimate samples: section 62 and Identification Code D, section 5[36]

The Act distinguishes between two kinds of body samples. One is "intimate samples" which (save for urine) may be taken only with written consent in advance and only by a doctor or dentist. The other cateogry is "non-intimate samples" which may exceptionally be taken without consent and by a police officer. Intimate samples are dealt with in section 62; non-intimate samples in section 63. The definition of both kinds of body samples is to be found in section 65.

---

[35] CJPOA, Sched. 10, para. 56, inserting a new subs. (7A) in s.61 of PACE—and Code D, paras. 3.1A and 3.8. For the equivalent changes in Northern Ireland see Appendix 4, p. 532 below [Article 9(2)(3)].
[36] See N.I. PACE Order, Art. 62 and Code D, s.5.

Certain changes in the powers regarding intimate and non-intimate samples were made in the Criminal Justice and Public Order Act 1994 (CJPOA)—mainly on the basis of recommendations of the Runciman Royal Commission. The Royal Commission wanted to see a considerable extension of the taking of samples, especially in view of advances in the technology of DNA evidence.[37]

Intimate samples may only be taken if an officer of the rank of superintendent or above gives permission *and* written consent is given by the suspect or an appropriate adult.

In the 1984 Act, intimate samples were defined as samples of blood, semen, other tissue fluid, urine, saliva, pubic hair or a swab taken from a person's body orifice. Neither swab nor sample is defined in the Act. In Northern Ireland a sample of saliva and a swab taken from someone's mouth have been treated as non-intimate samples and could therefore be taken without consent.[38] The Runciman Royal Commission recommended that the police should be permitted to pluck a sample of hair (other than pubic hair) without consent, that saliva be re-classified as a non-intimate sample to enable mouth swabs to be taken forcibly if necessary, and that intimate samples be permitted to be taken not just for serious arrestable offences but for less serious offences. The Runciman Commission also accepted the police suggestion that dental impressions should be classified as intimate samples.[39] The Government acted on these recommendations in the Criminal Justice and Public Order Act 1994. In regard to intimate samples, section 54(3)(b) of the 1994 Act[40] now permits such samples to be taken in regard to any recordable offence.[41] Saliva was removed from the definition of intimate samples and dental impressions were added to the definition (subs. (5)(a) and Code D, para. 5.11(a)). A dental impression can only be taken by a registered dentist (subs. (5)(b) and Code D, para. 5.3).[42]

The 1994 Act also added a new situation where an intimate sample may be taken.[43] This is where the accused is not in police detention and in the course of investigation two or more non-intimate samples suitable for the same means of analysis have been taken from him which have proved insufficient.[44] It must have the authorisation of an officer of the rank of superintendent or above and the person concerned (or an appropriate adult on his behalf) must give written consent.

The detailed guidelines regarding DNA samples and the National DNA database are set out in Home Office Circular No. 16/95, the relevant parts of which are printed in full in Appendix 5, pp. 536–541 below. It is clear that the police believe that DNA evidence will be of very great importance. They anticipate that the database will eventually hold some 5 million records.

There is no legal requirement that the superintendent who gives authority must be independent of the investigation, though if he is much involved in

---

[37] See Runciman Report, pp. 14–16.

[38] Criminal Justice Act 1988, s.149 and Sched. 14, para. 6.

[39] Runciman Report, pp. 14–15. Dental impressions were not defined as either intimate nor non-intimate samples under PACE though Code D, para. 5.1 said that, like intimate samples, they could only be taken by a registered practitioner and with the suspect's consent.

[40] See also Code D, para. 5.1(i).

[41] For the equivalent change in Northern Ireland see Appendix 4, p. 532 below [Art. 10(3)(b)].

[42] For the equivalent change in Northern Ireland see Appendix 4, p. 532 below [Art. 10(7)(b)].

[43] CJPOA s.54(2) adding a new subs. (1A) to s.62 of PACE. See also Code D, para. 5.1A. For the equivalent change in Northern Ireland see Appendix 4, p. 532 below [Art. 10(2)].

[44] For definition of an insufficient sample see Code D, Note 5B, p. 496 below.

the case it might be wise to seek authority from another superintendent who is less involved. (The same is true in regard to the need for a superintendent's authority under sections 56, 58 and 61 of the Act.) The superintendent can only give authority if he has reasonable grounds for believing that the sample will tend to confirm or disprove the suspect's involvement in the offence (subs. (2)). In the case of persons arrested under the Prevention of Terrorism (Temporary Provisions) Act 1989, such authorisation can also be given where the officer is satisfied that it is necessary to determine whether the person is or has been concerned in the commission, preparation or instigation of acts of terrorism or whether he is subject to an exclusion order.[45] The police officer's authorisation, if given orally in advance, must be confirmed in writing as soon as practicable (subs. (3)).

The question asking the suspect whether he is prepared to consent to provide an intimate sample can be put by any officer—it does not need to be a superintendent.[46] If he agrees, it requires the authority of the superintendent to carry out the procedure. The suspect must be told that the authorisation has been given and the grounds for it. He must also state the nature of the offence in which it is suspected that he is involved. He must be warned that a refusal to provide an intimate sample may harm his case in any proceedings brought against him (Code D, para. 5.2). Note 5A suggests that appropriate words might: "You do not have to [provide this sample] but I must warn you that if you refuse without good cause, your refusal may harm your case if it comes to trial." He must also be reminded of his right to free legal advice and this reminder must be recorded in the custody record form (para. 5.2).

PACE originally provided that refusal to provide an intimate sample could also be taken as corroboration of other evidence against that person (subs. (10)). That provision was however repealed by the 1994 CJPOA.[47] A record must be made as soon as possible of the authorisation, the grounds and the fact of consent. If the sample is taken at a police station, this must be put into the custody record (subss. (7) and (8)). Save in the case of urine, only a doctor or registered dentist may take an intimate sample (subs. (9)). The 1994 CJPOA added a new requirement that if an intimate sample is taken at a police station, the suspect must be informed that it may be the subject of a "speculative search" against other records (see s.65, p. 384 below) and the fact that he has been so informed must be recorded as soon as practicable after the sample has been taken.[48] A sample taken in the course of one investigation can be compared with a sample taken in another investigation relating to a completely different offence.[49]

Subsection (11) (as amended) makes it clear that the taking of samples of blood and urine in connection with offences of drink and driving under the Road Traffic Act 1988, ss.4 to 11 are not affected.

[45] New s.62(12) of PACE was added by the CJPOA, Sched. 10, para. 62(4)(a). It refers to new ss.15(11) and (12) of, and para. 7(6A) and (6B) of Sched. 5 to the 1989 Act. These were added to the 1989 Act by CJPOA, Sched. 10, para. 62(2) and (3). For the equivalent change in Northern Ireland see Appendix 4, p. 532 below [Art. 10(8)].

[46] In previous editions of this book I suggested otherwise. I am indebted to Mr Martyn Levett, of counsel, for drawing my attention to this error.

[47] See Sched. 11. It appeared however that the corroboration provision was to remain in the Northern Ireland law.

[48] CJPOA, Sched. 10, para. 57 inserting a new subs. (7A) in s.62 of PACE. For the equivalent change in Northern Ireland see Appendix 4, p. 532 below [Art. 10(5)].

[49] *Kelt, The Times,* December 15, 1993, C.A.

Taking non-intimate samples: section 63 and Identification Code D, section 5[50]

Section 63 deals with non-intimate samples. A non-intimate sample (defined in section 65)[51] means (a) a sample of hair[52] other than pubic hair[53]; (b) a sample taken from a nail or from under a nail; (c) a swab from any part of the body including the mouth but not from a body orifice; (d) saliva; (e) a footprint or similar impression of a part of the body other than hands. In certain circumstances a non-intimate sample can be taken compulsorily.

Normally written consent is required. But an officer of the rank of superintendent or above can authorise compulsory taking of a non-intimate sample where the offence in question is "a recordable one"[54] and there are reasonable grounds for believing that the sample will tend to confirm or disprove the suspect's involvement. In such a situation an officer must inform the suspect that authorisation for taking the sample compulsorily has been given, and the grounds and the nature of the offence in which it is suspected, that he is involved (subss. (6) and (7)). The reason for taking the sample without consent must be recorded as soon as practicable.

The CJPOA added a similar new requirement to that for intimate samples, that if a non-intimate sample is taken, with or without consent, the person must be informed that it may be the subject of a "speculative search" against other records (see below) and the fact that he has been so informed must be recorded as soon as practicable.[55]

Originally a non-intimate sample, like an intimate sample, could only be taken from someone in police detention or who was in police custody on the authority of a court. As has been seen, the CJPOA, has now added a new possibility of taking samples from persons not in custody. This applies to non-intimate samples as well. Section 63 of PACE has been amended[56] to include a new case (subs. (3A)) where someone has been charged with a recordable offence, whether or not he is in police custody, and either no non-intimate sample has been taken from him or a sample was taken but it proved not suitable for the same means of analysis or insufficient[57] for such analysis. A non-intimate sample may also be taken from someone, whether or not he is in custody, who has been convicted after April 10, 1995 of a

---

[50] See N.I. PACE Order, Art. 63 and Code D, section 5.

[51] As amended by s.55 of the Criminal Justice and Public Order Act 1994. For the equivalent change in Northern Ireland see Appendix 4, p. 532 below [Art. 11(2)].

[52] See *Cooke, The Times*, August 10, 1994, C.A. (A sample of hair plucked from the suspect's head without his consent was held to be validly admitted in evidence.)

[53] Where hair samples are taken for the purpose of DNA analysis the suspect should be allowed "a reasonable choice as to what part of the body he wishes the hairs to be taken from". When hairs are plucked they should be plucked individually unless the suspect prefers otherwise and no more should be plucked than is reasonably necessary. (Code D, note 5C.) The Northern Ireland PACE Order, Art. 63 states that a non-intimate sample of hair may be taken by cutting or plucking hairs with their roots so long as no more are taken than is necessary for analysis. (CJPOA, 1994 Sched. 9, para. 39—to become Art. 63A(2) by virtue of the 1995 amending Order, Art. 12.)

[54] PACE originally required it to be a serious arrestable offence but this was changed to a recordable offence by the CJPOA, s.55(3) and Code D, para. 5.5. For the equivalent change in Northern Ireland see Appendix 4, pp. 532–533 below [Art. 11(3)].

[55] CJPOA, Sched. 10, para. 58 inserting a new subs. (8B) in s.63 of PACE and Code D, paras. 5.10 and 5.11A. For the equivalent change in Northern Ireland see Appendix 4, pp. 532–533 below [Art. 11(4)].

[56] By CJPOA, s.55(2). See also Code D, para. 5.5. For the equivalent change in Northern Ireland see Appendix 5, p. 532 below [Art. 11(2)].

[57] For definition see Code D, note 5B.

recordable offence. For the equivalent change in Northern Ireland see Appendix 4, pp. 532–533 below [Art. 11(2)].

In any of these situations the person must be told the reason and the reason must be recorded in the custody record.[58]

These provisions apply also to suspects under the Prevention of Terrorism (Temporary Provisions) Act 1989 (see CJPOA, Sched. 10, para. 62 and for Northern Ireland see Appendix 4, p. 533 below [Art. 11(7)].

Fingerprints and samples: miscellaneous supplementary provisions: section 63A

The CJPOA s.56 added a substantial new section (s.63A) to PACE. This first clarified the power to check fingerprints and samples against existing records (subs. (1)). Such a search is defined as a "speculative search".[59] The new section then provides that hairs, other than pubic hairs, may be plucked as well as cut, so long as no more is taken than is reasonably considered to be necessary for a sufficient sample (subs. (2) and see also Code D, paras. 5.11(b)(i) and note 5C). It permits the exercise of powers to take samples in prisons (subs. (3)). For the equivalent change in Northern Ireland see Appendix 4, p. 533 below [Art. 12].

Power to require someone to attend a police station to give a sample The section also creates a power for a person not in police detention to be required to attend at a police station for the purpose of providing a sample. The pre-condition is that (a) he must have been charged with a recordable offence or informed that he will be reported for such an offence, or (b) he has been convicted of a recordable offence and either he has not had a sample taken or one was taken but it was found not to be suitable for the same means of analysis, or the sample proved insufficient (s.63A(4)). The period allowed for those in category (a) is one month from the date of charge or from the date when the officer is informed that the sample is not suitable or not sufficient. The time allowed for those in category (b) is one month from the date of conviction or one month from the date when the officer is told that the sample is unsuitable or insufficient (s.63A(5)). The person must be given at least seven days notice but the police can direct the time at which or between what times he should attend (s.63A(6)). A person who fails to attend can be arrested for such failure (s.63A(7)). For the equivalent change in Northern Ireland see Appendix 4, p. 533 below [Art. 12].

Taking of photographs: Identification Code D, section 4[60]

There is no judicial decision that determines whether the taking of photographs of suspects by the police without consent is unlawful. The Philips Royal Commission recommended[61] that photographing of suspects should be on the same basis as fingerprinting both in regard to the means for getting written consent and in regard to the rules regarding authorisation and safeguards where no written consent was forthcoming.

---

[58] CJPOA s.55(4) adding new subs. (8A) to s.63 of PACE. See also Code D, paras. 5.9 and 5.11B. For the equivalent change in Northern Ireland see Appendix 4, p. 533 below [Art. 11(4)].
[59] CJPOA, s.58 amending s.65 of PACE.
[60] See N.I. PACE Order, Code D, s.4.
[61] Philips Report, para. 3.133.

There is nothing in the Act on the subject. But Code D provides that, save as stated, no photograph of a suspect may be taken at a police station without his written consent. If the suspect is under 16 the consent must be that of his parent or guardian (paras. 1.11 and 4.1).

Photographs may be taken without his consent however if he is arrested at the same time as other persons (or when it is likely that others will be arrested) and it is considered necessary to make a photographic record to establish who was arrested, at what time and what place (para. 4.2(i)). A photograph may also be taken without consent if the suspect has been charged with or reported for a recordable offence and has not yet been released or brought before a court (para. 4.2(ii)). It may also be taken without consent where the person concerned has been convicted of a recordable offence and his photograph is not already on record as a result of the two previous provisions. This power only applies where the person is in custody as a result of another power such as where he has been arrested for fingerprinting under section 27 of PACE.

But a new and much more general basis for photographs was introduced in the 1995 revision of Code D—where an officer of superintendent or above authorises it, "having reasonable grounds for suspecting the involvement of the person in a criminal offence and where there is identification evidence in relation to that offence" (para. 4.2(iv)).

Force may not be used to take a photograph (para. 4.3).

Note 4A warns that the admissibility and value of identification evidence may be compromised if a potential witness in an identification procedure sees any photographs of the suspect otherwise in accordance with the provisions of Code D, para. 4.2(iii)). The grounds for taking the photographs must be recorded and the suspect must be told of his right to witness the destruction of the photographs.

In January 1995 a High Court judge held that the police were entitled to send "mug shot" photographs to local shops to assist them to identify troublemakers. He ruled that police who made reasonable use of suspects' photographs for the purpose of the prevention and detection of crime had a public interest defence to any action brought against them by the persons whose photographs had been circulated in that way.[62]

Destruction of fingerprints, samples and photographs: section 64 and Identification Code D, paragraphs 3.1, 3.4[63]

The Philips Royal Commission recommended[64] that fingerprints and samples taken must be destroyed if the person concerned is cleared. Section 64 gives effect to this recommendation. It provides that subject to new subsection (3A) (see below) fingerprints and samples, whether taken with consent or under compulsion, must be destroyed as soon as practicable after the suspect has been cleared of the offence. For this purpose he is to be treated as having been cleared if it is decided neither to prosecute nor formally to caution him; or if the offence is indictable and he is not sent for trial; or if he is tried for the offence and is acquitted. If fingerprints are destroyed, any copies that have been made must also be destroyed (subs.

---

[62] *Hellewell v. Chief Constable of Derbyshire, The Times*, January 13, 1995 (*per* Laws J.).
[63] See N.I. PACE Order, Art. 64 and Code D, ss.3 and 4.
[64] Philips Report, para. 3.131.

(5)) and if the data is held on computer, access to the data must be made impossible.[65] A person who asks to be allowed to be present to witness the destruction has a right to do so (subs. (6))[66] if he asks within *five days*[67] of being cleared (Code D, para. 3.1). The rules regarding destruction of fingerprints and body samples do not apply to terrorism cases. (See Code D, para. 1.16.)

Under Code D (para. 4.4) the same applies to photographs. But there is one important and new difference between the provisions for destruction of fingerprints and photographs. According to the 1995 revised Code D, para. 4.4(a), photographs need not be destroyed even though the suspect is cleared, or charged but not prosecuted, where he has a previous conviction for a recordable offence. The Home Office Circular on PACE (No. 88/1985) stated (para. 40) that persons must be informed of the right to witness destruction of the photogaphs at the time that fingerprints or photographs are taken and this is now in Code D (see paras. 3.1, 4.1). (In his commentary on the new comparable provisions for Northern Ireland, Mark Gelowitz said that the destruction provisions in paragraph 9 of Schedule 14 to the Criminal Justice Act 1988 apply to the sample but not to the actual DNA fingerprints, thus making the safeguard valueless.)[68]

Destruction of samples (DNA)

Where someone is entitled to have samples destroyed, information derived from them cannot be used in evidence against him nor can they be used for the purposes of any investigation. This provision was added to PACE by the Criminal Justice and Public Order Act 1994 (CJPOA).[69]

The CJPOA also dealt with the problem created by samples taken from DNA testing in the course of an investigation involving more than one person where one (or more) is acquitted and one (or more) is convicted. In that situation the sample need not be destroyed. This is because in the case of such samples it may be physically impossible to destroy the sample concerning those who were acquitted without also destroying the sample(s) relating to those who were convicted.[70] But again it is specifically provided that the information derived from the sample cannot be used either in evidence against the person who was acquitted or for the purposes of any investigation of an offence.[71]

Definitions relating to fingerprints and samples: section 65[72]

Section 65 of PACE defined "appropriate consent", "fingerprints", "intimate sample", "non-intimate sample" and "the terrorism provisions".

---

[65] Criminal Justice Act 1988, s.149. The equivalent provision for Northern Ireland is in the N.I. PACE Order, Art. 64(5), (6).
[66] As amended by the Criminal Justice Act 1988, s.148.
[67] Under the original Code D it was a period of two months.
[68] M. Gelowitz, [1989] Crim.L.R. 198.
[69] New s.64(3B) of PACE added by CJPOA, s.57(3). For the equivalent change in Northern Ireland see Appendix 4, p. 533 below [Art. 13(3)(3B)].
[70] This explanation was given by the Home Office Minister in the Committee stage of the Bill—see House of Commons, *Hansard*, Standing Committee B, February 3, 1994, col. 524.
[71] New s.64(3A) of PACE added by CJPOA, s.57(3). The equivalent change in Northern Ireland see Appendix 4, p. 533 below [Art. 13(3)(3A)].
[72] See N.I. PACE Order, Art. 53.

As has been seen the 1994 CJPOA slightly changed the definitions of "intimate" and "non-intimate" samples partly to reflect the re-definition of saliva and mouth swabs (now both non-intimate samples) and dental impressions (now as intimate sample), and partly to improve the drafting. The words and phrases defined in section 65 have been enlarged by CJPOA section 58(4) to include "registered dentist", "speculative search" and "sufficient" and "insufficient" in relation to the quantity or quality of samples. Section 59(1) of the CJPOA adds a further new definition to section 65—of "intimate search" which is defined as a physical examination of a person's body orifices other than his mouth. Subsection (2) states that in section 32, which gives the police power to search a person on arrest, the police are permitted to search a person's mouth. For the equivalent change in Northern Ireland see Appendix 4, p. 532 below [Arts. 5 and 8].

QUESTIONS AND ANSWERS

THE SUSPECT'S RIGHTS IN THE POLICE STATION

1. For how long can the police keep someone incommunicado in the police station?

Where someone is in custody in a police station he has the right "to have one friend or relative or other person who is known to him or who is likely to take an interest in his welfare told, *without delay*—except to the extent that delay is permitted" (s.56(1), italics supplied).

The Code states that if that person cannot be contacted, the suspect may choose up to two alternatives. If they too cannot be contacted the custody officer has discretion to allow further attempts until the information has been conveyed.

The right not to be held incommunicado applies every time one is taken to a new police station.

2. In what circumstances can the police delay the suspect's right to have someone informed as to his whereabouts?

Both the Act and Code C specify the circumstances in which delay is permitted. The Code sets these out in Annex B. Annex B is based on the identical provisions in the Act itself. Delay is permissible for a limited period if,

  (1) the suspect is detained in connection with a serious arrestable offence; and

  (2) an officer of the rank of superintendent or above reasonably believes that exercise of the right:
    (a) would lead to interference with or harm to witnesses or interference with or physical harm to other persons; or
    (b) would lead to the alerting of others suspected of involvement; or
    (c) would hinder the recovery of the proceeds of the crime.

But if these grounds cease to apply the person must be asked as soon as practicable if he wishes to exercise the right and action must then be taken on any affirmative response. The maximum period of delay is 36 hours.

3. If someone rings the police station asking about the detainee must he be told where he is?

Code C (para. 5.5) provides that when an inquiry is made as to the whereabouts of a detained person by his friends or relatives, the information "shall be given, if he agrees and if Annex B does not apply". But note 5D says that "in some circumstances it may not be appropriate to use the telephone to disclose information". The meaning of this *caveat* is unclear.

4. Does the right not to be held incommunicado apply also to persons held as suspects under the anti-terrorism legislation?

Under the previous law, suspects held under the Prevention of Terrorism (Temporary Provisions) Act had no right to make contact with the outside world while they were held for anything up to one week. But as a result of Lord Jellicoe's 1983 Report into the working of the Act this was changed by PACE. A suspect held under the Prevention of Terrorism (Temporary Provisions) Act 1989 cannot be denied the right to have someone informed of his arrest for longer than 48 hours. The grounds for delaying the exercise of this right are the same as those set out in Annex B that apply to suspects in serious arrestable offence cases. But there are in addition two further grounds on which a superintendent may authorise delay: if he has reasonable grounds for believing the notification will lead to interference with the gathering of information relating to acts of terrorism or that it will, by altering any person, make it more difficult to prevent an act of terrorism or to secure the arrest, prosecution or conviction of someone involved in terrorism.

5. Can detained persons demand to have visits or to make phone calls, send letters or cables?

Code C has provisions on all these matters. It states that detained persons may receive visits at the custody officer's discretion and that he should exercise his discretion as to visits "in the light of the availability of sufficient manpower to supervise a visit and any possible hindrance to the investigation" (note 5B). The detained person may also speak on the telephone to one person—unless an officer of the rank of inspector or above delays or denies such a call by applying the provisions of Annex B. This can be done not only in serious arrestable offence cases but also when the offence being investigated is merely an arrestable one. Whether or not the call is at public expense is at the discretion of the custody officer. A police officer may listen to what is said unless the call is to a solicitor. He may terminate the call if it is being abused. If the person does not speak English, an interpreter may make a call for him. The person should be cautioned that what he says in any letter, call or message may be listened to and given in evidence.

A detained person should be supplied on request with writing materials. Any letter or other message should be sent at his expense as soon as practicable unless Annex B applies. All letters except those to solicitors may be read by the police.

The only suspects who have an absolute and unqualified right to make a call and to have visits are those from abroad. The Code says that a foreign national or a citizen of a Commonwealth country "may communicate at any time with his High Commission, Embassy or Consulate" (para. 7.1). In regard to visits, the Code states that "consular officers may visit one of their nationals who is in police detention to talk to him and, if required, to arrange for legal advice". Such visits should take place out of hearing of a police officer (para. 7.3).

Note 7A states that the rules regarding foreign and Commonwealth detainees cannot be suspended even though Annex B applies.

6. In what circumstances can a suspect get a lawyer in the police station?

The Philips Royal Commission hoped to see a dramatic improvement in the suspect's access to legal advice in the police station. The Government broadly implemented its recommendations.

A suspect under arrest at a police station has a right to ask to see a solicitor privately. This is an absolute right, though if the crime being investigated is a serious arrestable offence the police can sometimes delay giving access to the lawyer. This is only permitted however in the rare situation where a superintendent reasonably believes that allowing access to that lawyer could lead to accomplices being alerted or evidence being destroyed. He should then permit access to another lawyer. The maximum period of delay is 36 hours or in terrorism cases 48 hours. If the reasons for delay cease, the suspect should be asked whether he wishes to exercise his right.

If the suspect has asked for a solicitor but he has not yet arrived, questioning can begin only if: (1) a superintendent reasonably believes that to delay would involve an immediate risk of harm to persons or serious loss of or damage to property; or (2) a superintendent reasonably believes that to wait for the solicitor to arrive would unreasonably delay the inquiry; or (3) the suspect indicates in writing or on tape that he has changed his mind and that the interview may be started without waiting for the solicitor. But an officer of the rank of inspector, having inquired into the matter, must assent.

Annex B (para. 3) specifically makes it clear that access to a solicitor cannot be denied or delayed on the ground that the solicitor might advise the suspect to say nothing.

7. How in practice does a suspect go about trying to find the name of a local solicitor?

The Code provides that if he does not know the name of a solicitor to contact, the detainee should (1) be told of the availability of the local Duty Solicitor scheme, and (2) be provided with a list of local solicitors who have indicated their willingness to act in such situations.

There are two basic duty solicitor systems—the rota system where an identifiable solicitor is on duty and a panel arrangement where the national telephone service can telephone the duty solicitors in the order in which they appear on the panel until one willing to advise the suspect is found. The advantage of the rota system is that the central telephone service only has to contact one solicitor; the disadvantage is that that solicitor has to hold himself available to go to the police station for the whole period for which he is on duty. The advantage of the panel system is that the solicitors can carry on with their ordinary routine and it is economical since it does not involve the payment of stand-by fees. On the other hand it often involves a delay in finding a solicitor who is available.

The duty solicitor system is operated by the Automobile Association covering England and Wales. The police are now required initially to contact the duty solicitor via the A.A. to ensure complete statistical coverage.

8. How could suspects in the police station expect to pay for the help of lawyers?

Advice and assistance by solicitors in police stations are exempted from the normal requirement of a means test and a graduated contribution. The service in other words is free of charge at public expense. The same is true of the services of solicitors at hearings before magistrates on applications by the police for warrants of further detention.

9. If the detained person wants a lawyer and one has been called, can the police start questioning him before the lawyer arrives?

A person who has asked for legal advice "may not be interviewed or continue to be interviewed until he has received it". But, as has been seen, there are three exceptions. The first is where Annex B (alerting accomplices, etc.) applies. The second is where an officer of the rank of superintendent or above has reasonable grounds to believe that there is an immediate risk of harm to persons or serious loss of or damage to the property, or that waiting for the arrival of the solicitor would cause unreasonable delay to the investigation (but when the danger has passed, questioning may not continue until the person has received the legal advice he asked for). The third is where the suspect, having first asked for legal advice, changes his mind, the interview can start provided an officer of the rank of inspector or above agrees and the suspect's change of mind is recorded on tape or in writing (Code C, para. 6.6).

10. Can the solicitor remain during the interview with the detained person?

The Code states that the solicitor can be asked to withdraw if an officer of the rank of superintendent or above considers that by his misconduct he is preventing the proper putting of questions to his client (Code C, paras. 6.9–6.11 and note 6D). The superintendent should consider whether a report to the Law Society is appropriate.

11. If the solicitor sends his clerk or legal executive does he count as a solicitor for these purposes?

The Code previously stated that the word "solicitor" meant someone qualified to practice as a solicitor. But the 1995 revision of the Code has considerably changed the position. Under the new definition, in Code C, para. 6.12 "solicitor" in this context also includes a trainee solicitor (formerly called "articled clerks") and "a duty solicitor representative or an accredited representative included on the register of representatives maintained by the Legal Aid Board". (See p. 137 above.)

A clerk who does not qualify under these heads should nevertheless be admitted to the police station to provide advice on behalf of his firm "unless an officer of the rank of inspector or above considers that such a visit will hinder the investigation of crime and directs otherwise" (Code C, para. 6.12). The Divisional Court held in the *Robinson* case (p. 137 above) that it is up to the inspector on the spot to decide whether any individual clerk should be admitted and that it is his subjective judgment which is decisive.

12. What is the position if a solicitor sent by a friend or relative arrives at the police station but the suspect has not asked for a solicitor?

Neither the Act nor the original Codes dealt explicitly with the point but there are now two provisions which deal with the matter. The general provision (in Code C, para. 6.15) is that unless Annex B applies, (even if he previously declined legal advice) the suspect must be informed if a solicitor comes to see him and he must be asked if he wants to see the solicitor.

13. At what point must the person in the police station be told of his rights?

The answer depends on whether he is there voluntarily or under arrest. If he is not under arrest he must be told of his rights only when he is cautioned. If he is under arrest he must be told of his rights when he first comes to the police station or, if he comes voluntarily but is then arrested, at that time. (It is the custody officer's duty to consider whether he ought to be detained as soon as practicable after he arrives at the police station, or, if he has been arrested at the station, as soon as practicable after his arrest.)

14. Of what rights must he be informed?

He must be told: (1) the grounds of his detention; (2) of the right to have someone informed of his detention; (3) of the right to consult a copy of the Codes; (4) of the right to free legal advice. He must be told of these rights orally and must also be given a notice setting them out together with a statement that he is entitled to ask for a copy of the custody record form, providing he does so within 12 months. He must also now be given a notice of his entitlements whilst a detainee (see p. 176).

A person who is at the police station voluntarily and who has been cautioned must be told of the same rights but he must also be told that he has a right to leave if he wishes.

15. To what extent do the rules make special provision for the needs of the young, those with mental handicaps, the deaf, those who cannot speak English, etc.?

There are special rules in Code C for each of these groups.

(1) *The young*. Code C (para. 3.9; note 3C) provides that when a child or

young person has been arrested an "appropriate adult" must be informed. This means his parent or guardian or if he is in care, the local authority or the voluntary organisation he is with. Failing the parent or guardian the information should be communicated to a representative of the social services department of the local authority or to another responsible adult who is not a police officer.

The custody officer has a specific duty (under Code C, para. 3.7) to discover the person responsible for the juvenile's welfare. It may be his parent or guardian (or if he is in care, the care authority or organisation). It may be anyone who has assumed responsibility for his welfare. That person must be informed as soon as practicable that the juvenile has been arrested, why he was arrested and where he is detained. The concept of the person responsible for the juvenile's welfare (who may or may not be the appropriate adult) was a new one in the 1991 revision of the Codes.

The custody officer should as soon as possible inform the appropriate adult of the grounds of detention and his whereabouts and should ask the adult to come to the police station (para. 3.9). The information about the suspect's right to legal advice and to inform someone else of his arrest and to consult the Codes must be given to the juvenile in the adult's presence, or if not must be given to him when he arrives at the police station (para. 3.11). If the appropriate adult is already at the police station when information about his rights is given to the juvenile as required in paragraphs 3.1 to 3.4 of the Code, then it must be given in the appropriate adult's presence. If the adult comes later it must be given to the juvenile again in his presence. (The same applies to other categories of persons for whom an appropriate adult has to be called.)

When the appropriate adult arrives at the police station the juvenile must be informed that he is there and that he has the right to consult privately with the adult *at any time* (para. 3.12; emphasis supplied).

The Code (para. 11.14) states categorically that "A juvenile ... whether suspected or not must not be interviewed or asked to provide or sign a written statement in the absence of the appropriate adult unless paragraph 11.1 or Annex C applies." Annex C, para. 1 sets out the circumstances in which a juvenile (or other person at risk such as someone who is mentally disordered, mentally handicapped, deaf, or under the influence of drink or drugs) may exceptionally be interviewed, even though the adult is not there: "If, and only if, an officer of the rank of superintendent or above considers that delay will lead to the consequences set out in paragraph 11.1—such as interference or harm to evidence or harm to persons or alerting of accomplices or hindering the recovery of property. Questioning in those circumstances "may not continue once sufficient information to avert the immediate risk has been obtained" (Annex C, para. 2).

If the adult thinks that the juvenile needs legal advice the police are required to treat this as a request for a lawyer by the juvenile himself (para. 3.13).

Juveniles may only be interviewed at school "in exceptional circumstances" and then only when the principal or his nominee agree (para. 11.15). Every effort should be made to notify both the parent(s) or other person responsible for the juvenile's welfare *and* the appropriate adult if this is someone different. If waiting for the appropriate adult would cause unreasonable delay, the principal or his nominee can act as appropriate adult (*ibid.*) in which case the head teacher or his nominee should agree and be present (para. 11.15). Note for guidance 1C states that a person, including a parent or guardian, should not be an appropriate adult if he is suspected of involvement in the offence, or is the victim, or a witness, or is involved in the investigation, or has "received admissions". (An estranged parent should not be the appropriate adult if the juvenile objects "expressly and specifically" (note 1C).) Police are warned that juveniles (like the mentally handicapped and the mentally ill) are "particularly prone in certain circumstances to provide information which is unreliable, misleading or self-incriminating" and that it is important to obtain corroboration of any facts admitted whenever possible (note 11B). A juvenile should not be arrested at school unless this is unavoidable, in which case the head teacher or his nominee must be informed (note 11C).

A juvenile should not be placed in police cells unless no other secure accommodation is available or the custody officer considers that it is not practicable to supervise him if he is not in a cell. He may not however be placed in a cell with an adult (para. 8.8).

An intimate search of a juvenile may only take place in the presence of an appropriate adult of the same sex, unless the juvenile signifies that he would prefer it to be done in the adult's absence and the adult agrees (Code C, Annex A(a), para. 5).

(2) *The mentally disordered and the mentally handicapped.* The rules in the Code for the mentally disordered and the mentally handicapped are similar to those for juveniles (Code C, note 1G). An appropriate adult must be notified that such a person is in the police station (Code C, para. 3.9). The "appropriate adult" would be a relative or guardian responsible for his care, someone experienced in dealing with such people not employed by the police, failing whom some other responsible adult not employed by the police (Code C, para. 1.7). It may in some circumstances be better if the appropriate adult is someone who has experience or training in the case of the mentally disordered or mentally handicapped than a relative lacking such qualifications. But if the person has a preference that should be respected if practicable (Note 1E).

Just as in the case of the juvenile, the custody officer must call the appropriate adult to the police station and must give the same information. The prohibitions on interviewing a mentally disordered person on his own are the same as for juveniles—subject to the exceptions in Annex C. The whole lengthy list of provisions affecting the treatment of the mentally disordered and mentally handicapped is to be found in Annex E to Code C.

(3) *The deaf.* Code C (para. 13.5) states that if a person is deaf or there is doubt about his hearing ability he must not be interviewed in the absence of an interpreter unless he agrees in writing or paragraph 11.1 or Annex C (see pp. 470, 482 below) applies. The principle relates equally where the appropriate adult is deaf (para. 13.6). The interviewing officer shall ensure that the interpreter makes a note of the interview at the time for use in the event of his being called to give evidence. The suspect should be given an opportunity to read and sign it as correct or to indicate any respects in which he considers it to be inaccurate. Such an interpreter is provided free of charge at public expense.

(4) *Those who cannot speak or understand English.* Code C (para. 13.2)

states that if someone has difficulty in understanding English and either the police officer does not speak the person's own language or the suspect wishes to have an interpreter to be present, "he must not be interviewed in the absence of a person capable of acting as interpreter". The only exception is again where paragraph 11.1 or Annex C (above) applies.

The interviewing officer must ensure that the interpreter makes a note at the time of the interview in the language of the person being interviewed and that he certifies its accuracy. The suspect should be given a chance to read it and to sign it as accurate or to indicate the respects in which he considers it to be inaccurate (para. 13.3).

If the suspect makes a statement in a language other than English the interpreter should take down the statement in the language in which it is made; the person making the statement should be invited to sign the statement; and an official English translation should be made in due course (para. 13.4).

Interpreters must be provided at public expense and all reasonable efforts must be made to make this clear to the detainee (para. 13.8).

If a person is charged, arrangements have to be made as soon as practicable to have the interpreter explain the offence and any other information given by the custody officer.

(5) *The blind*. If a person is blind or visually handicapped or can not read the custody officer should ensure that someone appropriate is called to the police station to help him in checking any documentation and to sign any document on his behalf if the blind person so wishes (para. 3.14).

16. Does the suspect have to answer questions put to him by the police?

A police officer has the right to ask any questions and the Code states that citizens have a civic duty to "help police officers to prevent crime and discover offenders" (Code C, note 1B). But the citizen has no legal duty to answer; a person detained in the police station, like everyone else in the community, has a "right of silence". The purpose of the caution is precisely to remind him of this right.

Until 1995 the caution told the suspect "You do not have to say anything unless you wish to do so but what you say may be given in evidence." When the case came to court neither the prosecution nor the judge could suggest that silence was evidence of guilt.

However the position has now changed. Under the Criminal Justice and Public Order Act 1994 both the prosecution and the judge *are* allowed to suggest to the jury that silence can be evidence of guilt. So the caution has had to be changed. It still tells the suspect that he is entitled to be silent. It has not become a criminal offence to be silent. The right to be silent remains but the suspect must now be warned that silence might be penalised by the jury drawing adverse inferences.

17. What is the wording of the new caution?

The new caution is: "You do not have to say anything. But it may harm your defence if you do not mention when questioned something which you later rely on in court. Anything you do say may be given in evidence." Minor variations in the way the caution is put are permitted. If the suspect does not understand the caution, the officer should try to explain it in his own words.

In fact the new provisions go further. They permit adverse inferences to be drawn from a failure by the suspect to answer specific police questions about objects, marks or substances on or about his person or at the place where he was arrested or failure to account for his presence at the scene of the crime. For such an inference to be drawn the officer must first however have told the suspect in ordinary language:

(a) what offence he is investigating;
(b) what fact he is asking the suspect to account for;
(c) that he believes this fact may be due to the suspect being involved in the offence; and
(d) that a court may draw a proper inference from his silence.

(For more details see the separate chapter on the topic, pp. 303–323 below.)

18. When does a person have to be cautioned?

The caution has to be given to a "person whom there are grounds to suspect of an offence" before any questions or further questions are put to him "regarding his involvement or suspected involvement in that offence if his answers or his silence (*i.e.* failure or refusal to answer a question or to answer satisfactorily) may be given in evidence to a court." (Code C, para. 10.1.)

But the person need not be cautioned if he is being questioned just to establish his identity or his ownership of a vehicle or "the proper and effective conduct of a search"—providing that it does not consist of questions about his possible involvement in a criminal offence.

THE EXERCISE OF POLICE POWERS IN THE POLICE STATION

19. What rules restrict the police in questioning the suspect?

There are rules in the Code about interviews with a suspect;
(1) In any 24 hour period a continuous period of eight hours must be allowed for rest, free from questioning, or travel. If possible, this period should be at night (Code C, para. 12.2).
(2) There is no rule as to the maximum length of an interview[73] but there

---

[73] The Home Office study by Brown *et al.* (1992, pp. 89–90) based on nearly 7,000 interviews showed that the average length of an interview is of the order of half an hour—31 minutes in the 1990 sample and 26 minutes in the 1991 sample. Many arrests did not involve questioning at all. Over 40 per cent of those detained were not interviewed. Only 8 per cent of the two samples were questioned more than once.

Brown (1993) showed that in terrorism cases PTA detainees were typically interviewed two or three times and on average interviews lasted 59 minutes (pp. 29–30). However a possible reason for the fact of longer interviews in terrorism cases may be that they are generally contemporaneously noted whereas ordinary interviews are tape-recorded. On average each P.T.A. detainee was interviewed for a total of three hours and eight minutes (p. 31). But this average was skewed by a small number of exceptional cases including one where questioning went on for a total of 21 hours. But in 49 per cent questioning went on for less than two hours and in 62 per cent for less than three hours. (In 10 per cent there was no questioning at all.) It went on for longer than three hours in only 27 per cent of the 251 cases (Table 4.2, p. 31).

are rules as to meal breaks. Breaks should be made at recognised meal times. In addition there should be short breaks for light refreshment at intervals of approximately two hours (*ibid.*, para. 12.7). The 1995 revised Code (note 12C) says that meal breaks should normally last at least 45 minutes and shorter breaks every two hours should last at least 15 minutes. If breaks are delayed, they should be longer. But breaks can be delayed in the interviewing officer's discretion if there are reasonable grounds for believing that the break would involve a risk of harm to persons, or serious loss of or damage to property; or would unnecessarily delay the person's release from custody; or would otherwise prejudice the investigation (*ibid.*). Two light and one main meal should be provided in any 24 hour period.

(3) Persons being questioned should not be required to stand whilst being questioned (*ibid.*, para. 12.5).

(4) If it is necessary to take a person's clothing for investigatory or health and hygiene reasons, adequate replacement clothing must be provided. A person may not be interviewed unless adequate clothing has been offered to him (*ibid.*, para. 8.5).

(5) No officer should try to obtain answers to questions or to elicit a statement "by the use of oppression" (*ibid.* para. 11.3).

(6) An officer should not indicate, save in answer to a direct question, what action will be taken by the police if the detainee answers questions, makes a statement or refuses to do so. If the person directly asks the officer such a question, "then the officer may inform the person what action he proposes to take in that event provided that that action is itself proper and warranted". (Code C, 11.3). It would therefore appear to be proper for instance for the officer in answer to a question to say to the suspect "If you make a statement I will let you go home, or let you off the more serious charges or not pursue charges against your wife etc." (This represents a major shift in the rules; see further pp. 303–315 below.)

20. In what circumstances can the police fingerprint the detainee?

There are four situations in which a person's fingerprints can be taken under section 61:

(1) With consent at a police station in writing from the suspect (s.61(1) and (2)).

(2) Without consent if authorised by a superintendent if he has reasonable grounds for suspecting the person's involvement in a criminal offence and that the fingerprints will prove or disprove his involvement. (s.61(3)(a) and (4).)

(3) Without consent at a police station if charged or reported for a recordable offence and fingerprints have not been taken in the course of the investigation (s.61(3)(b)).

(4) Without consent if convicted of a recordable offence (s.61(6)).

Fingerprints can also be taken compulsorily under PACE by virtue of section 27 where the person has been convicted of a recordable offence, has not been in police detention and has not had his fingerprints taken during the investigation or since the conviction. He can be required to attend at a police station for the purposes of being fingerprinted.

21. Can a suspect in the police station be photographed?

Normally a person who has been arrested but not convicted must give his consent to be photographed. Moreover the consent is required by the Code to be written. But a photograph can be taken without the person's consent if he is arrested at the same time as other persons and a photograph is necessary to establish who was arrested, at what time or at what place or under para. 4.2(ii) if he is charged with a recordable offence. Force may not be used however in the taking of a photograph.

All copies and negatives of the photograph must be destroyed if he is not charged or if he is tried but acquitted. Again he must be given the chance of witnessing their destruction if he wishes. But the photographs need not be destroyed if the suspect has one or more previous convictions for a recordable offence.

22. In what circumstances can the suspect's personal clothes and effects be taken from him?

A detained person may retain clothing and personal effects at his own risk unless the custody officer considers that he may use them to cause harm to himself or others, or interfere with evidence, or damage property or effect an escape or they are needed as evidence. In that event the custody officer can withhold such articles as he considers necessary. He must tell the person why.

23. In what circumstances can a search take place of body orifices?

A search of body orifices (an "intimate search") may only take place where an officer of the rank of superintendent or above has reasonable grounds for believing that the arrested person has concealed on him something which could be used to cause physical injury to himself or others and that it cannot be found without an intimate search. With one exception it cannot be a search for evidence of crime. The exception is where a superintendent reasonably believes that the suspect has on him hard drugs (Class A drugs) which he intended to supply to others or to export. The search should in principle be carried out by a doctor or nurse but in an urgent case, if a superintendent thinks it is not practicable, it can be done by a police officer providing he is of the same sex as the person being searched and provided that no officer of the opposite sex is present. But this is not so with searches for drugs. They can only be carried out by a doctor or nurse and cannot be done in a police station. Anything found in the course of an intimate search can be used in evidence.

24. Can a doctor or nurse be compelled to carry out a search of body orifices where the suspect refuses to consent?

The answer is No. It is for them to decide whether or not to conduct an intimate search in such circumstances. Most such searches are conducted by police surgeons. Note that consent to such a search by the suspect is not essential and force could therefore be used to carry out the search— presumably even if it is being carried out by a medical practitioner or nurse.

25. When can a person be asked to provide a bodily sample?

Previously an intimate and a non-intimate sample could only be asked for if the offence was a serious arrestable offence. Now under the Criminal Justice and Public Order Act 1994 they can be asked for in connection with any recordable (*i.e.* imprisonable) offence. The change is to give more opportunity in particular for DNA testing.

26. Does taking a sample require consent?

Taking an intimate sample always requires written consent—though failure to give consent can lead to the jury being invited to draw adverse inferences from the refusal. It also requires the authority of an officer at least of the rank of superintendent. Save in the case of urine, an intimate sample must be taken by a doctor or registered dentist.

Taking a non-intimate sample should also, if possible, not be done without the suspect's consent. But an officer of the rank of superintendent can authorise the taking of a non-intimate sample if there are reasonable grounds for believing that it will tend to confirm or disprove the suspect's involvement in the offence.

27. What are intimate and non-intimate samples?

An intimate sample is blood, semen or other tissue fluid, urine, pubic hair or a swab taken from a person's body orifice, and dental impressions. Saliva was classified as an intimate sample but it was re-classified as from April 1995 as a non-intimate sample.

A non-intimate sample is a sample of hair other than pubic hair, a sample taken from a nail or under a nail, a swab taken from a part of the body other than a body orifice, saliva and a footprint.

PART VI

THE CODES OF PRACTICE

Codes of practice: sections 66–67 and the Codes[1]

The Philips Royal Commission on Criminal Procedure said that all aspects of the treatment of suspects in custody should be statutory. This would involve the use of primary legislation on some matters. But the rules to regulate the facilities to be provided for, and the treatment to be accorded to suspects and the rules to govern the conduct and recording of interviews should, it thought, be contained in subordinate legislation. "This should be made by the Home Secretary with consultation as appropriate, and subject to the approval of Parliament by affirmative resolution."[2]

The actual method adopted in the Act, however, somewhat different.

The Act required the Secretary of State, subject to Parliament's approval, to issue Codes of Practice in relation to:

   (i) search of the person and of vehicles without an arrest;
  (ii) the detention, treatment, questioning and identification of persons; and
 (iii) searches of premises and seizure of property found in searches of persons or premises (s.66(1)).

As has been seen above, there is an equivalent duty in respect of the tape recording of interviews with suspects (s.60).

The Home Secretary, having prepared and published drafts of any Codes of Practice, must consider any representations made on them. He must lay a draft of the Code before both Houses of Parliament. After he has done this—and no time limit is specified—he "may bring the code into operation by order made by statutory instrument" (s.67(4)). Such an order must be approved by a resolution of each House of Parliament (subs. (5)). The same procedure must be followed for any subsequent revision of the whole or any part of the Codes (subs. (7)).

This procedure therefore contemplates two separate stages. The first is publishing of draft Codes. This in fact proved to be a very lengthy process of "open government". Each version of the Codes went through successive drafts as a result of comments from a wide range of organisations and individuals. By the time that Parliament considered them they had already

---

[1] See N.I. PACE Order, Arts. 65, 66.
[2] Philips Report, para. 4.116.

been extensively amended and re-amended. The preliminary stage of publishing drafts therefore proved very important in practice.

The second stage is laying them before Parliament and the order bringing them into force.

For the House of Commons debate on the original Codes see *Hansard*, December 5, 1985, Cols. 484–521 (by a curious coincidence Parliament approved the Codes of Practice for Northern Ireland precisely four years later on December 5, 1989). But one of the ironies of the process of bringing the Codes into existence is that parliamentarians are the group least able to influence the content of the Codes since the debate on the draft Codes cannot lead to them being amended.[3]

The reason given by the Home Office for not following the Royal Commission's recommendation that the Codes be in the form of a statutory instrument, was that it proved an unworkable proposal in the light of the need to make the Codes self-contained. The object was to produce a custody officer's booklet which would give him a comprehensive guide to the various aspects of his duties. Some of the material in the Code it was thought should come from the statute so as to reduce the need to refer to two documents. It was felt that it would be impossible to have a statutory instrument that repeated parts of the primary legislation in different language.

A second reason for having a Code rather than a statutory instrument was that the language of a Code could be less formal and this would be valuable since it must be intelligible to police officers.

Thirdly, the Home Office considered that the underlying objectives for making the Codes statutory instruments could all be fulfilled by the procedure adopted in the Act. There could be a parliamentary debate on the content of the Codes and there would therefore be parliamentary accountability. True, there would be no opportunity to move amendments—but this would be the same with any statutory instrument.

Whether the Codes would have a higher status in the eyes of the police if they were statutory instruments is impossible to say. The ordinary police officer is not a close student of the niceties of the parliamentary system and is therefore not likely to be aware of the difference between the procedure for passing a statutory instrument as compared with the bringing into force of the Codes of Practice. It is possible that the words "statutory instrument" have more of the ring of law about them than the words "Code of Practice". But again the difference may not be very great.

The crux of the matter is whether the police treat the rules in the Codes of Practice as rules to which they must adhere. The Judges' Rules were not law and the judges over the years showed themselves somewhat lax in enforcing their provisions. Generally breaches of the Judges Rules were not regarded by the judges as a reason to exclude evidence or on appeal to quash a conviction.

In spite of this the Judges' Rules were undoubtedly regarded by the police as something of which they had to take account. They formed part of the material a police officer had to study and indeed master. The informal view of police officers tended to be that the Judges' Rules were a bit of a nuisance—which in itself indicates that they did have some real existence. If

---

[3] Parliamentary procedure does not permit amendments to be moved when delegated legislation is being debated.

they had been treated as wholly irrelevant they would have provoked little or no reaction amongst police officers.

One question is what consequences flow from a breach of the Codes of Practice. On this, section 67 states that a failure on the part of any person to observe any provision of a Code of Practice shall not of itself render him liable to any criminal or civil proceedings[4] (subs. (10)) but in any proceedings the Code of Practice shall be admissible and shall be taken into account if it is thought "by the court" to be relevant to any question arising in those proceedings (subs. (11)).[5] In other words, the extent to which a breach of the Codes results in evidence being excluded is a matter for the judges but they are obliged to take it into account. It will be seen from many of the cases referred to in this edition of the book that the courts have very frequently used breaches of the Codes as the basis for exclusion of evidence or the quashing of convictions. Commentators (including the writer) have been surprised, given their pre-PACE attitudes, at the way the judges have been prepared to "penalise" breaches of the Codes by the police in this way.

There is even one Court of Appeal decision which holds that the Codes have sufficient status to replace legal rules emerging from case law! The case, *McCay*,[6] raised the question of whether a police officer could tell the court in what way a witness had identified the accused at an identification parade. The witness himself had forgotten that he had said "It is number eight" on the parade. Obviously the police officer's statement was hearsay. The Court of Appeal upheld the trial judge's decision to allow the evidence in—either because it was original evidence as part of the *res gestae* or, if not, as an admissible exception to the hearsay rule. The Code, the Court said, had the full authority of Parliament, having been approved by both Houses of Parliament. The provisions of Code D had been complied with. If the words used by the witness were hearsay there was "statutory authority" (*sic*) for the words used to be admissible.

Professor Diane Birch in her commentary on the case[7] was surely correct to argue that the Court of Appeal's view was mistaken. It cannot be the case that the rules of admissibility of evidence have been abolished and that the courts need only look to see whether there has been compliance with the Codes. Nor does a resolution in both Houses of Parliament amount to "statutory authority". But the decision indicates how powerfully the concept of the Codes has begun to influence the judges.

Section 67(8) originally stated that a police officer "shall be liable to disciplinary proceedings" for any breach of the Codes. This section was however repealed by the Police and Magistrates' Courts Act, 1994, section 37(a). Very few disciplinary proceedings for breaches of PACE had in fact been brought.[8] Breaches of PACE will in future have to be dealt with under the new discipline regime details of which were not available when this book went to press. (See further p. 255 below.) As has been seen, section 67(11) permits a breach of PACE to be taken into account in any civil or criminal proceedings—which presumably includes police disciplinary proceedings.

---

[4] For an account of a successful action for damages for false imprisonment founded on breaches of PACE see however J. MacKenzie "Civil Liability for PACE breaches", New L.J., June 7, 1991, p. 788.
[5] This may include taken into account by the jury as well as by the judge—see *R. v. Kenny* [1992] Crim.L.R. 800, C.A.
[6] [1990] 1 W.L.R. 645 [1990] Crim.L.R. 338, C.A.
[7] [1990] Crim.L.R. 338, p. 340.
[8] See Report of the Runciman Royal Commission on Criminal Justice, 1993, Report, p. 48, para. 102.

Other forces

"Police force" for the purpose of section 67 is defined as "any body of constables". The journal *Police Review* published a letter from the Home Office explaining the meaning of this phrase:

"The term constable in the 1984 Act includes any sworn constable. It is not restricted to officers of forces established under the 1964 Act but includes any member of a body of constables maintained by an authority other than a police authority. It will be the case, of course, that the constabulary powers of these bodies are limited to the specific activities for which the officers are employed and outside these activities they will cease to have constabulary powers. This will be the case with, for example, the British Transport Police and the Mersey Tunnels Police (who are both maintained by statutory undertakers), as well as with those such as the Ministry of Defence Police (who are not) ... On a final point, I do not believe that the Royal Military Police officers are constables."[9]

The Philips Royal Commission took the view that the Codes should also apply to persons who are not constables who do a similar job.[10] The Act gave effect to this objective in section 67(9) which provides that "persons other than police officers who are charged with the duty of investigating offences or charging offenders shall in the discharge of that duty have regard to any relevant provision of such a code".

Again the same piece in the *Police Review* quoted the Home Office view on the meaning of this phrase: "Our view is that in using the words of the Judges Rules, section 67(9) of the Act does not change the position hitherto that charged with the duty means charged by law with the duty. This refers, for example, to local authority officials such as trading standards officers,[11] Post Office investigation officers, or central government officers such as DTI inspectors."[12] Customs' officers are also covered.[13] The Home Office opinion continued:

"Our advice in the case of people such as store detectives and security officers who take it upon themselves to investigate offences, is that they should have regard to the standards set out in the Codes so far as in common sense they are applicable to the work they do. These people, however, have no special powers of arrest, search, entry, or seizure. If they make an arrest under their citizen's powers, or question a suspect in order

---

[9] Alan Harding, *Police Review*, January 22, 1988, p. 185. Mr Harding was at the time the senior Home Office official dealing with PACE.

[10] Philips Report, para. 4.135.

[11] This was confirmed in *Dudley Metropolitan Council v. Debenhams plc, The Times*, August 16, 1994 (Div.Ct.). When trading standards officers attended at premises to see whether an offence under the Consumer Protection Act 1987 had been committed they were under a duty to enforce compliance and intended, if appropriate, to prosecute. The Divisional Court held that they had a power of entry under the 1987 Act if there were at that time reasonable grounds to suspect that an offence had been committed. But absent such grounds, the employee should have been told, as under Code B of PACE, that he was not obliged to comply with a request to hand over the relevant documents [ed.].

[12] But see *R. v. Seelig and Spens* (1991) 94 Cr.App.R. 17; *The Times*, May 13, 1991 in which the Court of Appeal held that DTI inspectors inquiring into the so-called Guiness affair under sections 432 and 442 of the Companies Act 1985 were *not* investigating offences within the meaning of section 67(9) and that the Codes therefore did not apply [ed].

[13] See section 114, p. 295 below and *Sanusi* [1992] Crim.L.R. 43, C.A.

to obtain evidence, they should observe the provisions of the Codes as far as they are applicable to ensure that, in any subsequent trial, a court will regard their behaviour as fair and reasonable. What we are talking about is essentially a matter of common sense. If a civilian (like a store detective) oversteps the mark in regard to a suspect and obtains evidence by means that would not be open to a police officer, then he must expect his evidence to be at risk in subsequent proceedings."[14]

It was held in *R. v. Director of Serious Fraud, ex p. Saunders*[15] that the Codes apply to the officers of the Serious Fraud Office.[16] The Pace Codes have been held to apply not only to store detectives[17] but also to commercial investigators—in that case employed by Ladbroke's betting shops.[18] The Court of Appeal held there that the Codes applied to commercial investigators in so far as they were charged with the duty of investigating offences.[19]

Note that relevant provisions of the Code have been held not to apply to the circumstances of the motorist being processed under the drink–drive provisions of the Road Traffic Act.[20] Thus a motorist under arrest on suspicion of driving or being in charge of a motor vehicle with excess alcohol can, before the police undertake the specimen procedure, be denied access to a lawyer,[21] and be refused the opportunity to read the PACE Codes.[22] It has also been held that the breathalyser procedure does not constitute an interview.[23] But section 78 of PACE does apply.[24]

Where the police operate undercover, or by means of bugging or other tricks and stratagems the courts have sometimes held that the PACE Codes apply and sometimes that they do not apply. (See pp. 242–244 below.)

The Northern Ireland PACE Order (Art. 66(22)) states that the Codes of Practice do not apply to persons arrested or detained under the Emergency Powers or Prevention of Terrorism legislation. However separate non-statutory guidance for terrorism cases was issued. There is no equivalent general exclusion of terrorism cases from the effect of the Codes of Practice in England and Wales. Indeed on the contrary. Code C specifically states (para. 1.11) that persons in police custody for the purposes of the Code include persons taken to a police station after being arrested under section 14 of the Prevention of Terrorism (Temporary Provisions) Act 1989 and

---

[14] *op. cit.*

[15] [1988] Crim.L.R. 837 (Div.Ct.).

[16] In *R. v. Director of Serious Fraud Office, ex p. Smith* [1993] A.C. 1 (H.L.) it was held that the general provisions of the Codes regarding questioning and cautioning of suspects gave way however to the explicit provisions of the Criminal Justice Act 1987 which established an inquisitorial regime for serious fraud investigations.

[17] See *R. v. Bayliss* (1993) 98 Cr.App.R. 235; [1994] Crim.L.R. 687, C.A. The Court of Appeal said it was possible for a store detective to be a person "charged with the duty of investigating offences" within the meaning of s.67(9). It was a question of fact in each case.

[18] *R. v. Twaites and Brown* (1991) 92 Cr.App.R. 106, [1990] Crim.L.R. 863, C.A.

[19] See also *Joy v. Federation Against Copyright Theft Ltd* [1993] Crim.L.R. 588 (Div.Ct.) where an investigator for FACT operating with a warrant under the Copyright, Designs and Patents Act 1988, s.107(c), was considered to be someone "charged with the duty of investigating offences".

[20] See generally D. Tucker, "Drink-Drivers' PACE Rights: A cause for concern" [1990] Crim.L.R. 177.

[21] *D.P.P. v. Billington* [1988] R.T.R. 231, [1988] 1 All E.R. 454, C.A.

[22] *D.P.P. v. Whalley* [1991] Crim.L.R. 211 (Div.Ct.); *D.P.P. v. Cornell* [1990] R.T.R. 254 (Div.Ct.).

[23] *D.P.P. v. Rouse and Davis* [1991] Crim.L.R. 911 (Div.Ct.).

[24] See for instance *Matto v. D.P.P.* [1987] R.T.R. 337 (Div.Ct.); *D.P.P. v. Godwin* [1991] R.T.R. 303 (Div.Ct.); *Andrews v. D.P.P.* [1992] R.T.R. 1 (Div.Ct.); *Hudson* [1992] R.T.R. 27 (Div.Ct.).

persons detained at a police station following examination at a port under Schedule 5 to the Act.

The Codes

The Philips Royal Commission did not itself draft the Codes of Practice. They were prepared by the Home Office. Five Codes of Practice have been promulgated.

Code A is on Stop and Search: Code B is on Search of Premises; Code C is on Detention and Questioning of Suspects; and Code D is on Identification; Code E is on Tape-Recording.

The first edition of Codes A to D came into force on January 1, 1986. These were supplemented by Code E in 1988. A second, revised edition of Codes A to D came into force on April 1, 1991. The latest revision affects all five Codes. A draft of the new Codes was published for consultation between August and November 1994. The revised Codes were laid before Parliament on January 30, 1995. They were approved in the House of Commons[25] and in the House of Lords[26] at the end of February and came into force on April 10, 1995.

The Codes make a distinction between the actual rules and "Notes for guidance" and "Annexes". The Annexes mainly collect in one place provisions that recur at various points in the main text and would have to be repeated several times. The Annexes are stated to be part of the Codes (Code C, para. 1.3). Notes for Guidance are described as not being provisions of the Code but "guidance to police officers and others about its application and interpretation" (C.1.3).

The notes for guidance are therefore technically of a lower status in terms of their authority. But they contain much of great importance and it is doubtful whether the distinction between the rules in the Codes and the principles in the notes for guidance is a clear one.

The Code states that the document containing the Codes, "must be readily available at all police stations for consultation by police officers, detained persons and members of the public" (Codes A, B, D, E, para. 1.1, Code C, para. 1.2). They are distributed by the Home Office to the police free of charge.

Research since the Act suggests that it is very rare for suspects to ask for a copy of the Codes.

The actual content of Codes A (Stop and Search), B (Search of Premises) and E (on Tape-Recording) has already been dealt with above. Codes C (on Detention) and D (on Identification) in so far as they have not previously been treated, are dealt with in this chapter.

Code C: The Code for the detention, treatment and questioning of persons suspected of crime[27] (the Detention Code)

Code C starts with the statement that "all persons in custody must be dealt with expeditiously and be released as soon as the need for detention has

---

[25] Police and Criminal Evidence Act 1984 (Codes of Practice) (No. 3) Order 1995, S.I. No. 450. See House of Commons, 1st Standing Committee on Statutory Instruments, February 21, 1995.
[26] See House of Lords, *Hansard*, February 23, 1995, Vol. 561, cols. 1274–1282.
[27] See also the Code itself, pp. 453–486 below.

ceased to apply" (para. 1.1). A new provision in the 1995 version of the Code (para. 1.1A) adds that the custody officer is required to perform his functions "as soon as is practicable" but that he will not be in breach of the code if there is justifiable delay and that every reasonable step has been taken to prevent delay. Note 1H specifies that this is intended to cover the situation where a large number of persons are brought into the police station at the same time, or the interview rooms are all being used or there are delays in contacting an appropriate adult, solicitor or interpreter. Those who are at the police station voluntarily should be treated "with no less consideration" than those in custody (note 1A).

The custody record: section 2[28]

The Code requires the custody officer to maintain a custody record for every arrested person for the details of all the relevant events of the detention (para. 2.1). All information that has to be recorded must be recorded "as soon as practicable, in the custody record unless otherwise specified" (para. 2.1). In the case of any action requiring the authority of an officer of a specified rank, his name and rank must be noted in the custody record (para. 2.2). In the case of terrorism, the warrant number and duty station is the equivalent (*ibid.*).

The custody officer is responsible for the accuracy and completeness of the record and for ensuring that the record or a copy accompanies a detained person if he is transferred to another station. The record should show the time and the reason for the transfer and the time a person is released from detention (para. 2.3).

A new provision in the 1995 revision of the Code states that a solicitor or appropriate adult must be allowed to consult the custody record of a detainee "*as soon as practicable after their arrival at the police station*" (para. 2.4, emphasis supplied). The detainee, the appropriate adult or legal representative who gives reasonable notice of a request to inspect the original custody record after the person has left police detention should be allowed to do so (*ibid.*).

All entries in custody records must be timed and signed by the maker (para. 2.6). In the case of a record entered on a computer this has to be timed and must identify the operator. The Act does not specifically deal with whether the custody officer may delegate the function of "making a record" to someone including a civilian computer operative but commonsense suggests that this increasingly normal practice would be held to be lawful. Obviously however the custody officer rather than the civilian employee would be accountable for any errors or deficiencies in the record. Any refusal by a person to sign a custody record when asked to do so in accordance with the provisions of the Code must itself be recorded (para. 2.7).

What must be recorded?

The items that must be stated in the custody record include: the grounds of detention (para. 3.17); the suspect's signature acknowledging receipt of a

---

[28] The section numbers of the N.I. Codes are not necessarily the same as those of the Codes for England and Wales. The revised N.I. Codes were due to become effective as from January 31, 1996.

notice of his rights, or the custody officer's note that he refused to sign (para. 3.2); any waiver by the suspect of his right to have legal advice (para. 3.5); the list of the suspect's effects, signed by him as correct or, if he refuses, with a note to that effect (para. 4.4); details of any intimate search or strip search, including the reason for it and its result (Annex A, para. 7); a statement of reasons for withholding articles from the suspect (para. 4.5); requests to inform a relative or friend of the fact of the arrest and any action taken on such a request, and details of any letters, messages or telephone calls made or received and of visits (para. 5.8)[29]; the ground for delaying notification by the suspect of a friend or relative of the fact of detention and his whereabouts (para. 5.8) (Annex B, para. 6); the time of any later grant of this right (para. 5.8); action taken on any request for legal advice (para. 6.16); the grounds for delaying access to legal advice (Annex B, paras. 6 and 7); the grounds for starting to interview a suspect who has been allowed to call a solicitor before the solicitor arrives (para. 6.17); when a foreigner or Commonwealth citizen is told of his right to inform his Embassy or High Commission and details of any call made on his behalf regarding the fact of his detention (para. 7.5); details of the times at which meals are served to the suspect (para. 8.11); the grounds why a child or young person is placed in police cells (para. 8.12); details of any complaint by a suspect regarding his treatment (para. 9.7); details of any medical treatment or action taken regarding a condition requiring medical attention (*ibid.* and 9.8), the record should also show what medication he claims he needs which he does not have with him (para. 9.9); the time and place of any caution[30] (para. 10.7); the time at which the suspect is handed over by the custody officer for questioning (para. 12.9); the grounds for delay of a required break in interviews (para. 12.11); action taken to call an interpreter and any waiver of the right not to be interviewed without one (para. 13.11); the grounds for delaying a review of detention (para. 15.4); the details of any such review (para. 15.6); any decision to interview a mentally disordered person or child or young person without waiting for a responsible person who has been asked to come to be with him (Annex C); the time at which the suspect is cautioned on being charged and details of anything he said (para. 16.7–8).

On release a person is entitled to a copy of any part of the custody record that the police are required to maintain (para. 2.4) and he must be told in writing of his right to have a copy (para. 3.2). After leaving the police station, he or his representative, on giving reasonable notice, should also be allowed to inspect the original (para. 2.5).

It has already been seen that the Home Office Circular on PACE advised that although strictly a custody record form was not required for some categories of detainees it might nevertheless be wise to keep such a record for administrative reasons. Categories of whom this could be true would be those held awaiting a court appearance on the authority of a production order, following a remand to prison custody, or during examination under the Prevention of Terrorism Act where the person has not been arrested.

---

[29] Brown *et al.* (1992, pp. 56–57) stated that in around a quarter of cases where a request was made the action taken was not recorded. They note that the outcome of requests is often lost when the task of carrying them out falls to beat officers or those conducting searches of premises or where initial attempts fail and further attempts are left to the next shift.

[30] This should be made in the officer's note book or in the interview record as appropriate.

Initial action: information to the person in detention

When a person is brought to a police station under arrest or is arrested at the police station having attended there voluntarily, Code C requires that the custody officer must inform him of the following rights and that they are continuing rights which need not be exercised immediately. The rights of which he must be told forthwith are:

(i) the right to have someone informed of his arrest in accordance with section 5 of the Code;

(ii) the right to consult privately with a solicitor and that independent legal advice is available free of charge; and

(iii) the right to consult the Codes of Practice (Code C, para. 3.1).

Note for guidance 3E states however that the right to consult the Codes does not entitle the person concerned unreasonably to delay, necessary investigate or administrative action while he is doing so.[31]

The custody officer must give the person a written notice setting out the above three rights, the right to a copy of the custody record and the caution in the terms prescribed in section 10 of the Code (para. 3.2). He must also give the person a copy of a notice explaining the arrangements for obtaining legal advice (*ibid*).[32]

The custody officer must also give the suspect a notice setting out "his entitlements" while in custody (para. 3.2). Note for guidance 3A explains that the "notice of entitlements" is intended to give detainees brief details of matters over and above the statutory rights set out in the "notice of rights". It covers such matters as visits and contact with outside parties, standards of physical comfort, food and drink, access to toilet and writing facilities, clothing, medical treatment and exercise. It also mentions the provisions relating to the conduct of interviews, when the appropriate adult should be available and the right to make representations on reviews of detention. It should be available in relevant languages (para. 3B).

He should then ask the person to sign the custody record to acknowledge receipt of these notices. The person should be asked to sign on the custody record to signify whether he wants legal advice at that point (para. 3.5). The custody officer must ensure that he signs in the right place.

If the custody officer authorises the person's detention he must inform him of the grounds as soon as practicable and in any event before he is questioned about any offence (para. 3.4).

The most recent Home Office study of the implementation of these rights[33] suggests that:

---

[31] See to same effect *D.P.P. v. Cornell* [1990] R.T.R. 254, holding that a motorist cannot prevent the police doing a breath, blood or urine test on the ground that he wants time to study the Codes. For critical comment see D. Tucker, "Drink-Drivers' PACE Rights: A cause for concern", [1990] Crim.L.R. 176.

[32] These notices are supposed to be available in a variety of languages. The Home Office Circular on PACE stated that National Form 7, providing the information that a custody officer had to give a detained person under this part of the Code, was to be translated into Arabic, Punjabi, Urdu, Hindi, Gujerati and Bengali with the Welsh Office translating it into Welsh. The 1995 revision of the Code added a requirement that it be available in "the principle European languages".

[33] Brown *et al.* (1992) summarised in Home Office Research and Statistics Department, Research Findings No. 5, March 1993.

(1) broadly, the information is communicated to suspects both in written and oral form—though when orally, not always as clearly as it might be[34];

(2) most suspects do not avail themselves of these rights[35];

(3) legal advice is sought and obtained more in serious than in less serious cases[36]; and

(4) the effectiveness of the system of rights for suspects works better since the April 1991 revisions in the Codes.[37]

Special groups

If the person does not understand English or appears to be deaf the custory officer should as soon as practicable call an interpreter and ask him to provide the information required to be given to the detained person (para. 3.6).

If the person is a juvenile, mentally handicapped or suffering from some "mental disorder"[38] (Code C, Note 1G) the custody officer must, as soon as practicable, inform the appropriate adult of the grounds for his detention and his whereabouts, and ask the adult to come to the police station to see the person. The information required to be given to the detained person under paragraphs 3.1 to 3.4 should be given in the presence of the appropriate adult (para. 3.11). If the juvenile is a ward of court the police can interview him without getting permission from the court, providing they follow the rules for interviewing juveniles.[39]

If, having been informed of the right to legal advice under paragraph 3.11, the appropriate adult considers that legal advice should be taken, the provisions of section 6 of the Code apply (para. 3.13). Note 3G says however that if the suspect wants legal advice, action should be taken immediately without waiting for the appropriate adult to arrive.

Again if the person is blind or "seriously visually handicapped or is unable to read," the custody officer should ensure that his solicitor, relative, the appropriate adult or some other suitable person is available to help check any documentation (para. 3.14).

On the position of special groups see further, p. 185, below.

---

[34] The researchers considered that information about rights was given too quickly, incompletely or incomprehensibly in about a quarter of the cases of adults and one third where the detainee was a juvenile (Brown *et al.* (1992, pp. 22–35)).

[35] Thus after the April 1991 revisions in the Codes, the proportion of suspects who (1) asked for legal advice was 32 per cent for adults and 26 per cent for juveniles, (2) asked for someone to be informed of the fact of their detention was 17 per cent for adults and 7 per cent for juveniles; (3) asked for a telephone call was 8 per cent, (4) asked for a copy of the Codes was 4 per cent. However, of those who did not want someone informed, 40 per cent said the relevant parties knew already. (See Brown *et al.* (1992), p. 55.) It should be remembered in this context that about 70 per cent of suspects have previous experience of arrest. "Many of this group clearly indicated that they were not interested in hearing about their rights; they knew what they were entitled to and could make a decision unaided" (Brown *et al.*, p. 37).

[36] See on this p. 139 above.

[37] See Brown *et al.* (1992) generally.

[38] "Mental disorder" is defined as "mental illness, arrested or incomplete development of mind, psychopathic disorder and any other disorder or disability of mind" (Note IG).

[39] *Re R, Re G, The Times*, March 29, 1990.

Conditions of detention: section 8

The Judges' Rules and Administrative Directions made a few but only rather general reference to the conditions of detention. Code C makes many very detailed new rules.

So far as practicable there should be no more than one person per cell (para. 8.1). Cells and bedding should be adequately heated and reasonably clean (paras. 8.2, 8.3). There should be access to toilet and washing facilities (para. 8.4). Replacement clothing should be of reasonable standard and no questioning must take place unless the suspect has been offered clothing (para. 8.5). There should be at least two light and one main meal per 24 hours and any dietary requirements should be met so far as possible (para. 8.6). Drinks should be provided at mealtimes and on reasonable request between mealtimes (para. 8.6). Brief outdoor exercise should be permitted if possible (para. 8.7).

A juvenile should not be placed in police cells unless there is no other secure accommodation available and the custody officer thinks that it is not practicable to supervise him if he is not put in a cell (para. 8.8).[40]

Reasonable force may be used by a police officer to secure compliance with reasonable instructions, to prevent the suspect's escape or to restrain him from causing injury to persons or damage to property or evidence (para. 8.9).

Persons detained are supposed to be visited every hour (para. 8.10) Juveniles and persons at risk should, if possible, be visited more often (note 8A). Those who are drunk should be visited at least every half an hour. Drunks should be roused and spoken to on each visit.[41] Such visits or rousing of drunks do not constitute an interruption in the suspect's rest period for the purposes of the rules regarding rest periods (see para. 12.2 below).

If any ill-treatment or unlawful force has been used, any officer who has notice of it should draw it to the attention of the custody officer who in turn must inform an officer of at least the rank of inspector not connected with the investigation. If it involves an assault or the use of force he in turn must summon a police surgeon to examine the suspect (para. 9.1). A complaint from the suspect to this effect must similarly be reported to an inspector or above (*ibid.*).

Medical treatment: section 9

The Code requires that appropriate action be taken by the custody officer to deal with any medical condition—whether or not the person in custody asks for it. The police surgeon should be called immediately if the suspect is injured or appears to be suffering from any physical or mental illness or does not show awareness or fails to respond normally to conversation (other than through being drunk). The section warns that a person who appears to be drunk may in fact be suffering from illness or the effects of drugs or some

---

[40] Dixon (1990) reported that in the force in which he conducted research this requirement was "fulfilled" by simply designating ordinary cells as "juvenile detention rooms".

[41] Para. 8.10. The requirement that drunks be roused on each visit was added in the April 1995 revision.

injury (note 9B).[42] The police "should therefore always call the police surgeon when in any doubt and act with all due speed" (note 9B). But Code C (note 9A) makes it clear that the need to call a police surgeon need not apply to minor ailments or injuries nor when a Mental Health Act assessment can be made without delay (9.2 and note 9A).

If the suspect says he needs medication for a serious condition such as heart disease, diabetes or epilepsy the advice of the police surgeon should be obtained (para. 9.6). If the suspect is thought to be a drug addict a police officer other than a police surgeon cannot administer drugs (para. 9.5). The 'Code, para. 9.5 previously said that a person could only be allowed to administer drugs to himself under the personal supervision of the police surgeon. In the April 1995 revised Code C this has been relaxed to the extent of allowing for self-administration of a drug by a suspect under supervision of the custody officer after consultation (which can be by telephone) with the police surgeon (*ibid.*).

Cautions: section 10

Prior to PACE, the questioning of suspects was subject to the Judges' Rules. These were rules formulated by a committee of the judges of the Queen's Bench Division for the guidance of the police. Their origin was a letter from the Lord Chief Justice to the Chief Constable of Birmingham in October 1906 responding to a request for such guidance. The Judges' Rules were reformulated in 1964[43] and again in 1978.

They provided that a suspect should be cautioned "as soon as a police officer has evidence which affords him reasonable grounds for suspecting that a person has committed an offence": "You are not obliged to saything unless you wish to do so but what you say may be put into writing and given in evidence."

This traditional caution[44] was carried into the PACE system.[45] Now however, as has been seen above, the rules regarding the caution have been significantly altered by the so-called abolition of the right to silence by the CJPOA Act 1994, section 33 (pp. 303–323 below). The suspect does still have to be cautioned about his right to silence but he must now be warned that silence may be the subject of adverse comment by both the prosecution and the judge both of whom may invite the jury to draw adverse inferences from silence.

The new caution is: "You do not have to say anything. But it may harm your defence if you do not mention when questioned something which you later rely on in court. Anything you do say may be given in evidence."

As already stated, where this is relevant, he must also be cautioned about the adverse inferences that may be drawn from his failure to account for objects, marks, or substances found on or about his person or his presence at the place where he was arrested at or about the time the crime

---

[42] It seems that this admonition is taken to heart at least in terrorism cases. Brown (1993, pp. 35–36) found that although only 19 detainees asked for medical attention the police called a doctor in 105. In Paddington Green it was standard practice to call the doctor every morning to monitor the detainee's fitness for detention and questioning (p. 36). Three-quarters of the terrorism suspects held for more than 24 hours were examined by a doctor at least once (*ibid.*).

[43] [1964] 1 All E.R. 237.

[44] Modified only by the removal of the words "be put into writing and" to take account of tape-recording.

[45] For case law on failure to give a caution see pp. 238, 240 below.

was allegedly committed. (This flows from sections 36 and 37 of the CJPOA.)

In order for an adverse inference to be drawn in regard to such marks, etc., the officer must first have told the person being questioned what offence he is investigating; what facts he is asking the suspect to account for; that he believes the suspect has taken part in the commission of the offence; that the court can draw a proper inference if he fails or refuses to account for that fact; and that a record is being made (para. 10.5B).

The duty to caution the suspect does not apply however where the interview is conducted by the Serious Fraud Office exercising its special inquisitorial powers under section 2 of the Criminal Justice Act 1987. Moreover this situation continues even after charge—*R. v. Director of Serious Fraud Office, ex p. Smith.*[46] Paragraph 10.1 of the 1995 revised Code states that a person need not be cautioned if questions are put solely for the purpose of establishing his identity or ownership of a vehicle, or to obtain information in accordance with any relevant statutory requirement (such as that under the Road Traffic Act to give his name and address), or in furtherance of the proper conduct of a search or to seek verification of a written record—for instance under para. 11.13.

When cautions must be given

The first caution must be administered when the officer "has grounds to suspect" a person of an offence (para. 10.1). The grounds are not even required to be reasonable. He need not be cautioned unless questions are put to him to obtain evidence that may be given in court. As has been seen, if he is questioned in order to establish his identity or ownership of a vehicle he would therefore not have to be cautioned. If questioning is interrupted and restarted the officer must ensure that the suspect knows that he is still under caution and, if there is any doubt, he should be cautioned again in full (para. 10.5). If a person cautioned is not under arrest the officer should tell him that that is the position, that he is free to leave if he pleases and that he may get free legal advice if he wishes (paras. 10.2 and 3.15). A person who is under arrest should be cautioned: before being asked questions or further questions for the purpose of obtaining evidence for use in court; when being arrested for any further offence; when being charged and when being told about someone else's written statement or answers to questions. (See also p. 143 above.)

If a juvenile or a person who is mentally disordered or handicapped is cautioned in the absence of the appropriate adult, the caution should be repeated in the adult's presence (para. 10.6).

Interviews: general: paragraph 11(a)

The revised Code C (para. 11.1) makes it clear that interviews with arrested persons are basically to be conducted at police stations (or other authorised place of detention).[47] The Code provides that interviews should

---

[46] [1993] A.C. 1; (1992) 95 Cr.App.R. 191; [1992] 3 W.L.R. 66; [1992] 3 All E.R. 456 (H.L.).
[47] In *Goddard* (May 18, 1993, Unreported) Case No. 91/5291/Z2 C.A., the Court of Appeal said that to interview a suspect after he has been arrested and prior to his arrival at the police station was improper. The conviction for possessing heroin was quashed.

only be conducted somewhere other than at a police station where the same risks (of interference with evidence, alerting of accomplices, etc.) exists as justify delay of access to legal advice under section 58(8). Such questioning outside the police station should cease once that risk has been averted. However, there is no doubt that sometimes suspects are questioned prior to arrival at the police station.[48]

The 1995 revised Code states that after reminding the suspect of his right to legal advice and cautioning him (para. 11.2), the interviewing officer "shall put to him any significant statement or silence which occurred before his arrival at the police station, and shall ask him whether he confirms or denies that earlier statement or silence and whether he wishes to add anything" (para. 11.2A). A significant statement or silence is defined as one which "appears capable of being used in evidence against the suspect, in particular a direct admission of guilt, or failure or refusal to answer a question or to answer it satisfactorily which might give rise to an inference under Part III of the Criminal Justice and Public Order Act 1994" (*ibid.*).

Code C confirms the traditional common law rule that no police officer may try to obtain answers to question by the use of oppression (para. 11.3). Nor may an officer indicate, save in response to a direct question, what action would be taken by the police if the suspect answered questions, made a statement or refused to do either. If asked a direct question however, as has been seen, the officer may answer—provided the action he refers to is "proper and warranted" (*ibid.*).

But as soon as the officer believes that a prosecution should be brought against the person he is interviewing and that there is sufficient evidence for it to succeed, he should ask the suspect if he has anything else to say.[49] If the suspect indicates that he has nothing more to say, the officer "shall without delay cease to question him about that offence". (para. 11.4). A caveat added in the 1991 revised Code states that this should not however be taken to prevent officers inviting suspects in revenue cases or in confiscation proceedings under the Criminal Justice Act 1988 or the Drug Trafficking Offences Act 1986, to complete a formal question and answer record after the interview is concluded (*ibid.*).

Interview records: paragraph 11(b)

The provisions about the recording of interviews have given rise to considerable difficulty, controversy and case law. The 1991 revised Code made some important changes in the provisions regarding recording of interviews to take account of these difficulties as revealed in the case law. It also defused some of the problems that had arisen in regard to the recording of interviews by the new requirement in paragraph 11.13 that "a written record shall also be made of any comments made by a suspected person, including unsolicited comments, which are outside the context of an

---

[48] Brown *et al.* (1992) based on replies from police officers showed: that in 1991 questioning of the suspect by the police outside the police station occurred in 10 per cent of cases, that the suspect made unsolicited comments in 16 per cent and that there was questioning and/or unsolicited comments in 24 per cent. The comparable figures for the 1990 sample were 19 per cent, 19 per cent and 35 per cent. (Table 6.1, p. 81) See also S. Moston and G. Stephenson (1993, p. 22) showing that 8 per cent of the sample were questioned before arrival at the police station.

[49] An earlier draft of this provision required questioning to cease when the suspect had said all he wished to say—without any procedure for finding out whether this was the case.

interview but which might be relevant as to the offence." This could presumably now include significant silence. Any such record must be timed and signed by the maker. Where the person has been arrested he must be given the opportunity of reading the record and of signing it as correct or of indicating the respects in which he considers it inaccurate (*ibid.*).

In regard to interviews properly so called, the first and basic provision is that set out in paragraph 11.5(a) that "An accurate record must be made of each interview with a person suspected of an offence, whether or not the interview takes place at a police station."

The record must state the place of the interview, the time it starts and ends, the time the record is made (if different), and breaks and the names of those present. It must be made on forms provided or in the officer's pocket book or be tape-recorded (para. 11.5(b)). The record has to be made during the course of the interview "unless in the investigating officer's view this would not be practicable or would interfere with conduct of the interview"[50] (para. 11.5(c)). It must be either a verbatim record or, failing that, an account which adequately and accurately summarises it.

An accurate record must be made, as has been seen *whether or not the interview takes place in a police station*. The only questions therefore are, first, whether the exchange between the officer and the citizen amounts to "an interview" (on which see below) and, secondly, whether it is practicable to make a contemporaneous record.

The requirement to record the names of all those present does not apply however to interviews under the Prevention of Terrorism legislation. Instead in such cases the record must state the warrant number and duty station of each officer (para. 11.6).

If a record is not made during the course of the interview, it must be made as soon as practicable afterwards (para. 11.7). Written records must be timed and signed by the maker (para. 11.8). If a record is not completed during the interview the reason for this must be recorded in the officer's notebook (para. 11.9). As has been seen, the police are equally under a duty to make a written record of "any comments made by a suspected person, including unsolicited comments, which are outside of an interview but which might be relevant to the offence" (Code C, para. 11.13). Any such record must equally be timed and signed by the maker.

Unless it is not practicable, the person interviewed must be given the opportunity to read the interview record and to sign it as correct or to indicate in what respects he considers it inaccurate (para. 11.10.) If the suspect cannot read or refuses to read the record or to sign it, the senior police officer present must read it to him and ask whether he wishes to sign it as correct or to state in what way it is not accurate. He must then record what happens as a result (*ibid.*). The same rule applies equally to written records made (under new paragraph 11.13) of anything said by the suspect which is not technically part of an interview.

Failure to comply with this requirement (formerly para. 12.12) has frequently led to evidence of admissions and confessions being excluded and even convictions quashed. The courts have treated it as a very important provision safeguarding the suspect. (For cases in which the issue came up see

---

[50] See *Langiert* [1991] Crim.L.R. 777, C.A.; *Chung* (1991) 92 Cr.App.R. 314, C.A.; *Park, The Times*, July 30, 1992, C.A.; *Davis* (November 10, 1992, Unreported) Case No. 90/0816/Y3, C.A.

pp. 239–240 below.) Curiously, considering how important the rule has become, it is not required that the suspect must be shown the record immediately or even as soon as practicable.

If the appropriate adult or the person's solicitor is present during the interview he should also be given an opportunity to read and sign the interview record or any written statement taken down by the police (para. 11.11).

Any refusal by a person to sign an interview record when asked to do so must itself be recorded (para. 11.12).

The police fail to keep proper records of interviews at the peril of having the fruits of the interview held inadmissible or worse, having the conviction quashed on appeal. The decision in the case of *Canale*[51] in November 1989 given in the Court of Appeal by the Lord Chief Justice stands as the clearest warning. C had been sentenced to six years imprisonment for conspiracy to rob. The court quashed his conviction because of what the Lord Chief Justice described as "flagrant, deliberate and cynical" breaches of the rules regarding keeping of records of interviews. He had allegedly made admissions during two separate interviews, neither of which had been contemporaneously recorded. Each was followed by another interview which was recorded in which he repeated his earlier admissions. At the trial he claimed that he had made false admissions as a result of a trick by the police.

The reasons given by the police officers for not having recorded the interviews was stated in each of their notebooks as "B.W." which they explained meant "Best Way." In their view it was best not to record contemporaneously. This Lord Lane said was not a reason. It "demonstrated a lamentable attitude towards the 1984 Act and the rules" and a "cynical disregard of the rules".

It was argued for the police that the real reason for not recording the interviews was that they wanted to get the suspect's stories "into apple pie order" before the contemporaneously recorded interviews "so that it would be easier for the jury to follow the eventual statements". The court doubted whether this was the truth. The police had also failed to show the record they eventually made to the suspect for him to initial as required by the rules.

The importance of the rules relating to contemporaneous noting of interviews "could scarcely be over-emphasized". The object, Lord Lane said, was two-fold: "to ensure as far as possible that the suspect's remarks were accurately recorded and that he had an opportunity, when he went through the contemporaneous record afterwards, of checking and initialling each answer; likewise, it was a vital protection for the police to ensure that it could not be suggested that they had induced the suspect to confess by improper approaches or improper promises." If the contemporaneous note was not made each of those laudable objects "was apt to be stultified". Its absence deprived the trial judge of vital evidence as to the circumstances of the admissions. Since there was no evidence against the defendant other than the admissions made in the various interviews and since they should have been excluded the court said it had no option but to quash the conviction.[52]

---

[51] [1990] 2 All E.R. 187, C.A.
[52] See, to similar effect, the Court of Appeal's decision in *Keenan* [1989] 3 All E.R. 598.

What is an interview?

The question what constitutes "an interview" for the purposes of the rules about interviewing and recording of interviews has caused some difficulty. The 1991 revision of Code C produced a confusing definition of "interview"[53] which was criticised both by the courts[54] and by the Runciman Royal Commission.[55] The Royal Commission recommended that this confusion be cleared up when Code C was next revised.

The April 1995 revised Code attempts in paragraph 11.1A to deal with the problem by a shorter and simpler definition: "An interview is the questioning of a person regarding his involvement or suspected involvement in a criminal offence or offences which, by virtue of paragraph 10.1 of Code C, is required to be carried out under caution."[56] Hopefully, this redraft will prove to have removed the main defect of the previous formula. But there may still be occasions when it becomes necessary to refer back to the previous case law. If so, the cases appear to establish the following propositions:

(1) The word "interview" is to be given a wide rather than a narrow interpretation.[57] The Court of Appeal said in *Matthews, Voss and Dennison* that "normally any discussion or talk between a suspect or prisoner and a police officer would amount to an interview, whether instigated by the suspect or prisoner or a police officer".

(2) The fact that the exchange consisted merely of a "quick chat" does not prevent it being an interview.[58]

(3) Where an officer asks a question which produces an incriminating response, the exchange can be an interview even though the officer had no real grounds for suspicion when he put the question.[59]

(4) The fact that the exchange takes place in the street or at the scene of the crime does not prevent it being an interview.[60]

(5) The fact that the questions put by the officer are designed to give the arrested person or suspect an opportunity to give an innocent explanation (as opposed to eliciting admissions) does not prevent the change being an interview. In *Maguire*[61] the Court of Appeal distinguished *Absolam* on the ground that the purpose of the questions there was to get an admission to a

---

[53] Note 11A stated: "An interview is the questioning of a person regarding his involvement or suspected involvement in a criminal offence or offences. Questioning a person only to obtain information or his explanation of the facts or in the ordinary course of the officer's duties, does not constitute an interview for the purposes of this Code. Neither does questioning which is confined to the proper and effective conduct of a search."

[54] *Cox* [1993] Crim.L.R. 382.

[55] See Runciman Report, p. 27, para. 10. Both pointed out that the second part of the definition conflicted with the first.

[56] Note that the statutory breathalyser procedure under sections 7 and 8 of the Road Traffic Act 1988 does not constitute an interview—Code C, para. 11.1A; *D.P.P. v. Billington* [1988] 1 All E.R. 434 (Div.Ct.); *D.P.P. v. Rouse, D.P.P. v. Davis* [1991] Crim.L.R. 911 (Div.Ct.).

[57] *R. v. Matthews, Voss, Dennison* (1990) 91 Cr.App.R. 43; [1990] Crim.L.R. 190, C.A.

[58] *R. v. Foster* [1987] Crim.L.R. 821 (Cr.Ct.). What mattered, the court said, was not the length of the exchange but its content. See also *Younis and Ahmed* [1990] Crim.L.R. 425, C.A.

[59] *R. v. Absolam* (1989) 88 Cr.App.R. 332 (C.A.). A, who had been arrested for threatening behaviour, was asked by the custody officer to empty his pockets. He did so. The officer, knowing that he had previous convictions for possession of cannabis, then said "Put the drugs on the table", whereupon A produced a bag containing cannabis from the inside of his trousers and admitted selling the drug. It was held that this exchange was an interview which should have been recorded contemporaneously. The conviction was quashed.

[60] *R. v. Maloney and Doherty* [1988] Crim.L.R. 523 (Cr.Ct.): 16 questions asked at the scene of the crime were held to be an interview which should have been recorded contemporaneously. See also *Fogah* [1989] Crim.L.R. 141.

[61] [1990] Crim.L.R. 815, C.A.

more serious offence, whereas in *Maguire* the questions were to give the arrested person the opportunity to give an innocent explanation of the facts. This basis of distinction seems unreal. The officer said: "Look, you've been caught. Now tell us the truth ... It's for your own good. Don't be stupid." As Professor Diane Birch, commenting on the decision said,[62] it is highly unlikely that the officer was not trying to get a confession from Maguire. But in any event the definition of an interview in the 1991 revised Code covers this precise situation. (The point should have been clear even under the previous Code since note 12A stated, in terms, that "The purpose of any interview is to obtain from the person concerned his explanation of the facts, and not necessarily to obtain an admission.")

(6) The fact that the suspect has asked for the interview to be "off the record" does not prevent it being an interview.[63] The Code does not allow for "off the record" conversations—even in the form of a "general chat"— though if the suspect is not warned of this, a resulting admission may be excluded on the ground that its admission would be unfair.[64]

(7) The fact that it is difficult in the particular circumstances to make a record does not prevent the exchange from being an interview. In *Fogah*,[65] for instance, a juvenile was questioned in the street a quarter of a mile from the scene of a robbery. The resulting admissions were excluded on the ground that no appropriate adult had been present at the interview—which, by definition, meant that the exchange counted as an interview even though it took place in the street.[66]

(8) If the meeting between the police officers and the suspect is wholly at his request, without any suggestion or inducement from them and the officers ask no questions but simple record what he tells them it is not an interview.[67] But this situation is probably very rare and should not be regarded as a basis for ignoring the rules for interviews. Certainly it is clear that there is a fine line between a "social visit" and an "interview".[68]

In view of the provisions of paragraph 11.13, the only safe course for the police is always to make a record of every significant exchange with an actual or potential suspect in regard to a criminal offence.

Questioning of mentally disordered or mentally handicapped persons, children and young persons: Sections 1 and 11

Persons at risk:

As has already been seen, the Code makes detailed provision for special safeguards for persons at risk and notably for juveniles and persons who

---

[62] *ibid.* p. 816.
[63] *R. v. Rosemary Saunders* [1988] Crim.L.R. 521 (Cr.Ct.).
[64] *Woodall & Ors* [1989] Crim.L.R. 288 (Cr.Ct.). See also *Barry Trussler* [1988] Crim.L.R. 446 (Cr.Ct.).
[65] [1989] Crim.L.R. 141.
[66] See to like effect *Brezeanu and Francis* [1989] Crim.L.R. 650, C.A. But see also *Vivian Parchment* [1989] Crim.L.R. 290 (Cr.Crt.) where the court held that it had not been practicable to record exchanges with the suspect, first after he emerged naked from a cupboard at his house during a police search, then while he was getting dressed and thirdly, in a moving police car on the way back to the police station.
[67] *Menard*, 158 J.P. 854, *The Times*, March 23, 1994, C.A.
[68] See *Williams (Mark Alexander)*, *The Times*, February 6, 1992. The police had visited the defendant in the cells after he had been charged and remanded by the magistrates. The trial judge allowed in the record of the conversation.

have some form of mental disability either because of mental disorder or mental handicap. Research suggests that juveniles may be almost one-fifth of all persons arrested. The mentally disordered or handicapped are around 1 per cent of those arrested.[69]

The provisions in the Code for questioning of persons with the handicap of mental disorder or youth broadly are a much fuller and greatly improved version of the equivalent provisions in the Judge's Rules and Administrative Directions. If "an officer has any suspicion or is told in good faith that a person of any age may be mentally disordered or mentally handicapped or *mentally incapable of understanding the significance of questions put to him* or his replies" he must treat him as such a person (para. 1.4, emphasis added). Similarly, in the absence of evidence to the contrary, he must treat someone as a juvenile if he appears to be under 17 (para. 1.5). In all such cases an "appropriate adult" (see below) must be informed and asked to come to be with the person in question unless Annex C applies (see below).

Note 11B states that although persons at risk are capable of proving reliable evidence they may "without knowing or wishing to do so, be particularly prone in certain circumstances to provide information which is unreliable, misleading or self-incriminating. Special care should therefore always be exercised in questioning such a person and the appropriate adult should be involved if there is any doubt about a person's age, mental state or capacity. Because of the risk of unreliable evidence it is also important to obtain corroboration of any facts admitted whenever possible."

Juveniles can only be interviewed at school in "exceptional circumstances" and then only when the head or his nominee agree (para. 11.15). It is stated to be preferable that a juvenile should not be arrested at his school unless this is unavoidable. The head or his nominee should be informed (note 11C).

"The appropriate adult"

In the case of someone who is mentally disordered or mentally handicapped this means a relative, guardian or other person responsible for his care, someone experienced in dealing with such cases not employed by the police, failing whom some other responsible adult who is not a police officer (para. 1.7(b)).[70] Note 1E suggests that it may in some circumstances be better if the appropriate adult is someone who has training or experience in care of the mentally disordered or mentally handicapped rather than a relative who lacks such qualifications. But the note says that "if the person himself prefers a relative to a better qualified stranger his wishes should if practicable be respected."

In the case of a juvenile, the appropriate adult means a parent or guardian

---

[69] See Brown *et al.* (1992) at p. 70.

[70] According to Brown *et al.* (1992, Table 5.1, p. 71), the appropriate adult for juveniles in 1991 was a parent in 59 per cent of cases, some other relative in 7 per cent, a social worker, children's home worker or the like in 28 per cent, and miscellaneous others or identity not known in the remaining 6 per cent. The proportion of cases in which it was a parent had gone down from 68 per cent in the 1990 sample; the proportion of cases in which it was a social worker had gone up from 18 per cent.

In regard to the mentally disordered or mentally handicapped relatives were the appropriate adult in only 22 per cent of cases. The proportion of cases where the role was played by a social worker or other professional person was far higher than for juveniles (p. 78).

or if he is in care, the local authority or a representative of its social services department or another responsible adult who is not a police officer (para. 1.7(a)). Note 1C in the 1991 revised Code addressed the problem of the parent who for one or another reason may not be suitable. So if the parent is involved in the offence either as victim or perpetrator or witness he or she should not be the "appropriate adult". In the 1995 revision of the Code this provision was made even stronger and broader. Note 1C now states categorically:

> "A person, including a parent or guardian, should not be an appropriate adult if he is suspected of involvement in the offence in question, is the victim, is a witness, is involved in the investigation or has received admissions prior to attending to act as the appropriate adult."

The estranged parent of a juvenile should equally not be asked to act as appropriate adult if the juvenile specifically objects to his presence.[71] Also, if a child in care admits an offence to a social worker (other than during the time that the social worker is acting as appropriate adult), another social worker should act as appropriate adult (1D).

If he is subject to a supervision order, his supervisor should, if possible, be told (para. 3.8). Where the juvenile is a ward of court an application to interview him or her must be made to the court but if the interview is urgent the parent, foster parent or "appropriate adult" should be informed and invited to attend or to nominate someone to be present (Practice Direction [1988] 2 All E.R. 1015).

In England and Wales a solicitor cannot act as the appropriate adult if he is present in a professional capacity (Code C, note 1F).

The role of the appropriate adult was dealt with specifically in the 1991 revised Code. Paragraph 11.16 states that the appropriate adult should be informed (presumably by the police) that he is not expected to act simply as an observer and that the purposes of his presence are, first, to advise the person being questioned and to observe whether the interview is being conducted properly and fairly, and secondly to facilitate communication with the person being interviewed. The Code also requires the custody officer to inform the suspect that the appropriate adult "is there to assist and advise him and that he can consult privately with the appropriate adult at any time" (para. 3.12). This requirement does not seem to be much honoured. (Brown *et al.* (1992) at p. 72.)

Experience shows that it is a difficult concept to make effective. The appropriate adult in the majority of cases is a parent, guardian or relative. He or she is by no means always favourably disposed towards the person being interviewed; quite commonly the appropriate adult sides with the police against the suspect.[72] Nor does the parent necessarily understand what his role is supposed to be, even if the police act on the

---

[71] In *D.P.P. v. B.*, *The Times*, January 2, 1990 the Divisional Court rejected a prosecution appeal after the magistrates had held a confession to be inadmissible, partly because the appropriate adult was an estranged father. Therefore there had not been an appropriate adult present. This was affirmed by the Court of Appeal: *sub nom. D.P.P. v. Blake* [1989] 1 W.L.R. 432.

[72] In *Jefferson, Skerritt, Readman and Keogh* [1993] Crim.L.R. 881, C.A. the court upheld a conviction even though the suspect's father had intervened repeatedly on the side of the police. Encouragement by an appropriate adult to tell the truth, it said, should not normally be stigmatised as a failure by the adult to perform his function.

above admonition.[73] What seems to be required is a form of notice that could be handed to the appropriate adult to specify concretely both his role and his rights.

As has been seen, save in an emergency, no interview is supposed to take place with a juvenile or a mentally disordered or mentally handicapped person (whether suspected of crime or not) without a responsible adult there (para. 11.14). An interview may however take place in the absence of the responsible adult or lawyer if an officer of the rank of superintendent or above reasonably believes that the delay in waiting for such a person will lead to interference with evidence or alerting of accomplices or hindering of recovery of the proceeds of crime (para. 11.1, Annex C, para. 1).[74] The notes for guidance warn that because of the risks of unreliable evidence, interviews should only be conducted without an appropriate adult being present in exceptional cases of need (Annex C, note C1).

Where a person who is mentally ill or mentally handicapped or a child is interviewed in the absence of a responsible adult because of a risk of harm to persons or serious loss or damage to property the interview may not continue in the absence of an accompanying adult once the risk of such harm has been averted (Annex C, para. 2).

All the provisions relating to the mentally disordered and mentally handicapped are conveniently set out in Annex E to Code C.

For an explanation of these and other aspects of the Act so far as they concern social workers see M. Haley and J. Andrew Swift, "P.A.C.E. and the Social Worker: A Step in the Right Direction", (1988) *Journal of Social Welfare Law*, p. 355. In regard to the mentally disordered see also P. Fennell, "The appropriate adult", *Law Soc.Gaz.*, May 19, 1993, p. 19.

The Runciman Royal Commission recommended the establishment of a Home Office Working Party to undertake a comprehensive review of the role and functions of the appropriate adult.[75]

The Home Office set up a Review Group on appropriate adults with wide membership in 1994. It published its report in June 1995. (The report is available from the chairman of the Review Group Mr Stephen Wells of F2 Division, the Home Office.) It made 13 recommendations. These included:

* That appropriate adults should be entitled to confidential interviews with suspects and that the relationship with the suspect should therefore be covered by legal privilege
* That the Codes should reflect guidance on which persons are suitable to play the role of appropriate adults in respect of particular suspects
* That a clear definition of the role of appropriate adult be included in the Codes

---

[73] Brown *et al.* (1992, at pp. 72–73) stated:

"[O]bservation of cases generally and interviews by observers with parents and juveniles confirm the view that in many cases parents are ill-equipped to fulfil the function envisaged by the Code. Few ... appeared to have much knowledge of police procedures or the law. Some were nervous or subdued at being in a police station and it was unlikely that they took any active part in interviews. Some ... appeared to be strongly on the police's side ... And others fell into completely the opposite camp and vehemently took sides against the police—hardly a facilitation of communication."

[74] In Brown (1992 at p. 73) the average time before the appropriate adult for juveniles came to the police station was two hours 23 minutes with a median of 84 minutes. Where the appropriate adult was a social worker it took longer.
[75] Recommendation 72 based on Report, paras. 81–86, pp. 42–44.

* The provision of guidance through leaflets, posters in police stations, incorporation into police training and guidance for professionals and others likely to act in this role
* The establishment of local appropriate adult panels.

Interviews in police stations: section 12

Code C makes detailed provisions for the physical circumstances in which suspects must be questioned.[76]

In any period of 24 hours the suspect is supposed to be given eight hours of rest, free from questioning, travel or other interruptions and, if possible, at night.[77] It may only be interrupted or delayed if there are reasonable grounds for believing that it would involve a risk of harm to persons or serious loss of or damage to property or would delay the release of the individual or "otherwise prejudice the outcome of the investigation" (para. 12.2). For someone who comes to the police station as a volunteer, the period of time is measured from arrival there, not from arrest (*ibid.*).

No one may be questioned if he cannot understand the significance of the questions through the effect of drink or drugs (para. 12.3). The only exception is where an officer of the rank of superintendent or above considers that delay would be likely to lead to interference with evidence, alerting of accomplices or hindering the recovery of the proceeds of crime (para. 11.1, Annex C, para. 1).

Interview rooms are supposed to be adequately heated, lit and ventilated (para. 12.4). The suspect should not be required to stand (para. 12.5). The interviewing officers should identify themselves and their rank, except that in terrorism cases each officer should identify himself by warrant number and rank rather than name (para. 12.6). In addition to meal breaks there should also be short breaks for refreshment approximately every two hours unless this would prejudice the investigation (para. 12.7).

Taking a statement: section 12 and Annex D

Traditionally, at the end of the process of relatively informal questioning, police officers prepare, or help the person being interviewed to prepare, a "statement". This is a summary of the salient features of the interview. Code C sets out in Annex D the procedure for the taking of such "written statements under caution" but the notes for guidance do also say that if the interview has been contemporaneously recorded and the record has been signed by the person interviewed or the interview has been tape-recorded, there is normally no need also for a statement under caution. In those circumstances such a statement should only be taken at the request of the person concerned (Code C, note 12A). This would normally be the case, but if Annex D applies the suspect should always be invited to write down himself what he wants to say. Before writing the statement he should be asked to write down and sign: "I make this statement of my own free will. I understand that I need not say anything but that it may harm my defence if I

---

[76] For comments on the scheme of the Code and a suggestion that the Code's interview safeguards do not sufficiently address the problem of unreliability see H. Fenwick, "Confessions, Recording Rules and Miscarriages of Justice: a Mistaken Emphasis?" [1993] Crim.L.R. 174.

[77] For a case in which breach of this provision resulted in a conviction being quashed see *R. v. Barry Trussler* [1988] Crim.L.R. 446 (Cr.Ct.).

do not mention when questioned about something which I later rely in court. This statement may be given in evidence." He should be allowed to write his statement "without any prompting except that a police officer may indicate to him which matters are material or question any ambiguity in the statement" (Annex D(a)3). If the suspect wishes the officer to write it for him he must so signify in written form ("I ... wish to make a statement. I want someone to write down what I say ...") and that he has been cautioned as above.

The rules in Annex D state specifically that if a police officer writes the statement, "he must take down the exact words spoken by the person making [the statement];" (para. 5). Faithful compliance with this admonition would transform the taking of statements as it has been done in the past since it plainly prohibits the very understandable practice of police officers of putting suspects' statements into a coherent, tidy form.

When the writing of the statement is finished, the person whose statement it is must be asked to read it and to make any corrections he wishes. He should then be asked to sign that he has read the statement, that he has been allowed to make corrections, that the statement is true and that he has made it of his own free will. If he cannot read or refuses to do so, the senior officer present should read it to him and ask whether he wishes to make any corrections and to sign. He should then certify on the statement that this is what has occurred (paras. 6 and 7).

Interpreters: section 13

The Administrative Directions accompanying the Judges' Rules referred to statements made by those who could not speak English being translated by an interpreter. But they did not positively require an interpreter to be called. Code C remedies this deficiency and states categorically that a person who has difficulty in understanding English shall not, save in urgent cases under Annex C, be interviewed except in the presence of someone who can act as interpreter (para. 13.2).

An interpreter called to assist a person with obtaining of legal advice should not be a police officer. In other situations he can be if the person being questioned, or the appropriate adult, agrees in writing or the interview is tape recorded (para. 13.9).

Interpreters are to be provided at public expense (and all reasonable steps must be made so to inform the person concerned) (para. 13.8).

Interpreting is not easy and the Home Office have accepted that the responsibility for finding competent interpreters lies to some extent on the police. The Home Office Circular on PACE (p. 8 above, paras. 61–62) stated that chief officers should ensure that the police have access to persons whose proficiency in interpretation is sufficiently high to enable them to carry out the task efficiently. The interpreter must be able to understand, speak, read and write both English and the other language to a standard that includes the specialised terms and procedures encountered in police interviews (such as "caution", "bail", etc.). He must be familiar with both cultural backgrounds and be able to translate and interpret accurately. He must also act in an impartial professional manner and respect confidentiality. Local Community Relations Councils may be able to provide lists of suitable interpreters.

The interpreter should take down a note of the interview in the language of the suspect and should certify its accuracy. Enough time must be allowed by the interviewing officer for a note to be made of each question and answer. The person interviewed should be given a chance of reading it or having it read to him and sign it as accurate or to indicate in what respects he considers it to be inaccurate (para. 13.3). If the suspect makes a statement in a language other than English the interpreter should take it down in that language, the person who made it should sign the statement and the interpreter should translate it into English (para. 13.4).

For a case in which the failure to comply with this requirement led to the exclusion of interviews admitting involvement in importation of £2.5 million worth of cannabis see *Bassil and Mouffareg*.[78]

Questioning of deaf persons: section 13

The Code also provides that where there is a doubt as to a person's hearing, he should be treated as deaf (para. 1.6). If he wishes, no interview should take place without an interpreter save in urgent cases under Annex C or if he agrees in writing (para. 13.5). If the deaf person is also mentally disordered or a child or young person the interpreter should be someone different from the appropriate adult. If the appropriate adult is deaf an interpreter should be called, unless he agrees in writing that the interview should proceed without one or Annex C applies (para. 13.6).

The Home Office Circular on PACE said (p. 8 above, para. 65) that, except where legal advice is given, a police officer may act as an interpreter for a deaf person—providing he is sufficiently proficient to have reached a recognised standard in interpreting. A police officer should obviously not act as interpreter if the deaf person has expressed a wish for an independent interpreter. The local authority's Social Services Department may be able to supply lists of interpreters who have the necessary skills and experience to act as interpreters for the deaf.

In *Raymond Maurice Clarke*[79] the Court of Appeal declined to grant leave to appeal to a defendant who turned out to have a severe hearing defect, although this had not been appreciated by the officer who questioned him. The police evidence was that he had in effect admitted the charge of attempted theft. The defence case was that no such conversation had taken place. The defence tried to have the conversation excluded on the ground that there had been a breach of the rule that a deaf person must not be interviewed without an interpreter being present. The trial judge had admitted the evidence. The Court of Appeal said that it could not be shown that there was a breach of the Code provision if the police officers were not aware of the fact that the person was deaf. A breach could only occur if the officers continued to interview a person after they realised that he was deaf or at least had doubts on the matter.

But it might still be possible to exclude the evidence under section 78 (see below) if it was established that there was in fact a serious impairment of hearing, which made it unfair to admit the evidence or, possibly, that it was unfair to admit the evidence even though the police officer had been unaware of the dangers.

[78] Legal Action, December 1990, p. 23. (Acton Crown Court.)
[79] [1989] Crim.L.R. 892, C.A.

Charging of persons in custody: section 16

As has been seen, the suspect must be charged as soon as there is enough evidence to charge him (s.37(7))—though revised Code C, paragraph 16.1 says that it is permissible to delay charging the suspect being investigated for more than one offence until the police decide whether to charge him for all the offences being investigated (but he should not be further questioned about offences already dealt with—Code C, para. 11.4).

The procedure for charging is dealt with in paragraph 16 of the Code. He must be brought to the custody officer who is responsible for the charging process. He must be cautioned (in terms of the new caution), given a written statement of the charge, the name of the officer in the case, of the police station and the police reference number. If the person is a juvenile or someone suffering from mental disorder or mental handicap, the appropriate adult should be present.

Questions about an offence may not normally be put after the suspect has been charged with that offence. But they can be put exceptionally not only (as before) to, "prevent harm or loss to some other person or to the public or for clearing up an ambiguity" but also "where it is in the interests of justice that the person should have put to him and have an opportunity to comment on information concerning the offence which has come to light since he was charged" (para. 16.5). Before being asked such questions he must be cautioned again. Questions and answers must be recorded contemporaneously in full and the record signed by the person and any third person present. If he refuses, the officer should sign (para. 16.8). If the questions are tape-recorded the provisions of Code E apply.

If an officer wants to tell a suspect who has been charged about someone else's statement he must simply show him a copy of the statement or of the record of the interview. He "shall say or do nothing to invite any reply or comment" save to caution him (para. 16.4).

Where the person charged is a juvenile whose continued detention is authorised by the custody officer, arrangements should be made for him to be taken into care by the local authority unless he certifies that this is impracticable or, where the juvenile is 12 or over, no secure accommodation is available and there is a risk of serious harm from that juvenile. (See p. 91 above.)

Code C, note 16B states that neither a juvenile's behaviour nor the nature of the offence with which he is charged provides grounds for the custody officer to retain him in police custody rather than to arrange for his transfer to the care of the local authority. Nor does the lack of secure accommodation make it impracticable to transfer the juvenile. "The availability of secure accommodation is only a factor in relation to a juvenile aged 12 or over when the local authority accommodation would not be adequate to protect the public from serious harm from the juvenile" (Code C, note 16B).

Code D: Identification

The Code of Practice on Identification of Persons by Police Officers replaced the previous instruction to police (Home Office Circular No. 109/1978 entitled "Identification parades and the use of photographs for identification"). Partly it repeated previous rules, partly it added to and expanded on them and partly it introduced new procedures. The revised versions of Code D in 1991 and 1995 added further new elements.

The preliminaries are virtually identical to those in Code C and deal with formal matters, statements as to the requirement of "appropriate adults", etc., for persons at risk such as juveniles, the mentally disordered and mentally handicapped, the blind, deaf, etc.

The substantive provisions of Code D begin with section 2.

Section 2 of the 1995 revised Code starts with an important new rule recommended by the Runciman Royal Commission[80]: "A record shall be made of the description of the suspect as first given by a potential witness" (para. 2.0). The record must be made *before* the witness takes part in any form of identification. It can be made in any form. Copies of the details given by the witness have to be made and given to the suspect his solicitor *before any identification procedure takes place (ibid.)*

The Code provides for different methods of identification depending on whether the suspect is or is not known to the police. Being "known to the police" is defined to mean that there is enough information known to the police to justify the arrest of a particular person for suspected involvement in the offence (note 2E).

1. Where the suspect is known to the police

The Code sets out four alternative methods to be used in cases involving disputed identification where the suspect is known to the police:

  (i) a parade;
  (ii) a group identification;
  (iii) a video film; and
  (iv) a confrontation.

The responsibility for making the necessary arrangements falls upon an officer not below the rank of inspector (called the "identification officer", referred to here as I.O.). The I.O. must be someone who is not involved in the investigation.

(i) Identification parades

Prior to 1995, Code D provided that an identification parade had to be held "if the suspect asks for one and it is practicable to hold one" (para. 2.3). It might not be practicable for instance because of "the unusual appearance of the suspect" and the resulting difficulty in getting a sufficient number of persons who resembled him (para. 2.4). A parade could also be held if the officer in charge thought it would be useful (para. 2.3). The suspect's consent was required in either case.

In the 1995 revised Code, the first part of paragraph 2.3 has been changed to the following: "Whenever a suspect disputes an identification, an identification parade *shall be held* if the suspect consents unless paragraphs 2.4 or 2.7 or 2.10 apply". (Emphasis supplied. Paragraph 2.4 deals, as before, with impracticability because of the suspect's unusual appearance. Para-

---

[80] Recommendation 4, based on Report, para. 10, p. 11.

graph 2.7 permits a group identification in certain circumstances (see below). Paragraph 2.10 permits the witness to be shown a video film of the suspect in certain circumstances (see below).)

The significant difference in the new rule is that whether the suspect asks or not is no longer the criterion. Providing he consents, a parade must be held in cases of disputed identification if it is practicable unless a group identification or video film are thought in the circumstances to be better.

It is to be noted that the courts have been very severe in interpreting the exception in paragraph 2.4 as to what makes a parade impracticable. "Impracticable" does not mean "inconvenient".[81]

The detailed procedures for running an identification parade are set out in Annex A to Code D (see p. 497 below). For a useful practical guide to the procedure under old Code D see two articles in *Police Review* October 14, 1988, p. 2134 and p. 2141.

For disturbing statistics as to the high "failure rate" in use of identification parades and advice to use a new video library system see "Video on parade", *Police Review*, March 10, 1995, p. 22.

An important new rule about identification parades in the April 1995 revision of the Code is that "a colour photograph video film of the parade shall be taken". (Annex A, para. 19.)[82] Previously, a video or photo of the parade had to be made only where it was held without a solicitor or friend of the suspect being present.

Another new rule is that before the parade the suspect and his solicitor must be given copies of any material released to the media for the purposes of identification of a suspect unless this would not be practicable or would unduly delay the investigation (Annex A, para. 2A). Where material has been released to the media, each witness must be asked after the parade whether he saw any broadcast or published film or photographs relating to the offence (*ibid.* para. 17A). This is in addition to the new rule noted above that before the parade the suspect and his solicitor must be told about the first description of the suspect given by the witness (*ibid.* para. 2A).

If a suspect refuses to take part in an identification parade or having agreed, fails to appear, arrangements should be made if practicable to allow the witnesses an opportunity of seeing the suspect in a group identification, a video identification or a confrontation (Code D, para. 2.6).

(ii) Group identification

A group identification is where the suspect is viewed amongst an informal group of people (Code D, para. 2.7). The 1995 revised Code states that it can take place either with the suspect's consent and co-operation or covertly where the suspect has refused to co-operate with a parade or group identification or has failed to appear. It can also be arranged where the officer in charge considers that it would be better than a parade—for instance because of a witness' fear (*ibid.*).

---

[81] See, for instance, *Gaynor* [1988] Crim.L.R. 242; *Britton and Richards* [1989] Crim.L.R. 144; *Ladlow, Moss, Green and Jackson* [1989] Crim.L.R. 219 (Div.Ct.); *Conway* (1990) Cr.App.R. 143, C.A.; [1990] Crim.L.R. 402, C.A.; *Brown* [1991] Crim.L.R. 368, C.A.; *Graham* [1994] Crim.L.R. 212, C.A.; *Rutherford and Palmer* (1994) 98 Cr.App.R. 141, C.A.; *Tomkinson v. D.P.P.* [1995] Crim.L.R. 60 (Div.Ct.).
[82] This was one of the recommendations of the Runciman Royal Commission: Recommendation 6 based on Report, para. 10, p. 11.

The previous version of the Code said that the procedure for group identification should so far as possible follow the procedure laid down in Annex A for identity parades. The 1995 revision has a new Annex E (with 43 paragraphs) setting out the procedure for group identifications. (The paragraph references below are to Annex E.)

The place where it is held is a matter for the I.O. though he may take into account representations made by or on behalf of the suspect (para. 3). The place should be somewhere where people are passing by or waiting around informally—such as an escalator, a shopping centre, queues on railway or bus stations, etc. The foyer of a magistrates' court could be such a place.[83] A record by photograph or video film should be taken of the place and, if possible, of the actual identification procedure (paras. 7–8).

The witness must not be told whether anyone else has made an identification (para. 15). Anything said to or by the witness regarding the identification should be said in the presence and hearing of the I.O., and, if present, the suspect's solicitor, appropriate adult, or friend (para. 16).

Witnesses must not be able to communicate with each other. They should be brought to the place one at a time. They should not see or be reminded of any photographs or description of the suspect (paras. 17, 18). If two or more suspects are involved, each should be the subject of separate identification procedures though they can take place consecutively on the same occasion (para. 21). Slightly different rules apply depending on whether the group being observed is moving (paras. 20–23) or stationary (paras. 24–28).

If the group identification is held covertly, the suspect has no right to have a solicitor or friend there but the procedure adopted should so far as possible be the same as where it is done with the suspect's consent (paras. 33, 34).

Group identifications should only take place in a police station for reasons of safety, security or because it is impracticable to hold them elsewhere (para. 36). It can be done behind a one-way mirror or other means where the witness can see without being seen (para. 37).

(iii) Video film identifications

The I.O. can show a witness a video film of a suspect if he considers "whether because of the refusal of the suspect to take part in an identification parade or group identification or other reasons, that this would in the circumstances be the most satisfactory course of action" (Code D, para. 2.10). The suspect should be asked for his consent but if consent is refused the I.O. can nevertheless proceed with a video identification if it is practicable to do so (para. 2.11).

Code D states that "a video identification must be carried out in accordance with Annex B" (para. 2.12). (For Annex B see p. 499 below.) Annex B relates to a video made after the offence.

The procedure set out in Annex B requires that the film must include the suspect and at least eight other people who so far as possible resemble him, or 12 if there are two suspects in the film (para. 3). The suspect and other persons should so far as possible be filmed in the same positions or carrying out the same activity and under identical conditions (para. 4). The suspect and his solicitor, friend or appropriate adult must be given a chance to see

---

[83] *Tiplady, The Times*, February 23, 1994, C.A.

the film before it is shown to witnesses, to make any objections (para. 7). The suspect cannot be present when the film is shown to witnesses but his solicitor can and he (or, if he is unrepresented, the suspect) must be given notice of the time and place of such showings (para. 8). If there is no representative of the suspect present the viewing should be recorded on video (*ibid.*).

Witnesses may not communicate with each other before viewing the film nor may they discuss the matter with the I.O. (para. 9). Only one witness may see the film at a time (para. 10). He should not be asked to make an identification until he has seen the film at least twice (para. 11).

The I.O. must be careful not to direct the witness' attention to any one individual on the film or to give any other indication of the suspect's identity (para. 12).

But increasingly video films will be available that have been made before or during the offence by cameras placed on buildings, in shops and pubs and other premises. This form of video was the subject of the Court of Appeal's decision in the case of *Jones, Dowling, Jones and Brown.*[84]

The offence involved an attack by a group of assailants in a pub. The victim was at first unable to name any of the attackers. The doorman said that one of the attackers was known to him by sight. Some weeks later, video equipment was installed in the pub. As a result, the doorman picked out from the video film the person known to him who was named by the police. The police also recognised three other persons. The video was then shown to the victim who picked out the same four persons. These four were convicted of the offence. The Court of Appeal rejected the argument that once the police had a name they should have employed one of the methods of identification listed in Code D. The prosecution argued that Code D only came into play when there was a dispute over identification and no such dispute could arise until the evidence had been challenged, or not accepted by the suspect. Until then the police were free to obtain other forms of identification evidence. The Court said that this submission was correct. There was no element of unfairness. The video film was equivalent to a street identification or to an informal group identification. The appeal showed that the modern practice of installing video cameras which routinely filmed places was a tool available to investigating police officers—and that their use was not governed by the express terms of Code D. But where the film was made after the offence the process involved three stages. First did the witness identify a person present when the film was made. Secondly, did the witness identify that person as having been present at the time of the offence. Thirdly, did the witness identify that person as having taken part in the crime itself.

Where the incident itself was recorded on video tape and it is shown to police and other witnesses, care must be taken to maximise the prospect of any recognition evidence being truly spontaneous and independent.

(iv) Confrontation

If neither a parade, nor a group identification nor a video identification can be arranged, the suspect may simply be confronted by a witness. Code D states that such a confrontation does not require the suspect's consent "but

---

[84] *The Times*, January 13, 1994, C.A.

may not take place unless none of the other procedures are practicable" (para. 2.13). A confrontation "must be carried out in accordance with Annex C". (For Annex C see p. 501 below.)

The suspect should be confronted independently by each witness who should be asked "Is this the person?" The confrontation should take place in the presence of the suspect's solicitor, friend or appropriate adult unless that would cause unreasonable delay (para. 3).

The confrontation should normally take place in the police station, either in a normal room or in one equipped with a screen allowing the witness to see without being seen. But a screen may only be used if the suspect's solicitor, friend or appropriate adult is present and the confrontation is recorded on video (para. 4).

Information to be given to suspects

Before any parade takes place or a group identification or video identification is arranged the suspect must be given basic information orally (para. 2.15) and by way of a written notice (para. 2.16). The information that must be communicated includes: that he is entitled to free legal advice; the procedure to be followed; that he does not have to take part but that his refusal may be given in evidence and that a covert identification can be made; that if he alters his appearance, that can be given in evidence and it may make a parade impracticable; that a video or photograph may be taken of the procedure. As has been seen, he must also be told that he or his solicitor will be given details of the description of the suspect first given by the witness. After being given time to read the notice setting out these matters, the suspect should be asked to sign a copy indicating whether he is willing to take part in one or other of the identification procedures (para. 2.16).

2. Cases where the suspect is not known to the police

Where the suspect is not known to the police the witness can be taken to a particular neighbourhood or place to see whether he can identify the person he said he saw (para. 2.17). The 1995 revision of the Code adds that before doing this however a description should first be made of any description given of the suspect by the witness (*ibid.*). Care must be taken not to direct the witness' attention to anyone.

Photographs, photofit, identikit or similar pictures can only be shown to the witness if the identity of the suspect is not known to the police or he is not available to stand on an identification parade. If that is the case the showing of such pictures to the witness must follow the procedure set out in Annex D to Code D. (For Annex D see p. 502 below.)

The witness must be shown not less than 12 photographs at a time (Annex D, para. 3). So far as practicable they should be of a similar type (*ibid.*). He should not be prompted in any way (para. 4).

If a witness makes a positive identification, that procedure should not be continued with other witnesses. Instead, unless there is no dispute about identification of the suspect, the witness and other witnesses should be asked to attend an identification parade or group or video identification (para. 5).

At any such subsequent procedure the suspect and his solicitor must be told that the witness(es) have previously seen pictures (para. 7).

The photographs used should be numbered and a separate photograph should be made of the frame or part of the album from which the witness made the identification (para. 8).

Showing films and photographs of incidents to the public at large

New provisions in the 1995 revision of Code D permit the showing of video films or photographs to the public at large or to police officers through the national or local media (Code D, para. 2.21A). But when such material is shown to potential witnesses (including police officers), it should be shown individually,[85] and so far as possible in accordance with the rules for Video Film Identification (para. 2.10, see above) or Identification by Photographs (para. 2.18, see above).

Where there is a broadcast or publication of such material, a copy of the material released to the media should be made and retained and the suspect or his solicitor should be allowed to view such material before any identification procedure is carried out providing this is practicable and would not unreasonably delay the investigation. Any witness must be asked whether he has seen any broadcast or published film or photograph and any reply must be recorded (para. 2.21B).

Conclusion

The cases show that the police must make genuine (and, if necessary, considerable) efforts to organise the best possible method of identification. (For a case where the conviction was quashed because the court held that an identity parade should have been held rather than a street identification see *Nagah*.[86])

Also the rules must be followed carefully. In *Gall*[87] the Court of Appeal quashed a conviction because the I.O. had come into the room, looked at the parade and then spoken to a witness before he came to the parade. The judge at the first trial had excluded the witness' identification evidence but at a retrial it had been allowed in on the ground that in the view of the judge there had been no breach of the rules. The Court of Appeal disagreed. The Court thought it was obvious that there had been a breach of the rule that the I.O. must have nothing to do with the parade. In *Quinn*[88] the Court of Appeal allowed an appeal and quashed a count carrying six years' imprisonment[89] on the ground that the witnesses were not asked to walk down the parade at least twice as required by paragraph 14 of Annex A of Code D. (For more cases on failures in identification procedures see pp. 239, 241 below.)

The cases show that the courts are capable of being very particular about compliance with the rules. On the other hand, sometimes they will overlook breaches of the Code rules. As the Court of Appeal said in *Grannell*[90] "It is

---

[85] See *Caldwell and Dixon, The Times*, June 8, 1993, C.A.
[86] (1991) 92 Cr.App.R. 344, C.A. By contrast see *Penny* (1992) 94 Cr.App.R. 345 where in similar circumstances the Court of Appeal dismissed the appeal.
[87] (1990) 90 Cr.App.R. 64; [1989] Crim.L.R. 745, C.A.
[88] *The Times*, March 15, 1994, C.A.
[89] Other counts involving consecutive six year sentences were not appealed so that the sentence was in effect cut from 12 years to six years.
[90] (1989) 90 Cr.App.R. 149.

important that the Code be followed but what is equally important is to see whether any unfairness arose from the failure to do so" (at p. 153).

Where identification is an issue, a dock identification on its own will not normally be acceptable unless the witness knows the accused.[91] However, the courts do not require Code D procedures when the witness "recognises" the suspect from prior knowledge of the person.[92] Also, Code D does not apply where the victim or witness identifies the suspect immediately after the crime.[93]

QUESTIONS AND ANSWERS

CODES OF PRACTICE

1. Must the Codes of practice be complied with?

The Codes of Practice have replaced the Judges' Rules. They are far more detailed than the Judges' Rules. They cover a far wider area. Whereas the Judges' Rules were promulgated by a committee of judges, the Codes of Practice are put out by the Home Office under authority of the 1984 Act which requires the Home Secretary to issue them and to bring them into force by a statutory instrument approved by affirmative resolution in both Houses of Parliament. Before that occurs they have been debated in both Houses.

The judges consulted no one before promulgating the Judges' Rules. The Codes of Practice by contrast have been exposed to a long period of public debate. They were redrafted several times.

Originally, any breach of PACE or the PACE Codes was automatically a breach of police discipline which made the officers concerned liable to disciplinary proceedings. In fact hardly any such proceedings were brought. The Criminal Justice and Public Order Act 1994 changed the position by abolishing the rule that breaches of PACE or the Codes were automatically a breach of discipline. The matter was to be dealt with by the new discipline system foreshadowed by the Home Secretary. At the time when the book went to press the details of the new system were however not available (see p. 255 below). It was anticipated that it would come into effect later in 1995.

---

[91] *Reid* [1994] Crim.L.R. 442, C.A. In *North Yorkshire Trading Standards Department v. Williams*, November 22, 1994 the Divisional Court said that dock identification was generally undesirable even where the prosecution had no power to require a defendant to attend an identification parade. The principles applicable to more serious cases should apply equally to trivial cases. If this created unacceptable difficulties for the prosecution it was a matter for Parliament. The prosecution's appeal was dismissed.

[92] See *Ryan* [1992] Crim.L.R. 50, C.A.—no identification parade necessary where the witness said she recognised the defendant as the brother of a classmate she had seen at the school gates two or three times. *Cf. Conway* (1991) 91 Cr.App.R. 143, C.A.—there should have been an identification parade where the defendant denied knowing two witnesses who claimed to know him. D had asked for a parade. The two witnesses made only a dock identification. In *Fergus* [1992] Crim.L.R. 363, C.A. the court said it was an "identification" not a "recognition" case.

[93] *Oscar* [1991] Crim.L.R. 778, C.A. D charged with burglary was arrested and identified within minutes of the offence. The Court of Appeal dismissed the appellant's contention that there should have been an identification parade. Where the arrest and the confrontation occurred within a few minutes of each other and shortly after the alleged offence, a formal identification parade would be valueless. It was not so much a matter of identification as of recognition. The judge had warned the jury about the dangers of confrontation evidence. See to like effect *Kelly* [1992] Crim.L.R. 181, C.A.

2. Can a breach of the Codes lead to criminal or civil proceedings?

Only if the breach is also a breach of the criminal or the civil law.

3. What effect therefore does a breach of the rules have on the criminal proceedings against the person himself?

The Act states that "in all criminal and civil proceedings, any [such] Code shall be admissible in evidence, and if any provision of such a Code appears to the court or tribunal conducting the proceedings to be relevant to any question arising in the proceedings it shall be taken into account in determining that question".

This means that the court may take such account of the breach of the Codes as it thinks right. It can exclude evidence obtained in breach of the Codes. This has often happened quite often (see pp. 238–245 below).

PART VII

DOCUMENTARY EVIDENCE IN CRIMINAL PROCEEDINGS

Evidence from documentary records: formerly section 68 and Schedule 3, now Part II, Criminal Justice Act 1988 and Schedule 2

Section 68 of PACE was designed to make admissible certain categories of written evidence which were previously barred under the rule against hearsay evidence. The hearsay evidence rule had already been liberalised by the Criminal Evidence Act 1965 which made certain trade and business records admissible. The 1965 Act had been passed in response to the House of Lords' decision in *Myers v. D.P.P.*[1] For the evidence to be admissible under the 1965 Act the records had to be compiled from information supplied by a person who had, or might reasonably have been expected to have had, personal knowledge of the matters dealt with, provided that the person was dead, unfit to testify, could not be identified or found or could not reasonably be expected to have any recollection of the information supplied.

The chief purpose of section 68 was to extend the scope of this exception to the hearsay rule to records in the public sector. It followed the recommendations of the Criminal Law Revision Committee in its 1972 11th Report.[2] It also drew on some of the concepts used in the Civil Evidence Act 1968. Section 68 had to be read in conjunction with Schedule 3 to PACE.

It provided in essence for the admissibility of any record compiled by a person acting under a duty to do so, subject to some fairly stringent prescribed conditions.[3] Now however, both section 68 and the Schedule have been replaced by Part II and Schedule 2 to the Criminal Justice Act 1988 which came into force in April 1989.[4] The aim of Part II was to establish a new scheme for the admissibility of documentary hearsay in criminal cases.[5] It classifies documents that can be admitted into three categories: first-hand hearsay; secondly, business documents; and thirdly, documents which may

---

[1] [1965] A.C. 1001.
[2] "Evidence (General)", Cmnd. 4991, 1972, para. 258.
[3] In *O'Loughlin and McLoughlin* (1987) 85 Cr.App.R. 157; [1988] 3 All E.R. 431 (Cr.Ct.) and *Martin* [1988] 1 W.L.R. 655 C.A. the court held that witness statements taken by police officers from members of the public were not admissible under s.68 because they were statements made by the witnesses themselves rather than by the officers and therefore were not made under a duty.
[4] For a valuable (and refreshingly outspoken) assessment of the then new law see D. J. Birch [1989] *Criminal Law Review*, 15–31. The writer acknowledges his indebtedness to Professor Diane Birch for throwing much valuable light on these provisions. See also in particular John Clegg "Documentary Evidence and the Criminal Justice Act", Law Soc. Gaz., December 14, 1988, p. 14 and C.E. Bazell, "Criminal Justice Act 1988", J.P.N. September 2, 1989, p. 599.
[5] The new provisions were influenced by the Report of the (Roskill) Committee on Fraud Trials, 1986, at pp. 66–78.

fall into either of the first two categories but which are prepared specifically for the purpose of criminal proceedings.

These provisions are printed in this book in place of section 68 and Schedule 3 at pages 386 and 416 respectively.[6] As originally placed before Parliament the aim of the Bill was to make such evidence admissible without the need to establish strict conditions of admissibility. The only real control was to have been a discretion in the court to exclude evidence which it was not in the interests of justice to admit. (In the case of statements made during a criminal investigation or for the purpose of criminal proceedings, the proposed test was somewhat more stringent, requiring the actual leave of the court for admissibility.) But a considerable parliamentary row led to various other tests and safeguards being added.[7]

For a full discussion of the law and the problems with the hearsay provisions in the Criminal Justice Act 1988 and PACE, section 69 see Law Commission Consultation Paper No. 138, *Evidence in Criminal Proceedings: Hearsay and Related Topics*, July 1995, pp. 41–59, 200–209. The Law Commission's Consultation Paper is summarised at the end of this part, pp. 211–213.

Brief summary

The provisions are complex—needlessly so.[8]

Section 23 makes any first-hand documentary evidence admissible provided that the maker is unavailable to give evidence for one of the reasons stated in the section. Section 24 makes admissible a statement in a document, created or received in the course of business, whether first-hand or not, provided that it is based on information supplied by a person who had or may reasonably be supposed to have had personal knowledge of the matters dealt with. There is no requirement that the statement was made under a duty nor that the maker be unavailable to testify, unless the statement was prepared for the purposes of pending or contemplated criminal proceedings, or of a criminal investigation.

These provisions are supplemented by sections 25–28 and by Schedule 2.

First-hand hearsay: section 23

Section 23(1) provides that a statement made by a person in a document is admissible in criminal proceedings as evidence of any fact of which direct oral evidence by him would be admissible.

Section 68 of PACE made it necessary to establish that the document was part of a record.[9] Under section 23 by contrast it is only necessary to show the

---

[6] The equivalent provisions for Northern Ireland are in the Criminal Justice (Evidence etc.) (Northern Ireland) Order 1988.

[7] See especially House of Lords, Vol. 489, *Hansard*, October 20, 1987. Cols. 74–57.

[8] For criticism of the complexity and lack of principle in these provisions see for instance J.R. Spencer, "Orality and the Evidence of Absent Witnesses", [1994] Crim.L.R. 628. For an account of the origins of the provisions see D. Wolchover, "Criminal Trials: Proof by Missing Witnesses", (1987) *New L.J.*, pp. 525, 805, 833; (1988) 139 *New L.J.* 202, 242, 261, 461.

Note also that the Criminal Justice Act 1991, Pt. III provided for the admissibility in substitution of the whole or part of evidence in chief of the evidence of children in the form of pre-recorded videotapes. The method was to insert a new s.32A into the Criminal Justice Act 1988.

[9] For consideration of what constitutes a record see *R. v. Governor of Pentonville Prison, ex p. Osman* [1990] 3 All E.R. 701, 725 (Div.Ct.); and *Iqbal* (1990) 91 Cr.App.R. 193 C.A.

existence of a document. "Document" is defined by Schedule 2, para. 5[10] to include maps, plans and the like, together with discs, tapes and films. A video film is therefore included (note however that if the film is original evidence it is admissible without the aid of s.23[11]). Statements made to police officers or to solicitors would now seem admissible.

"Statement" is defined by Schedule 2 so as to include "any representation of fact, whether made in words or otherwise".[12] The statement can be made by a person via someone else, provided he has signified his acceptance of the document as his statement.[13] Note that where a machine or computer observes a fact and records it, that record states a fact. It is evidence of what the machine recorded and that is what is printed out. But it is not a statement by a person. It does not record information supplied by another, and without human intervention it is not hearsay evidence.

The statement must be one of "any fact". It is not certain whether this includes statements of opinion.[14]

The effect of the requirement that the statement must be one of which "direct oral evidence by him [the maker] would be admissible" is that it must not be one that would for any reason be inadmissible.

Subsection (2) lists reasons for not calling the maker (M): that he is dead[15]; or unfit[16]; or abroad[17] and it is not reasonably practicable to secure his attendance[18]; or that he cannot be found in spite of all reasonable steps taken.[19] These provisions are more or less the same as those under section 68 of PACE. (The surprising argument that the conditions were cumulative was rejected by the Divisional Court in *Re Osman*.[20]) The difference is that under section 23 it is not possible to tender a person's statement on the ground that he cannot reasonably be expected to remember what he said, as it was under section 68(2)(a)(iii), though this is a ground of admissibility under section 24(4). Nor is M's statement admissible as it was under section 68(2)(b) where all reasonable steps had been taken to identify M but he could not be identified. It follows that documents prepared by unidentified workmen seem not to be admissible under section 23. The standard of proof laid on the

---

[10] Para. 5 inconveniently incorporates by reference the definitions in s.10 of the Civil Evidence Act 1968. It is unfortunate that the draftsman did not trouble to set them out.

[11] *Taylor v. Chief Constable of Cheshire* [1986] 1 W.L.R. 1479.

[12] Again Sched. 2 incorporates by reference s.10 of the Civil Evidence Act 1968.

[13] *Re D. (A Minor)* [1986] 2 F.L.R. 189 at 191.

[14] *Dass v. Masih* [1968] 1 W.L.R. 756; *Wallhead v. Ruston & Hornsby Ltd.* (1973) 14 K.I.R. 285. I am indebted for the point and the references to Professor Birch in her above mentioned article.

[15] See *Cole* (1990) 90 Cr.App.R. 478 C.A. and *Kennedy* [1992] Crim.L.R. 37 C.A.

[16] See *Samuel* [1992] Crim.L.R. 189 C.A.; *Moore* [1992] Crim.L.R. 882 C.A.; and *Gent* (1989) 89 Cr.App.R. 247 [1990] 1 All E.R. 364 C.A.

[17] A letter written by an employee of a foreign embassy is not admissible under this heading as the writer is not physically outside the United Kingdom—see *Jiminez-Paez* [1993] Crim.L.R. 596 C.A..

[18] See *Bray* (1989) 88 Cr.App.R. 354, [1988] Crim.L.R. 829 C.A.; *Case* [1991] Crim.L.R. 192 C.A.; and *De Orango and others* (1993) 96 Cr.App.R. 399; [1992] Crim.L.R. 180 C.A.

[19] *Herbert* (unreported), Case No. 90/3340/43 C.A.; *Russell and Russell* (unreported), Case No. 4466/D3/87 C.A. In *Russell* the second defendant was convicted of armed robberies and firearms offences. A building society pass book in his girl-friend's name had entries showing large sums paid in which corresponded with the dates of the robberies. The Court of Appeal held the pass book had been wrongly admitted because the cashier could have been identified and had not been. (However the court denied the appeal by applying the proviso.)

[20] [1988] Crim.L.R. 611.

prosecution under section 23(2) is the criminal burden.[21] By contrast, the standard of proof laid on the defence is only the civil burden of a balance of probabilities.[22]

A statement is admissible under section 23(2) if it is signed by the deceased or if he has clearly indicated by speech or otherwise that it is accurate.[23] The judge should be careful not to "give a pat on the back" to any witness whose evidence is disputed.[24] The judge must direct the jury regarding any weaknesses in the evidence.[25]

Subsection (3) which deals with the fearful witness adds a new provision that the statement was made to a police officer or someone else charged with investigating offices and that the maker "does not give oral evidence through fear or because he is kept out of the way.[26] The nature of the fear required is not specified. The fear can be expressed in the witness box—by the witness saying that he cannot now remember matters in regard to which he previously gave a statement.[27] The fact that the witness was in fear must be established by admissible evidence.[28]

It could be a matter observed by the court.[29] The witness can be in fear as a consequence of the material offence or of something said or done since the offence. It includes the witness who takes the oath but because of fear gives evidence that lacks any substance or relevance.[30]

Subsection (4) provides that section 23 does not render admissible a confession made by an accused person which would not be admissible under section 76 of PACE. Professor Birch in her article in the *Criminal Law Review* argues convincingly[31] that this subsection is otiose as having meaning only with an earlier version of the Bill.

Business documents: section 24

Section 68 made admissible records made under a duty. The new provisions in section 24 are much broader in not requiring any duty. It is only necessary to show that they were made in the course of business.

---

[21] In *O'Loughlin & McLoughlin* [1987] 85 Cr.App.R. 157 it was held that the similar words in s.13(3) of the Criminal Justice Act 1925 required the prosecution to prove beyond reasonable doubt and by the oath of a credible witness that procurement of the witnesses related by them to the police officer who testified to the court. See *Minors and Harper* (1989) 89 Cr.App.R. 102 C.A.; *R. v. Acton Justices, ex p. McMullen* (1991) 92 Cr.App.R. 98 (Div.Ct.). See also *Patel* (1992) 97 Cr.App.R. 294 C.A. See also *Case* n.18 above.
[22] *Mattey, Quinney, The Times,* October 13, 1994 C.A.
[23] *McGillivray* (1993) 97 Cr.App.R. 232 C.A. The court approved the decision of the trial judge to allow in an unsigned statement of the deceased taken by a police officer at his hospital bedside which he was unable to sign because of the severity of the burns which led to his death. At the *voir dire* the court heard evidence from the police officer and from a nurse who heard what the deceased said, saw the officer take it down in writing and heard him read it back to the deceased.
[24] *Churchill* (1992) 97 Cr.App.R. 232, [1993] Crim.L.R. 285 C.A.
[25] *Kenealy and Burrell* [1994] Crim.L.R. 50 C.A.
[26] Note that, whereas under s.13(3) the procurement of keeping the witness "out of the way" had to be by means of the accused or on his behalf, under s.23 it need only be shown that the witness is "kept out of the way". See now *R. v. Acton JJ., ex p. McMullen* n.21 above.
[27] *R. v. Ashford and Tenterden Justices, ex p. Hilden* (1993) 96 Cr.App.R. 92 C.A. s.23 could apply provided the witness had not already started to give oral evidence of significant relevance to the case. Popplewell J., said that where a witness gave some oral evidence but was prevented from giving further evidence through fear, that was a person who "does not give oral evidence through fear".
[28] The evidence of fear must be admissible. In *Neil v. North Antrim Magistrates' Court* [1992] 1 W.L.R. 1221 the House of Lords rejected as hearsay evidence by a police officer that the mother of two teenage witnesses said they were too afraid to give evidence.
[29] *ex p. Hilden,* n.27 above, *per* Popplewell J.
[30] *ibid.*
[31] *op. cit.* n.4, p. 201 above, p. 24.

Section 24 makes admissible, as evidence of any of which direct oral evidence would be admissible, statements in a document if (i) the document was created or received by a person in the course of a trade, business, profession or other occupation, or as the holder of a paid or unpaid office and (ii) the information in the document was supplied by a person (whether or not the maker of the statement) who had, or may reasonably be supposed to have had, personal knowledge of the matters dealt with. For consideration of the difficulties of the concepts used in section 24 of "maker", "creator", "supplier" and "receiver" see D. Birch, *op. cit.* n.4 above; D. McEvoy, "Police Documents as Admissible Hearsay" [1993] Crim.L.R. 480, J.C. Smith, "Sections 23 and 24 of the Criminal Justice Act 1988: Some Problems", [1994] Crim.L.R. 426; D. McEvoy, "A Reply", *ibid.*, p. 430.

The Court of Appeal said in *Foxley*[32] that the purpose of section 24 was "to enable the document to speak for itself". Parliament's intention "would be defeated if oral evidence was to be required in every case from a person who was either the creator or keeper of the document, or the supplier of the information contained in the document". The court held that the trial judge had been entitled to infer from the documents themselves that business documents coming from abroad had been created in the normal course of business.

Whereas under section 23 it must be shown that the evidence could have been the subject of direct oral evidence *by the maker*, there is no such requirement in section 24.

Subsection (2) provides that the information in a document may be supplied to the creator of the document indirectly providing that each intermediary receives the information in the course of a trade, business, profession or other occupation or is the holder of a paid or unpaid office. So if a witness to an accident gave the number of one of the cars to a housewife passing by, the note made by the housewife could not be admitted. If he gave it to someone working in an office at the scene of the incident it is arguable that it would be admissible under section 24 as made by him in the course of his occupation.[33]

Subsection (3) is the same as section 23(4) (above) but here it does have some meaning.

Subsection (4) states that where a statement was prepared for the purposes of criminal proceedings or a criminal investigation[34] it is necessary to embark on proof of grounds for the absence of the maker of the record. Such grounds are that the maker is dead, unfit to attend, or abroad where it is not practicable to have him attend; or he cannot be found after all reasonable steps have been taken to find him; or the statement was made to a police officer; or the person does not give evidence "through fear or because he is kept out of the way"; or finally that he cannot be expected to have any recollection of the matter because of the lapse of time and the circumstances in which the record was made. On this see *Carrington* [1994] Crim.L.R. 438 C.A. and *Rock* [1994] Crim.L.R. 843 C.A.

In *Field*[35] the prosecution sought to introduce a statement made by the

---

[32] *The Times*, February 5, 1995 C.A.
[33] The example is given by C.E. Bazell, "Criminal Justice Act 1988", *J.P.N.,* September 2, 1988, p. 559, 561.
[34] In *Hinds* [1993] Crim.L.R. 528 C.A. it was held that missing book reports prepared by the Post Office, and computer print-outs based on such reports, had been prepared as a matter of routine and therefore section 24(4) did not apply.
[35] [1993] Crim.L.R. 456 C.A.

two-year old victim in an interview with a police officer. The Court of Appeal thought *obiter* that the maker of the statement was not the child but the officer who made a statement incorporating that of the child. If that is correct it would mean that the person who is required to be unavailable, or fearful or unable to recollect is the officer rather than the potential witness—which is unlikely to have been intended by the legislature.[36]

Where the document is brought into existence for a reason not connected with criminal proceedings there is, therefore, no longer a need to prove, as a condition of admissibility, the non-availability of the maker of the statement.[37] But, understandably more stringent conditions of admissibility apply to documents brought into existence as part of the process of investigation or prosecution.

Discretion to exclude evidence: section 25

The court (whether magistrates' courts, crown court or Court of Appeal) can exclude evidence if it is of the opinion that this is in the interests of justice. It should take into account:

(a) the likelihood that it is authentic;
(b) the extent to which the evidence might be available from some other source;
(c) the relevance of the document; and
(d) any risk of unfairness to the accused, especially if the maker of the document does not attend the trial.

Since (d) speaks only of unfairness to the accused it would not apply to documents sought to be introduced by the defence. The exercise of this discretion has, predictably, given rise to inconsistency of approach.[38]

Statements prepared for the purpose of criminal proceedings or investigations: section 26

Where a statement admissible under either section 23 or 24 appears to the court to have been prepared in the course of a criminal investigation or for the purposes of pending or contemplated criminal proceedings, leave of the court is needed before the evidence can be adduced. The court must decide whether it is in the interests of justice to hear the statement. In considering the matter the court is required to have regard: (i) to the contents of the statement, (ii) to the risk of unfairness to the accused, particularly if he cannot refute what M says if M is not a witness; and (iii) to any other relevant circumstance.

In *Setz-Dempsey*[39] the Court of Appeal quashed a conviction on the

---

[36] In *Bedi and Bedi* (1992) 95 Cr.App.R. 21; [1992] Crim.L.R. 299 C.A. the Court of Appeal similarly thought, again *obiter*, that the maker of the statement was the credit card company's employee who received the information that a card had been lost rather than the loser who supplied the information. For criticism see Professor D. J. Birch in her commentary on the case, *op. cit., supra*, at p. 301. See now n.71, p. 213 below.

[37] The problem of establishing admissibility that wrecked the prosecution's case in cases such as *De Orango* [1992] Crim.L.R. 180 C.A. therefore no longer arises.

[38] See for instance *Blithing* (1983) 77 Cr.App.R. 86 C.A.; *Scott v. R.* [1989] A.C. 1242 (P.C.); *Neshet* [1990] Crim.L.R. 579 C.A.; *Samuel* [1988] Cr.App.R. 232 C.A.; *Moore* [1992] Crim.L.R. 882 C.A.; *Kennedy* [1992] Crim.L.R. 37 C.A.; *McGillivray* (1993) 37 Cr.App.R. 232 C.A.; *Setz-Dempsey* (1994) 98 Cr.App.R. 23 C.A.; *Batt and Batt* [1995] Crim.L.R. 240 C.A.

[39] n.38 above.

ground that the trial judge had wrongly allowed in hearsay evidence in the form of statements identifying the defendant from video clips when the maker of the statements was unable to remember the relevant events due to mental illness. The judge held the witness was unfit to attend within the meaning of section 23(2)(a) and declined to apply the discretion to exclude under section 25. The Court of Appeal held that as the statements were prepared for the purpose of criminal proceedings, section 26 rather than section 25 was applicable. The difference between the two sections was that under section 26 the court started from the position that it had to be satisfied that the interests of justice required the admission of the evidence. The fact that the witness could not be cross-examined was of the utmost significance. The fact that the judge had not considered the issue from the point of view required by section 26 meant the court had to allow the appeal.[40] In *Patel*[41] the inability of the police to interview the witness was held to be a significant matter. The onus being on the party who seeks to admit the documentary hearsay to satisfy the court that it should be admitted, the Court of Appeal held there that the trial judge had been right to take that into account when refusing to allow in an alibi statement of a witness who was abroad.[42]

There were three decisions on section 68 which held respectively that depositions and witness statements were not within that section: *O'Loughlin & McLoughlin*,[43] *Martin*[44] and *Cunningham*.[45] In any event it seems that the redrafting of the provisions has ensured that depositions and witness statements are both within Part II of the 1988 Act—as well as section 13 of the Criminal Justice Act 1925.[46] There is a large measure of overlap between the sections in regard to death or unfitness of a witness who has given a deposition but they are not identical. In particular, the position of a conditionally bound witness is dealt with by section 13(3) but not by section 23. The matter was considered but not decided in *Cole* (1990) 90 Cr.App.R. 478 C.A. See also *Blithing* (1983) 77 Cr.App.R. 86 C.A. and *Grafton* [1995] Crim.L.R. 61 C.A. As Professor John Smith in his comment on *O'Loughlin* said, there may be some untidiness in allowing them to be admissible under two different acts but there does not seem to be any satisfactory way of excluding them from the terms of Part II.

Proof of statements contained in documents: section 27

Section 27 allows a copy of a document to be admitted so long as proof of its authenticity is given to the court "in such manner as the court may

[40] For the proposition that courts should be slow to allow in documentary evidence of identification which is the principal element of the prosecution's case see also *Neill v. North-Antrim Magistrates' Court*, n.28 above. In *French and Gowhar, The Times*, March 25, 1993 the Court of Appeal allowed an appeal where the trial judge had admitted two out of three statements made by a witness at the first trial when he refused to come from abroad for the second trial. Under s.26(iii) the C.A. took into account the fact that the defendant had been in custody for 9 months, that the witness had been present for the original trial and that the prosecution had in a sense created the problem for itself by arguing at the first trial against severance of the counts.
[41] (1992) 97 Cr.App.R. 294; [1993] Crim.L.R. 291 C.A.
[42] See further *Cole*, n.15 above in which the Court of Appeal held that the fact that the defendant does not propose to give evidence or call witnesses to controvert a statement in a document does not relieve the court of its obligation to weigh up the question of unfairness to the accused of admitting the statement.
[43] [1988] 3 All E.R. 431 (Cr.Ct.).
[44] [1988] 1 W.L.R. 655 C.A.
[45] [1989] Crim.L.R. 435 C.A.
[46] For confirmation that this was the draftsman's intention see House of Commons, Standing Committee "H", February 16, 1988, Col. 104.

approve". It is immaterial for this purpose how many removes there are between a copy and the original. This is an overdue recognition of the contribution made to modern existence by the photocopier.

Exclusion of evidence: section 28

Subsection (1) is there mainly to avoid doubt. It provides that nothing in Part II shall prejudice: (a) the admissibility of a statement not made by a person while giving oral evidence in court which is admissible otherwise than by virtue of Part II; or (b) any power of a court to exclude at its discretion a statement admissible under Part II.

Subsection (2) states that Schedule 2 has effect to supplement Part II.

Documentary evidence—supplementary: Schedule 2

Schedule 2 contains provisions designed to protect the accused by securing rights he would have had if the witness had given oral instead of written evidence. So paragraph 1(a) preserves the right to produce evidence as to credibility of the witness, such as his prior convictions. Paragraph 1(c) preserves the right to introduce evidence of previous inconsistent statements. Paragraph 2 provides that a statement admitted under Part II is not capable of corroborating evidence given by the person making the statement. An accomplice's oral testimony could not therefore be corroborated by a statement admitted under Part II.

Evidence from computer records: section 69[47]

Section 69 provides for the admissibility of computer records subject to certain conditions.

Prior case law had disclosed serious confusion as to whether and when computer records were admissible in evidence.[48] There were certain statutory provisions making computer records admissible,[49] but apart from these, the courts had tended to allow computer generated information and to disallow computer stored information.

The purpose of section 69 and the Schedule was to put the admissibility of computer evidence on a more sure footing. They were based to a large extent on proposals of the Criminal Law Revision Committee in its 11th Report[50] and are broadly similar to section 5 of the Civil Evidence Act 1968.

Subsection (1) provides that statements in documents produced by computers shall not be admissible evidence of any fact contained in them of which direct oral evidence would be admissible unless the conditions in paragraphs (a) to (c) are satisfied.

"Computer" is not defined in the Act—deliberately, lest developments in technology make any definition obsolete.[51] In *Shepherd*[52] the House of Lords

---

[47] See N.I. PACE Order, Art. 68.
[48] See especially *Pettigrew* (1980) 71 Cr.App.R. 39 and J.C. Smith, "The Admissibility of Statements by Computer" [1981] Crim.L.R. 387.
[49] Under the Banking Act 1979, Sched. 6; Army Act 1955, s.198B; Air Force Act 1955, s.198B; Finance Act 1972, s.34; Finance Act 1980, s.16.
[50] *op. cit.* note 2 above, para. 250.
[51] See the warning against using other statutory definitions in Professor Diane' Birch's commentary on *Golizadeh* [1995] Crim.L.R. 232 C.A.
[52] [1993] A.C. 380; [1993] 2 W.L.R. 102; [1993] 1 E.R. 225 (H.L.).

held that it applied to a Marks & Spencer till roll. The till was connected to a central computer which fed in the date, time, customer number and till number on each till roll. The contents of the till roll were held to be the product of a computer. In *Blackburn*,[53] by contrast, the Court of Appeal said *obiter* that it would be extremely reluctant to accept that a word processor used as a typewriter was a computer for these purposes.

Paragraph (a) of sub-section (1) states that there should be no reasonable grounds for believing the statement to be inaccurate because of improper use of the computer. Paragraph (b) provides that the computer must have been operating properly at all material times, or if not, that any malfunction shall not have affected the accuracy or production of the statement. Paragraph (c) provides that any conditions specified in rules of court made under subsection (2) of section 69 shall be satisfied. Subsection (2) simply provides that the procedure and additional requirements for the admission of computer evidence may be governed by rules of court. But in fact no such rules have been made.

The rest of the rules regulating computer evidence are in Part II (paras. 8–12) and Part III (paras. 13–15) of Schedule 3 (pp. 416–417 below).

Paragraph 8 allows evidence by certificate for the purpose of identifying a document produced by the computer, giving details of how the document was produced and showing that the conditions in section 69(1) have been fulfilled. The certificate may be stated to the best of the knowledge and belief of the person making it.

Paragraph 9 provides that the court may nevertheless require oral evidence to be given of any of the matters mentioned in the certificate. The Criminal Law Revision Committee said that this clause was desirable because there was no equivalent to the provision in the Civil Evidence Act of notice to the other side of the intention to call hearsay evidence which gave the opponent the opportunity to require oral evidence to be given. ("The provision . . . seems desirable in the absence of a requirement to give notice and having regard to the higher standard of proof required for a conviction in criminal proceedings."[54]) Presumably the court would act at the request of either prosecution or defence, or of its own motion.

Paragraph 10 makes it an offence knowingly to make a false statement in a certificate under paragraph 8. Paragraph 11 is similar to paragraph 7 in Part I of the Schedule (and section 6(3) of the Civil Evidence Act 1968). It sets out considerations to be taken into account when estimating the weight to be given to evidence admissible under section 69.

Paragraph 14 provides that, when considering whether to admit a statement in evidence the court can draw any reasonable inferences from the circumstances in which the document came to be made. (This is similar to section 6(2) of the Civil Evidence Act 1968 and supersedes the corresponding provision in section 1(2) of the Criminal Evidence Act 1965.)

But before inferences can be drawn the document must have been properly admitted. See *Bermudez v. Chief Constable of Avon and Somerset*[55] where the Divisional Court quashed a conviction because the formalities for

---

[53] *The Times*, December 1, 1992 C.A. The court said that if documents produced by word-processors were covered by s.69, then the welcome reforms found in s.24 of the 1988 Act would be greatly diminished and marginalised. Now, with the almost universal use of word processors, if that were the case, almost every business document would become subject to s.69 which surely could not have been Parliament's intention.
[54] *op. cit.* n.2, p. 201 above, para. 259.
[55] [1988] Crim.L.R. 452 (Div.Ct.).

admitting forms in regard to breath testing had not been complied with. See also *R. v. Feest*[56] where the Court of Appeal held that when considering admissibility, in proper circumstances inferences could be drawn from the form of a document.

In *Shepherd*[57] the House of Lords held that if the prosecution wish to rely on a document produced by a computer the requirements of section 69 must always be complied with. The House of Lords overruled decisions[58] in which it was held that section 69 only applied to cases falling within section 68 involving documentary hearsay and decisions in which it was held not to apply where the computer merely performed functions of calculation. Lord Griffiths said there was no reason to suppose that Parliament intended the general language of section 69 to be read in a restricted sense. ("It is surely every bit as important that a document produced by a computer and tendered as proof of guilt should be reliable whether or not it contains hearsay.")[59]

The House of Lords in *Shepherd* stated that affirmative evidence is required that the computer was functioning properly. This cannot just be assumed to have been the case in the absence of evidence to the contrary.[60] There is however only very rarely a need to call a computer expert. In *Shepherd* it was held that, although the evidence must be tailored to the needs of the case, in the great majority of cases it is enough to produce someone who can say that he or she is familiar with what the computer is supposed to do and that it was doing it properly. If the witness is giving oral evidence under section 69 (as opposed to signing a certificate under para. 8(d) of Part II of Schedule 3), there is no need for the witness to be a person responsible for the operation of the computer. In *Shepherd* the witness was the store detective. The House of Lords held that she was competent to give such evidence orally. In *Minors and Harper*,[61] however, it was held that the witness, a revenue protection official, could not speak of her own knowledge as to the reliability of the computer. Her evidence was held to be inadmissible.[62]

Where there is a disputed issue as to the admissibility of a computer print-out, the issue should be dealt with in a trial within a trial. The judge must decide whether the foundation requirements have been fulfilled. The standard of proof is criminal (*R. v. Ewing*[63]).

Note that, according to *R. v. Lewis*,[64] counsel for the defendant may validly waive the requirements of section 68 and 69 or, more correctly, make proof of the requirements of the sections unnecessary.[65]

---

[56] [1987] Crim.L.R. 766 C.A.

[57] [1993] 1 All E.R. 225 (H.L.).

[58] Notably *Sophocleus v. Ringer* [1987] Crim.L.R. 422 *Minors, Harper* [1989] 1 W.L.R. 441; [1989] 2 All E.R. 208 C.A.; *Spiby* (1990) 91 Cr.App.R. 186 C.A.; *Neville* [1991] Crim.L.R. 288 C.A. Professor Sir John's criticism of these decisions, reiterated, as he said in his commentary on *Neville* "with increasing desperation", finally prevailed in *Shepherd*.

[59] *op. cit.* at p. 229.

[60] Decisions to the contrary such as *Spiby* n.58 *supra* and *R. v. Governor of Pentonville Prison, ex p. Osman* (1990) 90 Cr.App.R. 281, were overruled.

[61] n.58 above.

[62] But see *Darby v. D.P.P.*, *The Times*, November 4, 1994 (Div.Ct.)—GR Speedman speed trap is a computer but an ordinary police constable who was experienced and trained could give evidence that it was working.

[63] [1983] Q.B. 1037; 77 Cr.App.R. 47.

[64] [1989] Crim.L.R. 61 C.A.

[65] It was held in *Tobi v. Nicholas* [1987] Crim.L.R. 774 (Div.Ct.) that counsel could not waive a rule of evidence. But in *Lewis* counsel was admitting a fact. He was not therefore waiving the rules of proof but rather making proof unnecessary.

Microfilm copies: section 71[66]

Under the previous law microfilm copies of certain categories of documents were admissible under certain statutory provisions.[67] It seemed unclear whether other microfilm copies were admissible.

Section 71 is intended to put the matter beyond doubt. It provides that the contents of a document may be proved by the production of an enlargement of a microfilm copy of that document or part of it. The copy must be authenticated "in such manner as the court may approve". The microfilm copy is admissible whether or not the original document is still in existence.

Definitions: section 72[68]

Section 72(1) defines "copy", "statement" and proceedings". The first two have the same meanings as in part I of the Civil Evidence Act 1968. The expression "proceedings" if not further defined means criminal proceedings.

Subsection (2) saves any power of a court to exclude evidence at its discretion. It is similar to section 18(5)(a) of the Civil Evidence Act 1968. It includes exclusion of evidence by preventing questions from being put or by excusing the witness from answering questions already put or by directing the jury to disregard evidence.

Note—Law Commission proposes radical reform of hearsay law

In July 1995 the Law Commission published *Evidence in Criminal Proceedings: Hearsay and Related Topics* (Consultation Paper, No. 138). The Royal Commission on Criminal Justice had recommended that the hearsay rule be reformed and that the Law Commission be asked to tackle the question. The Home Secretary referred the matter to the Commission in April 1994. The Consultation Paper, which is 266 pages long, gave the Commission's provisional conclusions:

— It is right that the rules about hearsay in civil and criminal cases should continue to be different. The hearsay rule is part of the protections for the defendant to reduce the risk of a miscarriage of justice. Also whereas the fact finders in civil cases are judges, in criminal cases they are jurors and magistrates.

— All relevant evidence should be admissible unless there is a good reason for it to be treated as inadmissible.

— The law of hearsay "is complex and uncertain" yet it has to be applied "on the spot and off the cuff by recorders and assistant recorders, by stipendiary magistrates and lay magistrates, and by justices' clerks, not to mention the full-time professional judiciary" (para. 4.68).

—"The rule is excessively complex; this complexity leads to confusion, anomalies and wasted time, both for the court and for the parties. The rule results in the exclusion of cogent evidence even when it is the defence that seeks to adduce it . . . In many situations, whether or not hearsay evidence

---

[66] See N.I. PACE Order, Art. 69.
[67] Banking Act 1979, Sched. 6; Finance Act 1972, ss.34 and 39.
[68] See N.I. PACE Order, Art. 67.

will be admitted depends on the exercise of judicial discretion, which leads to inconsistency of decisions from one court to another." (para. 9.2)

— Change therefore was necessary.

— The main reason why hearsay evidence was inferior to non-hearsay evidence was that it could not be tested by cross examination. Also there was a danger that hearsay evidence could be manufactured—but the danger that first-hand hearsay would be manufactured was less than that second or third-hand hearsay would be. In the case of first-hand hearsay, the jury could be warned about the danger of relying on evidence that had not been tested by cross-examination and about the danger that the evidence had been manufactured. The system expected jurors and magistrates to understand many complex warnings in other fields of evidence "and we find it difficult to see why they should not understand the warnings about the weaknesses of first-hand hearsay" (para. 6.100).

— The hearsay rule should be defined to cover everything now within its ambit other than implied assertions. (The House of Lords decision in *Kearley* [1992] 2 A.C. 228 would therefore be reversed.)

The Consultation Paper then considered six options for reform:

(1) Abolish the rule altogether.
(2) Abolish the rule subject to a duty for the court to hear first-hand evidence, if it is available.[69]
(3) Make all hearsay prima facie inadmissible subject to a discretion to admit if it is sufficiently reliable and it is necessary in the interests of justice.[70]
(4) Keep the present rule subject to a discretion to admit, to be used in exceptional circumstances.
(5) Have categories of automatically admissible hearsay subject to the two general and established discretions to exclude prosecution evidence (at common law if its prejudicial effect outweighs its probative value and under PACE, s.78).
(6) The same as (5) but with a limited additional discretion as a safety-valve where the court is concerned that a miscarriage of justice might otherwise result.

The Commission's provisional view was that the last option was the best. It therefore proposed:

1. As a general rule hearsay evidence should remain inadmissible in criminal proceedings—subject to exceptions.
2. The exceptions should apply only to first hand oral or documentary hearsay, they should not apply to unidentified witnesses and they should not extend to evidence of any fact of which the witness's oral evidence would not be admissible.

---

[69] This "best evidence available" principle operates in Germany.
[70] This was recommended by the New Zealand Law Reform Commission in 1991.

3. The categories of automatic exception should be:
    (a) where the witness is dead, or too ill to attend the court;
    (b) where such steps have been taken as are reasonably practicable to secure his or her attendance but without success and (i) he is outside the United Kingdom or (ii) he cannot be found; or
    (c) where the witness refuses to give evidence (or to continue giving evidence) although physically in court.

4. None of the exceptions would apply where the party wishing to adduce the hearsay statement was responsible for the fact that the witness cannot or will not give evidence.

5. The following statutory exceptions should be preserved with appropriate amendment: Criminal Justice Act 1988, ss.24, 25, 26[71]; Criminal Justice Act 1967, s.9; Bankers' Books Evidence Act 1879, ss. 3 and 4; Criminal Justice Act 1972, s.46(1); and Criminal Appeal Act 1968, Sched. 2, paras. 1 and 1A.

6. Confessions should continue to be admissible against their makers, subject to s.76 of PACE and the existing discretions to exclude prosecution evidence.

7. There should be a further limited exception (the "safety-valve" provision) in the form of a residual discretion to admit hearsay evidence falling outside the recognised categories and the preserved exceptions which:
    (a) should extend to oral as well as documentary hearsay;
    (b) should extend to multiple hearsay as well as first hand-hand hearsay; and
    (c) should be available only if it appears to the court that (i) the evidence is so positively and obviously trustworthy that the opportunity to test it by cross-examination can safely be dispensed with, and (ii) the interests of justice require that it be admitted.

8. The rules should be the same for prosecution and defence.

9. A previous consistent statement should be admissible (a) to rebut any suggestion of afterthought; (b) as evidence of previous identification or description; (c) on accusation, save for prepared self-serving statements; or (d) where the witness cannot remember details in a statement which he made when the details were fresh in his memory and it would not be reasonable to expect him to remember the details.

10. Section 69 of PACE should be repealed without replacement. The parties would then be able to rely on the presumption of regularity—in the absence of evidence to the contrary the courts presume that mechanical instruments were in order at the material time.

---

[71] (1) In s.24 the "maker" should be the supplier *or* the recorder of the information. (2) The discretionary provisions in ss.25 and 26 should be abolished. (3) It should be made clear that statements made by witnesses to police officers are not within this exception. (See para. 11.59.)

PART VIII

EVIDENCE IN CRIMINAL PROCEEDINGS—GENERAL

Convictions and acquittals: sections 73 to 75[1]

The Criminal Law Revision Committee in its 11th Report recommended that the law on proof of convictions and acquittals in criminal cases should be tidied up, and sections 73–75 broadly follow the recommendations of the Committee.[2] But the reforms have produced their own serious problems which seem not to have been anticipated by the C.L.R.C.

Section 73 replaces statutory provisions which contain references to court procedures that are outdated.[3] It provides for proof of a conviction or acquittal by a certificate signed by the appropriate officer of the court, together with evidence identifying the person named in the certificate.[4]

There is also a saving for any other authorised manner of providing evidence of a conviction or acquittal—such as by a person present in court, or by means of fingerprints under section 39 of the Criminal Justice Act 1948, or written statements under sections 2 or 9 of the Criminal Justice Act 1967 or an admission under section 10 of the 1967 Act.

Section 74 amends the law on admissibility of convictions as evidence of the commission of an offence. In accordance with *Hollington v. Hewthorn*,[5] evidence that a person other than the accused had been convicted of an offence was not admissible for the purpose of proving that that person committed the offence. Thus in a trial for handling it could not be shown that the goods were stolen by introducing the conviction of the thief.

The rule was abolished for civil proceedings by the Civil Evidence Act 1968, s.11. The difficulties that the rule gave rise to were illustrated in *Spinks*.[6] S had been convicted of acting with intent to impede the arrest of F, having hidden the knife used by F in a stabbing. S's conviction was quashed on appeal because the only evidence at his trial that F had committed the offence was inadmissible and F's conviction for the stabbing was inadmissible because of the rule in *Hollington v. Hewthorn*.

The Criminal Law Revision Committee recommended in its 11th Report[7]

---

[1] See N.I. PACE Order, Arts. 71–73.
[2] *op. cit.* n.2, p. 201 above, paras. 217–220.
[3] Evidence Act 1851, s.13; Criminal Procedure Act 1865, s.6; and the Prevention of Crimes Act 1871, s.18.
[4] In *Hacker* [1994] 1 W.L.R. 1659; [1995] 1 All E.R. 45, the House of Lords held that the whole certificate is admissible even if it gives details of the defendant's previous conviction—subject to the judge's overriding discretion to exclude evidence if the prejudicial effect would outweigh the probative value. For commentary see R. Munday 159 *Justice of the Peace*, April 8, 22, 1995.
[5] [1943] K.B. 587.
[6] [1982] 1 All E.R. 587.
[7] *op. cit.* n.2, p. 201 above, para. 218.

that the rule in *Hollington v. Hewthorn* should be abolished for criminal cases as well. Section 74 follows the C.L.R.C.'s proposals in regard to convictions of persons other than the accused. In regard to the accused himself the section makes no change in the rules regarding the admissibility of his past misconduct. But it does alter the rules regarding his commission of a previous offence by allowing it to be proved by evidence of his conviction. The consequences of this have been surprising and unfortunate.

Subsection (1) states that the conviction of someone other than the accused is admissible as proof that he committed that offence whether or not any other evidence of the fact is given. So if A is charged with handling goods stolen by B, evidence that B was convicted of stealing the goods will be admissible to prove that they were stolen.

Subsection (2) provides that the person convicted shall be taken to have committed that offence unless the contrary is proved.

Subsection (3) deals with the position of the accused. Where evidence is admissible of the fact that he has committed an offence, in so far as that is relevant to a matter in issue other than a tendency to show a disposition to commit the kind of offence with which he is charged, the conviction shall be taken as proof that he committed that offence unless the contrary is proved. The section however specifically preserves the operation of any statute making a conviction or finding of fact conclusive for the purpose of other proceedings. It is also provided that the admissibility of any conviction which would be admissible apart from the clause, is not prejudiced (for a similar provision in regard to civil cases, see Civil Evidence Act 1968, s.11(3).).

The case law on section 74 has however given it an unexpectedly broad interpretation, especially through the application of the power to exclude "unfair" evidence under section 78. As has been seen, the main thrust of the C.L.R.C.'s recommendation was to help the prosecution where the guilt of the accused depends on a third party's guilt. But section 74 is not limited in this way. It simply provides that the conviction is admissible in evidence where it is "relevant to any issue" in the proceedings to establish the guilt of the convicted person.

The courts have found two meanings of the word "issue". The restricted meaning is an issue which is an essential ingredient in the offence charged. An example would be to establish against an alleged accessory that the principal committed the offence—see *Turner* [1991] Crim.L.R. 57 C.A.; *Fedrick* [1990] Crim.L.R. 403. The extended meaning is other matters that are less important such as evidential matters that come up in the course of the case.[8] So in *Golder*[9] D was charged with robbery. Convictions of two other men in respect of the same offence were said to be relevant for the purpose, first of showing that a robbery had occurred (the narrow meaning) and secondly, to show that facts allegedly narrated by D in a disputed confession which were consistent with the guilt of the other two were likely to be true (the extended use).[10]

Given that his out-of-court admission would not be admissible against the accused it is plainly unfair, at least in some circumstances, to allow a third person's conviction to be introduced as evidence against the accused. It is

---

[8] *R. v. Robertson* [1987] 1 Q.B. 920, 927 C.A.
[9] Heard and reported with *Robertson* above.
[10] See also *Grey* (1989) 88 Cr.App.Rep. 375 C.A.; *Castle* [1989] Crim.L.R. 567 C.A., *Steers* (January 12, 1993, Unreported), Case No. 91/2551/X3 C.A.

this unfairness which has led the courts to try to restrict the use of the section by use of section 78.[11] So where D and E are charged with conspiring together and E pleads guilty to conspiring with D, his conviction becomes admissible evidence from which the jury may infer that D must have conspired with E. Indeed, unless the contrary be proved, the facts on which the conviction was based, namely that D and E conspired together, are established. This in effect reverses the burden of proof which, as Professor Sir John Smith has said, "was surely never intended and is contrary to all principle".[12] In *Robertson* Lord Lane warned that "Section 74 is a provision which should be sparingly used".[13] But the courts have used section 78 to exclude the evidence where its impact would be too damning.[14]

In *Boyson*[15] the defendant had been convicted of importing a drug. Her three co-defendants pleaded guilty. A fourth, her co-habitee and later husband, was separately convicted of importing a different drug. All the pleas and convictions were admitted in the trial of the defendant under section 74. The Court of Appeal held that the trial judge had admitted the evidence under section 74 without having regard to fairness under section 78. This was wrong. In order to admit evidence of a co-accused's conviction or plea it was necessary to observe the following principles:

(1) the conviction must be clearly relevant in an issue in the case;
(2) section 74 should be sparingly used;
(3) the judge should consider the question of fairness under section 78 of the Act and whether the probative value of the conviction outweighs its prejudicial value; and
(4) the judge must direct the jury clearly as to the issues to which the conviction is and is not relevant.

The accused's conviction was irrelevant and prejudicial. The court said that it did not approve of the growing practice of allowing evidence to go before the jury which was irrelevant, inadmissible, prejudicial or unfair simply because it is convenient for the jury to have "the whole picture".[16] It dismissed the appeal however by applying the proviso.

In *Warner and Jones*[17] the Court of Appeal in effect appeared to condone proof of guilt by association. The defendants were convicted of conspiracy to supply heroin. The prosecution led evidence that a great number of persons briefly visited the second defendant's premises—and that eight of these had convictions for possession or supplying heroin. The Court of Appeal said the judge should have told the jury that the appellants were not to be convicted simply because of their association with such people but it held that it could

---

[11] *O'Connor* (1987) 85 Cr.App.R. 298 C.A.; *Curry* [1988] Crim.L.R. 527 C.A.; *Kempster* [1989] 1 W.L.R. 1125 C.A. Cf. *Robertson and Golder* [1987] 1 Q.B. 920; *Lunnon* (1988) 88 Cr.App.R. 71 C.A.; *Bennett* [1988] Crim.L.R. 686 C.A.; *Mattison* [1990] Crim.L.R., 117 C.A.
[12] [1988] Crim.L.R. 456 commenting on the Court of Appeal's decision in *Lunnon*. See also Professor's Smith's comment on *Curry* [1988] Crim.L.R. 527, 528. See also *Humphreys and Tully* [1993] Crim.L.R. 288 C.A.
[13] *op. cit.* n.8, p. 215 above, p. 928.
[14] For further commentary see, for instance, D. Birch [1989] Crim.L.R. 749–750 and R. Munday, "Proof of Guilt by Association and section 74 of the Police and Criminal Evidence Act 1984" [1990] Crim.L.R. 236.
[15] [1991] Crim.L.R. 274 C.A.
[16] See to like effect *Mattison* [1990] Crim.L.R. 117 C.A.; *Humphrey and Tully* n.12 above and *Hall* [1993] Crim.L.R. 527 C.A. In this respect *cf. Bennett* [1988] Crim.L.R. 686 C.A. and *Turpin* [1990] Crim.L.R. 514 C.A. It is suggested that *Boyson* represents the better view.
[17] (1993) 96 Cr.App.Rep. 324 (C.A.).

not be said that the first conviction was irrelevant to the question which was taking place.

Section 75 has supplementary provisions making admissible duly certified copies of documents to prove the facts of the offence including the information, complaint, indictment or charge sheet. Without such factual details it may be difficult to determine whether a previous conviction is or is not relevant. In *O'Connor*[18] the Court of Appeal held that where the conviction is admitted it comes in with all the detail contained in the relevant count of the indictment. In that case the first defendant was charged with conspiracy to obtain property by deception with the second defendant. The second defendant pleaded guilty to count one. The court said that it would be difficult to contend from that admission and the details that not only had the second defendant conspired with the first defendant but that the converse had also taken place. Moreover, it was not open to the defence to challenge what the second defendant had said in the first defendant's absence since he had not given evidence. This was most unfair and the evidence should have excluded under section 78. (But the court applied the proviso and therefore dismissed the appeal.)

Oral evidence is also admissible. Subsection (3) provides that certain enactments under which a conviction leading to probation or discharge is to be disregarded shall not affect the admissibility of the conviction for evidentiary reasons. The enactments in question prevent the conviction from counting as part of the criminal record for the purpose of sentencing.

Confessions: section 76[19]

The common law background and the C.L.R.C.

One of the most important sections in PACE is section 76 which made a major change in the law on confessions. Under the classic common law a confession was only admissible if the prosecution could show that it was voluntary, in the sense that it had not been induced "by fear of prejudice or hope of advantage exercised or held out by a person in authority".[20] Also a confession must not have been obtained by oppression.[21]

In the past the courts took this principle very seriously and interpreted it strictly against the police. Even the mildest threat or inducement had been held to make a resulting confession inadmissible. Thus in *Northam*,[22] a person charged with housebreaking was being questioned about his part in other offences. Before confessing he asked whether the other offence might be taken into consideration at his trial rather than being the subject of a separate trial. The Court of Appeal quashed the conviction because of the police officer's acceptance of this suggestion. In *Zaveckas*[23] the Court of Appeal quashed a conviction because the trial judge had admitted a confession made after the defendant asked the police officer whether he could have bail if he made a statement.

[18] (1986) 85 Cr.App.Rep. 298 (C.A.).
[19] See N.I. PACE Order, Art. 74—but Art. 74(a) excludes trials on indictment for scheduled cases under the Northern Ireland (Emergency Provisions) Act 1978, s.8, as amended, which provides a very similar test: see further below.
[20] *R. v. Ibrahim* [1914] A.C. 599 (P.C.).
[21] See especially *R. v. Prager* [1972] 1 All E.R. 1114 C.A.; *R. v. Priestly* (1966) 50 Cr.App.R. 183 C.C.A.
[22] (1967) 52 Cr.App.R. 97 C.A.
[23] (1970) 54 Cr.App.R. 202 C.A.

In its 1972 11th Report, the Criminal Law Revision Committee said that two reasons had been given for the rule. One was that a confession not made voluntarily might not be reliable (the "reliability principle"); and secondly, that the police should be discouraged from using improper methods to obtain a confession (the "disciplinary principle"). It thought that historically the reliability principle underlay the law. This was shown by the authorities and also by the fact that if the police discovered something such as a body or a gun as a result of an involuntary confession, the evidence of that fact was admissible.

After reviewing the case law, the Committee said that it was unsatisfactory.[24] It recommended that only threats or inducements likely to produce an unreliable confession or oppression should cause a confession to be inadmissible. It would be for the judge to imagine that he was present at the interrogation and to consider whether at that point the threat or inducement would have been likely to make a confession unreliable.

After the report of the C.L.R.C. in 1972 the case law on confessions moved somewhat in the direct of the Committee's proposals. In *D.P.P. v. Ping Lin*[25] the suspect, a drugs dealer, asked "If I help the police, will you help me?" The officer replied: "I can make no deal with you but if you show the judge that you have helped the police to trace bigger people I am sure he will bear it in mind when he sentences you." The House of Lords said that the prosecution had to show as a matter of fact that the threat or promise had not induced the confession. The judge had been entitled to hold the statement admissible.

In the later case of *Rennie*[26] this ruling was applied to a confession which the police officer actually admitted had been prompted by the suspect's fear that the police would otherwise interview and perhaps arrest other members of his family. The Lord Chief Justice said that the speculation of the police officer as to what prompted the confession was irrelevant and inadmissible. But he went on (at p. 388): "Even if the appellant had decided to admit his guilt because he hoped that if he did so the police would cease their inquiries into the part played by his mother, it does not follow that the confession should have been excluded."

The law did not require, Lord Lane said, that every confession should be excluded simply because it was prompted in part by some hope of advantage. The question was whether on a common sense view the statement had been made voluntarily, which in ordinary parlance meant "of one's own free will". This was a question of fact which should be approached by the judge much in the way that a jury would. The confession was held to be admissible.

Plainly the definition of voluntariness in *Rennie* was wholly different from that in cases like *Northam* and *Zaveckas*. Much of the bite in the rule had been removed.

The Philips Royal Commission

The Philips Royal Commission[27] criticised the voluntariness test as unrealistic. Even a trained psychologist present during questioning, it

---

[24] *op. cit.* n.2, p. 201 above, paras. 53–69.
[25] [1976] A.C. 574 (H.L.).
[26] [1982] 1 All E.R. 385 (C.A.).
[27] Philips Report, para. 4.73.

suggested, could not determine to what extent any particular confession was truly voluntary.[28] In the Commission's view it would be better to abandon the vain attempt to distinguish between voluntary and involuntary confessions and concentrate instead on the behaviour of the police officer. If the suspect was subjected to torture, violence, the threat of violence or inhuman or degrading treatment any subsequent confession should be inadmissible. This would mark society's "abhorrence of such conduct".[29] But any lesser breach of the rules of questioning should merely lead to the judge warning the jury of the danger of relying on the resulting confession if there was no independent evidence.[30]

Section 76(1)

Section 76(1) states that in any proceedings a confession made by an accused person may be given in evidence against him "so far as it is relevant to any matter in the proceedings and is not excluded by the court in pursuance of this section". At first sight this seems straightforward, but a serious question is raised as to what use, if any, can be made of the subsection by one accused against another. If they are running "cut-throat defences" in which each seeks to blame the other, can one use in evidence a confession made by the other, even though the confession has been obtained in circumstances which would otherwise make it inadmissible?

Curiously, it would seem that the answer may be yes. The court's power to exclude a confession under subsections (2) or (3) only applies where it is the prosecution which seeks to introduce the confession. If the prosecution does not do so, the co-accused would apparently be able to use the confession against its maker—as evidence of guilt as well as evidence going to credibility as a witness.[31] But if the court considered the result to be unfair it could still exclude the evidence under either section 78 or its residual discretion given by section 82(3) (see below).

Section 76(2): the basic scheme

The Act imposes two tests on admissibility for confessions which are in addition to the general tests on admissibility of all evidence contained in section 78 (p. 232 below) and section 82(3) (p. 250 below). The first is that the confession should not be the result of oppression (s.76(2)(a)) and the second is that it should not be the result of conduct likely to render a confession unreliable (s.76(2)(b)) In other words, the Philips Royal Commission's proposal that the voluntariness test be abandoned altogether was rejected—on the ground that the Royal Commission's approach did not provide adequate protection against the danger of an unreliable confession.

If it is represented to the court[32] that the confession was, or may have been, obtained either by oppression or in a way likely to make it unreliable, the

---

[28] The Commission based its view largely on the research of Dr Barrie Irving, "Police Interrogation: A Case Study of Current Practice" *Royal Commission Research Study No. 2* (1980).

[29] Philips Report, para. 4.132.

[30] Philips Report, para. 4.133.

[31] See to this effect the views of Mr Michael Hirst and Professor John Smith [1989] Crim.L.R. 603. See also *Beckford and Daley* [1991] Crim.L.R. 833 C.A., *Callan* [1994] Crim.L.R. 198 C.A. and *Brown and Ciarla* [1995] Crim.L.R. 328 C.A., and the commentaries on these cases following the respective reports.

[32] A mere suggestion in cross-examination is not enough: *R. v. Liverpool Juvenile Court, ex p. R.* [1988] Q.B. 1 (Div.Ct.).

court is directed by subsection (2) not to allow it to be given in evidence "except in so far as the prosecution proves to the court beyond reasonable doubt that the confession (notwithstanding that it may be true)[33] was not obtained as aforesaid".

The burden of proof in regard to both section 76(2)(a) and (b) is squarely on the prosecution. So in the case of *Parris, Abdullai and Miller* (known as the case of the "Cardiff Three") the Lord Chief Justice said: "It is sufficient to say that in our judgment, the Crown did not and could not discharge the burden upon them to prove beyond reasonable doubt that the confessions were not obtained by oppression or by interviews which were likely to render them unreliable."[34] It would therefore be wrong for the judge to say that he was unable to make up his mind as to the matter. If he could not make up his mind the prosecution had failed to discharge the burden of proof.[35]

The section specifically says the prosecution must affirmatively prove that the confession was not so obtained—"*notwithstanding that it may be true*". This means that the court cannot take into consideration the fact that the confession appears to be true.[36] In fact it seems that during the *voire dire* the defendant should not be asked any questions as to the truth of the confession.[37] If the truth of the confession is not to be taken into account, it is difficult to see any justification for asking such questions. Indeed, the asking of such questions must create a danger that the apparent truth of the confession will affect the judge's decision on admissibility.

Where the prosecution proposes to give a confession in evidence, the court may of its own motion require the prosecution to prove that the confession was not so obtained (subs. (3)).

The fact that the confession itself is held to be inadmissible does not affect the admissibility of (a) facts discovered as a result of the confession (such as the gun with the fingerprints on it)[38]; or (b) so much of the confession as is necessary to show that the accused speaks, writes or expresses himself in a particular way where this is relevant (subs. (4)).[39]

But evidence that a fact was discovered *as a result* of an inadmissible confession is only admissible if given by or on behalf of the accused (subss. (5) and (6)). It cannot be produced by the prosecution.

---

[33] When the Bill was first published it contained a provision that evidence could be admitted to prove the truth or falsity of the confession if the court thought that such evidence would assist in determining the issue of admissibility. This rejected the view of the majority of the Judicial Committee of the Privy Council in *Wong Kam-Ming v. The Queen* [1980] A.C. 247 in which it was held that on a *voire dire* as to the admissibility of an extra-judicial statement by an accused the prosecution could not cross-examine him as to the truth of the statement. The sole issue on the *voire dire*, the majority held, was whether the statement had been made voluntarily, and whether it was true was not relevant to that issue. The subsection adopted the minority view expressed by Lord Hailsham which reflects the decision in *Hammond* (1941) 28 Cr.App.R. 84 (C.C.A.). However, the Government was persuaded to drop this provision with the result that the majority view in *Wong Kam-Ming* stands after all.

[34] (1993) 97 Cr.App.Rep. 99, at 105 C.A.

[35] *Baker* (August 18, 1992, Unreported), Case No. 92/3437/Z3 C.A. See also *Jerome*, (February 1, 1994, Unreported) Case No. 91/3384/W3 C.A.

[36] *Cox* [1991] Crim.L.R. 276 C.A. The court said: "It is perfectly true that the judge must have regard to all the circumstances. But one of the matters to which he plainly cannot have regard is the truth of the statement."

[37] *Davis* [1990] Crim.L.R. 860 in which the Court of Appeal indicated that it approved of the view of the Privy Council in *Wong Kam-Ming* [1980] A.C. 247 that the defendant could not be questioned on the *voire dire* regarding the truth of the confession. See also *Tyrer* (1990) 90 Cr.App.R. 446 C.A.

[38] Preserving the common law rule in *Warwickshall* (1783) 1 Leach 263.

[39] As in the old case of *R. v. Voisin* [1918] 1 K.B. 531.

What is a confession?

Section 82(1) defines "confession" thus: "'confession' includes any statement wholly or partly adverse to the person who made it, whether made to a person in authority or not and whether made in words or otherwise."

Where admissions are "mixed" in that they contain self-serving parts they count as confessions and therefore section 76 must be satisfied. (In *Sharp*[40] the House of Lords held that such statements are evidence of the truth of the self-serving, as well as the incriminating parts.)

According to *Sat-Bhambra*[41] the statutory definition of "confession" does not include a statement which, when made was purely self-serving but which becomes adverse to the defendant at trial for example because it is inconsistent with his defence. Such statements need not therefore satisfy the conditions of section 76—though they may still be excluded under section 78 or at common law. In *Doolan*[42] it was held that the defendant's admission that he had been drinking with the victim on the evening of the robbery did amount to a confession.

It should be noted that even after the "abolition of the right to silence" silence presumably can not be brought within the concept of a "statement"—and therefore could not count as a confession that is subject to section 76.

The importance of confessions

It is clear that confessions and admissions remain a very important factor in criminal investigation. Pre-PACE studies estimated that over 60 per cent of interviews with suspects led to confessions. (Softley *et al.* (1980); Irving (1980)).

Post-PACE, the proportion has remained high: Irving and McKenzie (1989) showed a confession rate of 65 per cent in their 1986 and 46 per cent in the 1987 sample; Sanders *et al.* (1989) in a study of 250 cases in ten police stations had an admission rate of 54 per cent overall with 60 per cent where no legal advice was given and 44 per cent where legal advice was given; Moston and Stephenson (1992) based on 558 cases had an overall admission rate of 59 per cent, with 51 per cent in legal advice cases compared with 63 per cent in other cases; Moston *et al.* (1990) based on 1,067 C.I.D. cases in the Metropolitan Police District had a 41 per cent overall admission rate, with only 29 per cent in legal advice cases compared with 50 per cent in others. See also Evans (1993) in regard to confessions by juveniles.

"Oppression": Section 76(2)(a)

At common law, the word "oppression" was defined by the Court of Appeal very, and perhaps too, widely in *Prager*[43]: "questioning which by its nature, duration, or other attendant circumstances (including the fact of

---

[40] [1988] 1 W.L.R. 7.
[41] (1988) 88 Cr.App.R. 55; [1988] Crim.L.R. 453 C.A.; see further D.J. Birch, "The PACE Hots Up: Confessions and Confusions under the 1984 Act" [1989] Crim.L.R. 95, 115 and J. Kodowo Bentil, "Issues Concerning the Admissibility of Confession Evidence in a Criminal Trial," *J.P.N.*, November 25, 1989, p. 750, 752.
[42] (1988) Cr.App.Rep. 55 C.A.
[43] [1972] 1 W.L.R. 260 C.A.

custody) excites hope (such as the hope of release) or fears, or so affects the mind of the subject that his will crumbles and he speaks when otherwise he would have stayed silent."

"Oppression", according to subsection (8), "includes torture, inhuman or degrading treatment[43a] and the use or threat of violence." The use of the word "includes" means that this list is not intended to be exhaustive. The Northern Ireland (Emergency Provisions) Act 1978, s.8 (amended by s.5 of the 1987 Act of the same name) defines oppression in almost the same terms, except that there is no mention of the word "includes", so that the definition is closed rather than open ended.

The concept of "oppression" has been considered in several cases since the Act became law. In the first three cases the courts found that there had not been oppression.

In *Miller*[44] the Court of Appeal had to consider a confession by a paranoid schizophrenic who confessed to killing his girl friend. When first interviewed he consistently denied the allegation. Next day however he admitted it in a statement which contained both reliable and unreliable matter. Then he tried to retract the confession. At the trial it was argued on his behalf that the confession should be excluded under section 76(2)(a) because it had been obtained as a result of protracted and oppressive interviews which had caused him to suffer an episode of schizophrenic terror. Medical evidence was given that the style and length of questioning had produced a state of involuntary insanity in which his language reflected hallucinations and delusion. The judge refused to exclude the evidence. The defendant was found guilty of manslaughter.

On appeal it was contended for the defendant that oppression meant conduct which in fact produced the effects of oppression regardless of the police officer's intention or state of mind. The Court of Appeal rejected this view. The court held that although questions which were asked deliberately with the intention of producing a disordered state of mind would amount to oppression, the mere fact that questions addressed to the defendant triggered off hallucinations was not evidence of oppression. Here there has been no evidence of oppression "within the ordinary meaning of that word".[45]

In *Fulling*[46] the Court of Appeal held that it was not oppression for the police to tell the defendant that her lover had been having an affair with another woman which so affected her that she made a confession. The court held that the word "oppression" should be given its ordinary dictionary meaning as stated in the *Oxford English Dictionary*: "The exercise of authority or power in a burdensome, harsh or wrongful manner; unjust or cruel treatment of subjects, inferiors, etc.; the imposition of unreasonable or unjust burdens." The court cited a quotation from the OED: "There is not a word in our language which expresses more detestable wickedness than oppression."

It was argued for the appellant that the trial judge had been wrong to hold

---

[43a] The phrase comes from the European Convention on Human Rights. It was considered by the European Court in *Tyrer v. U.K.* 2 E.H.R.R. 1, 9–12; and *Ireland v. U.K.* 2 E.H.R.R. 25, 75–85. For a Northern Ireland view see *R. v. McCormick* [1977] N.I. 105.

[44] [1986] 1 W.L.R. 1191 C.A. For a valuable discussion of the case see M. Beaumont "Confessions and the Mentally Ill," *Law Soc. Gaz.*, September 3, 1986, p. 256.

[45] *op. cit.*, n.44 above, p. 1201.

[46] [1987] Q.B. 426, C.A.

that "oppression" necessarily involved some impropriety on the part of the police, but Lord Lane L.C.J. for the court said "We find it hard to envisage any circumstances in which such oppression would not entail impropriety on the part of the interrogator." The judge had therefore not erred.

In *Samuel*[47] the Court of Appeal recognised that denial of access to a solicitor might be oppression—though counsel for S had not suggested that that was such a case. See also *Emmerson*[48] where shouting and swearing at the suspect were held not to amount to oppressive conduct.

An early case in which the courts found oppression to have existed was *Davison*[49] a decision at the Central Criminal Court. D had been arrested at home at 6.30 a.m. for handling a stolen ring, the proceeds of an armed robbery. He was questioned at various stages during the course of the day both about that offence and a bullion robbery. Eventually he confessed. There were a whole series of breaches of the rules in the Act and the Code. The judge considered the Court of Appeal's ruling in *Fulling* that oppression "is the exercise of authority or power in ... a wrongful manner". Here there had been various wrongs including, in particular, unlawful detention.[50] The authority of the police was being exercised in a wrongful manner and it was therefore capable of amounting to oppression. The burden was on the Crown to prove that it had not amounted to oppression and this they had failed to do. Accordingly, all the evidence after the first interview had to be excluded under section 76(2)(a).

Commenting on the decision in the *Criminal Law Review*[51] Professor D.J. Birch suggested that the decision shows the significance of the word "wrongful" in the phrase "burdensome, harsh or wrongful" used by the Court of Appeal in *Fulling*. She suggested that it would be "unfortunate" however if every breach of the detention rules, even mandatory rules, were to be regarded as oppression. It would be more than unfortunate.[52] She was surely right to suggest that "wrongful" in the context of the phrase used in *Fulling* must mean some flagrant or deliberate breach of the rules. No doubt, as she suggests, a court would take into account the number and extent of breaches of the rules and whether they indicate incompetence or design. In *Davison* there might have been enough evidence of serious police miscon-duct to have justified a finding of oppression even if the narrower interpretation of the term was implied.

There are however now several decisions which give the police concrete guidance as to what *will* amount to oppression.[53] In the case of Timothy John West in 1988 the trial judge held the following to have been oppressive:
1) The police officer had interrupted the defendant on a large number of occasions before he had finished his replies. The officer interrupted the defendant vigorously and with a raised voice sometimes shouting rudely.
2) The officer used obscenity to interrupt the defendant to indicate that he

---

[47] [1988] Q.B. 615 at 629.
[48] (1991) 92 Cr.App.R. 284 C.A.
[49] [1988] Crim.L.R. 442.
[50] The police failed to release D after the first interview at which stage there was no evidence against him (breach of s.34). Also, he had never been arrested in connection with the bullion robbery (breach of s.31).
[51] [1988] Crim.L.R. 444–445.
[52] See now also *Parker* [1995] Crim.L.R. 233 C.A. and Professor Birch's commentary.
[53] In addition to those dealt with here in some detail see also *Madeley* (Unreported, March 18, 1992), C.A. (confession in interview excluded where officers insulted and bullied M and said that by remaining silent he was making matters worse for himself); and *Beales* [1991] Crim.L.R. 118 (Cr.Ct.) (deliberate misstatement of the evidence in order to mislead B "stepped into the realm" of oppression).

was lying. It was also used to show that the officer had a clear view that the defendant had committed the offences and would continue to question him until he admitted them.[54]

In *Paris, Abdullai and Miller*[55] (the "Cardiff Three" case) the Court of Appeal quashed the defendants' convictions for murder. The defendant Miller, who it turned out was on the borderline of mental handicap, made admissions after having denied the offence more than 300 times. Lord Taylor, the Lord Chief Justice, said the court had been horrified by the hectoring and bullying manner of the questioning on Tape No. 7, much of which had been conducted in the form of shouting at the accused and repeating accusations over and over again. ("The officers ... were not questioning him so much as shouting at him what they wanted him to say. Short of physical violence, it is hard to conceive a more hostile and intimidating approach to a suspect. It is impossible to convey on the printed page the pace, force and menace of the officer's delivery.") Miller had stood his ground and had made no admissions until the next interview an hour later, but the Lord Chief Justice said the court had no doubt that this was oppression.

In the Cardiff Three case the Lord Chief Justice drew attention also to other matters that supported counsel's argument that the conviction should be quashed on the ground that questioning had been oppressive. The officers had made it clear to Miller on many occasions that they would go on questioning him until "they got it right" meaning until he agreed with the version they were putting. Additional pressure was applied by telling Miller that he was talking drivel and rubbish and that his alibi had been blown away. ("The alibi had never been totally water-tight, but so far as it went, it was not, on the police information, blown away.") The prosecution's version of events was said to be supported by a number of witnesses which it was not. Miller had more than once been threatened with the prospect of a life sentence. The officers persistently suggested to Miller that he was "stoned" due to the effects of cocaine so as to persuade him that he might have been present even though he had no recollection of it. Counsel for Miller submitted that he had in effect been brain-washed over the 13 hours of questioning into repeating back to the officers facts they had asserted many times to him. For extended periods Miller had been crying and sobbing but he had been given no respite. Lord Taylor said that having considered the tenor and length of these interviews taken as a whole, "we are of opinion that they would have been oppressive and confessions obtained in consequence of them would have been unreliable even with a suspect of normal mental capacity".[56] In saying that the oppressive methods of conducting the interview would have made the confession unreliable the Court of Appeal indicated that when the oppression is bad enough there is overlap between section 76(2)(a) and 76(2)(b).

In the George Heron case in November 1993 the defendant was charged with the murder of seven-year old Nikki Allan. Mr Justice Mitchell at Leeds Crown Court ruled on the *voire dire* that confessions and admissions

---

[54] Transcript of decision of His Honour Judge Hutton at Gloucester Crown Court, April 22, 1988.

[55] n.34 above.

[56] Cp. *L* [1994] Crim.L.R. 839 C.A.—aggressive and hostile questioning held not to be either oppression or sufficient to render the confession unreliable. *Emmerson*, n.48 above is a similar case. It is always a question of the degree of pressure.

obtained from the defendant could not be admitted in evidence because they had been obtained through oppression. As a result the prosecution's case collapsed. Unlike the Cardiff Three case there had been no hectoring or shouting or aggressive language. Mr Justice Mitchell said[57]:

"But oppression may take more insidious forms. The hallmark of such forms contains, in my judgment, two elements, continuity and injustice ... Where these elements are combined and are systematically visited upon a suspect there is prima facie evidence of oppression ... The police, of course, are not prohibited from putting questions to a suspect merely because he chooses not to answer them. They are not required to accept any answer or answers a suspect chooses to give. Nor are they prohibited from being persistent, searching and robust in their questioning. If they do not believe what they are being told they are entitled to say so. Persistence must not, however, develop into bullying; robustness must not develop into insulting or gratuitously demeaning questions, nor must robustness be regarded as an acceptable label for what, in truth, is no more than a repetitive verbal pounding alleging the certainty of a suspect's guilt. The balance between questions and comment should be appropriate and comment should be kept to a minimum. Where the line is to be drawn between proper and robust persistence and oppressive interrogation, can only be identified in general terms."

There was no suggestion that Heron had been especially vulnerable or subject to any mental incapacity. He had had a legal executive with him throughout each of the 12 tapes of interviews. The PACE rules had been complied with. The judge allowed the first four tapes in as evidence. But he excluded the subsequent tapes on which Heron had made admissions and then confessed. A crucial factor the judge seems to have taken into account in ruling that the confessions were inadmissible on the grounds of oppression was the fact that the police repeatedly misrepresented the evidence as to identification by stating that there were witnesses who had seen him with the girl at critical times when there was in fact no clear identification. The judge said: "I have no hesitation in concluding that there came a time in that interview when the police began to act oppressively ... I regard it as oppressive to misrepresent repeatedly the evidence and/or the strength of the evidence in relation to a fact which, if true, would be a most compelling indicator of the defendant's responsibility for the child's death ... It was wrong, in the teeth of his constant denials to pound him with accusations of being a killer, pound him with sexual motives for taking her ... It was wrong, quite wrong, to tell him that it was in his interest to tell them the truth when they had made it all too clear that they regarded the truth that he was the killer. It was wrong, in the teeth of his denials about being the killer, to pound him with questions about why he had done it. This interview, in short, was a continuing injustice and at an early stage, in my judgment, it did become oppressive." He ruled that tapes five to eight recorded "a tale of continual injustice, such that it is, in my judgment, a tale of an insidious form of oppression". It amounted to an exercise in breaking the defendant's

---

[57] The quotations from the Heron judgment are taken from the transcript of the judgment of Mitchell J. at Leeds Crown Court on November 1, 1993.

resolve to make no admissions. "The means adopted to achieve that end meant, in effect, that regardless of the fact that his eventual confession may very well have been true, the prosecution were prevented from discharging the burden imposed upon them by the two limbs of Section 76(2)."

The cases together with answers to specific questions put to and answered by the trial judge in the case of Timothy West[58] permit the following general propositions about oppression. It would be oppressive to repeat a question dozens of times in order to gain an admission. It would be oppressive repeatedly to use abusive language, to shout at or bully the suspect, constantly to interrupt the suspect, or to pound him with allegations of guilt, with accusations that he is lying. It is legitimate to go over the same ground more than once but to do so for the umpteenth time becomes oppressive. It can also be oppressive to seek to break down the suspect's denials by false assertions as to the strength of the evidence held by the police.

Section 76(2)(b): unreliability

The second category of confession evidence that is wholly excluded is where it has been obtained "in consequence of anything said or done which was likely in the circumstances existing at the time, to render unreliable any confession which might be made by [the accused] in consequence thereof" (subs. (2)(b)).

This adopts the approach recommended by the Criminal Law Revision Committee that reliability should be the test. The fact that the section abandons the old approach of cases like *Northam* and *Zaveckas* (p. 217 above) is explicitly in Code C. As has been seen, this states that no police officer shall seek to obtain answers to questions by the use of oppression or "shall indicate, except in answer to a direct question, what action willl be taken on the part of the police if the person being interviewed answers questions, makes a statement or refuses to do either" (para. 11.3). However, if the suspect directly asks the officer "what action will be taken in the event of his answering questions, making a statement or refusing to do either, the officer may inform him what action he proposes to take in that event provided that the action is itself proper and warranted" (*ibid.*).

In other words, indications of threats or promises within the limits of what is lawful and proper will not render a confession inadmissible if they emerge as a result of questions from the suspect. This is a far cry from the traditional common law approach to these matters. But *Ping Lin* and *Rennie* (p. 218 above) could be said to have paved the way.

The proper interpretation of section 76(2)(b) has been considered in several reported cases. As will be seen, the courts have held that under section 76(2)(b) a confession can be excluded as unreliable even though there was no impropriety by the police, and even though the impropriety did not itself cause the confession.

"In consequence of anything said or done"

The section seems to require that the unreliability must arise as a result of the breaches of the law or the Codes—that there must be some causal

---

[58] See p. 223 above.

connection. Yet the court has on occasion applied subsection (2)(b) in circumstances where no such causal relationship could be said to exist between the breach of the rules and the confession. Thus in *Doolan*[59] the Court of Appeal held that the confession had been wrongly admitted after the police had failed to caution the suspect, failed to keep a contemporaneous record of the interview, failed to show him a subsequent note of the interview and failed to record the times of the interview. Only the first of these could logically have had any impact on the reliability of the confession (and that was something *not* done rather than something done) but the court cited subsection (2)(b) as the reason for holding that the evidence should have been excluded. (But see *Matthews, Voss, Dennison*.[60])

In *Goldenberg*[61] the Court of Appeal, as in *Matthews, Voss and Dennison*, took the view that there had to be a causal link between what was said and done and the resulting confession. The Court also held that the words "in consequence of anything said or done" meant said or done by someone other than the suspect. The court could not look at what the suspect himself had said or done. This seems too restrictive—and not required by the words of the subsection. However it may be that such a case could be dealt with adequately under the discretion to exclude evidence under section 78. In *Harvey*[62] the trial judge excluded a confession to a murder under section 76(2)(b) on the ground that it might have been made to protect the defendant's lesbian lover. The defendant was a woman of low I.Q., suffering from a psychopathic disorder aggravated by alcohol abuse. Nothing was "said or done" by the police to induce the confession.[63]

It is no longer necessary as it was at common law to confine the inquiry to what was done by persons in authority. (A confession similarly is defined in s.82(1) in such a way that a statement may be a confession, whether or not it is made to a person in authority.)

Examples:

Examples of things said or done which have been held to constitute grounds for holding a confession to be unreliable include: an offer of bail[64]; minimising the significance of a serious (sex) offence and suggesting that psychiatric help might be appropriate[65]; saying to a defendant who has previously denied the offence, "Do I gather that you are now admitting the offence?"[66]; falsely telling the suspect that his voice has been recognised on tape[67]; falsely telling the suspect that he has been identified by a witness,[68] indicating that the suspect will have to stay in the police station until the matter is cleared up.[69]

---

[59] [1988] Crim.L.R. 747 C.A.
[60] [1990] Crim.L.R. 190 C.A.
[61] [1988] Crim.L.R. 678 C.A.
[62] [1988] Crim.L.R. 241.
[63] See also *Crampton* (1991) 92 Cr.App.R. 369, [1991] Crim.L.R. 277 C.A., where the Court of Appeal thought that interviewing a suspect while he was withdrawing from heroin was not "doing or saying" anything within the concept of s.76(2)(b).
[64] *Barry* (1992) 95 Cr.App.R. 384 C.A.
[65] *Delaney* (1989) 88 Cr.App.R. 338 C.A.
[66] *Waters* [1989] Crim.L.R. 62 C.A.
[67] *Blake* [1989] 1 W.L.R. 432; Crim.L.R. 119 C.A.
[68] *Heron*, see text pp. 224–225 above.
[69] *Jasper* (April 25, 1994, Unreported) No. 93/6043/X5 C.A. *cf. Weeks* [1995] Crim.L.R. 52 C.A.

Examples of things *not* said or done which have been held to be grounds for holding a confession to be unreliable: failure to obtain a solicitor[70]; breaches in the provisions of Code C[71]; or failure to see that the suspect has an appropriate adult.[72] But such grounds will not *necessarily* result in the confession being held to be inadmissible.[73]

"Which was likely, in the circumstances existing at the time"

The test is objective and hypothetical. It is objective so that it is not what the police officers thought about the suspect's mental state but what it actually was.[74] It is hypothetical so that the court has to consider whether any confession which D might have made would be likely to be unreliable without taking into account whether in fact it was true.[75] The point was considered by the Criminal Law Revision Committee which produced the basic formula that has now been adopted. The essential feature of the test it thought "is that it applies not to the confession which the accused in fact made but to any confession which he might have made in consequence of the threat or inducement. On this scheme the judge should imagine that he was present at the interrogation and heard the threat or inducement. In the light of all the evidence given he will consider whether, at the point when the threat was uttered or the inducement offered, any confession which the accused might make as a result of it would be likely to be unreliable. If so, the confession would be inadmissible. For example, if the threat was to charge the suspect's wife jointly with him, the judge might think that a confession even of a serious offence would be likely to be unreliable. If there was a promise to release the accused on bail to visit a sick member of his family, the judge might think that this would be unlikely to render a confession of a serious offence unreliable but likely to do so in the case of a minor offence".[76] The mere fact that the police bring improper pressure (not amounting to oppression) to bear on the suspect would therefore not be enough. It must be improper pressure which would be likely to make the confession unreliable. There must be some likely causal link between the pressure and an unreliable confession.

When the same question was debated in Parliament, the Opposition moved an amendment that no one should be convicted on the basis of a confession obtained as a result of detention in which there had been any breach of Parts IV and V of the Act (dealing with Detention and the Questioning and Treatment of Persons by the Police), or from a juvenile or someone suffering from a mental disorder in response to police questioning

---

[70] *Trussler* [1988] Crim.L.R. 446 (Cr.Ct.); *McGovern* (1990) 92 Cr.App.R. 228 C.A.; *Chung* (1991) 92 Cr.App.R. 314 C.A.

[71] *Delaney* (1989) 88 Cr.App.R. 338 C.A.—"flagrant" breaches in regard to making a contemporaneous note; *Doolan* [1988] Crim.L.R. 747 C.A.—failure to caution as well as failure to make a record.

[72] See for instance *Everett* [1988] Crim.L.R. 826 C.A.; *Moss* (1990) 91 Cr.App.R. 371 C.A.; *Cox* [1991] Crim.L.R. 276 C.A.; *Morse* [1991] Crim.L.R. 195 (Cr.Ct.); *Glaves* [1993] Crim.L.R. 685 C.A.—in that case the evidence was excluded even though a solicitor had been present.

[73] See for instance *Waters* [1989] Crim.L.R. 62 C.A. where the Court of Appeal held that various breaches of Code did not render the confession unreliable. See to like effect *Maguire* (1990) 90 Cr.App.R. 115 C.A. In *Heath*, (Unreported), Case No. 1757/A3/88 the Court of Appeal held that wrongly denying access to a solicitor and wrongly delaying making notes did not render the admissions unreliable since they were made to a co-defendant. See also *Tyrer* (1990) 90 Cr.App.R. 446 C.A.

[74] *R. v. Everett* [1988] Crim.L.R. 826 C.A.

[75] See *Cox* [1991] Crim.L.R. 276 C.A.; and *McGovern* (1991) 92 Cr.App.R. 228 C.A.

[76] *op. cit.* n.2 above, p. 201, pp. 43–44.

without a responsible adult being present unless there was corroboration of the confession. The Government resisted the amendment, but the former Home Office Minister Mr Mellor said that in his view "most, if not all the circumstances set out in the amendment render the confession unreliable".[77]

In several cases the "circumstances existing at the time" have been held to be the fact that the suspect was highly suggestible or vulnerable by virtue of low I.Q. or mental incapacity.[78] In *Silcott, Braithwaite and Raghip* the Court of Appeal held that medical or psychiatric evidence as to the defendant's likely mental state at the time of the interview could be taken into account. (See to the same effect also *McKenzie*.[79]) But *cf. Heaton*[80] where the Court of Appeal (with Lord Chief Justice, Lord Taylor, presiding),[81] approved the decision of the trial judge not to permit evidence of a psychiatrist to the effect that H was not bright and was abnormally suggestible. Unless the evidence was based on scientific data or expert analysis outside the experience of the judge and jury a mere impression even of a highly qualified doctor was not admissible.

Professor D.J. Birch believes that the courts have failed to focus sufficiently on the question of reliability. The fact that Code provisions have been broken, she suggests, does not necessarily mean that a resultant confession is *likely* to be unreliable ("were the Criminal Law Revision Committee to report on developments to date they would surely repeat their criticisms, with breaches of the Code taking the place of threats or inducements as the obstacles to the proper consideration of reliability").[82]

Confessions can of course be challenged not only under section 76 but also under section 78 (p. 232 below) and section 82(3) (p. 250 below).

Procedure

In *Barry*[83] the Court of Appeal said the first step under section 76(2)(b) was to identify everything that had been said and done. The second stage was for the judge to consider whether anything said or done was likely to render unreliable anything said or done in consequence. The test was hypothetical. The third stage was for the judge to ask himself whether the prosecution had proved beyond reasonable doubt that the confession had not been made as a consequence of anything said or done.

If the prosecution case depends entirely on confession evidence and the defendant suffers from a significant degree of mental handicap, the trial judge should withdraw the case from the jury if the confessions are unconvincing to a point where a properly directed jury could not convict on them—see the Court of Appeal's important decision in *McKenzie*.[84]

Section 76 read literally requires that the issue of admissibility be determined before the evidence is given. The court must not allow the evidence to be given until its admissibility is established if it is represented by

[77] House of Commons, *Hansard*, Standing Committee, March 8, 1984, Col. 1657.
[78] See for instance *Everett* [1988] Crim.L.R. 826 C.A.; *Dutton, The Independent* December 5, 1988 C.A.; *Moss* (1989) 91 Cr.App.R. 371 C.A.; *Delaney* (1988) Cr.App.Rep. 338 C.A.; *Silcott, Braithwaite and Raghip, The Times* December 9, 1991.
[79] (1993) 96 Cr.App.R. 58 C.A.
[80] [1993] Crim.L.R. 593 C.A.
[81] Lord Taylor had presided also in *McKenzie* and in *Miller, Paris and Abdullai*.
[82] D.J. Birch, "The Evidence Provisions", N.I.L.Q., 1989, 411 at 419.
[83] (1992) 95 Cr.App.R. 384 C.A.
[84] (1993) 96 Cr.App.R. 58 C.A.

the defendant that the confession is inadmissible (subs. (2)); and the same applies where the court of its own motion requires proof of admissibility (subs. (3)). Subsections (2) and (3) both specify that this applies to "any proceedings".

In 1982 the Divisional Court said that a trial within a trial was not an appropriate procedure in a magistrates' court.[85] But whether it was intended by Parliament or not, PACE has changed this. The requirement of a trial within a trial has been held to apply not only to trials in the crown court but equally to those in magistrates' courts: *R. v. Liverpool Juvenile Court, ex p. R.*[86] The Divisional Court granted an application for judicial review after the justices had declined an application by the prosecution (supported by the defence) for the court to hold a trial within a trial to consider the admissibility of a confession. The Divisional Court ruled that a *voire dire* must be held if it was "represented" that a confession was inadmissible. The defendant's evidence could be confined to the issue of admissibility without prejudice to his right to be silent at the trial proper. The court was not concerned at that stage with the truth or otherwise of the confession. The defendant was entitled to a ruling on admissibility before or at the end of the prosecution's case. It should not be necessary to call the prosecution's evidence relating to the obtaining of a confession twice.

As to timing, until recently it seemed that the defendant had both a discretion as to whether to raise the issue of admissibility as a preliminary matter and, if so, a second opportunity of attacking the admissibility of the evidence when it came to making his own case. Thus in *ex p. R.*[87] the Divisional Court ruled that a trial within a trial would only take place before the close of the prosecution case if the defence made representations (or, presumably, if the court took the point under subs. (3)). If no such representation was made, the defence could raise the question of admissibility as much as that of weight at any subsequent stage of the trial. This was the position recognised pre-PACE in the decision of the Judicial Committee of the Privy Council of *Ajodha v. The State.*[88]

In the pre-PACE decision of *Watson*[89] the Court of Appeal held that a judge was not prevented from reconsidering a decision on admissibility taken at a trial within a trial. He retained control over the evidence to be submitted to the jury throughout the trial. So if at a later stage further evidence emerged relevant to the voluntariness of the confession it could be the basis of a ruling to exclude the evidence. But such occasions would obviously be rare.

Both these principles were rejected by the Court of Appeal in *Sat-Bhambra.*[90] The trial judge had ruled that six of 10 tapes of recorded conversations between the accused and Customs officers were inadmissible because of the possible effects of medication given to the defendant who was a diabetic. Four other tapes were admitted. Before the jury the doctor put his view about the accused's medical condition even more strongly than on the

[85] *F. v. Kent Chief Constable* [1982] Crim.L.R. 682 (Cr.Ct.).
[86] [1988] Q.B. 1; Crim.L.R. 572 Div.Ct. For comment see Robert Stevens, "Trials within Trials in the Magistrates' Courts: A Panoramic View", J.P.N., August 22, 1988, p. 531.
[87] *R. v. Liverpool Juvenile Court, ex p. R* [1988] Q.B. 1 Div.Ct.
[88] [1982] A.C. 202 (P.C.).
[89] [1980] 1 W.L.R. 991 C.A.
[90] (1988) 88 Cr.App.R 55; [1988] Crim.L.R. 453 C.A.

voire dire and the defence submitted that the evidence of the four tapes should also be excluded. The judge said that he was precluded from doing so by the terms of section 76. The Court of Appeal agreed. If a defendant wished to exclude a confession under section 76 he had to raise the issue before the confession was given in evidence. He could not do so afterwards. Once the judge had ruled on section 76, the section ceased to have effect—and (*obiter*) the same applied to section 78. *Watson*, the Court of Appeal ruled, had not survived PACE. The judge could however avoid injustice either by applying section 82(3) (see p. 250 below) or by directing the jury either to disregard the evidence or on weight. He could even discharge the jury and order a retrial.

It seems unsatisfactory that the court should lose its rights to reconsider the issue of admissibility after an initial ruling on the *voire dire*. It is to be hoped that the Court of Appeal will decide that its *obiter dictum* in *Sat-Bhambra* on the effect of section 78 was wrong and that *Watson* did survive PACE in the sense that a judge can still withdraw evidence from a jury (or in the case of the bench treat it as inadmissible) even after first admitting it.[91]

Confessions by mentally handicapped persons: section 77[92]

This section requires a judge in cases brought against persons who are mentally handicapped to warn the jury of the need for special caution before convicting such an accused in reliance on his confession. The judge has to give this warning where the case against the accused depends wholly or mainly on his confession where he is satisfied that the confession was not made in the presence of an independent person. A confession made to friends is not made to "independent persons" within the meaning of the section.[93] If the case is a summary one in a magistrates' court, the bench are required to treat it in the same way "as one in which there is a special need for caution before convicting the accused on his confession" (subs. (2)). There is no need for a section 77 warning however if the prosecution's case is equally strong without the confession.[94]

A person is mentally handicapped for the purposes of this section if the court is satisfied that he "is in a state of arrested or incomplete development of mind which includes significant impairment of intelligence and social

---

[91] A similar view was expressed forcibly by Professor J.C. Smith in a comment on the case: [1988] Crim.L.R. 454–455. Professor Smith argued that it was difficult to see why section 76 should be thought to have had this effect or why the common law position should be thought to have been changed. See to like effect Professor D.J. Birch commenting on *Millard* [1987] Crim.L.R. 196, 198 and J.K. Bentil, *op. cit.* n.41 above. But see *Davis* [1990] Crim.L.R. 860. In *Marshall (Mark)*, *The Times*, December 28, 1992, the Court of Appeal quashed the conviction on the ground of problems with the confession despite the fact that the defence failed to object to the confession evidence being given until the end of the prosecution's case. In *Sayer*, (Unreported), Case No. 72223/F3/86 the Court of Appeal said that trial had taken place before the decision in *Sat-Bhambra*. However where evidence was heard and then a submission was made the judge was not powerless. He had powers under s.82(3) "to take such decision as he thinks fit to ensure fairness both to the prosecution...and to the defendant".

[92] See N.I. PACE Order, Art. 75.

[93] *Bailey*, *The Times*, January 26, 1995 C.A. A conviction for murder and arson was quashed and a retrial ordered because the judge did not give the section 77 warning where the defendant had confessed first to friends and then later to the police.

[94] *Campbell*, [1995] Crim.L.R. 157 C.A.

functioning" (subs. (3)). Whereas the Codes of Practice generally treat the mentally handicapped and the mentally disordered in the same way, the section does not mention the mentally disordered at all. (This may have been simply due to oversight. The section was the result of a last minute amendment to the Bill.)

There have not been many cases on the interpretation of section 77—partly perhaps because cases that might have raised the issue of a section 77 warning have instead been dealt with as issues of admissibility under sections 76 or 78. In *Lamont*[95] however the Court of Appeal quashed a conviction for attempted murder and assault occasioning bodily harm where the judge had failed to give the warning. The defendant was mentally sub-normal with the reading age of a child of eight and an I.Q. of 73. There was little evidence of the offence other than his confession. The Court of Appeal said that giving the section 77 warning was "an essential part of a fair summing up". It substituted a verdict of assault occasioning bodily harm.

Exclusion of "unfair evidence": section 78[96]

The common law

The English common law tradition in regard to the exclusion of improperly obtained evidence, other than confessions, was that such evidence was basically admissible subject to a rarely exercised judicial discretion to exclude it. This approach was in marked contrast to that of the common law in regard to confession evidence where, as has been seen, the judges adopted a much more rigorous rule.

The leading authority was *Kuruma, Son of Kaniu v. R.*[97] in which, on an appeal from Kenya, the Judicial Committee of the Privy Council held that if evidence was relevant, it mattered not how it was obtained. The accused in that case had been convicted of being in unlawful possession of ammunition discovered during the course of a search by an officer of a lower rank than the rules required for such searches. But the Board recognised that a judge always had a discretion to exclude evidence in a criminal case if the rules of admissibility would operate unfairly against the accused. Lord Goddard C.J. said that if evidence was admissible "the court is not concerned with how the evidence was obtained" but he went on to say "no doubt in a criminal case the judge always has a discretion to disallow evidence if the strict rules of admissibility would operate unfairly against the accused ... If, for instance, some admission of some piece of evidence, *e.g.* a document, had been obtained from a defendant by a trick, no doubt the judge might properly rule it out".[98]

The continuing existence of the judicial discretion to exclude improperly obtained evidence was confirmed by the Divisional Court in *Jeffrey v. Black* in 1978.[99] The accused was arrested for the suspected theft of a sandwich in a

[95] [1989 Crim.L.R. 813 C.A.
[96] See N.I. PACE Order, Art. 76(2)(b) excludes trials on indictment for scheduled offences under the Northern Ireland (Emergency Provisions) Act 1978, s.8, but the tests under Art. 76 and s.8 are very similar: see *Mullan* [1988] N.I.J.B. 36 and D.J. Birch, "The Evidence Provisions", 1989 N.I.L.Q. 411, 427–429.
[97] [1955] A.C. 197.
[98] *ibid.* p. 204.
[99] [1978] 1 Q.B. 490 (Div.Ct.).

pub. The police then went to his home where they discovered drugs. The court held that this search had been unlawful since it was not for the offence for which he was arrested. But they went on to consider whether the evidence should nevertheless have been admitted. Lord Widgery, the Lord Chief Justice, said: "... the justices sitting in this case, like any other criminal tribunal in England sitting under the English law, have a general discretion to decline to allow any evidence to be called by the prosecution if they think it would be unfair or oppressive to allow that to be done. ... It is a discretion which every criminal judge has all the time in respect of all the evidence which is tendered by the prosecution."[1] The discretion, he went on, would be rarely used. "But if the case is exceptional, if the case is such that not only have the police officers entered without authority, but they have been guilty of trickery or they have misled someone, or they have been oppressive or they have been unfair, or in other respects they have behaved in a manner which is morally reprehensible, then it is open to the justices to apply their discretion and decline to allow the particular evidence to be let in as part of the trial."[2]

But in 1979 in *R. v. Sang*[3] the House of Lords drastically reduced the scope of the common law discretion to exclude improperly obtained evidence. Lord Diplock in the leading judgment said that there were dicta suggesting that the courts had a general discretion to exclude evidence. There were in fact no decisions that supported such dicta. The fountain-head for all subsequent dicta on the subject was Lord Goddard's statement in *Kuruma* (cited p. 232 above). But properly understood this was an example of evidence obtained unfairly from the accused which came within the category of protecting his right not to incriminate himself. *Payne*[4] was a similar case. The court there excluded the evidence of a doctor who said the accused had been drunk while driving, on the ground that the motorist had been told that the doctor would only be looking to see whether he was ill or injured. He was specifically assured by the police that the doctor would not be asked to give an opinion about his sobriety. Lord Parker C.J. said the doctor's evidence should be excluded as a matter of discretion on the basis that, if the motorist had known the true position, he might have refused to subject himself to examination. But apart from *Payne*, Lord Diplock said: "there never has been a case in which these courts have come across conduct so unfair, so tricky or so oppressive as to justify them in holding that the discretion ought to have been exercised in favour of exclusion."[5] The fact was that the common law discretion was not wide, but very narrow. The courts were not concerned with how evidence was obtained but merely with how it was used by the prosecution at the trial. Save in regard to confessions or admissions or evidence obtained directly from the accused himself, a judge had no discretion to exclude evidence simply on the ground that it had been improperly obtained. The only broad principle of exclusion was where the prejudicial effect of the evidence greatly outweighed its probative effect. It followed that if, as in *Sang*, evidence had been improperly obtained by use of an *agent provocateur* that was not a basis for discretionary exclusion.

---

[1] *ibid.* pp. 497–498.
[2] *ibid.*
[3] [1980] A.C. 402; [1979] 2 All E.R. 1222 (H.C.).
[4] [1963] 1 W.L.R. 637.
[5] [1980] A.C. 402 at 435; [1979] All E.R. 1222 at 1229.

The Philips Royal Commission and PACE

The Philips Royal Commission considered whether the courts ought to be given a broad exclusionary rule. It was invited by some witnesses to recommend some form of exclusionary rule of evidence. In the United States illegally obtained evidence is generally inadmissible and various bodies giving evidence to the Commission argued for the adoption of such a rule. But the Royal Commission was not persuaded. It said that experience in the United States did not suggest that such a rule significantly deterred improper police conduct. It could only affect the small numbers of cases in which the defendant ultimately pleaded not guilty. It operated many months after the event. The proper way to check police misconduct was through actions for damages or disciplinary action by the police themselves.[6] The Commission's views on this issue were much criticised in some quarters.[7]

Neither Mr Whitelaw's nor Mr Brittan's version of the Police and Criminal Evidence Bill initially addressed the problem. But at a very late stage the question suddenly surfaced as one of importance and the Government decided after all to react to the pressure that was developing. The initiative was taken by Lord Scarman who moved an amendment at the Committee stage in the House of Lords to give the courts a discretion to exclude evidence that had arguably been unlawfully obtained unless the prosecution could prove beyond reasonable doubt that it had been lawfully obtained or that the illegality was of no material significance or that the overriding interests of justice required that it be allowed in as evidence notwithstanding that it was obtained unlawfully.

The Lord Chancellor, Lord Hailsham, said that he was against the amendment but that there was a case for some form of discretion to be exercised by the judge when to admit the evidence would be unfair to the accused. On that basis Lord Scarman withdrew his amendment.[8]

On the Report stage in the House of Lords, Lord Scarman returned to the point with a similar, though slightly redrafted, amendment. But this time the Lord Chancellor himself proffered his own amendment which would have given the courts a discretion to exclude evidence but only where it was obtained from the accused himself. The court would have a discretion to exclude any evidence obtained from the accused if it appeared to the court, "that, having regard to all circumstances, including the circumstances in which the evidence was obtained, the admission of the evidence would be so prejudicial to the fairness of those proceedings that the court ought not to allow it to be given".

The House of Lords debated Lord Scarman's amendment first. Against the advice of the Lord Chancellor, it was approved by 125 votes to 118. In the light of the result Lord Hailsham's amendment was not debated.[9]

But, the Government decided not to accept Lord Scarman's amendment. Mr Leon Brittan, the then Home Secretary, told the House of Commons that

---

[6] Philips Report, paras. 4.123–4.128.
[7] See for instance J. Driscoll, "Excluding Illegally Obtained Evidence—Can we learn from the United States", *Legal Action Group Bulletin*, June, 1981, p. 131. See also generally J.D. Heydon, "Illegally Obtained Evidence" [1973] Crim.L.R. 690; A.J. Ashworth, "Excluding Evidence as Protecting Rights" [1977] Crim.L.R. 723. For a comparison with the U.S.A. see P. Hartman, "Admissibility of Evidence Obtained by Illegal Search and Seizure under the U.S. Constitution", (1965) 28 M.L.R. 298. See now also William J. Stuntz, "The American Exclusionary Rule and Defendants' Changing Rights" [1989] Crim.L.R. 117.
[8] House of Lords, *Hansard*, July 11, 1984, Cols. 931–948.
[9] House of Lords, *Hansard*, July 31, 1984, Cols. 635–675.

the reason was partly that it would lead to the acquittal of guilty persons for reasons that were insufficiently related to the fairness of the case and partly to avoid excessive burdens on the courts of "trials within trials".[10] Instead he brought forward a new Government amendment. This was broadly the same as the clause originally introduced by Lord Hailsham with the difference that the evidence covered by the clause was no longer limited to that obtained from the accused himself. The new clause became section 78 which provides: "In any proceedings the court may refuse to allow evidence on which the prosecution proposes to rely to be given if it appears to the court that, having regard to all the circumstances, including the circumstances in which the evidence was obtained, the admission of the evidence would have such an adverse effect on the fairness of the proceedings that the court ought not to admit it."

It is an irony that this absolutely last-minute addition to the Bill became by far the most used as well as the most important section of the Act. It is fitting that the person mainly responsible for its introduction should have been Lord Scarman.

In *Mason*[11] the Court of Appeal said that section 78 "in our opinion, does no more than to restate the power which judges had at common law before the 1984 Act was passed". It is difficult to see how this could have been right since it seems obvious that the formula in section 78 is significantly different from that laid down by the House of Lords in *Sang*.[12] In *Fulling* Lord Lane C.J. said that the 1984 Act was a codifying act and had to be looked at on its own wording.[13]

This view is supported by the fact that section 82(3) states: "Nothing in this Part of this Act shall prejudice any power of a court to exclude evidence (whether by preventing questions from being put or otherwise) at its discretion." The statutory scheme seems therefore to have been that section 82(3) preserved the common law exclusionary rule whilst section 78 gave the courts a broader power of exclusion than was recognised by Sang.

Lord Diplock said in *Sang* that there was not a single recorded case in which the Court of Criminal Appeal or the Court of Appeal Criminal Division had allowed an appeal on the ground that magistrates or the trial judge ought to have excluded evidence because the evidence had been obtained "unfairly or by trickery or in some other way that is morally reprehensible".[14] But in the years since January 1, 1986 there have been many such cases under section 78.

Some commentators took the view at the time that, given their historic marked reluctance to exclude improperly obtained evidence, the courts would be likely to interpret the section narrowly. Perhaps even serious impropriety by the police might not result in the evidence being excluded since judges might take the view that it did not affect the fairness of the *proceedings*.

In 1990 a Canadian commentator, Mark Gelowitz, suggested that almost

[10] House of Commons, *Hansard*, October 29, 1984, Cols. 1012–1013.
[11] [1988] 1 W.L.R. 139 at 144; [1987] 3 All E.R. 481 at 484 C.A.
[12] See however *Apicella* (1985) 82 Cr.App.R. 295 C.A. decided a month before PACE came into force. The C.A., giving a much broader interpretation to *Sang* than seemed correct, said that a court could exclude prosecution evidence if its admission would have "such an adverse effect on the fairness of the proceedings that the court ought not to admit it". This was virtually to anticipate section 78.
[13] [1987] Q.B. 426 at 431–432 C.A. See to the same effect the Court of Appeal's decisions in *Samuel* [1988] 2 W.L.R. 920 at 934; (1987) 87 Cr.App.R. 232 at 245 and *O'Leary* (1988) 87 Cr.App.R. 387 at 391.
[14] [1980] A.C. 402 at 435; [1979] 2 All E.R. 1222 at 1229.

the only use for section 78 was in regard to confession evidence and that on the basis of the post-PACE cases as at that date, the courts seemed unlikely to depart from their traditional unwillingness to exclude improperly obtained real evidence.[15] He was perfectly correct that most of the cases brought under section 78 were (and have remained) confession cases. Section 78 quickly became a kind of adjunct to section 76. The judges showed themselves prepared to apply either, with little concern to keep the sections distinct. Indeed there were far more confession cases dealt with under section 78 then under section 76.

"In the only cases in which the Court of Appeal has been invited to exclude non-confession evidence pursuant to section 78," Gelowitz said, "it has declined to do so".[16] Where lower courts had excluded probative real evidence they had done so on the basis of unsound principles and in a way that was inconsistent with the language of section 78.[17]

Gelowitz submitted that real evidence, however obtained, could *never* affect the fairness of the proceedings. "Real evidence, such as a gun carrying the accused's fingerprints, or drugs found on the accused's person, is neutral as between the accused and the Crown. It simply exists and tells its story unaided. Its essence and inculpatory effect is neither enhanced nor diminished by the manner of its acquisition. It is pure proof." This, he suggested, was the approach adopted in 1955 by Lord Goddard C.J. in *Kurama*. It was the same as the view taken in 1971 by the Supreme Court of Canada: "The allowance of admissible evidence relevant to the issue before the court and of substantial value may operate unfortunately for the accused, but not unfairly."[18] By contrast, evidence that a confession is unreliable or that it has been obtained through undue pressure *could* be said to operate unfairly against the accused. Mark Gelowitz suggested that section 78 would prove to be little different from the previous common law.

But now, only a few years later, this prediction can be seen to have been wrong. The cases show that English courts have completely abandoned the amoral common law tradition of receiving non-confession evidence regardless of how it was obtained. There have been many cases in which the courts have used section 78 to reject both confession and non-confession evidence because of the improper way it was obtained. There have not as yet been any cases involving "a gun with the fingerprints". The cases have concerned less dramatic matters. But the principle has been solidly established. As has already been seen, there have for instance been quite a number of cases in which the courts have rejected identification evidence because the police failed to comply with the PACE procedures—see p. 194 above and pp. 239, 240 below. Thus in *Gall*[19] a conviction for affray was quashed by the Court of Appeal because the investigating officer spoke to the identification officer at the identification parade, contrary to the rules of Code D.[20]

---

[15] Mark Gelowitz, "Section 78 of the Police and Criminal Evidence Act 1984: middle ground or no man's land?" 106 *Law Qtrly. Rev.* 327 (1990).

[16] *op. cit.* p. 329. He instanced *O'Leary* (1988) 87 Cr.App.R. 387 C.A.— identification evidence; and *Harwood* [1989] Crim.L.R. 285 C.A.—entrapment is no defence.

[17] He instanced *Fennelley* [1989] Crim.L.R. 142—heroin found after a stop and search which did not comply with the procedural requirements.

[18] *Wray* [1971] S.C.R. 272 at 293.

[19] (1990) 90 Cr.App.R. 64, [1989] Crim.L.R. 745 C.A.

[20] See also for instance *Conway* (1990) 91 Cr.App.R. 143, [1990] Crim.L.R. 402 C.A.; *Nagah* (1991) 92 Cr.App.R. 344, [1991] Crim.L.R. 55 C.A.; *Finley* [1993] Crim.L.R. 50 C.A.; *Kensett* (1993) 157 J.P. 1116 (Dir. Ct.); *Knowles* [1994] Crim.L.R. 217 C.A.; *Ladlow, Moss, Green and Jackson* [1989] Crim.L.R. 219 (Cr.Ct.).

But perhaps even stronger are the drink driving cases where the courts have rejected the scientific (*i.e.* even more "real") evidence of intoxication because of the way the evidence was obtained.[21] In *Sharpe*, for instance, there was dangerous driving, a police car chase and the defendant was found to be way over the alcohol limit. In spite of those strong facts, the Divisional Court quashed the conviction of driving with excess alcohol because the police, having followed him home, had dragged the motorist from his own driveway onto the road where he was required to undergo a breath test. Buckley J. said he put his decision "on the grounds of oppression by the police officers in their general conduct, in particular in his driveway".[22]

It cannot be said that the courts have articulated a consistent and all-embracing theory for the application of section 78. Various principles explaining the exercise of the discretion to exclude evidence have been suggested by academic commentators. These include the Reliability principle (to promote the reliability of evidence), the Disciplinary principle (to penalise the police for breaches of the rules as a way of promoting adherence to the rules), and the Protective principle (to protect the accused).[23] Many cases could be said to fall within those broad approaches—though there is little or no sign that the judges themselves deal with the problems in that way. The evidence from the cases is to the contrary.[24]

The writer believes rather that section 78 has become both established and accepted as a means for the courts to determine what breaches of the rules or improper conduct are unacceptable on a case by case basis without any clearly articulated theory. Usually, even when there has been some breach or impropriety the court allows the evidence in and even when it finds there to have been impropriety, the Court of Appeal usually ends by dismissing the appeal. But there have also been many cases, including non-confession cases, in which the appeal court has quashed a conviction because of such improprieties. In the great majority of such cases the court's chief concern seems to be that the verdict should be based on reliable evidence. But sometimes, the court is expressing a more fundamental concern directed not so much to the result in the particular case as to a view that the system demands a minimum of procedural correctness and moral integrity.[25]

To some extent the decisions of the courts applying section 78 can be systematised. Certain basic distinctions have emerged. But there remains (and will always remain) a significant and irreducible degree of discretion left to the court. Professor Diane Birch, writing about the entrapment cases, has suggested that "The more principled the discretion can be said to be, and the more its underlying aims can be articulated, the more consistent will be

---

[21] Compare the House of Lords' decision in *Fox* [1986] A.C. 281, given before PACE with *D.P.P. v. McGladrigan* (1991) 155 J.P. 785 (Div.Ct.), *D.P.P. v. Godwin* [1991] R.T.R. 303 (Div.Ct.) and *Sharpe (George Hugo) v. D.P.P.* (1993) 158 J.P. 595 (Div.Ct.). It seems clear that *Thomas* [1990] Crim.L.R. 269 (Div.Ct.) was wrongly decided in holding that section 78 could only be applied where there were *mala fides.*
[22] At p. 597. See to like effect the earlier case of *Matto v. D.P.P.* [1987] R.T.R. 337 (Div.Ct.). But see also two recent "real" evidence cases *Cooke* [1995] Crim.L.R. 497 (C.A.) and *Stewart* [1995] Crim.L.R. 500 (C.A.).
[23] See especially A.J. Ashworth, "Excluding Evidence as Protecting Rights" [1977] Crim.L.R. 723 and A.A.S. Zuckerman, *The Principles of Criminal Evidence* (1989).
[24] See also M. Hunter, "Judicial Discretion: Section 78 in Practice" [1994] Crim.L.R. 558 reporting on an empirical study in Leeds Crown Court. The judges she interviewed were unanimous in rejecting the idea that they considered any of these theoretical principles when deciding whether to exclude disputed evidence. The writer cannot say he is surprised at this finding which would probably be equally true of the Court of Appeal.
[25] See further Ian Dennis, "Reconstructing the Law of Criminal Evidence" [1989] 42 *Current Legal Problems* 21; and A.A.S. Zuckerman, "Illegally Obtained Evidence: Discretion as a Guardian of Legitimacy" [1987] 40 *Current Legal Problems* 55.

the decisions made under it."[26] She cites another academic view of the need to avoid the "mushiness and unpredictability of a general doctrine of exclusion for 'unfairness'".[27] Consistency in the application of a discretion to exclude evidence on the grounds of unfairness may be desirable but in the end it is unattainable. We will instead have to be content with the fact that the courts sometimes are prepared to give expression to their view that the unfairness was such as to require that the evidence be rejected.

By far the most common basis for the Court of Appeal to apply section 78 has been "significant and substantial" breaches of the PACE rules. There are now a very great number of such decisions—too many to include here. What follows is an indication of the case law under the different main headings.

Evidence held not admissible because of breaches of PACE and or the Codes

D not told his rights—*Gokan and Hassan,*[28] *Sanusi,*[29] *Absolam,*[30] *Oransaye*[31]

D not given access to a solicitor—*Samuel,*[31a] *Parris,*[32] *Walsh,*[33] *Chung,*[34] *Silcott*[35]

D not cautioned—*Doolan,*[36] *Sparks,*[37] *Hunt,*[38] *Okafor,*[39] *Bryce,*[40] *Weerdestyn*[41]

D not provided with an appropriate adult—*Fogah,*[42] *Dutton,*[43] *Coker and Marshall,*[44] *Weekes,*[45] *Glaves*[46]

---

[26] "Excluding evidence from entrapment: what is a 'fair cop'?" [1994] 47 *Current Legal Problems* 73, at p. 89.
[27] J.D. Heydon, "Entrapment and unfairly obtained evidence in the House of Lords" [1980] Crim.L.R. 129 at 134.
[28] [1990] Crim.L.R. 185 C.A.
[29] [1992] Crim.L.R. 43 C.A.
[30] (1988) Cr.App.R. 332 C.A.—*cf. Iroegbu* (1988) *The Times*, August 2, C.A.
[31] [1993] Crim.L.R. 722 C.A.
[31a] [1988] Q.B. 615; [1988] 2 W.L.R. 920 C.A.
[32] (1989) 89 Cr.App.R. 68; [1989] Cr.App.R. 214 C.A.
[33] (1989) 91 Cr.App.R. 161; [1989] Crim.L.R. 822 C.A.
[34] (1991) 92 Cr.App.R. 314; [1991] Crim.L.R. 622 C.A.
[35] *The Times*, December 9, 1991 C.A.
[36] [1988] Crim.L.R. 747 C.A. But the court applied the proviso.
[37] [1991] Crim.L.R. 128 C.A. But the court applied the proviso.
[38] [1992] Crim.L.R. 582 C.A. The court allowed the appeal.
[39] [1994] Crim.L.R. 221 C.A. But the court applied the proviso.
[40] (1992) 95 Cr.App.R. 230, [1992] 4 All E.R. 567, [1992] Crim.L.R. 728 C.A. Undercover police officer. The conviction was quashed for failure to caution.
[41] [1995] Crim.L.R. 239.
[42] (1989) 90 Cr.App.R. 115 C.A.
[43] (1988) *The Independent*, December 5, C.A.
[44] (August 6, 1990, Unreported) Case No. T900616 (C.C.C.). The police had no reason to suppose that the suspect was in the bottom 1 per cent of the intellectual range of the population. He gave long and coherent replies to proper and unoppressive questioning in regard to a rape charge. But the judge excluded his confession on the ground that the Code proceeds on the basis that without an appropriate adult confessions "are or maybe inherently unreliable". The judge said "Whatever ... the practical advantages may in reality [be] derive[d] from the presence of such adults, it is the intention and spirit of the legislation of Parliament which the courts must loyally observe".
[45] [1993] Crim.L.R. 211 C.A.
[46] [1993] Crim.L.R. 685 C.A.

Interview formalities not complied with—*Doolan,*[47] *Manji,*[48] *Chung,*[49] *Hunt,*[50] *Scott,*[51] *Townend,*[52] *Keenan,*[53] *Rowe,*[54] *Joseph,*[55] *Gizzi*[56]

Initial breach contaminates later interviews—*Canale,*[57] *Wilkinson,*[58] *Bryce,*[59] *McGovern,*[60] *Wood,*[61] *Ismail,*[62] *Neill,*[63] *Glaves,*[64] (*cf. Y v. D.P.P.,*[65] *Gillard,*[66] *Madeley,*[67] *Doran,*[68] *Barrell, Cooke and Cooke*[69])

Identification procedures not complied with: *Conway,*[70] *Payne and Quinn,*[71]

---

[47] n.36 above.

[48] [1990] Crim.L.R. 512 C.A.

[49] (1991) 92 Cr.App.R. 314 C.A.. The Court of Appeal found it "quite astonishing" that four officers had not between them managed to make a contemporaneous note of an interview with the defendant whilst his home was being searched. Held: that this (together with unlawful delay of access to a solicitor) could have made the confession unreliable (which could not have been the case) or the record unreliable (which is not relevant under s.76(2)(b)).

[50] n.38 above.

[51] [1991] Crim.L.R. 56 C.A.

[52] (Unreported), Case No. 5860/X2/88 C.A.

[53] (1990) 90 Cr.App.R. 1 [1989] Crim.L.R. 720 C.A. The court said that breaches must be "significant and substantial" to justify exclusion under sections 76 or 78. If the defendant intended not to give evidence if the officer's evidence was excluded, admitting it unfairly robbed him of his right to remain silent. Also by attacking the police evidence he put his character in evidence.

[54] [1994] Crim.L.R. 837 C.A—but the court applied the proviso.

[55] [1993] Crim.L.R. 206 C.A.

[56] (July 15, 1993, Unreported) Case No. 92/5227/Y5 C.A.

[57] (1989) 91 Cr.App.R. 1 [1990] Crim.L.R. 329 C.A. The court said the importance of the rules relating to contemporaneous noting of interviews could scarcely be over-emphasised. The object was twofold: "not merely to ensure, so far as possible that the suspect's remarks are accurately recorded and that he has an opportunity when he goes through the contemporaneous note afterwards of checking each answer and initialling each answer, but likewise it is protection for the police, to ensure, so far as is possible, that it cannot be suggested that they induced the suspect to confess by improper approaches or improper promises".

[58] (Unreported), Case No. 91/4143/WA C.A.

[59] n.40 above.

[60] (1991) 92 Cr.App.R. 228 C.A.

[61] [1994] Crim.L.R. 222 C.A. The court said that where there had been oppression or an inducement in an earlier interview, it may be more difficult for the prosecution to prove that it has not carried through to a later interview. But in the case of a person of normal intellect who has had the opportunity of a full discussion with his solicitor before the later interview, the crown may be able to discharge the burden.

[62] [1990] Crim.L.R. 109 C.A.

[63] [1994] Crim.L.R. 441 C.A. Fatal stabbing. The court held that the question whether later unobjectionable interviews are contaminated by breaches in earlier interviews is a question of fact and degree. Were the breaches of a fundamental and continuing character, and if so, was the accused given a sufficient opportunity to make an informed decision whether to retract what he had previously said?

[64] n.46 above.

[65] [1991] Crim.L.R. 917 C.A.

[66] (1991) 92 Cr.App.R. 61; [1991] Crim.L.R. 280 C.A.

[67] (March 18, 1992, Unreported) C.A.

[68] (February 6, 1990, Unreported), Case No. 88/7185/Y2 C.A.

[69] (February 21, 1992, Unreported), Case No. 89/3403/S C.A. There is no hard and fast rule that because earlier tapes are held inadmissible, the same will apply to later ones.

[70] (1990) 91 Cr.App.Rep. 143, [1990] Crim.L.R. 402 C.A. Conviction quashed because there was a dock identification rather than an identity parade. No reference was made either by counsel or the court to section 78. In *North Yorkshire Trading Standards Department v. Williams* November 22, 1994 the Divisional Court said that dock identification was generally undesirable even where the prosecution had no power to require a defendant to attend an identification parade. The principles applicable to more serious cases should apply equally to trivial cases. The prosecution's appeal was dismissed.

[71] *The Times,* March 15, 1995 C.A. Conviction quashed because of defects in identification procedure. The court said the judge could have admitted the evidence but he should have pointed out the breaches to the jury in his summing up. See however *Middlebrook* n.9 below, where the Court of Appeal said that it was not the function of the jury to supervise the Codes. It is not easy to see how these two positions regarding the role of the jury can be reconciled.

Brown,[72] *Graham,*[73] *Rutherford and Palmer,*[74] *Ventour*[75] *Coleman,*[76] *Gall,*[77] *Martin and Nicholls,*[78] *Finley*[79]

Sometimes however the courts are prepared in effect to condone or overlook breaches of the PACE rules:

Evidence held admissible despite breaches

No caution where one is required—*O'Shea,*[80] *Weekes,*[81] *de Sayrah,*[82] *Allison and Murray,*[83] *Pall,*[84] (*cf.* no caution where one is not required—*Konscol,*[85] *Shah,*[86] *Park,*[87] *Nesbeth,*[88] *Oni,*[89] *Purcell*[90])

Access to legal advice wrongly refused—*Alladice,*[91] *Dunford,*[92] *McGovern,*[93] *Oliphant*[94]

Interview formalities not complied with—*Langiert,*[95] *White,*[96] *Hoyte,*[97] *Walsh,*[98] *Dunn,*[99] *Bedford*[1]

---

[72] [1991] Crim.L.R. 368 C.A. Failure to hold identification parade was a breach of Code D. But appeal dismissed because of the cumulative strength of the evidence.

[73] [1994] Crim.L.R. 212 C.A. Failure to hold a parade was fatal. Conviction quashed.

[74] (1994) Cr.App.R. 141 C.A. Breach of Code D in not holding a parade. But appeal dismissed because of the strength of the evidence.

[75] (December 16, 1988, Unreported), Case No. 418/C1/88 C.A. Failure to hold parade and showing photograph before a confrontation resulted in conviction being quashed.

[76] (March 30, 1990, Unreported), Case No. 729/A2/88 C.A. A variety of breaches of Code D. Conviction quashed.

[77] (1990) 90 Cr.App.R. 64, [1989] Crim.L.R. 745 C.A. An officer concerned with the I.D. parade brought the witness to the parade, looked in and spoke to the identification officer. At first trial this breach of Code D2.2 resulted in the identification evidence being excluded. At the second trial it was allowed in. Held: should have been excluded.

[78] [1994] Crim.L.R. 218 C.A. Two black defendants identified by schoolboy victims of theft from the person in the court building where there were very few coloured youths. Held: Identifications were made in highly unsatisfactory conditions and a long time after the incidents. [NB DJB for text about identifications.]

[79] [1993] Crim.L.R. 50 C.A. Many breaches of the Code. Difficult to believe it was mere inefficiency, as opposed to deliberate flouting of the Code. It was bound to appear that justice did not seem to have been done.

[80] [1993] Crim.L.R. 950 C.A.

[81] (January 11, 1991, Unreported), Case No. 90/859/Y4 C.A.

[82] (June 25, 1990, Unreported), Case No. 89/5270/Y3 C.A.

[83] (October 25, 1988, Unreported), Case No. 1731/A1/88 C.A. (Both appellants knew they did not have to answer questions.)

[84] [1992] Crim.L.R. 126 C.A.

[85] (May 18, 1993, Unreported), Case No. 92/1352/Z2 C.A. (The interview took place abroad.)

[86] [1994] Crim.L.R. 128 C.A. (Insufficient reason to suspect at that stage.)

[87] *The Times,* July 30, 1992, C.A. (Insufficient reason to suspect at that stage.)

[88] (February 12, 1991, Unreported), Case No. 336/Y3/90. (Insufficient reason to suspect at that stage.)

[89] [1992] Crim.L.R. 183 C.A. (Just cautioned in respect of a different offence.)

[90] [1992] Crim.L.R. 806 C.A.

[91] (1988) 87 Cr.App.R. 380; [1988] Crim.L.R. 608 C.A.

[92] (1990) 91 Cr.App.R. 150; [1991] Crim.L.R. 370 C.A.

[93] (1991) 92 Cr.App.R. 228; [1991] Crim.L.R. 124 C.A.

[94] [1992] Crim.L.R. 40 C.A.

[95] [1991] Crim.L.R. 777 C.A.

[96] [1991] Crim.L.R. 779 C.A.

[97] [1994] Crim.L.R. 215 C.A.

[98] (1989) 91 Cr.App.R. 161 C.A. The court said that not every significant or substantial breach of the Code will result in the evidence being excluded under section 78. The court must always consider whether there would be such an adverse effect on the fairness of the proceedings that justice required the evidence to be excluded.

[99] (1990) 91 Cr.App.R. 237 C.A. The court found that there had been "serious and inexcusable breaches" but refused to apply s.78 because a solicitors' clerk had been present.

[1] (1991) 93 Cr.App.R. 113 C.A.

Identification evidence allowed in, despite breach of Code D: *Quinn*,[2] *McClay*,[3] *Ryan*,[4] *Grannell*[5]

The crux of the matter is always whether the court considers that the circumstances are such as to make admission of the evidence as unfair. But what is "unfair"? In *Sang*[6] the House of Lords, as has been seen, confined the common law discretion to exclude evidence to the situation where its prejudicial effect outweighs its probative value. This is the discretion preserved by section 82(3) of PACE—see p. 250 below.[7] The discretion under section 78 is clearly broader—if only in not being restricted to evidence obtained from the defendant. In *Christou*[8] the Court of Appeal said that the criteria of unfairness are the same whether the trial judge is exercising his discretion at common law (applying the discretion identified in *Sang* and confirmed in section 82(3)) or under section 78 of PACE: "What is unfair cannot sensibly be subject to different standards depending on the source of his discretion to exclude it." But the case law shows that section 78 has been given a much wider interpretation than was the case under the pre-PACE common law rules.

The meaning in section 78 of the word "may" refuse to allow in evidence was considered in *Middlebrook*.[9] The Court of Appeal said that once the court decided that evidence should not be allowed in because of the adverse effect on the fairness of the proceedings it had no choice as to admissibility. At that point the word "may" was the equivalent of "shall". But the crucial question for the trial court and the Court of Appeal remains whether the effect of the way in which the evidence was obtained *is* such as to make the proceedings so unfair as to require it to be excluded. This, unavoidably, is a matter of judgment on which reasonable people and reasonable judges may disagree.

The Court of Appeal has indicated that generally it will leave the matter to trial judges and will not interfere with the view they have taken unless no trial judge could reasonably have reached that view. In *Middlebrook* the Court of Appeal said that if a reasonable judge must have concluded that the evidence would produce unfairness, the Court of Appeal would set aside a

---

[2] [1990] Crim.L.R. 581 C.A. The charge was an I.R.A. murder of a police officer in 1975. The identification was 11 weeks later, in court when the defendant was being tried on other charges. The murder trial was in 1988 after the defendant had been extradited from the United States. The Court of Appeal said there were five relevant circumstances that the court should take into account when deciding whether to exclude identification evidence: 1) the possibility of difficulty for the defence in cross-examining; 2) the court should insist on the best possible identification evidence; 3) the denial of a parade was capable of being unfair but here the defendant had himself refused a parade; 4) the reasons for delay—here the delay was caused by the long fight over extradition; and 5) the nature of other evidence. *Mala fides* and breaches of the Codes were relevant but not necessarily decisive.

[3] (December 15, 1992, Unreported), Case No. 91/3142/W3 C.A. No I.D. parade, therefore a breach of Code D, but less important where the witness who identified D knew him previously.

[4] [1992] Crim.L.R. 187 C.A. Major breach of Code para. 2.2 in investigating officer being involved in setting up the parade but evidence allowed in because the defendant's interests had been sufficiently protected by his solicitor.

[5] (1989) 90 Cr.App.R. 149 C.A. The breach, consisting of an informal group identification in the foyer of the court, held not to be unfair.

[6] [1980] A.C. 402.

[7] For an application of the principle see *Johnson* [1995] Crim.L.R. 53 C.A.

[8] [1992] Q.B. 979 at 988; [1992] 4 All E.R. 559 at 564 C.A.

[9] (February 18, 1994, Unreported), Case No. 92/6701/Z2 C.A. Group identification instead of a parade as requested by the defendant.

ruling going the other way. This, in essence, is the well-known *Wednesbury* principle.

It is not necessary to establish that there has been a breach of PACE, let alone police misconduct. Thus in *Brine*[10] the Court of Appeal allowed the appeal because the trial judge had not taken into account the defendant's psychological pre-disposition to stress even though the police were unaware of this condition. But police misconduct does often come into the question. Sometimes the court has applied section 78 on account of some unacceptable trick or stratagem played by the police.

Evidence obtained by tricks, stratagems, undercover police work held inadmissible:

Mason[11]; *H*[12]; *Gary Blake*[13]; *Bryce*[14]; *George Heron*[15]; *Keith Hall*[16] and *Colin Stagg.*[17]

However there are many more cases when the courts have allowed in evidence obtained as a result of police tricks and stratagems, even sometimes where there was an element of entrapment[18]:

[10] [1992] Crim.L.R. 122 C.A.
[11] [1988] 1 W.L.R. 139; [1987] 3 All E.R. 481; (1988) 86 Cr.App.Rep. 349 C.A. Police falsely told D and his solicitor that D's fingerprints had been found at scene of crime. Held: subsequent confession not admissible especially it seems because of the deceit on the solicitor.
[12] [1987] Crim.L.R. 47 (Cr. Ct.). Police arranged for rape victim to lure alleged rapist into a taped telephone conversation. She specifically told him it was not being taped. Held: the conversation had to be excluded as an unfair trap.
[13] [1991] Crim.L.R. 119 (Cr.Ct.). Falsely told that his voice had been identified. Held: Inadmissible.
[14] See n.40, p. 238.
[15] See pp. 224–225 above.
[16] National newspapers, March 11, 1994. Waterhouse J. at Leeds Crown Court held inadmissible taped admissions regarding murder of first wife made to undercover WPC who had befriended him.
[17] See similarly the view of Ognall J. on the evidence of the undercover WPC who befriended Colin Stagg accused of the Wimbledon Common murder. She tried to get him to confess by sending him lurid sex material. Described by the judge as an attempt to incriminate him "by deceptive conduct of the grossest kind". See national newspapers September 15, 1994.
[18] See generally S. Sharpe, "Covert Police Operations and the Discretionary Exclusion of Evidence" [1994] Crim.L.R. 793; G. Robertson. "Entrapment Evidence: Manna from Heaven, or Fruit of the Poisoned Tree" *ibid.* at 805 and D. Birch, "Exluding evidence from entrapment: when is it a fair cop?" *Current Legal Problems*, 1994, pp. 73–100.

Evidence obtained by tricks, stratagems, undercover police work held admissible:

D.P.P. v. Marshall and Downes[19]; *Jelen and Katz*[20]; *Shaukat Ali*[21]; *Bailey and Smith*[22]; *Edwards*[23]; *Effik, Mitchell*[24]; *Christou, Wright*[25]; *Maclean and Kosten*[26]; *Smurthwaite, Gill*[27]; *Gill and Ranuana*[28]; *Gibbons and Winterburn*[29]; *Cadette*[30]; *Morley and Hutton*[31]

In *Smurthwaite*[32] the Court of Appeal said "the fact that the evidence had been obtained by entrapment, or by an agent provocateur, or by a trick does not of itself require the judge to exclude it". Everything will depend on the particular circumstances. The Court of Appeal said that in a case involving an undercover operation the judge would take into account various factors: "Was the officer acting as an agent provocateur in the sense that he was enticing the defendant to commit an offence he would not otherwise have committed? What was the nature of any entrapment? Does the evidence consist of admissions to a completed offence? How active or passive was the officer's role in obtaining the evidence? Is there an unassailable record of what occurred or is it strongly corroborated?"

Sometimes the court has to strike a balance between fairness to the defendant and fairness to the prosecution and the needs of law enforcement. Thus in the recent case of *Khan (Sultan)*[33] (involving the placing of a bug on

---

[19] [1988] 3 All E.R. 683; [1988] Crim.L.R. 750 C.A. Out-of-hours test purchases by plain-clothes officer of liquor from licensed premises. See to like effect *London Borough of Ealing v. Woolworths plc* [1995] Crim.L.R. 58 (Div.Ct.).

[20] (1990) 90 Cr.App.R. 456 C.A. Surreptitious tape-recording of a conversation between the defendant and a co-defendant allowed in. *H*, n.12 above, distinguished on the ground that here the inquiries were at an early stage.

[21] *The Times*, February 19, 1991 C.A. Police bugged interview room in police station after the defendant had been charged with murder and recorded an incriminatory conversation between D and his family.

[22] [1993] Crim.L.R. 681 C.A. Defendants in robbery cases tricked into believing that the cell in which they had been place was not bugged. Evidence of their conversation held to have been correctly admitted. The court said such stratagems should only be used in grave cases and nothing should be done oppressively or so as to render the admission unreliable.

[23] [1991] Crim.L.R. 45 C.A. Undercover drugs squad officers offered to buy drugs from drugs dealer. Ample evidence that he was involved in the conspiracy before the police came on the scene. (The charge was conspiracy to supply to persons unknown—not to the police officers.)

[24] (1992) 95 Cr.App.R. 427 C.A. Court of Appeal upheld trial judge's decision to allow in evidence of overheard incriminatory phone conversation on a cordless telephone between the defendant and a third person. Even if the interception was illegal under the Interception of Communications Act 1985, it was not unfair to admit it.

[25] (1992) 95 Cr.App.R. 264; [1992] Crim.L.R. 729 C.A. Police set up phoney jewellery business as a "sting fencing operation" and recorded transactions on film and tape. Held: Evidence admissible. They did not incite the crime, nor did they question the suspects. The judge could exclude the evidence where an undercover disguise was adopted in order to question the suspect without complying with the Code.

[26] [1993] Crim.L.R. 687 C.A. Importing cannabis. Defendant tricked into coming to this country and tricked into revealing his involvement in the offence. Held: He had applied himself to the ruse as in *Christou*.

[27] [1994] 1 All E.R. 898 C.A. two wives solicited undercover police officers as "hitmen" to murder their husbands. The conversations which were tape-recorded, were held to have been rightly admitted. There had been no incitement by the officer.

[28] [1989] Crim.L.R. 358 C.A. Conspiracy to murder Rajiv Gandhi. Conversations with undercover officers posing as I.R.A. members held inadmissible.

[29] *The Times*, July 19, 1993. Conspiracy to supply drugs. Conversation with undercover officers admitted in evidence even though not all were not taped. But the defence did not deny the content of the conversations—only their import.

[30] [1995] Crim.L.R. 229 C.A.

[31] [1994] Crim.L.R. 919 C.A.

[32] n.27 above, at 902–903.

[33] [1994] 4 All E.R. 426 C.A. The report states that the Appellate Committee of the House of Lords gave leave to appeal in October 1994.

the home of a suspected heroin dealer) there had been a civil trespass to the outside of the building and a breach of the Home Office Guidelines on covert police surveillance operations,[34] in that no proper records were kept, as well as an invasion of the homeowner's privacy which might be a breach of Article 8 of the European Convention on Human Rights.

The trial judge held that the breach of the Home Office Guidelines was not significant. ("Allowing for these matters I do not think that they, in my judgment at least, come anywhere near allowing me to exclude this evidence under s.78.") Lord Taylor, Lord Chief Justice, for the Court of Appeal said (at p. 436): "In our view this was a conclusion which the learned judge was entitled to reach." He drew attention to the fact that no crime had been incited, that there had been no deliberate deceit practised on the defendant, that no misleading information was advanced or pressure placed upon him to induce him to speak, nor had the police acted oppressively toward him. Also there was a clear record on tape of what had admittedly been said. This has been an important factor in several cases. There was also no question of a breach of any of the PACE Codes of Practice.

Lord Taylor said that it was true that there had been an intrusion into the privacy "of those who believed themselves to be secure from being overheard when they had the crucial conversation" (at p. 437). The appellant contended that it had previously been accepted that the fruits of covert surveillance could only be used for the prevention and detection of crime—as opposed to securing a conviction through its introduction in evidence. In the House of Lords' decision in *Preston*[35] Lord Mustill had referred to the fact that prior to 1984 it was agreed that in practice material intercepted by mail, telegraph or telephone was never used as evidence in court. Moreover, in the Interception of Communications Act 1985 Parliament had confirmed that that previous practice should continue in regard to the product of telephone and telegraph interceptions. Lord Mustill said that it was surprising that the 1984 Home Office Guidelines (para. 10) stated that there might be circumstances "in which material obtained through the use of equipment by the police for surveillance as a necessary part of a criminal investigation could appropriately be used in evidence at subsequent court proceedings".

But Lord Taylor said (at p. 435) that "there is a strong public interest in the detection of crime and in the use by the police of up-to-date technical devices in appropriate circumstances". The Home Office Guidelines only permitted the use of covert listening devices in serious crime and where other means of obtaining evidence and detection were unlikely to prove effective. The fact of trespass was of limited importance. There were already, and would be more, devices that could pick up even the most private conversation without the need for any trespass. The court said (at pp. 437–38): "There are, as Article 8 recognises, circumstances in which such intrusion is necessary and therefore justifiable in a democratic society."

Exclusion of evidence under section 78 is to prevent unfairness in regard to the *proceedings*. This can include a *sense* of unfairness to the defendant even though there may not have been any actual unfairness.[36]

---

[34] The Guidelines have never been published but they were placed in the House of Commons library. The text of the Guidelines was set out in the Court of Appeal's judgment.

[35] [1993] 4 All E.R. 638 (H.L.).

[36] *Gall* (1990) 90 Cr.App.R. 64 C.A.

The cases on section 78 seems to permit the following general propositions:

(1) *No general guidelines.* The courts have declined to lay down guidelines for the application of the section—each case has to be taken on its own facts.

Thus in *Samuel*[37] Hodgson J. said: "It is undesirable to attempt any general guidance as to the way in which a judge's discretion under section 78 or his inherent powers should be exercised. Circumstances vary infinitely." In *Parris*[38] Lord Lane C.J. said that a breach of the Act or Codes does not mean that any statement made by a defendant after such a breach would necessarily be ruled inadmissible. "Every case has to be determined on its own facts."[39] In *Jelen and Katz*[40] Auld J. said "The circumstances of each case are almost always different, and judges may well take different views in the proper exercise of their discretion even where the circumstances are similar."

Despite this, the courts will look at, and do cite, previous cases—especially decisions of the Court of Appeal.[41]

(2) *Wednesbury unreasonableness.* If the trial judge has found there to have been a breach of the rules or some other impropriety and has gone on to exercise his discretion under section 78, the Court of Appeal says that it will only interfere on the well-known *Wednesbury* principle,[42] *i.e.* if the discretion was exercised on wholly wrong grounds.[43] As a matter of impression, it may be said however that the Court of Appeal does seem somewhat readier to take a different view from that adopted by the trial judge in this area than in some others where the principle of *Wednesbury* unreasonableness comes into issue.

(3) *No discretion exercised by trial judge.* Different considerations apply where the judge has not exercised his discretion, or has directed his mind to the wrong issue. Thus, if the trial judge wrongly decides that there has been no breach he has, by definition, failed to apply his mind to the matter. In that situation the appeal court may exercise the discretion.[44]

(4) *Burden of proof.* It is not entirely clear where the burden of proof lies in regard to points raised under section 78.[45] There is nothing in section 78 equivalent to the provision in section 76 which requires the prosecution to establish that a confession was not obtained in breach of section 76(2)(a) or (b). The prosecution need not disprove unfairness.[46]

---

[37] [1988] Q.B. 615, 630; (1988) Cr.App.R. 232, 245 C.A.
[38] (1989) 89 Cr.App.R. 68, 72 C.A.
[39] At p. 72.
[40] (1990) 90 Cr.App.R. 456, 465 C.A.
[41] The Court of Appeal is less impressed with citation of first instance authorities—see *Grannell* (1990) 90 Cr.App.R. 149 C.A. in which Tucker J. said of such decisions "We do not find them of any assistance in deciding whether the trial judge ... exercised his discretion wrongly."
[42] *Associated Provincial Picture Houses Ltd v. Wednesbury Corporation* [1948] 1 K.B. 223.
[43] See for instance *Penny* [1992] Crim.L.R. 184 C.A. Failure to hold an identification parade. Even if there had been a breach of the Code it had to be shown that the judge was wholly wrong in the exercise of the section 78 discretion. See also *O'Leary* (1988) 87 Cr.App.R. 387, 391; and *Christou* [1992] Q.B. 979.
[44] *Samuel* C.A., n.31a, p. 238 above, *Alladice* C.A., n.91, p. 240 above and *Absolam* C.A. n.30, p. 238 above were all examples. See also *Parris* C.A., n.32, p. 238 above, *Keenan* C.A., n.53, p. 239 above and *Howden-Simpson* [1991] Crim.L.R. 49 C.A.
[45] In previous editions the writer's view (cited in *Archbold*, 1994, 15–366) was that the burden fell on the defence. In *Anderson* [1993] 447 C.A. the court said it was not entirely clear where the burden of proof lay.
[46] *Vel v. Owen* [1987] Crim.L.R. 496 (Div.Ct.).

On the other hand, the defence plainly have to persuade the court that there is a serious issue as to unfairness in regard to admissibility of the evidence in question. The prosecution will seek to persuade the court either that there was no breach of the rules or other impropriety, or if there was, that it was not "significant and substantial", or that even so, there was not sufficient reason for the evidence to be excluded.[47] The court must take into account fairness to the prosecution as well as to the defence.[48]

The court will probably uphold the defence position under section 78 only if it is persuaded a) that there was a breach of the rules or other impropriety, b) that it was significant and substantial, c) that it affects the proceedings unfairly as from the defence standpoint and d) that the unfairness is so great as to require that the evidence be excluded.[49] If this does not amount to the burden of proof being on the defence it seems remarkably close.

(5) *Voire dire.* Whereas under section 76 there has to be a trial within a trial (*voire dire*) in both Crown courts and magistrates' courts, this does not apply to challenges under section 78.[50] Where the challenge is under both sections, there has to be a *voire dire*. Where it is only under section 78 the Crown Court has a discretion,[51] though in the magistrates' court there is no need to hold a *voire dire* on a section 78 application.[52]

(6) *Extradition.* It has been held that section 78 does not apply to extradition proceedings—see *R. v. Governor of Belmarsh Prison and another, ex p. Francis, The Times,* April 12, 1995.

(7) *Not penalising the police.* The courts have made it clear that a decision to exclude evidence should not be made to penalise or to discipline the police.[53]

In summary, whether the court will apply section 78 depends on its overall assessment of all the relevant facts.

See generally Bernard Robertson, "The Looking Glass World of Section 78", New L.J. 1223; I. Dennis, "Reconstructing the Law of Criminal Evidence", (1989) *Current Legal Problems* 21; D.J. Birch, "The Evidence Provisions" 1989, N.I.L.Q., pp. 411, 422–431; M. Gelowitz, "Section 78 of the Police and Criminal Evidence Act 1984", 106 L.Q.R. 327 (1990); C.J.W. Allen, "Discretion and Security: Excluding Evidence under s.78(1) of the Police and Criminal Evidence Act 1984" 49 Camb.L.J. 80 (1990); David Feldman, "Regulating Treatment of Suspects in Police Stations: Judicial

---

[47] See *Ryan* [1992] Crim.L.R. 187 C.A.—major breach of Code D in regard to identification evidence. The court said that even quite serious breaches might not result in the evidence being excluded if they did not cause unjust prejudice to the accused.
[48] See for instance *McDonald* [1991] Crim.L.R. 122 C.A.
[49] In *Walsh* (1990) 91 Cr.App.R. 161, 163, the Court of Appeal said: "The task of the court is not merely to consider whether there would be an adverse effect on the fairness of the proceedings, but such an adverse effect that justice requires the evidence to be excluded."
[50] For Crown Court see *Beveridge* (1987) 85 Cr.App.R. 255 C.A.; for magistrates' courts see *Vel v. Owen* [1987] Crim.L.R. 496, *Liverpool Juvenile Court, ex p. R.* [1988] Q.B. 1 (Div.Ct.). See further R. Stevens, "Trials within trials in the magistrates' court: a panoramic view", J.P.N. August 22, 1987, p. 531.
[51] In *Manji* [1990] Crim.L.R. 512 C.A. it was held that the judge had been wrong to refuse an application for a trial within a trial as to whether the defendant had or had not been cautioned.
[52] *Vel v. Owen* n.50 above. See now also *Halawa v. Federation Against Copyright Theft* [1995] Crim.L.R. 409.
[53] *Mason* [1988] 1 W.L.R. 139 C.A.; *Delaney* (1989) 88 Crim.App.Rep. 338 C.A.

Interpretation of Detention Provisions in the Police and Criminal Evidence Act 1984" [1990] Crim.L.R. 452.

PACE AND THE NORTHERN IRELAND (EMERGENCY PROVISIONS) ACT

The exclusion of evidence in trials for scheduled offences in Northern Ireland is governed by section 8 of the Northern Ireland (Emergency Provisions) Act 1991.[54] The concept of evidence excluded on the grounds of oppression in section 8 is almost identical to that in section 76(2)(a) and (8) of PACE and Article 74(2)(a) and (8) of the Northern Ireland PACE Order. But section 8 has no separate test of unreliability equivalent to that in section 76(2)(b) and Article 74(2)(b). Indeed, the Northern Ireland courts adopted a tough stance in regard to confessions obtained as a result of psychological pressures falling short of oppression.[55] Issues of unreliability have been dealt with instead under the judicial discretion which, under the original section 8, had to be developed as a common law power but which is now in the amended section 11 of the 1991 Act.[56] The discretion is exercisable under section 11(3) where "it appears to the court and it is appropriate to do so in order to avoid unfairness to the accused or otherwise in the interests of justice". But, not surprisingly, considering that these are all scheduled offences, it seems that the Northern Ireland courts have not been as ready to exercise their judicial discretion to exclude evidence under section 8 as the courts in England and Wales under their very similar discretion under section 78.

Time for taking accused's evidence: section 79[57]

Under the previous law, the accused had to give evidence before hearing the evidence and cross-examination of any witnesses he intended to call.[58] The Criminal Law Revision Committee in its 11th Report recommended[59] that the court should have a discretion—for instance to allow a witness to be called before the accused who is to speak of an event before the matters about which the accused is to give evidence. Section 79 implemented this proposal. The accused gives evidence first "unless the court in its discretion otherwise directs".

Competence and compellability of accused's spouse: section 80[60]

Section 80 deals with the rules of the *incompetence* of the accused's spouse to give evidence (when she cannot give evidence even when willing to do so), and of the spouse's *compellability* (when she can be required to give

---

[54] Formerly 1928 Act, s.8 and 1987 Act, s.5.
[55] See for instance *Dillon* [1984] N.I. 292, 299 and *Cowan* [1987] 1 N.I.J.B. 15.
[56] See D. Greer,"The Admissibility of Confessions under the Northern Ireland (Emergency Provisions) Act" (1980) 31 N.I.L.Q. 205, 217 *et seq.* See also *McCormick* [1977] N.I. 105; *Llewellyn* [1984] 15 N.I.J.B. 21; and *Mullan* [1988] 10 N.I.J.B. 36, 42.
[57] See N.I. PACE Order, Art. 77.
[58] *R. v. Morrison* (1911) 6 Cr.App.R. 159; *R. v. Smith* (1968) 52 Cr.App.R. 224.
[59] *op. cit.*, n.2, p. 201 above, para. 107.
[60] See N.I. PACE Order, Art. 79.

evidence even though unwilling to do so). The Criminal Law Revision Committee in its 11th Report proposed changes in these rules and section 80 broadly adopted these recommendations.

Under the previous law the accused's spouse was generally not competent for the prosecution[61] (save when the charge was one of personal violence against her) but was always competent as a defence witness for the accused[62] and was competent as a defence witness for the spouse's co-accused but normally only with the spouse's consent.[63]

The C.L.R.C. said that it had no doubt that a wife should always be competent as a witness for the prosecution in all cases. "If she is willing to give evidence, we think that the law would be showing excessive concern for the preservation of marital harmony if it were to say that she must not do so."[64] Subsection (1) adopts this view, subject to an exception in subsection (4) where the spouse is jointly charged with the same offence. But this exception does not apply where he or she is no longer liable to be convicted for that offence by virtue of having pleaded guilty or otherwise.

Previously the spouse was competent but not compellable for the accused. The C.L.R.C. recommended[65] that the spouse should always be compellable as well as competent as a witness for the accused. Subsection (2) gives effect to this recommendation save for the same exception in subsection (4) where they are jointly charged.

There were few cases where the spouse was compellable for the prosecution. For some time it was thought that at common law a spouse was compellable against the marriage partner if the case involved violence against her (or him). But the House of Lords rejected this view in *Hoskyn v. Metropolitan Police Commissioner.*[66]

The C.L.R.C. proposed[67] that a wife should be compellable for the prosecution not only where the case involved violence against her but also in cases of violence towards children under the age of 16 belonging to the same household as the accused. Often in such cases the wife was in fear of her husband but wanted to give evidence against him. To make her compellable as a witness would make her position easier rather than more difficult. The Committee did not however go so far as to recommend compellability where the child was not from the same household.

The Act went beyond what the C.L.R.C. recommended. Subsection (3): (a) makes the spouse compellable for the prosecution where the case involves violence against him or her or against anyone who was under 16 at the time; or (b) where the offence is a sexual one against a person aged under 16 or (c) where it consists of attempting or conspiring to commit an offence within (a) or (b).[68] Again the same exception under subsection (4) applies for the case where the spouses are charged jointly.[69]

[61] There were certain statutory exceptions including the Evidence Act 1898, s.4(1); Sexual Offences Act 1956, s.39; Theft Act 1968, s.30.
[62] By virtue of the Criminal Evidence Act 1898, s.1.
[63] Also by virtue of the Criminal Evidence Act 1898, s.1.
[64] *op. cit.* n.2, p. 201 above, para. 148.
[65] *ibid.* para. 153.
[66] [1979] A.C. 474.
[67] *op. cit.* n.2, p. 201 above, para. 150.
[68] For comment on the slight difference of meaning between "involves" and "consists of" see *Cross on Evidence* (6th ed.) p. 199 and P. Creighton, "Spouse Competence and Compellability" [1990] Crim.L.R. 34, 38–39.
[69] For a critique of this extension of the law of compellability as either being too wide or too narrow see P.Creighton, *op. cit.* n.64 above, pp. 35–36.

The C.L.R.C. also dealt with the problem of one spouse as witness for the co-accused of the other spouse.

At common law a spouse was competent for the defence with the consent of the accused but was not generally compellable. In the view of the C.L.R.C.[70] the accused's co-accused regardless of the accused's consent. Subsection (1)(b) gives effect to this proposal.[71]

The section does not address the question of a defendant charged with more than one offence. The better view is probably that in such a case the wife could be compellable for one but not another, rather than that she becomes compellable for all by virtue of being compellable for one.[72]

It seemed that a divorced wife was not competent to give evidence about something that occurred during the marriage.[73] The C.L.R.C. proposed[74] that, after the marriage had been dissolved, former spouses should be both competent and compellable as if they had never been married. The Act accepts this proposal (subs. (5)). It applies to anything that occurred whilst they were married.[75] Following the views of the C.L.R.C. it does not apply however unless the marriage has been ended by divorce or annulment. Judicial separation is not enough.

The C.L.R.C. proposed[76] that the prohibition in section 1(b) of the Criminal Evidence Act 1898 of comment by the prosecution on the failure by the accused's spouse to give evidence should be abolished. But the Government rejected this recommendation and section 1(b) is expressly confirmed in subsection (8) of section 80.

The final subsection deals with the privilege of a witness not to answer questions about a communication made to the witness by his or her spouse during the marriage and the right to decline to say whether marital intercourse did or did not take place. The Law Reform Committee recommended in its 16th Report in 1967 that these privileges should be abolished for civil cases.[77] This was achieved by sections 16(3) and (4) of the Civil Evidence Act 1968 and the C.L.R.C. made the same recommendation in regard to criminal cases.[78] The Act gave effect to the recommendation in subsection (9).

Advance notice of the defence case: section 81[79]

Under the previous law the only requirement that the defendant reveal any part of his case in advance of the trial concerned an alibi defence. The Philips Royal Commission recommended[80] that the defence should be

---

[70] *op. cit.* n.2, p. 201 above, paras. 155.

[71] For a critique of this proposal see Creighton, *op. cit.* n.68 above, p. 37.

[72] See Creighton, *op. cit.* n.68 above, p. 40. See also *Woolgar* [1991] Crim.L.R. 545 C.A. and Professor John Smith's commentary at pp. 545–547.

[73] See *Algar* [1955] 1 Q.B. 279; *Lapworth* [1931] 1 K.B. 117.

[74] *op. cit.* n.2, p. 201 above, para. 156.

[75] In *Mathias and others* [1989] Crim.L.R. 64 the trial judge applied s.80(5) to a confession made by a co-defendant to his then wife before the Act came into force. Subsequently they were divorced. A month later in April 1988 she made a statement to the police in which she gave the details of the confession which also implicated two other co-defendants. The court allowed in the statement, subject to the replacement the names of the other co-defendants by letters of the alphabet so that the jury would not be prejudiced by having their names included.

[76] *op. cit.* n.2 above, p. 201, pp. 43–44.

[77] "Privilege in Civil Proceedings", Cmnd. 3472 (1967).

[78] *op. cit.* n.2, p. 201 above, para. 173.

[79] See N.I. PACE Order, Art. 80.

[80] Philips Report, para. 8.22.

required to give advance notice also of expert evidence so as to reduce the danger of surprise causing adjournments. The Philips Royal Commission said that obvious examples were defences depending on medical evidence or expert forensic evidence which the prosecution needs an opportunity to evaluate or on which it may wish to call its own expert witnesses.

The Act adopted this suggestion by granting powers for Crown Court Rules to be made to require either party to disclose to the other any expert evidence he proposes to adduce in the proceedings and to prohibit a party who fails to comply with such rules to adduce such evidence, save with leave of the court. The Rules may specify the kinds of expert evidence covered.

The Crown Court (Advance Notice of Expert Evidence) Rules (S.I. 1987 No. 716) came into effect in July 1987.[81] The rules provided for the disclosure, as soon as practicable after committal, of a statement in writing of any finding or opinion of an expert upon which a party proposes to rely. Rule 4 allows non-disclosure if there are reasonable grounds to believe that compliance with the rules might lead to intimidation of a potential witness. Subject to Rule 4, a party who fails to comply with the requirement of disclosure cannot adduce expert evidence without leave of the court.

Exclusion of evidence: section 82[82]

At the end of the interpretation section for Part VIII of the Act is the sentence: "Nothing in this part of this Act shall prejudice any power of a court to exclude evidence (whether by preventing questions from being put or otherwise) at its discretion."

The meaning of this subsection is far from clear. At the time of the passage of the Bill it was generally thought to have a rather narrow scope. This certainly is the clear implication of the reference to the power of the judge to protect a witness from objectionable questions. But what is the import of the phrase "or otherwise", which taken literally could be said to be very open-ended. Certainly it covers the court's power to instruct the jury to disregard evidence it has heard.

The general view now is that section 82(3) preserved the whole of the common law on the exclusion of evidence. On this view the admissibility of a confession can be challenged under section 76, or under section 78 or under this section; evidence other than a confession can be challenged under either section 78 or this section.

The main thrust of section 82(3) therefore is to retain the power allowed by the House of Lords in *Sang*[83] to exclude evidence if the prejudicial effect outweighs its probative value.[84] Judge Richard May has suggested[85] that another example would be in cases arising out of cross-examination of the accused under section 1(f) of the Criminal Evidence Act 1898. Another example is where evidence has already been given and where it therefore cannot be challenged under sections 76 or 78. This was specifically referred to by the Court of Appeal in *Sat-Bhambra*[86] in which Lord Lane C.J. said that

[81] The Northern Ireland equivalent was S.I. 1989 No. 394.
[82] See N.I. PACE Order, Art. 70.
[83] [1980] A.C. 402; see p. 233 above.
[84] See for instance *O'Leary* (1988) 87 Cr.App.R. 387 C.A.; *Eatough(J)* [1989] Crim.L.R. 289 (Cr.Ct.).
[85] Richard May, "Fair Play at Trial: an Interim Assessment of section 78 of the Police and Criminal Evidence Act 1984", [1988] Crim.L.R. 722, 726.
[86] [1988] Crim.L.R. 453 C.A. and see pp. 230–231 above.

a judge who could not exclude evidence under section 78 could still do so under his common law power preserved by section 82(3) "to prevent injustice".

QUESTIONS AND ANSWERS

CONFESSIONS

1. How did PACE alter the law regarding the admissibility of confessions?

The common law excluded confessions that (1) were obtained as a result of oppression; and (2) that could not be shown by the prosecution to have been voluntary.

"Oppression" was defined by the courts to have two aspects. First, that the presence or absence of oppression was a function of both the circumstances of the questioning and the characteristics of the defendant. Secondly, that oppressive questioning was questioning which by its nature or duration or other circumstances so affected the accused that his will crumbled.

The 1984 Act retains the rule that confessions which result from oppressive questioning must be excluded. The judge has no discretion. Oppression is defined in the Act as including "torture, inhuman or degrading treatment, and the use or threat of violence (whether or not amounting to torture)".

But the Act does alter the law as regards the "voluntariness" test. The old test was whether the confession had been obtained from the accused "by fear of prejudice or hope of advantage exercised or held out by a person in authority". The test under PACE is whether the confession was or may have been obtained "in consequence of anything said or done which was likely, in the circumstances existing at the time, to render unreliable any confession which might be made by him in consequence thereof".

Under the old test the judges were supposed to consider primarily whether there had been any threat or promise. Under PACE they have to consider the likely impact on the mind of the accused of all the circumstances at the time of his confession and evaluate whether they would be likely to have made the confession unreliable.

When a case poses this problem the burden of proof is firmly on the prosecution. The statute says if the question of the admissibility of the confession is raised "the court shall not allow the confession to be given in evidence against him except in so far as the prosecution proves to the court beyond reasonable doubt that the confession (notwithstanding that it may be true) was not obtained as aforesaid" (*i.e.* by oppression or in circumstances likely to make it unreliable). Indeed the Act has an unusual additional provision that even if the defence fail to make representations about the admissibility of the confession the court can require the prosecution to prove that the confession was not obtained in ways that would make it inadmissible.

2. What is the rule about the admissibility of real evidence (fingerprints, bloodstains, stolen goods etc.) found as a direct result of an inadmissible confession?

The Act continues the previous law that such real evidence is admissible even though the confession which led to its discovery is inadmissible. But no evidence can be given by the prosecution about how the inadmissible confession led to the discovery of the real evidence unless the *defence* state that that was what had happened.

3. In what circumstances will the court exclude evidence (other than confessions) obtained by improper means?

Under section 78 a court has the power in its absolute discretion to exclude any evidence where, having regard to the circumstances (including the way the evidence in question was obtained), it considers that its admission would have an unduly adverse effect on the fairness of the proceedings. So, if the court takes serious exception to the way that the prosecution have obtained any evidence it can rule that the evidence should not be admitted. It can also exclude evidence on the ground that the police have broken the rules of the Codes—sometimes even if there was no causal relationship between those breaches and the evidence obtained. The courts have used section 78 in this way in a very large number of cases.

THE EVIDENCE OF SPOUSES

1. In what circumstances can a spouse be compelled to give evidence against her spouse?

Under the previous law, one spouse could not be compelled to give evidence against the other spouse, even in a case where the charge arose from a violent attack by one on the other.

This rule was changed by PACE which provides that one spouse can be compelled to give evidence against the other spouse where the offence charged involves an assault on, injury or threat of injury to, the first spouse or against a person under 16 or a sexual offence against a person under 16.

2. When else is a spouse permitted to give evidence against her husband?

Under the old law, subject to a few exceptions, one spouse was generally not allowed to testify against the other. The only important exception was where the charge arose out of personal violence by the accused on the other spouse.

The Act changes the rule by making each spouse eligible ("competent") though not required ("compellable") to give evidence against the other.

3. Is one spouse compellable to give evidence for the other?

The old law generally did not treat one spouse as a compellable witness for the other. But this rule has been changed by the Act which makes husband and wife each compellable to give evidence for each other.

4. What happens if one spouse is charged together with the other?

The Act makes this an exception to the new rules. In other words a wife charged jointly with her husband is neither competent nor compellable to give evidence against him unless she is no longer liable to conviction because she pleaded guilty or for any other reason.

5. How are these rules affected by the fact that the spouses are divorced?

The old law took no notice of divorce. A spouse who had been divorced was in exactly the same position in regard to the question of competence and compellability as beforehand.

The Act changes this by providing that once spouses have been divorced they must be treated as if they had never been married. In other words they are free to give evidence even as to what occurred during the marriage—and can be compelled to do so for the prosecution where the case arises out of physical injury by one spouse on the other or on someone under 16.

PART IX

POLICE COMPLAINTS AND DISCIPLINE

The pre-PACE system for dealing with complaints against the police had three main elements. A chief officer who received a complaint against a member of his force had to record it and order that it be investigated either by an officer from another force, failing which by a chief superintendent (or in London a chief inspector). In practice, the chief constable's discipline and complaints functions, other than the actual hearing of charges, were delegated to the deputy chief constable.

Unless the chief officer was satisfied from the report that no criminal offence had been committed, he had to send the report to the Director of Public Prosecutions (D.P.P.). The D.P.P. then advised whether the officer should be charged with an offence. The chief officer had to consider in addition whether or not disciplinary charges should be brought. He also had to send the investigating officer's report to the Police Complaints Board, established in 1976, together with a memorandum stating whether he intended to institute disciplinary proceedings and, if not, why not. If the chief officer did not bring charges, the Board could recommend and, in the last resort, could direct that he do so. If charges were brought, the Board would decide whether the hearing should be by the chief officer or by a tribunal consisting of the chief officer with two members of the Board.

The system was therefore the same for all cases however trivial. One criticism advanced was that too much time of senior officers was deployed in investigating minor matters that could have been better dealt with less formally. Cases had to be referred to the D.P.P. even when the chief officer was clear in his own mind as to whether criminal charges should be brought. There were accusations that officers investigating complaints applied pressure on complainants to withdraw their allegations.[1] Another criticism against the system was that there were no real independent checks on the process of investigation. The D.P.P. was an independent check in regard to criminal prosecution and the Board could review decisions on disciplinary charges. But there was no independent review of the way in which the original complaint was investigated.

In October 1982 the Government published a White Paper, "Police Complaints Procedures"[2] in which it set out its proposals for changes to the complaints system. These were reflected in the Police and Criminal Evidence Bill introduced in November 1982. It would have changed the system in three main respects.

[1] See Brown (1987).
[2] Cmnd. 8681 (1982).

First, in regard to serious complaints, an "independent assessor" would have been appointed by the chairman or deputy chairman of the Police Complaints Board to supervise the inquiry made by an officer from another force.

Secondly, it proposed to make changes in regard to very minor complaints by introducing a new system of informal resolution that would not require full investigation of the complaint, where the officer would not face disciplinary proceedings and could make admissions without it going on his record.

Thirdly, it proposed changes in the rules requiring reference of cases to the D.P.P. which resulted in the Director being inundated with large numbers of relatively minor cases. The Bill proposed to give the chief officer a discretion as to whether to refer a case to the D.P.P. so that he would only have to refer cases whose gravity warranted such a reference.

During the Committee stage of the Bill this last provision was removed, against the wishes of the Government, by an alliance between the Opposition parties and Mr Eldon Griffiths, Tory backbencher representing the Police Federation.[3]

When Mr Brittan introduced the second Bill in October 1983, he accompanied it with a second White Paper, "Police Complaints and Discipline Procedures."[4] The second Bill adopted the previous changes in regard to the informal resolution of minor complaints. It restored the proposals to give the chief officer a discretion as to whether to refer a case to the D.P.P. But it made major changes in the arrangements for dealing with the most serious complaints—notably by setting up a new Police Complaints Authority to replace the old Police Complaints Board with powers itself to supervise the actual investigation of serious complaints.

There is no equivalent of this Part of PACE in the Northern Ireland PACE Order since it was previously enacted in Parts II and III of the Police (Northern Ireland) Order 1987. However, as will be seen, amendments to the 1987 Order are being introduced by the Police (Amendment) (Northern Ireland) Order 1995 which is dealt with here. The Northern Ireland Order was designed to effect for the Province a variety of changes made to PACE, including changes in regard to complaints against the police. The 1995 Order repeals almost the whole of the 1987 Order (*i.e.* Articles 4–20, 21(b), 22, 23 and 26).

Overhaul of the police discipline system: The system of police discipline has for decades been based on principles similar to those that apply in the criminal courts. In particular, the burden of proof has been the same that applies in a criminal case—proof beyond a reasonable doubt. This gave rise to problems. Already in its 1986 Annual Report the Police Complaints Authority (P.C.A.) drew attention to the lack of any procedure to deal with officers who had not infringed the police discipline Code but whose performance fell below acceptable standards. It also suggested that there was a need for a quicker, less rigid and less legalistic system for handling complaints against police officers. This was especially so where there was a complaint but no corroborating evidence. Some of these cases deserved a disciplinary hearing but charges would not be laid unless the case could be

---

[3] See House of Commons, *Hansard*, Standing Committee J. March 10, 1983, Col. 1227.
[4] "Police Complaints and Discipline Procedures." Cmnd. 9072 (1983).

proved to the high standard required. This, it said, brought the complaints system into disrepute, especially when the unsuccessful complaint was followed by a successful civil action arising from the same incident. It proposed a two-tier disciplinary system under which comparatively minor offences would be dealt with at police divisional level, leaving the Authority to concentrate on the more serious cases.

In April 1993 the then Home Secretary, Mr Kenneth Clarke, issued a Consultation Paper on "Police Personnel Procedures". This made radical proposals for changes in the police disciplinary system. In particular it proposed: a new separate procedure to deal with unsatisfactory performance; splitting the disciplinary system into two categories, unsatisfactory performance and misconduct; unsatisfactory performance to be dealt with internally as part of the normal personnel management process; misconduct to be dealt with under less formal and legalistic procedures; requiring officers to account for their actions in response to misconduct allegations; and removing the need to prove disciplinary charges to the criminal standard of proof save in the most serious cases.[5] Also the right to legal representation at disciplinary hearings would be withdrawn[6] and a police industrial tribunal instead of the Secretary of State would hear appeals against dismissal or demotion.[7]

In September 1993 the then Home Secretary, Mr Michael Howard, said that the proposed new misconduct procedure would deal only with cases where a police officer may have committed a criminal offence or breach of the Codes of Practice under PACE which was or could have been detrimental to a member of the public. All other instances of poor behaviour or poor performance would be dealt with under the new unsatisfactory performance procedures. The standard of proof required in misconduct hearings would be that in general employment legislation—whether it was reasonably believed that there had been misconduct. There would be a new requirement that an officer give a full and accurate account of his or her actions if required to do so by a senior officer.[8]

At the time this book went to press in Summer 1995 the final outcome regarding the new disciplinary system had not been published. The Police and Magistrates' Courts Act 1994 laid the ground for a complete revision of the discipline system by new regulations.[9] These were expected sometime in 1995. They were to be applied also to Northern Ireland—see Appendix 4, p. 533 below, [Arts. 14, 15].

In its 1994 third Triennial Review, the Police Complaints Authority said that it was concerned with the proposed narrower definition of misconduct, and the more so since the police had the sole power to decide whether to record a complaint.[10] If the decision were to handle the matter on an

---

[5] The Runciman Royal Commission on Criminal Justice recommended the lowering of the standard of proof for disciplinary matters. See Report, p. 48, para. 103(ii).

[6] As will be seen, the Government failed to achieve this—see p. 282 below.

[7] The Home Secretary, outlined his proposals at the Superintendents' Conference in September 1993. The Minister of State at the Home Office gave an account of the objectives on February 21, 1994—see House of Lords, *Hansard*, Vol. 552, cols. 441–442.

[8] Speech to Superintendents' Association, September 22, 1993, Home Office Press Notice.

[9] Section 18(2)(3) of the 1994 Act amending section 33 of the Police Act 1964 permits regulations to be made by the Secretary of State for "the conduct, efficiency and effectiveness of members of police forces and the maintenance of discipline", including "procedures for cases in which a member of a police force may be dealt with by dismissal, requirement to resign, reduction in rank, reduction in pay, fine, reprimand or caution".

[10] On this see section 84, p. 258 below.

unsatisfactory performance basis the independent complaints machinery would not be involved. This could be seen as "a weakening of the present civilian oversight".[11] The P.C.A. had therefore proposed that any complainant dissatisfied with the decision to treat his or her complaint as being about an officer's "performance" should have the right to ask for that decision to be reviewed by the Authority. ("We believe that retaining civilian oversight in this way is essential if the public are to have confidence in the complaints procedure and in the continued use of police officers to investigate allegations against their colleagues.")

The idea in the Government's Consultation Paper for a new police industrial tribunal was withdrawn. Instead it was decided to have a specially appointed police appeals tribunal—see p. 275 below.

Complaints supervision in relation to special constables and civilian employees in the police service: It is to be noted that the complaints system and its supervision by the Police Complaints Authority do not apply to actions by special constables and civilians employed in the police service. This is a serious issue. (A special constable has the same powers of arrest as a regular officer.) The Home Secretary Mr Michael Howard announced in 1993 that he intended to increase the number of special constables from 19,000 to a target of 30,000. This would mean a ratio of one to four special to regular officers. Likewise, more and more police tasks are handled by civilian employees. In its 1994 Triennial Review the P.C.A. recommended[12] that the existing system should be extended to cover these new developments.[13] The protection of the complaints procedure, it suggested, was "just as necessary whatever the type of uniform being worn by the people concerned".[14] It seems, however, that there are no current plans to make any change in this regard.

Establishment of the Police Complaints Authority: section 83

Section 83 of PACE replaced the Police Complaints Board with the new Police Complaints Authority ("the Authority" or "P.C.A."—not to be confused with the "police authority" or "the authority" or "the appropriate authority," see below). The Authority has two main functions. One is the powers in relation to the consideration of disciplinary charges held by the old Police Complaints Board. In its discipline function its powers are limited to matters concerning officers up to and including the rank of superintendent. Disciplinary matters involving officers above the rank of chief superintendent continue to be the province of the police authority for that area.

The Authority's second function is the supervision of investigations relating to the conduct of police officers of whatever rank and related disciplinary charges.

Schedule 4 of the Act referred to in subsection (2) of section 83 contains detailed provision as to the status, members, staff, proceedings and financial arrangements of the Authority. The provisions are virtually identical to

[11] Police Complaints Authority, *Triennial Review, 1991–94*, H.C. 396, 1994, p. 12.
[12] *ibid.* at p. 20.
[13] On the model of the agreements reached by the P.C.A. under section 96 with various non-Home Office police forces covering areas such as public transport, parks, ports, defence and atomic energy. See p. 275 below.
[14] *ibid.*

those that governed the Police Complaints Board (in the Schedule to the Police Act 1976). Only two matters call for mention here:

Appointment of chairman and members

Whereas the Chairman of the Police Complaints Board was appointed by the Prime Minister, the chairman of the Authority is appointed by the Queen. On the other hand, whereas members of the Board were all appointed by the Prime Minister, the members of the Authority other than the chairman are appointed by the Home Secretary (Sched. 4, para. 1(3)).

There are some 12–16 full-time members assisted by civil service staff. The P.C.A. is divided into "I" and "D" Divisions dealing respectively with investigations and discipline.

Regional offices

The Authority has the right, if it wishes, to set up regional offices in order to improve its capacity to produce a quick response in investigation (Sched. 4, para. 9(1)). It has not however done so.

Handling of complaints: Preliminary: section 84

Section 84 sets out the duties of chief officers of police on receiving a complaint against a member of their force. (See also s.86 below, in relation to complaints against officers above the rank of chief superintendent.)

Subsection (1) places a duty on the chief officer when he receives a complaint to take any steps that appear to him to be desirable for obtaining or preserving evidence relating to the offence. The 1983 White Paper[15] said that the first few hours after receipt of a complaint may often be vital, since evidence may have to be obtained which would be unavailable later. "It is essential that the need to refer cases to the Authority should not delay any necessary preliminary investigations."

The duty to take steps to preserve evidence therefore applies regardless of whether the complaint has been sent to the right place.

Under subsection (2) the chief officer must then decide whether he is "the appropriate authority" to deal with the matter. The appropriate authority is defined in subsection (4) as the police authority in relation to senior officers (above the rank of chief superintendent), the chief constable in relation to all other officers and in London the Commissioner of the Metropolitan force in relation to any officer of his force.

If he decides that he is not the appropriate authority, his duty is to send the complaint (or if it was made orally, details of it) to the appropriate authority and to inform the person by whom or on whose behalf the complaint was made that he has done so (subs. (3)). It is therefore his responsibility to see that a misdirected complaint gets to the right place.

Complaints consist of any complaint made about the conduct of an officer of his force submitted by a "member of the public" (subs. (4)(a)). The Police Complaints Authority (P.C.A.) in its first Triennial Review[16] said that a "member of the public," it thought, did not include a limited company,

[15] *op. cit.* n.4 above, p. 255, para. 13.
[16] *Triennial Review 1985–1988*, May 1988, H.C. 466.

public or local authorities, local police authorities, trades unions, or pressure groups and their representatives.[17]

The duty to recognise and record a complaint lies on the chief officer, not on the Authority. In its first Triennial Review the P.C.A. said that where an unacceptable complaint (*e.g.* from a limited company) had been recorded it had advised that it be de-recorded. It recommended that the last word about recording and de-recording should lie with itself rather than with the police[18] but the Government rejected this recommendation.[19] In its 1994 Triennial Report the P.C.A. said[20] that although it still thought that public confidence would be greater if it had the power to direct that a complaint be recorded, there had been too few problems to justify pressing for legislative change in this regard.

Another point identified in the first Triennial Review was the complaint which does not accurately define the precise scope of the conduct complained of—possibly because the complainant does not know that the police broke the Codes of Practice. The P.C.A. totally rejected the police view expressed by some chief officers that a complaint could only be investigated or made the subject of disciplinary proceedings if the complainant detailed the acts of misconduct of which the complaint was made. The purpose of the provisions was to "unearth police misconduct and deal with it".[21] The Authority had told chief officers that even if a ground of complaint uncovered by the investigation was not specified and recorded originally, there was nothing to prevent that being done later when the wrongdoing came to light. Sometimes it had met "illiberal resistance to this idea", and a determination to construe "complaint" as that only which the complainant originally articulated.[22] The P.C.A.'s view was that "complaint about the conduct" should be redefined to embrace all such matters arising out of or in connection with the incident complained of as the Authority might determine by investigation or otherwise.[23] The Home Secretary said in June 1989 that he accepted this recommendation and that regulations would make the necessary amendment.[24]

The provisions of Part IX of the Act do not apply however to complaints regarding the "direction or control of a police force" by the chief officer or someone on his behalf (subs. (5)). Such complaints continue to be dealt with through the police authority calling for a report from the chief constable under section 12(2) of the Police Act 1964.

But it is not entirely clear what is meant by "direction and control of a police force". The P.C.A. in its first Triennial Review said that some Forces saw in this exclusion clause an opportunity to withdraw from its supervision some quite minor tactical decisions by junior officers "which were so obviously wrong as to amount to neglect of duty".[25] So, for instance, taking a very large number of officers to search a small house where no violent resistance was expected seemed calculated to strike terror into the

---

[17] *ibid.* para. 1.1, p. 5.
[18] *ibid.* para. 1.6, p. 6.
[19] House of Commons, *Hansard*, Vol. 155, June 27, 1989, Col. 398.
[20] *Triennial Review 1991–94*, H.C. 396, May 1994, p. 7.
[21] *op. cit.* n.16, p. 258 above, para. 1.7, p. 7.
[22] *ibid.*
[23] *ibid.* para. 1.8, p. 7.
[24] *op. cit.* n.19 above, Col. 397.
[25] *op. cit.* n.16, p. 258 above, para. 1.9, p. 7.

occupants rather than to achieve a more effective search. But there were some forces that argued that this came within the concept of decisions that related to the "direction and control" of a force. Leading counsel advised the Authority that the phrase "direction and control" was limited to strategic and central command of an entire force by the chief officer and that it referred only to matters of high command and policy. This construction of the exclusion clause, the P.C.A. said in the first Triennial Review had "proved reasonably trouble-free in practice and no substantial disagreement has arisen from it".[26]

Another exception is that Part IX procedures do not apply if the conduct has already been the subject of criminal or disciplinary proceedings (subs. (6)). If the matter has already been investigated there is no point in registering and investigating it as a formal complaint.

Investigation of complaints: standard procedure: section 85

If the chief constable decides that he is the appropriate authority he must record the complaint (subs. (1)). This replaced the duty to record complaints placed on chief officers of police by section 49(1) of the Police Act 1964. Under the new arrangements in Northern Ireland, the chief constable is obliged to refer a complaint to the Independent Commission for Police Complaints as soon as he has recorded it (see Appendix 4, p. 533 below [Art. 18(1)]).

The chief officer must next determine whether the complaint ought to be investigated formally or whether it is suitable for informal resolution and may appoint an officer from his own force to assist him (subs. (2)). The original requirement in PACE (s.95(8)) that the officer so appointed be at least of the rank of chief inspector and at least of the rank as the officer complained against has been repealed.[27]

A complaint is not suitable for informal resolution unless the member of the public consents and the chief officer is satisfied that, even if proved, the conduct would not justify criminal or disciplinary proceedings (subs. (10)).

If, after attempts have been made to settle the matter informally, it appears to the chief officer that the complaint is not after all suitable for informal resolution or that informal resolution of the matter is impossible, he must appoint an officer from his own force or another force to conduct an investigation. If he requests an officer from another force, the request cannot be refused (subss. (5) and (7)). Unless the investigation is supervised by the Authority, the officer who conducts the investigation must report about it to the chief officer (subs. (9)). If the complaint is considered by the chief officer to be suitable for informal resolution he must (under subs. (4)) seek to have it resolved informally and may appoint an officer from his own force for the purpose.

Informal resolution of complaints

There is nothing about the *method* of informal resolution of complaints in the Act but the 1983 White Paper went into some detail about the new system. No fixed procedure was imposed on police officers. The Police

---

[26] *ibid.* para. 1.10, p. 7.
[27] Police and Magistrates' Courts Act 1994, Sched. 9.

organ, impairment of bodily function, a deep cut or a deep laceration" (subs. (4)) (or, more informally, as broken bones or wounds requiring three or more stitches).

The 1983 White Paper stated that such cases must be referred to the Authority "irrespective of whether [the chief officer] considers that police action was or could have been responsible".[56]

The duty to refer cases arises on the basis of an allegation. The P.C.A. said in its 1988 Annual Report[57] that sometimes a force delayed referring a complaint until the allegation had been verified. But this was a misreading of the Act.

Regulations specify other types of complaints which must also be notified to the Authority (subs. (1)(a)(ii)). The Police (Complaints) (Mandatory Referrals Etc.) Regulations 1985 (S.I. 1985 No. 673) specify that any complaint alleging assault occasioning actual bodily harm or an offence under section 1 of the Prevention of Corruption Act 1906 or a serious arrestable offence under PACE must be referred to the Authority.[58] But the complaints in this additional list do not have to be supervised by the Authority. It is given a discretion.

In addition, a chief officer is entitled but not required to notify the Authority about any other complaint (subs. (1)(b)). The White Paper envisaged that the chief officer would exercise this discretion in regard to any complaint which he thought should be brought to the attention of the Authority "whether by reason of the gravity of the allegation or other exceptional circumstances".[59]

In its first Triennial Review the P.C.A. recommended that all incidents in the course of which a firearm is discharged, whether accidentally or deliberately, should be within the category referred mandatorily.[60] Most such cases were referred under section 87(1) or section 88 (below). But there was no compulsion on chief officers to refer such cases in the absence of a complaint. Even if a complaint of negligent or improper discharge of a firearm was lodged, it was not mandatory on forces to refer it unless someone was hurt. The P.C.A. could call the case in under section 87(2) but that could only be done if there was a complaint in being. Some accidental discharges of firearms had not been referred to the Authority. Because of the general public interest in the use of firearms by the police it would be better if there could always be an independent presence at the examination of the incident.

In its second Triennial Report in 1991, the P.C.A. said it would not press the matter since in practice it seemed that all cases involving discharge of firearms by the police were referred.[61] In the same report it said that it would not press for extension of the duty of mandatory referral to cases deserving supervision because of their gravity or other exceptional circumstances when there was no complaint. Experience showed that such cases were referred under section 88.[62]

Regulations specify the time limits within which complaints requiring

[56] *op. cit.* n.3, p. 255 above, 1983, para. 14.
[57] *ibid.* para. 1.3, p. 8.
[58] See Reg. 4.
[59] *op. cit.* n.4, p. 255 above, para. 16.
[60] *op. cit.* n.16, p. 258 above, paras. 2.32–2.33, p. 23.
[61] *Triennial Review, 1988–91*, H.C. 352, 1991, para. 1.26.
[62] *ibid.* para. 1.13.

mandatory reference or notification must be referred to the Authority (subs. (3)). The White Paper stated that such references and notifications should be effected "as soon as practicable and normally not later than the day after the complaint is recorded".[63]

The regulations for mandatory referrals[64] require that where complaints are required to be referred, notification shall be given not later than the end of the day following the day on which it becomes clear that the complaint is one that must be referred to the P.C.A. The P.C.A.'s first Triennial Review said that if necessary police could contact the Authority by telex or fax out of working hours. Generally the time limit had been met but there had been cases where an unexplainable delay had occurred.[65]

The Authority has the power to require the appropriate authority to submit to them for consideration any complaint which it has not referred to them and that authority (defined in s.84) has to comply with such a request within specified time limits (subs. (2)). In this connection it is important that the Authority, unlike the Ombudsman, is permitted to receive complaints direct from members of the public, M.P.s, the Home Secretary or any other source. The Authority can also ask the chief officer to provide all such information as is necessary to enable it to determine whether it wishes to supervise the investigation into the matter.[66]

Reference of other allegations to the authority: section 88

Section 88 enables other matters indicating that an officer may have committed a criminal offence or may have behaved in a manner justifying disciplinary proceedings not contained in a complaint, to be referred to the Authority, for it to decide whether it ought to supervise the investigation. Such a case might arise for instance where a civil action has been brought against the police or because of a newspaper campaign or local or national notoriety. The appropriate authority has the right to refer such a case to the Authority in its discretion because of its gravity or exceptional circumstances.

The first Triennial Review of the P.C.A. said that from the outset forces made considerable use of section 88 to "draw the Authority into the investigation of matters which, by reason of their gravity or exceptional circumstances, seemed to call for supervision on behalf of the public even though no complaint had been made".[67] Sometimes these referrals were followed by complaints from members of the public arising out of the same incident. But the investigation under section 88 was usually more thorough and far-reaching. The resource implications of such inquiries were considerable ("sometimes a team of 12 or 15 officers may be engaged for upwards of a year in unravelling the tangled web of events and the report which they ultimately produce may run to dozens of volumes".)[68]

The P.C.A.'s Annual Report for 1993 said that forces had referred 69

---

[63] *op. cit.* n.4, p. 255 above, para. 13.
[64] *op. cit.* text to n.58 above, Reg. 4.
[65] *op. cit.* n.16, p. 258 above, para. 1.28, p. 11.
[66] *op. cit.* n.4, p. 255 above, para. 1.
[67] *op. cit.* n.16, p. 258 above, para. 1.32, p. 11.
[68] *ibid.* para. 1.33, p. 12.

cases under section 88 and that the Authority agreed to supervise all but five. This compared with 68 referrals and 60 supervised cases in 1992. (On supervision generally see section 89 below.)

Supervision of investigation by the Authority: section 89

Section 89 sets out the powers, duties and procedures of the P.C.A. in the supervision of complaints investigations.

There are two kinds of cases where supervision is mandatory. The first is where there has been a complaint alleging death or serious injury. The second is any other type of complaint specified in regulations made by the Secretary of State (subs. (1)).

The first Triennial Review proposed[69] that the P.C.A. should have a discretion to dispense with supervision in cases where they are satisfied on proper evidence that the injury sustained is minor, notwithstanding the definition of "serious injury" in section 87(4). At present the Authority was obliged to supervise investigations into fractures or impairment of bodily functions even when they were very minor. It should be given a discretion, whether the nature of the injury was apparent from the outset or only became so during the investigation. The Government accepted this recommendation in its statement of June 27, 1989.[70]

The House of Commons Home Affairs Committee recommended in its Fifth Report that the P.C.A. should be given a discretion in regard to all cases that are now required to be supervised mandatorily. The number of mandatory supervisions acted as a constraint on the number of discretionary supervisions that could be undertaken. Where the evidence clearly suggested that there was no need for very close scrutiny the P.C.A. should have the power not to supervise. This would not remove its duty to consider the report of the completed investigation.[71]

The Government's Reply to the Fifth Report said that the Government accepted the view "that some relaxation would be appropriate in the categories of case requiring mandatory supervision by the Authority. But the Government had no plans for early legislation "in view of the already heavy programme of legislation faced by Parliament."[72]

In its 1991 second Triennial Review the P.C.A. recommended that mandatory supervision of investigations be retained only in complaints involving death, leaving the Authority with absolute discretion to supervise as it thought fit in all other cases.[73] But the Home Secretary rejected this proposal as it gave the impression of down-grading complaints involving serious injury and in its 1994 Triennial Review the P.C.A. said[74] that, having reconsidered the matter it did not feel justified in pressing further for the change. Partly the problem would be eased by the new power to

---

[69] *op. cit.* n.16, p. 258 above, para. 2.31, pp. 22–23.
[70] *op. cit.* n.19, p. 259 above, Col. 397.
[71] "Annual Report of the Police Complaints Authority for 1988", H.C. 1988–89, 395–1, paras. 63–65.
[72] The Government Reply to the Fifth Report from the Home Affairs Committee Session 1988–89, H.C. 395–1, "The Annual Report of the Police Complaints Authority for 1988", Cmnd. 928, p. 4.
[73] Initially, both the Home Office and the House of Commons Home Affairs Committee supported this proposal but both changed their mind. See Home Affairs Committee, Fourth Report, 1991–92, H.C. 179, para. 14.
[74] *op. cit.* n.20, p. 259 above, at p. 8.

relinquish supervision where injuries proved to be less serious than originally alleged.

As has been seen, the Authority has a discretion as to whether or not to supervise in relation to any other lesser complaint or any matter referred to them under section 88. The test is simply whether they think that such supervision "is desirable in the public interest" (subs. (2)).

The P.C.A.'s annual report states the numbers of cases that are supervised. Broadly they represent about 10 per cent of all matters being dealt with but they usually represent close to 20–23 per cent of the 4,139 cases referred by police forces for possible supervision. In 1993 by far the greatest proportion (66 per cent) involved death or serious injury. The next highest category was assault occasioning bodily harm (15 per cent). The other categories were corruption (2 per cent), serious arrestable offence (5 per cent), other complaint referred voluntarily (4 per cent), other referral required by the P.C.A. (1 per cent) and voluntary referral under section 88 (7 per cent)—see P.C.A. Annual Report, 1993, pp. 19–25.

When the Authority have decided whether or not to exercise their discretionary power to supervise an investigation they must inform the appropriate authority accordingly (subs. (3)).

The Authority may require that it should approve the appointment of an investigating officer in a case it is to supervise (subs. (4)). It therefore has the right to select a particular individual name or to veto a name selected by the chief officer. The Authority may require that no appointment of an officer be made until it approves his name, or if one has already been made, that it be changed (*ibid.*).

Regulations have been made by the Secretary of State regarding the duty of the Authority to consult and obtain the consent of the D.P.P. before imposing requirements in relation to evidential matters (see subs. (5) and the White Paper, para. 26).[75] However, subject to such regulations, the Authority has the power to impose requirements as to how the investigation should be conducted. This can include requirements as to the resources to be deployed on an investigation not simply as to the manner of the inquiry. But the regulations require that any such requirement involving disposition of resources is subject to a duty to consult with the chief constable.[76]

Subsection (6) of section 89 requires the investigating officer to submit his report to the Authority in any case in which it has supervised and to send a copy to the chief officer concerned. Sometimes the report is a mere dozen or so pages; sometimes it runs into many volumes. It contains full details of the complaint, statement from witnesses, and, where appropriate, material such as diagrams, photographs, copies of the custody record, of police officers' notebooks, tape recordings and any other relevant information. The final document is the officer's response to the complaint which might be a written statement, contemporaneous notes of an interview or often a tape of such an interview. But a police officer must be advised of his right to say nothing and a few exercise this right.[77]

After considering this report the Authority must send "an appropriate statement" to the "appropriate authority" (subs. (7)). An appropriate

---

[75] See The Police (Complaints) (Mandatory Referrals Etc.) Regulations 1985, S.I. 1985, No. 673, Reg. 5(3).
[76] *ibid.* Reg. 5(4).
[77] P.C.A., *Annual Report*, 1988, para. 2.8, p. 12. This will change under the Home Secretary's new disciplinary system, see p. 287 below.

statement is defined in subsection (10) as one as to whether the investigation was or was not conducted to the Authority's satisfaction; specifying any way in which it was not so conducted; and dealing with such other matters as the Home Secretary may specify in regulations.

If it is practicable to do so, the Authority when submitting the appropriate statement under subsection (7) must send a copy of it to the officer whose conduct has been investigated (subs. (8)). Similarly, if the investigation is related to a complaint it must, if it is practicable, send a copy to the person by or on behalf of whom the complaint was brought (subs. (9)). In practice the Authority sends its report to the chief officer with enough copies for each officer involved.[78]

Lord Elton explained in the House of Lords what sort of things might make this "not practicable". "Complainants may move away and not be traceable; the investigation may fail to identify a particular officer; indeed investigation might reveal that the person concerned was not a police officer at all."[79] It is also conceivable that it might turn out that the alleged incident never occurred at all.

In its annual report for 1985 the P.C.A. said "we regard the letters we write to members of the public as one of our most important tasks".[80] It tried to write letters which were readily understandable and which contained a fair and balanced explanation of the outcome of the investigation. Sometimes, inevitably, the report left the matter unresolved—often because there was no way of reconciling the different accounts of an incident by the complainant and the officer(s) concerned. Many complainants thought that in such circumstances their complaint had been rejected. This was not the case. Merely it had not been possible to get to the bottom of the matter.

The Authority can, if it wishes, issue separate statements on the criminal and disciplinary aspects of an investigation (subs. (11)). No disciplinary proceeding charges may be brought before the Authority's statement has been submitted to the appropriate authority (subs. (12)). Similarly, neither the appropriate authority nor the Director of Public Prosecutions should normally start criminal proceedings before the appropriate statement has been submitted. But if the D.P.P. thinks there are exceptional circumstances which make it undesirable to wait, criminal proceedings can be brought before the Authority's statement has been submitted (subss. (13) and (14)).

The extent to which the supervising member is involved depends on the nature of the case. Some involve very close liaison with the Investigating Officer. Sometimes the supervising member is even present during the interviewing of witnesses. But in the majority of cases the P.C.A. has found it sufficient to maintain contact by telephone and letter with perhaps an occasional meeting with the Investigating Officer. Sometimes at the outset of the process of supervision there is some conference with the Investigating Officer so that the P.C.A. can satisfy itself that appropriate action has been taken to preserve the necessary evidence and to identify witnesses and suspects. The plan of the investigation is discussed and agreed. The P.C.A. also checks that sufficient resources will be available to support the investigation. Usually it is arranged that as statements are taken and evidence is collected it is submitted to the supervisory member for scrutiny.

[78] P.C.A., *Annual Report*, 1986, p. 8.
[79] House of Lords, *Hansard*, July 11, 1984, Col. 994.
[80] Para. 4.14, p. 19.

Sometimes arrangements are made for interim reports on progress to be made. The supervising member may recommend that a witness be re-interviewed, that further witnesses be seen or that further evidence be collected. Almost always such recommendations are accepted by the Investigating Officer and there is no need for the Authority to exercise its formal power to require some further action to be taken.[81]

The White Paper gave some further indications regarding the nature of supervision by the Authority. It would be able, after consulting with the chief officer, to require that an investigation team be augmented in respect of manpower, equipment or other resources.[82] It would have the right to give investigating officers "such reasonable directions as it considers necessary for the proper conduct of the investigation" (subject to the consent of the D.P.P. in matters concerning the collection of evidence for possible criminal proceedings).[83] These powers would enable it to require investigating officers "to account for their actions; to explain the strategy and tactics of their investigation; and to justify particular lines and depth of questioning and any apparent delay in the investigation".[84] The degree of supervision in any particular case would depend on the circumstances but it was expected "that consultation and advice, rather than formal directions will be the usual means by which the Authority will proceed".[85] The members of the Authority would be divided into two divisions—one for investigations and one for discipline cases. No one would consider the same case from the point of view of both functions.

If a member of the Authority had been directed to take direct responsibility for the conduct of an investigation he would have regular contact with the officer in charge of the investigation. He could if he wished visit the scene of the incident or inspect material evidence. But it would not be his function to become directly involved in the process of investigation itself. So he would not for example attend interviews conducted by the investigating officer.

The P.C.A.'s annual reports give details of its methods. The Report for 1988, for instance, said that each investigation was supervised personally by a member of the Authority. The P.C.A. ensured that the complainant was given every opportunity to make a full statement, nominate witnesses and draw attention to evidence which might support the complaint. Sometimes the complainant refused to provide a written statement, which usually hampered and sometimes completely prevented the investigation going forward. In the great majority of cases however, the P.C.A. found that the investigation produced "lucid and comprehensive reports".[86]

Research carried out at the Centre for Criminological Research, Oxford University by Mike Maguire and Claire Corbett[87] has shown that the P.C.A.'s account of its own supervision may however give a somewhat overly rosy impression of the extent of its "hands on" supervision.

---

[81] This description is taken from the 1985 Annual Report, pp. 11–12.
[82] *op. cit.* n.4, p. 255 above, para. 21.
[83] *ibid.* para. 22.
[84] *ibid.*
[85] *ibid.*
[86] The Police Complaints Authority, *Annual Report*, 1988, para. 1.8; 1989 Report, chap. 2.
[87] See Mike Maguire, "Complaints Against the Police: The British Experience", in *Complaints Against the Police: A Comparative Study*, ed. A. Goldsmith (Oxford University, 1990). See also M. Maguire, and C. Corbett, "Patterns and Profiles of Complaints Against the Police" in Morgan, R. and Smith D. (eds) *Coming to Terms with Policing* (Routledge, 1989) and especially M. Maguire and C. Corbett, *A Study of the Police Complaints System* (HMSO, 1991).

Close analysis of a sample of 100 supervised cases showed that: "Half of all cases had been dealt with entirely in the 'passive' mode, and nearly all the remainder in a moderately active fashion. Intensive participant styles of supervision were to be found in only a handful of cases. Members met investigating officers personally in only 18 of the 100 cases sampled, and in most of these there was only one meeting. Meetings with complainants, witnesses or other interested parties occurred in only four. Finally we could find only six cases in which members directed the police to pursue a particular line in the investigation."[88]

The cases in which the P.C.A. were most likely to take an active interest were those in which there was intense media interest—mainly section 88 cases, many of which had in fact been referred by the police themselves.

Active attention was more likely in cases where the P.C.A. had themselves selected the case than in cases they were obliged to take on.

The research attempted an assessment of the value of supervision. It concluded that the empirical evidence was somewhat inconclusive as to whether it made any difference to the outcome of cases. Taking only mandatory referral cases there was virtually no difference in the outcome of supervised and unsupervised cases. In cases where the Authority had a choice (which may have been affected by the possibility of a successful outcome), the statistical difference was greater. The greatest difference was in cases ending with "advice" to the officer.

But there was no difference in the satisfaction level as to the outcome among complainants as between supervised and unsupervised cases. A slightly higher proportion (26 per cent against 17 per cent) of those who had experienced supervision as against those who had not said they were very or fairly satisfied with the general handling of their case. More of those whose complaints had been supervised felt that their complaint had been treated seriously, that the investigation had been thorough and that they had been kept informed. But the differences were small and in any case the great majority of reactions of complainants were negative. Only 9 per cent believed that the Authority was independent of the police and 5 per cent that it was effective in its monitoring role!

Concerning complaints against the police generally, the research by Maguire and Corbett suggests that the great majority of complainants are dissatisfied with the system. Over two-thirds of complainants said they were dissatisfied and most were very dissatisfied. Those whose complaints are investigated formally are the most dissatisfied. Their criticisms are of delay, absence of an apology and the inadequacy of explanations for decisions reached. These were found regardless of whether the complaint was substantiated. At the root of the criticisms was a lack of communication with the complainant. Officers complained against were also critical of delays in the system.

In its first Triennial Review the P.C.A. urged that it be given additional powers of investigation equivalent to those available to the police under PACE, Part II and Schedule 1.[89] The call was supported by the House of Commons Home Affairs Committee in its Fourth Report in 1988.[90] But the

---

[88] *op. cit.* n.87, "Complaints Against the Police: The British Experience" at p. 195.
[89] *op. cit.* n.16, p. 258 above, paras. 2.12–15, pp. 18–19.
[90] House of Commons Home Affairs Committee, Fourth Report, "*Parliamentary Accountability of the Police Complaints Authority*", November 1988, H.C. 583, para. 21.

Government rejected the recommendation in the Home Secretary's statement of June 27, 1989[91] and in its Fifth Report the Home Affairs Committee said that "on reflection" it accepted the Home Secretary's decision that the additional powers were not necessary, at least for the time being.[92]

The Authority's role in regard to the investigation of the complaint ceases with the issue of its "appropriate statement". It is not involved in any criminal prosecution.

The Authority's statement is publicly available. Whilst not naming names or providing evidential details it can record such matters as the numbers of witnesses interviewed and statements recorded; the time taken; and the number and rank of officers involved in the investigation.[93] (On problems associated with publication of its reports see p. 276 below.)

The role of the D.P.P.

If a police officer investigating a complaint under the supervision of the Authority wishes to consult the D.P.P. he is entirely free to do so as before—but he must inform the Authority of this intention and of the result of such consultation. Normally the Authority would wish to be involved in such discussions and it would have the right to do so.[94] Where the Authority is intending to give advice short of a formal direction on any matter relating to the collection of evidence for possible criminal proceedings it should first ensure that such advice conforms to the policy of the D.P.P.[95] Where the Authority finds it necessary to give formal directions on such a matter the White Paper said that it would be important to define the relationship between the Authority and the D.P.P. with care. "The need here is to strike a balance between on the one hand the independent position of the D.P.P. and his responsibilities for prosecution policy, and on the other, the new Authority's role as guardian of the public interest in the investigation of a special category of case of concern also to the D.P.P."[96] The Authority is required by law to consult the D.P.P. before giving directions on evidential questions and his consent is required before such directions may be made.[97] If it ever happened that the D.P.P. refused his consent the Authority can make reference to the fact in the statement it issues at the end of the inquiry.

Steps to be taken after investigation of complaint—general: section 90

If the report received by the appropriate authority relates to a senior officer (under section 86(6) or 89(6)) it *has* to be sent to the D.P.P. unless the report "satisfies them that no criminal offence has been committed" (subs. (1)).

The 1984 Act provided that the chief officer had to consider first, whether the investigation showed that a criminal offence might have been committed, and second, whether the officer ought to be charged (subs. (3)). If so, he had to refer it to the D.P.P. (subs. (4)). The P.C.A.'s second Triennial Report

---

[91] *op. cit.* n.19, p. 259 above, Col. 398.
[92] *op. cit.* n.71, p. 267 above, para. 42.
[93] *op. cit.* n.4, p. 255 above, para. 27.
[94] *ibid.* para. 25.
[95] *ibid.*
[96] *ibid.* para. 26.
[97] *ibid.*

suggested that this gave the chief officer too much discretion.[98] The point was taken by the Home Office and the Police and Magistrates' Courts Act 1994 eliminated the discretion. Section 90 as amended[99] now requires a report to the D.P.P. whenever the chief officer determines that the report indicates that a criminal offence "may have been committed".

The D.P.P.'s approach to the question of whether to prosecute has provoked considerable controversy, because of the policy of taking into account the well-known difficulty of getting convictions of police officers.[1]

After the D.P.P. has dealt with the question of criminal charges the chief officer must in cases prescribed in regulations (to be made) send the Authority a memorandum stating whether he has preferred disciplinary charges and if not, his reasons for not doing so (subs. (5)).

But if the chief constable decides that no criminal offence was committed he has to send the Authority a memorandum to that effect stating whether he has brought or intends to bring disciplinary proceedings and, if not, his reasons (subs. (7)).

Where the investigation related to conduct which was the subject of a complaint that was not supervised by the Authority and it is a case in regard to which the regulations require a memorandum to be sent to the Authority, the chief officer must send the Authority a copy of the complaint and of the report of the investigation when he sends them his memorandum (subs. (9)). Otherwise there would be no way for the Authority to be sure of getting a copy.

If the chief officer states in his memorandum that he has started or intends to start disciplinary proceedings, subject to the provisions of section 93(6) below, he is required by subsection (10) actually to carry out this intention. The standard of proof for disciplinary charges is "beyond reasonable doubt", as for criminal charges.

Steps to be taken where accused has admitted charges: section 91

The provisions of section 91 of PACE (which required a report to be sent to the P.C.A. of the outcome of disciplinary proceedings and the officer pleaded guilty) were repealed by the Police and Magistrates' Courts Act 1994, Schedule 5, paragraph 28.

Powers of the Authority to direct reference of reports etc. to D.P.P.: section 92

Section 92 of the 1984 Act dealt with the duty of the P.C.A. to direct the chief constable to send to the D.P.P. reports concerning apparent criminal offences committed by officers below the rank of superintendent. With the change under the 1994 Act (s.90, see above) regarding criminal charges, section 92 was no longer necessary and it was accordingly repealed.[2]

---

[98] *op. cit.* n.61, p. 265 above, para. 1.14.
[99] By Police and Magistrates' Courts Act 1994, s.35.
[1] See especially Glanville Williams, "Letting off the guilty and prosecuting the innocent", [1985] Crim.L.R. 115 and L. Lustgarten, *The Governance of Police*, Sweet & Maxwell, 1986, pp. 139–140. Professor Williams said (at p. 116) that the D.P.P.'s policy meant that corrupt and violent policemen were not brought to book when others would be. Mr. Lustgarten argued (p. 140) that the policy represented "a flagrant violation of the rule of law".
[2] Police and Magistrates' Courts Act 1994, s.37(b).

Powers of the Authority as to disciplinary charges: section 93

Section 93 confers on the Authority the same powers to recommend and direct the bringing of disciplinary charges as the Police Complaints Board had under section 3 of the Police Act 1976.

Subsection (1) states that where a memorandum under section 90 indicates that the chief officer does not intend to bring disciplinary proceedings, the Authority may recommend that he bring such charges as it specifies.

If after the Authority has made such a recommendation and has consulted the chief officer, he still declines to bring proceedings, the Authority may direct him to do so (subs. (3)). Where the Authority give the chief officer a direction under section 93 they must give him written reasons (subs. (4)). The chief officer must comply with any such direction (subs. (5)). (There are only a handful of such cases per year.) Disciplinary charges brought either on the chief officer's initiative or following a recommendation or direction by the Authority cannot be withdrawn save with the leave of the Authority (subs. (2)). Directions given under this section can be withdrawn by the Authority.[3]

The chief officer must inform the Authority what steps he has taken in response to a recommendation or direction under the section and must furnish the P.C.A. with such further information as it may reasonably require (subs. (7)).

In its first Triennial Review the Authority suggested that there was an illogicality in the procedure laid down in the Act when the P.C.A. wish to use their powers to recommend or direct charges. At the initial stage it is required to make a formal recommendation and to consult the chief officer. If, after consultation, the chief officer is still unwilling to prefer charges, the P.C.A. may direct that charges be preferred and must furnish him with a written statement of their reasons. It would be more logical, it suggested, if the Authority gave their reasons for preferring charges at the stage of recommendations, when the chief officer must be consulted. The Act should be amended accordingly.[4] The Home Office statement of June 27, 1989 accepted this recommendation.[5] But in its 1994 Triennial Review the P.C.A. said[6] it did not after all intend to press for the change since in practice the issue presented no problem.

Disciplinary tribunals: section 94

Section 94 dealt with the establishment of disciplinary tribunals. The section was repealed by the 1994 Police and Magistrates' Courts Act 1994, section 37(c) and Schedule 9—as part of the overall reform of the disciplinary system.

Section 94 provided for disciplinary tribunals set up at the direction or on the recommendation of the P.C.A. to include two members of the Authority. The P.C.A. in its second Triennial Review suggested that it would be better if in such cases it did not provide members and this recommendation was

---

[3] See Police and Magistrates' Courts Act 1994, s.36(6).
[4] *op. cit.* n.16, p. 258 above, para. 1.42, p. 13.
[5] *op. cit.* n.19, p. 259 above, Col. 397.
[6] *op. cit.* n.20, p. 259 above, at p. 8.

accepted. Schedule 3 of the Police and Magistrates' Courts Act 1994 provides for two types of appeal tribunal, one for senior officers and the second for other officers. For senior officers a three person tribunal is appointed by the Home Secretary consisting of a member of another police authority, a person who has been either an Inspector of Constabulary or a former Commissioner of the Metropolitan force and a legally qualified chairman. For other officers the relevant police authority appoints a four person tribunal consisting of a legally qualified chairman, a member of the police authority, a serving or recently retired chief officer of another force, and a retired officer of "appropriate rank".

Information as to the manner of dealing with complaints: section 95

Section 95 requires police authorities and H.M. Inspectorate of Constabulary to keep themselves informed about the way in which complaints against police officers are dealt with. The provision is similar to, but not identical with, section 50 of the Police Act 1964. But whereas that spoke of "the manner in which complaints ... are dealt with by the chief officer of police", section 95 refers more generally to "the working of sections 84 and 93". The section contemplates in particular the arrangements for the handling of minor complaints by informal means.

Constabularies maintained by authorities other than police authorities: section 96

Section 96 is the equivalent of section 7 of the Police Act 1976 under which the Police Complaints Board had power to exercise its functions in relation to constables maintained by bodies other than police authorities.

Subsection (1) permits the Authority, with the approval of the Home Secretary, to make such arrangements. Subsection (2) permits the Home Secretary, where no such arrangements are in force, to make them by order after consulting with the Authority and with the body maintaining the constabulary in question (subs. (4)). Any such order must be by way of statutory instrument subject to the negative resolution procedure (subs. (5)).

The forces within the scheme are the British Transport Police, the Ministry of Defence Police, the Port of Liverpool Police, the Port of Tilbury (formerly the Port of London) Police, the Royal Parks Constabulary and the United Kingdom Atomic Energy Authority Constabulary. The Fourth Report of the House of Commons Home Affairs Committee said that the Home Office view was that in principle "any force whose members have direct contact with the public in circumstances which could give rise to complaints, should have those complaints dealt with by the Police Complaints Authority".[7] Most of the forces outside the purview of the P.C.A. fell within the responsibility of Government Departments other than the Home Office. But Home Office witnesses told the Committee that they felt it was their responsibility to coordinate the efforts to include all remaining forces within the established procedure. The Committee said that it supported this intention.[8]

[7] *op. cit.* n.90, p. 271 above, para. 18, p. vii.
[8] *ibid.*

A further anomaly was revealed when it became clear from evidence that the activities of the Cusoms and Excise, whose officers have powers of search and arrest analogous to those of the police, were not subject to the Authority. Since customs officers are not legally "constables" they fell outside Part IX of PACE. The Committee said it expected the Government to consider the introduction of machinery similar to that established for the police to cover "this sensitive area of law enforcement".[9]

Reports: section 97

Section 97 provides for the Authority to make Annual and Triennial Reports and special reports as requested by the Secretary of State or on its own initiative. The section is similar to section 8 of the Police Act 1976 save that section 97 requires all such reports to be laid before Parliament and published whereas section 8 required this only in regard to the annual reports.

The Authority must respond to requests for reports from the Home Secretary and may for that purpose carry out research (subs. (1)). It can report to the Home Secretary on any matter to which it wishes to draw his attention because of its gravity or other exceptional circumstances.

The Fourth Report of the Home Affairs Committee of the House of Commons proposed that the work of the Authority should become the subject of regular scrutiny by the Committee. This had been proposed by the P.C.A.'s Chairman, Sir Cecil Clothier, the former Ombudsman, and the Committee agreed with him that the model of the relationship between the Ombudsman and the Parliamentary Select Committee for Administration was a good one ("the Parliamentary Commissioner has added impetus in his investigations. Trends and problems can be identified and discussed in Parliament before they become acute. Public confidence in the complaints machinery is thereby enhanced").[10] A similar arrangement should be established between the P.C.A. and the Home Affairs Committee. No change in the law was needed. The Committee would each year review the annual report and as necessary the Triennial Review and other reports of the P.C.A. It would undertake inquiries into any matters that seemed to merit investigation—"either because they reveal difficulties for the Authority in discharging its functions or because they show trends in complaints about police activities".[11]

The requirement in subs. 97(4) for the P.C.A. to make a Triennial Report was abolished (at the suggestion of the P.C.A.) by the Police and Magistrates' Courts Act 1994, s.37(d).

Restriction on disclosure: section 98

Section 98 restricts the unauthorised disclosure of information received by the Authority in the performance of its duties subject to a fine on summary conviction not exceeding level 5 on the scale laid down by the Criminal Justice Act 1982.

This section has caused the Authority considerable difficulties and in its

[9] *ibid.* para. 19, p. vii.
[10] *op. cit.* n.90, p. 271 above, para. 12, pp. v–vi.
[11] *ibid.* para. 14, p. vi.

first Triennial Review it recommended that it required "radical overhaul".[12] The problem was partly that the section was "unreasonably restrictive of the Authority".[13] It permitted publication of "a summary or other general statement" but said that the informant or parties affected must not be identified, "even though in most cases calling for a public statement the whole world knows who they are from the start".[14] The Review recommended that the Authority should be given discretion to publish such information as is reasonably necessary to inform the public of the outcome of investigations, without derogating from the principle of confidentiality between the Authority, complainants and those who provide information.[15] (The same point was made by the Authority in its evidence to the House of Commons Home Affairs Committee on July 6, 1988. Its memorandum said: "Whilst we can issue a summary or general statement the apparent secretiveness about names, places and circumstances, enjoined on us by the Act, often on occasions when there had been full identification in the media of everyone concerned, makes us look woodenly bureaucratic and timid. We have often wished that we had been entrusted with a greater discretion about when and how much to tell the public about the results of investigations with which we have been intimately involved."[16]) The Home Secretary said in his statement of June 27, 1989, that he accepted the recommendation.[17] But the opportunity to do something about the issue in the Police and Magistrates' Act 1994 was not taken. In its 1994 Triennial Review the P.C.A. said[18] that this was disappointing.

On the other hand, there were problems both in regard to access to the information held by the Authority by other persons and in regard to the use made of reports from the Authority by chief officers.

The first of these issues raised the question of whether material held by the Authority could be disclosed to third persons. In its first Triennial Review the P.C.A. said "nearly everyone concerned, before, during and after the processing of the complaint, would like to rummage in our files and by no means only from idle curiosity. Interested persons include the complainant and officers complained against, their legal advisers and representatives, persons named in files as having been involved in some disreputable way in the matter investigated, the Crown Prosecution Service, chief officers and their representatives wishing to defend their force at inquests or in civil proceedings, police authorities and Coroner's officers".[19] But many of those who gave statements did so on the basis that they were speaking in confidence. Section 98 made it a criminal offence to disclose information obtained in the course of investigations save in specified circumstances, one of which was "for the purposes of any criminal, civil or disciplinary proceedings".[20] But this could not mean that any party to litigation could claim access to the Authority's files. The P.C.A.'s view, supported by

[12] *op. cit.* n.16, p. 258 above, para. 2.10, p. 18.
[13] On the model of the agreements reached by the P.C.A. under section 96 with various non-Home Office police forces covering areas such as public transport, parks, ports, defence and atomic energy. See p. 275 above.
[14] *ibid.*
[15] *ibid.* para. 2.11, p. 18.
[16] *op. cit.* n.90, p. 271 above, Fourth Report, Evidence, p. 3, para. 8.
[17] *op. cit.* n.19, p. 259 above, Col. 39.
[18] *op. cit.* n.16, p. 258 above, at p. 10.
[19] *op. cit.* n.20, p. 259 above, para. 2.1, p. 16.
[20] PACE, s.98(1)(b).

Treasury Counsel, was that the exception was inserted for the benefit of the Authority and not to create a right of inspection for others.[21]

Public interest immunity

But could the P.C.A. be required to produce documents by parties to litigation? The P.C.A. considered that it was protected from doing so by public interest immunity. It took the view, on advice from the Treasury Solicitor, that it would produce nothing from its files save by order of a court ruling that the interests of justice in a particular case overrode the interests of confidentiality.[22] In a series of decisions the courts held that documents coming into existence in consequence of an investigation of a complaint against the police under Part IX of PACE were subject to public interest immunity *as a class.*[23] The P.C.A.'s view was that the rule was needed, for otherwise complainants and their witnesses would be deterred from co-operating with a complaints investigation until a civil action was resolved. This, it suggested, would have a detrimental effect on the important public interest in investigation of alleged misconduct by police officers. This rule was however overturned in July 1994 by the House of Lords in the cases of *R. v. Chief Constable of the West Midlands Police, ex p. Wiley and R. v. Chief Constable of the Nottinghamshire Constabulary, ex p. Sunderland.*[24] In his long leading judgment, Lord Woolf said that the courts had gone wrong. A class claim to immunity was unjustified since it tended to defeat the object it was designed to achieve. But a "contents claim" to immunity might be sustained on the facts and circumstances of the particular case.

By the time the case came before the House of Lords the P.C.A. had changed its approach to the problem. The law lords were told that the P.C.A. no longer wished to uphold a blanket claim to immunity for all such documents (which it was still maintaining at the Court of Appeal stage of the case). It thought that a claim to immunity would still be necessary for the report of the investigating officer which provided it with an assessment of the quality and credibility of witnesses and with a recommendation. It would likewise be necessary to have immunity for sensitive internal police material relating for instance to policy and operational matters, or documents identifying informers. In his judgment Lord Woolf did not purport to decide this matter other than to say in general terms that an immunity based on the contents of the particular document might be upheld.

In January 1995 the Court of Appeal held that the actual reports prepared by investigating officers under Part IX of PACE *were* entitled to public interest immunity as a class.[25] But it said, this would not necessarily shut a litigant out if he could persuade the trial judge that on the facts of the case the public interest in disclosing the contents of the report or any part of it outweighed the public interest in preserving their confidentiality.

---

[21] *op. cit.* n.20, p. 259 above, para. 2.2, p. 16.
[22] *ibid.* para. 2.4.
[23] See in particular *Neilson v. Laugharne* [1981] Q.B. 736, [1981] 2 W.L.R. 537, [1981] 1 All E.R. 829 C.A.; *Hehir v. Comr. of Police of the Metropolis* [1982] 1 W.L.R. 715, [1982] 2 All E.R. 335 C.A.; *Makanjuola v. Comr. of Police of the Metropolis* [1992] 3 All E.R. 617 C.A.
[24] [1994] 3 All E.R. 420 H.L.
[25] *Taylor v. Chief Constable of Greater Manchester* [1995] 2 All E.R. 420.

One situation in which public interest immunity will never apply is where the documents in question show that a miscarriage of justice has or may have occurred. The public interest in that situation will always require disclosure in the first instance to the prosecution authorities, and after sentence to the authorities responsible for dealing with alleged miscarriages of justice.[26] Disclosure in such situations will also be authorised to the person concerned and his advisers and sometimes further.[27] Another such situation is where the dominant purpose of the investigation which results in documents coming into existence is something other than the complaint.[28] Documents arising from a complaint investigation can also be released to a coroner investigating a death.

In *Makanjuola* Bingham L.J. (as he then was) said that to claim public interest immunity was a duty that could not be waived and it therefore should be claimed, leaving it to the court to decide.[29] Lord Woolf in *ex p. Wiley* said he did not think that this meant that a Department of State or other agency of government such as the Attorney General had to claim immunity rather than disclosing documents it thought should be disclosed. But parties other than government departments were in a different position. ("The indiscriminate and indeed any disclosure of documents which are the subject of a class claim to immunity can undermine the class" at p. 438.) It is not clear on which side of this line Lord Woolf would have placed the P.C.A. or the C.P.S.

So far as the police are concerned, Lord Woolf said that if the courts had established that a class claim to immunity existed a chief constable should not make disclosure at least without consulting the P.C.A. and the Attorney General "and possibly the Home Secretary as well" (p. 439). If they agreed to disclosure, it would be unobjectionable. But if they were in doubt, the wisest course would be to bring the matter to the court.

Public interest immunity in collateral proceedings

Section 98 applies only to the P.C.A. It does not apply to chief officers. Therefore when a chief officer receives a report under section 89(6) it is not subject in his hands to the restraints on disclosure imposed by section 98 on the Authority. So far as PACE is concerned he could therefore disclose it to anyone.

In its first Triennial Review the P.C.A. said that in its view public interest immunity applied but it had the impression that "the nature of that protection is very little understood amongst police forces".[30] In particular they did not always appreciate that the immunity belonged to the public and not to the holder of the confidence and that therefore only a judge could absolve one from the obligation to maintain confidentiality. Moreover, there

---

[26] Hitherto C3 at the Home Office but under the provisions of the Criminal Appeal Act 1995 it will be the new Criminal Cases Review Commission. The police are instructed to draw such material to the notice of the C.P.S. or C3 by Home Office Guidance to Chief Officers on Police Complaints and Discipline Procedures, 1991, para. 4.29.

[27] See *ex p. Coventry Newspapers Ltd* [1993] Q.B. 278, [1992] 3 W.L.R. 916, [1993] 1 All E.R. 816 C.A. Disclosure was first ordered to the convicted person of all the documents in the possession of the P.C.A. as a result of its investigation. But subsequently the Court of Appeal allowed the convicted person to hand the documents to a newspaper to permit it to defend libel proceedings brought by two police officers in the case.

[28] See *Peach v. Comr. of Police of the Metropolis* [1986] Q.B. 1064, [1986] 2 All E.R. 1064 C.A.

[29] *op. cit.* n.23 above, at 623.

[30] *op. cit.* n.16, p. 258 above, para. 2.7, p. 17.

was a tendency to think that provided the person asking for access to confidential files was "official" it was permissible to hand them over.[31] Some chief officers regarded the file as much their property as that of the P.C.A. In one case referred to by the P.C.A. in its first Triennial Review, "this led to statements made to 'our' investigating officer reappearing in court in the hands of counsel for the Force complained about".[32] The statements were used to contradict opposing witnesses. "The apparent linkage between the Authority and the police force under investigation did lasting and wide-spread damage to our claim to independence."[33] The P.C.A. said that more recent developments gave it increased anxieties in this regard. Some forces had been advised by counsel that the P.C.A.'s report was theirs to use as they pleased. It could therefore be used to instruct their representatives in any subsequent legal proceedings. The Authority had also taken legal advice and had been advised differently. In one case litigation between the Authority and a Force had only narrowly been averted. But "a most difficult conflict of interest and of interpretation of the Act" remained to be solved.[34]

In *ex p. Wiley* the Court of Appeal held that the police could not make any use in collateral proceedings such as a civil action for damages of knowledge obtained from documents that were subject to public interest immunity. But in the House of Lords this view was rejected by Lord Woolf. To prohibit the use of such knowledge, he suggested, would be "impractical and artificial". He recognised that it might have the effect of creating unfairness as between the parties[35] but it would be "neither desirable nor practical to try and achieve a level playing field" (p. 447) by prohibiting use to be made of such knowledge for instance in the preparation or handling of litigation.

Commenting on the House of Lords ruling, the journal *Police*[36] said that solicitors for the Federation said the judgment "was likely to have a substantial impact on the conduct of civil proceedings by both plaintiff and defendant". It would help chief officers because it would enable them to use material gathered during a complaints investigation in defending civil actions. But plaintiffs in civil actions might seek access to such documentation and there were certain to be many disputes as to what documents might still be covered by public interest immunity either on a class basis or because of the contents of the particular document.

Officers who were the subject of disciplinary proceedings should note that whatever they said in answer to allegations could now be disclosed in civil proceedings brought by the complainant. This would be the more significant since the Home Secretary has indicated that under the new proposed new discipline arrangements officers will come under a general duty to give answers to questions put in regard to such matters by their senior officers.

The Federation's solicitors also thought that the new ruling could assist officers wanting to sue complainants for defamation—by enabling them to use the investigation file to demonstrate the complainant's malice and thereby destroy the defence of qualified privilege.

The P.C.A. had recommended that chief officers be restricted in the use of

---

[31] *ibid.*
[32] *ibid.* para. 2.5, p. 17.
[33] *ibid.*
[34] *ibid.* para. 2.6, p. 17.
[35] For an explanation of the advantages that such use could give see the judgment of Staughton L.J. in the Court of Appeal in *ex p. Wiley* [1994] 1 All E.R. 702.
[36] February 1995, p. 7.

their copy of a report of a supervised investigation to the purposes for which they received the report and that they be prohibited from publishing any part of it.[37] The Home Office response in its statement of June 27, 1989 said that this matter was being reserved for further discussion with the police and the Authority.[38] It remains to be seen whether the view expressed in this regard by Lord Woolf in *ex p. Wiley* proves to be acceptable to the P.C.A., the Home Office and the police.

Regulations: section 99

Section 99 empowers the Secretary of State to make regulations as to the procedures to be followed under Part IX (Complaints and Discipline), and requires him to make regulations in respect of certain other matters. The regulations that he is required to make concern: (a) the supply to a complainant and the officer concerned of a copy of or a record of the complaint; (b) procedures for the informal resolution of complaints; (c) procedures for allowing an officer to comment orally or in writing on a complaint against him which is to be resolved informally; (d) cases where the complaint is withdrawn and any provisions of the Act are not to apply; (e) to enable the Authority to dispense with any requirement of Part IX; (ea) to enable the Authority to give up the supervision of the investigation of a complaint[39]; (f) procedures for the reference or submission of complaints to the Authority; (g) the supply of information or documents to the Authority; (i) notification by the Authority to the person concerned of any action or decision taken in regard to whether disciplinary charges should be brought or an investigation report should be sent to the D.P.P.

Regulations—supplementary: section 100

Section 100 enables the Secretary of State to make special provision for special cases, *e.g.* special provision to deal with administrative and constitutional arrangements in the Metropolitan Police. Before making such regulations the Home Secretary must provide the Police Advisory Board for England and Wales with a draft and consider any representations made by the Board (subs. (2)).

Discipline regulations: section 101

Section 101 set out provisions to be included in police discipline regulations made by the Home Secretary. It largely re-enacted section 10 of the Police Act 1964 in regard to the making of regulations dealing with police discipline. The Police (Discipline) Regulations 1985 (S.I. 1985 No. 518) is the

---

[37] *op. cit.* n.16, p. 258 above, para. 2.11.
[38] *op. cit.* n.19, p. 259 above, Col. 398.
[39] This was added by the Police and Magistrates' Courts Act 1994, Sched. 5, para. 31 in response to the P.C.A.'s request. It suggested that it should have a discretion to cease supervision when a complainant's injury proved to be less serious than originally alleged.

main set of regulations dealing with the procedure for discipline cases. It was repealed by the Magistrates' Courts Act 1994 section 37(e) as part of the overall reform of the police discipline system.

Representation at disciplinary proceedings: section 102

The Government and the police have disagreed as to whether police officers should be entitled to legal representation in disciplinary proceedings. When PACE was first introduced, the Government's view was that representation should be by a fellow officer. But it was forced to accept legal representation in the more serious cases.[40] As has been seen (p. 256 above), the Government's recent decision to make major changes in the disciplinary procedures included the abolition of the right to legal representation. When the Police and Magistrates' Courts Bill was introduced it contained a provision to abolish the entitlement to legal representation. But the Government was again defeated on the issue.[41]

The text of the original section 102 has been recast in light of the intention to change the discipline system,[42] but the content is essentially the same as before. It allows legal representation of officers at police disciplinary hearings where the officer is at risk of demotion, requirement to resign or dismissal.

Subsection (1) provides that an officer of the rank of superintendent or below cannot be dismissed, required to resign or reduced in rank unless he has been given an opportunity to be legally represented by a barrister or solicitor (subs. (2)) at any disciplinary hearing. Otherwise he can be represented by a fellow officer.

Disciplinary appeals: section 103

Section 103 dealt with appeals to the Secretary of State in disciplinary hearings. The section was repealed by the Police and Magistrates' Courts Act 1994, schedule 9. Appeals will no longer go to the Secretary of State. They will be dealt with by the appeals tribunals established under the 1994 Act, schedule 3—see p. 256 above.

Restrictions on subsequent proceedings: section 104

Section 104(1) and (2) of the 1984 Act enacted the so-called "double jeopardy" rule under which a police officer who had been convicted or acquitted of a criminal offence could not be made liable to disciplinary charges which were in substance the same. The Runciman Royal Commission on Criminal Justice proposed that this rule be abolished.[43] ("In our view there is nothing wrong in principle in officers being subject to disciplinary proceedings in regard to matters for which they have been exonerated by the criminal courts ... The double jeopardy rule in our view has no valid application here because the proceedings are different and lead

---

[40] The Police Federation was backed by the Law Society and the National Council for Civil Liberties which proved an unbeatable, if improbable, coalition.
[41] For the debate, see House of Lords, *Hansard*, February 21, 1994, vol. 552, cols. 445–56.
[42] See Police and Magistrates' Courts Act 1994, Sched. 5, para. 33, substituting for section 102 a new version of the section.
[43] Runciman Report, paras. 98, pp. 47 and 103(1), p. 48.

to different results. A criminal case is to determine whether an officer has committed a criminal offence and deserves punishment as a criminal. The disciplinary proceedings are to establish whether the officer has been guilty of misconduct and is liable to penalties for a breach of the standards and values of the disciplined service of which he or she is a member. The police service should be able to deal with officers who misconduct themselves according to the standards of the service regardless of whether they have been convicted or acquitted by a jury."[44])

The Government accepted this view. When the Police and Magistrates' Courts Bill was first introduced it contained a provision repealing subsections (1) and (2) of section 104. The House of Lords, after a brief debate, passed an amendment by 107 votes to 100 to remove this provision.[45] But the Government insisted and restored the provision.[46] It would therefore now be possible for an officer to face disciplinary charges arising out of facts on which he had been exonerated by the criminal courts. The same change is being made in Northern Ireland—see Appendix 4, p. 535 below [Art. 30 and Schedule 2 repealing Article 22 of the 1987 Order].

Subsection (3) of section 104 restricts the admissibility of statements made during informal procedures to resolve a complaint—in the same way that "without prejudice" negotiations cannot be produced at any subsequent civil trial. The aim is to encourage honest apologies and admissions in the informal procedure. But if formal disciplinary proceedings are taken the accused officer should not be penalised by his previous honesty provided the admission related to the matter being resolved in the informal procedure (subs. (4)).

Guidance concerning discipline, complaints etc.: section 105

Section 105 puts onto a statutory basis the issuing of guidance by the Secretary of State to chief officers of police and police authorities[47] and requires them to have regard to it. It also empowers the Secretary of State to issue guidance to the P.C.A. on the same basis as his guidance to the Police Complaints Board under section 3(8) of the Police Act 1976.

QUESTIONS AND ANSWERS

COMPLAINTS AGAINST THE POLICE AND DISCIPLINARY MATTERS

1. What is the simplest way of describing the changes made to the complaints system by PACE?

PACE aimed to achieve some very significant reforms in the system. Instead of every complaint having to be investigated by a senior officer the most minor complaints were to be siphoned off through a form of local

---

[44] Runciman Report, para. 98, p. 47.
[45] House of Lords, *Hansard*, February 21, 1994, vol. 552, cols. 445–56. For a consideration of the arguments see M. Zander, "Stand firm on double jeopardy", *New Law J.*, March 4, 1994, p. 316.
[46] See Police and Magistrates' Courts Act 1994, s.37(f).
[47] Added by Police and Magistrates' Courts Act 1994, Sched. 5, para. 34.

informal settlement as recommended by Lord Scarman in his report on the Brixton riots. Also whereas before *all* complaints had to be investigated by superintendents, the Act applies to the rest of the country the practice previously available to the Metropolitan Force of using chief inspectors as investigators. Thirdly, the number of cases that have to be sent to the D.P.P. was drastically reduced by giving powers of decision over the most minor cases to chief officers. Fourthly, a new Police Complaints Authority (P.C.A.) replaced the old Police Complaints Board. The main difference was that it has far greater powers and duties of supervision over the handling of investigations into the most serious complaints and allegations against police officers. The Act also gave legal representation to police officers facing the most serious disciplinary charges.

2. What kind of complaints are subject to informal resolution?

Only complaints where the chief officer is satisfied that, even if proved, the conduct would not justify criminal or disciplinary proceedings. A chief inspector considers whether the complaint is suitable for informal resolution. The complainant has a veto over the decision to send to the complaint for informal settlement since he has to give his consent.

3. Does the informal settlement of a complaint go onto an officer's record?

No. The White Paper said as to this that "no entry of any kind relating to attempted or successful informal resolution will be made in the personal record of the accused officer" (para. 32).

4. Can admissions made by an officer during informal settlement discussions be used against him in subsequent disciplinary or criminal proceedings?

No. The White Paper said that no reference would be allowed in any subsequent formal proceedings to what any party said or did during the process of informal resolution. "In particular, no statement made by either the complainant or the accused officer will be admissible at criminal or disciplinary proceedings, or in a civil action brought by either party" (para. 32). This statement was implemented by section 104(3) of the Act. The only exception allowed is where the admission relates to something that was not for informal resolution.

5. Can an informal resolution ever be superseded by a formal investigation?

Yes. If during informal resolution it appears that the case is actually too serious for that procedure the informal process has to be terminated and a formal investigation commenced.

6. What happens if informal settlement does not work?

The Act states that if it appears that informal resolution is impossible or that it is for any other reason not suitable for that means of resolution, the chief officer must appoint an officer from his force to investigate the complaint formally. The case goes forward as a normal complaint.

7. What is the remit of the Police Complaints Authority?

It has three main functions. One is to supervise the investigation of the most serious complaints. Secondly it has the power to "call in" any other case where it believes that independent supervision would be appropriate. It also continues to have the role played by the old Board to consider whether disciplinary proceedings should have been, or should be, instituted.

8. What sorts of cases come to the Authority?

Some matters *must* be referred to the Authority; some *may* be referred to it; and some can be summoned by the Authority even though they are not referred.

Those that must be referred are:

(1) All complaints alleging that a police officer's conduct resulted in the death of or serious injury to some other person. (Serious injury is defined to mean "a fracture, damage to an internal organ, impairment of bodily function, a deep cut or a deep laceration".)

(2) All complaints of a description specified for this purpose by the Home Secretary in regulations. The kind of cases that are required to be notified in the regulations are any complaint alleging corruption, assault resulting in actual bodily harm which is not already covered by the first category and "other serious cases reflecting adversely on the reputation of the police" (para. 15).

The difference between these two categories of case is that the Authority is required to supervise the investigation of the first, whereas it can decide whether or not it thinks it right to supervise in the second type of case.

(3) The third class of matter that comes to the Authority is the case that is referred to it by the chief officer as a matter of his discretion. This might, for instance, be a matter of local or national notoriety where the chief officer thinks that it would be desirable to report the matter to the Authority. The chief officer has a discretion to refer either complaints or other matters which have not become actual complaints but which should be referred because of their gravity or exceptional circumstances.

In addition to these three categories of case which must or may be referred to the Authority there is also a very important reserve power for the authority to call for any matter that it wishes to consider. It has the power to inform a chief constable that it wants to consider a particular complaint together with the file and the chief officer is obliged to comply.

9. What are the powers and duties of the Authority?

Apart from those investigations which it *must* supervise, the Authority also has a duty to supervise any complaint or any matter referred to them "if they consider that it is desirable in the public interest". In other words they have a completely unfettered discretion.

The general function of the Authority, the White Paper said, would be "to ensure in the public interest that [investigations] are carried out expeditiously, thoroughly and impartially" (para. 18). It was given the powers of direction necessary to perform that function. The Authority is in a position, if it wishes, materially to influence the actual handling of the case.

At the end of any investigation which the Authority has supervised the investigating officer must submit a report on the investigation to the Authority. The Authority must then issue a statement (known, rather unhappily, as "an appropriate statement") indicating whether the investigation was or was not conducted to its satisfaction and if not, specifying any respect in which it was not.

The other principal function of the Authority is to review the exercise of discretion by chief officers as to whether or not to bring disciplinary charges. The Authority has the power to recommend to the chief officer that disciplinary charges should be brought. If after they have made such a recommendation and have consulted with the chief officer, he is still unwilling to prefer such charges, the Authority can direct him to prefer such charges as they may specify and the chief officer must comply with such a direction.

If the Authority consider that the officer in question ought to have been charged with a criminal offence it is their duty to instruct the chief officer to send the papers to the D.P.P. They do not however have any power to direct the D.P.P. to commence or to recommend the commencement of criminal proceedings. They can only require that the papers be sent to the D.P.P.

10. What is the role of the D.P.P.?

Under the previous law the D.P.P. had the function of considering all complaints save those where the chief officer was satisfied that no criminal offence had been committed. The Government's aim was to confine the D.P.P.'s function to the more serious cases which merited his attention. The formula changed somewhat as the Bill was amended but the final wording enshrined in the Act required the chief officer to consider whether the report of the investigating officer discloses a criminal offence with which the officer concerned *ought to be charged.* This formula has however now been changed by the Police and Magistrates' Courts Act 1994. Under the new formula the chief officer must send to the D.P.P. any report indicating that an officer in his force may have committed a criminal offence. He is no longer asked to consider whether it is an offence for which the officer ought to be charged. But otherwise the system for bringing criminal charges will not be altered.

11. What changes in the discipline system are contemplated by the Home Office?

The changes contemplated are very radical. The old system is in effect being largely scrapped and replaced by something much closer to what is normal in industry.

The Home Secretary intends to put in place a two-tier system. One tier for "misconduct" affecting the public will be for the more serious matters. It will be somewhat like the old system involving disciplinary charges, but there will be important new features. One concerns the burden of proof. Instead of a case having to be proved beyond a reasonable doubt as in a criminal court, it will only be necessary to establish that it is reasonably believed that there has been misconduct. Another new feature will be the requirement that an officer give a full and accurate account of his actions if required to do so. There will no longer be any right to silence in regard to disciplinary matters. (The right to silence in criminal matters will remain, subject to the same changes as will affect everyone under the new law which came into force in April 1995—see pp. 303–323 above). Another new feature is abolition of the right of appeal to the Home Secretary himself. Instead, there will be a right of appeal to a statutory tribunal. But the present right to legal representation remains.

The main changes will be in regard to the second-tier which will affect most matters previously dealt with by disciplinary procedures. In future this will be dealt with on the basis of "unsatisfactory performance" more like personnel management in private industry. It will be much less formal and legalistic. Its main objective will be to help officers to improve their standards. The Home Office Minister told the House of Lords that the concern of police managers hearing the case would be "to evaluate the evidence about the incident as a whole and to consider what the totality of the officer's conduct means for his future as a police officer. The issue will not be whether it is proved that he or she has committed a criminal offence, but whether, in the light of his or her actions, any corrective action needs to be taken by police managers".[48] "Only in cases where room for improvement seem minimal or where repetition of past actions could not be tolerated, would we expect the ultimate sanction of dismissal to apply."[49]

12. What is to happen to the "double jeopardy" rule?

The so-called double jeopardy rule prevented disciplinary proceedings being brought on the same facts against an officer who had been acquitted in a criminal case. The rule was abolished by the 1994 Police and Magistrates' Courts Act—as recommended by the Royal Commission on Criminal Justice. This means that in future a police officer can be disciplined for a matter in regard to which he has been acquitted in the criminal courts.

---

[48] House of Lords, *Hansard*, February 21, 1994, vol. 552, col. 442.
[49] *ibid.* col. 441.

PART X

POLICE—GENERAL

Arrangements for obtaining the views of the community on policing: section 106

Lord Scarman in his report on the Brixton riots[1] proposed that there should be appropriate procedures to enable the police to consult with members of local communities about the problems of policing. Section 106 gives effect to this recommendation without however, specifying what form the arrangements should take.

In June 1982, the Home Office gave administrative guidance to the police authorities and chief constables (and in the Metropolitan Police District to the police and each borough and district council) regarding the role and nature of local arrangements. The guidelines said the machinery to be set up should produce a two-way information flow, enabling chief constables and police authorities to take local views into account when doing their job. Membership should be flexible and wide ranging whilst not being so large as to be unwieldy. Local councillors and M.P.s should be part of the system and local services such as probation, education and social services, housing and recreation should also be represented. Some members could be nominated by organisations. At the very local level there should be opportunities for consultation at parish council level through regular meetings with beat officers and station officers. Neighbourhood consultation should be based on the local station. At police division level membership of the consultative body should be broadly based.

Section 106 was intended to strengthen the guidance by making the arrangements mandatory rather than optional. Subsection (1) requires that arrangements must be made in each police area "for obtaining the views of people in that area about matters concerning the policing of the area and for obtaining their co-operation with the police in preventing crime in the area". There are 43 police force areas for this purpose—the 41 areas served by individual forces set up under the Police Act 1964 plus the City of London and the Metropolitan Police District.

The arrangements have to be made by the police authority in consultation with the chief constable—except in the City of London and the Metropolitan area (subs. (2)). In the Metropolitan Police District, the arrangements have to be made not by the Home Secretary but by the Commissioner of the Metropolitan Police. Separate arrangements must after consultation with the local council be made for each London Borough, District and any part of

---

[1] Report on the Brixton Disorders of 10–12 April, Cmnd. 8427 (1981).

288

a District that is within its territory (there are 11 districts in the Metropolitan area in the counties of Essex, Hertfordshire and Surrey). The arrangements for each area can be different (subss. (4) to (7)).

During the Committee stage of the first Bill the Government moved an amendment stating that the Home Secretary may issue guidance to the Commissioner of the Metropolitan police regarding the arrangements to be made in the metropolis for consultation with the community and that "the Commissioner shall take account of any such guidance". Mr Whitelaw told the Committee that the purpose of the clause was to "enable the Home Secretary to establish policies, without involving him in the detailed arrangements in every area".[2] Home Office Circular 2/1985 issued in January 1985 provided guidance for the whole of the country outside London and separate guidance was issued at the same time by the Commissioner for the Metropolitan Police Area for London after taking into account guidance from the Home Secretary.

Subsection (10) gives the Home Secretary the power, if he has reason to believe that the arrangements in any area are inadequate, to require the police authority or Commissioner responsible for making the arrangements to submit a report to him about the arrangements. Having considered such a report, the Home Secretary could, under subsection (11), require the body or person who supplied the report to review the arrangements and submit a further report. There is, therefore, no actual power to direct the nature of the arrangements that should be set up. But reading between the lines of section 106, it was intended that the Home Secretary should have considerable power to "influence" the authority.

The section complemented the existing legislation on the administration of policing, namely the police authority's duties under section 4 of the Police Act 1964; the duties of the Commissioners under section 1 of the Metropolitan Police Act 1829 and section 14 of the Metropolitan Police Act 1839 respectively.

The guidance said that matters which could usefully be taken up in local consultation included: "discussion of the incidence of and police response to both crime generally and specific types of offence" and "the operation of police procedures and policy in relation to law enforcement". But consultative groups could not intervene in the enforcement of the criminal law. The deployment of police officers and the method of timing of police operations were a matter for the police. The timing and detail of discussions about those issues were also within the discretion of the police. There were some operational aspects of policing such as criminal investigations and security matters which it would be wrong to make the subject of local consultation. Nor could consultative groups be the forum for the pursuit of individual cases which might be under investigation or *sub judice*; nor for the discussion of allegations of crime or of complaints against police officers. But within these well established limits, "issues directly or indirectly concerned with the policing of the local community may be considered so that the decisions which are properly for the police can be more closely informed by the discussion of local needs".

On membership, the guidance recommended that groups should reflect as wide a range of community interests as was consistent with reasonably

---

[2] House of Commons, *Hansard*, Standing Committee J, March 22, 1983, Col. 1344.

effective working arrangements. In London, members should include M.P.s, members of the Greater London Council, (later to be abolished) and up to five local council members. But the police, local councillors, M.P.s, GLC councillors and members of statutory agencies should normally be fewer than the number of community representatives. Groups should encourage a regular turnover of members so that they could not be seen to be exclusive. Local umbrella organisations such as councils for voluntary service, community relations councils, trades councils and chambers of commerce might be able to help select suitable representatives or individual members for the consultative groups. Local representatives of services such as probation, education, social services, housing and recreation would also be suitable members.

In 1989 the Home Office issued Circular 62/1989, a report of an internal Home Office Review of police/community consultation arrangements under section 106. It stated that formal consultative machinery existed in all London boroughs and in most other parts of England and Wales.

Local elected representatives and police authority members were allocated places (other than in London where the police authority is the Home Secretary). M.P.s were also given automatic membership in nearly all cases. The police were usually represented by divisional or sub-divisional commanders or their deputies (ranks ranging from chief superintendent to chief inspector). Often a community liaison officer was also present. It was rare for home beat officers to be members.

Representation of the local community had been organised in a variety of ways. Some had only representatives of organisations; others allowed individuals to be members. In practice most groups had "experienced difficulties in attracting an active membership which [was] genuinely representative of the area they serve" (para. 21). In particular it had generally been found difficult to attract members from ethnic minority organisations. In some areas the local Community Relations Council or the local authority had distanced themselves from the consultation process and the organisations under their umbrellas had followed suit. There had also been difficulties in attracting membership from the under-25s. ("The general view ... was that young people in general, and disaffected young people in particular, were virtually impossible to attract to consultatve groups" (para. 23).)

The general impression formed was that the community representatives did not always represent a genuine cross-section of the local community. There was "a predominance of people well used to committees: professional and middle class white people, most of whom are in the 40-plus age range" (para. 24). Most groups held open meetings but in general very few members of the public attended unless a particular meeting was advertised as being about some local issue that had provoked interest.

The frequency of meetings varied from monthly to twice a year. Most groups met quarterly. In inner city areas meetings tended to be more frequent.

The policy authority generally played a critical role—supplying the chairman, convening groups, providing the constitution and often playing a leading role in compiling the agenda. In many areas the police too played a major part in identifying agenda items while in some areas the police seemed very ready to share information with the group, in others they were reluctant to do so.

In London most groups were serviced by others of the borough council with costs reimbursed out of the Metropolitan Police Fund. Outside London groups were serviced either by the police authority, by the police force or, in a few cases, by community volunteers.

The report said sufficient groups had been encountered that were establishing active roles "to have convinced us that the section 106 arrangements are, potentially at least, a most exciting and valuable method of involving people in the policing of their area". But there were also too many groups that were achieving very little. The report set out a long list of suggested "good practice guidelines".

Most of the research on the operation of the Scarman police consultative committees has been conducted by Professor Rod Morgan.[3] In the latest of his research reports (Morgan (1992)) Professor Morgan said that nationwide there were at least 400 such committees involving some 10,000 people as members (p. 178). His verdict was that they had however achieved little in regard to conflict resolution or crime prevention. ("Nor during our extensive fieldwork and countryside surveys could we find more than one or two slender examples of committees claiming to have achieved anything practically to solve a local problem, change the way an area was policed, or stimulate a sub-committee or community group to tackle a concern identified during PCC deliberations" (p. 180)). Nevertheless, he considered that they had had "a considerable and largely unrecognised impact on the shape of policing policy in the late 1980s" (p. 181). The committees had largely been co-opted to the police standpoint. Police middle-management devoted considerable efforts to working successfully with their consultative committees. The purpose they served was more symbolic than substantive (p. 183).

Police officers performing duties of higher rank: section 107[4]

Many sections in the Act require that an action or decision be made or taken by an officer of a specified rank. Section 107 provides for the situation where an officer of that rank may not be available and permits an officer of a lower rank to be "made up". The section provides that a chief inspector may act as a superintendent if properly authorised to do so by a chief superintendent and that a sergeant may act as an inspector if authorised to do so by a chief superintendent. There is no reference in the Act however for any special procedure to be followed for such "making up", nor for the authorisation to be in writing.

The rank of chief superintendent has been eliminated under the provisions of the Police and Magistrates' Courts Act 1994, section 7(c). The same Act therefore amends PACE section 108 by providing that authority to "make up" can be given by an officer above the rank of superintendent. Alternatively it can be a case of a chief inspector acting during the absence of a superintendent who has specifically authorised him to act during his absence.

The Home Office Circular on PACE (p. 8 above, para. 41) stated that the

---

[3] See in particular Morgan and Maggs (1985), Morgan (1987) and Morgan (1992).
[4] There is no equivalent provision in the N.I. PACE Order.

power in the section was supposed to be used only in specific situations to meet the particular needs of a situation and "does not provide for a blanket authority to be issued". According to the Circular, it would, for instance, be within the terms of the section for authority to be given to those chief inspectors who were Deputy Sub-Divisional Commanders to carry out the full duties of the Sub-Divisional Commander in the superintendent's absence. Other chief inspectors could not be so authorised.

In *Alladice*[5] the Court of Appeal dismissed an appeal brought, *inter alia*, on the ground that the officer who had denied him access to a solicitor was not qualified by rank to make the decision. Lord Lane C.J. for the court held that the officer was a Chief Inspector who had been given authority to exercise the necessary power by an acting Chief Superintendent. The holder of an acting rank was to be treated, so far as authority and powers were concerned, as if he were the holder of the substantive rank—"unless his appointment was a colourable pretence".

Deputy chief constables: section 108

Section 108 of PACE established the separate rank of deputy chief constable. The Sheehy Report (*Inquiry into Police Responsibilties & Rewards*, 1993, Cm2280) recommended the abolition of the rank. This was effected by the Police and Magistrates' Courts Act 1994, schedule 9.

Amendments relating to the Police Federations: section 109[6]

Subsections (a) and (b) amended section 44(1) of the Police Act 1964 to enable the Police Federations for England and Wales and for Scotland to represent their members at disciplinary hearings and at any appeals.

An accused officer at a disciplinary hearing may conduct his case either in person or by a fellow officer selected by him and known as his "friend". Although the Police Federation was technically barred by section 44 of the Police Act 1964 from representing an officer in its own right, in practice it often acted as the officer's friend. The Edmund-Davies Report[7] on the structure and role of the police staff associations recommended that they should be able to do so in their capacity as officers of the Federations.[8] The amendment gave effect to this recommendation. But if an official acts in this way he must be a serving police officer.

As has been seen, at the Committee stage of the first Bill the Government was defeated over an amendment to give police officers the right to be legally represented at disciplinary hearings.[9] When the new Bill was introduced in October 1983 this amendment had however been taken out. Legal representation is only permitted therefore on appeals from disciplinary proceedings.

Paragraph (c) of section 109 amended section 44(3) of the Police Act 1964 which gives the Secretary of State the power to make regulations regarding the constitution and proceedings of the Police Federations. The Edmund-Davies Report[10] recommended that the regulations should be amended to

---

[5] (1988) 87 Cr.App.R. 380; [1988] Crim.L.R. 608 C.A.
[6] There is no equivalent provision in the N.I. PACE Order.
[7] "Committee of the Inquiry on the Police", Cmnd. 7633 (1979).
[8] *ibid.* para. 333.
[9] See House of Commons, *Hansard*, Standing Committee J. March 22, 1983, Col. 1393.
[10] *op. cit.* n.7 above, paras. 97, 98 and 171.

give the Federations greater freedom to manage their affairs and this amendment was intended to achieve that result. It gave the Home Secretary the power to delegate to the Federations the power to make rules governing some aspects of their internal affairs.

The regulations continue to deal with such matters as the basic elements of the constitution, provisions on membership, the right to hold meetings and conduct Federation business in duty time, the voluntary nature of the subscriptions and restrictions on the use of Federation funds for political purposes. But the details of the constitution and provisions to govern the proceedings of the Federation can set out in their own rules.

Functions of special constables in Scotland: section 110[11]

Section 110 consists of two and a half lines which repealed section 17(6) of the Police (Scotland) Act 1967 (restriction on functions of special constables).

Regulations for police forces and police cadets—Scotland: section 111[12]

Section 110 provided for powers of delegation in regard to regulations affecting the government and administration of police forces in Scotland.

Metropolitan police officers: section 112[13]

Section 112 conferred the powers and privileges of a constable under the local law on an officer of the Metropolitan Police in Scotland or Northern Ireland when assigned to the protection of any person or property there. It filled a gap in the law affecting officers guarding, say, the Royal Family or Ministers who go with them to Scotland or Northern Ireland.

Officers in the Metropolitan Force get their powers under section 19 of the Police Act 1964. Those guarding Royal residences get their powers under section 7 of the Metropolitan Police Act 1839 which enables the Commissioner to administer an oath conferring the powers and privileges of a constable within the Royal Palaces and 10 miles surrounding them. But it was realised that section 7 of the 1839 Act did not extend to other parts of the country. Nor had there been any statutory authority for the carrying out by officers of the Metropolitan force of protection duties for members of the Royal Family or other public figures in Scotland and Northern Ireland.

---

[11] There is no equivalent in the N.I. PACE Order.
[12] There is no equivalent in the N.I. PACE Order.
[13] There is no equivalent in the N.I. PACE Order.

PART XI

MISCELLANEOUS AND SUPPLEMENTARY

Application of act to armed forces: section 113[1]

Section 113 provided for some parts of the Act to apply to the Armed Forces.

Subsection (1) permits the Secretary of State for Defence to apply any of the provisions of the Act relating to the investigation of offences (subject to any qualifications he may specify) to the investigation of offences under the Army Act 1955, the Air Force Act 1955 and the Naval Discipline Act 1957 and to persons under arrest under any of those Acts.

Subsections (3), (4) and (5) state that the Home Secretary shall issue suitably adapted Codes of Practice for persons other than police officers concerned with investigations in the armed services. They must be laid before Parliament, subject to the negative resolution procedure, rather than the affirmative procedure applicable to the Codes for the police.

Subsection (12) provides that the Secretary of State may modify the application of Parts VII (Documentary Evidence in Criminal Proceedings) and VIII (Evidence in Criminal Proceedings—General) in regard to court martials or a Standing Civilian Court which tries civilian personnel for offences against military law overseas.

In December 1985 the Secretary of State for Defence laid before Parliament the Police and Criminal Evidence Act 1984 (Application to Armed Forces) Order 1985 which became S.I. 1985 No. 1882. It came into force on January 1, 1986 (for text see Appendix 1 below).

The Order applied the following provisions of the Act subject to certain modifications:

Access to legal advice: (Art. 4) section 58 applies to persons being "interviewed in connection with a serious service office". (A "serious service offence" is defined in Art. 2 as an offence under any of the service Acts which cannot be dealt with summarily or which appears to a service policeman to be serious.) Article 5 made the duty solicitor provisions in section 59 applicable to such consultations.

Fingerprinting: article 6 applied section 61 of the Act with modifications so that fingerprints may be taken from a person in service custody without his consent, providing this has been duly authorised on the ground that there are reasonable grounds for believing that his fingerprints will tend to confirm or

---

[1] There is no equivalent to this section in the Northern Ireland PACE Order because under section 120 below it already applies.

disprove the individual's involvement in any offence under one of the service discipline Act.

Intimate samples: section 62 for the taking of intimate samples with consent applies, subject to modifications which adapt the provisions of the section to the service situation.

Other samples: article 8 made equivalent modifications to apply section 63 which provides that non-intimate samples may be taken without consent, providing there has been appropriate authorisation. Instead of the authority of a superintendent, the authority of a service policeman is sufficient.

Destruction of fingerprints and samples: article 9 provided for the application of section 64 with minor modifications.

Definitions: article 10 applied the definitions in sections 65 and 118—*e.g.* of "appropriate consent", "fingerprints", "intimate samples", "non-intimate sample", "the terrorism provisions", "terrorism", "arrestable offence" etc.

Use of force: article 11 applied the provision in section 117 as to use of reasonable force by a constable (*e.g.* when taking fingerprints and samples) to service policemen.

Extent: article 12 extended the provisions of the Order to any place where the service discipline Acts extend—except for the legal aid provisions which apply only to England and Wales.

Application of act to Customs and Excise: section 114

Many of the activities of the Customs and Excise are similar to those of the police. The section is broadly intended to apply the same regime to Customs officials as apply under the Act to the police, where and to the extent that this has been decreed by Treasury Order.

The Treasury made such an Order in 1985[2] which came into force on January 1, 1986—(for text see Appendix 2 below). Article 3 of the Order applied to officers of Customs and Excise provisions of PACE relating to the investigation of offences and detention of persons by the police subject to appropriate modifications. In *Sanusi* [1992] Crim.L.R. 43 C.A. it was held that quite apart from section 114, under section 67(9) of PACE, Customs officers have a duty to observe the provisions of Code C. Questioning by Customs officers of a person arriving at the airport can therefore be a PACE interview and accordingly be subject to the provisions of Code C. See to like effect *Weerdestyn*, [1995] Crim.L.R. 239, C.A. Schedule 2 to the Order substituted for words and phrases in PACE equivalent terms for Customs and for police ranks, the equivalent Customs and Excise ranks.

Article 4 stated that Customs officers do not have the power to charge a person with an offence, to release a person on bail or to detain him after he has been charged. Article 5 gives Customs officers the power to retain articles they have seized which are evidence of an offence and retain articles seized by others. It also distinguishes articles seized under PACE from goods seized and liable to forfeiture under Customs and Excise Acts and provided that the PACE sections on access and copying do not apply to goods seized under Customs laws.

Article 6 retained the previous power of Customs officers to obtain search

[2] The Police and Criminal Evidence Act 1984 (Application to Customs and Excise) Order 1985, (1985 No. 1800).

warrants where the material sought is acquired or created in the course of a trade, business or profession. So the rules under PACE regarding excluded material and special procedure material do not apply. It was felt not appropriate to require application to be made to a circuit judge in such cases. It follows that section 9 of PACE replacing existing powers to obtain a search warrant with Schedule 1 of PACE does not touch legislation for Customs and Excise.

Article 7 limits the right of a Customs officer to enter and search premises under section 18(1) of PACE to premises occupied or controlled by someone under arrest for a Customs offence which is also an arrestable offence.

Article 8 provided for the keeping and publication of records regarding persons held in Customs detention. Article 9 extended existing powers of intimate search to include searches by Customs officers for items which the detainee might use to cause physical injury to himself or others. Article 11 gave Customs officers, like police officers, the power to use reasonable force in exercising their power under the Act.

Note that there is no equivalent to section 114(1) in the N.I. PACE Order because it already applies by virtue of section 120(5) below.

Expenses: section 115

Section 115 made financial provision out of central funds for expenditure incurred under the Act. The Explanatory and Financial Memorandum attached to the Bill said that Parts I to VI might increase the workload of police and Customs and Excise officers. The size of the increase was not quantifiable but was unlikely to be large. Some £6 million had been set aside for increases in legal advice by persons in police custody as a result of sections 58 and 59.[3] The resource implications of tape-recording would have to await the field trials.

The total annual cost of the P.C.A. was expected to be around £0.75 million in the early years compared with £0.5 million for the Police Complaints Board.[4] The new rules for referring police discipline appeals to tribunals in section 103 would increase the cost of the appeals system by an estimated £0.15 million per year.

Meaning of "serious arrestable offence": section 116

The Philips Royal Commission recommended that the police should have additional powers to deal with what it termed "grave offences". It said that it thought that this category should cover the following broad categories of offences: serious offences against the person or serious sexual offences (murder, manslaughter, causing grievous bodily harm, armed robbery, kidnapping, rape); serious offences of damaging property (arson, causing explosions); serious dishonesty offences (counterfeiting, corruption, and burglary, theft and fraud where major amounts are involved); and a miscellaneous group (the supply, importation or exportation of controlled drugs, perversion of the course of justice and blackmail).[5]

---

[3] This proved to be a considerable underestimate: see p. 110 above. In 1994–95 the cost was £68m!
[4] The operating cost of the P.C.A. in 1993–94 was £4m.
[5] Philips Report, para. 3.5.

The Government did not, however, accept the recommendation that special powers should be so narrowly confined. Instead it defined a category of "serious arrestable offences".

Various sections in the Act give the police special powers when a "serious arrestable offence" is under consideration. This arises in section 4 (road checks); section 9 (orders and warrants issued by judges under Sched. 1); section 42 (authority to detain without charge for up to 36 hours); sections 43 and 44 (magistrates' warrants of further detention); section 56 (delay in allowing notification of a person's arrest); section 58 (delay in allowing access to legal advice); section 62 (authority to take an intimate sample); and section 63 (authority to take samples without consent).

When the first Bill was published the definition of a "serious arrestable offence" was simply that the person exercising a power under the Act considered the offence to be sufficiently serious to justify his exercising that power. This wholly circular definition was criticised from all sides and the Home Office made several attempts to find a more acceptable definition.

The eventual definition divided offences into two categories. One is that of offences that are so serious that they are always serious arrestable offences. These are listed in Schedule 5 Part I, Part II (p. 421 below). They include treason, murder, manslaughter, rape, kidnapping, incest or intercourse with a girl under 13; buggery with a person under 16[6]; indecent assault which amounts to gross indecency; possession of firearms with intent to injure; carrying firearms with criminal intent; use of firearms or imitation firearms to resist arrest; causing explosions likely to endanger life or property; hostage taking, hijacking and torture. Attempts or conspiracies are treated as if they were completed. Offences under sections 2, 8, 9, 10 or 11 of the Prevention of Terrorism (Temporary Provisions) Act 1989 are also always serious arrestable offences.[7] Causing death by dangerous driving and causing death by careless driving when under the influence of drink are both serious arrestable offences under section 116. Other offences specifically listed are endangering safety at aerodromes, hijacking of ships, seizing or exercising control of oil platforms at sea, hijacking of Channel Tunnel trains or seizing control of the tunnel itself. As has already been seen, making, having or distributing indecent photographs of children[8] and publication of obscene matter[9] have also now become serious arrestable offences.

The sexual offences in the list were added by the House of Commons on Report stage. Fears were expressed about the inclusion in the list of offences of indecent assault amounting to acts of gross indecency. The effect, it was said, could be to give the police the means of harassment of the homosexual community. The offence of committing an act of gross indecency with another man under section 13 of the Sexual Offences Act 1956 is only an arrestable offence if one is over 21 and the other is under 21. But if one is over 21 and the other is under 21, it could be a serious arrestable offence if there is an assault—and the fact of the assault would result from the incapacity of the person under 21 to give valid consent to what takes place.

---

[6] Originally it was "buggery with a boy under 16 or someone who has not consented". This was altered to the formula stated in the text by the Criminal Justice and Public Order Act (CJPOA) 1994, sched. 10, para. 59.
[7] The equivalent provisions in Northern Ireland are in the Northern Ireland (Emergency Provisions) Act 1987, ss.14 and 15.
[8] See PACE, sched. 5, para. 14 added by CJPOA, s.85(3). Section 85(3) of the CJPOA also makes the equivalent alteration to the Northern Ireland PACE Order.
[9] See PACE sched. 5, para. 15 added by CJPOA s.85(3).

Any other arrestable offence is serious only if its commission has led or is likely to lead to any of the consequences specified in subsection (6)—namely: (a) serious harm to the security of the State or public order; (b) serious interference with the administration of justice or with the investigation of offences; (c) the death of anyone; (d) serious injury to anyone; (e) substantial financial gain to anyone; and (f) serious financial loss to anyone in the sense that having regard to all the circumstances, it is serious, for the person suffering the loss. The definition of "loss" therefore takes into account the particular circumstances of the person in question. The application of this definition obliges the police officer to consider the matter from the point of view of the person who has suffered the loss—an exercise that is obviously fraught with difficulty. But the test is whether the loss is serious not whether it is felt to be serious by the person concerned. His feeling that the loss is serious is only evidence of whether it is in fact serious. Nevertheless the definition could result in the theft of £20 from an old age pensioner being a serious arrestable offence! But the converse is also true. In *McIvor (Neil)*[10] Lord Justice Lawton, sitting as a Deputy High Court judge, held that the theft of beagles worth £880 from a hunt was not a serious arrestable offence because that amount shared amongst the members was not serious. Similarly in *Smith (Eric)*[11] a robbery from Woolworths involving two video recorders valued at some £800, plus cash of £116 was thought by the trial judge probably not to be a serious arrestable offence because the financial gain to the robbers was not necessarily substantial and the store was large and might not regard the loss as serious.

Subsection (8) defines injury in such a way as to make it clear that it includes disease and impairment of a person's mental as well as physical condition. This is very imprecise but it would presumably include at last severe mental distress even though the physical abuse was minor (as in some sexual offences). However, if the judges were to hold that "impairment of a person's mental condition" covered also "upset" it would drive the proverbial coach and four through the definition.

Power of constables to use reasonable force: section 117

Early drafts of the Bill referred in a number of sections to the right of the police to exercise a power with reasonable force. At a certain point the draftsman must have decided that it would be better to deal with this issue in one brief section which would apply to all such powers. Section 117 permits the use of reasonable force where any provision of the Act confers a power on the police and does not provide that the power may only be used with consent.

The sections of the Act affected are:
   powers of search and detention for the purposes of a search (ss.1 and 2)
   entry and search of premises to execute a search warrant (s.16)
   entry and search premises to make an arrest (s.17)
   entry and search of premises following arrest for an arrestable offence

[10] [1987] Crim.L.R. 409.
[11] [1987] Crim.L.R. 579 Cr.Ct.

(s.18)
seizure of evidence (s.19)
arrest (ss.24, 25, 27, 31)
search of the person on arrest (s.32)
detention of a person at a station (ss.36 and 37)
search of a detained person at a police station (s.54)
intimate searches of detailed persons (s.55)
fingerprinting without consent (s.61)
taking a non-intimate sample without consent (s.63)

General interpretation: section 118

Section 118 defines or indicates the source of the definition for the following terms: "arrestable offence"; "designated police station"; "document"; "item subject to legal privilege"; "parent or guardian"; "premises"; "recordable offence"; "vessel".

The section also defines the term "police detention" as where a person has been taken to a police station after being arrested and is detained there or is detained elsewhere in the charge of a constable or, where he is arrested at a police station, after going there voluntarily (subs. (2)). There are various categories of persons at the police station who therefore seem to be outside the definition of "police detention". They include: someone attending voluntarily at the police station, persons arrested under section 136 of the Mental Health Act 1983 and persons in custody awaiting extradition or deportation. Also someone detained after an unlawful arrest which has not yet been cured is probably not within the definition of being in police detention. However, as has been seen, Code C, paragraph 1.10 states:

"This code applies to persons who are in custody at police stations whether or not they have been arrested for an offence and to those who have been removed to a police station as a place of safety under sections 135 and 136 of the Mental Health Act 1983. Section 15 of Code C[12] applies however solely to persons in police detention."

In Northern Ireland, the definition of police detention was to be expanded in 1995 to include persons produced to a police station from a custodial establishment—see Appendix 4, p. 531 below [Art. 3].

Amendments and repeals: section 119

Section 119 provided for consequential amendments in Schedule 6 and for the repeal of enactments mentioned in Schedule 7.

Extent: section 120

Section 120 detailed the sections which apply to the different parts of the United Kingdom.

---

[12] Reviews and Extensions of Detention.

Commencement: section 121

Section 121 dealt with commencement.

Short title: section 122

The short title of the Act is the Police and Criminal Evidence Act 1984.

THE RIGHT TO SILENCE

THE RIGHT TO SILENCE

In a recent case Lord Mustill in the House of Lords distinguished six separate meanings for "the right of silence"[1]:

"This expression arouses strong but unfocused feelings. In truth it does not denote any single right, but rather refers to a disparate group of immunities, which differ in nature, origin, incidence and importance, and also as to the extent to which they have already been encroached upon by statute. Amongst these may be identified:

(1) a general immunity, possessed by all persons and bodies, from being compelled on pain of punishment to answer questions posed by other persons or bodies;

(2) a general immunity, possessed by all persons and bodies, from being compelled on pain of punishment to answer questions the answers to which may incriminate them;

(3) a specific immunity, possessed by all persons under suspicion of criminal responsibility whilst being interviewed by police officers and others in similar positions of authority, from being compelled on pain of punishment to answer questions of any kind;

(4) a specific immunity, possessed by accused persons undergoing trial, from being compelled to give evidence, and from being compelled to answer questions put to them in the dock;

(5) a specific immunity, possessed by persons who have been charged with a criminal offence, from having questions material to the offence addressed to them by police officers or persons in a similar position of authority;

(6) a specific immunity (at least in certain circumstances, which it is unnecessary to explore) possessed by accused persons undergoing trial, from having adverse comment made on any failure (a) to answer questions before the trial, or (b) to give evidence at the trial."

The so-called "abolition of the right to silence" by the Criminal Justice and Public Order Act 1994 affects only the last of these meanings. The 1994 Act changes the traditional common law rule that has protected the accused from adverse comment at his trial in respect of silence when being questioned by the police and in respect of a refusal to go into the witness box.[2]

---

[1] *Smith v. Director of Serious Fraud Office* [1992] 3 All E.R. 456 at pp. 463–464. Lord Mustill also briefly identified the very different policy reasons underlying the different concepts implicit in the phrase—see pp. 464–465.

The phrase "the right *of* silence", used by Lord Mustill, and "the right *to* silence" are interchangeable. The latter is preferred here.

[2] For material dealing with the history, the extent, the exceptions, the empirical evidence, and the debate over this rule see M. Zander, *Cases and Materials on the English Legal System* (Butterworths, 6th ed., 1993) pp. 128–150. For a helpful and long bibliography regarding the right of silence see R. Leng, "The Right-to-Silence Debate" in D. Morgan and G. Stephenson, *Suspicion and Silence* (Blackstone, 1994), pp. 35–38.

The background

The Police and Criminal Evidence Act itself said nothing regarding the right to silence. The Philips Royal Commission had recommended by a majority that the right to silence be preserved. Philips rejected the view of the Criminal Law Revision Committee (CLRC) in its 11th Report in 1972[3] that the right to silence be abolished. The Commission gave two distinct reasons. One was the fear that additional pressure on suspects to say something might cause some innocent persons to make a false confession. The other was that such pressure was contrary to the principle that it was for the prosecution to prove its case and that it was, therefore, wrong to put the defendant under pressure to participate in the process by saying something in his own defence.[4] The Government accepted the Philips Royal Commission's recommendation. This was reflected in the provisions in Code C, paras. 10.1–4 regarding the caution. ("You do not have to say anything unless you wish to do so but what you say may be given in evidence.")

However in July 1987, the then Home Secretary, Mr Douglas Hurd, signalled that he took a different view. Giving the annual Police Foundation lecture he asked:

"Is it really in the interests of justice, for example, that experienced criminals should be able to refuse to answer all police questions secure in the knowledge that a jury will never hear of it?[5] Does the present law really protect the innocent whose interests will generally lie in answering questions frankly? Is it really unthinkable that the jury should be allowed to know about the defendant's silence and, in the light of other facts brought to light during a trial, be able to draw its own conclusions?"

He called for a public debate.

Less than a year later Mr Hurd seemed virtually to have made up his mind. He announced the setting up of a Home Office Working Group to consider not whether the right to silence should be abolished but "the precise form of the change in the law which would best achieve our purpose". Then, before the Working Group produced its report, the Government moved to abolish the right to silence in Northern Ireland not merely in relation to terrorist offences but for all offences.

---

[3] *Evidence (General)*, 1972, Cmnd. 491.

[4] "To use a suspect's silence as evidence against him seems to run counter to a central element in the accusatorial system." There was an inconsistency of principle "in requiring the onus of proof at trial to be upon the prosecution and to be discharged without any assistance from the accused, and yet in enabling the prosecution to use the accused's silence in the face of police questioning under caution as any part of the case against him at trial". (Philips Report, paras. 4.50–51).

[5] This was a factual error. The jury normally do learn of the fact that the suspect was silent—see M. Zander and P. Henderson, *The Crown Court Study*, Royal Commission on Criminal Justice, Research Study No. 19 (HMSO, 1993) p. 7, para. 1.2.5. Both prosecution and defence barristers agreed that in the overwhelming majority of cases where the defendant had been silent in response to police questions the jury learnt of it.

Northern Ireland

In October 1988 the Secretary of State for Northern Ireland laid before Parliament the draft Criminal Evidence (Northern Ireland) Order 1988 which was first approved[6] and then made on November 14 and came into force one month later.[7]

The Northern Ireland Order permits the court to draw adverse inferences from the accused's failure before being charged or on being charged to mention any fact relied on in his defence at trial. As recommended by the CLRC, the Order states that such silence can also be corroboration of other evidence.

The Northern Ireland Order in fact goes further. Where a person is arrested and there is on his person, clothing, footwear or otherwise in his possession or in any place where he was at the time of arrest "any object, substance or mark" and the officer reasonably believes that the presence of the object, substance or mark is suspicious he may request an explanation from the suspect. Failure to provide such an explanation can be the subject of adverse inferences by the court or jury and can again amount to corroboration (Art. 5).[8]

Similarly, if a person is found at the scene of the crime or at the time of the crime and his presence there reasonable seems suspicious he can be asked for an explanation. Failure to give such an explanation again can be made the subject of adverse inferences and can be corroboration of other evidence (Art. 6).

Home Office Working Group

The Report of the Home Office Working Group on the Right of Silence was published in July 1989.[9] It recommended changes that were similar but not identical to those already introduced for Northern Ireland.

It approved the recommendation of the CLRC in its 1972 Report that silence during police questioning should be capable of being the subject of adverse comment by the prosecution and the judge and adverse inference by the jury. The new rules should also apply to cases in magistrates' courts.

The primary inference which should be drawn from a defendant's failure to answer questions or to mention a fact later relied on at his trial was that the subsequent line of defence was untrue. It could also have an adverse effect on his general credibility. But unlike the position in Northern Ireland, silence would not be capable of being corroboration or otherwise constitute positive evidence of guilt.

Moreover, there would be certain additional safeguards not included in either the CLRC's Report or in the Northern Ireland Order.

The first is that statutory guidelines should specify the factors to be taken into account in relation to the inferences which may be drawn. The judge would have to invite the jury to consider: (1) whether the failure to mention a fact later relied on was capable of an innocent explanation; (2) whether the

---

[6] House of Commons, *Hansard*, Vol. 140, November 8, 1988, Cols. 184–2253; House of Lords, *Hansard*, Vol. 501, November 10, 1989, Cols. 774–803.

[7] S.I. 1988 No. 1987 (N.I. 20).

[8] The model for this provision was the Criminal Justice Act 1984 in Eire, ss.18 and 19.

[9] The report is obtainable from the Home Office Library, 50 Queen Anne's Gate, London SW1A 9AT, price £1. ISBN 0862524245.

defendant knew the fact at the time; (3) whether it was reasonable to expect him to have disclosed it at that stage having regard to all the circumstances including the extent of his then knowledge of the case against him; and (4) any other relevant factors.

The judge would also have to ask the jury to take into account: (1) whether the suspect had been cautioned or further cautioned; (2) whether the police had noted anything said by the suspect prior to a tape-recorded interview and whether the accused was allowed to sign the record; (3) whether the accused had received legal advice before the start of an interview; (4) whether the police had delayed legal advice for the suspect or whether he had declined it himself; (5) whether the provisions of the Codes of Practice had been complied with; and (6) whether the interview was tape recorded or whether there had been a contemporaneous note.

In magistrates' courts the court would have to apply the same guidelines before deciding what inferences they could draw from the accused's failure to mention a fact.

The Working Party also recommended that in serious cases where there is a risk of an ambush defence the judge should be given power to order advance disclosure of the defence case either on his own initiative or at the suggestion of the prosecution. Failure to comply with the requirements of advance disclosure should enable the judge and counsel to comment adversely and the jury to draw adverse inferences.

No action was however taken on the matter, no doubt because of the mounting concern relating to the notorious miscarriage of justice cases—the Guildford Four, the Maguires and the Birmingham Six. This culminated in the announcement by the Prime Minister, Mr John Major of the establishment of the Runciman Royal Commission on Criminal Justice on the day the Court of Appeal quashed the convictions of the Birmingham Six. The terms of reference of the Commission asked it to consider, *inter alia*: "(v) the opportunities available for an accused person to state his position on the matters charged and the extent to which the courts might draw adverse inferences from primary facts, the conduct of the accused, and any failure on his part to take advantage of an opportunity to state his position."

The Runciman Royal Commission and the Government's response

The Runciman Royal Commission, like the Philips Royal Commission, recommended by a majority (of 8–3) that the right to silence be preserved. The chief reason they gave was concern that abolition of the right to silence would increase the risk of miscarriages of justice: "The majority of us, however, believe that the possibility of an increase in the convictions of the guilty is outweighed by the risk that the extra pressure on suspects to talk in the police station and the adverse inferences invited if they do not may result in more convictions of the innocent."[10]

But the Government rejected the recommendation and preferred the view of the minority. Mr Michael Howard QC, the Home Secretary, announced his decision at the Conservative Party's annual conference on 6 October 1993. The decision was translated into legislative action in the Criminal Justice and Public Order Bill which received the Royal Assent in

[10] Runciman Royal Commission Report, 1993, p. 54, para. 22.

November 1994 (CJPOA). The right to silence provisions became effective on April 10, 1995 together with the revised Codes.[11]

The choice faced by the Government was whether to follow the Northern Ireland legislation or the variant proposed by the Home Office Working Group.[12] The Government opted essentially for the Northern Ireland model—with the important exception that it did not adopt the Northern Ireland rule that silence can be taken not merely as an indication of guilt but also as corroboration of other evidence.[13] On the other hand, the 1994 legislation which enacted the new right to silence provisions for England and Wales also changed the equivalent Northern Ireland provisions in a variety of ways to bring them into line with the English rules.[14] The most important change made was to provide that adverse inferences can be drawn from silence under police questioning only if the suspect has first been cautioned[15]—see p. 308 below. The 1994 Act also abolishes the Northern Ireland procedure for calling the defendant into the witness box and replaces it with the less intrusive procedure applicable in England[16]—see p. 313 below.

The provisions regarding silence in the fact of questioning by the police are sections 34, 36 and 37 of the 1994 Act. The drawing of adverse inferences from silence in the court is dealt with in section 35. (The text below deals first with sections 34, 36 and 37 and then with section 35.) Section 38 deals with "Interpretation and savings".

Section 39 gives the Secretary of State the power to apply any or all of the provisions of sections 34 to 38 (subject to whatever modifications he may specify), to disciplinary or other proceedings in the armed forces—"wherever the proceedings take place". This includes both summary proceedings and courts martial. It also includes proceedings before a Standing Civilian Court. Section 39 requires an order to be made by statutory instrument. It was the intention that the Commencement Order bringing sections 34 to 38 into effect as from April 10, 1995 would also activate section 39.

For the text of sections 34 to 39 see Appendix 6, p. 542 below.

Failure to mention facts when questioned or charged: CJPOA, section 34

Section 34 applies to silence while being questioned under caution (s.34(1)(a)).[17] It also applies to silence on being charged (s.34(1)(b)). The

---

[11] For an extended account of the modern debate over the right of silence see M. Zander, "Abolition of the Right of Silence, 1972–1994" in ed. D. Morgan and G. Stephenson, *Suspicion and Silence*, Blackstone, 1994. That paper also reviews the empirical evidence as to whether the reform is likely to "work" from a police point of view. In the same book see also Roger Leng, "The Right-to-Silence debate" and see further R. Leng *The Right to Silence in Police Interrogation: A Study of Some of the issues underlying the Debate*, Royal Commission on Criminal Justice Research Study No. 10 (London, HMSO, 1993).

[12] For a consideration of the differences between the two see M. Zander, "How will the right to silence be abolished?", *New L.J.*, December 3, 1993, p. 1710.

[13] The corroboration provisions in the 1988 Northern Ireland Order, are Art. 3(2)(ii), Art. 4(4)(b), Art. 5(2)(ii) and Art. 6(2)(ii).

[14] See Criminal Justice and Public Order Act, sched. 10, para. 61 amending the Criminal Evidence (Northern Ireland) Order 1988.

[15] *ibid.* para. 61(2).

[16] *ibid.* para. 61(3)(b).

[17] As to when a caution is required see Code C, para. 10.1, 10.3, 10.5 and 10.6. The requirement that the defendant must first have been cautioned was introduced into the Bill by a Government amendment largely because of an intervention by the Lord Chief Justice—see House of Lords, *Hansard*, May 23, 1994, vol. 555, col. 523.

questioning must be by a constable trying to discover whether or by whom the offence has been committed (s.34(1)(a)). The silence consists of failure to mention a fact relied on in his defence which "in the circumstances existing at the time the accused could reasonably have been expected to mention when so questioned [or] charged".

Section 34(2) states that, where the subsection applies, such inferences may be drawn from the failure as appear proper. The subsection applies to a court or jury determining whether the accused is guilty of the offence charged (s.34(2)(d)). It also applies to applications by the defendant to dismiss charges that are to be transferred to the Crown Court and considering whether there is a case to answer (s.34(2)(a)(b)(c)).

As has been seen, the new caution to take account of the change in the law is in the following terms—

"You do not have to say anything. But it may harm your defence if you do not mention when questioned something which you later rely on in court. Anything you do say may be given in evidence."[18]

This new caution is somewhat longer than the old caution.[19] It remains to be seen what difficulties of comprehension it creates.[20] In the JUSTICE report, "Right of Silence Debate: The Northern Ireland experience" (May 1994), the authors interviewed 12 experienced solicitors. They were unanimous "that suspects do not understand the caution under the Order when it is read to them by the police and that only a small minority, estimated at around 5 per cent, actually appreciate its significance". This was despite the fact "that clients will usually claim that they have understood it when asked".[21] This is consistent with the research conducted for the Runciman Royal Commission by Dr Ghisli Gudjonsson.[22]

As has been seen, adverse inferences can only be drawn if the silence was while "being questioned under caution by a constable trying to discover whether or by whom the offence had been committed" (s.34(1)(a)). It should be remembered that under Code C, para. 11A an interview is now defined simply as "the questioning of a person regarding his involvement in a criminal offence" and under para. 11.1 a suspect must normally not be interviewed about the relevant offence except at a police station". But it is inevitable that some questioning will take place outside the police station.[23]

From a police point of view it will become of value to caution the suspect

---

[18] The caution in Northern Ireland is to be amended to bring it into line with the new caution in England and Wales. In the June 1995 draft version it was in fact slightly neater: "You do not have to say anything, but I must caution you that if you do not mention when questioned something which you later rely on in court, it may harm your defence. If you do say anything it may be given in evidence."

[19] The new 37 word caution is a considerable improvement on an earlier draft which had 58 words.

[20] For evidence that many suspects could not understand the old "Notice to Detained Persons" which included the caution, see G.H. Gudjonsson, "Understanding the notice to detained persons", *Law Soc. Gaz.*, 28 November 1990, pp. 24, 27; Gudjonsson *et al.*, *Persons at Risk during Interviews in Police Custody: The identification of Vulnerabilities*, Royal Commission on Criminal Justice Research Study No. 12 (HMSO, London, 1993); and G.H. Gudjonsson, "Psychological Vulnerability: Suspects at Risk" in ed. D. Morgan and G. Stephenson, *Suspicion & Silence* (Blackstone, 1994).

[21] p.14.

[22] See n.20 above. The research found that only about half the suspects (52 per cent) understood the right to remain silent.

[23] See as to this S.J. Moston and G.M. Stephenson, *The Questioning and Interviewing of Suspects outside the Police Station*, Royal Commission on Criminal Justice Research Study No. 22 (HMSO, 1993).

at the earliest possible time—so that any subsequent silence can be taken into account by the court. This is liable to lead to disputes as to whether the accused was in fact cautioned in the street, or wherever he was first questioned, and whether he did or did not fail to mention a relevant fact. (Instead of allegedly being "verballed",[24] the suspect may therefore claim that he was "non-verballed".) The courts will have to decide what constitutes "questioning" for this purpose.[25] One issue here is whether, and in what circumstances, the courts will seek to discourage questioning outside the police station by holding that "being questioned under caution" connotes a degree of formality and access to rights, especially of having legal advice, that are not available outside the police station.[26]

The parliamentary history of the CJPOA shows that the Government resisted an amendment seeking to limit the new right of silence provisions to questioning in the police station.[27] Nevertheless, the Court of Appeal is unlikely to be supportive of a new development by the police of questioning outside the police station in order to take advantage of the right to silence provisions when the consequence must be a weakening of the rules designed to have questioning take place in the more controlled and therefore protective environment of the police station. Perhaps the courts will develop a concept of a need for "informed silence". The problem is especially serious in regard to children and juveniles who are not supposed to be interviewed save with the support of an appropriate adult. The new rule about drawing adverse inferences from silence under questioning applies to them as much as to adults. The same is the case with adverse inferences under ss.36 and 37 but, curiously, if the defendant is under 14, adverse inferences cannot be drawn under s.35 from failure to go into the witness box. The basis of the distinction drawn is not clear.

Sometimes the courts may find the solution to the dilemma in the requirement that adverse inferences can only be drawn if the suspect could reasonably have been expected to mention the fact later relied on at his trial. Often it would not have been reasonable to have expected the suspect to have mentioned the fact prior to having had the opportunity of taking legal advice.

Inferences can only be drawn in regard to facts relied on at the trial. They therefore cannot be drawn under section 34 if the defendant said nothing pre-trial and then neither gives evidence nor calls evidence at the trial—see comment by Professor D.J. Birch on *Mitchell* [1995] Crim.L.R. 146, 148. But inferences might be drawn under section 35 in regard to the failure to give evidence—see below.

Section 34(3) says that "subject to any directions by the court, evidence tending to establish the failure [to mention facts] may be given before or after evidence tending to establish the fact which the accused is alleged to have failed to mention". In other words, the facts of silence as to a relevant

---

[24] A slang term for being the victim of a false allegation by the police that he has said something.

[25] The issue of what constitutes "questioning" for the purposes of the new rules regarding the right of silence is likely to replace the question of what constitutes an "interview" for the purposes of the rules regarding the recording of interviews, on which there was much confusing case law.

[26] *cf.* the Court of Appeal's decision in *Keenan* [1989] 3 All E.R. 598 holding inadmissible under s.78 an interview in the street because the police had not complied with the rules about recording an interview.

[27] See House of Lords, *Hansard*, May 23, 1994, vol. 555, cols. 495–506. In fact, the amendment moved by Lord Ackner would have required both prior legal advice and tape-recording before silence could be taken as evidence of guilt. The amendment was however not pressed to a vote.

fact may emerge from prosecution witnesses or from cross-examination of the accused. It would seem that it cannot be brought out by examination-in-chief of prosecution witnesses unless there is some indication that a fact is relied on by the defence which was not mentioned at the time of police questioning. But this could be a fact suggested to a prosecution witness in the course of cross-examination by the defence. Also, section 34(5) states that the section does not prejudice the admissibility in evidence, as before, of the silence of the accused or of any other reaction to what is said in his presence about the matter under investigation. The arresting or investigating officer would therefore still be able to state in evidence that the defendant was silent or replied "No comment" to questions put, whether before and after he had been cautioned.

It is not the case that adverse inferences will always be appropriate. The CLRC in its 1972 report said:

"What, if any, inferences are proper will depend on the circumstances. In a straightforward case of interrogation by the police where the accused has no reason for withholding his story (apart from the fact that he has not had time to invent it or that he hopes to spring it on the court at his trial) an adverse inference will clearly be proper and, we think, should readily be drawn. Obviously there may be reasons for silence consistent with innocence. For example the accused may be shocked by the accusation and unable at first to remember some fact which would clear him.[28] Again, to mention an exculpatory fact might reveal something embarassing to the accused, such as that he was in the company of a prostitute. Or he may wish to protect a member of his family. It will be for the court (or with the help of the judge's direction) for the jury to decide whether in all the circumstances they are justified in drawing an adverse inference."[29]

The Lord Chief Justice made it clear during the Committee stage in the House of Lords that the courts would be especially vigilant to protect the vulnerable or the very young from adverse inferences that it would be unfair to draw from silence. But, he suggested, on the whole the vulnerable were not the ones most likely to be silent. ("By and large, these defendants respond freely to police questioning" and indeed "say all kinds of things that are inappropriate".[30])

"We are not talking about silence in their cases. The evidence before the Royal Commission also showed, and judicial experience confirms, that it is the most experienced criminals charged with very serious offences[31] who most frequently decline to answer any questions. It is against them that these clauses principally, and in my view properly, are directed.[32]

---

[28] It will be in the experience of jurors that a shock often causes temporary confusion. (ed.)
[29] *op. cit.*, para. 35.
[30] House of Lords, *Hansard*, May 23, 1994, vol. 555, col. 521.
[31] The only evidence that to the writer's knowledge supports this conclusion in fact emerged *after* the Runciman Royal Commission reported, in the form of a study conducted by ACPO. The sample was drawn in September 1993 and was based on 3,600 suspects from eight force areas. It showed that 47 per cent of suspects with five or more convictions exercised the right to silence as against 15 per cent of suspects with no criminal record. (For further details and some reservations as to the methodology of the study see R. Leng, "The Right to Silence Debate" in D. Morgan and G. Stephenson, *Suspicion and Silence* (Blackstone, 1994) pp. 25–28.)
[32] *op. cit.* n.30 above.

The new rules apply to questioning not only by police officers but also by "persons (other than constables) charged with the duty of investigating offences or charging offenders as it applies in relation to questioning by constables" (s.34(4)). This is the same wording as is used in section 67(9) of PACE regarding the applicability of the Codes to persons other than police officers (see p. 171 above).[33]

Revised Code C, para. 112A states that at the beginning of an interview at the police station the interviewing officer after cautioning the suspect shall put to him any significant statement or silence (*i.e.* of failure or refusal to answer a question or refusal to answer it satisfactorily) which occurred before the start of the interview and shall ask him whether he confirms or denies that earlier statement or silence and whether he wishes to add anything.

Failure or refusal to account for objects, substances or marks: CJPOA, section 36

Section 36 deals with the failure or refusal of the accused to answer police questions about objects, substances or marks on his person, clothing or footwear, or in his possession, or at the place where he is arrested. Where a police officer reasonably believes that the presence of the object, substance or mark may be attributable to the person's participation in the commission of an offence actually specified by the officer and he tells the person and asks him to account for the object, substance or mark, failure to do so may result in adverse inferences being drawn by the court or the jury (s.36(1)(2)). The same is true in regard to the condition of clothing or footwear (s.36(3)). But the person must first be warned in ordinary language what may be the consequences of a failure or refusal to answer such questions (s.36(4)). The revised Code C for England and Wales does not prescribe a set form of words but it states (para. 10.5B) that for an inference to be drawn in this regard the interviewing officer must first tell the suspect (a) what offence he is investigating; (b) what fact he is asking the suspect to account for; (c) that he believes this fact may be due to the suspect's involvement in the offence in question; (d) that a court may draw proper inference from his silence; and (e) that a record is being made of the interview and that it may be given in evidence.[34]

Section 36 does not apply unless the accused was under arrest at the time when he failed to explain the object, substance or mark (s.36(1)(a)). Whether adverse inferences will be drawn depends on the same considerations as in regard to failure to mention facts later relied on by the defendant in his defence (see above). By what may be a slip in the drafting of this section (and the next), the questions to, and cautioning of the suspect must have been by the officer who made the arrest. Section 34 (1)(a)(b) and (c)

---

[33] For the Northern Ireland equivalent see Art. 3(4).

[34] In Northern Ireland there is a set form of words. The June 1995 draft (Code C, para. 10.6) was rather a mouthful: "When you were arrested on (date) at (time) at (place) for the offence of ... there was on your person/in or on your clothing (or footwear) in your possession/in the place where you were at the time of your arrest a (state the object/substance or mark). I believe this may be due to your involvement in this offence. You do not have to say anything about this (object, substance or mark), but I must caution you that if you fail or refuse to mention when questioned, something which you later rely on in court, it may harm your defence. If you do say anything it may be given in evidence. I now ask you to account for (state the object/substance/mark). Have you anything you wish to say?" Para. 10.7 was similar in regard to explaining one's presence at the scene of the crime.

specifically draw a distinction between the arresting officer and any other officer. It will be difficult for the courts to avoid that inconvenient construction of the words of the section if the point is taken for the defence.

Failure or refusal to account for presence at a particular place: CJPOA, section 37

Section 37 deals in terms similar to those of section 36 with the suspect's failure or refusal to answer police questions regarding his presence "at a place at or about the time the offence for which he was arrested is alleged to have been committed". The investigating officer must reasonably believe that his presence at that place and at that time may be attributable to his having participated in the commission of the offence. Otherwise the requirements are the same as in section 36.[35]

Effect of accused's silence at trial: CJPOA, section 35

The defendant has the right not to give evidence. Previously, if he exercised that right, the Criminal Evidence Act 1898, section 1 provided that "the failure of any person charged with an offence ... to give evidence shall not be made the subject of any comment by the prosecution". But no such prohibition was imposed on the judge. The extent of the judge's right to comment was considered recently by the Court of Appeal in *Martinez-Tobon*.[36] Giving judgment, the Lord Chief Justice cited the standard direction approved by the Judicial Studies Board:

> "The defendant does not have to give evidence. He is entitled to sit in the dock and require the prosecution to prove its case. You must not assume that he is guilty because he has not given evidence. The fact that he has not given evidence proves nothing one way or the other. It does nothing to establish his guilt. On the other hand, it means that there is no evidence from the defendant to undermine, contradict, or explain the evidence put before you by the prosecution."

But the Court of Appeal had on occasion approved comments going beyond the conventional direction. The Court said that provided the essentials of the conventional direction were given, the judge might go beyond that where the defence case alleged facts that (a) were at variance with the prosecution's evidence or additional to it and exculpatory, and (b) must, if true, be within the defendant's knowledge. The court approved the particular comment to which the defence had taken exception.

In its 1972 Report, the CLRC recommended that the defendant should be put under pressure to give evidence:

> "In our opinion the present law and practice are much too favourable to the defence. We are convinced that, when a prima facie case has been made against the accused, it should be regarded as incumbent on him to give evidence in all ordinary cases. We have no doubt that the prosecution should be entitled, like the judge, to comment on his failure to do so. The

---

[35] For the Northern Ireland equivalent see Art. 6.
[36] [1994] 1 W.L.R. 388; [1994] 2 All E.R. 90.

present prohibition of comment seems to us wrong in principle and entirely illogical."[37]

The CJPOA, section 35 implements this recommendation.

When the Bill was first introduced it included a provision following the CLRC's suggestion that the accused should actually be called by the court to give evidence.[38] The judges, led by the Lord Chief Justice, made it clear that they were not happy with this procedure which they suggested would have the effect of bringing the judge too much into the arena. The Government eventually introduced an amendment which provides that at the close of the prosecution's evidence the court shall—"satisfy itself (in the case of proceedings on indictment, in the presence of the jury) that the accused is aware that the stage has been reached at which evidence can be given for the defence and that he can, if he wishes, give evidence and that, if he chooses not to give evidence, or, having been sworn, without good cause refuses to answer any question, it will be permissible for the court or jury to draw such inferences as appear proper from his failure to give evidence or his refusal, without good cause, to answer any question" (CJPOA, s.35(2)). Good cause for refusal to answer questions may exist under statute or by virtue of privilege or if the court exercising its discretion excuses it (subs. (5)).

The court may draw such inferences from a refusal to go into the witness box as appear proper (s.35(3)). The procedure does not apply if the defendant's legal representative informs the court that the accused will give evidence or, where he is unrepresented, he says so himself. Nor does the procedure apply if the defendant is under 14[39] nor where it appears to the court that "the physical or mental condition of the accused makes it undesirable for him to give evidence" (s.35(1)(b)). Failure to give evidence does not however render the accused liable to proceedings for contempt of court (s.35(4)). The new procedure applies only when the case is tried on indictment where the defendant was arraigned after the commencement of the section and in cases tried by magistrates where the court began to receive evidence after the commencement of the section (s.35(7)).

The procedure

The actual mechanics of the new procedure were laid down in Practice Direction (Crown Court: Evidence: Advice to defendant) [1995] 1 W.L.R. 657, [1995] 2 All E.R. 499 issued on April 10, 1995 the day the new provisions came into force. Issuing the Practice Direction, the Lord Chief Justice said that if the defendant was legally represented and chose to gave evidence, his legal representative should indicate this intention in open court. The case then proceeds in the normal way.

If the court is not so informed or it is informed that the accused does not intend to give evidence, the judge should in the presence of the jury inquire of the lawyer in the following terms: "Have you advised your client that the

---

[37] *op. cit.*, para. 110.
[38] This has until now been the procedure in Northern Ireland—see Criminal Evidence (Northern Ireland) Order, 1988, Art. 4. As has been seen however, the Northern Ireland procedure will now be the same as that in England and Wales—see CJPOA, sched. 10, para. 61(3)(b).
[39] Where the defendant's age is material it shall for these purposes be taken to be "that which appears to the court to be his age" (s. 35(6)).

stage has now been reached at which he may give evidence and if he chooses not to do so or, having been sworn, without good cause refuses to answer any questions, the jury may draw such inferences as appear proper from his failure to do so."

If the legal representative replies to the judge that the accused has been so advised, the case proceeds. If he or she says that the accused has not been so advised, the judge should briefly adjourn the case for that to be done.

If the accused is unrepresented,[40] the judge should at the conclusion of the · prosecution's case and in the presence of the jury say to the defendant: "You have heard the evidence against you. Now is the time for you to make your defence. You may give evidence on oath, and be cross-examined like any other witness. If you do not give evidence, or having been sworn, without good cause refuse to answer any question the jury may draw such inferences as appear proper. That means they may hold it against you. You may also call any witness or witnesses whom you have arranged to attend court. Afterwards you may also, if you wish, address the jury by arguing your case from the dock. But you cannot at that stage give evidence. Do you now intend to give evidence?"

It is obviously impossible to predict whether section 35 will result in more defendants going into the witness box. The Crown Court Study carried out for the Runciman Royal Commission suggested that about one quarter of defendants in contested cases in the Crown Court currently do not give evidence.[41]

Interpretation and savings for sections 34, 35, 36 and 37: section 38

Section 38 first defines "legal representative" and "place". It then makes it clear that reference to an offence in sections 34(2), 35(3) and 37(2) includes any other offence of which the accused could be convicted on that charge.

Subsection (3) establishes the fundamental point that a person cannot be convicted solely on the basis of inferences drawn from silence (*i.e.* a failure or refusal such as is mentioned in ss.34(2), 35(3), 36(2) or 37(2)). There must always be some positive prosecution evidence. The same applies equally to transfer of proceedings to the Crown Court (subs. (3) and (4)).[42]

Subsection (5) makes it clear that the new provisions do not affect the operation of any enactment which provides that any answer or evidence[43] given by a person in certain circumstances is not admissible in evidence against him or someone else in civil or criminal proceedings. An obvious example is the provision in section 2 of the Criminal Justice Act 1987 regarding statements made to the Serious Fraud Office.

Subsection (6) states that "nothing in sections 34, 35, 36 or 37 prejudices any power of a court, in any proceedings, to exclude evidence (whether by preventing questions being put or otherwise) at its discretion". This appears to be the same reservation of the judge's overall discretion to exclude

---

[40] Fewer than 1 per cent of defendants in the Crown Court are unrepresented.
[41] M. Zander and P. Henderson, *The Crown Court Study*, Royal Commission on Criminal Justice Research Study No. 19 (HMSO, 1993) p. 114, para. 4.5.1.
[42] Including the decision whether to dismiss charges of serious fraud under sections 4 and 6 of the Criminal Justice Act 1987 and charges of violent or sexual offences involving a child under section 53 and sched. 6, para. 5 of the Criminal Justice Act 1991.
[43] This is stated to mean giving evidence in any manner "whether by furnishing information, making discovery, producing documents or otherwise" (subs. (5)).

evidence as is the subject of section 82(3) of PACE—discussed at p. 250 above.

Commencement

The new provisions in regard to the inferences to be drawn from silence came into force as from April 10, 1995. They do not have retrospective effect and therefore apply only to a failure or refusal under the provisions that occurs after that date.[44]

How will solicitors advise their clients?

The police obviously hope that the change in the law relating to silence will mean less silence in the police station and in the face of police questioning generally. It remains to be seen whether that hope is realised. The Law Society has issued guidance to solicitors and their clerks as to how they should respond to the new law in regard to the right to silence and the new caution.[45] Having set out the text of CJPOA, sections 34, 36 and 37, the advice begins—"You should not be panicked into thinking that these changes mean that you have to adopt a completely different approach to formulating your advice to a client. In practical terms, the changes make little difference to the actual advice you give."

If the client admits his or her guilt but the adviser is unsure whether the police have sufficient evidence, "the safest advice remains unchanged: your client should remain silent". Even if the client is likely in due course to be advised to plead guilty "you must be satisfied that there are significant mitigation advantages to him or her admitting guilt which are verifiable at this early stage in the proceedings".

Experience would show how judges exercise their discretion to disallow comment to be made about a suspect's silence. "The less articulate a client is, the less capable he or she is of understanding and making a reasoned choice about whether to remain silent or not and the less able he or she is of giving a good account in interview, the more likely that a judge will not allow comment to be made."

The risk of talking to the police had to be balanced against the risk of being wrongfully convicted after remaining silent. Talking to the police would pose a greater risk of wrongful conviction if, for example, the client:

- "was in an emotional, highly compliant and highly suggestible state of mind at the time of the interview"; or
- "was confused and liable to make mistakes which could be inter-preted—incorrectly—as deliberate lies at any subsequent trial"; or
- "forgot important details, distrusted his or her memory, responded inappropriately to negative feedback by the police, went along with their suggestive questioning and, as a result damaged his or her case in court";
- "used loose expressions, unaware of the possible adverse interpret-ations which could be placed upon them at trial"; or

---

[44] See ss.34(6), 35(7) and 37(6).
[45] "Changes in the Law Relating to Silence: Advice to practitioners from the Criminal Law Committee of the Law Society", *Criminal Practitioners Newsletter*, October 1994, issued before the CJPOA became law. Extracts are used here with the Law Society's consent.

- "there was some other reason, particularly psychological, why he or she might be expected to perform badly during the interview; or
- "previous experience of the police officers concerned leads you to believe that the conduct of the interview may be unfair or may place undue pressure on your client".

There must be many clients who would fall within one or more of these categories.

The Law Society says that there should be no adverse comment on silence where there is an innocent explanation for the accused having remained silent. Innocent explanations could include: where the suspect wanted to protect others or where the suspect was reluctant to admit having done something that though not illegal was discreditable, potentially damaging, indiscreet or embarrassing. Another reason for silence was where the police failed to disclose adequate information about the case so that the adviser was unable to advise, where the suspect did not understand the police questions or it was not apparent to the suspect at the time that the fact which he or she failed to mention would later become relevant to the defence. It may also be reasonable not to volunteer information about matters about which the police ask no questions. Another reason for advising silence might be in response to improper or abusive questioning by the police.[46]

The client who is advised to be silent under police questioning may still be advised to make a statement when being charged. The section distinguishes between inferences from silence when being questioned (s.34(1)(a)) and inferences from silence on being charged or officially informed that one might be prosecuted (s.34(1)(b)). If the suspect makes a full statement on being charged he does not expose himself to questioning and he can be presented to the jury as someone who was prepared at an early stage to set out his position.

The Law Society says that if the solicitor advises silence, that fact and the reasons for it should be recorded both in writing and on the tape of the police interview with the client. The client should be warned that a consequence of remaining silent is that he may later be advised to waive client confidentiality so that the adviser can give evidence in court as to having advised the client to be silent and the reasons for it. For that purpose the adviser should keep full notes.

One thing that is certain is that the need for a solicitor in the police station will increase as a result of the change in the rules regarding silence. Solicitors will find it necessary more often to go to the police station, to stay during the interview and even to be there when the client is charged. A rise in the cost of the scheme for legal advice in police stations is therefore to be anticipated.

On the problems for the lawyers see also Helen Fenwick, "Curtailing the Right to Silence, Access to Legal Advice and Section 78" [1995] Crim.L.R. 132–6.

Advice to the police

It is not only the lawyers who have received advice as to the new law. The police have also had guidance. Neil Addison, formerly a barrister employed by the CPS, writing in *Police Review* on April 14, 1995—the week when the

---

[46] See further *Becoming Skilled*, the resource book of the Police Station Skills for Legal Advisers Kit published by the Law Society 1994.

right to silence changes took effect—said that instead of getting annoyed over the Law Society's advice about silence the police should work to minimise and, if possible, to outflank the legal advice.

If the changes were to be of real value, "investigating officers will have to alter their tactics in interviews". In the past, because silence counted for nothing, the purpose of an interview had been to get a confession. It was therefore not surprising that police officers had sometimes become aggressive in their interviewing of unco-operative suspects. Now however silence could count and it therefore did not any longer matter so much whether the suspect answered. His response could be made to count against him either way.

Police officers would have to plan their interviews beforehand and have a list of points to be covered. The vital thing was to ensure that the suspect was asked about as many aspects of the matter as possible. Since silence only "counted" in relation to matters in regard to which questions had been asked, the suspect should be told the date, time and place of the offence and asked whether he was at that place, on that date, at that time. Maps and plans should be available so that suspects could not argue later that they were unsure as to the place. The police should be precise and clear in their questions. They should sound and be reasonable in their questioning. If for instance the officer was sarcastic in his response to the suspect's silence, the defence might be able to argue that the officer's manner was the reason for the silence.

If the suspect said that on legal advice he intended to say nothing, the officer should repeat the new caution and say that he would proceed with the interview and that it would be for the court to draw its own conclusions about the suspect's response. "On no account", Addison suggests, "should officers enter into legal debate with solicitors". The officer should maintain a firm but low-key response. "The police now have a situation where whatever a suspect does—lie, tell the truth or remain silent—can be evidence providing the interview is conducted properly."

The effect of legal advice to be silent or not to give evidence

If the defendant claims that he was silent or decided not to give evidence on the basis of legal advice, it is obviously open to the defence to argue in its closing speech at the trial that the jury (or magistrates) should not draw adverse inferences when the defendant was simply doing what his lawyers advised. In many cases jurors (and magistrates) will find that to be a persuasive argument.

But the defence can equally use this argument to invite the court to *rule* that no such inferences can be drawn. During the Committee stage of the Bill the Home Office Minister Mr D. Maclean said:

"Nothing in the Bill would bar a court from drawing an adverse inference just because the defendant acted or said that he acted on legal advice. It will be for the courts to decide what, if any, inference to draw. A solicitor's advice would be negligent if it ignored the Bill's effects. It would be a solicitor's duty to assess the situation and decide what was in the client's best interests, taking the Bill into account."[47]

---

[47] House of Commons, Standing Committee B, February 1, 1994, col. 407.

That seems plainly to be correct.[48] But that does not mean that the judge would have to leave the matter to the jury. Wherever appropriate he could rule that no adverse inference can properly be drawn. The judge might rule that the fact that the defendant was following legal advice was sufficient reason to prevent any adverse inference properly being drawn.

Judicial attitude to the new provisions—the Northern Ireland experience

There is as yet little basis for forming a view as to how English judges are likely to interpret the new right to silence provisions. A JUSTICE publication ("Right of silence Debate: The Northern Ireland Experience", May 1994) reported on judicial interpretation of the comparable provisions in the Province. The report was based on transcripts of unreported cases heard in the Belfast Crown Court and on appeal by the Northern Ireland Court of Appeal during the period March 1989 to February 1994. They all involved scheduled offences which were tried before Diplock courts—*i.e.* without a jury. There is no way of knowing whether the fact that they all involved terrorism may have affected the attitude of the judges. On the Northern Ireland case law up to 1992 see also Amnesty International, "United Kingdom: Fair trial concerns in Northern Ireland: the right to silence", November 1992, pp. 10–18.[49]

The JUSTICE report (p. 23) states that "initially the judges took a cautious approach to the drawing of adverse inference's from the accused's silence at trial". In *McDonnell* (March 1989) Mr Justice Nicholson refused the prosecution's invitation to draw inferences from the accused's refusal to testify on the ground that Article 4 of the Criminal Evidence (Northern Ireland) Order 1988 (the equivalent provision to s. 35 of the CJPOA) was not to be used to bolster a weak prosecution case. ("There must be other evidence which at least established the probable guilt of the accused.") In *Smyth* (October 1989) Lord Justice Kelly said that the decision of the accused not to testify might justify a finding of guilt where the weight of the prosecution case "just rests on the brink of the necessary standard of proof".

But the attitude of the Northern Ireland judges appeared to have changed. In *Kane and others* (March 30, 1990) one defendant, Kelly, denied being involved in the killing of two British soldiers who drove their car into a funeral procession of an IRA supporter. At first he said nothing but later he made a short statement which he declined to sign. He admitted that he had been at the funeral but said he took no part in the attack on the soldiers. Carswell J. found on the basis of video evidence that he took part both in the attack on the car and in taking one of the soldiers to where they were shot. He regarded the evidence regarding Kelly of a film taken from a helicopter of the actual execution style killings to be of doubtful quality but he used Kelly's failure to give evidence as part of the reason to find that he took part in the actual killings.

---

[48] This presumably is the meaning of an *obiter dictum* in an unreported Northern Ireland Court of Appeal case *Connolly and McCartney* (1991): "I should not regard it as reasonable for a person being interviewed to fail to mention facts simply because he had been advised by a solicitor to remain silent. If that failure is objectively unreasonable it does not in my opinion become reasonable merely because a solicitor gives his client ill judged advice." (*per* Carswell J.). But whether advice to remain silent was "objectively unreasonable" could plainly be a matter of dispute.

[49] The report was published by Amnesty's International Secretariat, 1 Easton Street, London WC1X 8DJ.

"In my opinion, the court is entitled to place together and consider in sum the evidence of the film taken outside Casement Park up to the point when the soldiers were taken inside, the film taken when the taxi was leaving, the heli-tele film of events inside Casement Park, the falsity of Kelly's statement and his refusal to give evidence. When that is done, I am satisfied that Kelly not only took part in bringing Corporal Wood to Casement Park, but took part as an active participant in the events that occurred inside."

The Court of Appeal held on the facts that Kelly could be clearly identified from the hele-tele film as having been present in Casement Park and therefore did not need to use adverse inferences from Kelly's failure to testify at trial in upholding the conviction.

The relaxation of the requirement of the strength of the prosecution's evidence was demonstrated even more clearly in *McLernon* (December 1990). Lord Justice Kelly drew adverse inferences from the defendant's silence both before trial and at trial. He said that his words in *Smyth* were not intended to restrict the court's discretion: "In certain cases a refusal to give evidence under the Article may well in itself with nothing more increase the weight of a prima facie case to the weight of proof beyond a reasonable doubt." In January 1991, in the case of Kevin Murray, Lord Justice Kelly held that failure to testify reduced the defendant's credibility. This ruling was upheld by the Court of Appeal and by the House of Lords—*Murray*.[50] The defendant was charged with the attempted murder of a part-time member of the Ulster Defence Regiment. While his home was being searched he had made a short statement about the shooting. After his arrest he had remained silent and he did not testify at his trial. There was forensic evidence which could, but did not necessarily link the defendant to the crime. The trial judge placed most emphasis on the defendant's failure to testify and it was the inference he drew from that that led to the appeal.

Lord Slynn gave the leading judgment with which all four of the other law lords (Lords Templeman, Oliver, Jauncey and Mustill) agreed. The defence argued that the Northern Ireland Order was only declaratory of the common law and did not permit inferences that could not have been drawn at common law. Lord Slynn, like the Court of Appeal below, rejected this view.[51] The accused could not be compelled to give evidence but if he did not, he risked the consequences:

"Those consequences are not simply, as the defendant contends, that specific inferences can be drawn from specific facts. They include in a proper case the drawing of an inference that the accused is guilty of the events with which he is charged. This does not mean that the court can conclude simply because the accused does not give evidence that he is guilty. In the first place the prosecutor must establish a prima facie case—a case for him to answer.[52]

Secondly, the judge or jury may draw only such inferences as are proper.

[50] [1994] 1 W.L.R. 1.
[51] He did so by reference to the words of the 11th Report of the Criminal Law Revision Committee, 1972, para. 110. It is clear that the 11th Report will be much cited in coming years in the courts.
[52] *op. cit.*, n.50, above, at p. 11.

("There must be some basis derived from the circumstances which justify the inference."[53])

> "If there is no prima facie shown by the prosecution there is no case to answer. Equally, if parts of the prosecution case had so little evidential value that they called for no answer, a failure to deal with those specific matters cannot justify an inference of guilt. On the other hand, if aspects of the evidence taken alone or in combination with other facts clearly call for an explanation which the accused ought to be in a position to give, if an explanation exists, then a failure to give any explanation may *as a matter of common sense* allow the drawing of an inference that there is no explanation and that the accused is guilty."[54]

Here parts of the circumstantial evidence and certainly the cumulative effect of the circumstantial evidence had called for answer. The prosecution established a clear prima facie case and the trial judge had been entitled "in the circumstances of the case and as a matter of common sense, to infer that there was no innocent explanation to the prima facie case and that the defendant was guilty".

In a separate concurring opinion Lord Mustill said that a prima facie case in this context meant a case that was strong enough to go to a jury—"*i.e.* a case consisting of direct evidence which, if believed and combined with legitimate inferences based upon it, could lead a properly directed jury to be satisfied beyond reasonable doubt ... that each of the essential elements of the offence is proved". The prosecutor must have erected a case which, absent rebuttal, the fact-finder may accept as proved.[55]

> "At this stage the trial is in a state of balance ... If in such circumstances the defendant does not go on oath to say that the witnesses who have spoken to his actions are untruthful or unreliable, or that an inference which appears on its face to be plausible is in reality unsound for reasons within his personal knowledge, the fact-finder may suspect that the defendant does not tell his story because he has no story to tell, or none which will stand up to scrutiny; and this suspicion may be sufficient to convert a provable prosecution case into one which is proved ... [T]he fact finder is entitled as a matter of common sense to draw his own conclusions if a defendant who is faced with evidence which does call for an answer fails to come forward and provide it. So also if the defendant seeks to outflank the case for the prosecution by means of a 'positive' defence—as for example where he replies in relation to a charge of murder that although he did kill the deceased he acted under provocation. If he does not give evidence in support of his allegation there will in very many cases be a legitimate inference that the defence is untrue."[56]

---

[53] *ibid.*

[54] *ibid.* Emphasis supplied.

[55] Query whether this applies in the same way where a magistrates' court is considering an application to dismiss the proceedings rather than approve transfer to the Crown Court or a court is hearing a submission that there is no case to answer. An adverse inference from silence under s.34 of the CJPOA (Art. 3 of the Northern Ireland Order) may lift a prosecution case over those hurdles even though it is not sufficient to establish guilt.

[56] *op. cit.*, n.50 above, at pp. 4–5.

It is predictable that the phrase from these two opinions which will be quoted by the courts as authoritative again and again is that the fact-finder is entitled to draw such inferences as are suggested by the application of common sense. The view of the juror on the Clapham Omnibus as to whether silence was suspicious in the particular context of the case will be decisive.[57]

Is abolition of the right of silence a breach of the European Convention on Human Rights?

The question whether "abolition of the right of silence" in the Northern Ireland Order (and therefore also in the comparable new English legislation) constitutes a breach of the European Convention on Human Rights is already before the European Court of Human Rights in Strasburg. The first case to test the issue was brought by John Murray.[58] Murray was charged with conspiracy to murder, aiding and abetting with others the imprisonment of a police informer L and of belonging to the IRA. Murray had been at the house where L was imprisoned by the IRA. L identified him as a person who was there and said that after the police arrived to rescue him Murray had been pulling tape out of a cassette player. Murray said nothing when questioned. No witness was called on his behalf and he gave no evidence. In finding him guilty of aiding and abetting the false imprisonment of L, the judge said that he drew strong inferences of guilt from the fact that he said nothing when being questioned by the police and from the fact that he declined to give evidence.

Murray was given an eight-year sentence. The Northern Ireland Court of Appeal dismissed his appeal. It said that, given the evidence of his presence in the house and of his attempt to destroy the evidence of the kidnapping in the form of the tape and the absence of any explanation, it was inevitable that the judge would draw very strong inferences against him.

Murray's petition to Strasburg[59] raised two issues. One was that he had been denied access to a solicitor. The other was that the 1988 Northern Ireland Order infringed his rights under Article 6, paragraphs 1 and 2 of the Convention.[60]

In June 1994 the European Commission decided by 15 votes to 2 that there was no violation of Article 6 paragraphs 1 or 2 as regards the right of silence. (It also found by 13 votes to 4 that there had been a violation of the Convention guarantee of access to a lawyer.) The Commission referred the case to the European Court.

It was argued for Murray that the drawing of adverse inferences from silence had the effect of transferring to him the burden of proof which was

[57] In the *Crown Court Study, op. cit.*, n.41 above, the judges in cases where the accused had been silent in response to police questioning were asked: "If you had been a member of the jury, how would you have interpreted the defendant's silence?" They were offered three alternative answers—"Probably adversely, the silence seemed suspicious", "Probably not adversely, the silence was explicable" and "Don't know". There were 180 responses. In 41 per cent the judges answered "Probably adversely", in 42 per cent they answered "Probably not adversely", and in 17 per cent they answered "Don't know".

[58] The defendant in the House of Lords case referred to above was Kevin Sean Murray. The fact that the defendant in both cases was named Murray is a pure coincidence. The cases are completely separate.

[59] Application No. 18731/91.

[60] Art. 6, para. 1 states that in a criminal case the defendant "is entitled to a fair and public hearing within a reasonable time by an independent and impartial tribunal established by law. Art. 6, para. 2 states that "Everyone charged with a criminal offence shall be presumed innocent until proved guilty according to law."

inconsistent with the presumption of innocence guaranteed in Art. 6, paragraph 2 of the Convention. The Government, arguing the contrary, pointed to the fact that the law required that the prosecution make a prima facie case before any adverse inferences could be drawn. The Order merely allowed the trier of fact to draw such inferences as common sense dictated. The burden of proof rested throughout on the prosecution.

In its Report, the European Commission on Human Rights drew attention to the fact that the right to silence was not expressly guaranteed in the provisions of Article 6 of the Convention. In *Funke*[61] the Court had held, in the context of a prosecution for refusal to disclose incriminating documents at the request of the customs authorities, that the "special features of customs law ... cannot justify such an infringement of the right of anyone 'charged with a criminal offence', within the meaning of this expression in Article 6, to remain silent and not to contribute to incriminating himself". The Commission said that in that passage the Court appeared to have found that the right to silence and the privilege against self-incrimination were "an inherent part of the protection given to an accused under Article 6, paragraph 1".

In the case of *Saunders*[62] the Commission had found a violation of Article 6, paragraph 1 where the applicant had been compelled under threat of penalty to make incriminating statements to Department of Trade and Industry Inspectors and that information given to them had been used against him in a subsequent criminal prosecution.[63] The Commission in that case said:

> "In the Commission's opinion, the privilege against self-incrimination is an important element in safeguarding an accused from oppression and coercion during criminal proceedings. The very basis of a fair trial presupposes that the accused is afforded the opportunity of defending himself against the charges brought against him. The position of the defence is undermined if the accused is under compulsion, or has been compelled, to incriminate himself."

In *Murray* the United Kingdom Government argued that there was no question of the defendant being forced to provide incriminating information subject to penalties by fine or imprisonment. The defendant was fully entitled to exercise his right to silence and faced no penalty for doing so. The applicant contended that the right to silence became worthless if silence was evidence for the prosecution. The accused was left with no reasonable choice between testifying and not testifying.

The Report said the Commission agreed with the Government's argument "to the extent that it accepted that the right to silence may not be unqualified" (p. 13). The essential issue under Article 6 was whether the applicant received a fair trial which depended on an overall assessment of the case as a whole. No penalty had been imposed on the defendant for exercising his right to silence but he was under indirect pressure from the threat of adverse inferences.

The Commission said it accepted the Government's view that the burden

---

[61] Series A, no. 256–A, 1993.
[62] *Ernest Saunders*, (No. 19187/01) Comm.Rep. 10.5.94.
[63] The case known as Guinness 1.

of proof remained throughout on the prosecution. The judge was not required to draw any adverse inferences. In Northern Ireland in Diplock Court trials the judge gave a reasoned judgment as to why he drew such inferences and what weight he gave them. There *was* a prima facie case against him. It concluded (p. 14): "The Commission finds that the adverse inferences drawn against him as a result were a formal expression of the inevitable doubt that no innocent explanation for conduct may exist where an accused against whom considerable suspicion already lies fails to offer any innocent explanation."

The Commission also considered the significance of the fact that he had been advised by a solicitor to be silent both in the police station and in court. By the time he first had this advice he had already been silent under police questioning. If therefore he had subsequently answered questions or given evidence, adverse inferences could still have been drawn in regard to his initial silence. "On this view the applicant's position was irrevocably prejudiced from his initial silence when cautioned by the police in the first hours of his detention" (p. 15). But there was no suggestion in this case that the applicant failed to understand the significance of the warnings he was given about the consequences of exercising his right to silence. Nor was the Commission impressed by the argument that if the accused had given evidence on oath he would have faced the possibility of being charged with perjury. It thought this possibility too remote. It did not think his conduct had been influenced by fear of prosecution for perjury. The Commission's treatment of the right to silence issue concluded (p. 15):

"The Commission is of the opinion that the provisions of the 1988 Order constitute a formalised system which aims at allowing common sense implications to play an open role in the assessment of evidence. The Commission finds no indication on the facts of this case that it deprived the applicant of the right to silence or that the consequences which flowed from his exercise of that right were unfair."

It will be noted that, like the House of Lords in its *Murray* case, the Commission referred to the significance of "common sense". See further: J.D. Jackson, "Interpreting the Silence Provisions: The Northern Ireland Cases" [1995] *Criminal Law Review*, 587–601; Rosemary Pattenden, "Inferences from Silence", *ibid.*, 602–611; Peter Mirfield, "Two Side-Effects of Sections 34 to 37 of the Criminal Justice and Public Order Act 1994", *ibid.*, 612–624.

POLICE AND CRIMINAL EVIDENCE ACT 1984

POLICE AND CRIMINAL EVIDENCE ACT 1984

[as amended]

CHAPTER 60.   N.I. equivalent*

* The Police and Criminal Evidence (Northern Ireland) Order 1989, S.I. 1989 No. 1341 (N.I. 12).

* Repealed by the Children Act 1989, Sched. 15.

* Repealed by the Legal Aid Act 1988 s.45, Sched. 6.

Part VI

Codes of Practice—General

Part VII   VIII

Documentary Evidence in Criminal Proceedings

* Repealed and replaced by Pt. II of the Criminal Justice Act; see pp. 386–389 below.

Part VIII   IX

Evidence in Criminal Proceedings—General

Convictions and acquittals

Confessions

Part VIII—Supplementary

Part IX

Police Complaints and Discipline

The Police Complaints Authority

Police and Criminal Evidence Act 1984

Handling of complaints etc.

* Police (Amendment) (Northern Ireland) Order 1995 (Draft).
** Repealed by the Police and Magistrates' Courts Act 1994, Sched. 5, para. 28 and Sched. 9.
*** Repealed by the Police and Magistrates' Courts Act 1994, s.37 and Sched. 9.

Amendments of discipline provisions

* Repealed by the Police and Magistrates' Courts Act 1994, s.37 and Sched. 9.
** Repealed by the Police and Magistrates' Courts Act 1994, Sched. 9.

General

* Police (Amendment) (Northern Ireland) Order 1995 (Draft).
** Repealed by the Police and Magistrates' Courts Act 1994, s.37 and Sched. 9.

PART X

POLICE—GENERAL

PART XI

MISCELLANEOUS AND SUPPLEMENTARY

PART I[1]

POWERS TO STOP AND SEARCH

Power of constable to stop and search persons, vehicles etc.

  1.—(1) A constable may exercise any power conferred by this section—
    (a) in any place to which at the time when he proposes to exercise the power the public or any section of the public has access, on payment or otherwise, as of right or by virtue of express or implied permission; or
    (b) in any other place to which people have ready access at the time when he proposes to exercise the power but which is not a dwelling.
  (2) Subject to subsection (3) to (5) below, a constable—
    (a) may search—
      (i) any person or vehicle;
      (ii) anything which is in or on a vehicle,
    for stolen or prohibited articles or any article to which subsection (8A) below applies; and
    (b) may detain a person or vehicle for the purpose of such a search.
  (3) This section does not give a constable power to search a person or vehicle or anything in or on a vehicle unless he has reasonable grounds for suspecting that he will find stolen or prohibited articles or any article to which subsection (8A) below applies.

---

[1] The Northern Ireland Order has a Pt. I consisting of two articles. Art. 1 deals with Title and commencement; Art. 2 deals with General Interpretation of PACE, s.118.

(4) If a person is in a garden or yard occupied with and used for the purposes of a dwelling or on other land so occupied and used, a constable may not search him in the exercise of the power conferred by this section unless the constable has reasonable grounds for believing—

    (a) that he does not reside in the dwelling; and

    (b) that he is not in the place in question with the express or implied permission of a person who resides in the dwelling.

(5) If a vehicle is in a garden or yard or other place occupied with and used for the purposes of a dwelling or on other land so occupied and used a constable may not search the vehicle or anything in it or on it in the exercise of the power conferred by this section unless he has reasonable grounds for believing—

    (a) that the person in charge of the vehicle does not reside in the dwelling; and

    (b) that the vehicle is not in the place in question with the express or implied permission of a person who resides in the dwelling.

(6) If in the course of such a search a constable discovers an article which he has reasonable grounds for suspecting to be a stolen or prohibited article (or an article to which subsection (8A) below applies), he may seize it.

(7) An article is prohibited for the purposes of this Part of this Act if it is—

    (a) an offensive weapon; or

    (b) an article—

        (i) made or adapted for use in the course of or in connection with an offence to which this sub-paragraph applies; or

        (ii) intended by the person having it with him for such use by him or by some other person.

(8) The offences to which subsection (7)(b)(i) above applies are—

    (a) burglary;

    (b) theft;

    (c) offences under section 12 of the Theft Act 1968 (taking motor vehicle or other conveyance without authority); and

    (d) offences under section 15 of that Act (obtaining property by deception).

(8A) This subsection applies to any article in relation to which a person has committed, or is committing or is going to commit an offence under section 139 of the Criminal Justice Act 1988.[2]

---

[2] Subs. (8A) was added by the Criminal Justice Act 1988, s.140. Section 139 of that Act created a new offence of carrying an article with a blade in a public place—

Articles with blades or points and offensive weapons

139.—(1) Subject to subsections (4) and (5) below, any person who has an article to which this section applies with him in a public place shall be guilty of an offence.

(2) Subject to subsection (3) below, this section applies to any article which has a blade or is sharply pointed except a folding penknife.

(3) This section applies to a folding pocketknife if the cutting edge of its blade exceeds 3 inches.

(4) It shall be a defence for a person charged with an offence under this section to prove that he had good reason or lawful authority for having the article with him in a public place.

(5) Without prejudice to the generality of subsection (4) above, it shall be a defence for a person charged with an offence under this section to prove that he had the article with him—

    (a) for use at work;

    (b) for religious reasons; or

    (c) as part of any national costume.

(6) A person guilty of an offence under subsection (1) above shall be liable on summary conviction to a fine not exceeding level 3 on the standard scale.

(7) In this section "public place" includes any place to which at the material time the public have or are permitted access, whether on payment or otherwise.

(8) This section shall not have effect in relation to anything done before it comes into force. See to same effect Northern Ireland PACE Order, Art. 3(9) (ed.).

(9) In this Part of this Act—
"offensive weapon" means any article—
    (a) made or adapted for use for causing injury to persons; or
    (b) intended by the person having it with him for such use by him or by some other person.

Provisions relating to search under section 1 and other powers

2.—(1) A constable who detains a person or vehicle in the exercise—
    (a) of the power conferred by section 1 above; or
    (b) of any other power—
        (i) to search a person without first arresting him; or
        (ii) to search a vehicle without making an arrest,
need not conduct a search if it appears to him subsequently—
        (i) that no search is required; or
        (ii) that a search is impracticable.
(2) If a constable contemplates a search, other than a search of an unattended vehicle, in the exercise—
    (a) of the power conferred by section 1 above; or
    (b) of any other power, except the power conferred by section 6 below and the power conferred by section 27(2) of the Aviation Security Act 1982—[3]
        (i) to search a person without first arresting him; or
        (ii) to search a vehicle without making an arrest,
it shall be his duty, subject to subsection (4) below, to take reasonable steps before he commences the search to bring to the attention of the appropriate person—
        (i) if the constable is not in uniform, documentary evidence that he is a constable; and
        (ii) whether he is in uniform or not, the matters specified in subsection (3) below,
and the constable shall not commence the search until he has performed that duty.
(3) The matters referred to in subsection (2)(ii) above are—
    (a) the constable's name and the name of the police station to which he is attached[4];
    (b) the object of the proposed search;
    (c) the constable's grounds for proposing to make it; and
    (d) the effect of section 3(7) or (8) below, as may be appropriate.
(4) A constable need not bring the effect of section 3(7) or (8) below to the attention of the appropriate person if it appears to the constable that it will not be practicable to make the record in section 3(1) below.
(5) In this section "the appropriate person" means—
    (a) if the constable proposes to search a person, that person; and
    (b) if he proposes to search a vehicle, or anything in or on a vehicle, the person in charge of the vehicle.
(6) On completing a search of an unattended vehicle or anything in or on such a vehicle in the exercise of any such power as is mentioned in subsection (2) above a constable shall leave a notice—
    (a) stating that he has searched it;
    (b) giving the name of the police station to which he is attached;
    (c) stating that an application for compensation for any damage caused by the search may be made to that police station; and

---

[3] The Northern Ireland PACE Order, Art. 4(3)(b) also excluded searches under ss.15, 16 and 20 of the Northern Ireland (Emergency Provisions) Act. See now sections 19, 20 and 26 of the 1991 Act.
[4] The Northern Ireland PACE Order, Art. 4(4)(a) substitutes the officer's number for his name.

(d) stating the effect of section 3(8) below.

(7) The constable shall leave the notice inside the vehicle unless it is not reasonably practicable to do so without damaging the vehicle.

(8) The time for which a person or vehicle may be detained for the purposes of such a search is such time as is reasonably required to permit a search to be carried out either at the place where the person or vehicle was first detained or nearby.

(9) Neither the power conferred by section 1 above nor any other power to detain and search a person without first arresting him or to detain and search a vehicle without making an arrest is to be construed—

> (a) as authorising a constable to require a person to remove any of his clothing in public other than an outer coat, jacket or gloves[5];
> or
> (b) as authorising a constable not in uniform to stop a vehicle.

(10) This section and section 1 above apply to vessels, aircraft and hovercraft as they apply to vehicles.

Duty to make records concerning searches

3.—(1) Where a constable has carried out a search in the exercise of any such power as is mentioned in section 2(1) above, other than a search—

> (a) under section 6 below; or
> (b) under section 27(2) of the Aviation Security Act 1982,

he shall make a record of it in writing unless it is not practicable to do so.

(2) If—

> (a) a constable is required by subsection (1) above to make a record of a search; but
> (b) it is not practicable to make the record on the spot,

he shall make it as soon as practicable after the completion of the search.

(3) The record of a search of a person shall include a note of his name, if the constable knows it, but a constable may not detain a person to find out his name.

(4) If a constable does not know the name of a person whom he has searched, the record of the search shall include a note otherwise describing that person.

(5) The record of a search of a vehicle shall include a note describing the vehicle.

(6) The record of a search—

> (a) shall state—
>> (i) the object of the search;
>> (ii) the grounds for making it;
>> (iii) the date and time when it was made;
>> (iv) the place where it was made;
>> (v) whether anything, and if so what, was found;
>> (vi) whether any, and if so what, injury to a person or damage to property appears to the constable to have resulted from the search; and
> (b) shall identify the constable making it.

(7) If a constable who conducted a search of a person made a record of it, the person who was searched shall be entitled to a copy of the record if he asks for one before the end of the period specified in subsection (9) below.

(8) If—

> (a) the owner of a vehicle which has been searched or the person who was in charge of the vehicle at the time when it was searched

---

[5] The Northern Ireland PACE Order, Art. 4(10)(a), adds headgear.

asks for a copy of the record of the search before the end of the period specified in subsection (9) below; and

(b) the constable who conducted the search made a record of it, the person who made the request shall be entitled to a copy.

(9) The period mentioned in subsections (7) and (8) above is the period of 12 months beginning with the date on which the search was made.

(10) The requirements imposed by this section with regard to records of searches of vehicles shall apply also to records of searches of vessels, aircraft and hovercraft.

Road checks

4.—(1) This section shall have effect in relation to the conduct of road checks by police officers for the purpose of ascertaining whether a vehicle is carrying—

(a) a person who has committed an offence other than a road traffic offence or a vehicle[5a] excise offence;

(b) a person who is a witness to such an offence;

(c) a person intending to commit such an offence; or

(d) a person who is unlawfully at large.

(2) For the purposes of this section a road check consists of the exercise in a locality of the power conferred by section 163[6] of the Road Traffic Act 1988[7] in such a way as to stop during the period for which its exercise in that way in that locality continues all vehicles or vehicles selected by any criterion.

(3) Subject to subsection (5) below, there may only be such a road check if a police officer of the rank of superintendent or above authorises it in writing.

(4) An officer may only authorise a road check under subsection (3) above—

(a) for the purpose specified in subsection (1)(a) above, if he has reasonable grounds—

(i) for believing that the offence is a serious arrestable offence; and

(ii) for suspecting that the person is, or is about to be, in the locality in which vehicles would be stopped if the road check were authorised;

(b) for the purpose specified in subsection (1)(b) above, if he has reasonable grounds for believing that the offence is a serious arrestable offence;

(c) for the purpose specified in subsection (1)(c) above, if he has reasonable grounds—

(i) for believing that the offence would be a serious arrestable offence; and

(ii) for suspecting that the person is, or is about to be in the locality in which vehicles would be stopped if the road check were authorised;

(d) for the purpose specified in subsection (1)(d) above, if he has reasonable grounds for suspecting that the person is, or is about to be, in that locality.

(5) An officer below the rank of superintendent may authorise such a road check if it appears to him that it is required as a matter of urgency for one of the purposes specified in subsection (1) above.

[5a] Amended by the Vehicle Excise and Registration Act 1994, Sched. 3, para. 19.

[6-7] Amended by the Road Traffic (Consequential Provisions) Act 1988, Sched. 3, para. 27.

(6) If an authorisation is given under subsection (5) above, it shall be the duty of the officer who gives it—
(a) to make a written record of the time at which he gives it; and
(b) to cause an officer of the rank of superintendent or above to be informed that it has been given.

(7) The duties imposed by subsection (6) above shall be performed as soon as it is practicable to do so.

(8) An officer to whom a report is made under subsection (6) above may, in writing, authorise the road check to continue.

(9) If such an officer considers that the road check should not continue, he shall record in writing—
(a) the fact that it took place; and
(b) the purpose for which it took place.

(10) An officer giving an authorisation under this section shall specify the locality in which vehicles are to be stopped.

(11) An officer giving an authorisation under this section, other than an authorisation under subsection (5) above—
(a) shall specify a period, not exceeding seven days, during which the road check may continue; and
(b) may direct that the road check—
(i) shall be continuous; or
(ii) shall be conducted at specified times, during that period.

(12) If it appears to an officer of the rank of superintendent or above that a road check ought to continue beyond the period for which it has been authorised he may, from time to time, in writing specify a further period, not exceeding seven days, during which it may continue.

(13) Every written authorisation shall specify—
(a) the name of the officer giving it;
(b) the purpose of the road check; and
(c) the locality in which vehicles are to be stopped.

(14) The duties to specify the purposes of a road check imposed by subsections (9) and (13) above include duties to specify any relevant serious arrestable offence.

(15) Where a vehicle is stopped in a road check, the person in charge of the vehicle at the time when it is stopped shall be entitled to obtain a written statement of the purpose of the road check, if he applies for such a statement not later than the end of the period of twelve months from the day on which the vehicle was stopped.

(16) Nothing in this section affects the exercise by police officers of any power to stop vehicles for purposes other than those specified in subsection (1) above.

Reports of recorded searches and of road checks

5.—(1) Every annual report—
(a) under section 12 of the Police Act 1964; or
(b) made by the Commissioner of Police of the Metropolis,
shall contain information—
(i) about searches recorded under section 3 above which have been carried out in the area to which the report relates during the period to which it relates; and
(ii) about road checks authorised in that area during that period under section 4 above.

(2) The information about searches shall not include information about specific searches but shall include—
(a) the total numbers of searches in each month during the period to which the report relates—

    (i) for stolen articles;
    (ii) for offensive weapons or articles to which section 1(8A) above applies, and
    (iii) for other prohibited articles;
  (b) the total number of persons arrested in each such month in consequence of searches of each of the descriptions specified in paragraph (a)(i) to (iii) above.

(3) The information about road checks shall include information—
  (a) about the reason for authorising each road check; and
  (b) about the result of each of them.

Statutory undertakers etc.

6.—(1) A constable employed by statutory undertakers may stop, detain and search any vehicle before it leaves a goods area included in the premises of the statutory undertakers.

(2) In this section—
    "goods area" means any area used wholly or mainly for the storage or handling of goods.

(3) For the purposes of section 6 of the Public Stores Act 1875, any person appointed under the Special Constables Act 1923 to be a special constable within any premises which are in the possession or under the control of British Nuclear Fuels Limited shall be deemed to be a constable deputed by a public department and any goods and chattels belonging to or in the possession of British Nuclear Fuels Limited shall be deemed to be Her Majesty's Stores.

(4) In the application of subsection (3) above to Northern Ireland, for the reference to the Special Constables Act 1923 there shall be substituted a reference to paragraph 1(2) of Schedule 2 to the Emergency Laws (Miscellaneous Provisions) Act 1947.

Part I—Supplementary[8]

7.—(1) The following enactments shall cease to have effect—
  (a) section 8 of the Vagrancy Act 1824;
  (b) section 66 of the Metropolitan Police Act 1839;
  (c) section 11 of the Canals (Offences) Act 1840;
  (d) section 19 of the Pedlars Act 1871;
  (e) section 33 of the County of Merseyside Act 1980; and
  (f) section 42 of the West Midlands County Council Act 1980.

(2) There shall also cease to have effect—
  (a) so much of any enactment contained in an Act passed before 1974, other than—
    (i) an enactment contained in a public general Act; or
    (ii) an enactment relating to statutory undertakers, as confers power on a constable to search for stolen or unlawfully obtained goods; and
  (b) so much of any enactment relating to statutory undertakers as provides that such a power shall not be exercisable after the end of a specified period.

(3) In this Part of this Act "statutory undertakers" means persons authorised by any enactment to carry on any railway, light railway, road transport, water transport, canal, inland navigation, dock or harbour undertaking.

[8] Note drafting differences in Northern Ireland PACE Order, Art. 9(2).

Police and Criminal Evidence Act 1984

PART II

POWERS OF ENTRY, SEARCH AND SEIZURE

Search warrants

Power of the justice of the peace to authorise entry and search of premises

8.—(1) If on an application made by a constable a justice of the peace is satisfied that there are reasonable grounds for believing—

    (a) that a serious arrestable offence has been committed; and

    (b) that there is material on premises specified in the application which is likely to be of substantial value (whether by itself or together with other material) to the investigation of the offence; and

    (c) that the material is likely to be relevant evidence; and

    (d) that it does not consist of or include items subject to legal privilege, excluded material or special procedure material; and

    (e) that any of the conditions specified in subsection (3) below applies,

he may issue a warrant authorising a constable to enter and search the premises.

(2) A constable may seize and retain anything for which a search has been authorised under subsection (1) above.

(3) The conditions mentioned in subsection (1)(e) above are—

    (a) that it is not practicable to communicate with any person entitled to grant entry to the premises;

    (b) that it is practicable to communicate with a person entitled to grant entry to the premises but it is not practicable to communicate with any person entitled to grant access to the evidence;

    (c) that entry to the premises will not be granted unless a warrant is produced;

    (d) that the purpose of a search may be frustrated or seriously prejudiced unless a constable arriving at the premises can secure immediate entry to them.

(4) In this Act "relevant evidence", in relation to an offence, means anything that would be admissible in evidence at a trial for the offence.

(5) The power to issue a warrant conferred by this section is in addition to any such power otherwise conferred.

Special provisions as to access[9]

9.—(1) A constable may obtain access to excluded material or special procedure material for the purposes of a criminal investigation by making an application under Schedule 1 below and in accordance with that Schedule.

(2) Any Act (including a local Act) passed before this Act under which a search of premises for the purposes of a criminal investigation could be authorised by the issue of a warrant to a constable shall cease to have effect so far as it relates to the authorisation of searches—

    (a) for items subject to legal privilege; or

    (b) for excluded material; or

    (c) for special procedure material consisting of documents or records other than documents.

---

[9] Note drafting differences in Northern Ireland PACE Order, Art. 11(2) and (3).

Meaning of "items subject to legal privilege"

10.—(1) Subject to subsection (2) below, in this Act "items subject to legal privilege" means—

    (a) communications between a professional legal adviser and his client or any person representing his client made in connection with the giving of legal advice to the client;

    (b) communications between a professional legal adviser and his client or any person representing his client or between such an adviser or his client or any such representative and any other person made in connection with or in contemplation of legal proceedings and for the purposes of such proceedings; and

    (c) items enclosed with or referred to in such communications and made—

      (i) in connection with the giving of legal advice; or

      (ii) in connection with or in contemplation of legal proceedings and for the purposes of such procedings,

when they are in the possession of a person who is entitled to possession of them.

(2) Items held with the intention of furthering a criminal purpose are not items subject to legal privilege.

Meaning of "excluded material"

11.—(1) Subject to the following provisions of this section, in this Act "excluded material" means—

    (a) personal records which a person has acquired or created in the course of any trade, business, profession or other occupation or for the purposes of any paid or unpaid office and which he holds in confidence;

    (b) human tissue or tissue fluid which has been taken for the purposes of diagnosis or medical treatment and which a person holds in confidence;

    (c) journalistic material which a person holds in confidence and which consists—

      (i) of documents; or

      (ii) of records other than documents.

(2) A person holds material other than journalistic material in confidence for the purposes of this section if he holds it subject—

    (a) to an express or implied undertaking to hold it in confidence; or

    (b) to a restriction on disclosure or an obligation of secrecy contained in any enactment, including an enactment contained in an Act passed after this Act.

(3) A person holds journalistic material in confidence for the purposes of this section if—

    (a) he holds it subject to such an undertaking, restriction or obligation; and

    (b) it has been continuously held (by one or more persons) subject to such an undertaking, restriction or obligation since it was first acquired or created for the purposes of journalism.

Meaning of "personal records"

12. In this Part of this Act "personal records" means documentary and other records concerning an individual (whether living or dead) who can be identified from them, and relating—

    (a) to his physical or mental health;

    (b) to spiritual counselling or assistance given or to be given to him;

    (c) to counselling or assistance given or to be given to him, for the purposes of his personal welfare, by any voluntary organisation or by any individual who—

        (i) by reason of his office or occupation has responsibilities for his personal welfare; or

        (ii) by reason of an order of a court, has responsibilities for his supervision.

Meaning of "journalistic material"

13.—(1) Subject to subsection (2) below, in this Act "journalistic material" means material acquired or created for the purposes of journalism.

(2) Material is only journalistic material for the purposes of this Act if it is in the possession of a person who acquired or created it for the purposes of journalism.

(3) A person who receives material from someone who intends that the recipient shall use it for the purposes of journalism is to be taken to have acquired it for those purposes.

Meaning of "special procedure material"

14.—(1) In this Act "special procedure material" means—

    (a) material to which subsection (2) below applies; and

    (b) journalistic material, other than excluded material.

(2) Subject to the following provisions of this section, this subsection applies to material, other than items subject to legal privilege and excluded material, in the possession of a person who—

    (a) acquired or created it in the course of any trade, business, profession or other occupation or for the purpose of any paid or unpaid office and

    (b) holds it subject—

        (i) to an express or implied undertaking to hold it in confidence; or

        (ii) to a restriction or obligation such as is mentioned in section 11(2)(b) above.

(3) Where material is acquired—

    (a) by an employee from his employer and in the course of his employment; or

    (b) by a company from an associated company,

it is only special procedure material if it was special procedure material immediately before the acquisition.

(4) Where material is created by an employee in the course of his employment, it is only special procedure material if it would have been special procedure material had his employer created it.

(5) Where material is created by a company on behalf of an associated company, it is only special procedure material if it would have been special procedure material had the associated company created it.

(6) A company is to be treated as another's associated company for the purposes of this section if it would be so treated under section 302 of the Income and Corporation Taxes Act 1970.

Search warrants—safeguards[10]

15.—(1) This section and section 16 below have effect in relation to the issue to constables under any enactment, including an enactment contained

---

[10] Note drafting changes in Northern Ireland PACE Order, Art. 17(1), (3), (4) and (8).

in an Act passed after this Act, of warrants to enter and search premises, and an entry on or search of premises under a warrant is unlawful unless it complies with this section and section 16 below.

(2) Where a constable applies for any such warrant, it shall be his duty—
  (a) to state—
      (i) the ground on which he makes the application; and
      (ii) the enactment under which the warrant would be issued;
  (b) to specify the premises which it is desired to enter and search; and
  (c) to identify, so far as is practicable, the articles or persons to be sought.

(3) An application for such a warrant shall be made ex parte and supported by an information in writing.

(4) The constable shall answer on oath any question that the justice of the peace or judge hearing the application asks him.

(5) A warrant shall authorise an entry on one occasion only.

(6) A warrant—
  (a) shall specify—
      (i) the name of the person who applies for it;
      (ii) the date on which it is issued;
      (iii) the enactment under which it is issued; and
      (iv) the premises to be searched; and
  (b) shall identify, so far as is practicable, the articles or person to be sought.

(7) Two copies shall be made of a warrant.

(8) The copies shall be clearly certified as copies.

Execution of warrants[11]

16.—(1) A warrant to enter and search premises may be executed by any constable.

(2) Such a warrant may authorise persons to accompany any constable who is executing it.

(3) Entry and search under a warrant must be within one month from the date of its issue.

(4) Entry and search under a warrant must be at a reasonable hour unless it appears to the constable executing it that the purposes of a search may be frustrated on an entry at a reasonable hour.

(5) Where the occupier of premises which are to be entered and searched is present at the time when a constable seeks to execute a warrant to enter and search them, the constable—
  (a) shall identify himself to the occupier and, if not in uniform, shall produce to him documentary evidence that he is a constable;
  (b) shall produce the warrant to him; and
  (c) shall supply him with a copy of it.

(6) Where—
  (a) the occupier of such premises is not present at the time when a constable seeks to execute such a warrant; but
  (b) some other person who appears to the constable to be in charge of the premises is present,
subsection (5) above shall have effect as if any reference to the occupier were a reference to that other person.

(7) If there is no person present who appears to the constable to be in charge of the premises, he shall leave a copy of the warrant in a prominent place on the premises.

---

[11] Note drafting changes in Northern Ireland PACE Order, Art. 18(5)(c), (7), (10) and (11).

(8) A search under a warrant may only be a search to the extent required for the purpose for which the warrant was issued.

(9) A constable executing a warrant shall make an endorsement on it stating—

    (a) whether the articles or persons sought were found; and

    (b) whether any articles were seized, other than articles which were sought.

(10) A warrant which—

    (a) has been executed; or

    (b) has not been executed within the time authorised for its execution, shall be returned—

        (i) if it was issued by a justice of the peace, to the clerk to the justices for the petty sessions area for which he acts; and

        (ii) if it was issued by a judge, to the appropriate officer of the court from which he issued it.

(11) A warrant which is returned under subsection (10) above shall be retained for 12 months from its return—

    (a) by the clerk to the justices, if it was returned under paragraph (i) of that subsection; and

    (b) by the appropriate officer, if it was returned under paragraph (ii).

(12) If during the period for which a warrant is to be retained the occupier of the premises to which it relates asks to inspect if, he shall be allowed to do so.

Entry and search without search warrant

Entry for purpose of arrest etc.[12]

17.—(1) Subject to the following provisions of this section, and without prejudice to any other enactment, a constable may enter and search any premises for the purpose—

    (a) of executing—

        (i) a warrant of arrest issued in connection with or arising out of criminal proceedings; or

        (ii) a warrant of commitment issued under section 76 of the Magistrates' Courts Act 1980;

    (b) of arresting a person for an arrestable offence;

    (c) of arresting a person for an offence under—

        (i) section 1 (prohibition of uniforms in connection with political objects) . . .[13] of the Public Order Act 1936;

        (ii) any enactment contained in sections 6 to 8 or 10 of the Criminal Law Act 1977 (offences relating to entering and remaining on property);

        (iii) s.4 of the Public Order Act 1986 (fear or provocation of violence)[14];

        (iv) section 76 of the Criminal Justice and Public Order Act 1994 (failure to comply with interim possession order)[14a];

    (d) of recapturing a person who is unlawfully at large and whom he is pursuing[14aa]; or

    (e) of saving life or limb or preventing serious damage to property.

(2) Except for the purpose specified in paragraph (e) of subsection (1) above, the powers of entry and search conferred by this section—

---

[12] Note drafting change in Northern Ireland PACE Order, Art. 19(1)(c).

[13] Words deleted by Public Order Act 1986, Sched. 2, para. 7.

[14a] Added by the Criminal Justice and Public Order Act 1994, Sched. 10, para. 53(a).

[14aa] As amended for Northern Ireland, see Appendix 4, p. 532 below [Art. 7].

    (a) are only exercisable if the constable has reasonable grounds for believing that the person whom he is seeking is on the premises; and

    (b) are limited, in relation to premises consisting of two or more separate dwellings, to powers to enter and search—

        (i) any parts of the premises which the occupiers of any dwelling comprised in the premises use in common with the occupiers of any other such dwelling; and

        (ii) any such dwelling in which the constable has reasonable grounds for believing that the person whom he is seeking may be.

(3) The powers of entry and search conferred by this section are only exercisable for the purposes specified in subsection (1)(c)(ii) or (iv)[14b] above by a constable in uniform.

(4) The power of search conferred by this section is only a power to search to the extent that is reasonably required for the purpose for which the power of entry is exercised.

(5) Subject to subsection (6) below, all the rules of common law under which a constable has power to enter premises without a warrant are hereby abolished.

(6) Nothing in subsection (5) above affects any power of entry to deal with or prevent a breach of the peace.

Entry and search after arrest

18.—(1) Subject to the following provisions of this section, a constable may enter and search, any premises occupied or controlled by a person who is under arrest for an arrestable offence, if he has reasonable grounds for suspecting that there is on the premises evidence other than items subject to legal privilege, that relates—

    (a) to that offence; or

    (b) to some other arrestable offence which is connected with or similar to that offence.

(2) A constable may seize and retain anything for which he may search under subsection (1) above.

(3) The power to search conferred by subsection (1) above is only a power to search to the extent that is reasonably required for the purpose of discovering such evidence.

(4) Subject to subsection (5) below, the powers conferred by this section may not be exercised unless an officer of the rank of inspector or above has authorised them in writing.

(5) A constable may conduct a search under subsection (1) above—

    (a) before taking the person to a police station; and

    (b) without obtaining an authorisation under subsection (4) above, if the presence of that person at a place other than a police station is necessary for the effective investigation of the offence.

(6) If a constable conducts a search by virtue of subsection (5) above, he shall inform an officer of the rank of inspector or above that he has made the search as soon as practicable after he has made it.

(7) An officer who—

    (a) authorises a search; or

    (b) is informed of a search under subsection (6) above, shall make a record in writing—

[14b] Amended by the Criminal Justice and Public Order Act 1994, Sched. 10, para. 53(b).

(i) of the grounds for the search; and

(ii) of the nature of the evidence that was sought.

(8) If the person who was in occupation or control of the premises at the time of the search is in police detention at the time the record is to be made, the officer shall make the record as part of his custody record.[15]

Seizure etc.

General power of seizure etc.

19.—(1) The powers conferred by subsections (2), (3), and (4) below are exercisable by a constable who is lawfully on any premises.

(2) The constable may seize anything which is on the premises if he has reasonable grounds for believing—

(a) that it has been obtained in consequence of the commission of an offence; and

(b) that it is necessary to seize it in order to prevent it being concealed, lost, damaged, altered or destroyed.

(3) The constable may seize anything which is on the premises if he has reasonable grounds for believing—

(a) that it is evidence in relation to an offence which he is investigating or any other offence; and

(b) that it is necessary to seize it in order to prevent the evidence being concealed, lost, altered or destroyed.

(4) The constable may require any information which is contained in a computer and is accessible from the premises to be produced in a form in which it can be taken away and in which it is visible and legible if he has reasonable grounds for believing—

(a) that—

(i) it is evidence in relation to an offence which he is investigating or any other offence; or

(ii) it has been obtained in consequence of the commission of an offence; and

(b) that it is necessary to do so in order to prevent it being concealed, lost, tampered with or destroyed.

(5) The powers conferred by this section are in addition to any power otherwise conferred.

(6) No power of seizure conferred on a constable under any enactment (including an enactment contained in an Act passed after this Act) is to be taken to authorise the seizure of an item which the constable exercising the power has reasonable grounds for believing to be subject to legal privilege.

Extension of powers of seizure to computerised information

20.—(1) Every power of seizure which is conferred by an enactment to which this section applies on a constable who has entered premises in the exercise of a power conferred by an enactment shall be construed as including a power to require any information contained in a computer and accessible from the premises to be produced in a form in which it can be taken away and in which it is visible and legible.

(2) This section applies—

(a) to any enactment contained in an Act passed before this Act;

---

[15] The Northern Ireland PACE Order, Art. 20 has an extra para. (9) to take account of the fact that Ministry of Defence police in the province have no rank two above constable.

(b) to sections 8 and 18 above;

(c) to paragraph 13 of Schedule 1 to this Act; and

(d) to any enactment contained in an Act passed after this Act.

Access and copying

21.—(1) A constable who seizes anything in the exercise of a power conferred by any enactment, including an enactment contained in an Act passed after this Act, shall, if so requested by a person showing himself—

(a) to be the occupier of premises on which it was seized; or

(b) to have had custody or control of it immediately before the seizure,

provide that person with a record of what he seized.

(2) The officer shall provide the record within a reasonable time from the making of the request for it.

(3) Subject to subsection (8) below, if a request for permission to be granted access to anything which—

(a) has been seized by a constable; and

(b) is retained by the police for the purpose of investigating an offence,

is made to the officer in charge of the investigation by a person who had custody or control of the thing immediately before it was so seized or by someone acting on behalf of such a person the officer shall allow the person who made the request access to it under the supervision of a constable.

(4) Subject to subsection (8) below, if a request for a photograph or copy of any such thing is made to the officer in charge of the investigation by a person who had custody or control of the thing immediately before it was so seized, or by someone acting on behalf of such a person, the officer shall—

(a) allow the person who made the request access to it under the supervision of a constable for the purpose of photographing or copying it; or

(b) photograph or copy it, or cause it to be photographed or copied.

(5) A constable may also photograph or copy, or have photographed or copied, anything which he has power to seize, without a request being made under subsection (4) above.

(6) Where anything is photographed or copied under subsection (4)(b) above, the photograph or copy shall be supplied to the person who made the request.

(7) The photograph or copy shall be so supplied within a reasonable time from the making of the request.

(8) There is no duty under this section to grant access to, or to supply a photograph or copy of, anything if the officer in charge of the investigation for the purposes of which it was seized has reasonable grounds for believing that to do so would prejudice—

(a) that investigation;

(b) the investigation of an offence other than the offence for the purposes of investigating which the thing was seized; or

(c) any criminal proceedings which may be brought as a result of—

(i) the investigation of which he is in charge; or

(ii) any such investigation as is mentioned in paragraph (b) above.

Retention

22.—(1) Subject to subsection (4) below, anything which has been seized by a constable or taken away by a constable following a requirement made by virtue of section 19 or 20 may be retained so long as is necessary in all the circumstances.

(2) Without prejudice to the generality of subsection (1) above—

    (a) anything seized for the purposes of a criminal investigation may be retained, except as provided by subsection (4) below,—

        (i) for use as evidence at a trial for an offence; or

        (ii) for forensic examination or for investigation in connection with an offence; and

    (b) anything may be retained in order to establish its lawful owner, where there are reasonable grounds for believing that it has been obtained in consequence of the commission of an offence.

(3) Nothing seized on the ground that it may be used—

    (a) to cause physical injury to any person;

    (b) to damage property;

    (c) to interfere with evidence; or

    (d) to assist in escape from police detention or lawful custody,

may be retained when the person from whom it was seized is no longer in police detention or the custody of a court or is in the custody of a court but has been released on bail.

(4) Nothing may be retained for either of the purposes mentioned in subsection (2)(a) above if a photograph or copy would be sufficient for that purpose.

(5) Nothing in this section affects any power of a court to make an order under section 1 of the Police (Property) Act 1897.

Supplementary

Meaning of "premises" etc.

23. In this Act—

    "premises" includes any place and, in particular, includes—

    (a) any vehicle, vessel, aircraft or hovercraft;

    (b) any offshore installation; and

    (c) any tent or movable structure; and

    "offshore installation" has the meaning given to it by section 1 of the Mineral Workings (Offshore Installations) Act 1971.

PART III

ARREST

Arrest without warrant for arrestable and other offences

24.—(1) The powers of summary arrest conferred by the following subsections shall apply—

    (a) to offences for which the sentence is fixed by law;

    (b) to offences for which a person of 21 years of age or over (not previously convicted) may be sentenced to imprisonment for a term of five years (or might be so sentenced but for the restrictions imposed by section 33 of the Magistrates' Courts Act 1980); and

    (c) to the offences to which subsection (2) below applies,

and in this Act "arrestable offence" means any such offence.

(2) The offences to which this subsection applies are—

    (a) offences for which a person may be arrested under the customs and excise Acts, as defined in section 1(1) of the Customs and Excise Management Act 1979;

(b) offences under the Official Secrets Act 1920 that are not arrestable offences by virtue of the term of imprisonment for which a person may be sentenced in respect of them;

(bb) offences under any provision of the Official Secrets Act 1989 except section 8(1), (4) or (5)[15a];

(c) offences under section ...[16] 22 (causing prostitution of women) or 23 (procuration of girl under 21) of the Sexual Offences Act 1956;

(d) offences under section 12(1) (taking motor vehicle or other conveyance without authority etc.) or 25(1) (going equipped for stealing, etc.) of the Theft Act 1968; and

(e) any offence under the Football (Offences) Act 1991[17];

(f) an offence under section 2 of the Obscene Publications Act 1959 (publication of obscene matter);

(g) an offence under section 1 of the Protection of Children Act 1978 (indecent photographs and pseudo-photographs of children)[17a];

(h) an offence under section 166 of the Criminal Justice and Public Order Act 1994 (sale of tickets by unauthorised persons)[17b];

(i) an offence under section 19 of the Public Order Act 1986 (publishing, etc. material intended or likely to stir up racial hatred)[17c];

(j) an offence under section 167 of the Criminal Justice and Public Order Act 1994 (touting for hire car services).[17d]

(3) Without prejudice to section 2 of the Criminal Attempts Act 1981, the powers of summary arrest conferred by the following subsections shall also apply to the offences of—

(a) conspiring to commit any of the offences mentioned in subsection (2) above;

(b) attempting to commit any such offence [other than an offence under section 12(1) of the Theft Act 1968][18];

(c) inciting, aiding, abetting, counselling or procuring the commission of any such offence,

and such offences are also arrestable offences for the purposes of this Act.

(4) Any person may arrest without a warrant—

(a) anyone who is in the act of committing an arrestable offence;

(b) anyone whom he has reasonable grounds for suspecting to be committing such an offence.

(5) Where an arrestable offence has been committed, any person may arrest without a warrant—

(a) anyone who is guilty of the offence;

(b) anyone whom he has reasonable grounds for suspecting to be guilty of it.

(6) Where a constable has reasonable grounds for suspecting that an arrestable offence has been committed, he may arrest without a warrant anyone whom he has reasonable grounds for suspecting to be guilty of the offence.

(7) A constable may arrest without a warrant—

(a) anyone who is about to commit an arrestable offence;

[15a] Added by the Official Secrets Act 1989, s.11(1).
[16] Words repealed by the Sexual Offences Act 1985, s.5(3).
[17] Substituted by the Football (Offences) Act 1991, s.5(1).
[17a] Added by the Criminal Justice and Public Order Act 1994, s.85(2). See also s.85(4) and (5) which made an equivalent addition to the Northern Ireland PACE Order, s.26.
[17b] Added by the Criminal Justice and Public Order Act 1994, s.166(4).
[17c] Added by the Criminal Justice and Public Order Act 1994, s.155.
[17d] Added by the Criminal Justice and Public Order Act 1994 s.167(7).
[18] The words in square brackets were added by the Criminal Justice Act 1988, Sched. 15, para. 98.

(b) anyone whom he has reasonable grounds for suspecting to be about to commit an arrestable offence.

General arrest conditions

25.—(1) Where a constable has reasonable grounds for suspecting that any offence which is not an arrestable offence has been committed or attempted, or is being committed or attempted, he may arrest the relevant person if it appears to him that service of a summons is impracticable or inappropriate because any of the general arrest conditions is satisfied.

(2) In this section, "the relevant person" means any person whom the constable has reasonable grounds to suspect of having committed or having attempted to commit the offence or of being in the course of committing or attempting to commit it.

(3) The general arrest conditions are—

(a) that the name of the relevant person is unknown to, and cannot be readily ascertained by, the constable;

(b) that the constable has reasonable grounds for doubting whether a name furnished by the relevant person as his name is his real name;

(c) that—

(i) the relevant person has failed to furnish a satisfactory address for service; or

(ii) the constable has reasonable grounds for doubting whether an address furnished by the relevant person is a satisfactory address for service;

(d) that the constable has reasonable grounds for believing that arrest is necessary to prevent the relevant person—

(i) causing physical harm to himself or any other person;

(ii) suffering physical injury;

(iii) causing loss of or damage to property;

(iv) committing an offence against public decency; or

(v) causing an unlawful obstruction of the highway;

(e) that the constable has reasonable grounds for believing that arrest is necessary to protect a child or other vulnerable person from the relevant person.

(4) For the purposes of subsection (3) above an address is a satisfactory address for service if it appears to the constable—

(a) that the relevant person will be at it for a sufficiently long period for it to be possible to serve him with a summons; or

(b) that some other person specified by the relevant person will accept service of a summons for the relevant person at it.

(5) Nothing in subsection (3)(d) above authorises the arrest of a person under sub-paragraph (iv) of that paragraph except where members of the public going about their normal business cannot reasonably be expected to avoid the person to be arrested.

(6) This section shall not prejudice any power of arrest conferred apart form this section.

Repeal of statutory powers of arrest without warrant or order

26.—(1) Subject to subsection (2) below, so much of any Act (including a local Act) passed before this Act as enables a constable[19]—

---

[19] In the Northern Ireland PACE Order the words "(including a local act)" are removed.

(a) to arrest a person for an offence without a warrant; or

(b) to arrest a person otherwise than for an offence without a warrant or an order of a court,

shall cease to have effect.

(2) Nothing in subsection (1) above affects the enactments specified in Schedule 2 to this Act.

Fingerprinting of certain offenders

27.—(1) If a person—

(a) has been convicted of a recordable offence;

(b) has not at any time been in police detention for the offence; and

(c) has not had his fingerprints taken—

    (i) in the course of the investigation of the offence by the police; or

    (ii) since the conviction;

any constable may at any time not later than one month after the date of the conviction require him to attend a police station in order that his fingerprints may be taken.

(2) A requirement under subsection (1) above—

(a) shall give the person a period of at least 7 days within which he must so attend; and

(b) may direct him to so attend at a specified time of day or between specified times of day.

(3) Any constable may arrest without warrant a person who has failed to comply with a requirement under subsection (1) above.

(4) The Secretary of State may by regulations make provision for recording in national police records convictions for such offences as are specified in the regulations.

(5) Regulations under this section shall be made by statutory instrument and shall be subject to annulment in pursuance of a resolution of either House of Parliament.

Information to be given on arrest

28.—(1) Subject to subsection (5) below, when a person is arrested otherwise than by being informed that he is under arrest, the arrest is not lawful unless the person arrested is informed that he is under arrest as soon as is practicable after his arrest.

(2) Where a person is arrested by a constable subsection (1) above applies regardless of whether the fact of the arrest is obvious.

(3) Subject to subsection (5) below, no arrest is lawful unless the person arrested is informed of the ground for the arrest at the time of, or as soon as is practicable after, the arrest.[20]

(4) Where a person is arrested by a constable, subsection (3) above applies regardless of whether the ground for the arrest is obvious.

(5) Nothing in this section is to be taken to require a person to be informed—

(a) that he is under arrest; or

(b) of the ground for the arrest,

if it was not reasonably practicable for him to be so informed by reason of his having escaped from arrest before the information could be given.

---

[20] The Northern Ireland PACE Order, Art. 30(3) excluded arrests by the army under s.14(2) of the Northern Ireland (Emergency Provisions) Act 1978. See now section 18(2) of the 1991 Act.

Voluntary attendance at police station etc.

29. Where for the purpose of assisting with an investigation a person attends voluntarily at a police station or at any other place where a constable is present or accompanies a constable to a police station or any such other place without having been arrested—

    (a) he shall be entitled to leave at will unless he is placed under arrest;

    (b) he shall be informed at once that he is under arrest if a decision is taken by a constable to prevent him from leaving at will.

Arrest elsewhere than at police station

30.—(1) Subject to the following provisions of this section, where a person

    (a) is arrested by a constable for an offence; or

    (b) is taken into custody by a constable after being arrested for an offence by a person other than a constable;

at any place other than a police station he shall be taken to a police station by a constable as soon as practicable after the arrest.

(2) Subject to subsections (3) and (4) below, the police station to which an arrested prson is taken under subsection (1) above shall be a designated police station.

(3) A constable to whom this subsection applies may take an arrested person to any police station unless it appears to the constable that it may be necessary to keep the arrested person in police detention for more than six hours.

(4) Subsection (3) above applies—

    (a) to a constable who is working in a locality covered by a police station which is not a designated police station; and

    (b) to a constable belonging to a body of constables maintained by an authority other than a police authority.

(5) Any constable may take an arrested person to any police station if—[21]

    (a) either of the following conditions is satisfied—

        (i) the constable has arrested him without the assistance of any other constable and no other constable is available to assist him;

        (ii) the constable has taken him into custody from a person other than a constable without the assistance of any other constable and no other constable is available to assist him; and

    (b) it appears to the constable that he will be unable to take the arrested person to a designated police station without the arrested person injuring himself, the constable or some other person.

(6) If the first police station to which an arrested person is taken after his arrest is not a designated police station he shall be taken to a designated police station not more than six hours after his arrival at the first police station unless he is released previously.

(7) A person arrested by a constable at a place other than a police station shall be released if a constable is satisfied, before the person arrested reaches a police station, that there are no grounds for keeping him under arrest.

(8) A constable who releases a person under subsection (7) above shall record the fact that he has done so.

---

[21] The Northern Ireland PACE Order, Art. 32(6), (7) and (8), adds the danger to the suspect or officer of an unacceptable risk of injury. He can be held on a superintendent's authority.

(9) The constable shall make the record as soon as is practicable after the release.

(10) Nothing in subsection (1) above shall prevent a constable delaying taking a person who has been arrested to a police station if the presence of that person elsewhere is necessary in order to carry out such investigations as it is reasonable to carry out immediately.

(11) Where there is a delay in taking a person who has been arrested to a police station after his arrest, the reasons for the delay shall be recorded when he first arrives at a police station.

(12) Nothing in subsection (1) above shall be taken to affect—

    (a) paragraphs 16(3) or 18(1) of Schedule 2 to the Immigration Act 1971;

    (b) section 34(1) of the Criminal Justice Act 1972; or

    (c) section 15(6) and (9) of the Prevention of Terrorism (Temporary Provisions) Act 1989 and paragraphs 7(4) and 8(4) and (5) of Schedule 2 and paragraphs 6(6) and 7(4) and (5) of Schedule 5 to that Act.[22]

(13) Nothing in subsection (9) above shall be taken to affect paragraph 18(3) of Schedule 2 to the Immigration Act 1971.

Arrest for further offence

31. Where—

    (a) a person—

        (i) has been arrested for an offence; and

        (ii) is at a police station in consequence of that arrest; and

    (b) it appears to a constable that, if he were released from that arrest, he would be liable to arrest for some other offence,

he shall be arrested for that offence.

Search upon arrest

32.—(1) A constable may search an arrested person, in any case where the person to be searched has been arrested at a place other than a police station, if the constable has reasonable grounds for believing that the arrested person may present a danger to himself or others.

(2) Subject to subsections (3) to (5) below, a constable shall also have power in any such case—

    (a) to search the arrested person for anything—

        (i) which he might use to assist him to escape from lawful custody; or

        (ii) which might be evidence relating to an offence; and

    (b) to enter and search any premises in which he was when arrested or immediately before he was arrested for evidence relating to the offence for which he has been arrested.

(3) The power to search conferred by subsection (2) above is only a power to search to the extent that is reasonably required for the purpose of discovering any such thing or any such evidence.

(4) The powers conferred by this section to search a person are not to be construed as authorising a constable to require a person to remove any of his clothing in public other than an outer coat, jacket or gloves,[23] but they do authorise a search of a person's mouth.[23a]

(5) A constable may not search a person in the exercise of the power

---

[22] The new text of para. 12(c) was substituted for the original version by the Prevention of Terrorism (Temporary Provisions) Act 1989, Sched. 8, para. 6(2).

[23] The Northern Ireland PACE Order, Art. 34(4) added headgear.

[23a] Added by the Criminal Justice and Public Order Act 1994, s.59(2).

conferred by subsection (2)(a) above unless he has reasonable grounds for believing that the person to be searched may have concealed on him anything for which a search is permitted under that paragraph.

(6) A constable may not search premises in the exercise of the power conferred by subsection (2)(b) above unless he has reasonable grounds for believing that there is evidence for which a search is permitted under that paragraph on the premises.

(7) In so far as the power of search conferred by subsection (2)(b) above relates to premises consisting of two or more separate dwellings, it is limited to a power to search—

    (a) any dwelling in which the arrest took place or in which the person arrested was immediately before his arrest; and

    (b) any parts of the premises which the occupier of any such dwelling uses in common with the occupiers of any other dwellings comprised in the premises.

(8) A constable searching a person in the exercise of the power conferred by subsection (1) above may seize and retain anything he finds, if he has reasonable grounds for believing that the person searched might use it to cause physical injury to himself or to any other person.

(9) A constable searching a person in the exercise of the power conferred by subsection (2)(a) above may seize and retain anything he finds, other than an item subject to legal privilege, if he has reasonable grounds for believing—

    (a) that he might use it to assist him to escape from lawful custody; or

    (b) that it is evidence of an offence or has been obtained in consequence of the commission of an offence.

(10) Nothing in this section shall be taken to affect the power conferred by section 15(3), (4) and (5) of the Prevention of Terrorism (Temporary Provisions) Act 1989.[24]

Execution of warrant not in possession of constable

33. In section 125 of the Magistrates' Courts Act 1980[25]—

    (a) in subsection (3), for the words "arrest a person charged with an offence" there shall be substituted the words "which this subsection applies";

    (b) the following subsection shall be added after that subsection—

        "(4) The warrants to which subsection (3) above applies are—

        (a) a warrant to arrest a person in connection with an offence;

        (b) without prejudice to paragraph (a) above, a warrant under section 186(3) of the Army Act 1955, section 186(3) of the Air Force Act 1955, section 105(3) of the Naval Discipline Act 1957 or Schedule 5 to the Reserve Forces Act 1980 (desertion etc.);

        (c) a warrant under—

          (i) section 102 or 104 of the General Rate Act 1967 (insufficiency of distress);

          (ii) section 18(4) of the Domestic Proceedings and Magistrates' Courts Act 1978 (protection of parties to marriage and children of family); and

          (iii) section 55, 76, 93 or 97 above.".

---

[24] As amended by the Prevention of Terrorism (Temporary Provisions) Act 1989, Sched. 8, para. 6(3).

[25] This provision was not needed in Northern Ireland as it was already dealt with by the Magistrates' Courts (Northern Ireland) Order, Art. 158.

PART IV

DETENTION

Detention—conditions and duration

Limitations on police detention

34.—(1) A person arrested for an offence shall not be kept in police detention except in accordance with the provisions of this Part of this Act.

(2) Subject to subsection (3) below, if at any time a custody officer—

(a) becomes aware, in relation to any person in police detention, that the grounds for the detention of that person have ceased to apply; and

(b) is not aware of any other grounds on which the continued detention of that person could be justified under the provisions of this Part of this Act,

it shall be the duty of the custody officer, subject to subsection (4) below, to order his immediate release from custody.

(3) No person in police detention shall be released except on the authority of a custody officer at the police station where his detention was authorised or, if it was authorised at more than one station, a custody officer at the station where it was last authorised.

(4) A person who appears to the custody officer to have been unlawfully at large when he was arrested is not to be released under subsection (2) above.

(5) A person whose release is ordered under subsection (2) above shall be released without bail unless it appears to the custody officer—[26]

(a) that there is need for further investigation of any matter in connection with which he was detained at any time during the period of his detention; or

(b) that proceedings may be taken against him in respect of any such matter,

and if it so appears, he shall be released on bail.

(6) For the purposes of this Part of this Act a person arrested under section 6(5) of the Road Traffic Act 1988[27] is arrested for an offence.

(7) For the purpose of this Part of this Act a person who returns to a police station to answer to bail or is arrested under section 46A below shall be treated as arrested for an offence and the offence in connection with which he was granted bail shall be deemed to be that offence.[27a]

Designated police stations

35.—(1) The chief officer of police for each police area shall designate the police stations in his area which, subject to section 30(3) and (5) above, are to be the stations in that area to be used for the purpose of detaining arrested persons.

(2) A chief officer's duty under subsection (1) above is to designate police stations appearing to him to provide enough accommodation for that purpose.

---

[26] Note drafting changes in Northern Ireland PACE Order, Art. 35(5), (6) and (7).

[27] Amended by the Road Traffic (Consequential Provisions) Act 1988, Sched. 3, para. 27.

[27a] Added by the Criminal Justice and Public Order Act 1994, s.29(3). For the equivalent change in Northern Ireland see Appendix 4, p. 532 below [Art. 7].

(3) Without prejudice to section 12 of the Interpretation Act 1978 (continuity of duties) a chief officer—

(a) may designate a station which was not previously designated; and

(b) may direct that a designation of a station previously made shall cease to operate.

(4) In this Act "designated police station" means a police station for the time being designated under this section.

Custody officers at police stations

36.—(1) One or more custody officers shall be appointed for each designated police station.

(2) A custody officer for a designated police station shall be appointed—

(a) by the chief officer of police for the area in which the designated police station is situated; or

(b) by such other police officer as the chief officer of police for that area may direct.

(3) No officer may be appointed a custody officer unless he is of at least the rank of sergeant.

(4) An officer of any rank may perform the functions of a custody officer at a designated police station if a custody officer is not readily available to perform them.

(5) Subject to the following provisions of this section and to section 39(2) below, none of the functions of a custody officer in relation to a person shall be performed by an officer who at the time when the function falls to be performed is involved in the investigation of an offence for which that person is in police detention at that time.

(6) Nothing in subsection (5) above is to be taken to prevent a custody officer—

(a) performing any function assigned to custody officers—

(i) by this Act; or

(ii) by a code of practice issued under this Act;

(b) carrying out the duty imposed on custody officers by section 39 below;

(c) doing anything in connection with the identification of a suspect; or

(d) doing anything under sections 7 and 8[28] of the Road Traffic Act 1988.[29]

(7) Where an arrested person is taken to a police station which is not a designated police station, the functions in relation to him which at a designated police station would be the functions of a custody officer shall be performed—

(a) by an officer who is not involved in the investigation of an offence for which he is in police detention, if such an officer is readily available; and

(b) if no such officer is readily available, by the officer who took him to the station or any other officer.

(8) References to a custody officer in the following provisions of this Act include references to an officer other than a custody officer who is performing the functions of a custody officer by virtue of subsection (4) or (7) above.

(9) Where by virtue of subsection (7) above an officer of a force maintained by a police authority who took an arrested person to a police

---

[28] Amended by the Road Traffic (Consequential Provisions) Act 1988, Sched. 3, para. 27.

[29] In Northern Ireland PACE Order, Art. 37(6)(d) the equivalent reference is to Arts. 144, 146 and 147 of the Road Traffic (Northern Ireland) Order 1981.

station is to perform the functions of a custody officer in relation to him, the officer shall inform an officer who—
    (a) is attached to a designated police station; and
    (b) is of at least the rank of inspector,
that he is to do so.

(10) The duty imposed by subsection (9) above shall be performed as soon as it is practicable to perform it.

Duties of custody officer before charge

37.—(1) Where—
    (a) a person is arrested for an offence—
        (i) without a warrant; or
        (ii) under a warrant not endorsed for bail,
    (b) ...[30]

the custody officer at each police station where he is detained after his arrest shall determine whether he has before him sufficient evidence to charge that person with the offence for which he was arrested and may detain him at the police station for such period as is necessary to enable him to do so.

(2) If the custody officer determines that he does not have such evidence before him, the person arrested shall be released either on bail or without bail, unless the custody officer has reasonable grounds for believing that his detention without being charged is necessary to secure or preserve evidence relating to an offence for which he is under arrest or to obtain such evidence by questioning him.

(3) If the custody officer has reasonable grounds for so believing, he may authorise the person arrested to be kept in police detention.

(4) Where a custody officer authorises a person who has not been charged to be kept in police detention, he shall, as soon as is practicable, make a written record of the grounds for the detention.

(5) Subject to subsection (6) below, the written record shall be made in the presence of the person arrested who shall at that time be informed by the custody officer of the grounds for his detention.

(6) Subsection (5) above shall not apply where the person arrested is, at the time when the written record is made—
    (a) incapable of understanding what is said to him;
    (b) violent or likely to become violent; or
    (c) in urgent need of medical attention.

(7) Subject to section 41(7) below, if the custody officer determines that he has before him sufficient evidence to charge the person arrested with the offence for which he was arrested, the person arrested—
    (a) shall be charged; or
    (b) shall be released without charge, either on bail or without bail.

(8) Where—
    (a) a person is released under subsection (7)(b) above; and
    (b) at the time of his release a decision whether he should be prosecuted for the offence for which he was arrested has not been taken,
it shall be the duty of the custody officer so to inform him.

(9) If the person arrested is not in a fit state to be dealt with under subsection (7) above, he may be kept in police detention until he is.

(10) The duty imposed on the custody officer under subsection (1) above shall be carried out by him as soon as practicable after the person arrested arrives at the police station or, in the case of a person arrested at the police station, as soon as practicable after the arrest.

---

[30] Repealed by the Criminal Justice and Public Order Act 1994, s.29(4) and Sched. 11.

(11) ....[31]
(12) ....[31a]
(13) ....[31b]
(14) ....[31c]
(15) In this Part of this Act—
"arrested juvenile" means a person arrested with or without a warrant who appears to be under the age of 17 ...,[31d]
"endorsed for bail" means endorsed with a direction for bail in accordance with section 117(2) of the Magistrates' Courts Act 1980.

Duties of custody officer after charge

38.—(1) Where a person arrested for an offence otherwise than under a warrant endorsed for bail is charged with an offence, the custody officer shall, subject to section 25 of the Criminal Justice and Public Order Act 1994, order his release from police detention, either on bail or without bail, unless—

    (a) if the person arrested is not an arrested juvenile—

        (i) his name or address cannot be ascertained or the custody officer has reasonable grounds for doubting whether a name or address furnished by him as his name or address is his real name or address;

        (ii) the custody officer has reasonable grounds for believing that the person arrested will fail to appear in court to answer bail;

        (iii) in the case of a person arrested for an imprisonable offence, the custody officer has reasonable grounds for believing that the detention of the person arrested is necessary to prevent him from committing an offence[31e];

        (iv) in the case of a person arrested for an offence which is not an imprisonable offence, the custody officer has reasonable grounds for believing that the detention of the person arrested is necessary to prevent him from causing physical injury to any other person or from causing loss of or damage to property;

        (v) the custody officer has reasonable grounds for believing that the detention of the person arrested is necessary to prevent him from interfering with the administration of justice or with the investigation of offences of a particular offence; or

        (vi) the custody officer has reasonable grounds for believing that the detention of the person arrested is necessary for his own protection[31f];

    (b) if he is an arrested juvenile—

        (i) any of the requirements of paragraph (a) above is satisfied; or

        (ii) the custody officer has reasonable grounds for believing that he ought to be detained in his own interests.

(2) If the release of a person arrested is not required by subsection (1) above, the custody officer may authorise him to be kept in police detention.

---

[31] Repealed by the Criminal Justice Act 1991, s.72 and Sched. 13.
[31a] Repealed by the Criminal Justice Act 1991, s.72 and Sched. 13.
[31b] Repealed by the Criminal Justice Act 1991, s.72 and Sched. 13.
[31c] Repealed by the Criminal Justice Act 1991, s.72 and Sched. 13.
[31d] Words repealed by the Children Act 1989, Sched. 15.
[31e] Added by the Criminal Justice and Public Order Act 1994, Sched. 10, para. 54.
[31f] Substituted and added by the Criminal Justice and Public Order Act 1994, s.28(2).

(2A) The custody officer, in taking the decisions required by subsection (1)(a) and (b) above (except (a)(i) and (vi) and b(ii)), shall have regard to the same considerations as those which a court is required to have regard to in taking the corresponding decisions under paragraph 2 of Part I of Schedule 1 to the Bail Act 1976.[31g]

(3) Where a custody officer authorises a person who has been charged to be kept in police detention he shall, as soon as practicable, make a written record of the grounds for the detention.

(4) Subject to subsection (5) below the written record shall be made in the presence of the person charged who shall at that time be informed by the custody officer of the grounds for his detention.

(5) Subsection (4) above shall not apply where the person charged is, at the time when the written record is made—

    (a) incapable of understanding what is said to him;

    (b) violent or likely to become violent; or

    (c) in urgent need of medical attention.

(6) Where a custody officer authorises an arrested juvenile to be kept in police detention under subsection (1) above, the custody officer shall, unless he certifies—

    (a) that, by reason of such circumstances as are specified in the certificate, it is impracticable for him to do so; or

    (b) in the case of an arrested juvenile who has attained the age of 12 years, that no secure accommodation is available and that keeping him in other local authority accommodation would not be adequate to protect the public from serious harm from him,

secure that the arrested juvenile is moved to local authority accommodation.

(6A) In this section—[32]

    "local authority accommodation" means accommodation provided by or on behalf of a local authority (within the meaning of the Children Act 1989);

    "secure accommodation" means accommodation provided for the purpose of restricting liberty;

    "sexual offence" and "violent offence" have the same meanings as in Part I of the Criminal Justice Act 1991;

and any reference, in relation to an arrested juvenile charged with a violent or sexual offence, to protecting the public from serious harm from him shall be construed as a reference to protecting members of the public from death or serious personal injury, whether physical or psychological, occasioned by further such offences committed by him.[32a]

(6B) Where an arrested juvenile is moved to local authority accommodation under subsection (b) above, it shall be lawful for any person acting on behalf of the authority to detain him.[32b]

(7) A certificate made under subsection (6) above in respect of an arrested juvenile shall be produced to the court before which he is first brought thereafter.

(7A) In this section "imprisonable offence" has the same meaning as in Schedule 1 to the Bail Act 1976.[32c]

(8) In this Part of this Act "local authority" has the same meaning as in the Children Act 1989.[32d]

[31g] Added by the Criminal Justice and Public Order Act 1994, s.28(3).

[32] Substituted by the Criminal Justice Act 1991, s.59 and amended by the Criminal Justice and Public Order Act 1994, s.24.

[32a] Added by the Children Act 1989, Sched. 13, para. 53(2) and then substituted by the Criminal Justice Act 1991, s.59.

[32b] Added by the Children Act 1989, Sched. 13, para. 53(2).

[32c] Added by the Criminal Justice and Public Order Act 1994, s.28(4).

[32d] Amended by the Children Act 1989, Sched. 13, para. 53(3).

Responsibilities in relation to persons detained

39.—(1) Subject to subsections (2) and (4) below, it shall be the duty of the custody officer at a police station to ensure—

    (a) that all persons in police detention at that station are treated in accordance with this Act and any code of practice issued under it and relating to the treatment of persons in police detention; and

    (b) that all matters relating to such persons which are required by this Act or by such codes of practice to be recorded are recorded in the custody records relating to such persons.

(2) If the custody officer, in accordance with any code of practice issued under this Act, transfers or permits the transfer of a person in police detention

    (a) to the custody of a police officer investigating an offence for which that person is in poice detention;

    (b) to the custody of an officer who has charge of that person outside the police station,

the custody officer shall cease in relation to that person to be subject to the duty imposed on him by subsection (1)(a) above; and it shall be the duty of the officer to whom the transfer is made to ensure that he is treated in accordance with the provisions of this Act and of any such codes of practice as are mentioned in subsection (1) above.

(3) If the person detained is subsequently returned to the custody of the custody officer, it shall be the duty of the officer investigating the offence to report to the custody officer as to the manner in which this section and the codes of practice have been complied with while that person was in his custody.

(4) If an arrested juvenile is moved to local authority accommodation[32e] under section 38(6) above, the custody officer shall cease in relation to that person to be subject to the duty imposed on him by subsection (1) above.

    (5) ....[32f]

    (6) Where—

    (a) an officer of higher rank than the custody officer gives directions relating to a person in police detention; and

    (b) the directions are at variance—

        (i) with any decision made or action taken by the custody officer in the performance of a duty imposed on him under this Part of this Act; or

        (ii) with any decision or action which would but for the directions have been made or taken by him in the performance of such a duty,

the custody officer shall refer the matter at once to an officer of the rank of superintendent or above who is responsible for the police station for which the custody officer is acting as custody officer.

Review of police detention

40.—(1) Reviews of the detention of each person in police detention in connection with the investigation of an offence shall be carried out periodically in accordance with the following provisions of this section—

    (a) in the case of a person who has been arrested and charged, by the custody officer; and

    (b) in the case of a person who has been arrested but not charged, by an officer of at least the rank of inspector who has not been directly involved in the investigation.

[32e] As amended by the Children Act 1989, Sched. 13, para. 54.
[32f] Repealed by the Children Act 1989, Sched. 15.

(2) The officer to whom it falls to carry out a review is referred to in this section as a "review officer".

(3) Subject to subsection (4) below—

    (a) the first review shall be not later than six hours after the detention was first authorised;

    (b) the second review shall be not later than nine hours after the first;

    (c) subsequent reviews shall be at intervals of not more than nine hours.

(4) A review may be postponed—

    (a) if, having regard to all the circumstances prevailing at the latest time for it specified in subsection (3) above, it is not practicable to carry out the review at that time;

    (b) without prejudice to the generality of paragraph (a) above—

        (i) if at that time the person in detention is being questioned by a police officer and the review officer is satisfied that an interruption of the questioning for the purpose of carrying out the review would prejudice the investigation in connection with which he is being questioned; or

        (ii) if at that time no review officer is readily available.

(5) If a review is postponed under subsection (4) above it shall be carried out as soon as practicable after the latest time specified for it in subsection (3) above.

(6) If a review is carried out after postponement under subsection (4) above, the fact that it was so carried out shall not affect any requirement of this section as to the time at which any subsequent review is to be carried out.

(7) The review officer shall record the reasons for any postponement of a review in the custody record.

(8) Subject to subsection (9) below, where the person whose detention is under review has not been charged before the time of the review, section 37(1) to (6) above shall have effect in relation to him, but with the substitution—

    (a) of references to the person whose detention is under review for references to the person arrested; and

    (b) of references to the review officer for references to the custody officer;

(9) Where a person has been kept in police detention by virtue of section 37(9) above, section 37(1) to (6) shall not have effect in relation to him but it shall be the duty of the review officer to determine whether he is yet in a fit state.

(10) Where the person whose detention is under review has been charged before the time of the review, section 38(1) to (6) above shall have effect in relation to him, but with the substitution of references to the person whose detention is under review for references to the person arrested.

(11) Where—

    (a) an officer of higher rank than the custody officer gives directions relating to a person in police detention;

    (b) the directions are at variance—

        (i) with any decision made or action taken by the review officer in the performance of a duty imposed on him under this Part of this Act; or

        (ii) with any decision or action which would but for the directions have been made or taken by him in the performance of such a duty,

the review officer shall refer the matter at once to an officer of the rank of superintendent or above who is responsible for the police station for which the review officer is acting as review officer in connection with the detention.

(12) Before determining whether to authorise a person's continued detention the review officer shall give—
   (a) that person (unless he is asleep); or
   (b) any solicitor representing him who is available at the time of the review,
an opportunity to make representations to him about the detention.

(13) Subject to subsection (14) below, the person whose detention is under review or his solicitor may make representations under subsection (12) above either orally or in writing.

(14) The review officer may refuse to hear oral representations from the person whose detention is under review if he considers that he is unfit to make such representations by reason of his condition or behaviour.

Limits on period of detention without charge

41.—(1) Subject to the following provisions of this section and to sections 42 and 43 below, a person shall not be kept in police detention for more than 24 hours without being charged.

(2) The time from which the period of detention of a person is to be calculated (in this Act referred to as "the relevant time")—
   (a) in the case of a person to whom this section applies, shall be—[33]
      (i) the time at which that person arrives at the relevant police station, or
      (ii) the time 24 hours after the time of that person's arrest, whichever is the earlier;
   (b) in the case of a person arrested outside England and Wales, shall be
      (i) the time at which that person arrives at the first police station to which he is taken in the police area in England or Wales in which the offence for which he was arrested is being investigated; or
      (ii) the time 24 hours after the time of that person's entry into England and Wales, whichever is the earlier.
   (c) in the case of a person who—
      (i) attends voluntarily at a police station; or
      (ii) accompanies a constable to a police station without having been arrested, and is arrested at the police station, the time of his arrest;
   (d) in any other case, except when subsection (5) below applies, shall be the time at which the person arrested arrives at the first police station to which he is taken after his arrest.

(3) Subsection (2)(a) above applies to a person if—
   (a) his arrest is sought in one police area in England and Wales;
   (b) he is arrested in another police area; and
   (c) he is not questioned in the area in which he is arrested in order to obtain evidence in relation to an offence for which he is arrested,
and in sub-paragraph (i) of that paragraph "the relevant police station" means the first police station to which he is taken in the police area in which his arrest was sought.

(4) Subsection (2) above shall have effect in relation to a person arrested under section 31 above as if every reference in it to his arrest or his being arrested were a reference to his arrest or his being arrested for the offence for which he was originally arrested.

(5) If—[34]

---

[33] Not relevant in Northern Ireland where the whole province is treated as one police area.
[34] Not relevant in Northern Ireland where the whole province is treated as one police area.

(a) a person is in police detention in a police area in England and Wales ("the first area"); and

(b) his arrest for an offence is sought in some other police area in England and Wales ("the second area"); and

(c) he is taken to the second area for the purposes of investigating that offence, without being questioned in the first area in order to obtain evidence in relation to it,

the relevant time shall be—

(i) the time 24 hours after he leaves the place where he is detained in the first area; or

(ii) the time at which he arrives at the first police station to which he is taken in the second area,

whichever is the earlier.

(6) When a person who is in police detention is removed to hospital because he is in need of medical treatment, any time during which he is being questioned in hospital or on the way there or back by a police officer for the purpose of obtaining evidence relating to an offence shall be included in any period which falls to be calculated for the purposes of this Part of this Act, but any other time while he is in hospital or on his way there or back shall not be so included.

(7) Subject to subsection (8) below, a person who at the expiry of 24 hours after the relevant time is in police detention and has not been charged shall be released at that time either on bail or without bail.

(8) Subsection (7) above does not apply to a person whose detention for more than 24 hours after the relevant time has been authorised or is otherwise permitted in accordance with section 42 or 43 below.

(9) A person released under subsection (7) above shall not be re-arrested without a warrant for the offence for which he was previously arrested unless new evidence justifying a further arrest has come to light since his release[; but this subsection does not prevent an arrest under section 46A below.][34a]

Authorisation of continued detention

42.—(1) Where a police officer of the rank of superintendent or above who is responsible for the police station at which a person is detained has reasonable grounds for believing that—

(a) the detention of that person without charge is necessary to secure or preserve evidence relating to an offence for which he is under arrest or to obtain such evidence by questioning him;

(b) an offence for which he is under arrest is a serious arrestable offence; and

(c) the investigation is being conducted diligently and expeditiously,

he may authorise the keeping of that person in police detention for a period expiring at or before 36 hours after the relevant time.

(2) Where an officer such as is mentioned in subsection (1) above has authorised the keeping of a person in police detention for a period expiring less than 36 hours after the relevant time, such an officer may authorise the keeping of that person in police detention for a further period expiring not more than 36 hours after that time if the conditions specified in subsection (1) above are still satisfied when he gives the authorisation.

(3) If it is proposed to transfer a person in police detention to another police area, the officer determining whether or not to authorise keeping him in detention under subsection (1) above shall have regard to the distance and the time the journey would take.[35]

[34a] The words in square brackets were added by the Criminal Justice and Public Order Act 1994, s.29(4)(b).

[35] Not relevant in Northern Ireland where the whole province is treated as one police area.

(4) No authorisation under subsection (1) above shall be given in respect of any person—
    (a) more than 24 hours after the relevant time; or
    (b) before the second review of his detention under section 40 above has been carried out.

(5) Where an officer authorises the keeping of a person in police detention under subsection (1) above, it shall be his duty—
    (a) to inform that person of the grounds for his continued detention; and
    (b) to record the grounds in that person's custody record.

(6) Before determining whether to authorise the keeping of a person in detention under subsection (1) or (2) above, an officer shall give—
    (a) that person; or
    (b) any solicitor representing him who is available at the time when it falls to the officer to determine whether to give the authorisation,
an opportunity to make representations to him about the detention.

(7) Subject to subsection (8) below, the person in detention or his solicitor may make representations under subsection (6) above either orally or in writing.

(8) The officer to whom it falls to determine whether to give the authorisation may refuse to hear oral representations from the person in detention if he considers that he is unfit to make such representations by reason of his condition or behaviour.

(9) Where—
    (a) an officer authorises the keeping of a person in detention under subsection (1) above; and
    (b) at the time of the authorisation he has not yet exercised a right conferred on him by section 56 or 58 below,
the officer—
    (i) shall inform him of that right;
    (ii) shall decide whether he should be permitted to exercise it;
    (iii) shall record the decision in his custody record; and
    (iv) if the decision is to refuse to permit the exercise of the right, shall also record the grounds for the decision in that record.

(10) Where an officer has authorised the keeping of a person who has not been charged in detention under subsection (1) or (2) above, he shall be released from detention, either on bail or without bail, not later than 36 hours after the relevant time, unless—
    (a) he has been charged with an offence; or
    (b) his continued detention is authorised or otherwise permitted in accordance with section 43 below.

(11) A person released under subsection (10) above shall not be re-arrested without a warrant for the offence for which he was previously arrested unless new evidence justifying a further arrest has come to light since his release; but this subsection does not prevent an arrest under section 46A below.[35a]

Warrants of further detention

43.—(1) Where, on an application on oath made by a constable and supported by an information, a magistrates' court is satisfied that there are reasonable grounds for believing that the further detention of the person to whom the application relates is justified, it may issue a warrant of further detention authorising the keeping of that person in police detention.

[35a] Added by the Criminal Justice and Public Order Act 1994, s.29(4)(b).

(2) A court may not hear an application for a warrant of further detention unless the person to whom the application relates—

(a) has been furnished with a copy of the information; and

(b) has been brought before the court for the hearing.

(3) The person to whom the application relates shall be entitled to be legally represented at the hearing and, if he is not so represented, but wishes to be so represented—

(a) the court shall adjourn the hearing to enable him to obtain representation; and

(b) he may be kept in police detention during the adjournment.

(4) A person's further detention is only justified for the purposes of this section or section 44 below if—

(a) his detention without charge is necessary to secure or preserve evidence relating to an offence for which he is under arrest or to obtain such evidence by questioning him;

(b) an offence for which he is under arrest is a serious arrestable offence; and

(c) the investigation is being conducted diligently and expeditiously.

(5) Subject to subsection (7) below, an application for a warrant of further detention may be made—

(a) at any time before the expiry of 36 hours after the relevant time; or

(b) in a case where—

(i) it is not practicable for the magistrates' court to which the application will be made to sit at the expiry of 36 hours after the relevant time; but

(ii) the court will sit during the 6 hours following the end of that period,

at any time before the expiry of the said 6 hours.

(6) In a case to which subsection (5)(b) above applies—

(a) the person to whom the application relates may be kept in police detention until the application is heard; and

(b) the custody officer shall make a note in that person's custody record—

(i) of the fact that he was kept in police detention for more than 36 hours after the relevant time; and

(ii) of the reason why he was so kept.

(7) If—

(a) an application for a warrant of further detention is made after the expiry of 36 hours after the relevant time; and

(b) it appears to the magistrates' court that it would have been reasonable for the police to make it before the expiry of that period,

the court shall dismiss the application.

(8) Where on an application such as is mentioned in subsection (1) above a magistrates' court is not satisfied that there are reasonable grounds for believing that the further detention of the person to whom the application relates is justified, it shall be its duty—

(a) to refuse the application; or

(b) to adjourn the hearing of it until a time not later than 36 hours after the relevant time.

(9) The person to whom the application relates may be kept in police detention during the adjournment.

(10) A warrant of further detention shall—

(a) state the time at which it is issued;

(b) authorise the keeping in police detention of the person to whom it relates for the period stated in it.

(11) Subject to subsection (12) below, the period stated in a warrant of further detention shall be such period as the magistrates' court thinks fit, having regard to the evidence before it.

(12) The period shall not be longer than 36 hours.

(13) If it is proposed to transfer a person in police detention to a police area other than that in which he is detained when the application for a warrant of further detention is made, the court hearing the application shall have regard to the distance and the time the journey would take.[36]

(14) Any information submitted in support of an application under this section shall state—

    (a) the nature of the offence for which the person to whom the application relates has been arrested;

    (b) the general nature of the evidence on which that person was arrested;

    (c) what inquiries relating to the offence have been made by the police and what further inquiries are proposed by them;

    (d) the reasons for believing the continued detention of that person to be necessary for the purposes of such further inquiries.

(15) Where an application under this section is refused the person to whom the application relates shall forthwith be charged or, subject to subsection (16) below, released, either on bail or without bail.

(16) A person need not be released under subsection (15) above—

    (a) before the expiry of 24 hours after the relevant time; or

    (b) before the expiry of any longer period for which his continued detention is or has been authorised under section 42 above.

(17) Where an application under this section is refused, no further application shall be made under this section in respect of the person to whom the refusal relates, unless supported by evidence which has come to light since the refusal.

(18) Where a warrant of further detention is issued, the person to whom it relates shall be released from police detention, either on bail or without bail, upon or before the expiry of the warrant unless he is charged.

(19) A person released under subsection (18) above shall not be re-arrested without a warrant for the offence for which he was previously arrested unless new evidence justifying a further arrest has come to light since his release; but this subsection does not prevent an arrest under section 46A below.[36a]

Extension of warrants of further detention

44.—(1) On an application on oath made by a constable and supported by an information a magistrates' court may extend a warrant of further detention issued under section 43 above if it is satisfied that there are reasonable grounds for believing that the further detention of the person to whom the application relates is justified.

(2) Subject to subsection (3) below, the period for which a warrant of further detention may be extended shall be such period as the court thinks fit, having regard to the evidence before it.

(3) The period shall not—

    (a) be longer than 36 hours; or

    (b) end later than 96 hours after the relevant time.

(4) Where a warrant of further detention has been extended under subsection (1) above, or further extended under this subsection, for a period ending before 96 hours after the relevant time, on an application such as is

---

[36] Not relevant in Northern Ireland where the whole province is treated as one police area.
[36a] Added by the Criminal Justice and Public Order Act 1994, s.29(4)(b).

mentioned in that subsection a magistrates' court may further extend the warrant if it is satisfied as there mentioned; and subsections (2) and (3) above apply to such further extensions as they apply to extensions under subsection (1) above.

(5) A warrant of further detention shall, if extended or further extended under this section, be endorsed with a note of the period of the extension.

(6) Subsections (2), (3) and (14) of section 43 above shall apply to an application made under this section as they apply to an application made under that section.

(7) Where an application under this section is refused, the person to whom the application relates shall forthwith be charged or, subject to subsection (8) below, released, either on bail or without bail.

(8) A person need not be released under subsection (7) above before the expiry of any period for which a warrant of further detention issued in relation to him has been extended or further extended on an earlier application made under this section.

Detention before charge—supplementary

45.—(1) In sections 43 and 44 of this Act "magistrates' court" means a court consisting of two or more justices of the peace sitting otherwise than in open court.

(2) Any reference in this Part of this Act to a period of time or a time of day is to be treated as approximate only.

Detention—miscellaneous

Detention after charge

46.—(1) Where a person—[37]
    (a) is charged with an offence; and
    (b) after being charged—
        (i) is kept in police detention; or
        (ii) is detained by a local authority in pursuance of arrangements made under section 38(6) above,
he shall be brought before a magistrates' court in accordance with the provisions of this section.

(2) If he is to be brought before a magistrates' court for the petty sessions area in which the police station at which he was charged is situated, he shall be brought before such a court as soon as is practicable and in any event not later than the first sitting after he is charged with the offence.

(3) If no magistrates' court for that area is due to sit either on the day on which he is charged or on the next day, the custody officer for the police station at which he was charged shall inform the clerk to the justices for the area that there is a person in the area to whom subsection (2) above applies.

(4) If the person charged is to be brought before a magistrates' court for a petty sessions area other than that in which the police station at which he was charged is situated, he shall be removed to that area as soon as is practicable and brought before such a court as soon as is practicable after his arrival in the area and in any event not later than the first sitting of a magistrates' court for that area after his arrival in the area.

(5) If no magistrates' court for that area is due to sit either on the day on which he arrives in the area or on the next day—
    (a) he shall be taken to a police station in the area; and

---

[37] Note Northern Ireland PACE Order, Art. 47 is slightly redrafted to take account of the fact that there is no "first sitting" of a magistrates' court in Northern Ireland and it is therefore not necessary to specify a period within which magistrates' courts will be held.

(b) the custody officer at that station shall inform the clerk to the justices for the area that there is a person in the area to whom subsection (4) applies.

(6) Subject to subsection (8) below, where a clerk to the justices for a petty sessions area has been informed—

(a) under subsection (3) above that there is a person in the area to whom subsection (2) above applies; or

(b) under subsection (5) above that there is a person in the area to whom subsection (4) above applies,

the clerk shall arrange for a magistrates' court to sit not later than the day next following the relevant day.

(7) In this section "the relevant day"—

(a) in relation to a person who is to be brought before a magistrates' court for the petty sessions area in which the police station at which he was charged is situated, means the day on which he was charged; and

(b) in relation to a person who is to be brought before a magistrates' court for any other petty sessions area, means the day on which he arrives in the area.

(8) Where the day next following the relevant day is Christmas Day, Good Friday or a Sunday, the duty of the clerk under subsection (6) above is a duty to arrange for a magistrates' court to sit not later than the first day after the relevant day which is not one of those days.

(9) Nothing in this section requires a person who is in hospital to be brought before a court if he is not well enough.

46A.—(1) A constable may arrest without a warrant any person who, having been released on bail under this Part of this Act subject to a duty to attend at a police station, fails to attend at that police station at the time appointed for him to do so.

(2) A person who is arrested under this section shall be taken to the police station appointed as the place at which he is to surrender to custody as soon as practicable after the arrest.

(3) For the purpose of—

(a) section 30 above (subject to the obligation in subsection (2) above), and

(b) section 31 above,

and arrest under this section shall be treated as an arrest for an offence.[37a]

Bail after arrest

47.—(1) Subject to subsection (2) below, a release on bail of a person under this Part of this Act shall be a release on bail granted in accordance with sections 3, 3A, 5 and 5A of the Bail Act 1976 as they apply to bail granted by a constable.[38]

(1A) The normal powers to impose conditions of bail shall be available to him where a custody officer releases a person on bail under section 38(1) above (including that subsection as applied by section 40(10) above) but not in any other cases.

In this subsection "the normal powers to impose conditions of bail" has the meaning given in section 3(6) of the Bail Act 1976.[38a]

[37a] s.46A was added by the Criminal Justice and Public Order Act 1994, s.29(2). For the equivalent change in Northern Ireland see Appendix 4, p. 532 below [Art. 7].

[38] Note that the Northern Ireland PACE Order, Art. 48 is redrafted to amalgamate the bail provisions of Art. 130 of the Magistrates' Courts (Northern Ireland) Order 1981 with those of Art. 48. Amended by the Criminal Justice and Public Order Act 1994, s.27(1)(a).

[38a] s.1A was added by the Criminal Justice and Public Order Act 1994, s.27(1)(b).

(2) Nothing in the Bail Act 1976 shall prevent the rearrest without warrant of a person released on bail subject to a duty to attend at a police station if new evidence justifying a further arrest has come to light since his release.

(3) Subject to subsection (4) below, in this Part of this Act references to "bail" are references to bail subject to a duty—

    (a) to appear before a magistrates' court at such time and such place; or

    (b) to attend at such police station at such time,

as the custody officer may appoint.

(4) Where a custody officer has granted bail to a person subject to a duty to appear at a police station, the custody officer may give notice in writing to that person that his attendance at the police station is not required.

(5) ....[38b]

(6) Where a person who has been granted bail and either has attended at the police station in accordance with the grant of bail or has been arrested under section 46A above is detained at a police station,[38c] any time during which he was in police detention prior to being granted bail shall be included as part of any period which falls to be calculated under this Part of this Act.

(7) Where a person who was released on bail subject to a duty to attend at a police station is re-arrested, the provisions of this Part of this Act shall apply to him as they apply to a person arrested for the first time; but this subsection does not apply to a person who is arrested under section 46A above or has attended a police station in accordance with the grant of bail (and who accordingly is deemed by section 34(7) above to have been arrested for an offence).[38d]

(8) In the Magistrates' Courts Act 1980—

    (a) the following section shall be substituted for section 43—

        "Bail on arrest

        43.—(1) Where a person has been granted bail under the Police and Criminal Evidence Act 1984 subject to a duty to appear before a magistrates' court, the court before which he is to appear may appoint a later time as the time at which he is to appear and may enlarge the recognizances of any sureties for him at that time.

        (2) The recognizance of any surety for any person granted bail subject to a duty to attend at a police station may be enforced as if it were conditioned for his appearance before a magistrates' court for the petty sessions area in which the police station named in the recognizance is situated."; and

    (b) the following subsection shall be substituted for section 117(3)—

        "(3) Where a warrant has been endorsed for bail under subsection (1) above—

        (a) where the person arrested is to be released on bail on his entering into a recognizance without sureties, it shall not be necessary to take him to a police station, but if he is so taken, he shall be released from custody on his entering into the recognizance; and

        (b) where he is to be released on his entering into a recognizance with sureties, he shall be taken to a police station on his arrest, and the custody officer there shall (subject to his approving any surety tendered in com-

---

[38b] Repealed by the Criminal Justice and Public Order Act 1994, s.29(4)(c) and Sched. 11.
[38c] Amended by the Criminal Justice and Public Order Act 1994, s.29(4)(d).
[38d] Added by the Criminal Justice and Public Order Act 1994, s.29(4)(e).

pliance with the endorsement) release him from custody as directed in the endorsement."[39]

Remands to police custody

48. In section 128 of the Magistrates' Courts Act 1980—
  (a) in subsection (7) for the words "the custody of a constable" there shall be substituted the words "detention at a police station";
  (b) after subsection (7) there shall be inserted the following subsection—
      "(8) Where a person is committed to detention at a police station under subsection (7) above—
        (a) he shall not be kept in such detention unless there is a need for him to be so detained for the purposes of inquiries into other offences;
        (b) if kept in such detention, he shall be brought back before the magistrates' court which committed him as soon as that need ceases;
        (c) he shall be treated as a person in police detention to whom the duties under section 39 of the Police and Criminal Evidence Act 1984 (responsibilities in relation to persons detained) relate;
        (d) his detention shall be subject to periodic review at the times set out in section 40 of that Act (review of police detention)."

Police detention to count towards custodial sentence

49.—(1) In subsection (1) of section 67 of the Criminal Justice Act 1967 (computation of custodial sentences) for the words from "period", in the first place where it occurs, to "the offender" there shall be substituted the words "relevant period, but where he".
  (2) The following subsection shall be inserted after that subsection—
      "(1A) In subsection (1) above "relevant period" means—
        (a) any period during which the offender was in police detention in connection with the offence for which the sentence was passed; or
        (b) any period during which he was in custody—
            (i) by reason only of having been committed to custody by an order of a court made in connection with any proceedings relating to that sentence or the offence for which it was passed or any proceedings from which those proceedings arose; or
            (ii) by reason of his having been so committed and having been concurrently detained otherwise than by order of a court."
  (3) The following subsections shall be added after subsection (6) of that section—
      "(7) A person is in police detention for the purposes of this section—
        (a) at an time when he is in police detention for the purposes of the Police and Criminal Evidence Act 1984; and
        (b) at any time when he is detained under section 12 of the Prevention of Terrorism (Temporary Provisions) Act 1984.[39]

---

[39] The Northern Ireland PACE Order, Art. 49(3) substitutes s.14 of the Prevention of Terrorism (Temporary Provisions) Act 1989.

(8) No period of police detention shall be taken into account under this section unless it falls after the coming into force of section 49 of the Police and Criminal Evidence Act 1984."

Records of detention

50.—(1) Each police force shall keep written records showing on an annual basis—
- (a) the number of persons kept in police detention for more than 24 hours and subsequently released without charge;
- (b) the number of applications for warrants of further detention and the results of the applications; and
- (c) in relation to each warrant of further detention—
    - (i) the period of further detention authorised by it;
    - (ii) the period which the person named in it spent in police detention on its authority; and
    - (iii) whether he was charged or released without a charge.

(2) Every annual report—
- (a) under section 12 of the Police Act 1964; or
- (b) made by the Commissioner of Police of the Metropolis,

shall contain information about the matters mentioned in subsection (1) above in respect of the period to which the report relates.

Savings

51. Nothing in this Part of this Act shall affect—
- (a) the powers conferred on immigration officers by section 4 of and Schedule 2 to the Immigration Act 1971 (administrative provisions as to control on entry etc.);
- (b) the powers conferred by or by virtue of section 14 of the Prevention of Terrorism (Temporary Provisions) Act 1989[40] or Schedule 2 or 5 to that Act (powers of arrest and detention and control of entry and procedure for removal);
- (c) any duty of a police officer under—
    - (i) section 129, 190 or 202 of the Army Act 1955 (duties of governors of prisons and others to receive prisoners, deserters, absentees and persons under escort);
    - (ii) section 129, 190 or 202 of the Air Force Act 1955 (duties of governors of prisons and others to receive prisoners, deserters, absentees and persons under escort); or
    - (iii) section 107 of the Naval Discipline Act 1957 (duties of governors of civil prisons etc.); or
    - (iv) paragraph 5 of Schedule 5 to the Reserve Forces Act 1980 (duties of governors of civil prisons); or
- (d) any right of a person in police detention to apply for a writ of habeas corpus or other prerogative remedy.

Children

52.[41] . . . .[41a]

---

[40] Amended by the Prevention of Terrorism (Temporary Provisions) Act 1989, Sched. 8, para. 6(4).
[41] The Northern Ireland PACE Order, Art. 52 states that Pt. V does not apply to a child "apparently under 14."
[41a] Repealed by the Children Act 1989, Sched. 15.

PART V

QUESTIONING AND TREATMENT OF PERSONS BY POLICE

Abolition of certain powers of constables to search persons

53.—(1) Subject to subsection (2) below, there shall cease to have effect any Act (including a local Act) passed before this Act in so far as it authorises—

(a) any search by a constable of a person in police detention at a police station; or

(b) an intimate search of a person by a constable,

and any rule of common law which authorises a search such as is mentioned in paragraph (a) or (b) above is abolished.

[Subsection (2) was repealed by the Prevention of Terrorism (Temporary Provisions) Act 1989, Sched. 9.]

Searches of detained persons

54.—(1) The custody officer at a police station shall ascertain and record or cause to be recorded everything which a person has with him when he is—

(a) brought to the station after being arrested elsewhere or after being committed to custody by an order or sentence of a court; or

(b) arrested at the station or detained there, as a person falling within section 34(7), under section 37 above.[42]

(2) In the case of an arrested person the record shall be made as part of his custody record.

(3) Subject to subsection (4) below, a custody officer may seize and retain any such thing or cause any such thing to be seized and retained.

(4) Clothes and personal effects may only be seized if the custody officer—

(a) believes that the person from whom they are seized may use them—

(i) to cause physical injury to himself or any other person;

(ii) to damage property;

(iii) to interfere with evidence; or

(iv) to assist him to escape; or

(b) has reasonable grounds for believing that they may be evidence relating to an offence.

(5) Where anything is seized, the person from whom it is seized shall be told the reason for the seizure unless he is—

(a) violent or likely to become violent; or

(b) incapable of understanding what is said to him.

(6) Subject to subsection (7) below, a person may be searched if the custody officer considers it necessary to enable him to carry out his duty under subsection (1) above and to the extent that the custody officer considers necessary for that purpose.

(6A) A person who is in custody at a police station or is in police detention otherwise than at a police station may at any time be searched in order to ascertain whether he has with him anything which he could use for any of the purposes specified in subsection (4)(a) above.

(6B) Subject to subsection (6C) below, a constable may seize and retain, or cause to be seized and retained, anything found on such a search.

(6C) A constable may only seize clothes and personal effects in the circumstances specified in subsection (4) above.[43]

---

[42] Amended by the Criminal Justice and Public Order Act 1994, Sched. 10, para. 55.

[43] ss.(6A) to (6C) were added by the Criminal Justice Act, 1988, s.147(b).

(7) An intimate search may not be conducted under this section.

(8) A search under this section shall be carried out by a constable.

(9) The constable carrying out a search shall be of the same sex as the person searched.

Intimate searches

55.—(1) Subject to the following provisions of this section if an officer of at least the rank of superintendent has reasonable grounds for believing—

    (a) that a person who has been arrested and is in police detention may have concealed on him any thing which

        (i) he could use to cause physical injury to himself or others; and

        (ii) he might so use while he is in police detention or in the custody of a court; or

    (b) that such a person—

        (i) may have a Class A drug concealed on him; and

        (ii) was in possession of it with the appropriate criminal intent before his arrest,

he may authorise an intimate[44] search of that person.

(2) An officer may not authorise an intimate search of a person for anything unless he has reasonable grounds for believing that it cannot be found without his being intimately searched.

(3) An officer may given an authorisation under subsection (1) above orally or in writing but, if he gives it orally, he shall confirm it in writing as soon as is practicable.

(4) An intimate search which is only a drug offence search shall be by way of examination by a suitably qualified person.

(5) Except as provided by subsection (4) above, an intimate search shall be by way of examination by a suitably qualified person unless an officer of at least the rank of superintendent considers that this is not practicable.

(6) An intimate search which is not carried out as mentioned in subsection (5) above shall be carried out by a constable.

(7) A constable may not carry out an intimate search of a person of the opposite sex.

(8) No intimate search may be carried out except—

    (a) at a police station;

    (b) at a hospital;

    (c) at a registered medical practitioner's surgery; or

    (d) at some other place used for medical purposes.

(9) An intimate search which is only a drug offence search may not be carried out at a police station.

(10) If an intimate search of a person is carried out, the custody record relating to him shall state—

    (a) which parts of his body were searched; and

    (b) why they were searched.

(11) The information required to be recorded by subsection (10) above shall be recorded as soon as practicable after the completion of the search.

(12) The custody officer at a police station may seize and retain anything which is found on an intimate search of a person, or cause any such thing to be seized and retained—

    (a) if he believes that the person from whom it is seized may use it—

        (i) to cause physical injury to himself or any other person;

        (ii) to damage property;

---

[44] "an intimate" replaced "such a" in the original—which was plainly a drafting error; see Criminal Justice Act 1988, Sched. 15, para. 99.

   (iii) to interfere with evidence; or

   (iv) to assist him to escape; or

  (b) if he has reasonable grounds for believing that it may be evidence relating to an offence.

 (13) Where anything is seized under this section, the person from whom it is seized shall be told the reason for the seizure unless he is

  (a) violent or likely to become violent; or

  (b) incapable of understanding what is said to him.

 (14) Every annual report—

  (a) under section 12 of the Police Act 1964; or

  (b) made by the Commissioner of Police of the Metropolis,

shall contain information about searches under this section which have been carried out in the area to which the report relates during the period to which it relates.

 (15) The information about such searches shall include—

  (a) the total number of searches;

  (b) the number of searches conducted by way of examination by a suitably qualified person;

  (c) the number of searches not so conducted but conducted in the presence of such a person; and

  (d) the result of the searches carried out.

 (16) The information shall also include, as separate items—

  (a) the total number of drug offence searches; and

  (b) the result of those searches.

 (17) In this section—

 "the appropriate criminal intent" means an intent to commit an offence under—

  (a) section 5(3) of the Misuse of Drugs Act 1971 (possession of controlled drug with intent to supply to another); or

  (b) section 68(2) of the Customs and Excise Management Act 1979 (exportation etc. with intent to evade a prohibition or restriction);

 "Class A drug" has the meaning assigned to it by section 2(1)(b) of the Misuse of Drugs Act 1971;

 "drug offence search" means an intimate search for a Class A drug which an officer has authorised by virtue of subsection (1)(b) above; and

 "suitably qualified person" means—

  (a) a registered medical practitioner; or

  (b) a registered nurse.[45]

Right to have someone informed when arrested

 56.—(1) Where a person has been arrested and is being held in custody in a police station or other premises, he shall be entitled, if he so requests, to have one friend or relative or other person who is known to him or who is likely to take an interest in his welfare told, as soon as is practicable except to the extent that delay is permitted by this section, that he has been arrested and is being detained there.

 (2) Delay is only permitted—

  (a) in the case of a person who is in police detention for a serious arrestable offence; and

  (b) if an officer of at least the rank of superintendent authorises it.

---

[45] The Northern Ireland PACE Order, Art. 56(17)(b) expands the definition of nurse.

(3) In any case the person in custody must be permitted to exercise the right conferred by subsection (1) above within 36 hours from the relevant time, as defined in section 41(2) above.

(4) An officer may give an authorisation under subsection (2) above orally or in writing but, if he gives it orally, he shall confirm it in writing as soon as is practicable.

(5) Subject to subsection (5A) below, an officer may only authorise delay where he has reasonable grounds for believing that telling the named person of the arrest—

    (a) will lead to interference with or harm to evidence connected with a serious arrestable offence or interference with or physical injury to other persons; or

    (b) will lead to the alerting of other persons suspected of having committed such an offence but not yet arrested for it; or

    (c) will hinder the recovery of any property obtained as a result of such an offence.

(5A) An officer may also authorise delay where the serious arrestable offence is a drug trafficking offence or an offence to which Part VI of the Criminal Justice Act 1988 applies (offences in respect of which confiscation orders under that Part may be made) and the officer has reasonable grounds for believing—

    (a) where the offence is a drug trafficking offence, that the detained person has benefited from drug trafficking and that the recovery of the value of that person's proceeds of drug trafficking will be hindered by telling the named person of the arrest; and

    (b) where the offence is one to which Part VI of the Criminal Justice Act 1988 applies, that the detained person has benefited from the offence and that the recovery of the value of the property obtained by that person from or in connection with the offence or of the pecuniary advantage derived by him from or in connection with it will be hindered by telling the named person of the arrest.[46]

(6) If a delay is authorised—

    (a) the detained person shall be told the reason for it; and

    (b) the reason shall be noted on his custody record.

(7) The duties imposed by subsection (6) above shall be performed as soon as is practicable.

(8) The rights conferred by this section on a person detained at a police station or other premises are exercisable whenever he is transferred from one place to another, and this section applies to each subsequent occasion on which they are exercisable as it applies to the first such occasion.

(9) There may be no further delay in permitting the exercise of the right conferred by subsection (1) above once the reason for authorising delay ceases to subsist.

(10) In the foregoing provisions of this section references to a person who has been arrested include references to a person who has been detained under the terrorism provisions and "arrest" includes detention under those provisions.

(11) In its application to a person who has been arrested or detained under the terrorism provisions—

    (a) subsection (2)(a) above shall have effect as if for the words "for a serious arrestable offence" there were substituted the words "under the terrorism provisions";

---

[46] Subs. (5A) was added by the Drug Trafficking Offences Act 1986, s.32. It was amended by the Criminal Justice Act 1988, s.99.

(b) subsection (3) above shall have effect as if for the words from "within" onwards there were substituted the words "before the end of the period beyond which he may no longer be detained without the authority of the Secretary of State"; and

(c) subsection (5) above shall have effect as if at the end there were added "or

    (d) will lead to interference with the gathering of information about the commission, preparation or instigation of acts of terrorism; or

    (e) by alerting any person, will make it more difficult—

        (i) to prevent an act of terrorism; or

        (ii) to secure the apprehension, prosecution or conviction of any person in connection with the commission, preparation or instigation of an act of terrorism."

Additional rights of children and young persons who are arrested

57. The following subsections shall be substituted for section 34(2) of the Children and Young Persons Act 1933—

"(2) Where a child or young person is in police detention, such steps as are practicable shall be taken to ascertain the identity of a person responsible for his welfare.

(3) If it is practicable to ascertain the identity of a person responsible for the welfare of the child or young person, that person shall be informed, unless it is not practicable to do so—

(a) that the child or young person has been arrested;

(b) why he has been arrested; and

(c) where he is being detained.

(4) Where information falls to be given under subsection (3) above, it shall be given as soon as it is practicable to do so.

(5) For the purposes of this section the persons who may be responsible for the welfare of a child or young person are—

(a) his parent or guardian; or

(b) any other person who has for the time being assumed responsibility for his welfare.

(6) If it is practicable to give a person responsible for the welfare of the child or young person the information required by subsection (3) above, that person shall be given it as soon as it is practicable to do so.

(7) If it appears that at the time of his arrest a supervision order, as defined in section 11 of the Children and Young Persons Act 1969, is in force in respect of him, the person responsible for his supervision shall also be informed as described in subsection (3) above as soon as it is reasonably practicable to do so.[47]

(8) The reference to a parent or guardian in subsection (5) above is—

(a) in the case of a child in the care of a local authority, a reference to that authority; and

(b) in the case of a child or young person in the care of a voluntary organisation in which parental rights and duties with respect to him are vested by virtue of a resolution under section 64(1) of the Child Care Act 1980, that organisation.

(9) The rights conferred on a child or young person by subsections (2) to (8) above are in addition to his rights under section 56 of the Police and Criminal Evidence Act 1984.

(10) The reference in subsection (2) above to a child or young person who is in police detention includes a reference to a child or young

---

[47] The Northern Ireland PACE Order, Art. 58(7) adds reference also to a probation order.

person who has been detained under the terrorism provisions, and in subsection (3) above "arrest" includes such detention.

(11) In subsection (10) above "the terrorism provisions" has the meaning assigned to it by section 65 of the Police and Criminal Evidence Act 1984".

Access to legal advice

58.—(1) A person arrested and held in custody in a police station or other premises shall be entitled, if he so requests, to consult a solicitor privately at any time.

(2) Subject to subsection (3) below, a request under subsection (1) above and the time at which it was made shall be recorded in the custody record.

(3) Such a request need not be recorded in the custody record of a person who makes it at a time while he is at a court after being charged with an offence.

(4) If a person makes such a request, he must be permitted to consult a solicitor as soon as is practicable except to the extent that delay is permitted by this section.

(5) In any case he must be permitted to consult a solicitor within 36 hours from the relevant time, as defined in section 41(2) above.

(6) Delay in compliance with a request is only permitted—
>   (a) in the case of a person who is in police detention for a serious arrestable offence; and
>   (b) if an officer of at least the rank of superintendent authorises it.

(7) An officer may give an authorisation under subsection (6) above orally or in writing but, if he gives it orally, he shall confirm it in writing as soon as is practicable.

(8) Subject to subsection (8A) below, an officer may only authorise delay where he has reasonable grounds for believing that the exercise of the right conferred by subsection (1) above at the time when the person in police detention desires to exercise it—
>   (a) will lead to interference with or harm to evidence connected with a serious arrestable offence or interference with or physical injury to other persons; or
>   (b) will lead to the alerting of other persons suspected of having committed such an offence but not yet arrested for it; or
>   (c) will hinder the recovery of any property obtained as a result of such an offence.

(8A) An officer may also authorise delay where the serious arrestable offence is a drug trafficking offence or an offence to which Part VI of the Criminal Justice Act 1988 applies and the officer has reasonable grounds for believing—
>   (a) where the offence is a drug trafficking offence, that the detained person has benefited from drug trafficking and that the recovery of the value of that person's proceeds of drug trafficking will be hindered by the exercise of the right conferred by subsection (1) above; and
>   (b) where the offence is one to which Part VI of the Criminal Justice Act 1988 applies, that the detained person has benefited from the offence and that the recovery of the value of the property obtained by that person from or in connection with the offence or of the pecuniary advantage derived by him from or in connection with it will be hindered by the exercise of the right conferred by subsection (1) above.[48]

---

[48] Subs. (8A) (like s.56(5A)) was added by the Drug Trafficking Offences Act 1986, s.32 and was amended by the Criminal Justice Act 1988, s.99.

(9) If delay is authorised—
    (a) the detained person shall be told the reason for it; and
    (b) the reason shall be noted on his custody record.

(10) The duties imposed by subsection (9) above shall be performed as soon as is practicable.

(11) There may be no further delay in permitting the exercise of the right conferred by subsection (1) above once the reason for authorising delay ceases to subsist.

(12) The reference in subsection (1) above to a person who is in police detention includes a reference to a person who has been detained under the terrorism provisions.

(13) In the application of this section to a person who has been arrested or detained under the terrorism provisions—
    (a) subsection (5) above shall have effect as if for the words from "within" onwards there were substituted the words "before the end of the period beyond which he may no longer be detained without the authority of the Secretary of State";
    (b) subsection (6)(a) above shall have effect as if for the words "for a serious arrestable offence" there were substituted the words "under the terrorism provisions"; and
    (c) subsection (8) above shall have effect as if at the end there were added "or
    (d) will lead to interference with the gathering of information about the commission, preparation or instigation of acts of terrorism; or
    (e) by alerting any person, will make it more difficult—
        (i) to prevent an act of terrorism; or
        (ii) to secure the apprehension, prosecution or conviction of any person in connection with the commission, preparation or instigation of an act of terrorism."

(14) If an officer of appropriate rank has reasonable grounds for believing that, unless he gives a direction under subsection (15) below, the exercise by a person arrested or detained under the terrorism provisions of the right conferred by subsection (1) above will have any of the consequences specified in subsection (8) above (as it has effect by virtue of subsection (13) above), he may give a direction under that subsection.

(15) A direction under this subsection is a direction that a person desiring to exercise the right conferred by subsection (1) above may only consult a solicitor in the sight and hearing of a qualified officer of the uniformed branch of the force of which the officer giving the direction is a member.

(16) An officer is qualified for the purpose of subsection (15) above if—
    (a) he is of at least the rank of inspector; and
    (b) in the opinion of the officer giving the direction he has no connection with the case.

(17) An officer is of approriate rank to give a direction under subsection (15) above if he is of at least the rank of Commander or Assistant Chief Constable.

(18) A direction under subsection (15) above shall cease to have effect once the reason for giving it ceases to subsist.

Legal aid for persons in police stations

59. . . . . [49]

---

[49] The whole of s.59 was repealed under Legal Aid Act 1988, s.45, Sched. 6 as from April 1, 1989. See S.I. 1989 No. 288.

Tape-recording of interviews

60.—(1) It shall be the duty of the Secretary of State—
- (a) to issue a code of practice in connection with the tape-recording of interviews of persons suspected of the commission of criminal offences which are held by police officers at police stations; and
- (b) to make an order requiring the tape-recording of interviews of persons suspected of the commission of criminal offences, or of such descriptions of criminal offences as may be specified in the order, which are so held, in accordance with the code as it has effect for the time being.

(2) An order under subsection (1) above shall be made by statutory instrument and shall be subject to annulment in pursuance of a resolution of either House of Parliament.

Fingerprinting

61.—(1) Except as provided by this section no person's fingerprints may be taken without the appropriate consent.

(2) Consent to the taking of a person's fingerprints must be in writing if it is given at a time when he is at a police station.

(3) The fingerprints of a person detained at a police station may be taken without the appropriate consent—
- (a) if an officer of at least the rank of superintendent authorises them to be taken; or
- (b) if—
  - (i) he has been charged with a recordable offence or informed that he will be reported for such an offence; and
  - (ii) he has not had his fingerprints taken in the course of the investigation of the offence by the police.

(4) An officer may only give an authorisation under subsection (3)(a) above if he has reasonable grounds—
- (a) for suspecting the involvement of the person whose fingerprints are to be taken in a criminal offence; and
- (b) for believing that his fingerprints will tend to confirm or disprove his involvement.

(5) An officer may give an authorisation under subsection (3)(a) above orally or in writing but, if he gives it orally, he shall confirm it in writing as soon as is practicable.

(6) Any person's fingerprints may be taken without the appropriate consent if he has been convicted of a recordable offence.

(7) In a case where by virtue of subsection (3) or (6) above a person's fingerprints are taken without the appropriate consent—
- (a) he shall be told the reason before his fingerprints are taken; and
- (b) the reason shall be recorded as soon as is practicable after the fingerprints are taken.

(7A) If a person's fingerprints are taken at a police station, whether with or without the appropriate consent—
- (a) before the fingerprints are taken, an officer shall inform him that they may be the subject of a speculative search; and
- (b) the fact that the person has been informed of this possibility shall be recorded as soon as is practicable after the fingerprints have been taken.[49a]

(8) If he is detained at a police station when the fingerprints are taken, the

---

[49a] Added by the Criminal Justice and Public Order Act 1994, Sched. 10, para. 56(a). For the equivalent change in Northern Ireland see Appendix 4, p. 532 below [Art. 9(2)].

reason for taking them and, in the case falling within subsection (7A) above, the fact referred to in paragraph (b) of that subsection[49b] shall be recorded on his custody record.

(9) Nothing in this section—

    (a) affects any power conferred by paragraph 18(2) of Schedule 2 to the Immigration Act 1971; or

    (b) *except as provided in section 15(10) of, and paragraph 7(6) of Schedule 5 to, the Prevention of Terrorism (Temporary Provisions) Act 1989*, applies to a person arrested or detained under the terrorism provisions.[50]

Intimate samples[51]

62.—(1) An intimate sample may be taken from a person in police detention only—

    (a) if a police officer of at least the rank of superintendent authorises it to be taken; and

    (b) if the appropriate consent is given.

(1A) An intimate sample may be taken from a person who is not in police detention but from whom, in the course of the investigation of an offence, two or more non-intimate samples suitable for the same means of analysis have been taken which have proved insufficient—

    (a) if a police officer of at least the rank of superintendent authorises it to be taken; and

    (b) if the appropriate consent is given.[51a]

(2) An officer may only give an authorisation under subsection (1) or (1A) above [51b] if he has reasonable grounds—

    (a) for suspecting the involvement of the person from whom the sample is to be taken in a recordable offence[51c]; and

    (b) for believing that the sample will tend to confirm or disprove his involvement.

(3) An officer may give an authorisation under subsection (1) or (1A)[51d] above orally or in writing but, if he gives it orally, he shall confirm it in writing as soon as is practicable.

(4) The appropriate consent must be given in writing.

(5) Where—

    (a) an authorisation has been given; and

    (b) it is proposed that an intimate sample shall be taken in pursuance of the authorisation,

an officer shall inform the person from whom the sample is to be taken—

        (i) of the giving of the authorisation; and

        (ii) of the grounds for giving it.

[49b] Amended by the Criminal Justice and Public Order Act 1994, Sched. 10, para. 56(b). For the equivalent change in Northern Ireland see Appendix 4, p. 532 below [Art. 9(3)].

[50] The words in italics in s.61(9)(b) were added by the Prevention of Terrorism (Temporary Provisions) Act 1989, s.25(1) and Sched. 8, para. 6(5). The 1989 Act, s.15(10) and Sched. 5, para. 7(6) extends this subs. to investigations under s.14 of the 1989 Act and inquiries as to whether the suspect is subject to an exclusion order and to port and border controls.

[51] For the comparable Northern Ireland provisions see Criminal Justice Act 1988, Sched. 14 and see also Appendix 4, p. 532 below [Art. 10].

[51a] Added by the Criminal Justice and Public Order Act 1994, s.54(2). For the equivalent change in Northern Ireland see Appendix 4, p. 532 below [Art. 10(2)].

[51b] Amended by the Criminal Justice and Public Order Act 1994, s.54(3)(a) and (b). For the equivalent change in Northern Ireland see Appendix 4, p. 532 below [Art. 10(3)].

[51c] Amended by the Criminal Justice and Public Order Act 1994, s.54(3)(a) and (b). For the equivalent change in Northern Ireland see Appendix 4, p. 532 below [Art. 10(3)].

[51d] Amended by the Criminal Justice and Public Order Act 1994, s.54(4). For the equivalent change in Northern Ireland see Appendix 4, p. 532 below [Art. 10(4)].

(6) The duty imposed by subsection (5)(ii) above includes a duty to state the nature of the offence in which it is suspected that the person from whom the sample is to be taken has been involved.

(7) If an intimate sample is taken from a person—
    (a) the authorisation by virtue of which it was taken;
    (b) the grounds for giving the authorisation; and
    (c) the fact that the appropriate consent was given,
shall be recorded as soon as is practicable after the sample is taken.

(7A) If an intimate sample is taken from a person at a police station—
    (a) before the sample is taken, an officer shall inform him that it may be the subject of a speculative search; and
    (b) the fact that the person has been informed of this possibility shall be recorded as soon as practicable after the sample has been taken.[51e]

(8) If an intimate sample is taken from a person detained at a police station, the matters required to be recorded by subsection (7) or (7A)[51f] above shall be recorded in his custody record.

(9) An intimate sample, other than a sample of urine or a dental impression, may only be taken from a person by a medical practitioner and a dental impression may only be taken by a registered dentist.[51g]

(10) Where the appropriate consent to the taking of an intimate sample from a person was refused without good cause, in any proceedings against that person for an offence—
    (a) the court, in determining—
        (i) whether to grant an application for dismissal made by that person under section 6 of the Magistrates' Courts Act 1980 (application for dismissal of charge in course of proceedings with a view to transfer for trial); or[51h]
        (ii) whether there is a case to answer; and
    (aa) a judge, in deciding whether to grant an application made by the accused under—
        (i) section 6 of the Criminal Justice Act 1987 (application for dismissal of charges of serious fraud it respect of which notice of transfer has been given under section 4 of that Act); or
        (ii) paragraph 5 of Schedule 6 to the Criminal Justice Act 1991 (application for dismissal of charge of violent or sexual offence involving child in respect of which notice of transfer has been given under section 53 of that Act); and[51i]
    (b) the court or jury, in determining whether that person is guilty of the offence charged,
may draw such inferences from the refusal as appear proper; . . . .[51j]

(11) Nothing in this section affects sections 4 to 11 of the Road Traffic Act 1988.[52]

(12) Nothing in this section, except as provided in section 15(11) and (12)

[51e] Added by the Criminal Justice and Public Order Act 1994, Sched. 10, para. 57(a). For the equivalent change in Northern Ireland see Appendix 4, p. 532 below [Art. 10(5)].

[51f] Amended by the Criminal Justice and Public Order Act 1994, Sched. 10, para. 57(b). For the equivalent change in Northern Ireland see Appendix 4, p. 532 below [Art. 10(6)].

[51g] Amended by the Criminal Justice and Public Order Act 1994, s.54(5)(a) and (b). For the equivalent change in Northern Ieland see Appendix 4, p. 532 below [Art. 10(7)].

[51h] Substituted for the original by the Criminal Justice and Public Order Act 1994, Sched. 4, para. 58. For the equivalent change in Northern Ireland see Appendix 4, p. 532 below [Art. 10(7)].

[51i] Added by the Criminal Justice and Public Order Act 1994, Sched. 9, para. 24.

[51j] Repealed by the Criminal Justice and Public Order Act 1994, Sched. 11.

[52] Amended by the Road Traffic (Consequential Provisions) Act 1988, s.4, Sched. 3, para. 27 and in Northern Ireland by the Road Traffic (Amendment) (Northern Ireland) Order 1991, Arts. 143–152A.

of, and paragraph 7(6A) and (6B) of Schedule 5 to, the Prevention of Terrorism (Temporary Provisions) Act 1989, applies to a person arrested or detained under the terrorism provisions.[52a]

Other samples

　　63.—(1) Except as provided by this section a non-intimate sample may not be taken from a person without the appropriate consent.

　　(2) Consent to the taking of a non-intimate sample must be given in writing.

　　(3) A non-intimate sample may be taken from a person without the appropriate consent if—

　　　　(a)　he is in police detention or is being held in custody by the police on the authority of a court[53]; and

　　　　(b)　an officer of at least the rank of superintendent authorises it to be taken without the appropriate consent.

　　(3A) A non-intimate sample may be taken from a person (whether or not he falls within subsection (3)(a) above) without the appropriate consent if—

　　　　(a)　he has been charged with a recordable offence or informed that he will be reported for such an offence; and

　　　　(b)　either he has not had a non-intimate sample taken from him in the course of the investigation of the offence by the police or he has had a non-intimate sample taken from him but either it was not suitable for the same means of analysis or, though so suitable, the sample proved insufficient.

　　(3B) A non-intimate sample may be taken from a person without the appropriate consent if he has been convicted of a recordable offence.[53a]

　　(4) An officer may only give an authorisation under subsection (3) above if he has reasonable grounds—

　　　　(a)　for suspecting the involvement of the person from whom the sample is to be taken in a recordable offence[53b]; and

　　　　(b)　for believing that the sample will tend to confirm or disprove his involvement.

　　(5) An officer may give an authorisation under subsection (3) above orally or in writing but, if he gives it orally, he shall confirm it in writing as soon as is practicable.

　　(6) Where—

　　　　(a)　an authorisation has been given; and

　　　　(b)　it is proposed that a non-intimate sample shall be taken in pursuance of the authorisation,

an officer shall inform the person from whom the sample is to be taken—

　　　　　　(i)　of the giving of the authorisation; and

　　　　　　(ii)　of the grounds for giving it.

　　(7) The duty imposed by subsection (6)(ii) above includes a duty to state the nature of the offence in which it is suspected that the person from whom the sample is to be taken has been involved.

　　(8) If a non-intimate sample is taken from a person by virtue of subsection (3) above—

　　　　(a)　the authorisation by virtue of which it was taken; and

　　　　(b)　the grounds for giving the authorisation,

[52a] Added by the Criminal Justice and Public Order Act 1994, Sched. 10, para. 62(4)(a).

[53] The words "or is being held in custody by the police on the authority of a court" are not in the Northern Ireland PACE Order, Art. 63(3)(a) as there is no provision in Northern Ireland for a person charged with an offence to be remanded by a court into police custody.

[53a] Added by the Criminal Justice and Public Order Act, 1994, s.55(2).

[53b] Amended by the Criminal Justice and Public Order Act 1994, s.55(3).

shall be recorded as soon as is practicable after the sample is taken.

(8A) In a case where by virtue of subsection (3A) or (3B) a sample is taken from a person without the appropriate consent—

    (a) he shall be told the reason before the sample is taken; and

    (b) the reason shall be recorded as soon as practicable after the sample is taken.[53c]

(8B) If a non-intimate sample is taken from a person at a police station, whether with or without the appropriate consent—

    (a) before the sample is taken, an officer shall inform him that it may be the subject of a speculative search; and

    (b) the fact that the person has been informed of this possibility shall be recorded as soon as practicable after the sample has been taken.[53d]

(9) If a non-intimate sample is taken from a person detained at a police station, the matters required to be recorded by subsection (8) or (8A) or (8B)[53e] above shall be recorded in his custody record.

(10) Subsection (3B) above shall not apply to persons convicted before the date on which that subsection comes into force.[53f]

(10) Nothing in this section, except as provided in section 15(13) and (14) of, and paragraph 7(6C) and (6D) of Schedule 5 to, the Prevention of Terrorism (Temporary Provisions) Act 1989, applies to a person arrested or detained under the terrorism provisions.[53g]

63A.—(1) Fingerprints or samples or the information derived from samples taken under any power conferred by this Part of this Act from a person who has been arrested on suspicion of being involved in a recordable offence may be checked against other fingerprints or samples or the information derived from other samples contained in records held by or on behalf of the police or held in connection with or as a result of an investigation of an offence.

(2) Where a sample of hair other than pubic hair is to be taken the sample may be taken either by cutting hairs or by plucking hairs with their roots so long as no more are plucked than the person taking the sample reasonably considers to be necessary for a sufficient sample.

(3) Where any power to take a sample is exercisable in relation to a person the sample may be taken in a prison or other institution to which the Prison Act 1952 applies.

(4) Any constable may, within the allowed period, require a person who is neither in police detention nor held in custody by the police on the authority of a court to attend a police station in order to have a sample taken where—

    (a) the person has been charged with a recordable offence or informed that he will be reported for such an offence and either he has not had a sample taken from him in the course of the investigation of the offence by the police or he has had a sample so taken from him but either it was not suitable for the same means of analysis or, though so suitable, the sample proved insufficient; or

    (b) the person has been convicted of a recordable offence and either he has not had a sample taken from him since the conviction or he has had a sample taken from him (before or after his conviction) but either it was not suitable for the same means of analysis or, though so suitable, the sample proved insufficient.

[53c] Added by the Criminal Justice and Public Order Act 1994, s.55(4).
[53d] Added by the Criminal Justice and Public Order Act 1994, Sched. 10, para. 58(a).
[53e] Amended by the Criminal Justice and Public Order Act 1994, s.55(5) and Sched. 10, para. 58(b).
[53f] Added by the Criminal Justice and Public Order Act 1994, s.55(6).
[53g] Added by the Criminal Justice and Public Order Act 1994, Sched. 10, para. 62(4)(b).

(5) The period allowed for requiring a person to attend a police station for the purpose specified in subsection (4) above is—

    (a) in the case of a person falling within paragraph (a), one month beginning with the date of the charge or one month beginning with the date on which the appropriate officer is informed of the fact that the sample is not suitable for the same means of analysis or has proved insufficient, as the case may be;

    (b) in the case of a person falling within paragraph (b), one month beginning with the date of the conviction or one month beginning with the date on which the appropriate officer is informed of the fact that the sample is not suitable for the same means of analysis or has proved insufficient, as the case may be.

(6) A requirement under subsection (4) above—

    (a) shall give the person at least 7 days within which he must so attend; and

    (b) may direct him to attend at a specified time of day or between specified times of day.

(7) Any constable may arrest without a warrant a person who has failed to comply with a requirement under subsection (4) above.

(8) In this section "the appropriate officer" is—

    (a) in the case of a person falling within subsection (4)(a), the officer investigating the offence with which that person has been charged or as to which he was informed that he would be reported;

    (b) in the case of a person falling within subsection (4)(b), the officer in charge of the police station from which the investigation of the offence of which he was convicted was conducted.[53h]

Destruction of fingerprints and samples

64.—(1) If—

    (a) fingerprints or samples are taken from a person in connectin with the investigation of an offence; and

    (b) he is cleared of that offence,

they must, except as provided in subsection (3A) below,[53i] be destroyed as soon as is practicable after the conclusion of the proceedings.

(2) If—

    (a) fingerprints or samples are taken from a person in connection with such an investigation; and

    (b) it is decided that he shall not be prosecuted for the offence and he has not admitted it and has been dealt with by way of being cautioned by a constable,

they must, except as provided in subsection (3A) below,[53j] be destroyed as soon as is practicable after that decision is taken.

(3) If—

    (a) fingerprints or samples are taken from a person in connection with the investigation of an offence; and

    (b) that person is not suspected of having committed the offence,

they must, except as provided in subsection (3A) below,[53k] be destroyed as soon as they have fulfilled the purpose for which they were taken.

(3A) Samples which are required to be destroyed under subsection (1), (2) or (3) above need not be destroyed if they were taken for the purpose of the same investigation of an offence of which a person from whom one was taken has been convicted, but the information derived from the sample of

---

[53h] Added by the Criminal Justice and Public Order Act 1994, s.56.
[53i-k] Amended by the Criminal Justice and Public Order Act 1994, s.57(2).

any person entitled (apart from this subsection) to its destruction under subsection (1), (2) or (3) above shall not be used—
    (a) in evidence against the person so entitled; or
    (b) for the purposes of any investigation of an offence.

(3B) Where samples are required to be destroyed under subsections (1), (2) or (3) above, and subsection (3A) above does not apply, information derived from the sample of any person entitled to its destruction under subsection (1), (2) or (3) above shall not be used—
    (a) in evidence against the person so entitled; or
    (b) for the purposes of any investigation of an offence.[531]

(4) Proceedings which are discontinued are to be treated as concluded for the purposes of this section.

(5) If fingerprints are destroyed—
    (a) any copies of the fingerprints shall also be destroyed; and
    (b) any chief officer of police controlling access to computer data relating to the fingerprints shall make access to the data impossible, as soon as it is practicable to do so.[54]

(6) A person who asks to be allowed to witness the destruction of his fingerprints or copies of them shall have a right to witness it.

(6A) If—
    (a) subsection (5)(b) above falls to be complied with; and
    (b) the person to whose fingerprints the data relate asks for a certificate that it has been complied with,
such a certificate shall be issued to him, not later than the end of the period of three months beginning with the day on which he asks for it, by the responsible chief officer of police or a person authorised by him or on his behalf for the purposes of this section.

(6B) In this section—
    "chief officer of police" means the chief officer of police for an area mentioned in Schedule 8 to the Police Act 1964; and
    "the responsible chief officer of police" means the chief officer of police in whose area the computer data were put on to the computer.[55]

(7) Nothing in this section—
    (a) affects any power conferred by paragraph 18(2) of Schedule 2 to the Immigration Act 1971; or
    (b) applies to a person arrested or detained under the terrorism provisions.

Fingerprints and samples—supplementary

65. In this Part of this Act—
    "appropriate consent" means—
        (a) in relation to a person who has attained the age of 17 years, the consent of that person;
        (b) in relation to a person who has not attained that age but has attained the age of 14 years, the consent of that person and his parent or guardian; and
        (c) in relation to a person who has not attained the age of 14 years, the consent of his parent or guardian;
    "drug trafficking" and "drug trafficking offence" have the same meaning as in the Drug Trafficking Act 1994"[56];

---

[531] Added by the Criminal Justice and Public Order Act 1994, s.57(3).

[54-55] This amended version of subs. (5) and the new (6A) and (6B) were introduced by the Criminal Justice Act 1988, s.148.

[56] Added by the Drug Trafficking Act 1994, Sched. 1, para. 8.

"fingerprints" includes palm prints;

"intimate sample" means

    (a) a sample of blood, semen or any other tissue fluid, urine or pubic hair;

    (b) a dental impression;

    (c) a swab taken from a person's body orifice other than the mouth[57];

"intimate search" means a search wich consists of the physical examination of a person's body orifices other than the mouth[57a];

"non-intimate sample" means—

    (a) a sample of hair other than pubic hair;

    (b) a sample taken from a nail or from under a nail;

    (c) a swab taken from any part of a person's body including the mouth but not any other body orifice;

    (d) saliva;

    (e) a footprint or a similar impression of any part of a person's body other than a part of his hand[57b];

"registered dentist" has the same meaning as in the Dentists Act 1984;

"speculative search", in relation to a person's fingerprints or samples, means such a check against other fingerprints or samples or against information derived from other samples as is referred to in section 63A(1) above;

"sufficient" and "insufficient", in relation to a sample, means sufficient or insufficient (in point of quantity or quality) for the purpose of enabling information to be produced by the means of analysis used or to be used in relation to the sample.[57c]

"the terrorism provisions" means—

    (a)[58]Section 14(1) of the Prevention of Terrorism (Temporary Provisions) Act 1989 and any provision of Schedule 2 or 5 to that Act conferring a power of arrest or detention; and

"terrorism" has the meaning assigned to it by section 20(1) of that Act, and references in this Part to any person's proceeds of drug trafficking are to be construed in accordance with the Drug Trafficking Offences Act 1986.

PART VI

CODES OF PRACTICE—GENERAL

Codes of practice

66. The Secretary of State shall issue codes of practice in connection with—

    (a) the exercise by police officers of statutory powers—

        (i) to search a person without first arresting him; or

---

[57] Added by the Criminal Justice and Public Order Act 1994, s.58(2) and (3). For the equivalent change in Northern Ireland see Appendix 4, p. 532 below [Art. 8(2)].

[57a] Added by the Criminal Justice and Public Order Act 1994, s.59(1). For the equivalent change in Northern Ireland see Appendix 4, p. 532 below [Art. 5(2)].

[57b] Added by the Criminal Justice and Public Order Act 1994, s.58(2) and (3). For the equivalent change in Northern Ireland see Appendix 4, p. 532 below [Art. 8(3)].

[57c] Added by the Criminal Justice and Public Order Act 1994, s.58(4). For the equivalent change in Northern Ireland see Appendix 4, p. 532 below [Art. 8(4)].

[58] Amended by the Prevention of Terrorism (Temporary Provisions) Act 1989, Sched. 8, para. 6(6).

      (ii) to search a vehicle without making an arrest;
  (b) the detention, treatment, questioning and identification of persons by police officers;
  (c) searches of premises by police officers; and
  (d) the seizure of property found by police officers on persons or premises.

Codes of practice—supplementary

67.—(1) When the Secretary of State proposes to issue a code of practice to which this section applies, he shall prepare and publish a draft of that code, shall consider any representations made to him about the draft and may modify the draft accordingly.

(2) This section applies to a code of practice under Section 60 or 66 above.

(3) The Secretary of State shall lay before both Houses of Parliament a draft of any code of practice prepared by him under this section.

(4) When the Secretary of State has laid the draft of a code before Parliament, he may bring the code into operation by order made by statutory instrument.

(5) No order under subsection (4) above shall have effect until approved by a resolution of each House of Parliament.

(6) An order bringing a code of practice into operation may contain such transitional provisions or savings as appear to the Secretary of State to be necessary or expedient in connection with the code of practice thereby brought into operation.

(7) The Secretary of State may from time to time revise the whole or any part of a code of practice to which this section applies and issue that revised code, and the foregoing provisions of this section shall apply (with appropriate modifications) to such a revised code as they apply to the first issue of a code.

(8) ... [58a]

(9) Persons other than police officers who are charged with the duty of investigating offences or charging offenders shall in the discharge of that duty have regard to any relevant provision of such a code.

(10) A failure on the part
  (a) of a police officer to comply with any provision of such a code; or
  (b) of any person other than a police officer who is charged with the duty of investigating offences or charging offenders to have regard to any relevant provision of such a code in the discharge of that duty,
shall not of itself render him liable to any criminal or civil proceedings.

(11) In all criminal and civil proceedings any such code shall be admissible in evidence, and if any provision of such a code appears to the court or tribunal conducting the proceedings to be relevant to any question arising in the procedings it shall be taken into account in determining that question.

(12) In this section "criminal proceedings" includes—[59]
  (a) proceedings in the United Kingdom or elsewhere before a court-martial constituted under the Army Act 1955, or the Air Force Act 1955 or the Naval Discipline Act 1957 or a disciplinary court constituted under section 50 of the said Act of 1957;
  (b) proceedings before the Courts-Martial Appeal Court; and
  (c) proceedings before a Standing Civilian Court.

[58a] Repealed by the Police and Magistrates' Courts Act 1994, s.37 and Sched. 9.
[59] The equivalent provision in the Northern Ireland PACE Order, Art. 66(11) applies only to Northern Ireland proceedings. Para. (12) of the order states that the Codes do not apply to terrorism cases.

PART VII

DOCUMENTARY EVIDENCE IN CRIMINAL PROCEEDINGS

Evidence from documentary records

68.—[s.68 was repealed and replaced by Part II of the Criminal Justice Act 1988. Part I of Schedule 3 to the Police and Criminal Evidence Act, which accompanied the provisions of s.68, has been replaced by Schedule 2 to the Criminal Justice Act 1988.[60] Both are included here for convenience. The equivalent Northern Ireland provisions are in the Criminal Justice (Evidence etc.) (Northern Ireland) Order 1989.]

Part II

Documentary Evidence in Criminal Proceedings

First-hand hearsay

23.—(1) Subject—
  (a) to subsection (4) below;
  (b) to paragraph 1A of Schedule 2 to the Criminal Appeal Act 1968 (evidence given orally at original trial to be given orally at retrial); and
  (c) to section 69 of the Police and Criminal Evidence Act 1984 (evidence from computer records),
a statement made by a person in a document shall be admissible in criminal proceedings as evidence of any fact of which direct oral evidence by him would be admissible if—
      (i) the requirements of one of the paragraphs of subsection (2) below are satisfied; or
      (ii) the requirements of subsection (3) below are satisfied.
(2) The requirements mentioned in subsection (1)(i) above are—
  (a) that the person who made the statement is dead or by reason of his bodily or mental condition unfit to attend as a witness;
  (b) that—
      (i) the person who made the statement is outside the United Kingdom; and
      (ii) it is not reasonably practicable to secure his attendance; or
  (c) that all reasonable steps have been taken to find the person who made the statement, but that he canot be found.
(3) The requirements mentioned in subsection (1)(ii) above are—
  (a) that the statement was made to a police officer or some other person charged with the duty of investigating offences or charging offenders; and
  (b) that the person who made it does not give oral evidence through fear or because he is kept out of the way.
(4) Subsection (1) above does not render admissible a confession made by an accused person that would not be admissible under section 76 of the Police and Criminal Evidence Act 1984.

[60] Pt. II of and Sched. 2 to the Criminal Justice Act 1988 both came into force in April 1989; see S.I. 1989/264 (c.8).

Business etc. documents

24.—(1) Subject—

(a) to subsections (3) and (4) below;

(b) to paragraph 1A of Schedule 2 to the Criminal Appeal Act 1968; and

(c) to section 60 of the Police and Criminal Evidence Act 1984,

a statement in a document shall be admissible in criminal proceedings as evidence of any fact of which oral evidence would be admissible, if the following conditions are satisfied—

(i) the document was created or received by a person in the course of a trade, business, profession or other occupation, or as the holder of a paid or unpaid office; and

(ii) the information contained in the document was supplied by a person (whether or not the maker of the statement) who had, or may reasonably be supposed to have had, personal knowledge of the matters dealt with.

(2) Subsection (1) above applies whether the information contained in the document was supplied directly but, if it was supplied indirectly, only if each person through whom it was supplied received it—

(a) in the course of a trade, business, profession or other occupation; or

(b) as the holder of a paid or unpaid office.

(3) Subsection (1) above does not render admissible a confession made by an accused person that would not be admissible under section 76 of the Police and Criminal Evidence Act 1984.

(4) A statement prepared otherwise than in accordance with section 3 of the Criminal Justice (International Cooperation) Act 1990[60a] or an order under paragraph 6 of Schedule 13 to this Act or under section 30 or 31 below for the purposes—

(a) of pending or contemplated criminal proceedings; or

(b) of a criminal investigation,

shall not be admissible by virtue of subsection (1) above unless—

(i) the requirements of one of the paragraphs of subsection (2) of section 23 above are satisfied; or

(ii) the requirements of subsection (3) of that section are satisfied; or

(iii) the person who made the statement cannot reasonably be expected (having regard to the time which has elapsed since he made the statement and to all the circumstances) to have any recollection of the matters dealt with in the statement.

Principles to be followed by Court

25.—(1) If, having regard to all the circumstances—

(a) the Crown Court—

(i) on a trial on indictment;

(ii) on an appeal from a magistrates' court; ...[60b]

(iii) on the hearing of an application under section 6 of the Criminal Justice Act 1987 (applications for dismissal of charges of fraud transferred from magistrates' court to Crown Court); or

(iv) on the hearing of an application under paragraph 5 of Schedule 6 to the Criminal Justice Act 1991 (applications for

---

[60a] Substituted by the Criminal Justice (International Co-operation) Act 1990, Sched. 4, para. 6.
[60b] Repealed by the Criminal Justice and Public Order Act 1994, Sched. 11.

> *dismissal of charges in certain cases involving children transferred from magistrates' court to Crown Court); or[60c]*
>
> (b) *the criminal division of the Court of Appeal; or*
>
> (c) *a magistrates' court on a trial of an information,*

is of the opinion that in the interests of justice a statement which is admissible by virtue of section 23 or 24 above nevertheless ought not to be admitted, it may direct that the statement shall not be admitted.

(2) Without prejudice to the generality of subsection (1) above, it shall be the duty of the court to have regard—

> (a) *to the nature and source of the document containing the statement and to whether or not, having regard to its nature and source and to any other circumstances that appear to the court to be relevant, it is likely that the document is authentic;*
>
> (b) *to the extent to which the statement appears to supply evidence which would otherwise not be readily available;*
>
> (c) *to the relevance of the evidence that it appears to supply to any issue which is likely to have to be determined in the proceedings; and*
>
> (d) *to any risk, having regard in particular to whether it is likely to be possible to controvert the statement if the person making it does not attend to give oral evidence in the proceedings, that its admission or exclusion will result in unfairness to the accused or, if there is more than one, to any of them.*

Statements in documents that appear to have been prepared for purposes of criminal proceedings or investigations

26. *Where a statement which is admissible in criminal proceedings by virtue of section 23 or 24 above appears to the court to have been prepared, otherwise than in accordance with section 3 of the Criminal Justice (International Cooperation) Act 1990[60d] or an order under paragraph 6 of Schedule 13 to this Act or under section 30 or 31 below, for the purposes—*

> (a) *of pending or contemplated criminal proceedings; or*
>
> (b) *of a criminal investigation,*

the statement shall not be given in evidence in any criminal proceedings without the leave of the court, and the court shall not give leave unless it is of the opinion that the statement ought to be admitted in the interests of justice; and in considering whether its admission would be in the interests of justice, it shall be the duty of the court to have regard—

> (i) *to the contents of the statement;*
>
> (ii) *to any risk, having regard in particular to whether it is likely to be possible to controvert the statement if the person making it does not attend to give oral evidence in the proceedings, that its admission or exclusion will result in unfairness to the accused or, if there is more than one, to any of them; and*
>
> (iii) *to any other circumstances that appear to the court to be relevant.*

Proof of statements contained in documents

27. *Where a statement contained in a document is admissible as evidence in criminal proceedings, it may be proved—*

[60c] Inserted by the Criminal Justice and Public Order Act 1994, Sched. 9, para. 31.
[60d] Substituted by the Criminal Justice (International Co-operation) Act 1990, Sched. 4, para. 6.

> (a) by the production of that document; or
> (b) (whether or not that document is still in existence) by the production of a copy of that document, or of the material part of it,

authenticated in such manner as the court may approve; and it is immaterial for the purposes of this subsection how many removes there are between a copy and the original.

Documentary evidence—supplementary

28.—(1) *Nothing in this Part of this Act shall prejudice—*
> (a) the admissibility of a statement not made by a person while giving oral evidence in court which is admissible otherwise than by virtue of this Part of this Act.

(2) *Schedule 2 to this Act shall have effect for the purpose of supplementing this Part of this Act.*

Evidence from computer records

69.—(1) In any proceedings, a statement contained in a document produced by a computer shall not be admissible as evidence of any fact stated therein unless it is shown—
> (a) that there are no reasonable grounds for believing that the statement is inaccurate because of improper use of the computer;
> (b) that at all material times the computer was operating properly, or if not, that any respect in which it was not operating properly or was out of operation was not such as to affect the production of the document or the accuracy of its contents; and
> (c) that any relevant conditions specified in rules of court under subsection (2) below are satisfied.[61]

(2) Provision may be made by rules of court requiring that in any proceedings where it is desired to give a statement in evidence by virtue of this section such information concerning the statement as may be required by the rules shall be provided in such form and at such time as may be so required.[62]

Provisions supplementary to sections 68 and 69

70.—(1) Part I of Schedule 3 to this Act shall have effect for the purpose of supplementing section 68 above. [As has been seen, Part I of Schedule 3 has been replaced by Schedule 2 to the Criminal Justice Act 1988; see p. 416 below.]

(2) Part II of that Schedule shall have effect for the purpose of supplementing section 69 above.

(3) Part III of that Schedule shall have effect for the purpose of supplementing both sections.

Microfilm copies

71. In any proceedings the contents of a document may (whether or not the document is still in existence) be proved by the production of an enlargement of a microfilm copy of that document or of the material part of it, authenticated in such manner as the court may approve.

[61-62] The words "rules of court" do not appear in the Northern Ireland PACE Order, Art. 68(1) and (2) because of a drafting amendment to (2) and the new (3).

Part VII—supplementary

72.—(1) In this Part of this Act—

"copy" and "statement" have the same meanings as in Part I of the Civil Evidence Act 1968; and

"proceedings" means criminal proceedings, including—

    (a) proceedings in the United Kingdom or elsewhere before a court martial constituted under the Army Act 1955 or the Air Force Act 1955

    (b) proceedings in the United Kingdom or elsewhere before the Courts-Martial Appeal Court—

        (i) on an appeal from a court-martial so constituted or from a court-martial constituted under the Naval Discipline Act 1957; or

        (ii) on a reference under section 34 of the Courts-Martial (Appeals) Act 1968; and

    (c) proceedings before a Standing Civilian Court.

(2) Nothing in this Part of this Act shall prejudice any power of any court to exclude evidence (whether by preventing questions from being put or otherwise) at its discretion.

PART VIII

EVIDENCE IN CRIMINAL PROCEEDINGS—GENERAL

Convictions and acquittals

Proof of convictions and acquittals

73.—(1) Where in any proceedings the fact that a person has in the United Kingdom been convicted or acquitted of an offence otherwise than by a Service court is admissible in evidence, it may be proved by producing a certificate of conviction or, as the case may be, of acquittal relating to that offence, and proving that the person named in the certificate as having been convicted or acquitted of the offence is the person whose conviction or acquittal of the offence is to be proved.

(2) For the purposes of this section a certificate of conviction or of acquittal—

    (a) shall, as regards a conviction or acquittal on indictment, consist of a certificate, signed by the clerk of the court where the conviction or acquittal took place, giving the substance and effect (omitting the formal parts) of the indictment and of the conviction or acquittal; and

    (b) shall, as regards a conviction or acquittal on a summary trial, consist of a copy of the conviction or of the dismissal of the information, signed by the clerk of the court where the conviction or acquittal took place or by the clerk of the court, if any, to which a memorandum of the conviction or acquittal was sent;

and a document purporting to be a duly signed certificate of conviction or acquittal under this section shall be taken to be such a certificate unless the contrary is proved.

(3) References in this section to the clerk of a court include references to his deputy and to any other person having the custody of the court record.

(4) The method of proving a conviction or acquittal authorised by this section shall be in addition to and not to the exclusion of any other authorised manner of proving a conviction or acquittal.

Conviction as evidence of commission of offence

74.—(1) In any proceedings the fact that a person other than the accused has been convicted of an offence by or before any court in the United Kingdom or by a Service court outside the United Kingdom shall be admissible in evidence for the purpose of proving, where to do so is relevant to any issue in those proceedings, that that person committed that offence, whether or not any other evidence of his having committed that offence is given.

(2) In any proceedings in which by virtue of this section a person other than the accused is proved to have been convicted of an offence by or before any court in the United Kingdom or by a Service court outside the United Kingdom, he shall be taken to have committed that offence unless the contrary is proved.

(3) In any proceedings where evidence is admissible of the fact that the accused has committed an offence, in so far as that evidence is relevant to any matter in issue in the proceedings for a reason other than a tendency to show in the accused a disposition to commit the kind of offence with which he is charged, if the accused is proved to have been convicted of the offence—

(a) by or before any court in the United Kingdom; or

(b) by a Service court outside the United Kingdom,

he shall be taken to have committed that offence unless the contrary is proved.

(4) Nothing in this section shall prejudice—

(a) the admissibility in evidence of any conviction which would be admissible apart from this section; or

(b) the operation of any enactment whereby a conviction or a finding of fact in any proceedings is for the purposes of any other proceedings made conclusive evidence of any fact.

Provisions supplementary to section 74

75.—(1) Where evidence that a person has been convicted of an offence is admissible by virtue of section 74 above, then without prejudice to the reception of any other admissible evidence for the purpose of identifying the facts on which the conviction was based—

(a) the contents of any document which is admissible as evidence of the conviction; and

(b) the contents of the information, complaint, indictment or charge-sheet on which the person in question was convicted,

shall be admissible in evidence for that purpose.

(2) Where in any proceedings the contents of any document are admissible in evidence by virtue of subsection (1) above, a copy of that document, or of the material part of it, purporting to be certified or otherwise authenticated by or on behalf of the court or authority having custody of that document shall be admissible in evidence and shall be taken to be a true copy of that document or part unless the contrary is shown.

(3) Nothing in any of the following—

(a) section 13 of the Powers of Criminal Courts Act 1973 (under which a conviction leading to probation or discharge is to be disregarded except as mentioned in that section);

(b) section 392 of the Criminal Procedure (Scotland) Act 1975 (which makes similar provision in respect of convictions on indictment in Scotland); and

(c) section 8 of the Probation Act (Northern Ireland) 1950 (which corresponds to section 13 of the Powers of Criminal Courts Act

1973) or any legislation which is in force in Northern Ireland for the time being and corresponds to that section,
shall affect the operation of section 74 above; and for the purposes of that section any order made by a court of summary jurisdiction in Scotland under section 182 or section 183 of the said Act of 1975 shall be treated as a conviction.

(4) Nothing in section 74 above shall be construed as rendering admissible in any proceedings evidence of any conviction other than a subsisting one.

Confessions

Confessions

76.—(1) In any proceedings a confession made by an accused person may be given in evidence against him in so far as it is relevant to any matter in issue in the proceedings and is not excluded by the court in pursuance of this section.

(2) If, in any proceedings where the prosecution proposes to give in evidence a confession made by an accused person, it is represented to the court that the confession was or may have been obtained—

(a) by oppression of the person who made it; or

(b) in consequence of anything said or done which was likely, in the circumstances existing at the time, to render unreliable any confession which might be made by him in consequence thereof,

the court shall not allow the confession to be given in evidence against him except in so far as the prosecution proves to the court beyond reasonable doubt that the confession (notwithstanding that it may be true) was not obtained as aforesaid.

(3) In any proceedings where the prosecution proposes to give in evidence a confession made by an accused person, the court may of its own motion require the prosecution, as a condition of allowing it to do so, to prove that the confession was not obtained as mentioned in subsection (2) above.

(4) The fact that a confession is wholly or partly excluded in pursuance of this section shall not affect the admissibility in evidence—

(a) of any facts discovered as a result of the confession; or

(b) where the confession is relevant as showing that the accused speaks, writes or expresses himself in a particular way, of so much of the confession as is necessary to show that he does so.

(5) Evidence that a fact to which this subsection applies was discovered as a result of a statement made by an accused person shall not be admissible unless evidence of how it was discovered is given by him or on his behalf.

(6) Subsection (5) above applies—

(a) to any fact discovered as a result of a confession which is wholly excluded in pursuance of this section; and

(b) to any fact discovered as a result of a confession which is partly so excluded, if that fact is discovered as a result of the excluded part of the confession.

(7) Nothing in Part VII of this Act shall prejudice the admissibility of a confession made by an accused person.

(8) In this section "oppression" includes torture, inhuman or degrading treatment, and the use or threat of violence (whether or not amounting to torture).

Confessions by mentally handicapped persons

77.—(1) Without prejudice to the general duty of the court at a trial on indictment to direct the jury on any matter on which it appears to the court appropriate to do so, where at such a trial—

   (a) the case against the accused depends wholly or substantially on a confession by him; and

   (b) the court is satisfied—

      (i) that he is mentally handicapped; and

      (ii) that the confession was not made in the presence of an independent person,

the court shall warn the jury that there is special need for caution before convicting the accused in reliance on the confession, and shall explain that the need arises because of the circumstances mentioned in paragraphs (a) and (b) above.

(2) In any case where at the summary trial of a person for an offence it appears to the court that a warning under subsection (1) above would be required if the trial were on indictment, the court shall treat the case as one in which there is a special need for caution before convicting the accused on his confession.

(3) In this section—

   "independent person" does not include a police officer or a person employed for, or engaged on police purposes;

   "mentally handicapped", in relation to a person, means that he is in a state of arrested or incomplete development of mind which includes significant impairment of intelligence and social functioning; and

   "police purposes" has the meaning assigned to it by section 64 of the Police Act 1964.

Miscellaneous

Exclusion of unfair evidence

78.—(1) In any proceedings the court may refuse to allow evidence on which the prosecution proposes to rely to be given if it appears to the court that, having regard to all the circumstances, including the circumstances in which the evidence was obtained, the admission of the evidence would have such an adverse effect on the fairness of the proceedings that the court ought not to admit it.

(2) Nothing in this section shall prejudice any rule of law requiring a court to exclude evidence.[63]

Time for taking accused's evidence

79. If at the trial of any person for an offence—

   (a) the defence intends to call two or more witnesses to the facts of the case; and

   (b) those witnesses include the accused,

the accused shall be called before the other witness or witnesses unless the court in its discretion otherwise directs.

Competence and compellability of accused's spouse

80.—(1) In any proceedings the wife or husband of the accused shall be competent to give evidence—

   (a) subject to subsection (4) below, for the prosecution; and

   (b) on behalf of the accused or any person jointly charged with the accused.

(2) In any proceedings the wife or husband of the accused shall, subject to

---

[63] The Northern Ireland PACE Order, Art. 76(2)(b) stated that this provision also excluded statements to which s.8(1) of the Northern Ireland (Emergency Provisions) Act 1978 applies. See now s.11 of the 1991 Act.

subsection (4) below, be compellable to give evidence on behalf of the accused.

(3) In any proceedings the wife or husband of the accused shall, subject to subsection (4) below, be compellable to give evidence for the prosecution or on behalf of any person jointly charged with the accused if and only if—

    (a) the offence charged involves an assault on, or injury or a threat of injury to, the wife or husband of the accused or a person who was at the material time under the age of sixteen; or

    (b) the offence charged is a sexual offence alleged to have been committed in respect of a person who was at the material time under that age; or

    (c) the offence charged consists of attempting or conspiring to commit, or of aiding, abetting, counselling, procuring or inciting the commission of, an offence falling within paragraph (a) or (b) above.

(4) Where a husband and wife are jointly charged with an offence neither spouse shall at the trial be competent or compellable by virtue of subsection (1)(a), (2) or (3) above to give evidence in respect of that offence unless that spouse is not, or is no longer, liable to be convicted of that offence at the trial as a result of pleading guilty or for any other reason.

(5) In any proceedings a person who has been but is no longer married to the accused shall be competent and compellable to give evidence as if that person and the accused had never been married.

(6) Where in any proceedings the age of any person at any time is material for the purposes of subsection (3) above, his age at the material time shall for the purposes of that provision be deemed to be or to have been that which appears to the court to be or to have been his age at that time.

(7) In subsection (3)(b) above "sexual offence" means an offence under the Sexual Offences Act 1956, the Indecency with Children Act 1960, the Sexual Offences Act 1967, section 54 of the Criminal Law Act 1977 or the Protection of Children Act 1978.

(8) The failure of the wife or husband of the accused to give evidence shall not be made the subject of any comment by the prosecution.

(9) Section 1(d) of the Criminal Evidence Act 1898 (communications between husband and wife) and section 43(1) of the Matrimonial Causes Act 1965 (evidence as to marital intercourse) shall cease to have effect.

Advance notice of expert evidence in Crown Court

    81.—(1) Crown Court Rules may make provision for—

    (a) requiring any party to proceedings before the Court to disclose to the other party or parties any expert evidence which he proposes to adduce in the proceedings; and

    (b) prohibiting a party who fails to comply in respect of any evidence with any requirement imposed by virtue of paragraph (a) above from adducing that evidence without the leave of the court.

(2) Crown Court Rules made by virtue of this section may specify the kinds of expert evidence to which they apply and may exempt facts or matters of any description specified in the rules.

Part VIII—Supplementary

Interpretation of Part VIII

    82.—(1) In this Part of this Act—

    "confession" includes any statement wholly or partly adverse to the person who made it, whether made to a person in authority or not and whether made in words or otherwise;

"court-martial" means a court-martial constituted under the Army Act 1955, the Air Force Act 1955 or the Naval Discipline Act 1957 or a disciplinary court constituted under section 50 of the said Act of 1957;

"proceedings" means criminal proceedings, including—

    (a) proceedings in the United Kingdom or elsewhere before a court-martial constituted under the Army Act 1955 or the Air Force Act 1955;

    (b) proceedings in the United Kingdom or elsewhere before the Courts-Martial Appeal Court—

        (i) on an appeal from a court-martial so constituted or from a court-martial constituted under the Naval Discipline Act 1957; or

        (ii) on a reference under section 34 of the Courts-Martial (Appeals) Act 1968; and

    (c) proceedings before a Standing Civilian Court; and

"Service court" means a court-martial or a Standing Civilian Court.

(2) In this Part of this Act references to conviction before a Service court are references—

    (a) as regards a court-martial constituted under the Army Act 1955 or the Air Force Act 1955, to a finding of guilty which is, or falls to be treated as, a finding of the court duly confirmed;

    (b) as regards—

        (i) a court-martial; or

        (ii) a disciplinary court,

    constituted under the Naval Discipline Act 1957, to a finding of guilty which is, or falls to be treated as, the finding of the court;

and "convicted" shall be construed accordingly.[64]

(3) Nothing in this Part of this Act shall prejudice any power of a court to exclude evidence (whether by preventing questions from being put or otherwise) at its discretion.

PART IX

POLICE COMPLAINTS AND DISCIPLINE

The Police Complaints Authority

Establishment of the Police Complaints Authority

83.—(1) There shall be an authority, to be known as "the Police Complaints Authority" and in this Act referred to as "the Authority".

(2) Schedule 4 to this Act shall have effect in relation to the Authority.

(3) The Police Complaints Board is hereby abolished.

Handling of complaints etc.

Preliminary

84.—(1) Where a complaint is submitted to the chief officer of police for a police area, it shall be his duty to take any steps that appear to him to be

---

[64] The words "and 'convicted' shall be construed accordingly" do not appear in the Northern Ireland PACE Order, Art. 70(2)(b). They are not necessary in light of s.35 of the Interpretation Act (Northern Ireland) 1954.

desirable for the purpose of obtaining or preserving evidence relating to the conduct complained of.

(2) After performing the duties imposed on him by subsection (1) above, the chief officer shall determine whether he is the appropriate authority in relation to the officer against whom the complaint was made.

(3) If he determines that he is not the appropriate authority, it shall be his duty—

> (a) to send the complaint or, if it was made orally, particulars of it, to the appropriate authority, and
>
> (b) to give notice that he has done so to the person by or on whose behalf the complaint was made.

(4) In this Part of this Act—

> "complaint" means any complaint about the conduct of a police officer which is submitted—
>
> > (a) by a member of the public; or
> >
> > (b) on behalf of a member of the public and with his written consent;
>
> "the appropriate authority" means—
>
> > (a) in relation to an officer of the metropolitan police, the Commissioner of Police of the Metropolis; and
> >
> > (b) in relation to an officer or any other police force—
> >
> > > (i) if he is a senior officer, the police authority for the force's area; and
> > >
> > > (ii) if he is not a senior officer, the chief officer of the force;
>
> "senior officer" means an officer holding a rank above the rank of …[64a] superintendent.
>
> "disciplinary proceedings" means proceedings identified as such by regulations under section 33 of the Police Act 1964.[64b]

(5) Nothing in this Part of this Act has effect in relation to a complaint in so far as it relates to the direction or control of a police force by the chief officer or the person performing the functions of the chief officer.

(6) If any conduct to which a complaint wholly or partly relates is or has been the subject of criminal or disciplinary proceedings, none of the provisions of this Part of this Act which relate to the recording and investigation of complaints have effect in relation to the complaint in so far as it relates to that conduct.

Investigation of complaints: standard procedure

85.—(1) If a chief officer determines that he is the appropriate authority in relation to an officer, about whose conduct a complaint has been made and who is not a senior officer, he shall record it.

(2) After doing so he shall consider whether the complaint is suitable for informal resolution and may appoint an officer from his force to assist him.

(3) If it appears to the chief officer that the complaint is not suitable for informal resolution, he shall appoint an officer from his force or some other force to investigate it formally.

(4) If it appears to him that it is suitable for informal resolution, he shall seek to resolve it informally and may appoint an officer from his force to do so on his behalf.

(5) If it appears to the chief officer, after attempts have been made to resolve a complaint informally—

> (a) that informal resolution of the complaint is impossible; or
>
> (b) that the complaint is for any other reason not suitable for informal resolution,

---

[64a] Amended and added by the Police and Magistrates' Courts Act 1994, Sched. 5, para. 24.
[64b] Amended and added by the Police and Magistrates' Courts Act 1994, Sched. 5, para. 24.

he shall appoint an officer from his force or some other force to investigate it formally.

(6) An officer may not be appointed to investigate a complaint formally if he has previously been appointed to act in relation to it under subsection (4) above.

(7) If a chief officer requests the chief officer of some other force to provide an officer of his force for appointment under subsection (3) or (5) above, that chief officer shall provide an officer to be so appointed.

(8) ...[64c]

(9) Unless investigation is supervised by the Authority under section 89 below, the investigating officer shall submit his report on the investigation to the chief officer.

(10) A complaint is not suitable for informal resolution unless—

    (a) the member of the public concerned gives his consent; and

    (b) the chief officer is satisfied that the conduct complained of, even if proved, would not justify criminal or disciplinary proceedings.[64d]

Investigation of complaints against senior officers

86.—(1) Where a complaint about the conduct of a senior officer—

    (a) is submitted to the appropriate authority; or

    (b) is sent to the appropriate authority under section 84(3) above,

it shall be the appropraite authority's duty to record it and, subject to subsection (2) below, to investigate it.

(2) The appropriate authority may deal with the complaint according to the appropriate authjority's discretion, if satisfied that the conduct complained of, even if proved, would not justify criminal or disciplinary proceedings.[64e]

(3) In any other case the appropriate authority shall appoint an officer from the appropriate authority's force or from some other force to investigate the complaint.

(4) A chief officer shall provide an officer to be appointed, if a request is made to him for one to be appointed under subsection (3) above.

(5) No officer may be appointed unless he is of at least the rank of the officer against whom the complaint is made.

(6) Unless an investigation under this section is supervised by the Authority under section 89 below, the investigating officer shall submit his report on it to the appropriate authority.

References of complaints to Authority

87.—(1) The appropriate authority—

    (a) shall refer to the Authority—

        (i) any complaint alleging that the conduct complained of resulted in the death of or serious injury to some other person; and

        (ii) any complaint of a description specified for the purposes of this section in regulations made by the Secretary of State, and

    (b) may refer to the Authority any complaint which is not required to be referred to them.

(2) The Authority may require the submission to them for consideration of any complaint not referred to them by the appropriate authority, and it

---

[64c] Repealed by the Police and Magistrates' Courts Act 1994, Sched. 5, para. 25 and Sched. 9.
[64d] Amended by the Police and Magistrates' Courts Act 1994, Sched. 5, para. 25 and Sched. 9.
[64e] Amended by the Police and Magistrates' Courts Act 1994, Sched. 5, para. 26.

shall be the appropriate authority's duty to comply with any such requirement not later than the end of a period specified in regulations made by the Secretary of State.

(3) Where a complaint falls to be referred to the Authority under subsection (1)(a) above, it shall be the appropriate authority's duty to refer it to them not later than the end of a period specified in such regulations.

(4) In this Part of this Act "serious injury" means a fracture, damage to an internal organ, impairment of bodily function, a deep cut or a deep laceration.

References of other matters to Authority

88. The appropriate authority may refer to the Authority any matter which—
  (a) appears to the appropriate authority to indicate that an officer may have committed a criminal offence or behaved in a manner which would justify disciplinary proceedings[64f]; and
  (b) is not the subject of a complaint,
if it appears to the appropriate authority that it ought to be referred by reason—
      (i) of its gravity; or
      (ii) of exceptional circumstances.

Supervision of investigations by Authority

89.—(1) The Authority shall supervise the investigation—
  (a) of any complaint alleging that the conduct of a police officer resulted in the death or a serious injury to some other person; and
  (b) of any other description of complaint specified for the purposes of this section in regulations made by the Secretary of State.

(2) The Authority shall supervise the investigation—
  (a) of any complaint the investigation of which they are not required to supervise under subsection (1) above; and
  (b) of any matter referred to them under section 88 above,
if they consider that it is desirable in the public interest that they should supervise that investigation.

(3) Where the Authority have made a determination under this section, it shall be their duty to notify it to the appropriate authority.

(4) Where an investigation is to be supervised by the Authority they may require—
  (a) that no appointment shall be made under section 85(3) or 86(3) above unless they have given notice to the appropriate authority that they approve the officer whom that authority propose to appoint; or
  (b) if such an appointment has already been made and the Authority are not satisfied with the officer appointed, that—
      (i) the appropriate authority shall, as soon as is reasonably practicable, select another officer and notify the Authority that they propose to appoint him; and
      (ii) the appointment shall not be made unless the Authority give notice to the appropriate authority that they approve that officer.

(5) It shall be the duty of the Secretary of State by regulations to provide

---

[64f] Amended by the Police and Magistrates' Courts Act 1994, s.34.

that the Authority shall have power, subject to any restrictions or conditions specified in the regulations, to impose requirements as to a particular investigation additional to any requirements imposed by virtue of subsection (4) above and it shall be the duty of a police officer to comply with any requirement imposed on him by virtue of the regulations.

(6) At the end of an investigation which the Authority have supervised, the investigating officer—

    (a) shall submit a report on the investigation to the Authority and

    (b) shall send a copy to the appropriate authority.

(7) After considering a report submitted to them under subsection (6) above the Authority shall submit an appropriate statement to the appropriate authority.

(8) If it is practicable to do so, the Authority, when submitting the appropriate statement under subsection (7) above, shall send a copy to the officer whose conduct has been investigated.

(9) If—

    (a) the investigation related to a complaint; and

    (b) it is practicable to do so,

the Authority shall also send a copy of the appropriate statement to the person by or on behalf of whom the complaint was made.

(10) In subsection (7) above "appropriate statement" means a statement—

    (a) whether the investigation was or was not conducted to the Authority's satisfaction;

    (b) specifying any respect in which it was not so conducted; and

    (c) dealing with any such other matters as the Secretary of State may be regulations provide.

(11) The power to issue an appropriate statement includes power to issue separate statements in respect of the disciplinary and criminal aspects of an investigation.

(12) No disciplinary proceedings[64g] shall be brought before the appropriate statement is submitted to the appropriate authority.

(13) Subject to subsection (14) below, neither the appropriate authority nor the Director of Public Prosecutions shall bring criminal proceedings before the appropriate statement is submitted to the appropriate authority.

(14) The restriction imposed by subsection (13) above does not apply if it appears to the Director that there are exceptional circumstances which make it undesirable to wait for the submission of the appropriate statement.

Steps to be taken after investigation—general

90.—(1) It shall be the duty of the appropriate authority, on receiving—

    (a) a report concerning the conduct of a senior officer which is submitted to them under section 86(6) above; or

    (b) a copy of a report concerning the conduct of a senior officer which is sent to them under section 89(6) above.

to send a copy of the report to the Director of Public Prosecutions unless the report satisfies them that no criminal offence has been committed.

(2) Nothing in the following provisions of this section or in sections 91 to 93 below has effect in relation to senior officers.

(3) On receiving—

    (a) a report concerning the conduct of an officer who is not a senior officer which is submitted to him under section 85(9) above; or

---

[64g] Amended by the Police and Magistrates' Courts Act 1994, Sched. 5, para. 27.

      (b) a copy of a report concerning the conduct of such an officer which is sent to him under section 89(6) above—

it shall be the duty of a chief officer of police—

          (i) to determine whether the report indicates that a criminal offence may have been committed by a member of the police force for his area; ...[64h]

(4) If the chief officer—

      (a) determines that the report does indicate that a criminal offence may have been committed by a a member of the police force for his area; ...[64i]

he shall send a copy of the report to the Director of Public Prosecutions.

(5) In such cases as may be prescribed by regulations made by the Secretary of State[64j] after the Director has dealt with the question of criminal proceedings, the chief officer shall send the Authority a memorandum, signed by him and stating whether he has brought (or proposes to bring) disciplinary proceedings in respect of the conduct which was the subject of the investigation and, if not, giving his reasons.[64k]

(6) ....[64l]

(7) In such cases as may be prescribed by regulations made by the Secretary of State[64m] if the chief officer considers that the report does not indicate that a criminal offence may have been committed by a member of the police force for his area, he shall send the Authority a memorandum to that effect, signed by him and stating whether he has brought (or proposes to bring) disciplinary proceedings in respect of the conduct which was the subject of the investigation and, if not, giving his reasons.[64n]

(8) ....[64o]

(9) Where the investigation—

      (a) related to conduct which was the subject of a complaint; and

      (b) was not supervised by the authority,

then, if the chief officer is required by virtue of regulations under subsections (5) or (7) above to send the Authority a memorandum, he shall at the same time send them a copy of the complaint, or of the record of the complaint, and a copy of the report of the investigation.[64p]

(10) Subject to section 93(6) below—

      (a) if a chief officer's memorandum states that he proposes to bring disciplinary proceedings, it shall be his duty to bring and proceed with them; and[64q]

      (b) if such a memorandum states that he has brought such proceedings,[64r] it shall be his duty to proceed with them.

Steps to be taken where accused has admitted charges

    91. ....[64s]

Powers of Authority to direct reference of reports etc. to Director of Public Prosecutions

    92. ....[64t]

[64h-i] Repealed by the Police and Magistrates' Courts Act 1994, s.35 and Sched. 9.
[64j-k] Amended by the Police and Magistrates' Courts Act 1994, s.35(4).
[64l] These words cease to have effect by way of the Police and Magistrates' Courts Act 1994, s.35 and Sched. 9.
[64m-n] Amended by the Police and Magistrates' Courts Act 1994, s.35(6).
[64o] Repealed by the Police and Magistrates' Courts Act 1994, s.35 and Sched. 9.
[64p] Amended by the Police and Magistrates' Courts Act 1994, s.34(8).
[64q-r] Amended by the Police and Magistrates' Courts Act 1994, s.35(9).
[64s] Repealed by the Police and Magistrates' Courts Act 1994, Sched. 5, para. 28 and Sched. 9.
[64t] Repealed by the Police and Magistrates' Courts Act 1994, s.37 and Sched. 9.

Powers of Authority as to disciplinary charges

93.—(1) Where a memorandum under section 90 above states that a chief officer of police has not brought disciplinary proceedings or does not propose to do so, the Authority may recommend him to bring such proceedings.[64u]

(2) Subject to subsection (6) below, a chief officer may not discontinue disciplinary proceedings that he has brought[64v] in accordance with a recommendation under subsection (1) above.

(3) If after the Authority have made a recommendation under this section and consulted the chief officer he is still unwilling to bring disciplinary proceedings, they may direct him to do so.[64w]

(4) Where the Authority give a chief officer a direction under this section, they shall furnish him with a written statement of their reasons for doing so.

(5) Subject to subsection (6) below, it shall be the duty of a chief officer to comply with[64x] such a direction.

(6) The authority may withdraw a direction given under this section.[64y]

(7) A chief officer shall—

    (a) advise the Authority of what action he has taken in response to a recommendation or direction under this section, and

    (b) furnish the Authority with such other information as they may reasonably require for the purpose of discharging their functions under this section.[64z]

(8) ....[64za]

Disciplinary tribunals

94. ....[65]

Information as to the manner of dealing with complaints

95. Every police authority in carrying out their duty with respect to the maintenance of an efficient and effective[65a] police force, and inspectors of constabulary in carrying out their duties with respect to the efficiency and effectiveness[65b] of any police force, shall keep themselves informed as to the working of sections 84 to 93 above in relation to the force.

Constabularies maintained by authorities other than police authorities

96.—(1) An agreement for the establishment in relation to any body of constables maintained by an authority other than a police authority of procedures corresponding or similar[65c] to any of those established by or by virtue of this Part of this Act may, with the approval of the Secretary of State, be made between the Authority and the authority maintaining the body of constables.

(2) Where no such procedures are in force in relation to any body of constables, the Secretary of State may by order establish such procedures.

(3) An agreement under this section may at any time be varied or terminated with the approval of the Secretary of State.

(4) Before making an order under this section the Secretary of State shall consult—

[64u–za] Amended by the Police and Magistrates' Courts Act 1994, s.36.
[65] Repealed by the Police and Magistrates' Courts Act 1994, s.37 and Sched. 9. See now Sched. 3.
[65a–b] Amended by the Police and Magistrates' Courts Act 1994, Sched. 5, para. 29.
[65c] Amended by the Police and Magistrates' Courts Act 1994, Sched. 5, para. 30.

(a) the Authority; and

(b) the authority maintaining the body of constables to whom the order would relate.

(5) The power to make orders under this section shall be exercisable by statutory instrument; and any statutory instrument containing such an order shall be subject to annulment in pursuance of a resolution of either House of Parliament.

(6) Nothing in any other enactment shall prevent an authority who maintain a body of constables from carrying into effect procedures established by virtue of this section.

(7) No such procedures shall have effect in relation to anything done by a constable outside England and Wales.

Reports

97.—(1) The Authority shall, at the request of the Secretary of State, report to him on such matters relating generally to their functions as the Secretary of State may specify, and the Auhority may for that purpose carry out research into any such matters.

(2) The Authority may make a report to the Secretary of State on any matters coming to their notice under this Part of this Act to which they consider that his attention should be drawn by reason of their gravity or of other exceptional circumstances; and the Authority shall send a copy of any such report to the police authority and to the chief officer of police of any police force which appears to the Authority to be concerned or, if the report concerns any such body of constables as is mentioned in section 96 above, to the authority or body maintaining it and the officer having the direction and the control of it.

(3) As soon as practicable after the end of each calendar year the Authority shall make to the Secretary of State a report on the discharge of their functions during that year.

(4) ....[65d]

(5) The Secretary of State shall lay before Parliament a copy of every report received by him under this section and shall cause every such report to be published.

(6) The Authority shall send to every police authority—

(a) a copy of every report made by the Authority under subsection (3) above; and

(b) any statistical or other general information which relates to the year dealt with by the report and to the area of that authority and which the Authority consider should be brought to the police authority's attention in connection with their functions under section 95 above.

Restriction on disclosure of information

98.—(1) No information received by the Authority in connection with any of their functions under section 84 to 97 above or regulations made by virtue of section 99 below shall be disclosed by any person who is or has been a member, officer or servant of the Authority except—

(a) to the Secretary of State or to a member, officer or servant of the Authority or, so far as may be necessary for the proper discharge of the functions of the Authority, to other persons;

(b) for the purposes of any criminal, civil or disciplinary proceedings; or

---

[65d] Repealed by the Police and Magistrates' Courts Act 1994, s.37 and Sched. 9.

(c) in the form of a summary or other general statement made by the Authority which does not identify the person from whom the information was received or any person to whom it relates.

(2) Any person who discloses information in contravention of this section shall be guilty of an offence and liable on summary conviction to a fine of an amount not exceeding level 5 on the standard scale....[65e]

Regulations

99.—(1) The Secretary of State may make regulations as to the procedure to be followed under this Part of this Act.

(2) It shall be the duty of the Secretary of State to provide by regulations—

(a) that, subject to such exceptions as may be specified by the regulations, a chief officer of police shall furnish, in accordance with such procedure as may be so specified, a copy of, or of the record of, a complaint against a member of the police force for his area—

(i) to the person by or on behalf of whom the complaint was made; and

(ii) to the officer against whom it was made;

(b) procedures for the informal resolution of complaints of such descriptions as may be specified in the regulations, and for giving the person who made the complaint a record of the outcome of any such procedure if he applies for one within such period as the regulations may provide;

(c) procedures for giving a police officer against whom a complaint is made which falls to be resolved informally an opportunity to comment orally or in writing on the complaint;

(d) for cases in which any provision of this Part of this Act is not to apply where a complaint, other than a complaint which falls to be resolved by an informal procedure, is withdrawn or the complainant indicates that he does not wish any further steps to be taken;

(e) for enabling the Authority to dispense with any requirement of this Part of this Act;

(ea) for enabling the Authority to relinquish the supervision of the investigation of any complaint or other matter[65f];

(f) procedures for the reference or submission of complaints or other matters to the Authority;

(g) for the time within which the Authority are to give a notification under section 89(3) above;

(h) that the Authority shall be supplied with such information or documents of such description as may be specified in the regulations at such time or in such circumstances as may be so specified;

(j) that any action or decision of the Authority which they take in consequence of their receipt of a memorandum under section 90 above shall be notified if it is an action or decision of a description specified in the regulations, to the person concerned and that, in connection with such a notification, the Authority shall have power to furnish him with any relevant information;

(k) that chief officers of police shall have power to delegate any functions conferred on them by or by virtue of the foregoing provisions of this Part of this Act....[65g]

[65e] Repealed by the Statute Law (Repeals) Act 1993, Sched. 1.
[65f] Added by the Police and Magistrates' Courts Act 1994, Sched. 5, para. 31.
[65g] Words repealed by the Police and Magistrates' Courts Act 1994, Sched. 9.

Regulations—supplementary

100.—(1) Regulations under this Part of this Act may make different provision for different circumstances and may authorise the Secretary of State to make provision for any purposes specified in the regulations.

(2) Before making regulations under this Part of this Act the Secretary of State shall furnish a draft of the regulations to the Police Advisory Board for England and Wales, and take into consideration any representations made by that Board.

(3) Any power to make regulations under this Part of this Act shall be exercisable by statutory instrument.

(4) Subject to subsection (5) below, regulations under this Part of this Act shall be subject to annulment in pursuance of a resolution of either House of Parliament.

(5) Regulations to which this subsection applies shall not be made unless a draft of them has been approved by resolution of each House of Parliament.

(6) Subsection (5) above applies to regulations made by virtue—

   (aa) of section 90(5) or (7) above;

   (a) of section 87(1)(a)(ii) or 89(1)(b) or (5) above;

   (b) of section 99(2)(b), (e) or (ea).[65h]

Amendments of discipline provisions

Discipline regulations

101. .....[65i]

Representation at disciplinary hearings

102.—(1) A police officer of the rank of superintendent or below may not be dismissed, required to resign or reduced in rank by a decision taken in proceedings under regulations made in accordance with section 33(3)(a) of the Police Act 1964 unless he has been given an opportunity to elect to be legally represented at any hearing held in the course of those proceedings.

(2) Where an officer makes an election to which subsection (1) above refers, he may be represented at the hearing, at his option, either by counsel or by a solicitor.

(3) Except in a case where an officer of the rank of superintendent or below has been given an opportunity to elect to be legally represented and has so elected, he may be represented at the hearing only by another member of a police force.

(4) Regulations under section 33 of the Police Act 1964 shall specify—

   (a) a procedure for notifying an officer of the effect of subsections (1) to (3) above,

   (b) when he is to be notified of the effect of those subsections, and

   (c) when he is to give notice whether he wishes to be legally represented at the hearing.

(5) If an officer—

   (a) fails without reasonable cause to give notice in accordance with the regulations that he wishes to be legally represented; or

   (b) gives notice in accordance with the regulations that he does not wish to be legally represented,

he may be dismissed, required to resign or reduced in rank without his being legally represented.

(6) If an officer has given notice in accordance with the regulations that he

---

[65h] Amended by the Police and Magistrates' Courts Act 1994, Sched. 5, para. 32.

[65i] Repealed by the Police and Magistrates' Courts Act 1994, s.37 and Sched. 9.

wishes to be legally represented, the case against him may be presented by counsel or a solicitor whether or not he is actually so represented.[65j]

Disciplinary appeals

103. .... [65k]

General

Restrictions on subsequent proceedings

104.—(1) .... [65l]

(2) .... [65m]

(3) Subject to subsection (4) below, no statement made by any person for the purpose of the informal resolution of a complaint shall be admissible in any subsequent criminal, civil or disciplinary proceedings.

(4) A statement is not rendered inadmissible by subsection (3) above if it consists of or includes an admission relating to a matter which does not fall to be resolved informally.

Guidelines concerning discipline, complaints etc.

105.—(1) The Secretary of State may issue guidance to police authorities,[65n] to chief officers of police and to other police officers concerning the discharge of their functions—

(a) under this Part of this Act, and

(b) under regulations made under section 33 of the Police Act 1964 in relation to the matters mentioned in subsection (2)(e) of that section[65o];

and police authorities and[65p] police officers shall have regard to any such guidance in the discharge of their functions.

(2) Guidance may not be issued under subsection (1) above in relation to the handling of a particular case.

(3) A failure on the part of a police authority or a police officer to have regard to any guidance issued under subsection (1) above shall be admissible in evidence on any appeal from a decision taken in proceedings under regulations made in accordance with subsection (3) of section 33 of the Police Act 1964.[65q]

(4) In discharging their functions under section 93 above the Authority shall have regard to any guidance given to them by the Secretary of State with respect to such matters[65r] repealed as are for the time being the subject of guidance under subsection (1) above, and shall have regard in particular, but without prejudice to the generality of this subsection, to any such guidance as to the principles to be applied in cases that involve any question of criminal proceedings .... [65s]

(5) The report of the Authority under section 97(3) above shall contain a statement of any guidance given to the Authority under subsection (4) above during the year to which the report relates.

[65j] The new text of s.102 was substituted for the original version by the Police and Magistrates' Courts Act 1994, Sched. 5, para. 33.

[65k] Repealed by the Police and Magistrates' Courts Act 1994, Sched. 9.

[65l-m] Repealed by the Police and Magistrates' Courts Act 1994, s.37 and Sched. 9.

[65n-p] Substituted and amended by the Police and Magistrates' Courts Act 1994, Sched. 5, para. 34.

[65q] Substituted by the Police and Magistrates' Courts Act 1994, Sched. 5, para. 34.

[65r-s] Repealed by the Police and Magistrates' Courts Act 1994, Sched. 5, para. 34 and Sched. 9.

PART X

POLICE—GENERAL

Arrangements for obtaining the views of the community on policing

106.—(1) Arrangements shall be made in each police area for obtaining the views of people in that area about matters concerning the policing of the area and for obtaining their co-operation with the police in preventing crime in the area.

(2) Except as provided by subsections (3) to (7) below, arrangements for each police area shall be made by the police authority after consulting the chief constable as to the arrangements that would be appropriate.

(3) The Secretary of State shall issue guidance to the Commissioner of Police of the Metropolis concerning arrangements for the Metropolitan Police District; and the Commissioner shall make such arrangements after taking account of that guidance.

(4) The Commission shall make separate arrangements—
    (a) for each London borough;
    (b) for each district which falls wholly within the Metropolitan Police District; and
    (c) for each part of a district which falls partly within that District.

(5) The Commissioner shall consult the council of each London borough as to the arrangements that would be appropriate for the borough.

(6) The Commissioner shall consult the council of each such district as is mentioned in subsection (4)(b) above as to the arrangements that would be appropriate for the district.

(7) The Commissioner shall consult the council of each such district as is mentioned in subsection (4)(c) above as to the arrangements that would be appropriate for the part of the district for which it falls to him to make arrangements.

(8) The Common Council of the City of London shall issue guidance to the Commissioner of Police for the City of London concerning arrangements for the City; and the Commissioner shall make such arrangements after taking account of that guidance.

(9) A body or person whose duty it is to make arrangements under this section shall review the arrangements so made from time to time.

(10) If it appears to the Secretary of State that arrangements in a police area are not adequate for the purposes set out in subsection (1) above, he may require the body or person whose duty it is to make arrangements in that area to submit a report to him concerning the arrangements.

(11) After considering the report the Secretary of State may require the body or person who submitted it to review the arrangements and submit a further report to him concerning them.

(12) A body or person whose duty it is to make arrangements shall be under the same duties to consult when reviewing arrangements as when making them.

Police officers performing duties of higher rank

107.—(1) For the purpose of any provision of this Act or any other Act under which a power in respect of the investigation of offences or the treatment of persons in police custody is exercisable only by or with the authority of a police officer of at least the rank of superintendent, an officer of the rank of chief inspector shall be treated as holding the rank of superintendent if

   (a) he has been authorised by an officer holding a rank above the rank of superintendent to exercise the power or, as the case may be, to give his authority for its exercise, or

   (b) he is acting during the absence of an officer holding the rank of superintendent who has authorised him, for the duration of that absence, to exercise the power or, as the case may be, to give his authority for its exercise.[65t]

(2) For the purpose of any provsion of this Act or any other Act under which such a power is exercisable only by or with the authority of an officer of at least the rank of inspector, an officer of the rank of sergeant shall be treated as holding the rank of inspector if he has been authorised by an officer of at least the rank of superintendent[65u] to exercise the power or, as the case may be, to give his authority for its exercise.

Deputy chief constables

108.—(1) The office of deputy chief constable is hereby abolished.

(2) ....[65v]

(3) ....[65w]

(4) In section 5 of the Police (Scotland) Act 1967—

   (a) in subsection (1), after the word "a" there shall be inserted the words "person holding the rank of";

   (b) subsection (3) shall be omitted; and

   (c) in subsection (5), for the words from the beginning to "of", in the second place where it occurs, there shall be substituted the words "Appointments or promotions to the rank of deputy chief constable or."

(5) The following section shall be inserted after that section—

"Deputy chief constables—supplementary

5A.—(1) Any police force may include more than one person holding the rank of deputy chief constable, but only if the additional person or persons holding that rank—

   (a) was a deputy chief constable before a period—

      (i) of central service; or

      (ii) of overseas service, as defined in section 3 of the Police (Overseas Service) Act 1945; or

      (iii) of service in pursuance of an appointment under section 10 of the Overseas Development and Co-operation Act 1980 as an officer to whom that section applied; or

   (b) became a deputy chief constable by virtue of section 23(2) of this Act.

(2) If there is more than one person in a police force who holds the rank of deputy chief constable, one of the persons who hold it shall be designated as the officer having the powers and duties conferred on a deputy chief constable by section 5(1) of this Act.

(3) A person shall be designated under subsection (2) of this section by the police authority after consultation with the chief constable and subject to the approval of the Secretary of State."

(6) In ...[65x] section 23(2) of the Police (Scotland) Act 1967 (under ...[65y] which a chief constable affected by an amalgamation holds the rank of

---

[65t-u] Amended by the Police and Magistrates' Courts Act 1994, Sched. 5, para. 35.

[65v-w] Repealed by the Police and Magistrates' Courts Act 1994, Sched. 9.

[65x-y] Repealed by the Police and Magistrates' Courts Act 1994, Sched. 9.

assistant chief constable) for the word "assistant" thee shall be substituted the word "deputy".

Amendments relating to Police Federations

109. In section 44 of the Police Act 1964—
    (a) in subsection (1), for the word "and", in the last place where it occurs, there shall be substituted the words "affecting individuals, except as provided by subsection (1A) below, and questions of";

    (b) the following subsections shall be inserted after that subsection—

        "(1A) A Police Federation may represent a member of a police force at any disciplinary proceedings or on an appeal from any such proceedings.

        (1B) Except on an appeal to the Secretary of State or as provided by section 102 of the Police and Criminal Evidence Act 1984, a member of a police force may only be represented under subsection (1A) above by another member of a police force."; and

    (c) in subsection (3), after the word "Federations", in the first place where it occurs, there shall be inserted the words "or authorise the Federations to make rules concerning such matters relating to their constitution and proceedings as may be spcified in the regulations.".

Functions of special constables in Scotland

110. Subsection (6) of section 17 of the Police (Scotland) Act 1967 (restriction on functions of special constables) is hereby repealed.

Regulations for Police Forces and Police Cadets—Scotland

111.—(1) In section 26 of the Police (Scotland) Act 1967 (regulations as to government and administration of police forces)—
    (a) after subsection (1) there shall be inserted the following subsection—

        "(1A) Regulations under this section may authorise the Secretary of State, the police authority or the chief constable to make provision for any purpose specified in the regulations."; and

    (b) at the end there shall be inserted the following subsection—

        "(10) Any statutory instrument made under this section shall be subject to annulment in pursuance of a resolution of either House of Parliament."

(2) In section 27 of the said Act of 1967 (regulations for police cadets) in subsection (3) for the word "(9)" there shall be substituted the words "(1A), (9) and (10)."

Metropolitan police officers

112.—(1) An officer belonging to the metropolitan police force who is assigned to the protection of any person or property in Scotland shall in the discharge of that duty have the powers and privileges of a constable of a police force maintained under the Police (Scotland) Act 1967.

(2) An officer belonging to the metropolitan police force who is assigned to the protection of any person or property in Northern Ireland shall in the discharge of that duty have the powers and privileges of a constable of the Royal Ulster Constabulary.

PART XI

MISCELLANEOUS AND SUPPLEMENTARY

Application of Act to Armed Forces

113.—(1) The Secretary of State may by order direct that any provision of this Act which relates to the investigation of offences conducted by police officers or to persons detained by the police shall apply, subject to such modifications as he may specify, to investigations of offences conducted under the Army Act 1955, the Air Force Act 1955 or the Naval Discipline Act 1957 or to persons under arrest under any of those Acts.

(2) Section 67(9) above shall not have effect in relation to investigations of an offence under the Army Act 1955, the Air Force Act 1955 or the Naval Discipline Act 1957.

(3) The Secretary of State shall issue a code of practice or a number of such codes, for persons other than police officers who are concerned with enquiries into offences under the Army Act 1955, the Air Force Act 1955 or the Naval Discipline Act 1957.

(4) Without prejudice to the generality of subsection (3) above, a code issued under that subsection may contain provisions, in connection with enquiries into such offences, as to the following matters—

    (a) the tape-recording of interviews;

    (b) searches of persons and premises; and

    (c) the seizure of things found on searches.

(5) If the Secretary of State lays before both Houses of Parliament a draft of a code of practice under this section, he may by order bring the code into operation.

(6) An order bringing a code of practice into operation may contain such transitional provisions or savings as appear to the Secretary of State to be necessary or expedient in connection with the code of practice thereby brought into operation.

(7) The Secretary of State may from time to time revise the whole or any part of a code of practice issued under this section and issue that revised code, and the foregoing provisions of this section shall apply (with appropriate modifications) to such a revised code as they apply to the first issue of a code.

(8) A failure on the part of any person to comply with any provision of a code of practice issued under this section shall not of itself render him liable to any criminal or civil proceedings except those to which this subsection applies.

(9) Subsection (8) applies—

    (a) to proceedings under any provision of the Army Act 1955 or the Air Force Act 1955 other than section 70; and

    (b) to proceedings under any provision of the Naval Discipline Act 1957 other than section 42.

(10) In all criminal and civil proceedings any such code shall be admissible in evidence, and if any provision of such a code appears to the court or tribunal conducting the proceedings to be relevant to any question arising in the proceedings it shall be taken into account in determining that question.

(11) In subsection (10) above "criminal proceedings" includes—

    (a) proceedings in the United Kingdom or elsewhere before a court-martial constituted under the Army Act 1955, the Air Force Act 1955 or the Naval Discipline Act 1957 or a disciplinary court constituted under section 50 of the said Act of 1957;

    (b) proceedings before the Courts-Martial Appeal Court; and

    (c) proceedings before a Standing Civilian Court.

(12) Parts VII and VIII of this Act have effect for the purposes of proceedings—
    (a) before a court-martial constituted under the Army Act 1955 or the Air Force Act 1955
    (b) before the Courts-Martial Appeal Court; and
    (c) before a Standing Civilian Court,
subject to any modifications which the Secretary of State may by order specify.

(13) An order under this section shall be made by statutory instrument and shall be subject to annulment in pursuance of a resolution of either House of Parliament.

Application of Act to Customs and Excise

114.—(1) "Arrested", "arresting", "arrest" and "to arrest" shall respectively be substituted for "detained", "detaining", "detention" and "to detain" wherever in the customs and excise Acts, as defined in section 1(1) of the Customs and Excise Management Act 1979, those words are used in relation to persons.

(2) The Treasury may by order direct—
    (a) that any provision of this Act which relates to the investigation of offences by police officers or to persons detained by the police shall apply, subject to such modifications as the order may specify, to investigations by officers of Customs and Excise of offences which relate to assigned matters, as defined in section 1 of the Customs and Excise Management Act 1979, or to persons detained by such officers; and
    (b) that, in relation to investigations of offences conducted by officers of Customs and Excise,
        (i) this Act shall have effect as if the following section were inserted after section 14—
        "Exception for customs and excise
        14A. Material in the possession of a person who acquired or created it in the course of any trade, business, profession or other occupation or for the purpose of any paid or unpaid office and which relates to an assigned matter, as defined in section 1 of the Customs and Excise Management Act 1979, is neither excluded material nor special procedure material for the purposes of any enactment such as is mentioned in section 9(2) above."; and
        (ii) section 55 above shall have effect as if it related only to things such as are mentioned in subsection (1)(a) of that section.
    and
    (c) that in relation to customs detention (as defined in any order made under this subsection) the Bail Act 1976 shall have effect as if references in it to a constable were references to an officer of Customs and Excise of such grade as may be specified in the order.[65z]

(3) Nothing in any order under subsection (2) above shall be taken to limit any powers exercisable under section 164 of the Customs and Excise Management Act 1979.

(4) In this section "officers of Customs and Excise" means officers commissioned by the Commissioners of Customs and Excise under section 6(3) of the Customs and Excise Management Act 1979.

[65z] (c) was added by the Criminal Justice Act 1988, s.150 as from date to be appointed.

(5) An order under this section shall be made by statutory instrument and shall be subject to annulment in pursuance of a resolution of either House of Parliament.

Expenses

115. Any expenses of a Minister of the Crown incurred in consequence of the provisions of this Act, including any increase attributable to those provisions in sums payable under any other Act, shall be defrayed out of money provided by Parliament.

Meaning of "serious arrestable offence"

116.—(1) This section has effect for determining whether an offence is a serious arrestable offence for the purposes of this Act.

(2) The following arrestable offences are always serious—
    (a) an offence (whether at common law or under any enactment) specified in Part I of Schedule 5 to this Act; and
    (aa) ...[66]
    (b) an offence under an enactment specified in Part II of that Schedule;
    (c) any of the offences mentioned in paragraphs (a) to (f) of section 1(3) of the Drug Trafficking Act 1994.[66a]

(3) Subject to subsections (4) and (5) below, any other arrestable offence is serious only if its commission
    (a) has led to any of the consequences specifed in subsection (6) below; or
    (b) is intended to lead to any of those consequences.

(4) An arrestable offence which consists of making a threat is serious if carrying out the threat would be likely to lead to any of the consequences specified in subsection (6) below.

(5) An offence under section 2, 8, 9, 10 or 11 of the Prevention of Terrorism (Temporary Provisions) Act 1989 is always a serious arrestable offence for the purposes of section 56 or 58 above; and an attempt or conspiracy to commit any such offence is also always a serious arrestable offence for those purposes.[67]

(6) The consequences mentioned in subsections (3) and (4) above are—
    (a) serious harm to the security of the State or to public order;
    (b) serious interference with the administration of justice or with the investigation of offences or of a particular offence;
    (c) the death of any person;
    (d) serious injury to any person;
    (e) substantial financial gain to any person; and
    (f) serious financial loss to any person.

(7) Loss is serious for the purposes of this section if, having regard to all the circumstances, it is serious for the person who suffers it.

(8) In this section "injury" includes any disease and any impairment of a person's physical or mental condition.

Power of constable to use reasonable force

117. Where any provision of this Act—
    (a) confers a power on a constable; and
    (b) does not provide that the power may only be exercised with the consent of some person, other than a police officer,

---

[66] Repealed by the Drug Trafficking Act 1994, Sched. 1, para. 9 and Sched. 3.
[66a] Added by the Drug Trafficking Act 1994, Sched. 1, para. 9.
[67] Amended by the Prevention of Terrorism (Temporary Provisions) Act 1989, Sched. 8, para. 6(7).

the officer may use reasonable force, if necessary, in the exercise of the power.

General interpretation

118.—(1) In this Act—

"arrestable offence" has the meaning assigned to it by section 24 above;

"designated police station" has the meaning assigned to it by section 35 above;

"document" has the same meaning as in Part I of the Civil Evidence Act 1968;

"intimate search" ...[67a];

"item subject to legal privilege" has the meaning assigned to it by section 10 above;

"parent or guardian" means—

(a) in the case of a child or young person in the care of a local authority, that authority; ...[67b]

"premises" has the meaning assigned to it by section 23 above;

"recordable offence" means any offence to which regulations under section 27 above apply;

"vessel" includes any ship, boat, raft or other apparatus constructed or adapted for floating on water.

(2) A person is in police detention for the purposes of this Act if

(a) he has been taken to a police station after being arrested for an offence or after being arrested under section 14 of the Prevention of Terrorism (Temporary Provisions) Act 1989 or under paragraph 6 of Schedule 5 to that Act by an examining officer who is a constable[68]; or

(b) he is arrested at a police station after attending voluntarily at the station or accompanying a constable to it; and—

(a) is detained there; or

(b) is detained elsewhere in the charge of a constable,

except that a person who is at a court after being charged is not in police detention for those purposes.

Amendments and repeals

119.—(1) The enactments mentioned in Schedule 6 to this Act shall have effect with the amendments there specified.

(2) The enactments mentioned in Schedule 7 to this Act (which include enactments already obsolete or unnecessary) are repealed to the extent specified in the third column of that Schedule.

(3) The repeals in Parts II and IV of Schedule 7 to this Act have effect only in relation to criminal proceedings.

Extent

120.—(1) Subject to the following provisions of this section, this Act extends to England and Wales only.

(2) The following extend to Scotland only—

section 108(4) and (5);

[67a] Repealed by the Criminal Justice and Public Order Act 1994, Sched. 11.

[67b] Repealed by the Children Act 1989, Sched. 15.

[68] Amended by the Prevention of Terrorism (Temporary Provisions) Act 1989, Sched. 8, para. 6(8).

section 110;
section 111;
section 112(1); and
section 119(2), so far as it relates to the provisions of the Pedlars Act 1871 repealed by Part VI of Schedule 7.
(3) The following extend to Northern Ireland only—
section 6(4); and
section 112(2).
(4) The following extend to England and Wales and Scotland—
section 6(1) and (2);
section 7;
section 83(2), so far as it relates to paragraph 8 of Schedule 4;
section 108(1) and (6);
section 109; and
section 119(2), so far as it relates to section 19 of the Pedlars Act 1871.
(5) The following extend to England and Wales, Scotland and Northern Ireland—
section 6(3);
section 83(2), so far as it relates to paragraph 7(1) of Schedule 4; and
section 114(1).
(6) So far as they relate to proceedings before courts-martial and Standing Civilian Courts, the relevant provisions extend to any place at which such proceedings may be held:
(7) So far as they relate to proceedings before the Courts-Martial Appeal Court, the relevant provisions extend to any place at which such proceedings may be held.
(8) In this section "the relevant provisions" means—
  (a) subsection (11) of section 67 above;
  (b) subsection (12) of that section so far as it relates to subsection (11);
      (c) Parts VII and VIII of this Act except paragraph 10 of Schedule 3;
  (d) subsections (2), (8) to (12) of section 113 above; and
  (e) subsection (13) of that section, so far as it relates to an order under subsection (12).
(9) Except as provided by the foregoing provisions of this section, section 113 above extends to any place to which the Army Act 1955, the Air Force Act 1955 or the Naval Discipline Act 1957 extends.
(9A) Section 119(1), so far as it relates to any provision amended by Part II of Schedule 6, extends to any place to which that provision extends.
(10) Section 119(2), so far as it relates—
  (a) to any provision contained in—
      the Army Act 1955;
      the Air Force Act 1955;
      the Armed Forces Act 1981, or
      the Value Added Tax Act 1983,
  (b) to any provision mentioned in Part VI of Schedule 7, other than section 18 of the Pedlars Act 1871,
extends to any place to which that provision extends.
(11) So far as any of the following—
section 115;
in section 118; the definition of "document";
this section;
section 121, and
section 122,
has effect in relation to any other provision of this Act, it extends to any place to which that provision extends.

Commencement

121.—(1) This Act, except section 120 above, this section and section 122 below, shall come into operation on such day as the Secretary of State may by order made by statutory instrument appoint, and different days may be so appointed for different provisions and for different purposes.

(2) Different days may be appointed under this section for the coming into force of section 60 above in different areas.

(3) When an order under this section provides by virtue of subsection (2) above that section 60 above shall come into force in an area specified in the order, the duty imposed on the Secretary of State by that section shall be construed as a duty to make an order under it in relation to interviews in that area.

(4) An order under this section may make such transitional provision as appears to the Secretary of State to be necessary or expedient in connection with the provisions thereby brought into operation.

Short title

122. This Act may be cited as the Police and Criminal Evidence Act 1984.

SCHEDULES

Section 9   **SCHEDULE 1**

SPECIAL PROCEDURE

Making of orders by circuit judge

1. If on an application made by a constable a circuit judge is satisfied that one or other of the sets of access conditions is fulfilled, he may make an order under paragraph 4 below.

2. The first set of access conditions is fulfilled if—
  (a) there are reasonable grounds for believing—
    (i) that a serious arrestable offence has been committed;
    (ii) that there is material which consists of special procedure material or includes special procedure material and does not also include excluded material on premises specified in the application;
    (iii) that the material is likely to be of substantial value (whether by itself or together with other material) to the investigation in connection with which the application is made; and
    (iv) that the material is likely to be relevant evidence;
  (b) other methods of obtaining the material—
    (i) have been tried without success; or
    (ii) have not been tried because it appeared that they were bound to fail; and
  (c) it is in the public interest, having regard—
    (i) to the benefit likely to accrue to the investigation if the material is obtained; and
    (ii) to the circumstances under which the person in possession of the material holds it, that the material should be produced or that access to it should be given.

3. The second set of access conditions is fulfilled if—
  (a) there are reasonable grounds for believing that there is material which consists of or includes excluded material or special procedure material on premises specified in the application;
  (b) but for section 9(2) above a search of the premises for that material could have been authorised by the issue of a warrant to a constable under an enactment other than this Schedule; and
  (c) the issue of such a warrant would have been appropriate.

4. An order under this paragraph is an order that the person who appears to the circuit judge to be in possession of the material to which the application relates shall—

    (a) produce it to a constable for him to take it away; or

    (b) give a constable access to it,

not later than the end of the period of seven days from the date of the order or the end of such longer period as the order may specify.

5. Where the material consists of information contained in a computer,

    (a) an order under paragraph 4(a) above shall have effect as an order to produce the material in a form in which it can be taken away and in which it is visible and legible, and

    (b) an order under paragraph 4(b) above shall have effect as an order to give a constable access to the material in a form in which it is visible and legible.

6. For the purposes of sections 21 and 22 above material produced in pursuance of an order under paragraph 4(a) above shall be treated as if it were material seized by a constable.

Notices of applications for orders

7. An application for an order under paragraph 4 above shall be made inter partes.

8. Notice of an application for such an order may be served on a person either by delivering it to him or by leaving it as his proper address or by sending it by post to him in a registered letter or by the recorded delivery service.

9. Such a notice may be served—

    (a) on a body corporate, by serving it on the body's secretary or clerk or other similar officer; and

    (b) on a partnership, by serving it on one of the partners.

10. For the purposes of this Schedule, and of section 7 of the Interpretation Act 1978 in its application to this Schedule, the proper address of a person, in the case of secretary or clerk or other similar officer of a body corporate, shall be that of the registered or principal office of that body, in the case of a partner of a firm shall be that of the principal office of the firm, and in any other case shall be the last known address of the person to be served.

11. Where notice of an application for an order under paragraph 4 above has been served on a person, he shall not conceal, destroy, alter or dispose of the material to which the application relates except—

    (a) with the leave of a judge; or

    (b) with the written permission of a constable,

until—

      (i) the application is dismissed or abandoned; or

      (ii) he has complied with an order under paragraph 4 above made on the application.

Issue of warrants by circuit judge

12. If on an application made by a constable a circuit judge—

    (a) is satisfied—

      (i) that either set of access conditions is fulfilled; and

      (ii) that any of the further conditions set out in paragraph 14 below is also fulfilled; or

    (b) is satisfied—

      (i) that the second set of access conditions is fulfilled; and

      (ii) that an order under paragraph 4 above relating to the material has not been complied with,

he may issue a warrant authorising a constable to enter and search the premises.

13. A constable may seize and retain anything for which a search has been authorised under paragraph 12 above.

14. The further conditions mentioned in paragraph 12(a)(ii) above are—

    (a) that it is not practicable to communicate with any person entitled to grant entry to the premises to which the application relates;

    (b) that it is practicable to communicate with a person entitled to grant entry to the premises but it is not practicable to communicate with any person entitled to grant access to the material;

    (c) that the material contains information which—

      (i) is subject to a restriction or obligation such as is mentioned in section 11(2)(b) above; and

(ii) is likely to be disclosed in breach of it if a warrant is not issued;

(d) that service of a notice of an application for an order under paragraph 4 above may seriously prejudice the investigation.

15.—(1) If a person fails to comply with an order under paragraph 4 above, a circuit judge may deal with him as if he had committed a contempt of the Crown Court.

(2) Any enactment relating to contempt of the Crown Court shall have effect in relation to such a failure as if it were such a contempt.

Costs

16. The costs of any application under this Schedule and of anything done or to be done in pursuance of an order made under it shall be in the discretion of the judge.

Section 26   **SCHEDULE 2**

PRESERVED POWERS OF ARREST[69]

1892 c.43.	Section 17(2) of the Military Lands Act 1892.
1911 c.27.	Section 12(1) of the Protection of Animals Act 1911.
1920 c.55.	Section 2 of the Emergency Powers Act 1920.
1936 c.6.	Section 7(3) of the Public Order Act 1936.
1952 c.52.	Section 49 of the Prison Act 1952.
1952 c.67.	Section 13 of the Visiting Forces Act 1952.
1955 c.18.	Sections 186 and 190B of the Army Act 1955.
1955 c.19.	Sections 186 and 190B of the Air Force Act 1955.
1957 c.53.	Sections 104 and 105 of the Naval Discipline Act 1957.
1959 c.37.	Section 1(3) of the Street Offences Act 1959.
1969 c.54.	Section 32 of the Children and Young Persons Act 1969. As amended by the Children Act 1989, Sched. 13, para. 55.
1971 c.77.	Section 24(2) of the Immigration Act 1971 and paragraphs 17, 24 and 33 of Schedule 2 and paragraph 7 of Schedule 3 to that Act.
...[70]	
1976 c.63.	Section 7 of the Bail Act 1976.
1977 c.45.	Sections 6(6), 7(11), 8(4), 9(7) and 10(5) of the Criminal Law Act 1977.
...	The previous entry relating to the Child Care Act 1980 was repealed by the Children Act 1989, Sched. 15.
1980 c.9.	Schedule 5 to the Reserve Forces Act 1980.
1981 c.22.	Sections 60(5) and 61(1) of the Animal Health Act 1981.
1983 c.2.	Rule 36 in Schedule 1 to the Representation of the People Act 1983.[71]
1983 c.20.	Sections 18, 35(10), 36(8), 38(7), 136(1) and 138 of the Mental Health Act 1983.
...[72]	
1984 c.47.	Section 5(5) of the Repatriation of Prisoners Act 1984.

Section 68   **SCHEDULE 3**

PROVISIONS SUPPLEMENTARY TO SECTIONS 68 AND 69

PART I

[Part I and paragraph 13 of the Schedule were repealed by the Criminal Justice Act 1988, Sched. 16. They are replaced by Schedule 2 to the 1988 Act which accompanies sections 23 to 28 of the 1988 Act and is set out below in italics:]

[69] Note a number of additional preserved powers of arrest in Sched. 2 to the Northern Ireland PACE Order.
[70] [The previous entry relating to the Road Traffic Act 1972 was repealed by the Road Traffic (Consequential Provisions) Act 1988, Sched. 1.]
[71] Added by Representation of the People Act 1985, s.25.
[72] [The previous entry relating to the Prevention of Terrorism (Temporary Provisions) Act 1984 was repealed by the 1989 Act of the same name, Sched. 9.]

DOCUMENTARY EVIDENCE—SUPPLEMENTARY

1. Where a statement is admitted as evidence in criminal proceedings by virtue of Part II of this Act—

    (a) any evidence which, if the person making the statement had been called as a witness, would have been admissible as relevant to his credibility as a witness shall be admissible for that purpose in those proceedings;

    (b) evidence may, with the leave of the court, be given of any matter which, if that person had been called as a witness, could have been put to him in cross-examination as relevant to his credibility as a witness but of which evidence could not have been adduced by the cross-examining party; and

    (c) evidence tending to prove that that person, whether before or after making the statement, made (whether orally or not) some other statement which is inconsistent with it shall be admissible for the purpose of showing that he has contradicted himself.

2. A statement which is given in evidence by virtue of Part II of this Act shall not be capable of corroborating evidence given by the person making it.

3. In estimating the weight, if any, to be attached to such a statement regard shall be had to all the circumstances from which any inference can reasonably be drawn as to its accuracy or otherwise.

4. Without prejudice to the generality of any enactment conferring power to make them—

    (a) Crown Court Rules;

    (b) Criminal Appeal Rules; and

    (c) rules under section 144 of the Magistrates' Courts Act 1980,

may make such provision as appears to the authority making any of them to be necessary or expedient for the purposes of Part II of this Act.

5. Expressions used in Part II of this Act and in Part I of the Civil Evidence Act 1968 are to be construed in Part II of this Act in accordance with section 10 of that Act.

6. In Part II of this Act "confession" has the meaning assigned to it by section 82 of the Police and Criminal Evidence Act 1984.

PART II

PROVISIONS SUPPLEMENTARY TO SECTION 69

8. In any proceedings where it is desired to give a statement in evidence in accordance with section 69 above, a certificate—

    (a) identifying the document containing the statement and describing the manner in which it was produced;

    (b) giving such particulars of any device involved in the production of that document as may be appropriate for the purpose of showing that the document was produced by a computer;

    (c) dealing with any of the matters mentioned in subsection (1) of section 69 above; and

    (d) purporting to be signed by a person occupying a responsible position in relation to the operation of the computer,

shall be evidence of anything stated in it; and for the purposes of this paragraph it shall be sufficient for a matter to be stated to the best of the knowledge and belief of the person stating it.

9. Notwithstanding paragraph 8 above, a court may require oral evidence to be given of anything of which evidence could be given by a certificate under that paragraph.

10. Any person who in a certificate tendered under paragraph 8 above in a magistrates' court, the Crown Court or the Court of Appeal makes a statement which he knows to be false or does not believe to be true shall be guilty of an offence and liable—

    (a) on conviction on indictment to imprisonment for a term not exceeding two years or to a fine or to both;

    (b) on summary conviction to imprisonment for a term not exceeding six months or to a fine not exceeding the statutory maximum ...[72a] or to both.

11. In estimating the weight, if any, to be attached to a statement regard shall be had to all the circumstances from which any inference can reasonably be drawn as to the accuracy or otherwise of the statement and, in particular—

    (a) to the question whether or not the information which the information contained in the statement reproduces or is derived from was supplied to the relevant computer, or

---

[72a] Repealed by the Statute Law (Repeals) Act 1993, Sched. 1.

recorded for the purpose of being supplied to it, contemporaneously with the occurrence or existence of the facts dealt with in that information; and

(b) to the question whether or not any person concerned with the supply of information to that computer, or with the operation of that computer or any equipment by means of which the document containing the statement was produced by it, had any incentive to conceal or misrepresent the facts.

12. For the purposes of paragraph 11 above information shall be taken to be supplied to a computer whether it is supplied directly or (with or without human intervention) by means of any appropriate equipment.

PART III

[As stated above, paragraph 13 was repealed by the Criminal Justice Act 1988, Sched. 16.]

14. For the purpose of deciding whether or not a statement is so admissible the court may draw any reasonable inference—

(a) from the circumstances in which the statement was made or otherwise came into being; or

(b) from any other circumstances, including the form and contents of the document in which the statement is contained.

15. Provision may be made by rules of court for supplementing the provisions of section 68 or 69 above or this Schedule.

Section 83   **SCHEDULE 4**

THE POLICE COMPLAINTS AUTHORITY

PART I—GENERAL

Constitution of Authority

1.—(1) The Police Complaints Authority shall consist of a chairman and not less than 8 other members.

(2) The chairman shall be appointed by Her Majesty.

(3) The other members shall be appointed by the Secretary of State.

(4) The members of the Authority shall not include any person who is or has been a constable in any part of the United Kingdom.

(5) Persons may be appointed as whole-time or part-time members of the Authority.

(6) The Secretary of State may appoint not more than two of the members of the Authority to be deputy chairmen.[72b]

Incorporation and status of Authority

2.—(1) The Authority shall be a body corporate.

(2) It is hereby declared that the Authority are not to be regarded as the servant or agent of the Crown or as enjoying any status, privilege or immunity of the Crown; and the Authority's property shall not be regarded as property of or property held on behalf of the Crown.

Members

3.—(1) Subject to the following provisions of this Schedule, a person shall hold an office to which he is appointed under paragraph 1(2), (3) or (6) above in accordance with the terms of his appointment.

(2) A person shall not be appointed to such an office for more than 3 years at a time.

(3) A person may at any time resign such an office.

(4) The Secretary of State may at any time remove a person from such an office if satisfied that—

(a) he has without reasonable excuse failed to carry out his duties for a continuous period of 3 months beginning not earlier than 6 months before that time; or

(b) he has been convicted of a criminal offence; or

[72b] Substituted by the Police and Magistrates' Courts Act 1994, Sched. 5, para. 36.

(c) he has become bankrupt or made an arrangement with his creditors; or

(d) he is incapacitated by physical or mental illness; or

(da) he has acted improperly in relation to his duties, or[72c]

(e) he is otherwise unable or unfit to perform his duties.

4. The Secretary of State may pay, or make such payments towards the provision of, such remuneration, pensions, allowances or gratuities to or in respect of persons appointed to office under paragraph 1(2), (3) or (6) above or any of them as, with the consent of the Treasury, he may determine.

5. Where a person ceases to hold such an office otherwise than on the expiry of his term of office, and it appears to the Secretary of State that there are special circumstances which make it right for that person to receive compensation, the Secretary of State may, with the consent of the Treasury, direct the Authority to make to the person a payment of such amount as, with the consent of the Treasury, the Secretary of State may determine.

Staff

6. The Authority may, after consultation with the Secretary of State, appoint such officers and servants as the Authority think fit, subject to the approval of the Treasury as to numbers and as to remuneration and other terms and conditions of service.

7.—(1) Employment by the Authority shall be included among the kinds of employment to which a superannuation scheme under section 1 of the Superannuation Act 1972 can apply, and accordingly in Schedule 1 to that Act, at the end of the list of "Other Bodies' there shall be inserted—

"Police Complaints Authority."

(2) Where a person who is employed by the Authority and is by reference to that employment a participant in a scheme under section 1 of the said Act of 1972 is appointed to an office under paragraph 1(2), (3) or (6) above, the Treasury may determine that his service in that office shall be treated for the purposes of the scheme as service as an employee of the Authority; and his rights under the scheme shall not be affected by paragraph 4 above.

8. The Employer's Liability (Compulsory Insurance) Act 1969 shall not require insurance to be effected by the Authority.

Power of Authority to set up regional offices

9.—(1) If it appears to the Authority that it is necessary to do so in order to discharge their duties efficiently, the Authority may, with the consent of the Secretary of State and the Treasury, set up a regional office in any place in England and Wales.

(2) The Authority may delegate any of their functions to a regional office.

Proceedings

10.—(1) Subject to the provisions of this Act, the arrangements for the proceedings of the Authority (including the quorum for meetings) shall be such as the Authority may determine.

(2) The arrangements may, with the approval of the Secretary of State, provide for the discharge, under the general direction of the Authority, of any of the Authority's functions by a committee or by one or more of the members, officers or servants of the Authority.

11. The validity of any proceedings of the Authority shall not be affected—

(a) by any defect in the appointment

(i) of the chairman;

(ii) ...[72d]

(iii) of any other member or

(b) by any vacancy

(i) in the office of chairman;

(ii) among the other members; ...[72e]

Finance

12. The Secretary of State shall pay to the Authority expenses incurred or to be incurred by the Authority under paragraphs 5 and 6 above and, with the consent of the Treasury, shall pay

[72c] Added, by the Police and Magistrates' Courts Act 1994, Sched. 5, para. 36.
[72d-e] Repealed by the Police and Magistrates' Courts Act 1994, Sched. 9.

to the Authority such sums as the Secretary of State thinks fit for enabling the Authority to meet other expenses.

13.—(1) It shall be the duty of the Authority—
    (a) to keep proper accounts and proper records in relation to the accounts;
    (b) to prepare in respect of each financial year of the Authority a statement of accounts in such form as the Secretary of State may direct with the approval of the Treasury; and
    (c) to send copies of the statement to the Secretary of State and the Comptroller and Auditor General before the end of the month of August next following the financial year to which the statement relates.

(2) The Comptroller and Auditor General shall examine, certify and report on each statement received by him in pursuance of this paragraph and shall lay copies of each statement and of his report before Parliament.

(3) The financial year of the Authority shall be the 12 months ending on 31st March.

PART II

TRANSITIONAL

Information received by Police Complaints Board

14.—(1) No information received by the Police Complaints Board in connection with any complaint shall be disclosed by any person who has been a member, officer or servant of the Board except—
    (a) to the Secretary of State or to a member, officer or servant of the Authority or, so far as may be necessary for the proper discharge of the functions of the Authority, to other persons; or
    (b) for the purposes of any criminal, civil or disciplinary proceedings.

(2) Any person who discloses information in contravention of this paragraph shall be guilty of an offence and liable on summary conviction to a fine of an amount not exceeding level 5 on the standard scale. . . .[72f]

Property, rights and liabilities

15.—(1) On the day on which section 83 above comes into operation all property, rights and liabilities which immediately before that day were property, rights and liabilities of the Police Complaints Board shall vest in the Authority by virtue of this paragraph and without further assurance.

(2) Section 12 of the Finance Act 1895 (which requires Acts to be stamped as conveyances on sale in certain cases) shall not apply to any transfer of property effected by this paragraph.

Proceedings

16. Proceedings in any court to which the Police Complaints Board is a party and which are pending immediately before the date on which section 83 above comes into operation may be continued on and after that day by the Authority.

Payments to former members of Police Complaints Board

17. Where a person—
    (a) ceases to be a member of the Police Complaints Board by reason of its abolition; and
    (b) does not become a member of the Authority,
the Secretary of State may, with the consent of the Treasury, make to the person a payment of such amount as, with the consent of the Treasury, the Secretary of State may determine.

General

18. Paragraphs 14 to 17 above are without prejudice to the generality of section 121(4) above.

[72f] Repealed by the Statute Law (Repeals) Act 1993, Sched. 1.

Section 116   **SCHEDULE 5**

SERIOUS ARRESTABLE OFFENCES

PART I

OFFENCES MENTIONED IN SECTION 116(2)(a)

1. Treason.
2. Murder.
3. Manslaughter.
4. Rape.
5. Kidnapping.
6. Incest with a girl under the age of 13.
7. Buggery with a person under the age of 16.[72g]
8. Indecent assault which constitutes an act of indecency.

PART II

OFFENCES MENTIONED IN SECTION 116(2)(b)

Explosive Substances Act 1883 (c.3)

1. Section 2 (causing explosion likely to endanger life or property).

Sexual Offences Act 1956 (c.69)

2. Section 5 (intercourse with a girl under the age of 13).

Firearms Act 1968 (c.27)

3. Section 16 (possession of firearm with intent to injure).
4. Section 17(1) (use of firearms and imitation firearms to resist arrest).
5. Section 18 (carrying firearms with criminal intent).

Road Traffic Act 1972 (c.20)

6. [Repealed by the Road Traffic (Consequential Provisions) Act 1988, Sched. 1]

Taking of Hostages Act 1982 (c.28)

7. Section 1 (hostage-taking).

Aviation Security Act 1982 (c.36)

8. Section 1 (hijacking).

Criminal Justice Act 1988 (c.33)

9. Section 134 (torture).[73]

Road Traffic Act 1988 (c.52)

Section 1 (causing death by dangerous[73a] driving).[74]
Section 3A (causing death by careless driving when under the influence of drink or drugs).[74a]

[72g] Substituted by the Criminal Justice and Public Order Act 1994, Sched. 10, para. 59.
[73] Added by the Criminal Justice Act 1988, Sched. 15. s.102.
[73a] Amended by the Road Traffic Act 1991, Sched. 4, para. 39.
[74] Added by the Road Traffic (Consequential Provisions) Act 1988, Sched. 3, para. 27.
[74a] Amended by the Road Traffic Act 1991, Sched. 4, para. 39.

Aviation and Maritime Security Act 1990 (c.31)

11. Section 1 (endangering safety at aerodromes).
12. Section 9 (hijacking of ships).
13. Section 10 (seizing or exercising control of fixed platforms).[74b]

Channel Tunnel (Security) Order 1994 No.

14. Article 4 (hijacking of Channel Tunnel trains).
15. Article 5 (seizing or exercising control of the tunnel system).[74c]

Protection of Children Act 1978 (c.37)

16. Section 1 (indecent photographs and pseudo-photographs of children).

Obscene Publications Act 1959 (c.66)

17. Section 2 (publication of obscene matter).[74d]

Section 119   **SCHEDULE 6**

CONSEQUENTIAL AMENDMENTS

PART I

ENGLAND AND WALES

Game Act 1831 (32)

1. The following section shall be inserted after section 31 of the Game Act 1831—
"Powers of constables in relation to trespassers
   31A. The powers conferred by section 31 above to require a person found on land as mentioned in that section to quit the land and to tell his Christian name, surname, and place of abode shall also be exercisable by a police constable."

Metropolitan Police Act 1839 (c.47)

2. In section 39 of the Metropolitan Police Act 1839 (fairs within the metropolitan police district) after the word "amusement" there shall be inserted the words "shall be guilty of an offence."

Railway Regulation Act 1840 (c.97)

3. In section 16 of the Railway Regulation Act 1840 (persons obstructing officers of railway company or trespassing upon railway) for the words from "and" in the third place where it occurs to "justice," in the third place where it occurs there shall be substituted the words ", upon conviction by a magistrates' court, at the discretion of the court,".

[74b] Added by the Aviation and Maritime Security Act 1990, Sched. 3.
[74c] Added by the Channel Tunnel (Security) Order 1994 (S.I. 1994 No. 570), Sched. 3.
[74d] Added by the Criminal Justice and Public Order Act 1994, s.85(3). The equivalent addition to the Northern Ireland PACE Order was made by s.85(6).

London Hackney Carriages Act 1843 (c.86)

4. In section 27 of the London Hackney Carriages Act 1843 (no person to act as driver of carriage without consent of proprietor) for the words after "constable" there shall be substituted the words "if necessary, to take charge of the carriage and every horse in charge of any person unlawfully acting as a driver and to deposit the same in some place of safe custody until the same can be applied for by the proprietor."

Town Gardens Protection Act 1863 (c.13)

5. In section 5 of the Town Gardens Protection Act 1863 (penalty for injuring garden) for the words from the beginning to "district" there shall be substituted the words "Any person who throws any rubbish into any such garden, or trespasses therein, or gets over the railings or fence, or steals or damages the flowers or plants, or commits any nuisance therein, shall be guilty of an offence and".

Parks Regulation Act 1872 (c.15)

6. The following section shall be substituted for section 5 of the Parks Regulation Act 1872 (apprehension of offender whose name or residence is not known)—
  "5. Any person who—
      (a) within the view of a park constable acts in contravention of any of the said regulations in the park where the park constable has jurisdiction; and
      (b) when required by any park constable or by any police constable to give his name and address gives a false name or false address,
  shall be liable on summary conviction to a penalty of an amount not exceeding level 1 on the standard scale, as defined in section 75 of the Criminal Justice Act 1982."

Dogs (Protection of Livestock) Act 1953 (c.28)

7. In the Dogs (Protection of Livestock) Act 1953 the following section shall be inserted after section 2—
  "Power of justice of the peace to authorise entry and search
      2A. If on an application made by a constable a justice of the peace is satisfied that there are reasonable grounds for believing—
      (a) that an offence under this Act has been committed; and
      (b) that the dog in respect of which the offence has been committed is on premises specified in the application,
  he may issue a warrant authorising a constable to enter and search the premises in order to identify the dog."

Army Act 1955 (c.18)

Air Force Act 1955 (c.19)

8. The following subsection shall be substituted for section 195(3) of the Army Act 1955 and section 195(3) of the Air Force Act 1955—
  "(3) A constable may seize any property which he has reasonable grounds for suspecting of having been the subject of an offence against this section."

Sexual Offences Act 1956 (c.69)

9. At the end of section 41 of the Sexual Offences Act 1956 (power to arrest in cases of soliciting by men) there shall be added the words "but a constable may only do so in accordance with section 25 of the Police and Criminal Evidence Act 1984."

Game Laws (Amendment) Act 1960 (c.30)

10. In subsection (1) of section 2 of the Game Laws (Amendment) Act 1960 (power of police to enter on land) for the words "purpose of exercising any power conferred on him by the foregoing section" there shall be substituted the words "purpose—
      (a) of exercising in relation to him the powers under section 31 of the Game Act 1831 which section 31A of that Act confers on police constables; or

(b) of arresting him in accordance with section 25 of the Police and Criminal Evidence Act 1984."

11. In subsection (1) of section 4 of that Act (enforcement powers) for the words from "under", in the first place where it occurs, to "thirty-one" there shall be substituted the words ", in accordance with section 25 of the Police and Criminal Evidence Act 1984, for an offence under section one or section nine of the Night Poaching Act 1828, or under section thirty".

Betting, Gaming and Lotteries Act 1963 (c.2)

12. The following subsection shall be substituted for subsection (2) of section 8 of the Betting, Gaming and Lotteries Act 1963 (prohibition of betting in streets and public places)—
"(2) Where a person is found committing an offence under this section, any constable may seize and detain any article liable to be forfeited under this section."

Deer Act 1963 (c.36)

13. ...[74e]

Police Act 1964 (c.48)

14. ...[74f]
15. ...[74g]
16. ...[74h]

Criminal Law Act 1967 (c.58)

17. The following subsection shall be inserted after section 4(1) of the Criminal Law Act 1967—
"(1A) In this section and section 5 below 'arrestable offence' has the meaning assigned to it by section 24 of the Police and Criminal Evidence Act 1984."

Theatres Act 1968 (c.54)

18. In section 15(1) of the Theatres Act 1968 (powers of entry and inspection) for the words "fourteen days" there shall be substituted the words "one month".

Children and Young Persons Act 1969 (c.54)

19. In the Children and Young Persons Act 1969—
(a) in section 28(4), for the words "a police officer not below the rank of inspector or by the police officer in charge of" there shall be substituted the words "the custody officer at"; and
(b) the following section shall be substituted for section 29—
"Recognisance on release of arrested child or young person
29. A child or young person arrested in pursuance of a warrant shall not be released unless he or his parent or guardian (with or without sureties) enters into a recognisance for such amount as the custody officer at the police station where he is detained considers will secure his attendance at the hearing of the charge; and the recognisance entered into in pursuance of this section may, if the custody officer thinks fit, be conditioned for the attendance of the parent or guardian at the hearing in addition to the child or young person."

Immigration Act 1971 (c.77)

20. In section 25(3) of the Immigration Act 1971 for the words "A constable or" there shall be substituted the word "An".

[74e] Repealed by the Deer Act 1991, Sched. 4.
[74f-g] Repealed by the Police and Magistrates' Courts Act 1994, Sched. 9.
[74h] Repealed by the Police Officers (Central Service) Act 1989, Sched.

Criminal Justice Act 1972 (c.71)

21. In subsection (1) of section 34 of the Criminal Justice Act 1972 (powers of constable to take drunken offender to treatment centre) for the words from the beginning to "section the" there shall be substituted the words "On arresting an offender for an offence under—
   (a) section 12 of the Licensing Act 1872; or
   (b) section 91(1) of the Criminal Justice Act 1967,
a".

Child Care Act 1980 (c.5)

22. In subsection (1)(b) of section 73 of the Child Care Act 1980 (provisions as to places of safety etc.) for the words "section 29(3) of the Children and Young Persons Act 1969" there shall be substituted the words "section 38(7) of the Police and Criminal Evidence Act 1984."

Deer Act 1980 (c.49)

23. ...[74i]

Animal Health Act 1981 (c.22)

24. In subsection (5) of section 60 of the Animal Health Act 1981 (enforcement powers) for the words "a constable or other officer" there shall be substituted the words "an officer other than a constable."

Wildlife and Countryside Act 1981 (c.69)

25. In subsection (2) of section 19 of the Wildlife and Countryside Act 1981 (enforcement powers) after the words "subsection (1)" there shall be inserted the words "or arresting a person in accordance with section 25 of the Police and Criminal Evidence Act 1984 for such an offence".

Mental Health Act 1983 (c.20)

26. In section 135(4) of the Mental Health Act 1983 for the words "the constable to whom it is addressed", in both places where they occur, there shall be substituted the words "a constable."

Prevention of Terrorism (Temporary Provisions) Act 1984 (c.8)

27. [Paragraph 27 was repealed by the Prevention of Terrorism (Temporary Provisions) Act 1989, Sched. 9 (ed.)]

PART II

OTHER AMENDMENTS

Army Act 1955 (c.18)

28.—(1) The Army Act 1955 shall be amended as follows.
(2) In section 99—
   (a) in subsection (1), after the word "below" there shall be inserted the words "and to service modifications"; and
   (b) the following subsections shall be inserted after that subsection—
      "(1A) In this section 'service modifications' means such modifications as the Secretary of State may by regulations made by statutory instrument prescribe, being modifications which appear to him to be necessary or proper for the purposes of proceedings before a court-martial; and it is hereby declared that in this section—
'rules' includes rules contained in or made by virtue of an enactment; and
'enactment' includes an enactment contained in an Act passed after this Act.
(1B) Regulations under subsection (1A) above may not modify section 99A below.

[74i] Repealed by the Deer Act 1991, Sched. 4.

(1C) Regulations under subsection (1A) above shall be subject to annulment in pursuance of a resolution of either House of Parliament."

(3) In section 99A(1) for the word "Section" there shall be substituted the words "Without prejudice to section 99 above, section".

(4) The following section shall be inserted after section 200—

"False statements in computer record certificates

200A.—(1) Any person who in a certificate tendered under paragraph 8 of Schedule 3 to the Police and Criminal Evidence Act 1984 (computer records) in evidence before a court-martial makes a statement which he knows to be false or does not believe to be true shall be guilty of an offence and liable—

(a) on conviction on indictment to imprisonment for a term not exceeding two years or to a fine or to both;

(b) on summary conviction to imprisonment for a term not exceeding six months or to a fine not exceeding the statutory maximum or to both.

(2) In this section 'statutory maximum' has the meaning given by section 74 of the Criminal Justice.Act 1982."

Air Force Act 1955 (c.19)

29.—(1) The Air Force Act 1955 shall be amended as follows.

(2) In section 99—

(a) in subsection (1), after the word "below" there shall be inserted the words "and to service modifications"; and

(b) the following subsections shall be inserted after that subsection—

"(1A) In this section 'service modifications' means such modifications as the Secretary of State may by regulations made by statutory instrument prescribe, being modifications which appear to him to be necessary or proper for the purposes of proceedings before a court-martial; and it is hereby declared that in this section—

'rules' includes rules contained in or made by virtue of an enactment; and

'enactment' includes an enactment contained in an Act passed after this Act.

(1B) Regulations under subsection (1A) above may not modify section 99A below.

(1C) Regulations under subsection (1A) above shall be subject to annulment in pursuance of a resolution of either House of Parliament."

(3) In section 99A(1) for the word "Section" there shall be substituted the words "Without prejudice to section 99 above, section."

(4) The following section shall be inserted after section 200—

"False statements in computer record certificates

200A.—(1) Any person who in a certificate tendered under paragraph 8 of Schedule 3 to the Police and Criminal Evidence Act 1984 (computer records) in evidence before a court-martial makes a statement which he knows to be false or does not believe to be true shall be guilty of an offence and liable—

(a) on conviction on indictment to imprisonment for a term not exceeding two years or to a fine or to both;

(b) on summary conviction to imprisonment for a term not exceeding six months or to a fine not exceeding the statutory maximum or to both.

(2) In this section "statutory maximum" has the meaning given by section 74 of the Criminal Justice Act 1982."

Police (Scotland) Act 1967 (c.77)

30. In section 6(2) of the Police (Scotland) Act 1967 (constables below rank of assistant chief constable) for the words "an assistant chief constable or a constable holding the office of deputy chief constable" there shall be substituted the words "a deputy chief constable or an assistant chief constable".

31. In section 7(1) of that Act (ranks) after the words "chief constable," there shall be inserted the words "deputy chief constable".

32. In section 26(7) of that Act (disciplinary authority) immediately before the words "deputy chief constable" there shall be inserted the word "any".

33. In section 31(2) of that Act (compulsory retirement of chief constable etc.) for the words "the deputy or an assistant chief constable" there shall be substituted the words "a deputy or assistant chief constable".

Courts-Martial (Appeals) Act 1968 (c.20)

34.—(1) The following section shall be inserted after section 37 of the Courts-Martial (Appeals) Act 1968—
"False statements in computer record certificates.
    37A.—(1) Any person who in a certificate tendered under paragraph 8 of Schedule 3 to the Police and Criminal Evidence Act 1984 (computer records) in evidence before the Appeal Court makes a statement which he knows to be false or does not believe to be true shall be guilty of an offence and liable—
    (a) on conviction on indictment to imprisonment for a term not exceeding two years or to a fine or to both;
    (b) on summary conviction to imprisonment for a term not exceeding six months or to a fine not exceeding the statutory maximum or to both.
    (2) Proceedings for an offence under this section committed outside the United Kingdom may be taken, and the offence may for all incidental purposes be treated as having been committed, in any place in the United Kingdom.
    (3) In this section 'statutory maximum' has the meaning given by section 74 of the Criminal Justice Act 1982."

House of Commons Disqualification Act 1975 (c.24)

Northern Ireland Assembly Disqualification Act 1975 (c.25)

35. In Part II of Schedule 1 to the House of Commons Disqualification Act 1975 and Part II of Schedule 1 to the Northern Ireland Assembly Disqualification Act 1975 (bodies of which all members are disqualified under those Acts) there shall be inserted at the appropriate place in alphabetical order—
    "The Police Complaints Authority."

Armed Forces Act 1976 (c.52)

36. The following paragraph shall be inserted after paragraph 17 of Schedule 3 to the Armed Forces Act 1976 (Standing Civilian Courts)—
    "17A. Section 200A of that Act (false statements in computer record certificates) shall have effect as if the reference to a court-martial in subsection (1) included a reference to a Standing Civilian Court."

Customs and Excise Management Act 1979 (c.2)

37. The following subsection shall be substituted for section 138(4) of the Customs and Excise Management Act 1979—
    "(4) Where any person has been arrested by a person who is not an officer—
    (a) by virtue of this section; or
    (b) by virtue of section 24 of the Police and Criminal Evidence Act 1984 in its application to the Customs and Excise Acts,
the person arresting him shall give notice of the arrest to an officer at the nearest convenient office of customs and excise."
38. In section 161 of that Act—
    (a) in subsection (3), for the words from "that officer" to the end of the subsection that there shall be substituted the words "any officer and any person accompanying an officer to enter and search the building or place named in the warrant within one month from that day"; and
    (b) in subsection (4), for the words "person named in a warrant under subsection (3) above" there shall be substituted the words "other person so authorised".

Betting and Gaming Duties Act 1981 (c.63)

39. In the following provisions of the Betting and Gaming Duties Act 1981, namely—
    (a) section 15(2);
    (b) paragraph 16(1) of Schedule 1;
    (c) paragraph 17(1) of Schedule 3; and
    (d) paragraph 17(1) of Schedule 4,
for the words "fourteen days" there shall be substituted the words "one month".

Car Tax Act 1983 (c.53)

40. In paragraph 7(3) of Schedule 1 to the Car Tax Act 1983 for the words "fourteen days" there shall be substituted the words "one month".

Value Added Tax Act 1983 (c.55)

41. ....[74j]

Section 119   **SCHEDULE 7**

REPEALS

PART I

ENACTMENTS REPEALED IN CONSEQUENCE OF PARTS I TO V

Chapter	Short title	Extent of repeal
5 Geo. 4. c.83.	Vagrancy Act 1824	Section 8 Section 13
1 & 2 Will. 4. c.32.	Game Act 1831.	In section 31, the words "or for any police constable".
2 & 3 Vict. c.47.	Metropolitan Police Act 1839.	Section 34. In section 38, the words from "it" to "and" in the sixth place where it occurs. In section 39, the words "to take into custody". In section 47, the words "take into custody" and the words ", and every person so found". In section 54, the words from "And" to the end of the section. In section 62, the words from "may" in the first place where it occurs to "and" in the second place where it occurs. Sections 63 to 67.
3 & 4 Vict. c.50.	Canals (Offences) Act 1840.	The whole Act.
5 & 6 Vict. c.55.	Railway Regulation Act 1842.	In section 17, the words "or for any special constable duly appointed".
8 & 9 Vict. c.20.	Railways Clauses Consolidation Act 1845.	In section 104, the words "and all constables, gaolers, and police officers,".
10 & 11 Vict. c.89.	Town Police Clauses Act 1847.	In section 15, the words "may be taken into custody, without a warrant, by any constable, or" and the words from "Provided" to the end of the section. In section 28, the words from "and" in the first place where it occurs to "offence" in the second place where it occurs.
14 & 15 Vict. c.19.	Prevention of Offences Act 1851.	Section 11.
23 & 24 Vict. c.32.	Ecclesiastical Courts Jurisdiction Act 1860.	In section 3, the words "constable or".
24 & 25 Vict. c.100.	Offences against the Person Act 1861.	In section 65, the words "in the daytime".
34 & 35 Vict. c.96.	Pedlars Act 1871.	Sections 18 and 19.
35 & 36 Vict.c.93.	Pawnbrokers Act 1872.	In section 36, the words ", within the hours of business".

[74j] Repealed by the Value Added Tax Act 1994, Sched. 15.

Chapter	Short title	Extent of repeal
38 & 39 Vict. c.17.	Explosives Act 1875.	In section 78, the words "a constable, or".
52 & 53 Vict. c.18.	Indecent Advertisements Act 1889.	Section 6.
52 & 53 Vict. c.57.	Regulation of Railways Act 1889.	In section 5(2), the words "or any constable".
8 Edw. 7. c.66.	Public Meeting Act 1908.	In section 1, in subsection (3) the words from "and" in the sixth place where it occurs to the end of the subsection.
1 & 2 Geo. 5. c.28.	Official Secrets Act 1911.	In section 9(1), the words "named therein".
15 & 16 Geo. 5. c.71.	Public Health Act 1925.	Section 74(2) and (3).
23 & 24 Geo. 5. c.12.	Children and Young Persons Act 1933.	Section 10(2). Section 13(1) and (2). In section 40, in subsection (1) the words "named therein" and in subsection (4) the words "addressed to and".
11 & 12 Geo. 6. c.58.	Criminal Justice Act 1948.	Section 68.
1 & 2 Eliz. 2. c.14.	Prevention of Crime Act 1953.	Section 1(3).
3 & 4 Eliz. 2. c.28.	Children and Young Persons (Harmful Publications) Act 1955.	In section 3(1), the words "named therein".
4 & 5 Eliz. 2. c.69.	Sexual Offences Act 1956.	Section 40. In section 43(1), the word "named".
5 & 6 Eliz. 2. c.53.	Naval Discipline Act 1957.	In section 106(1), the words from "may" in the first place where it occurs to "and".
7 & 8 Eliz. 2. c.66.	Obscene Publications Act 1959.	In section 3(1), the words ", within fourteen days from the date of the warrant,".
8 & 9 Eliz. 2. c.36.	Game Laws (Amendment) Act 1960.	Section 1.
1963 c.2.	Betting, Gaming and Lotteries Act 1963.	In section 51(1), the words "at any time within fourteen days from the time of the issue of the warrant" and the words "arrest and".
1963 c.36.	Deer Act 1963.	Section 5(1)(c).
1964 c.26.	Licensing Act 1964.	Section 187(5).
1967 c.58.	Criminal Law Act 1967.	Section 2.
1968 c.27.	Firearms Act 1968.	In section 46(1), the words "named therein". Section 50.
1968 c.52.	Caravan Sites Act 1968.	Section 11(5).
1968 c.60.	Theft Act 1968.	Section 12(3). Section 26(2).
1968 c.65.	Gaming Act 1968.	Section 5(2). In section 43, in subsection (4), the words "at any time within fourteen days from the time of the issue of the warrant", and in subsection (5)(b), the words "arrest and".
1970 c.30.	Conservation of Seals Act 1970.	Section 4(1)(a).
1971 c.38.	Misuse of Drugs Act 1971.	Section 24.
1971 c.77.	Immigration Act 1971.	In Schedule 2, in paragraph 17(2), the words "acting for the police area in which the premises are situated," and the words "at any time or times within one month from the date of the warrant".

Chapter	Short title	Extent of repeal
1972 c.20.	Road Traffic Act 1972.	Section 19(3). Section 164(2).
1972 c.27.	Road Traffic (Foreign Vehicles) Act 1972.	Section 3(2).
1972 c.71.	Criminal Justice Act.	Section 34(3).
1973 c.57.	Badgers Act 1973.	Section 10(1)(b).
1974 c.6.	Biological Weapons Act 1974.	In section 4(1), the words "named therein".
1976 c.32.	Lotteries and Amusements Act 1976.	In section 19, the words "at any time within 14 days from the time of the issue of the warrant".
1976 c.58.	International Carriage of Perishable Foodstuffs Act 1976.	Section 11(6).
1977 c.45.	Criminal Law Act 1977.	Section 11. Section 62.
1979 c.2.	Customs and Excise Management Act 1979.	In section 138, in subsections (1) and (2), the words "or constable".
1980 c.43.	Magistrates' Courts Act 1980.	Section 49.
1980 c.49.	Deer Act 1980.	Section 4(1)(c).
1980 c.66.	Highways Act 1980.	Section 137(2).
1980 c.x.	County of Merseyside Act 1980.	Section 33.
1980 c.xi.	West Midlands County Council Act 1980.	Section 42.
1981 c.14.	Public Passenger Vehicles Act 1981.	Section 25(2).
1981 c.22.	Animal Health Act 1981.	In section 60, subsection (3), in subsection (4) the words "or apprehending", and in subsection (5) the words "constable or" in the second place when they occur.
1981 c.42.	Indecent Displays (Control) Act 1981.	Section 2(1). In section 2(3), the words "within fourteen days from the date of issue of the warrant".
1981 c.47.	Criminal Attempts Act 1981.	Section 9(4).
1981 c.69.	Wildlife and Countryside Act 1981.	Section 19(1)(c).
1982 c.48.	Criminal Justice Act 1982.	Section 34.
1983 c.2.	Representation of the People Act 1983.	In section 97(3), the words from "and" in the fifth place where it occurs to "him" in the third place where it occurs. ...[75]
1983 c.20.	Mental Health Act 1983.	In section 135, in subsections (1) and (2), the words "named in the warrant".

[75] Words deleted by Representation of the People Act 1985, s.28, Sched. 5.

PART II

ENACTMENTS REPEALED IN RELATION TO CRIMINAL PROCEEDINGS IN CONSEQUENCE OF
PART VII

Chapter	Short title	Extent of repeal
1971 c.liv.	Cornwall County Council Act 1971.	Section 98(4).
1972 c.xlvii.	Hampshire County Council Act 1972.	Section 86(2).

PART III

ENACTMENTS REPEALED GENERALLY IN CONSEQUENCE OF PART VII

Chapter	Short title	Extent of repeal
3 & 4 Eliz. 2. c.18.	Army Act 1955.	In section 198(1), the words "of this section and of sections 198A and 198B of this Act". Sections 198A and 198B.
3 & 4 Eliz. 2. c.19.	Air Force Act 1955.	In section 198(1), the words "of this section and of sections 198A and 198B of this Act". Sections 198A and 198B.
1965 c.20.	Criminal Evidence Act 1965.	The whole Act.
1969 c.48.	Post Office Act 1969.	In section 93(4), the words "the Criminal Evidence Act 1965 and". In Schedule 4, paragraph 77.
1981 c.55.	Armed Forces Act 1981.	Section 9.
1981 c.xviii.	County of Kent Act 1981.	Section 82.
1983 c.55.	Value Added Tax Act 1983.	In Schedule 7, paragraph 7(7) and (8).

PART IV

ENACTMENTS REPEALED IN RELATION TO CRIMINAL PROCEEDINGS IN CONSEQUENCE OF PART
VIII

Chapter	Short title	Extent of repeal
14 & 15 Vict. c.99.	Evidence Act 1851.	Section 13.
28 & 29 Vict. c.18.	Criminal Procedure Act 1865.	In section 6 the words from "and a certificate" onwards.
34 & 35 Vict. c.112.	Prevention of Crimes Act 1871.	Section 18 except the words "A previous conviction in any one part of the United Kingdom may be proved against a prisoner in any other part of the United Kingdom.".

PART V

ENACTMENTS REPEALED GENERALLY IN CONSEQUENCE OF PART VIII

Chapter	Short title	Extent of repeal
16 & 17 Vict. c.83.	Evidence (Amendment) Act 1853.	Section 3.
46 & 47 Vict. c.3.	Explosive Substances Act 1883.	Section 4(2).
58 & 59 Vict. c.24.	Law of Distress Amendment Act 1895.	Section 5.
61 & 62 Vict. c.36.	Criminal Evidence Act 1898.	In section 1, the words "and the wife or husband, as the case may be, of the person so charged", the words (in paragraph (b)) "or the wife or husband, as the case may be, of the person so charged" and paragraphs (c) and (d). Section 4. In section 6(1), the words from "notwithstanding" to the end. The Schedule.
4 & 5 Geo. 5. c.58.	Criminal Justice Administration Act 1914.	Section 28(3).
19 & 20 Geo. 5. c.34.	Infant Life (Preservation) Act 1929.	Section 2(5).
23 & 24 Geo. 5. c.12.	Children and Young Persons Act 1933.	Section 15. Section 26(5).
4 & 5 Eliz. 2. c.69.	Sexual Offences Act 1956.	Section 12(2) and (3). Section 15(4) and (5). Section 16(2) and (3). Section 39. In Schedule 3 the entry relating to section 15 of the Children and Young Persons Act 1933.
8 & 9 Eliz. 2. c.33.	Indecency with Children Act 1960.	In section 1, subsection (2) and in subsection (3) the words "except in section 15 (which relates to the competence as a witness of the wife or husband of the accused)".
1965 c.72.	Matrimonial Causes Act 1965.	Section 43(1).
1968 c.60.	Theft Act 1968.	Section 30(3).
1970 c.55.	Family Income Supplements Act 1970.	Section 12(5).
1973 c.38.	Social Security Act 1973.	In Schedule 23, paragraph 4.
1975 c.14.	Social Security Act 1975.	Section 147(6).
1975 c.16.	Industrial Injuries and Diseases (Old Cases) Act 1975.	Section 10(4).
1975 c.61.	Child Benefit Act 1975.	Section 11(8).
1976 c.71.	Supplementary Benefits Act 1976.	Section 26(5).
1977 c.45.	Criminal Law Act 1977.	In section 54(3) the words "subsection (2) (competence of spouse of accused to give evidence)."
1978 c.37.	Protection of Children Act 1978.	Section 2(1).
1979 c.18.	Social Security Act 1979.	Section 16.

Chapter	Short title	Extent of repeal
1980 c.43.	Magistrates' Courts Act 1980.	In Schedule 7, paragraph 4.
1982 c.24.	Social Security and Housing Benefits Act 1982.	Section 21(6).

PART VI

MISCELLANEOUS REPEALS

Chapter	Short title	Extent of repeal
2 & 3 Vict. c.47.	Metropolitan Police Act 1839.	Section 7.
34 & 35 Vict. c.96.	Pedlars Act 1871.	In section 18, the words from "or" where secondly occurring to "Act," and the words from "and forthwith" to the end of the section.
1964 c.48.	Police Act 1964.	Section 49. Section 50.
1967 c.77.	Police (Scotland) Act 1967.	Section 5(3) and section 17(6).
1972 c.11.	Superannuation Act 1972.	In Schedule 1, the reference to the Police Complaints Board.
1975 c.24.	House of Commons Disqualification Act 1975.	In Part II of Schedule 1, the entry relating to the Police Complaints Board.
1975 c.25.	Northern Ireland Assembly Disqualification Act 1975.	In Part II of Schedule 1, the entry relating to the Police Complaints Board.
1976 c.46.	Police Act 1976.	Section 1(1) to (4). Sections 2 to 13. Section 14(2). In the Schedule, paragraphs 1 to 3, in paragraph 4, the words "remuneration" and "allowances" and paragraphs 5 to 13.

CODES OF PRACTICE

CODES OF PRACTICE

E CODE OF PRACTICE ON TAPE RECORDING OF INTERVIEWS WITH
SUSPECTS

A. CODE OF PRACTICE FOR THE EXERCISE BY POLICE OFFICERS OF STATUTORY POWERS OF STOP AND SEARCH

1 General

1.1   This code of practice must be readily available at all police stations for consultation by police officers, detained persons and members of the public.

1.2   The notes for guidance included are not provisions of this code, but are guidance to police officers and others about its application and interpretation. Provisions in the annexes to the code are provisions of this code.

1.3   This code governs the exercise by police officers of statutory powers to search a person without first arresting him or to search a vehicle without making an arrest. The main stop and search powers to which this code applies at the time the code was prepared are set out in *Annex A*, but that list should not be regarded as definitive.

1.4   This code does not apply to the following powers of stop and search:
  (i) Aviation Security Act 1982, s27(2);
  (ii) Police and Criminal Evidence Act 1984, s6(1) (which relates specifically to powers of constables employed by statutory undertakers on the premises of the statutory undertakers).

1.5   This code applies to stops and searches under powers:
  (a) requiring reasonable grounds for suspicion that articles unlawfully obtained or possessed are being carried;
  (b) authorised under section 60 of the Criminal Justice and Public Order Act 1994 based upon a reasonable belief that incidents involving serious violence may take place within a locality;
  (c) authorised under section 13A of the Prevention of Terrorism (Temporary Provisions) Act 1989 as amended by section 81 of the Criminal Justice and Public Order Act 1994;
  (d) exercised under paragraph 4(2) of Schedule 5 to the Prevention of Terrorism (Temporary Provisions) Act 1989.

[See *Note 1A*]

(a) Powers requiring reasonable suspicion

1.6   Whether a reasonable ground for suspicion exists will depend on the circumstances in each case, but there must be some objective basis for it. An officer will need to consider the nature of the article suspected of being carried in the context of other factors such as the time and the place, and the behaviour of the person concerned or those with him. Reasonable suspicion may exist, for example, where information has been received such as a description of an article being carried or of a suspected offender; a person is seen acting covertly or warily or attempting to hide something; or a person is carrying a certain type of article at an unusual time or in a place where a number of burglaries or thefts are known to have taken place recently. But the decision to stop and search must be based on all the facts which bear on the likelihood that an article of a certain kind will be found.

1.7 Reasonable suspicion can never be supported on the basis of personal factors alone. For example, a person's colour, age, hairstyle or manner of dress, or the fact that he is known to have a previous conviction for possession of an unlawful article, cannot be used alone or in combination with each other as the sole basis on which to search that person. Nor may it be founded on the basis of stereotyped images of certain persons or groups as more likely to be committing offences.

1.7A Where a police officer has reasonable grounds to suspect that a person is in innocent possession of a stolen or prohibited article or other item for which he is empowered to search, the power of stop and search exists notwithstanding that there would be no power of arrest. However every effort should be made to secure the person's co-operation in the production of the article before resorting to the use of force.

(b) Authorisation under section 60 of the Criminal Justice and Public Order Act 1994

1.8 Authority to exercise the powers of stop and search under section 60 of the Criminal Justice and Public Order Act 1994 may be given where it is reasonably believed that incidents involving serious violence may take place in a locality, and it is expedient to use these powers to prevent their occurrence. Authorisation should normally be given by an officer of the rank of superintendent or above, in writing, specifying the locality in which the powers may be exercised and the period of time for which they are in force. Authorisation may be given by an inspector or chief inspector if he reasonably believes that violence is imminent and no superintendent is available. In either case the period authorised shall be no longer than appears reasonably necessary to prevent, or try to prevent incidents of serious violence, and it may not exceed 24 hours. A superintendent or the authorising officer may direct that the period shall be extended for a further six hours if violence has occurred or is suspected to have occurred and the continued use of the powers is considered necessary to prevent further violence. That direction must also be given in writing at the time or as soon as practicable afterwards. [See *Notes 1F and 1G*]

(c) Authorisation under section 13A of the Prevention of Terrorism (Temporary Provisions) Act 1989, as amended by section 81 of the Criminal Justice and Public Order Act 1994

1.8A Authority to exercise the powers of stop and search under section 13A of the Prevention of Terrorism (Temporary Provisions) Act 1989 may be given where it appears expedient to do so to prevent acts of terrorism. Authorisation must be given by an officer of the rank of assistant chief constable (or equivalent) or above, in writing, specifying where the powers may be exercised and the period of time for which they are to remain in force. The period authorised may not exceed 28 days. Further periods of up to 28 days may be authorised. [See *Notes 1F and 1G*]

Notes for guidance

 1A It is important to ensure that powers of stop and search are used responsibly by those who exercise them and those who authorise their use. An officer should bear in mind that he may be required to justify the authorisation or use of the powers to a senior officer and in court, and that misuse of the powers is likely to be harmful to the police effort in the long term and can lead to mistrust of the police by the community. Regardless of the power exercised all police officers should be careful to ensure that the selection and treatment of those questioned or searched is based upon objective factors and not upon personal prejudice. It is also particularly important to ensure that any person searched is treated courteously and considerately.

1B This code does not affect the ability of an officer to speak to or question a person in the ordinary course of his duties (and in the absence of reasonable suspicion) without detaining him or exercising any element of compulsion. It is not the purpose of the code to prohibit such encounters between the police and the community with the co-operation of the person concerned and neither does it affect the principle that all citizens have a duty to help police officers to prevent crime and discover offenders.

1C [Not used]

1D Nothing in this code affects

    a. the routine searching of persons entering sports grounds or other premises with their consent, or as a condition of entry; or

    b. the ability of an officer to search a person in the street with his consent where no search power exists. In these circumstances an officer should always make it clear that he is seeking the consent of the person concerned to the search being carried out by telling the person that he need not consent and that without his consent he will not be searched.

1E If an officer acts in an improper manner this will invalidate a voluntary search. Juveniles, people suffering from a mental handicap or mental disorder and others who appear not to be capable of giving an informed consent should not be subject to a voluntary search.

1F It is for the authorising officer to determine the period of time during which the powers mentioned in paragraph 1.5(b) and (c) may be exercised. The officer should set the minimum period he considers necessary to deal with the risk of violence or terrorism. A direction to extend the period authorised under the powers mentioned in paragraph 1.5(b) may be given only once. Thereafter further use of the powers requires a new authorisation.

1G It is for the authorising officer to determine the geographical area in which the use of the powers are to be authorised. In doing so he may wish to take into account factors such as the nature and venue of the anticipated incident, the numbers of people who may be in the immediate area of any possible incident, their access to surrounding areas and the anticipated level of violence. The officer should not set a geographical area which is wider than that he believes necessary for the purpose of preventing anticipated violence or terrorism.

2 Action before a search is carried out

(a) Searches requiring reasonable suspicion

2.1 Where an officer has the reasonable grounds for suspicion necessary to exercise a power of stop and search he may detain the person concerned for the purposes of and with a view to searching him. There is no power to stop or detain a person against his will in order to find grounds for a search.

2.2 Before carrying out a search the officer may question the person about his behaviour or his presence in circumstances which give rise to the suspicion, since he may have a satisfactory explanation which will make a search unnecessary. If, as a result of any questioning preparatory to a search, or other circumstances which come to the attention of the officer, there cease to be reasonable grounds for suspecting that an article is being carried of a kind for which there is a power of stop and search, no search may take place. [See *Note 2A*]

2.3   The reasonable grounds for suspicion which are necessary for the exercise of the initial power to detail may be confirmed or eliminated as a result of the questioning of a person detained for the purposes of a search (or such questioning may reveal reasonable grounds to suspect the possession of a different kind of unlawful article from that originally suspected); but the reasonable grounds for suspicion without which any search or detention for the purposes of a search is unlawful cannot be retrospectively provided by such questioning during his detention or by his refusal to answer any question put to him.

(b) All searches

2.4   Before any search of a detained person or attended vehicle takes place the officer must take reasonable steps to give the person to be searched or in charge of the vehicle the following information:

    (i) his name (except in the case of enquiries linked to the investigation of terrorism, in which case he shall give his warrant or other identification number) and the name of the police station to which he is attached;
    (ii) the object of the search; and
    (iii) his grounds or authorisation for undertaking it.

2.5   If the officer is not in uniform he must show his warrant card. In doing so in the case of enquiries linked to the investigation of terrorism, the officer need not reveal his name. Stops and searches under the powers mentioned in paragraphs 1.5(b) and (c) may be undertaken only by a constable in uniform.

2.6   Unless it appears to the officer that it will not be practicable to make a record of the search, he must also inform the person to be searched (or the owner or person in charge of a vehicle that is to be searched, as the case may be) that he is entitled to a copy of the record of the search if he asks for it within a year. If the person wishes to have a copy and is not given one on the spot, he shall be advised to which police station he should apply.

2.7   If the person to be searched, or in charge of a vehicle to be searched, does not appear to understand what is being said, or there is any doubt about his ability to understand English, the officer must take reasonable steps to bring the information in paragraphs 2.4 and 2.6 to his attention. If the person is deaf or cannot understand English and has someone with him then the officer must try to establish whether that person can interpret or otherwise help him to give the required information.

Note for guidance

2A   In some circumstances preparatory questioning may be unnecessary, but in general a brief conversation or exchange will be desirable as a means of avoiding unsuccessful searches. Where a person is lawfully detained for the purpose of a search, but no search in the event takes place, the detention will not thereby have been rendered unlawful.

3 Conduct of the search

3.1   Every reasonable effort must be made to reduce to the minimum the embarrassment that a person being searched may experience.

3.2   The co-operation of the person to be searched shall be sought in every case, even if he initially objects to the search. A forcible search may be made only if it has been established that the person is unwilling to co-operate (*e.g.* by opening a bag) or resists. Although force may only be used as a last resort, reasonable force may be used if necessary to conduct a search or to detain a person or vehicle for the purposes of a search.

3.3   The length of time for which a person or vehicle may be detained will depend on the circumstances, but must in all circumstances, be reasonable and not extend beyond the time taken for the search. Where the exercise of the power requires reasonable suspicion, the thoroughness and extent of a search must depend on what is suspected of being carried, and by whom. If the suspicion relates to a particular article which is seen to be slipped into a person's pocket, then, in the absence of other grounds for suspicion or an opportunity for the article to be moved elsewhere, the search must be confined to that pocket. In the case of a small article which can readily be concealed, such as a drug, and which might be concealed anywhere on the person, a more extensive search may be necessary. In the case of searches mentioned in paragraph 1.5(b), (c) and (d), which do not require reasonable grounds for suspicion, the officer may make any reasonable search to find what he is empowered to search for. [See *Note 3B*]

3.4   The search must be conducted at or nearby the place where the person or vehicle was first detained.

3.5   Searches in public must be restricted to superficial examination of outer clothing. There is no power to require a person to remove any clothing in public other than an outer coat, jacket or gloves. Where on reasonable grounds it is considered necessary to conduct a more thorough search (*e.g.* by requiring a person to take off a T-shirt or headgear), this shall be done out of public view for example, in a police van or police station if there is one nearby. Any search involving the removal of more than an outer coat, jacket, gloves, headgear or footwear may only be made by an officer of the same sex as the person searched and may not be made in the presence of anyone of the opposite sex unless the person being searched specifically requests it. [See *Note 3A*]

3.5A   Where a pedestrian is stopped under section 13A of the Prevention of Terrorism (Temporary Provisions) Act 1989, a search may be made of anything carried by him. The pedestrian himself must not be searched under this power. This would not prevent a search being carried out under other powers if, in the course of a search of anything carried by the pedestrian, the police officer formed reasonable grounds for suspicion.

Notes for guidance

   3A   A search in the street itself should be regarded as being in public for the purposes of paragraph 3.5 above, even though it may be empty at the time a search begins. Although there is no power to require a person to do so, there is nothing to prevent an officer from asking a person to voluntarily remove more than an outer coat, jacket or gloves in public.

   3B   As a search of a person in public should be superficial examination of outer clothing, such searches should be completed as soon as possible.

4 Action after a search is carried out

(a) General

4.1   An officer who has carried out a search must make a written record unless it is not practicable to do so, on account of the numbers to be searched or for some other operational reason, *e.g.* in situations involving public disorder.

4.2   The records must be completed as soon as practicable – on the spot unless circumstances (*e.g.* other immediate duties or very bad weather) make this impracticable.

4.3   The record must be made on the form provided for this purpose (the national search record).

4.4   In order to complete the search record the officer shall normally seek the name, address and date of birth of the person searched, but under the search procedures there is no obligation on a person to provide these details and no power to detain him if he is unwilling to do so.

4.5   The following information must always be included in the record of a search even if the person does not wish to identify himself or give his date of birth:

   (i) the name of the person searched, or (if he withholds it) a description of him;

  (ii) a note of the person's ethnic origin:

 (iii) when a vehicle is searched, a description of it, including its registration number; [See *Note 4B*]

 (iv) the object of the search;

  (v) the grounds for making it;

 (vi) the date and time it was made;

 (vii) the place where it was made;

(viii) its results;

 (ix) a note of any injury or damage to property resulting from it;

  (x) the identity of the officer making it (except in the case of enquiries linked to the investigation of terrorism, in which case the record shall state the officer's warrant or other identification number and duty station). [See *Note 4A*]

4.6   A record is required for each person and each vehicle searched. However, if a person is in a vehicle and both are searched, and the object and grounds of the search are the same, only one record need be completed.

4.7   The record of the grounds for making a search must, briefly but informatively, explain the reason for suspecting the person concerned, whether by reference to his behaviour or other circumstances; or in the case of those searches mentioned in paragraph 1.5(b), (c) and (d) by stating the authority provided to carry out such a search.

4.7A   The driver (but not any passengers) of a vehicle which is stopped in accordance with the powers mentioned in paragraphs 1.5(b) and (c) may obtain a written statement to that effect within 12 months from the day the vehicle was searched. A written statement may be similarly obtained by a pedestrian if he is stopped in accordance with the powers mentioned in paragraph 1.5(b) and (c) (see paragraph 2.6). The statement may form part of the national search record or be supplied on a separate document. [See *Note 4C*]

(b) Unattended vehicles

4.8   After searching an unattended vehicle, or anything in or on it, an officer must leave a notice in it (or on it, if things in or on it have been searched without opening it) recording the fact that it has been searched.

4.9   The notice shall include the name of the police station to which the officer concerned is attached and state where a copy of the record of the search may be obtained and where any application for compensation should be directed.

4.10   The vehicle must if practicable be left secure.

Notes for guidance

4A   Where a search is conducted by more than one officer the identity of all the officers engaged in the search must be recorded on the search record.

4B   Where a vehicle has not been allocated a registration number (e.g. a rally car or a trials motorbike) that part of the requirements under 4.5(iii) does not apply.

4C   In paragraph 4.7A, a written statement means a record that a person or vehicle was stopped under the powers contained in paragraph 1.5(b) and (c) of this code.

ANNEX A   SUMMARY OF MAIN STOP AND SEARCH POWERS
[See paragraph 1.3]

Power	Object of search	Extent of search	Where exercisable
Unlawful articles general			
1. Public Stores Act 1875, s.6	HM Stores stolen or unlawfully obtained	Persons, vehicles and vessels	Anywhere where the constabulary powers are exercisable
2. Firearms Act 1968, s.47	Firearms	Persons and vehicles	A public place, or anywhere in the case of reasonable suspicion of offences of carrying firearms with criminal intent or trespassing with firearms
3. Misuse of Drugs Act 1971, s.23	Controlled drugs	Persons and vehicles	Anywhere
4. Customs and Excise Management Act 1979, s.163	Goods: (a) on which duty has not been paid. (b) being unlawfully removed, imported or exported; (c) otherwise liable to forfeiture to HM Customs and Excise	Vehicles and vessels only	Anywhere
5. Aviation Security Act 1982, s.27(1)	Stolen or unlawfully obtained goods	Airport employees and vehicles carrying airport employees or aircraft or any vehicle in a cargo area whether or not carrying an employee	Any designated airport
6. Police and Criminal Evidence Act 1984, s.1	Stolen goods: articles for use in certain Theft Act offences; offensive weapons, including bladed or sharply-pointed articles (except folding pocket knives with a bladed cutting edge not exceeding 3 inches)	Persons and vehicles	Where there is public access
Police and Criminal Evidence Act 1984, s.6(3) (by a constable of the United Kingdom Atomic Energy Authority Constabulary in respect of property owned or controlled by British Nuclear Fuels plc)	HM Stores (in the form of goods and chattels belonging to British Nuclear Fuels plc)	Persons, vehicles and vessels	Anywhere where the constabulary powers are exercisable
7. Sporting events (Control of Alcohol etc) Act 1985, s.7	Intoxicating Liquor	Persons, coaches and trains	Designated sports grounds or coaches and trains travelling to or from a designated sporting event
8. Crossbows Act 1987, s.4	Crossbows or parts of crossbows (except crossbows with a draw weight of less than 1.4 kilograms)	Persons and vehicles	Anywhere except dwellings
Evidence of game and wildlife offences			
9. Poaching Prevention Act 1862, s.2	Game or poaching equipment	Persons and vehicles	A public place

Power	Object of search	Extent of search	Where exercisable
10. Deer Act 1991, s.12	Evidence of offences under the Act	Persons and vehicles	Anywhere except dwellings
11. Conservation of Seals Act 1970, s.4	Seals or hunting equipment	Vehicles only	Anywhere
12. Badgers Act 1992, s.11	Evidence of offences under the Act	Persons and vehicles	Anywhere
13. Wildlife and Countryside Act 1981, s.19	Evidence of wildlife offences	Persons and vehicles	Anywhere except dwellings
Other			
14. Prevention of Terrorism (Temporary Provisions) Act 1989, s.15(3)	Evidence of liability to arrest under section 14 of the Act	Persons	Anywhere
15. Prevention of Terrorism (Temporary Provisions) Act 1989, s.13A as inserted by section 81 of the Criminal Justice and Public Order Act 1994	Articles which could be used for a purpose connected with the commission preparation of instigation of acts of terrorism	Persons and vehicles	Anywhere within the area or locality authorised under subsection (1)
16. Prevention of Terrorism (Temporary Provisions) Act 1989, paragraph 4(2) of Schedule 5	Anything relevant to determining if a person being examined fails within paragraph 2(a) to (c) of Schedule 5	Persons, vehicles, vessels etc	At designated ports and airports
17. Section 60 Criminal Justice and Public Order Act 1994	Offensive weapons or dangerous instruments to prevent incidents of serious violence	Persons and vehicles	Anywhere within a locality authorised under subsection (1)

B. CODE OF PRACTICE FOR THE SEARCHING OF PREMISES BY POLICE OFFICERS AND THE SEIZURE OF PROPERTY FOUND BY POLICE OFFICERS ON PERSONS OR PREMISES

1 General

1.1   This code of practice must be readily available at all police stations for consultation by police officers, detained persons and members of the public.

1.2   The notes for guidance included are not provisions of this code, but are guidance to police officers and others about its application and interpretation.

1.3   This code applies to searches of premises:

    (a) undertaken for the purposes of an investigation into an alleged offence, with the occupier's consent, other than searches made in the following circumstances:
- routine scenes of crime searches
- calls to a fire or a burglary made by or on behalf of an occupier or searches following the activation of fire or burglar alarms
- searches to which paragraph 4.4 applies
- bomb threat calls;

    (b) under powers conferred by sections 17, 18 and 32 of the Police and Criminal Evidence Act 1984;

    (c) undertaken in pursuance of a search warrant issued in accordance with section 15 of, or Schedule 1 to the Police and Criminal Evidence Act 1984, or section 15 of, or Schedule 7 to the Prevention of Terrorism (Temporary Provisions) Act 1989.

'Premises' for the purpose of this code is defined in section 23 of the Police and Criminal Evidence Act 1984. It includes any place and, in particular, any vehicle, vessel, aircraft, hovercraft, tent or movable structure. It also includes any offshore installation as defined in section 1 of the Mineral Workings (Offshore Installations) Act 1971.

1.3A   Any search of a person who has not been arrested which is carried out during a search of premises shall be carried out in accordance with Code A.

1.3B   This code does not apply to the exercise of a statutory power to enter premises or to inspect goods, equipment or procedures if the exercise of that power is not dependent on the existence of grounds for suspecting that an offence may have been committed and the person exercising the power has no reasonable grounds for such suspicion.

2 Search warrants and production orders

(a) Action to be taken before an application is made

2.1   Where information is received which appears to justify an application, the officer concerned must take reasonable steps to check that the information is accurate, recent and has not been provided maliciously or irresponsibly. An application may not be made on the basis of information from an anonymous source where corroboration has not been sought. [See *Note 2A*]

2.2   The officer shall ascertain as specifically as is possible in the circumstances the nature of the articles concerned and their location.

2.3   The officer shall also make reasonable enquiries to establish what, if anything, is known about the likely occupier of the premises and the nature of the premises themselves; and whether they have been previously searched and if so how recently; and to obtain any other information relevant to the application.

2.4   No application for a search warrant may be made without the authority of an officer of at least the rank of inspector (or, in the case of urgency where no officer of this rank is readily available, the senior officer on duty). No application for a production order or warrant under Schedule 7 to the Prevention of Terrorism (Temporary Provisions) Act 1989, may be made without the authority of an officer of at least the rank of superintendent.

2.5   Except in a case of urgency, if there is reason to believe that a search might have an adverse effect on relations between the police and the community then the local police/community liaison officer shall be consulted before it takes place. In urgent cases, the local police/community liaison officer shall be informed of the search as soon as practicable after it has been made. [See *Note 2B*]

(b) Making an application

2.6   An application for a search warrant must be supported by an information in writing, specifying:
   (i) the enactment under which the application is made;
  (ii) the premises to be searched and the object of the search; and
 (iii) the grounds on which the application is made (including, where the purpose of the proposed search is to find evidence of an alleged offence, an indication of how the evidence relates to the investigation).

2.7   An application for a search warrant under paragraph 12(a) of Schedule 1 to the Police and Criminal Evidence Act 1984, or under Schedule 7 to the Prevention of Terrorism (Temporary Provisions) Act 1989, shall also, where appropriate, indicate why it is believed that service of notice of an application for a production order may seriously prejudice the investigation.

2.8   If an application is refused, no further application may be made for a warrant to search those premises unless supported by additional grounds.

Notes for guidance

2A *The identity of an informant need not be disclosed when making an application, but the officer concerned should be prepared to deal with any questions the magistrate or judge may have about the accuracy of previous information provided by that source or any other related matters.*

2B *The local police/community consultative group, where it exists, or its equivalent, should be informed as soon as practicable after a search has taken place where there is reason to believe that it might have had an adverse effect on relations between the police and the community.*

3 Entry without warrant

(a) Making an arrest etc.

3.1   The conditions under which an officer may enter and search premises without a warrant are set out in section 17 of the Police and Criminal Evidence Act 1984.

(b) Search after arrest of premises in which arrest takes place or in which the arrested person was present immediately prior to arrest

3.2   The powers of an officer to search premises in which he has arrested a person or where the person was immediately before he was arrested are as set out in section 32 of the Police and Criminal Evidence Act 1984.

(c) Search after arrest of premises other than those in which arrest takes place

3.3   The specific powers of an officer to search premises occupied or controlled by a person who has been arrested for an arrestable offence are as set out in section 18 of the Police and Criminal Evidence Act 1984. They may not (unless subsection (5) of section 18 applies) be exercised unless an officer of the rank of inspector or above has given authority in writing. That authority shall (unless wholly impracticable) be given on the Notice of Powers and Rights (see paragraph 5.7(1)). The record of the search required by section 18(7) of the Act shall be made in the custody record, where there is one. In the case of enquiries linked to the investigation of terrorism, the authorising officer shall use his warrant or other identification number.

4 Search with consent

4.1   Subject to paragraph 4.4 below, if it is proposed to search premises with the consent of a person entitled to grant entry to the premises the consent must, if practicable, be given in writing on the Notice of Powers and Rights before the search takes place. The officer must make enquiries to satisfy himself that the person is in a position to give such consent. [See *Notes 4A and 4B* and paragraphs 5.7(i)]

4.2   Before seeking consent the officer in charge of the search shall state the purpose of the proposed search and inform the person concerned that he is not obliged to consent and that anything seized may be produced in evidence. If at the time the person is not suspected of an offence, the officer shall tell him so when stating the purpose of the search.

4.3   An officer cannot enter and search premises or continue to search premises under 4.1 above if the consent has been given under duress or is withdrawn before the search is completed.

4.4   It is unnecessary to seek consent under paragraphs 4.1 and 4.2 above where in the circumstances this would cause disproportionate inconvenience to the person concerned. [See *Note 4C*]

Notes for guidance

4A *In the case of a lodging house or similar accommodation a search should not be made on the basis solely of the landlord's consent unless the tenant, lodger or occupier is unavailable and the matter is urgent.*

4B *Where it is intended to search premises under the authority of a warrant or a power of entry and search without warrant, and the co-operation of the occupier of the premises is obtained in accordance with paragraph 5.4 below, there is no additional requirement to obtain written consent as at paragraph 4.1 above.*

4C *Paragraph 4.4 is intended in particular to apply to circumstances where it is reasonable to assume that innocent occupiers would agree to, and expect that, police should take the proposed action. Examples are where a suspect has fled from the scene of a crime or to evade arrest and it is necessary quickly to check surrounding gardens and readily accessible places to see whether he is hiding; or where police have arrested someone in the night after a pursuit and it is necessary to make a brief check of gardens along the route of the pursuit to see whether stolen or incriminating articles have been discarded.*

5 Searching of premises: general considerations

(a) Time of searches

5.1   Searches made under warrant must be made within one calendar month from the date of issue of the warrant.

5.2   Searches must be made at a reasonable hour unless this might frustrate the purpose of the search. [See *Note 5A*]

5.3   A warrant authorises an entry on one occasion only.

(b) Entry other than with consent

5.4   The officer in charge shall first attempt to communicate with the occupier or any other person entitled to grant access to the premises by explaining the authority under which he seeks entry to the premises and ask the occupier to allow him to enter, unless:
  (i) the premises to be searched are known to be unoccupied;
 (ii) the occupier and any other person entitled to grant access are known to be absent; or
(iii) there are reasonable grounds for believing that to alert the occupier or any other person entitled to grant access by attempting to communicate with him would frustrate the object of the search or endanger the officers concerned or other people.

5.5   Where the premises are occupied the officer shall identify himself (by warrant or other identification number in the case of inquiries linked to the investigation of terrorism) and, if not in uniform, show his warrant card (but in so doing in the case of enquiries linked to the investigation of terrorism, the officer need not reveal his name); and state the purpose of the search and the grounds for undertaking it, before a search begins, unless sub-paragraph 5.4(iii) applies.

5.6 Reasonable force may be used if necessary to enter premises if the officer in charge is satisfied that the premises are those specified in any warrant, or in exercise of the powers described in 3.1 to 3.3 above, and where:
  (i) the occupier or any other person entitled to grant access has refused a request to allow entry to his premises;
  (ii) it is impossible to communicate with the occupier or any other person entitled to grant access; or
  (iii) any of the provisions of 5.4(i) to (iii) apply.

(c) Notice of powers and rights

5.7 If an officer conducts a search to which this code applies he shall, unless it is impracticable to do so, provide the occupier with a copy of a notice in a standard format:
  (i) specifying whether the search is made under warrant, or with consent, or in the exercise of the powers described in 3.1 to 3.3 above (the format of the notice shall provide for authority or consent to be indicated where appropriate – see 3.3 and 4.1 above);
  (ii) summarising the extent of the powers of search and seizure conferred in the Act;
  (iii) explaining the rights of the occupier, and of the owner of property seized in accordance with the provisions of 6.1 to 6.5 below, set out in the Act and in this code;
  (iv) explaining that compensation may be payable in appropriate cases for damages caused in entering and searching premises, and giving the address to which an application for compensation should be directed;
  (v) stating that a copy of this code is available to be consulted at any police station.
5.8 If the occupier is present, copies of the notice mentioned above, and of the warrant (if the search is made under warrant) shall if practicable be given to the occupier before the search begins, unless the officer in charge of the search reasonably believes that to do so would frustrate the object of the search or endanger the officers concerned or other people. If the occupier is not present, copies of the notice, and of the warrant where appropriate, shall be left in a prominent place on the premises or appropriate part of the premises and endorsed with the name of the officer in charge of the search (except in the case of enquiries linked to the investigation of terrorism, in which case the officer's warrant or other identification number shall be given), the name of the police station to which he is attached and the date and time of the search. The warrant itself shall be endorsed to show that this has been done.

(d) Conduct of searches

5.9 Premises may be searched only to the extent necessary to achieve the object of the search, having regard to the size and nature of whatever is sought. A search under warrant may not continue under the authority of that warrant once all the things specified in it have been found, or the officer in charge of the search is satisfied that they are not on the premises.
5.10 Searches must be conducted with due consideration for the property and privacy of the occupier of the premises searched, and with no more disturbance than necessary. Reasonable force may be used only where this is necessary because the co-operation of the occupier cannot be obtained or is insufficient for the purpose.
5.11 If the occupier wishes to ask a friend, neighbour or other person to witness the search then he must be allowed to do so, unless the officer in charge has reasonable grounds for believing that this would seriously hinder the investigation or

endanger the officers concerned or other people. A search need not be unreasonably delayed for this purpose.

(e) Leaving premises

5.12   If premises have been entered by force the officer in charge shall before leaving them, satisfy himself that they are secure either by arranging for the occupier or his agent to be present or by any other appropriate means.

(f) Search under Schedule 1 to the Police and Criminal Evidence Act 1984

5.13   An officer of the rank of inspector or above shall take charge of and be present at any search made under a warrant issued under Schedule 1 to the Police and Criminal Evidence Act 1984 or under Schedule 7 to the Prevention of Terrorism (Temporary Provisions) Act 1989. He is responsible for ensuring that the search is conducted with discretion and in such a manner as to cause the least possible disruption to any business or other activities carried on in the premises.

5.14   After satisfying himself that material may not be taken from the premises without his knowledge, the officer in charge of the search shall ask for the documents or other records concerned to be produced. He may also, if he considers it to be necessary, ask to see the index to files held on the premises, if there is one; and the officers conducting the search may inspect any files which, according to the index, appear to contain any of the material sought. A more extensive search of the premises may be made only if the person responsible for them refuses to produce the material sought, or to allow access to the index; if it appears that the index is inaccurate or incomplete; or if for any other reason the officer in charge has reasonable grounds for believing that such a search is necessary in order to find the material sought. [See *Note 5B*]

Notes for guidance

5A   *In determining at what time to make a search, the officer in charge should have regard, among other considerations, to the time of day at which the occupier of the premises is likely to be present, and should not search at a time when he, or any other person on the premises, is likely to be asleep unless not doing so is likely to frustrate the purpose of the search.*

5B   *In asking for documents to be produced in accordance with paragraph 5.14 above, officers should direct the request to a person in authority and with responsibility for the documents.*

5C   *If the wrong premises are searched by mistake, everything possible should be done at the earliest opportunity to allay any sense of grievance. In appropriate cases assistance should be given to obtain compensation.*

6 Seizure and retention of property

(a) Seizure

6.1   Subject to paragraph 6.2 below, an officer who is searching any premises under any statutory power or with the consent of the occupier may seize:
   (a) anything covered by a warrant; and
   (b) anything which he has reasonable grounds for believing is evidence of an offence or has been obtained in consequence of the commission of an offence.

Items under (b) may be seized where this is necessary to prevent their concealment, alteration, loss, damage or destruction.

6.2   No item may be seized which is subject to legal privilege (as defined in section 10 of the Police and Criminal Evidence Act 1984).

6.3   An officer who decides that it is not appropriate to seize property because of an explanation given by the person holding it, but who has reasonable grounds for believing that it has been obtained in consequence of the commission of an offence by some person, shall inform the holder of his suspicions and shall explain that, if he disposes of the property, he may be liable to civil or criminal proceedings.

6.4   An officer may photograph or copy, or have photographed or copied, any document or other article which he has power to seize in accordance with paragraph 6.1 above.

6.5   Where an officer considers that a computer may contain information which could be used in evidence, he may require the information to be produced in a form which can be taken away and in which it is visible and legible.

(b) Retention

6.6   Subject to paragraph 6.7 below, anything which has been seized in accordance with the above provisions may be retained only for as long as is necessary in the circumstances. It may be retained, among other purposes:

  (i)   for use as evidence at a trial for an offence;

  (ii) for forensic examination or for other investigation in connection with an offence; or

  (iii) where there are reasonable grounds for believing that it has been stolen or obtained by the commission of an offence, in order to establish its lawful owner.

6.7   Property shall not be retained in accordance with 6.6(i) and (ii) (*i.e.* for use as evidence or for the purposes of investigation) if a photograph or copy would suffice for those purposes.

(c) Rights of owners etc.

6.8   If property is retained the person who had custody or control of it immediately prior to its seizure must on request be provided with a list or description of the property within a reasonable time.

6.9   He or his representative must be allowed supervised access to the property to examine it or have it photographed or copied, or must be provided with a photograph or copy, in either case within a reasonable time of any request and at his own expense, unless the officer in charge of an investigation has reasonable grounds for believing that this would prejudice the investigation of an offence or any criminal proceedings. In this case a record of the grounds must be made.

Note for guidance

6A   Any person claiming property seized by the police may apply to a magistrates' court under the Police (Property) Act 1897 for its possession, and should, where appropriate, be advised of this procedure.

7 Action to be taken after searches

7.1   Where premises have been searched in circumstances to which this code applies, other than in the circumstances covered by the exceptions to paragraph 1.3(a), the officer in charge of the search shall, on arrival at a police station, make or have made a record of the search. The record shall include:

  (i)   the address of the premises searched;

  (ii) the date, time and duration of the search;

(iii) the authority under which the search was made. Where the search was made in the exercise of a statutory power to search premises without warrant, the record shall include the power under which the search was made; and where the search was made under warrant, or with written consent, a copy of the warrant or consent shall be appended to the record or kept in a place identified in the record;

(iv) the names of all the officers who conducted the search (except in the case of enquiries linked to the investigation of terrorism, in which case the record shall state the warrant or other identification number and duty station of each officer concerned);

(v) the names of any people on the premises if they are known;

(vi) either a list of any articles seized or a note of where such a list is kept and, if not covered by a warrant, the reason for their seizure;

(vii) whether force was used, and, if so, the reason why it was used;

(viii) details of any damage caused during the search, and the circumstances in which it was caused.

7.2 Where premises have been searched under warrant, the warrant shall be endorsed to show:

(i) whether any articles specified in the warrant were found;

(ii) whether any other articles were seized;

(iii) the date and time at which it was executed;

(iv) the names of the officers who executed it (except in the case of enquiries linked to the investigation of terrorism, in which case the warrant or other identification number and duty station of each officer concerned shall be shown);

(v) whether a copy, together with a copy of the Notice of Powers and Rights was handed to the occupier; or whether it was endorsed as required by paragraph 5.8, and left on the premises together with the copy notice and, if so, where.

7.3 Any warrant which has been executed or which has not been executed within one calendar month of its issue shall be returned, if it was issued by a justice of the peace, to the clerk to the justices for the petty sessions area concerned or, if issued by a judge, to the appropriate officer of the court from which he issued it.

8 Search registers

8.1 A search register shall be maintained at each sub-divisional police station. All records which are required to be made by this code shall be made, copied, or referred to in the register.

C. CODE OF PRACTICE FOR THE DETENTION, TREATMENT AND QUESTIONING OF PERSONS BY POLICE OFFICERS

1 General

1.1 All persons in custody must be dealt with expeditiously, and released as soon as the need for detention has ceased to apply.

1.1A A custody officer is required to perform the functions specified in this code as soon as is practicable. A custody officer shall not be in breach of this code in the event of delay provided that the delay is justifiable and that every reasonable step is taken to prevent unnecessary delay. The custody record shall indicate where a delay has occurred and the reason why. [See *Note 1H*]

1.2 This code of practice must be readily available at all police stations for consultation by police officers, detained persons and members of the public.

1.3 The notes for guidance included are not provisions of this code, but are guidance to police officers and others about it application and interpretation. Provisions in the annexes to this code are provisions of this code.

1.4 If an officer has any suspicion, or is told in good faith, that a person of any age may be mentally disordered or mentally handicapped, or mentally incapable of understanding the significance of questions put to him or his replies, then that person shall be treated as a mentally disordered or mentally handicapped person for the purposes of this code. [See *Note 1G*]

1.5 If anyone appears to be under the age of 17 then he shall be treated as a juvenile for the purposes of this code in the absence of clear evidence to show that he is older.

1.6 If a person appears to be blind or seriously visually handicapped, deaf, unable to read, unable to speak or has difficulty orally because of a speech impediment, he shall be treated as such for the purposes of this code in the absence of clear evidence to the contrary.

1.7 In this code 'the appropriate adult' means:
    (a) in the case of a juvenile:
        (i) his parent or guardian (or, if he is in care, the care authority or voluntary organisation. The term 'in care' is used in this code to cover all cases in which a juvenile is 'looked after' by a local authority under the terms of the Children Act 1989);
        (ii) a social worker;
        (iii) failing either of the above, another responsible adult aged 18 or over who is not a police officer or employed by the police.
    (b) in the case of a person who is mentally handicapped:
        (i) a relative, guardian or other person responsible for his care or custody;
        (ii) someone who has experience of dealing with mentally disordered or mentally handicapped people but who is not a police officer or employed by the police (such as an approved social worker as defined by the Mental Health Act 1983 or a specialist social worker); or
        (iii) failing either of the above, some other responsible adult aged 18 or over who is not a police officer or employed by the police.
        [See *Note 1E*]

1.8 Whenever this code requires a person to be given certain information he does not have to be given it if he is incapable at the time of understanding what is said to him or is violent or likely to become violent or is in urgent need of medical attention, but he must be given it as soon as practicable.

1.9 Any reference to a custody officer in this code includes an officer who is performing the functions of a custody officer.

1.10 Subject to paragraph 1.12, this code applies to people who are in custody at police stations in England and Wales whether or not they have been arrested for an offence and to those who have been removed to a police station as a place of safety under sections 135 and 136 of the Mental Health Act 1983. Section 15 (reviews and extensions of detention) however applies solely to people in police detention, for example those who have been brought to a police station under arrest for an offence or have been arrested at a police station for an offence after attending there voluntarily.

1.11 People in police custody include anyone taken to a police station after being arrested under section 14 of the Prevention of Terrorism (Temporary Provisions) Act 1989 or under paragraph 6 of Schedule 5 to that Act by an examining officer who is a constable.

1.12   This code does not apply to the following groups of people in custody:
   (i) people who have been arrested by officers from a police force in Scotland exercising their powers of detention under section 137(2) of the Criminal Justice and Public Order Act 1994 (Cross Border powers of arrest etc.);
   (ii) people arrested under section 3(5) of the Asylum and Immigration Appeals Act 1993 for the purpose of having their fingerprints taken;
   (iii) people who have been served a notice advising them of their detention under powers contained in the Immigration Act 1971;
   (iv) convicted or remanded prisoners held in police cells on behalf of the Prison Service under the Imprisonment (Temporary Provisions) Act 1980);

but the provisions on conditions of detention and treatment in sections 8 and 9 of this code must be considered as the minimum standards of treatment for such detainees.

Notes for guidance

1A Although certain sections of this code (e.g. section 9 – treatment of detained persons) apply specifically to people in custody at police stations, those there voluntarily to assist with an investigation should be treated with no less consideration (e.g. offered refreshments at appropriate times) and enjoy an absolute right to obtain legal advice or communicate with anyone outside the police station.

1B This code does not affect the principle that all citizens have a duty to help police officers to prevent crime and discover offenders. This is a civic rather than a legal duty; but when a police officer is trying to discover whether, or by whom, an offence has been committed he is entitled to question any person from whom he thinks useful information can be obtained, subject to the restrictions imposed by this code. A person's declaration that he is unwilling to reply does not alter this entitlement.

1C A person, including a parent or guardian, should not be an appropriate adult if he is suspected of involvement in the offence in question, is the victim, is a witness, is involved in the investigation or has received admissions prior to attending to act as the appropriate adult. If the parent of a juvenile is estranged from the juvenile, he should not be asked to act as the appropriate adult if the juvenile expressly and specifically objects to his presence.

1D If a juvenile admits an offence to or in the presence of a social worker other than during the time that the social worker is acting as the appropriate adult for that juvenile, another social worker should be the appropriate adult in the interest of fairness.

1E In the case of people who are mentally disordered or mentally handicapped, it may in certain circumstances be more satisfactory for all concerned if the appropriate adult is someone who has experience or training in their care rather than a relative lacking such qualifications. But if the person himself prefers a relative to a better qualified stranger or objects to a particular person as the appropriate adult, his wishes should if practicable be respected.

1EE A person should always be given an opportunity, when an appropriate adult is called to the police station, to consult privately with a solicitor in the absence of the appropriate adult if they wish to do so.

1F A solicitor or lay visitor who is present at the police station in that capacity may not act as the appropriate adult.

1G The generic term 'mental disorder' is used throughout this code. 'Mental disorder' is defined in section 1(2) of the Mental Health Act 1983 as 'mental illness, arrested or incomplete development of mind, psychopathic disorder and any other disorder or disability of mind'. It should be noted that 'mental disorder' is different from 'mental handicap' although the two are dealt with similarly throughout this code. Where the custody officer has any doubt as to the mental state or capacity of a person detained an appropriate adult should be called.

1H Paragraph 1.1A is intended to cover the kinds of delays which may occur in the processing of detained persons because, for example, a large number of suspects are brought into the police station simultaneously to be placed in custody, or interview rooms are all being used, or where there are difficulties in contacting an appropriate adult, solicitor or interpreter.

1I It is important that the custody officer reminds the appropriate adult and the detained person of the right to legal advice and records any reasons for waiving it in accordance with section 6 of this code.

2 Custody records

2.1 A separate custody record must be opened as soon as practicable for each person who is brought to a police station under arrest or is arrested at the police station having attended there voluntarily. All information which has to be recorded under this code must be recorded as soon as practicable in the custody record unless otherwise specified. Any audio or video recording made in the custody area is not part of the custody record.

2.2 In the case of any action requiring the authority of an officer of a specified rank, his name and rank must be noted in the custody record. The recording of names does not apply to officers dealing with people detained under the Prevention of Terrorism (Temporary Provisions) Act 1989. Instead the record shall state the warrant or other identification number and duty station of such officers.

2.3 The custody officer is responsible for the accuracy and completeness of the custody record and for ensuring that the record or a copy of the record accompanies a detained person if he is transferred to another police station. The record shall show the time of and reason for transfer and the time a person is released from detention.

2.4 A solicitor or appropriate adult must be permitted to consult the custody record of a person detained as soon as practicable after their arrival at the police station. When a person leaves police detention or is taken before a court, he or his legal representative or his appropriate adult shall be supplied on request with a copy of the custody record as soon as practicable. This entitlement lasts for 12 months after his release.

2.5 The person who has been detained, the appropriate adult, or the legal representative shall be permitted to inspect the original custody record after the person has left police detention provided they give reasonable notice of their request. A note of any such inspection shall be made in the custody record.

2.6 All entries in custody records must be timed and signed by the maker. In the case of a record entered on a computer this shall be timed and contain the operator's identification. Warrant or other identification numbers shall be used rather than names in the case of detention under the Prevention of Terrorism (Temporary Provisions) Act 1989.

2.7 The fact and time of any refusal by a person to sign a custody record when asked to do so in accordance with the provisions of this code must itself be recorded.

3 Initial action

(a) Detained persons: normal procedure

3.1 When a person is brought to a police station under arrest or is arrested at the police station having attended there voluntarily, the custody officer must tell him clearly of the following rights and of the fact that they are continuing rights which may be exercised at any stage during the period in custody.

    (i) the right to have someone informed of his arrest in accordance with section 5 below;

 (ii) the right to consult privately with a solicitor and the fact that independent legal advice is available free of charge; and

 (iii) the right to consult these codes of practice.

  [See *Note 3E*]

3.2 In addition the custody officer must give the person a written notice setting out the above three rights, the right to a copy of the custody record in accordance with paragraph 2.4 above and the caution in the terms prescribed in section 10 below. The notice must also explain the arrangements for obtaining legal advice. The custody officer must also give the person an additional written notice briefly setting out his entitlements while in custody. [See *Notes 3A and 3B*] The custody officer shall ask the person to sign the custody record to acknowledge receipt of these notices and any refusal to sign must be recorded on the custody record.

3.3 A citizen of an independent Commonwealth country or a national of a foreign country (including the Republic of Ireland) must be informed as soon as practicable of his rights of communication with his High Commission, Embassy or Consulate. [See *Section 7*]

3.4 The custody officer shall note on the custody record any comment the person may make in relation to the arresting officer's account but shall not invite comment. If the custody officer authorises a person's detention he must inform him of the grounds as soon as practicable and in any case before that person is then questioned about any offence. The custody officer shall note any comment the person may make in respect of the decision to detain him but, again, shall not invite comment. The custody officer shall not put specific questions to the person regarding his involvement in any offence, nor in respect of any comments he may make in response to the arresting officer's account or the decision to place him in detention. Such an exchange is likely to constitute an interview as defined by paragraph 11.1A and would require the associated safeguards included in section 11. [See also paragraph 11.13 in respect of unsolicited comments.]

3.5 The custody officer shall ask the detained person whether at this time he would like legal advice (see paragraph 6.5). The person shall be asked to sign the custody record to confirm his decision. The custody officer is responsible for ensuring that in confirming any decision the person signs in the correct place.

3.5A If video cameras are installed in the custody area, notices which indicate that cameras are in use shall be prominently displayed. Any request by a detained person or other person to have video cameras switched off shall be refused.

(b) Detained persons: special groups

3.6 If the person appears to be deaf or there is doubt about his hearing or speaking ability or ability to understand English, and the custody officer cannot establish effective communication, the custody officer must as soon as practicable call an interpreter and ask him to provide the information required above. [See Section 13]

3.7 If the person is a juvenile, the custody officer must, if it is practicable, ascertain the identity of a person responsible for his welfare. That person may be his parent or guardian (or, if he is in care, the care authority or voluntary organisation) or any other person who has, for the time being, assumed responsibility for his welfare. That person must be informed as soon as practicable that the juvenile has been arrested, why he has been arrested and where he is detained. This right is in addition to the juvenile's right in section 5 of the code not to be held incommunicado. [See *Note 3C*]

3.8 In the case of a juvenile who is known to be subject to a supervision order, reasonable steps must also be taken to notify the person supervising him.

3.9 If the person is a juvenile, is mentally handicapped or appears to be suffering from a mental disorder, then the custody officer must, as soon as practicable, inform the appropriate adult (who in the case of a juvenile may or may not be a person responsible for his welfare, in accordance with paragraph 3.7 above) of the grounds for his detention and his whereabouts and ask the adult to come to the police station to see the person.

3.10 It is imperative that a mentally disordered or mentally handicapped person who has been detained under section 136 of the Mental Health Act 1983 shall be assessed as soon as possible. If that assessment is to take place at the police station, an approved social worker and a registered medical practitioner shall be called to the police station as soon as possible in order to interview and examine the person. Once the person has been interviewed and examined and suitable arrangements have been made for his treatment or care, he can no longer be detained under section 136. The person should not be released until he has been seen by both the approved social worker and the registered medical practitioner.

3.11 If the appropriate adult is already at the police station, then the provisions of paragraphs 3.1 to 3.5 above must be compiled within his presence. If the appropriate adult is not at the police station when the provisions of paragraphs 3.1 to 3.5 above are complied with, then these provisions must be complied with again in the presence of the appropriate adult once that person arrives.

3.12 The person shall be advised by the custody officer that the appropriate adult (where applicable) is there to assist and advise him and that he can consult privately with the appropriate adult at any time.

3.13 If, having been informed of the right to legal advice under paragraph 3.11 above, either the appropriate adult or the person detained wishes legal advice to be taken, then the provisions of section 6 of this code apply. [See *Note 3G*]

3.14 If the person is blind or seriously visually handicapped or is unable to read, the custody officer shall ensure that his solicitor, relative, the appropriate adult or some other person likely to take an interest in him (and not involved in the investigation) is available to help in checking any documentation. Where this code requires written consent or signification then the person who is assisting may be asked to sign instead if the detained person so wishes. [See *Note 3F*]

(c) Persons attending a police station voluntarily

3.15 Any person attending a police station voluntarily for the purpose of assisting with an investigation may leave at will unless placed under arrest. If it is decided that he should not be allowed to leave than he must be informed at once that he is under arrest and brought before the custody officer, who is responsible for ensuring that he is notified of his rights in the same way as other detained persons. If he is not placed under arrest but is cautioned in accordance with section 10 below, the officer who gives the caution must at the same time inform him that he is not under arrest, that he is not obliged to remain at the police station but if he remains at the police station he may obtain free and independent legal advice if he wishes. The officer shall point that the right to legal advice includes the right to speak with a solicitor on the telephone and ask him if he wishes to do so.

3.16 If a person who is attending the police station voluntarily (in accordance with paragraph 3.15) asks about his entitlement to legal advice, he shall be given a copy of the notice explaining the arrangements for obtaining legal advice. [See paragraph 3.2]

(d) Documentation

3.17 The grounds for a person's detention shall be recorded, in his presence if practicable.

3.18 Action taken under paragraphs 3.6 to 3.14 shall be recorded.

Notes for guidance

3A The notice of entitlements is intended to provide detained persons with brief details of their entitlements over and above the statutory rights which are set out in the notice of rights. The notice of entitlements should list the entitlements contained in this code, including visits and contact with outside parties (including special provisions for Commonwealth citizens and foreign nationals), reasonable standards of physical comfort, adequate food and drink, access to toilets and washing facilities, clothing, medical attention, and exercise where practicable. It should also mention the provisions relating to the conduct of interviews, the circumstances in which an appropriate adult should be available to assist the detained person and his statutory rights to make representation whenever the period of his detention is reviewed.

3B In addition to the notices in English, translations should be available in Welsh, the main ethnic minority languages and the principal European languages whenever they are likely to be helpful.

3C If the juvenile is in the care of a local authority or voluntary organisation but is living with his parents or other adults responsible for his welfare then, although there is no legal obligation on the police to inform them, they as well as the authority or organisation should normally be contacted unless suspected of involvement in the offence concerned. Even if a juvenile in care is not living with his parents, consideration should be given to informing them as well.

3D Most local authority Social Services Departments can supply a list of interpreters who have the necessary skills and experience to interpret for deaf people at police interviews. The local Community Relations Council may be able to provide similar information in cases where the person concerned does not understand English. [See section 13]

3E The right to consult the codes of practice under paragraph 3.1 above does not entitle the person concerned to delay unreasonably any necessary investigative or administrative action while he does so. Procedures requiring the provision of breath, blood or urine specimens under the terms of the Road Traffic Act 1988 need not be delayed.

3F Blind or seriously visually handicapped people may be unwilling to sign police documents. The alternative of their representative signing on their behalf seeks to protect the interests of both police and detained people.

3G The purpose of paragraph 3.13 is to protect the rights of a juvenile, mentally disordered or mentally handicapped person who may not understand the significance of what is being said to him. If such a person wishes to exercise the right to legal advice the appropriate action should be taken straightaway and not delayed until the appropriate adult arrives.

4 Detained persons' property

(a) Action

4.1   The custody officer is responsible for:
  (a) ascertaining:
      (i) what property a detained person has with him when he comes to the police station (whether on arrest, re-detention on answering to bail, commitment to prison custody on the order or sentence of a court, lodgement at the police station with a view to his production in court from such custody, arrival at a police station on transfer from detention at another police station or from hospital or on detention under section 135 or 136 of the Mental Health Act 1983);
      (ii) what property he might have acquired for an unlawful or harmful purpose while in custody;

(b) the safekeeping of any property which is taken from him and which remains
            at the police station.
To these ends the custody officer may search him or authorise his being searched to
the extent that he considers necessary (provided that a search of intimate parts of the
body or involving the removal of more than outer clothing may be made only in
accordance with *Annex A* to this code). A search may be only carried out by an officer
of the same sex as the person searched. [See *Note 4A*]

4.2   A detained person may retain clothing and personal effects at his own risk
unless the custody officer considers that he may use them to cause harm to himself or
others, interfere with evidence, damage property or effect an escape or they are
needed as evidence. In this event the custody officer may withhold such articles as he
considers necessary. If he does so he must tell the person why.

4.3   Personal effects are those items which a person may lawfully need or use or
refer to while in detention but do not include cash or other items of value.

(b) Documentation

4.4   The custody officer is responsible for recording all property brought to the
police station which a detained person had with him, or had taken from him on arrest.
The detained person shall be allowed to check and sign the record of property as
correct. Any refusal to sign shall be recorded.

4.5   If a detained person is not allowed to keep any article of clothing or personal
effects the reason must be recorded.

Notes for guidance

4A   *Section 54(1) of PACE and paragraph 4.1 require a detained person to be
searched where it is clear that the custody officer will have continuing duties in
relation to that person or where that person's behaviour or offence makes an
inventory appropriate. They do not require every detained person to be
searched. Where, for example, it is clear that a person will only be detained for a
short period and is not to be placed in a cell, the custody officer may decide not to
search him. In such a case the custody record will be endorsed 'not searched',
paragraph 4.4 will not apply, and the person will be invited to sign the entry.
Where the person detained refuses to sign, the custody officer will be obliged to
ascertain what property he has on him in accordance with paragraph 4.1.*

4B   *Paragraph 4.4 does not require the custody officer to record on the custody
record property in the possession of the person on arrest, if by virtue of its
nature, quantity or size, it is not practicable to remove it to the police station.*

4C   *Paragraph 4.4 above is not to be taken as requiring that items of clothing worn
by the person be recorded unless withheld by the custody officer in accordance
with paragraph 4.2.*

5 Right not to be held incommunicado

(a) Action

5.1   Any person arrested and held in custody at a police station or other premises
may on request have one person known to him or who is likely to take an interest in
his welfare informed at public expense of his whereabouts as soon as practicable. If
the person cannot be contacted the person who has made the request may choose up
to two alternatives. If they too cannot be contacted the person in charge of detention

or of the investigation has discretion to allow further attempts until the information has been conveyed. [See *Notes 5C and 5D*]

5.2   The exercise of the above right in respect of each of the persons nominated may be delayed only in accordance with *Annex B* to this code.

5.3   The above right may be exercised on each occasion that a person is taken to another police station.

5.4   The person may receive visits at the custody officer's discretion. [See *Note 5B*]

5.5   Where an enquiry as to the whereabouts of the person is made by a friend, relative or person with an interest in his welfare, this information shall be given, if he agrees and if *Annex B* does not apply. [See *Note 5D*]

5.6   Subject to the following condition, the person shall be supplied with writing materials on request and allowed to speak on the telephone for a reasonable time to one person [See *Notes 5A and 5E*]. Where an officer of the rank of Inspector or above considers that the sending of a letter or the making of a telephone call may result in:

(a) any of the consequences set out in the first and second paragraphs of *Annex B* and the person is detained in connection with an arrestable or a serious arrestable offence, for which purpose, any reference to a serious arrestable offence in *Annex B* includes an arrestable offence; or

(b) either of the consequences set out in paragraph 8 of *Annex B* and the person is detained under the Prevention of Terrorism (Temporary Provisions) Act 1989;

that officer can deny or delay the exercise of either or both these privileges. However, nothing in this section permits the restriction or denial of the rights set out in paragraphs 5.1 and 6.1.

5.7   Before any letter or message is sent, or telephone call made, the person shall be informed that what he says in any letter, call or message (other than in the case of a communication to a solicitor) may be read or listened to as appropriate and may be given in evidence. A telephone call may be terminated if it is being abused. The costs can be at public expense at the discretion of the custody officer.

(b) Documentation

5.8   A record must be kept of:

(a) any request made under this section and the action taken on it;

(b) any letters, messages or telephone calls made or received or visits received; and

(c) any refusal on the part of the person to have information about himself or his whereabouts given to an outside enquirer. The person must be asked to countersign the record accordingly and any refusal to sign shall be recorded.

Notes for guidance

5A *An interpreter may make a telephone call or write a letter on a person's behalf.*

5B *In the exercise of his discretion the custody officer should allow visits where possible in the light of the availability of sufficient manpower to supervise a visit and any possible hindrance to the investigation.*

5C *If the person does not know of anyone to contact for advice or support or cannot contact a friend or relative, the custody officer should bear in mind any local voluntary bodies or other organisations who might be able to offer help in such cases. But if it is specifically legal advice that is wanted, then paragraph 6.1 below will apply.*

5D *In some circumstances it may not be appropriate to use the telephone to disclose information under paragraphs 5.1 and 5.5 above.*

461

5E　The telephone call at paragraph 5.6 is in addition to any communication under paragraphs 5.1 and 6.1.

6 Right to legal advice

(a) Action

6.1　Subject to the provisos in *Annex B* all people in police detention must be informed that they may at any time consult and communicate privately, whether in person, in writing or by telephone with a solicitor, and that independent legal advice is available free of charge from the duty solicitor. [See paragraph 3.1 and *Note 6B* and *Note 6J*]

6.2　[Not used]

6.3　A poster advertising the right to have legal advice must be prominently displayed in the charging area of every police station. [See *Note 6H*]

6.4　No police officer shall at any time do or say anything with the intention of dissuading a person in detention from obtaining legal advice.

6.5　The exercise of the right of access to legal advice may be delayed only in accordance with *Annex B* to this code. Whenever legal advice is requested (and unless *Annex B* applies) the custody officer must act without delay to secure the provision of such advice to the person concerned. If, on being informed or reminded of the right to legal advice, the person declines to speak to a solicitor in person, the officer shall point out that the right to legal advice includes the right to speak with a solicitor on the telephone and ask him if he wishes to do so. If the person continues to waive his right to legal advice the officer shall ask him the reasons for doing so, and any reasons shall be recorded on the custody record or the interview record as appropriate. Reminders of the right to legal advice must be given in accordance with paragraphs 3.5, 11.2, 15.3, 16.4 and 16.5 of this code and paragraphs 2.15(ii) and 5.2 of Code D. Once it is clear that a person neither wishes to speak to a solicitor in person nor by telephone he should cease to be asked his reasons. [See *Note 6K*]

6.6　A person who wants legal advice may not be interviewed or continue to be interviewed until he has received it unless:

(a)　*Annex B* applies; or

(b)　an officer of the rank of superintendent or above has reasonable grounds for believing that:

　　(i)　delay will involve an immediate risk of harm to persons or serious loss of, or damage to, property; or

　　(ii)　where a solicitor, including a duty solicitor, has been contacted and has agreed to attend, awaiting his arrival would cause unreasonable delay to the process of investigation; or

(c)　the solicitor nominated by the person, or selected by him from a list:

　　(i)　cannot be contacted; or

　　(ii)　has previously indicated that he does not wish to be contacted; or

　　(iii)　having been contacted, has declined to attend:

and the person has been advised of the Duty Solicitor Scheme but has declined to ask for the duty solicitor, or the duty solicitor is unavailable. [In these circumstances the interview may be started or continued without further delay provided that an officer of the rank of Inspector or above has given agreement for the interview to proceed in those circumstances – see *Note 6B*]

(d)　the person who wanted legal advice changes his mind. In these circumstances the interview may be started or continued without further delay provided that the person has given his agreement in writing or on tape to being interviewed without receiving legal advice and that an officer of the rank of Inspector or above, having inquired into the person's reasons for his change of mind, has given authority for the interview to proceed. Confirmation of the person's agreement, his change of mind, his reasons where given and the name of the authorising officer shall be recorded in the taped or written interview record at the beginning or re-commencement of interview. [See *Note 6I*]

6.7   Where 6.6(b)(i) applies, once sufficient information to avert the risk has been obtained, questioning must cease until the person has received legal advice unless 6.6(a), (b)(ii), (c) or (d) apply.

6.8   Where a person has been permitted to consult a solicitor and the solicitor is available (*i.e.* present at the station or on his way to the station or easily contactable by telephone) at the time the interview begins or is in progress, the solicitor must be allowed to be present while he is interviewed.

6.9   The solicitor may only be required to leave the interview if his conduct is such that the investigating officer is unable properly to put questions to the suspect. [See *Notes 6D* and *6E*]

6.10   If the investigating officer considers that a solicitor is acting in such a way, he will stop the interview and consult an officer not below the rank of superintendent, if one is readily available, and otherwise an officer not below the rank of inspector who is not connected with the investigation. After speaking to the solicitor, the officer who has been consulted will decide whether or not the interview should continue in the presence of that solicitor. If he decides that it should not, the suspect will be given the opportunity to consult another solicitor before the interview continues and that solicitor will be given an opportunity to be present at the interview.

6.11   The removal of a solicitor from an interview is a serious step and, if it occurs, the officer of superintendent rank or above who took the decision will consider whether the incident should be reported to the Law Society. If the decision to remove the solicitor has been taken by an officer below the rank of superintendent, the facts must be reported to an officer of superintendent rank or above who will similarly consider whether a report to the Law Society would be appropriate. Where the solicitor concerned is a duty solicitor, the report should be both to the Law Society and to the Legal Aid Board.

6.12   In Codes of Practice issued under the Police and Criminal Evidence Act 1984, 'solicitor' means a solicitor who holds a current practising certificate, a trainee solicitor, a duty solicitor representative or an accredited representative included on the register of representatives maintained by the Legal Aid Board. If a solicitor wishes to send a non-accredited or probationary representative to provide advice on his behalf, then that person shall be admitted to the police station for this purpose unless an officer of the rank of inspector or above considers that such a visit will hinder the investigation of crime and directs otherwise. (Hindering the investigation of a crime does not include giving proper legal advice to a detained person in accordance with *Note 6D*.) Once admitted to the police station, the provisions of paragraphs 6.6 to 6.10 apply.

6.13   In exercising his discretion under paragraph 6.12, the officer should take into account in particular whether the identity and status of the non-accredited or probationary representative have been satisfactorily established; whether he is of suitable character to provide legal advice (a person with a criminal record is unlikely to be suitable unless the conviction was for a minor offence and is not of recent date); and any other matters in any written letter of authorisation provided by the solicitor on whose behalf the person is attending the police station. [See *Note 6F*]

6.14   If the inspector refuses access to a non-accredited or probationary representative or a decision is taken that such a person should not be permitted to remain at an interview, he must forthwith notify a solicitor on whose behalf the non-accredited or probationary representative was to have acted or was acting, and give him an opportunity to make alternative arrangements. The detained person must also be informed and the custody record noted.

6.15   If a solicitor arrives at the station to see a particular person, that person must (unless *Annex B* applies) be informed of the solicitor's arrival whether or not he is being interviewed and asked whether he would like to see him. This applies even if the person concerned has already declined legal advice or having requested it, subsequently agreed to be interviewed without having received advice. The solicitor's attendance and the detained person's decision must be noted in the custody record.

(b) Documentation

6.16   Any request for legal advice and the action taken on it shall be recorded.

6.17   If a person has asked for legal advice and an interview is begun in the absence of a solicitor or his representative (or the solicitor or his representative has been required to leave an interview), a record shall be made in the interview record.

Notes for guidance

6A   *In considering whether paragraph 6.6(b) applies, the officer should where practicable ask the solicitor for an estimate of the time that he is likely to take in coming to the station, and relate this information to the time for which detention is permitted, the time of day (i.e. whether the period of rest required by paragraph 12.2 is imminent) and the requirements of other investigations in progress. If the solicitor says that he is on his way to the station or that he will set off immediately, it will not normally be appropriate to begin an interview before he arrives. If it appears that it will be necessary to begin an interview before the solicitor's arrival he should be given an indication of how long the police would be able to wait before paragraph 6.6(b) applies so that he has an opportunity to make arrangements for legal advice to be provided by someone else.*

6B   *A person who asks for legal advice should be given an opportunity to consult a specific solicitor or another solicitor from that solicitor's firm or the duty solicitor. If advice is not available by these means, or he does not wish to consult the duty solicitor, the person should be given an opportunity to choose a solicitor from a list of those willing to provide legal advice. If this solicitor is unavailable, he may choose up to two alternatives. If these attempts to secure legal advice are unsuccessful, the custody officer has discretion to allow further attempts until a solicitor has been contacted and agrees to provide legal advice. Apart from carrying out his duties under Note 6B, a police officer must not advise the suspect about any particular firm of solicitors.*

6C   *[Not used]*

6D   *A detained person has a right to free legal advice and to be represented by a solicitor. The solicitor's only role in the police station is to protect and advance the legal rights of his client. On occasions this may require the solicitor to give advice which has the effect of his client avoiding giving evidence which strengthens a prosecution case. The solicitor may intervene in order to seek clarification or to challenge an improper question to his client or the manner in which it is put, or to advise his client not to reply to particular questions, or if he wishes to give his client further legal advice. Paragraph 6.9 will only apply if the solicitor's approach or conduct prevents or unreasonably obstructs proper questions being put to the suspect or his response being recorded. Examples of unacceptable conduct include answering questions on a suspect's behalf or providing written replies for him to quote.*

6E   *In a case where an officer takes the decision to exclude a solicitor, he must be in a position to satisfy the court that the decision was properly made. In order to do this he may need to witness what is happening himself.*

6F   *If an officer of at least the rank of inspector considers that a particular solicitor or firm of solicitors is persistently sending non-accredited or probationary representatives who are unsuited to provide legal advice, he should inform an officer of at least the rank of superintendent, who may wish to take the matter up with the Law Society.*

6G   *Subject to the constraints of* Annex B, *a solicitor may advise more than one client in an investigation if he wishes. Any question of a conflict of interest is for*

464

the solicitor under his professional code of conduct. If, however, waiting for a solicitor to give advice to one client may lead to unreasonable delay to the interview with another, the provisions of paragraph 6.6(b) may apply.

6H *In addition to a poster in English advertising the right to legal advice, a poster or posters containing translations into Welsh, the main ethnic minority languages and the principal European languages should be displayed wherever they are likely to be helpful and it is practicable to do so.*

6I *Paragraph 6.6(d) requires the authorisation of an officer of the rank of inspector or above, to the continuation of an interview, where a person who wanted legal advice changes his mind. It is permissible for such authorisation to be given over the telephone, if the authorising officer is able to satisfy himself as to the reason for the person's change of mind and is satisfied that it is proper to continue the interview in those circumstances.*

6J *Where a person chooses to speak to a solicitor on the telephone, he should be allowed to do so in private unless this is impractical because of the design and layout of the custody area or the location of telephones.*

6K *A person is not obliged to give reasons for declining legal advice and should not be pressed if he does not wish to do so.*

7 Citizens of Independent Commonwealth countries or foreign nationals

(a) Action

7.1 Any citizen of an Independent Commonwealth country or a national of a foreign country (including the Republic of Ireland) may communicate at any time with his High Commission, Embassy or Consulate. He must be informed of this right as soon as practicable. He must also be informed as soon as practicable of his right, upon request to have his High Commission, Embassy or Consulate told of his whereabouts and the grounds for his detention. Such a request should be acted upon as soon as practicable.

7.2 If a person is detained who is a citizen of an Independent Commonwealth or foreign country with which a bilateral consular convention or agreement is in force requiring notification of arrest, the appropriate High Commission, Embassy or Consulate shall be informed as soon as practicable, subject to paragraph 7.4 below. The countries to which this applies as at 1 January 1995 are listed in *Annex F.*

7.3 Consular officers may visit one of their nationals who is in police detention to talk to him and, if required, to arrange for legal advice. Such visits shall take place out of the hearing of a police officer.

7.4 Notwithstanding the provisions of consular conventions, where the person is a political refugee (whether for reasons of race, nationality, political opinion or religion) or is seeking political asylum, a consular officer shall not be informed of the arrest of one of his nationals or given access or information about him except at the person's express request.

(b) Documentation

7.5 A record shall be made when a person is informed of his rights under this section and of any communications with a High Commission, Embassy or Consulate.

Note for guidance

7A *The exercise of the rights in this section may not be interfered with even though Annex B applies.*

8 Conditions of detention

(a) Action

8.1   So far as is practicable, not more than one person shall be detained in each cell.

8.2   Cells in use must be adequately heated, cleaned and ventilated. They must be adequately lit, subject to such dimming as is compatible with safety and security to allow people detained overnight to sleep. No additional restraints shall be used within a locked cell unless absolutely necessary, and then only suitable handcuffs. In the case of a mentally handicapped or mentally disordered person, particular care must be taken when deciding whether to use handcuffs. [See *Annex E* paragraph 13]

8.3   Blankets, mattresses, pillows and other bedding supplied shall be of a reasonable standard and in a clean and sanitary condition. [See *Note 8B*]

8.4   Access to toilet and washing facilities must be provided.

8.5   If it is necessary to remove a person's clothes for the purposes of investigation, for hygiene or health reasons or for cleaning, replacement clothing of a reasonable standard of comfort and cleanliness shall be provided. A person may not be interviewed unless adequate clothing has been offered to him.

8.6   At least two light meals and one main meal shall be offered in any period of 24 hours. [See *Note 8C*] Drinks should be provided at meal times and upon reasonable request between meal times. Whenever necessary, advice shall be sought from the police surgeon on medical and dietary matters. As far as practicable, meals provided shall offer a varied diet and meet any special dietary needs or religious beliefs that the person may have; he may also have meals supplied by his family or friends at his or their own expense. [See *Note 8B*]

8.7   Brief outdoor exercise shall be offered daily if practicable.

8.8   A juvenile shall not be placed in a police cell unless no other secure accommodation is available and the custody officer considers that it is not practicable to supervise him if he is not placed in a cell or the custody officer considers that a cell provides more comfortable accommodation than other secure accommodation in the police station. He may not be placed in a cell with a detained adult.

8.9   Reasonable force may be used if necessary for the following purposes:
   (i) to secure compliance with reasonable instructions, including instructions given in pursuance of the provisions of a code of practice; or
   (ii) to prevent escape, injury, damage to property or the destruction of evidence.

8.10   People detained shall be visited every hour, and those who are drunk, at least every half hour. A person who is drunk shall be roused and spoken to on each visit. [See *Note 8A*] Should the custody officer feel in any way concerned about the person's condition, for example because he fails to respond adequately when roused, then the officer shall arrange for medical treatment in accordance with paragraph 9.2 of this code.

(b) Documentation

8.11   A record must be kept of replacement clothing and meals offered.

8.12   If a juvenile is placed in a cell, the reason must be recorded.

Notes for guidance

8A   Whenever possible juveniles and other people at risk should be visited more frequently.

8B   The provisions in paragraphs 8.3 and 8.6 respectively regarding bedding and a varied diet are of particular importance in the case of a person detained under the Prevention of Terrorism (Temporary Provisions) Act 1989, immigration detainees and others who are likely to be detained for an extended period.

8C   Meals should so far as practicable be offered at recognised meal times.

9 Treatment of detained persons

(a) General

9.1   If a complaint is made by or on behalf of a detained person about his treatment since his arrest, or it comes to the notice of any officer that he may have been treated improperly, a report must be made as soon as practicable to an officer of the rank of inspector or above who is not connected with the investigation. If the matter concerns a possible assault or the possibility of the unnecessary or unreasonable use of force then the police surgeon must also be called as soon as practicable.

(b) Medical treatment

9.2   The custody officer must immediately call the surgeon (or, in urgent cases – for example, where a person does not show signs of sensibility or awareness – must send the person to hospital or call the nearest available medical practitioner) if a person brought to a police station or already detained there:
(a)   appears to be suffering from physical illness or a mental disorder; or
(b)   is injured; or
(c)   [Not used]
(d)   fails to respond normally to questions or conversation (other than through drunkenness alone); or
(e)   otherwise appears to need medical attention.
This applies even if the person makes no request for medical attention and whether or not he has already had medical treatment elsewhere (unless brought to the police station direct from hospital). It is not intended that the contents of this paragraph should delay the transfer of a person to a place of safety under section 136 of the Mental Health Act 1983 where that is applicable. Where an assessment under that Act is to take place at the police station, the custody officer has discretion not to call the police surgeon so long as he believes that the assessment by a registered medical practitioner can be undertaken without undue delay. [See *Note 9A*]

9.3   If it appears to the custody officer, or he is told, that a person brought to the police station under arrest may be suffering from an infectious disease of any significance he must take steps to isolate the person and his property until he has obtained medical directions as to where the person should be taken, whether fumigation should take place and what precautions should be taken by officers who have been or will be in contact with him.

9.4   If a detained person requests a medical examination the police surgeon must be called as soon as practicable. He may in addition be examined by a medical practitioner of his own choice at his own expense.

9.5   If a person is required to take or apply any medication in compliance with medical directions, but prescribed before the person's detention, the custody officer should consult the police surgeon prior to the use of the medication. The custody officer is responsible for the safekeeping of any medication and for ensuring that the person is given the opportunity to take or apply medication which the police surgeon has approved. However no police station may administer medicines which are also controlled drugs subject to the Misuse of Drugs Act 1971 for this purpose. A person may administer a controlled drug to himself only under the personal supervision of the police surgeon. The requirement for personal supervision will have been satisfied if the custody officer consults the police surgeon (this may be done by telephone) and both the police surgeon and the custody officer are satisfied that, in all the circumstances, self administration of the controlled drug will not expose the detained person, police officers or anyone to the risk of harm or injury. If so satisfied, the police surgeon may authorise the custody officer to permit the detained person to administer the controlled drug. If the custody officer is in any doubt, the police surgeon should be asked to attend. Such consultation should be noted in the custody record.

9.6 If a detained person has in his possession or claims to need medication relating to a heart condition, diabetes, epilepsy or a condition of comparable potential seriousness then, even though paragraph 9.2 may not apply, the advice of the police surgeon must be obtained.

(c) Documentation

9.7 A record must be made of any arrangements made for an examination by a police surgeon under paragraph 9.1 above and of any complaint reported under that paragraph together with any relevant remarks by the custody officer.

9.8 A record must be kept of any request for a medical examination under paragraph 9.4, of the arrangements for any examinations made, and of any medical directions to the police.

9.9 Subject to the requirements of section 4 above the custody record shall include not only a record of all medication that a detained person has in his possession on arrival at the police station but also a note of any such medication he claims he needs but does not have with him.

Notes for guidance

9A *The need to call a police surgeon need not apply to minor ailments or injuries which do not need attention. However, all such ailments or injuries must be recorded in the custody record and any doubt must be resolved in favour of calling the police surgeon.*

9B *It is important to remember that a person who appears to be drunk or behaving abnormally may be suffering from illness or the effects of drugs or may have sustained injury (particularly head injury) which is not apparent, and that someone needing or addicted to certain drugs may experience harmful effects within a short time of being deprived of their supply. Police should therefore always call the police surgeon when in any doubt, and act with all due speed.*

9C *If a medical practitioner does not record his clinical findings in the custody record, the record must show where they are recorded.*

10 Cautions

(a) When a caution must be given

10.1 A person whom there are grounds to suspect of an offence must be cautioned before any questions about it (or further questions if it is his answers to previous questions which provide the grounds for suspicion) are put to him regarding his involvement or suspected involvement in that offence if his answers or his silence (*i.e.* failure or refusal to answer a question or to answer satisfactorily) may be given in evidence to a court in a prosecution. He therefore need not be cautioned if questions are put for other purposes, for example, solely to establish his identity or his ownership of any vehicle or to obtain information in accordance with any relevant statutory requirement (see paragraph 10.5C) or in furtherance of the proper and effective conduct of a search, (for example to determine the need to search in the exercise of powers of stop and search or to seek co-operation while carrying out a search) or to seek verification of a written record in accordance with paragraph 11.13.

10.2   Whenever a person who is not under arrest is initially cautioned or is reminded that he is under caution (see paragraph 10.5) he must at the same time be told that he is not under arrest and is not obliged to remain with the officer (see paragraph 3.15).

10.3   A person must be cautioned upon arrest for an offence unless:

(a) it is impracticable to do so by reason of his condition or behaviour at the time; or

(b) he has already been cautioned immediately prior to arrest in accordance with paragraph 10.1 above.

(b) Action: general

10.4   The caution shall be in the following terms:

'You do not have to say anything. But it may harm your defence if you do not mention when questioned something which you later rely on in court. Anything you do say may be given in evidence.'

Minor deviations do not constitute a breach of this requirement provided that the sense of the caution is preserved. [See *Note 10C*]

10.5   When there is a break in questioning under caution the interviewing officer must ensure that the person being questioned is aware that he remains under caution. If there is any doubt the caution shall be given again in full when the interview resumes. [See *Note 10A*]

Special warnings under sections 36 and 37 of the Criminal Justice and Public Order Act 1994

10.5A   When a suspect who is interviewed after arrest fails or refuses to answer certain questions, or to answer them satisfactorily, after due warning, a court or jury may draw such inferences as appear proper under sections 36 and 37 of the Criminal Justice and Public Order Act 1994. This applies when:

(a) a suspect is arrested by a constable and there is found on his person, or in or on his clothing or footwear, or otherwise in his possession, or in the place where he was arrested, any objects, marks or substances, or marks on such objects, and the person fails or refuses to account for the objects, marks or substances found; or

(b) an arrested person was found by a constable at a place at or about the time the offence for which he was arrested, is alleged to have been committed, and the person fails or refuses to account for his presence at that place.

10.5B   For an inference to be drawn from a suspect's failure or refusal to answer a question about one of these matters or to answer it satisfactorily, the interviewing officer must first tell him in ordinary language:

(a) what offence he is investigating;

(b) what fact he is asking the suspect to account for;

(c) that he believes this fact may be due to the suspect's taking part in the commission of the offence in question;

(d) that a court may draw a proper inference if he fails or refuses to account for the fact about which he is being questioned;

(e) that a record is being made of the interview and that it may be given in evidence if he is brought to trial.

10.5C   Where, despite the fact that a person has been cautioned, failure to co-operate may have an effect on his immediate treatment, he should be informed of any relevant consequences and that they are not affected by the caution. Examples are when his refusal to provide his name and address when charged may render him liable to detention, or when his refusal to provide particulars and information in accordance with a statutory requirement, for example, under the Road Traffic Act 1988, may amount to an offence or may make him liable to arrest.

(c) Juveniles, the mentally disordered and the mentally handicapped

10.6   If a juvenile or a person who is mentally disordered or mentally handi-capped is cautioned in the absence of the appropriate adult, the caution must be repeated in the adult's presence.

(d) Documentation

10.7   A record shall be made when a caution is given under this section, either in the officer's pocket book or in the interview record as appropriate.

Notes for guidance

10A   *In considering whether or not to caution again after a break, the officer should bear in mind that he may have to satisfy a court that the person understood that he was still under caution when the interview resumed.*
10B   *[Not used]*
10C   *If it appears that a person does not understand what the caution means, the officer who has given it should go on to explain it in his own words.*
10D   *[Not used]*

11 Interviews: general

(a) Action

11.1A   An interview is the questioning of a person regarding his involvement or suspected involvement in a criminal offence or offences which, by virtue of paragraph 10.1 of Code C, is required to be carried out under caution. Procedures undertaken under section 7 of the Road Traffic Act 1988 do not constitute interviewing for the purpose of this code.

11.1   Following a decision to arrest a suspect he must not be interviewed about the relevant offence except at a police station or other authorised place of detention unless the consequent delay would be likely:
  (a) to lead to interference with or harm to evidence connected with an offence or interference with or physical harm to other people; or
  (b) to lead to the alerting of other people suspected of having committed an offence but not yet arrested for it; or
  (c) to hinder the recovery of property obtained in consequence of the commission of an offence.
Interviewing in any of these circumstances shall cease once the relevant risk has been averted or the necessary questions have been put in order to attempt to avert that risk.

11.2   Immediately prior to the commencement or re-commencement of any interview at a police station or other authorised place of detention, the interviewing officer shall remind the suspect of his entitlement to free legal advice and that the interview can be delayed for him to obtain legal advice (unless the exceptions in paragraph 6.6 or *Annex C* apply). It is the responsibility of the interviewing officer to ensure that all such reminders are noted in the record of interview.

11.2A   At the beginning of an interview carried out in a police station, the interviewing officer, after cautioning the suspect, shall put to him any significant statement or silence which occurred before his arrival at the police station, and shall ask him whether he confirms or denies that earlier statement or silence and whether he wishes to add anything. A 'significant' statement or silence is one which appears capable of being used in evidence against the suspect, in particular a direct admission of guilt, or failure or refusal to answer a question or to answer it satisfactorily, which might give rise to an inference under Part III of the Criminal Justice and Public Order Act 1994.

11.3   No police officer may try to obtain answers to questions or to elicit a statement by the use of oppression. Except as provided for in paragraph 10.5C, no police officer shall indicate, except in answer to a direct question, what action will be taken on the part of the police if the person being interviewed answers questions, makes a statement or refuses to do either. If the person asks the officer directly what action will be taken in the event of his answering questions, making a statement or refusing to do either, then the officer may inform the person what action the police propose to take in that event provided that action is itself proper and warranted.

11.4   As soon as a police officer who is making enquiries of any person about an offence believes that a prosecution should be brought against him and that there is sufficient evidence for it to succeed, he shall ask the person if he has anything further to say. If the person indicates that he has nothing more to say the officer shall without delay cease to question him about that offence. This should not, however, be taken to prevent officers in revenue cases or acting under the confiscation provisions of the Criminal Justice Act 1988 or the Drug Trafficking Offences Act 1986 from inviting suspects to complete a formal question and answer record after the interview is concluded.

(b) Interview records

11.5
   (a)   An accurate record must be made of each interview with a person suspected of an offence, whether or not the interview takes place at a police station.
   (b)   The record must state the place of the interview, the time it begins and ends, the time the record is made (if different), any breaks in the interview and the names of all those present; and must be made on the forms provided for this purpose or in the officer's pocket book or in accordance with the code of practice for the tape-recording of police interviews with suspects (Code E).
   (c)   The record must be made during the course of the interview, unless in the investigating officer's view this would not be practicable or would interfere with conduct of the interview, and must constitute either a verbatim record of what has been said or, failing this, an account of the interview which adequately and accurately summarises it.

11.6   The requirement to record the names of all those present at any interview does not apply to police officers interviewing people detained under the Prevention of Terrorism (Temporary Provisions) Act 1989. Instead the record shall state the warrant or other identification number and duty station of such officers.

11.7   If an interview record is not made during the course of the interview it must be made as soon as practicable after its completion.

11.8   Written interview records must be timed and signed by the maker.

11.9   If an interview record is not completed in the course of the interview the reason must be recorded in the officer's pocket book.

11.10   Unless it is impracticable the person interviewed shall be given the opportunity to read the interview record and to sign it as correct or to indicate the respects in which he considers it inaccurate. If the interview is tape-recorded the arrangements set out in Code E apply. If the person concerned cannot read or refuses to read the record or to sign it, the senior police officer present shall read it to him and ask him whether he would like to sign it as correct (or make his mark) or to indicate the respects in which he considers it inaccurate. The police officer shall then certify on the interview record itself what has occurred. [See *Note 11D*]

11.11   If the appropriate adult or the person's solicitor is present during the interview, he shall also be given an opportunity to read and sign the interview record (or any written statement taken down by a police officer).

11.12   Any refusal by a person to sign an interview record when asked to do so in accordance with the provisions of the code must itself be recorded.

11.13   A written record shall also be made of any comments made by a suspected person, including unsolicited comments, which are outside the context of an interview but which might be relevant to the offence. Any such record must be timed and signed by the maker. Where practicable the person shall be given the opportunity to read that record and to sign it as correct or to indicate the respects in which he considers it inaccurate. Any refusal to sign shall be recorded. [See *Note 11D*]

(c) Juveniles, mentally disordered people and mentally handicapped people

11.14   A juvenile or a person who is mentally disordered or mentally handicapped, whether suspected or not, must not be interviewed or asked to provide or sign a written statement in the absence of the appropriate adult unless paragraph 11.1 or *Annex C* applies.

11.15   Juveniles may only be interviewed at their places of education in exceptional circumstances and then only where the principal or his nominee agrees. Every effort should be made to notify both the parent(s) or other person responsible for the juvenile's welfare and the appropriate adult (if this is a different person) that the police want to interview the juvenile and reasonable time should be allowed to enable the appropriate adult to be present at the interview. Where awaiting the appropriate adult would cause unreasonable delay and unless the interviewee is suspected of an offence against the educational establishment, the principal or his nominee can act as the appropriate adult for the purposes of the interview.

11.16   Where the appropriate adult is present at an interview, he shall be informed that he is not expected to act simply as an observer; and also that the purposes of his presence are, first, to advise the person being questioned and to observe whether or not the interview is being conducted properly and fairly, and secondly, to facilitate communication with the person being interviewed.

Notes for guidance

11A   [Not used]

11B   It is important to bear in mind that, although juveniles or people who are mentally disordered or mentally handicapped are often capable of providing reliable evidence, they may, without knowing or wishing to do so, be particularly prone in certain circumstances to provide information which is unreliable, misleading or self-incriminating. Special care should therefore always be exercised in questioning such a person, and the appropriate adult should be involved, if there is any doubt about a person's age, mental state or capacity. Because of the risk of unreliable evidence it is also important to obtain corroboration of any facts admitted whenever possible.

11C   It is preferable that a juvenile is not arrested at his place of education unless this is unavoidable. Where a juvenile is arrested at his place of education, the principal or his nominee must be informed.

11D   When a suspect agrees to read records of interviews and of other comments and to sign them as correct, he should be asked to endorse the record with words such as 'I agree that this is a correct record of what was said' and add his signature. Where the suspect does not agree with the record, the officer should record the details of any disagreement and then ask the suspect to read these details and then sign them to the effect that they accurately reflect his disagreement. Any refusal to sign when asked to do so shall be recorded.

12 Interviews in police stations

(a) Action

12.1   If a police officer wishes to interview, or conduct enquiries which require the presence of a detained person, the custody officer is responsible for deciding whether to deliver him into his custody.

12.2   In any period of 24 hours a detained person must be allowed a continuous period of at least 8 hours for rest, free from questioning, travel or any interruption by police officers in connection with the investigation concerned. This period should normally be at night. The period of rest may not be interrupted or delayed, except at the request of the person, his appropriate adult or his legal representative, unless there are reasonable grounds for believing that it would:
  (i) involve a risk of harm to people or serious loss of, or damage to, property; or
  (ii) delay unnecessarily the person's release from custody; or
  (iii) otherwise prejudice the outcome of the investigation.

If a person is arrested at a police station after going there voluntarily, the period of 24 hours runs from the time of his arrest and not the time of arrival at the police station. Any action which is required to be taken in accordance with section 8 of this code, or in accordance with medical advice or at the request of the detained person, his appropriate adult or his legal representative, does not constitute an interruption to the rest period such that a fresh period must be allowed.

12.3   A detained person may not be supplied with intoxicating liquor except on medical directions. No person, who is unfit through drink or drugs to the extent that he is unable to appreciate the significance of questions put to him and his answers, may be questioned about an alleged offence in that condition except in accordance with *Annex C.* [See *Note 12B*]

12.4   As far as practicable interviews shall take place in interview rooms which must be adequately heated, lit and ventilated.

12.5   People being questioned or making statements shall not be required to stand.

12.6   Before the commencement of an interview each interviewing officer shall identify himself and any other officers present by name and rank to the person being interviewed, except in the case of people detained under the Prevention of Terrorism (Temporary Provisions) Act 1989 when each officer shall identify himself by his warrant or other identification number and rank rather than his name.

12.7   Breaks from interviewing shall be made at recognised meal times. Short breaks for refreshment shall also be provided at intervals of approximately two hours, subject to the interviewing officer's discretion to delay a break if there are reasonable grounds for believing that it would:
  (i) involve a risk of harm to people or serious loss of, or damage to property;
  (ii) delay unnecessarily the person's release from custody; or
  (iii) otherwise prejudice the outcome of the investigation.
[See *Note 12C*]

12.8   If in the course of the interview a complaint is made by the person being questioned or on his behalf concerning the provisions of this code then the interviewing officer shall:
  (i) record it in the interview record; and
  (ii) inform the custody officer, who is then responsible for dealing with it in accordance with section 9 of this code.

(b) Documentation

12.9   A record must be made of the time at which a detained person is not in the custody of the custody officer, and why; and of the reason for any refusal to deliver him out of that custody.

12.10   A record must be made of any intoxicating liquor supplied to a detained person, in accordance with paragraph 12.3 above.

12.11   Any decision to delay a break in an interview must be recorded, with grounds, in the interview record.

12.12   All written statements made at police stations under caution shall be written on the forms provided for the purpose.

12.13   All written statements made under caution shall be taken in accordance with *Annex D* to this code.

Notes for guidance

12A   *If the interview has been contemporaneously recorded and the record signed by the person interviewed in accordance with paragraph 11.10 above, or has been tape recorded, it is normally unnecessary to ask for a written statement. Statements under caution should normally be taken in these circumstances only at the person's express wish. An officer may, however, ask him whether or not he wants to make such a statement.*

12B   *The police surgeon can give advice about whether or not a person is fit to be interviewed in accordance with paragraph 12.3 above.*

12C   *Meal breaks should normally last at least 45 minutes and shorter breaks after two hours should last at least 15 minutes. If the interviewing officer delays a break in accordance with paragraph 12.7 of this code and prolongs the interview, a longer break should then be provided. If there is a short interview, and a subsequent short interview is contemplated, the length of the break may be reduced if there are reasonable grounds to believe that this is necessary to avoid any of the consequences in paragraph 12.7(i) to (iii).*

13 Interpreters

(a) General

13.1   Information on obtaining the services of a suitably qualified interpreter for the deaf or for people who do not understand English is given in *Note for guidance 3D*.

(b) Foreign languages

13.2   Except in accordance with paragraph 11.1 or unless *Annex C* applies, a person must not be interviewed in the absence of a person capable of acting as interpreter if:
   (a) he has difficulty in understanding English;
   (b) the interviewing officer cannot speak the person's own language; and
   (c) the person wishes an interpreter to be present.

13.3   The interviewing officer shall ensure that the interpreter makes a note of the interview at the time in the language of the person being interviewed for use in the event of his being called to give evidence, and certifies its accuracy. He shall allow sufficient time for the interpreter to make a note of each question and answer after each has been put or given and interpreted. The person shall be given an opportunity to read it or have it read to him and sign it as correct or to indicate the respects in which he considers it inaccurate. If the interview is tape-recorded the arrangements set out in Code E apply.

13.4   In the case of a person making a statement in a language other than English:
  (a) the interpreter shall take down the statement in the language in which it is made;
  (b) the person making the statement shall be invited to sign it; and
  (c) an official English translation shall be made in due course.

(c) Deaf people and people with a speech handicap

13.5   If a person appears to be deaf or there is doubt about his hearing or speaking ability, he must not be interviewed in the absence of an interpreter unless he agrees in writing to be interviewed without one or paragraph 11.1 or *Annex C* applies.

13.6   An interpreter shall also be called if a juvenile is interviewed and the parent or guardian present as the appropriate adult appears to be deaf or there is doubt about his hearing or speaking ability, unless he agrees in writing that the interview should proceed without one or paragraph 11.1 or *Annex C* applies.

13.7   The interviewing officer shall ensure that the interpreter is given an opportunity to read the record of the interview and to certify its accuracy in the event of his being called to give evidence.

(d) Additional rules for detained persons

13.8   All reasonable attempts should be made to make clear to the detained person that interpreters will be provided at public expense.

13.9   Where paragraph 6.1 applies and the person concerned cannot communicate with the solicitor, whether because of language, hearing or speech difficulties, an interpreter must be called. The interpreter may not be a police officer when interpretation is needed for the purposes of obtaining legal advice. In all other cases a police officer may only interpret if he first obtains the detained person's (or the appropriate adult's) agreement in writing or if the interview is tape-recorded in accordance with Code E.

13.10   When a person is charged with an offence who appears to be deaf or there is doubt about his hearing or speaking ability or ability to understand English, and the custody officer cannot establish effective communication, arrangements must be made for an interpreter to explain as soon as practicable the offence concerned and any other information given by the custody officer.

(e) Documentation

13.11   Action taken to call an interpreter under this section and any agreement to be interviewed in the absence of an interpreter must be recorded.

Note for guidance

13A   *If the interpreter is needed as a prosecution witness at the person's trial, a second interpreter must act as the court interpreter.*

14 Questioning: special restrictions

14.1   If a person has been arrested by one police force on behalf of another and the lawful period of detention in respect of that offence has not yet commenced in accordance with section 41 of the Police and Criminal Evidence Act 1984 no questions may be put to him about the offence while he is in transit between the forces except in order to clarify any voluntary statement made by him.

14.2 If a person is in police detention at a hospital he may not be questioned without the agreement of a responsible doctor. [See *Note 14A*]

Note for guidance

> *14A If questioning takes place at a hospital under paragraph 14.2 (or on the way to or from a hospital) the period concerned counts towards the total period of detention permitted.*

15 Reviews and extensions of detention

(a) Action

15.1 The review officer is responsible under section 40 of the Police and Criminal Evidence Act 1984 (or, in terrorist cases, under Schedule 3 to the Prevention of Terrorism (Temporary Provisions) Act 1989) for determining whether or not a person's detention continues to be necessary. In reaching a decision he shall provide an opportunity to the detained person himself to make representations (unless he is unfit to do so because of his condition or behaviour) or to his solicitor or to the appropriate adult if available at the time. Other people having an interest in the person's welfare may make representations at the review officer's discretion.

15.2 The same people may make representations to the officer determining whether further detention should be authorised under section 42 of the Act or under Schedule 3 to the 1989 Act. [See *Note 15A*]

15.2A After hearing any representations, the review officer or officer determining whether further detention should be authorised shall note any comment the person may make if the decision is to keep him in detention. The officer shall not put specific questions to the suspect regarding his involvement in any offence, nor in respect of any comments he may make in response to the decision to keep him in detention. Such an exchange is likely to constitute an interview as defined by paragraph 11.1A and would require the associated safeguards included in section 11. [See also paragraph 11.13]

(b) Documentation

15.3 Before conducting a review the officer must ensure that the detained person is reminded of his entitlements to free legal advice (see paragraph 6.5). It is the responsibility of the review officer to ensure that all such reminders are noted in the custody record.

15.4 The grounds for and extent of any delay in conducting a review shall be recorded.

15.5 Any written representations shall be retained.

15.6 A record shall be made as soon as practicable of the outcome of each review and application for a warrant of further detention or its extension.

Notes for guidance

> *15A If the detained person is likely to be asleep at the latest time when a review of detention or an authorisation of continued detention may take place, the appropriate officer should bring it forward so that the detained person may make representations without being woken up.*
>
> *15B An application for a warrant of further detention or its extension should be made between 10 a.m. and 9 p.m., and if possible during normal court hours. It will not be practicable to arrange for a court to sit specially outside the hours of 10 a.m. to 9 p.m. If it appears possible that a special sitting may be needed (either at a weekend, Bank/Public Holiday or on a weekday outside normal court hours but between 10 a.m. and 9 p.m.) then the clerk to the justices should*

be given notice and informed of this possibility, while the court is sitting if possible.

15C *If in the circumstances the only practicable way of conducting a review is over the telephone then this is permissible, provided that the requirements of section 40 of the Police and Criminal Evidence Act 1984 or of Schedule 3 to the Prevention of Terrorism (Temporary Provisions) Act 1989 are observed. However, a review to decide whether to authorise a person's continued detention under section 42 of the 1984 Act must be done in person rather than over the telephone.*

16 Charging of detained persons

(a) Action

16.1   When an officer considers that there is sufficient evidence to prosecute a detained person, and that there is sufficient evidence for a prosecution to succeed, and that the person has said all that he wishes to say about the offence, he shall without delay (and subject to the following qualification) bring him before the custody officer who shall then be responsible for considering whether or not he should be charged. When a person is detained in respect of more than one offence it is permissible to delay bringing him before the custody officer until the above conditions are satisfied in respect of all the offences (but see paragraph 11.4). Any resulting action shall be taken in the presence of the appropriate adult if the person is a juvenile or mentally disordered or mentally handicapped.

16.2   When a detained person is charged with or informed that he may be prosecuted for an offence he shall be cautioned in the following terms:
'You do not have to say anything. But it may harm your defence if you do not mention now something which you later rely on in court. Anything you do say may be given in evidence.'

16.3   At the time a person is charged he shall be given a written notice showing particulars of the offence with which he is charged and including the name of the officer in the case (in terrorist cases, the officer's warrant or other identification number instead), his police station and the reference number for the case. So far as possible the particulars of the charge shall be stated in simple terms, but they shall also show the precise offence in law with which he is charged. The notice shall begin with the following words:
'You are charged with the offence(s) shown below. You do not have to say anything. But it may harm your defence if you do not mention now something which you later rely on in court. Anything you do say may be given in evidence.'
If the person is a juvenile or is mentally disordered or mentally handicapped the notice shall be given to the appropriate adult.

16.4   If, at any time after a person has been charged with or informed that he may be prosecuted for an offence, a police officer wishes to bring to the notice of that person any written statement made by another person or the content of an interview with another person, he shall hand to that person a true copy of any such written statement or bring to his attention the content of the interview record, but shall say or do nothing to invite any reply or comment save to warn him that he does not have to say anything but that anything he does say may be given in evidence and to remind him of his right to legal advice in accordance with paragraph 6.5 above. If the person cannot read then the officer may read it to him. If the person is a juvenile or mentally disordered or mentally handicapped the copy shall also be given to, or the interview record brought to the attention of, the appropriate adult.

16.5   Questions relating to an offence may not be put to a person after he has been charged with that offence, or informed that he may be prosecuted for it, unless they are necessary for the purpose of preventing or minimising harm or loss to some other person or to the public or for clearing up an ambiguity in a previous answer or statement, or where it is in the interests of justice that the person should have put to him and have an opportunity to comment on information concerning the offence which has come to light since he was charged or informed that he might be prosecuted. Before any such questions are put to him, he shall be warned that he does not have to say anything but that anything he does say may be given in evidence and reminded of his right to legal advice in accordance with paragraph 6.5 above. [See *Note 16A*]

16.6   Where a juvenile is charged with an offence and the custody officer authorises his continued detention he must try to make arrangements for the juvenile to be taken into care of a local authority to be detained pending appearance in court unless he certifies that it is impracticable to do so, or, in the case of a juvenile of at least 12 years of age, no secure accommodation is available and there is a risk to the public of serious harm from that juvenile, in accordance with section 38(6) of the Police and Criminal Evidence Act 1984, as amended by Section 59 of the Criminal Justice Act 1991 and section 24 of the Criminal Justice and Public Order Act 1994. [See *Note 16B*]

(b) Documentation

16.7   A record shall be made of anything a detained person says when charged.

16.8   Any questions put after charge and answers given relating to the offence shall be contemporaneously recorded in full on the forms provided and the record signed by that person or, if he refuses, by the interviewing officer and any third parties present. If the questions are tape-recorded the arrangements set out in Code E apply.

16.9   If it is not practicable to make arrangements for the transfer of a juvenile into local authority care in accordance with paragraph 16.6 above the custody officer must record the reasons and make out a certificate to be produced before the court together with the juvenile.

Notes for guidance

16A   *The service of the Notice of Intended Prosecution under sections 1 and 2 of the Road Traffic Offenders Act 1988 does not amount to informing a person that he may be prosecuted for an offence and so does not preclude further questioning in relation to that offence.*

16B   *Except as provided for in 16.6 above, neither a juvenile's behaviour nor the nature of the offence with which he is charged provides grounds for the custody officer to decide that it is impracticable to seek to arrange for his transfer to the care of the local authority. Similarly, the lack of secure local authority accommodation shall not make it impracticable for the custody officer to transfer him. The availability of secure accommodation is only a factor in relation to a juvenile aged 12 or over when the local authority accommodation would not be adequate to protect the public from serious harm from the juvenile. The obligation to transfer a juvenile to local authority accommodation applies as much to a juvenile charged during the daytime as it does to a juvenile to be held overnight, subject to a requirement to bring the juvenile before a court under section 46 of the Police and Criminal Evidence Act 1984.*

ANNEX A

Intimate and Strip Searches [See Paragraph 4.1]

A. Intimate Search

1.   An 'intimate search' is a search which consists of the physical examination of a person's body orifices other than the mouth.

(a) Action

Body orifices other than the mouth may be searched only if an officer of the rank of superintendent or above has reasonable grounds for believing:

    (a) that an article which could cause physical injury to the detained person or others at the police station has been concealed; or

    (b) that the person has concealed a Class A drug which he intended to supply to another or to export; and

    (c) that in either case an intimate search is the only practicable means of removing it.

The reasons why an intimate search is considered necessary shall be explained to the person before the search takes place.

3.   An intimate search may only be carried out by a registered medical practitioner or registered nurse, unless an officer of at least the rank of superintendent considers that this is not practicable and the search is to take place under sub-paragraph 2(a) above.

4.   An intimate search under sub-paragraph 2(a) above may take place only at a hospital, surgery, other medical premises or police station. A search under sub-paragraph 2(b) may take place only at a hospital, surgery or other medical premises.

5.   An intimate search at a police station of a juvenile or a mentally disordered or mentally handicapped person may take place only in the presence of an appropriate adult of the same sex (unless the person specifically requests the presence of a particular adult of the opposite sex who is readily available). In the case of a juvenile the search may take place in the absence of the appropriate adult only if the juvenile signifies in the presence of the appropriate adult that he prefers the search to be done in his absence and the appropriate adult agrees. A record shall be made of the juvenile's decision and signed by the appropriate adult.

6.   Where an intimate search under sub-paragraph 2(a) above is carried out by a police officer, the officer must be of the same sex as the person searched. Subject to paragraph 5 above, no person of the opposite sex who is not a medical practitioner or nurse shall be present, nor shall anyone whose presence is unnecessary but a minimum of two people, other than the person searched, must be present during the search. The search shall be conducted with proper regard to the sensitivity and vulnerability of the person in these circumstances.

(b) Documentation

7.   In the case of an intimate search the custody officer shall as soon as practicable record which part of the person's body were searched, who carried out the search, who was present, the reasons for the search and its result.

8.   If an intimate search is carried out by a police officer, the reason why it was impracticable for a suitably qualified person to conduct it must be recorded.

B. Strip Search

A strip search is a search involving the removal of more than outer clothing.

(a) Action

10.   A strip search may take place only if it is considered necessary to remove an article which a person would not be allowed to keep, and the officer reasonably

considers that the person might have concealed such an article. Strip searches shall not be routinely carried out where there is no reason to consider that articles have been concealed.

The conduct of strip searches

11.   The following procedures shall be observed when strip searches are conducted:
   (a) a police officer carrying out a strip search must be of the same sex as the person searched;
   (b) the search shall take place in an area where the person being searched cannot be seen by anyone who does not need to be present, nor by a member of the opposite sex (except an appropriate adult who has been specifically requested by the person being searched);
   (c) except in cases of urgency, where there is a risk of serious harm to the person detained or to others, whenever a strip search involves exposure of intimate parts of the body, there must be at least two people present other than the person searched, and if the search is of a juvenile or a mentally disordered or mentally handicapped person, one of the people must be the appropriate adult. Except in urgent cases as above, a search of a juvenile may take place in the absence of the appropriate adult only if the juvenile signifies in the presence of the appropriate adult that he prefers the search to be done in his absence and the appropriate adult agrees. A record shall be made of the juvenile's decision and signed by the appropriate adult. The presence of more than two people, other than an appropriate adult, shall be permitted only in the most exceptional circumstances.
   (d) the search shall be conducted with proper regard to the sensitivity and vulnerability of the person in these circumstances and every reasonable effort shall be made to secure the person's co-operation and minimise embarrassment. People who are searched should not normally be required to have all their clothes removed at the same time, for example, a man shall be allowed to put on his shirt before removing his trousers, and a woman shall be allowed to put on her blouse and upper garments before further clothing is removed;
   (e) where necessary to assist the search, the person may be required to hold his or her arms in the air or to stand with his or her legs apart and to bend forward so that a visual examination may be made of the genital and anal areas provided that no physical contact is made with any body orifice;
   (f) if, during a search, articles are found, the person shall be asked to hand them over. If articles are found within any body orifice other than the mouth, and the person refuses to hand them over, their removal would constitute an intimate search, which must be carried out in accordance with the provisions of Part A of this Annex;
   (g) a strip search shall be conducted as quickly as possible, and the person searched allowed to dress as soon as the procedure is complete.

(b) Documentation

12.   A record shall be made on the custody record of a strip search including the reason it was considered necessary to undertake it, those present and any result.

ANNEX B

Delay in Notifying Arrest or Allowing Access to Legal Advice

A. Persons detained under the Police and Criminal Evidence Act 1984

(a) Action

1.   The rights set out in sections 5 or 6 of the code or both may be delayed if the person is in police detention in connection with a serious arrestable offence, has not yet been charged with an offence and an officer of the rank of superintendent or above has reasonable grounds for believing that the exercise of either right:
>   (i) will lead to interference with or harm to evidence connected with a serious arrestable offence or interference with or physical injury to other people; or
>   (i) will lead to the alerting of other people suspected of having committed such an offence but not yet arrested for it; or
> (iii) will hinder the recovery of property obtained as a result of such an offence.
[See *Note B3*]

2.   These rights may also be delayed where the serious arrestable offence is either:
>   (i) a drug trafficking offence and the officer has reasonable grounds for believing that the detained person has benefited from drug trafficking, and that the recovery of the value of that person's proceeds of drug trafficking will be hindered by the exercise of either right or;
>   (ii) an offence to which Part VI of the Criminal Justice Act 1988 (covering confiscation orders) applies and the officer has reasonable grounds for believing that the detailed person has benefited from the offence, and that the recovery of the value of the property obtained by that person from or in connection with the offence, or if the pecuniary advantage derived by him from or in connection with it, will be hindered by the exercise of either right.

3.   Access to a solicitor may not be delayed on the grounds that he might advise the person not to answer any questions or that the solicitor was initially asked to attend the police station by someone else, provided that the person himself then wishes to see the solicitor. In the latter case the detained person must be told that the solicitor has come to the police station at another person's request, and must be asked to sign the custody record to signify whether or not he wishes to see the solicitor.

4.   These rights may be delayed only for as long as is necessary and, subject to paragraph 9 below, in no case beyond 36 hours after the relevant time as defined in section 41 of the Police and Criminal Evidence Act 1984. If the above grounds cease to apply within this time, the person must as soon as practicable be asked if he wishes to exercise either right, the custody record must be noted accordingly, and action must be taken in accordance with the relevant section of the code.

5.   A detained person must be permitted to consult a solicitor for a reasonable time before any court hearing.

(b) Documentation

6.   The grounds for action under this Annex shall be recorded and the person informed of them as soon as practicable.

7.   Any reply given by a person under paragraphs 4 or 9 must be recorded and the person asked to endorse the record in relation to whether he wishes to receive legal advice at this point.

B. Persons detained under the Prevention of Terrorism (Temporary Provisions) Act 1989

(a) Action

8.   The rights set out in sections 5 or 6 of this code or both may be delayed if paragraph 1 above applies or if an officer of the rank of superintendent or above has reasonable grounds for believing that the exercise of either right:
    (a) will lead to interference with the gathering of information about the commission, preparation or instigation of acts of terrorism; or
    (b) by alerting any person, will make it more difficult to prevent an act of terrorism or to secure the apprehension, prosecution or conviction of any person in connection with the commission, preparation or instigation of an act of terrorism.

9.   These rights may be delayed only for as long as is necessary and in no case beyond 48 hours from the time of arrest. If the above grounds cease to apply within this time, the person must as soon as practicable be asked if he wishes to exercise either right, the custody record must be noted accordingly, and action must be taken in accordance with the relevant section of this code.

10.   Paragraphs 3 and 5 above apply.

(b) Documentation

11.   Paragraphs 6 and 7 above apply.

Notes for guidance

B1   Even if Annex B applies in the case of a juvenile, or a person who is mentally disordered or mentally handicapped, action to inform the appropriate adult (and the person responsible for a juvenile's welfare, if that is a different person) must nevertheless be taken in accordance with paragraph 3.7 and 3.9 of this code.

B2   In the case of Commonwealth citizens and foreign nationals see Note 7A.

B3   Police detention is defined in section 118(2) of the Police and Criminal Evidence Act 1984.

B4   The effect of paragraph 1 above is that the officer may authorise delaying access to a specific solicitor only if he has reasonable grounds to believe that specific solicitor will, inadvertently or otherwise, pass on a message from the detained person or act in some other way which will lead to any of the three results in paragraph 1 coming about. In these circumstances the officer should offer the detained person access to a solicitor (who is not the specific solicitor referred to above) on the Duty Solicitor Scheme.

B5   The fact that the grounds for delaying notification of arrest under paragraph 1 above may be satisfied does not automatically mean that the grounds for delaying access to legal advice will also be satisfied.

ANNEX C

Vulnerable Suspects: Urgent Interviews at Police Stations

1.   When an interview is to take place in a police station or other authorised place of detention if, and only if, an officer of the rank of superintendent or above considers

that delay will lead to the consequences set out in paragraph 11.1(a) to (c) of this Code:

(a) a person heavily under the influence of drink or drugs may be interviewed in that state; or

(b) a juvenile or a person who is mentally disordered or mentally handicapped may be interviewed in the absence of the appropriate adult; or

(c) a person who has difficulty in understanding English or who has a hearing disability may be interviewed in the absence of an interpreter.

2. Questioning in these circumstances may not continue once sufficient information to avert the immediate risk has been obtained.

3. A record shall be made of the grounds for any decision to interview a person under paragraph 1 above.

Note for guidance

C1 *The special groups referred to in this Annex are all particularly vulnerable. The provisions of the Annex, which override safeguards designed to protect them and to minimise the risk of interviews producing unreliable evidence, should be applied only in exceptional cases of need.*

ANNEX D

Written Statements Under Caution [See Paragraph 12.13]

(a) Written by a person under caution

1. A person shall always be invited to write down himself what he wants to say.

2. Where the person wishes to write it himself, he shall be asked to write out and sign, before writing what he wants to say, the following:

'I make this statement of my own free will. I understand that I do not have to say anything but that it may harm my defence if I do not mention when questioned something which I later rely on in court. This statement may be given in evidence.'

3. Any person writing his own statement shall be allowed to do so without any prompting except that a police officer may indicate to him which matters are material or question any ambiguity in the statement.

(b) Written by a police officer

4. If a person says that he would like someone to write it for him, a police officer shall write the statement, but, before starting, he must ask him to sign, or make his mark, to the following:

'I, ..., wish to make a statement. I want someone to write down what I say. I understand that I do not have to say anything but that it may harm my defence if I do not mention when questioned something which I later rely on in court. This statement may be given in evidence.'

5. Where a police officer writes the statement, he must take down the exact words spoken by the person making it and he must not edit or paraphrase it. Any questions that are necessary (*e.g.* to make it more intelligible) and the answers given must be recorded contemporaneously on the statement form.

6. When the writing of a statement by a police officer is finished the person making it shall be asked to read it and to make any corrections, alterations or additions he wishes. When he has finished reading it he shall be asked to write and sign or make his mark on the following certificate at the end of the statement:

'I have read the above statement, and I have been able to correct, alter or add anything I wish. This statement is true. I have made it of my own free will.'

7.   If the person making the statement cannot read, or refuses to read it, or to write the above mentioned certificate at the end of it or to sign it, the senior police officer present shall read it to him and ask him whether he would like to correct, alter or add anything and to put his signature or make his mark at the end. The police officer shall then clarify on the statement itself what has occurred.

ANNEX E

Summary of Provisions Relating to Mentally Disordered and Mentally Handicapped People

1.   If an officer has any suspicion, or is told in good faith, that a person of any age may be mentally disordered or mentally handicapped, or mentally incapable of understanding the significance of questions put to him or his replies, then that person shall be treated as mentally distorted or mentally handicapped for the purposes of this code. [See paragraph 1.4]

2.   In the case of a person who is mentally disordered or mentally handicapped, 'the appropriate adult' means:

    (a)   a relative, guardian or some other person responsible for his care or custody;

    (b)   someone who has experience of dealing with mentally disordered or mentally handicapped people but is not a police officer or employed by the police; or

    (c)   failing either of the above, some other responsible adult aged 18 or over who is not a police officer or employed by the police.

[See paragraph 1.7(b)]

3.   If the custody officer authorises the detention of a person who is mentally handicapped or appears to be suffering from a mental disorder he must as soon as practicable inform the appropriate adult of the grounds for the person's detention and his whereabouts, and ask the adult to come to the police station to see the person. If the appropriate adult is already at the police station when information is given as required in paragraphs 3.1 to 3.5 the information must be given to the detained person in the appropriate adult's presence. If the appropriate adult is not at the police station when the provisions of 3.1 to 3.5 are complied with then these provisions must be complied with again in the presence of the appropriate adult once that person arrives. [See paragraphs 3.9 and 3.11]

4.   If the appropriate adult, having been informed of the right to legal advice, considers that legal advice should be taken, the provisions of section 6 of the code apply as if the mentally disordered or mentally handicapped person had requested access to legal advice. [See paragraph 3.13 and *Note E2*]

5.   If a person brought to a police station appears to be suffering from mental disorder or is incoherent other than through drunkenness alone, or if a detained person subsequently appears to be mentally disordered, the custody officer must immediately call the police surgeon or, in urgent cases, send the person to hospital or call the nearest available medical practitioner. It is not intended that these provisions should delay the transfer of a person to a place of safety under section 136 of the Mental Health Act 1983 where that is applicable. Where an assessment under that Act is to take place at the police station, the custody officer has discretion not to call the police surgeon so long as he belies that the assessment by a registered medical practitioner can be undertaken without undue delay. [See paragraph 9.2]

6.   It is imperative that a mentally disordered or mentally handicapped person who has been detained under section 136 of the Mental Health Act 1983 should be assessed as soon as possible. If that assessment is to take place at the police station, an approved social worker and a registered medical practitioner shall be called to the

police station as soon as possible in order to interview and examine the person. Once the person has been interviewed and examined and suitable arrangements have been made for his treatment or care, he can no longer be detained under section 136. The person shall not be released until he has been seen by both the approved social worker and the registered medical practitioner. [See paragraph 3.10]

7.   If a mentally disordered or mentally handicapped person is cautioned in the absence of the appropriate adult, the caution must be repeated in the appropriate adult's presence. [See paragraph 10.6]

8.   A mentally disordered or mentally handicapped person must not be interviewed or asked to provide or sign a written statement in the absence of the appropriate adult unless the provisions of paragraph 11.1 or *Annex C* of this code apply. Questioning in these circumstances may not continue in the absence of the appropriate adult once sufficient information to avert the risk has been obtained. A record shall be made of the grounds for any decision to begin an interview in these circumstances. [See paragraphs 11.1 and 11.14 and *Annex C*]

9.   Where the appropriate adult is present at an interview, he shall be informed that he is not expected to act simply as an observer; and also that the purposes of his presence are, first, to advise the person being interviewed and to observe whether or not the interview is being conducted properly and fairly, and, secondly, to facilitate communication with the person being interviewed. [See paragraph 11.16]

10.   If the detention of a mentally disordered or mentally handicapped person is reviewed by a review officer or a superintendent, the appropriate adult must, if available at the time, be given an opportunity to make representations to the officer about the need for continuing detention. [See paragraphs 15.1 and 15.2]

11.   If the custody officer charges a mentally disordered or mentally handicapped person with an offence or takes such other action as is appropriate when there is sufficient evidence for a prosecution this must be done in the presence of the appropriate adult. The written notice embodying any charge must be given to the appropriate adult. [See paragraphs 16.1 to 16.3]

12.   An intimate or strip search of a mentally disordered or mentally handicapped person may take place only in the presence of the appropriate adult of the same sex, unless the person specifically requests the presence of a particular adult of the opposite sex. A strip search may take place in the absence of an appropriate adult only in cases of urgency where there is a risk of serious harm to the person detained or to others. [See *Annex A*, paragraphs 5 and 11(c)]

13.   Particular care must be taken when deciding whether to use handcuffs to restrain a mentally disordered or mentally handicapped person in a locked cell. [See paragraph 8.2]

Notes for guidance

E1   *In the case of mentally disordered or mentally handicapped people, it may in certain circumstances be more satisfactory for all concerned if the appropriate adult is someone who has experience or training in their care rather than a relative lacking such qualifications. But if the person himself prefers a relative to a better qualified stranger or objects to a particular person as the appropriate adult, his wishes should if practicable be respected. [See Note 1E]*

E2   *The purpose of the provision at paragraph 3.13 is to protect the rights of a mentally disordered or mentally handicapped person who does not understand the significance of what is being said to him. If the person wishes to exercise the right to legal advice, the appropriate action should be taken and not delayed until the appropriate adult arrives. [See Note 3G] A mentally disordered or mentally handicapped person should always be given an opportunity, when an appropriate adult is called to the police station, to consult privately with a solicitor in the absence of the appropriate adult if he wishes to do so. [See Note 1EE]*

E3 It is important to bear in mind that although mentally disordered or mentally handicapped people are often capable of providing reliable evidence, they may, without knowing or wishing to do so, be particularly prone in certain circumstances to provide information which is unreliable, misleading or self-incriminating. Special care should therefore always be exercised in questioning such a person, and the appropriate adult involved, if there is any doubt about a person's mental state or capacity. Because of the risk of unreliable evidence, it is important to obtain corroboration of any facts admitted whenever possible. [See Note 11B]

E4 Because of the risks referred to in Note E3, which the presence of the appropriate adult is intended to minimise, officers of superintendent rank or above should exercise their discretion to authorise the commencement of an interview in the adult's absence only in exceptional cases, where it is necessary to avert an immediate risk of serious harm. [See paragraph 11.1 and Annex C and Note C1]

ANNEX F   COUNTRIES WITH WHICH BILATERAL CONSULAR CONVENTIONS OR AGREEMENTS REQUIRING NOTIFICATION OF THE ARREST AND DETENTION OF THEIR NATIONALS ARE IN FORCE AS AT 1 JANUARY 1995

Armenia	Kyrgyzstan
Austria	Macedonia
Azerbaijan	Mexico
Belarus	Moldova
Belgium	Mongolia
Bosnia-Hercegovina	Norway
Bulgaria	Poland
China*	Romania
Croatia	Russia
Cuba	Slovak Republic
Czech Republic	Slovenia
Denmark	Spain
Egypt	Sweden
France	Tajikistan
Georgia	Turkmenistan
German Federal Republic	Ukraine
Greece	USA
Hungary	Uzbekistan
Kazakhstan	Yugoslavia

* Police are required to inform Chinese officials of arrest/detention in the Manchester consular district only. This comprises Derbyshire, Durham, Greater Manchester, Lancashire, Merseyside, North South and West Yorkshire, and Tyne and Wear.

D. CODE OF PRACTICE FOR THE IDENTIFICATION OF PERSONS BY POLICE OFFICERS

1 General

1.1   This code of practice must be readily available at all police stations for consultation by police officers, detained persons and members of the public.

1.2   The notes for guidance included are not provisions of this code, but are guidance to police officers and others about its application and interpretation. Provisions in the Annexes to the code are provisions of this code.

1.3　If an officer has any suspicion, or is told in good faith, that a person of any age may be mentally disordered or mentally handicapped, or mentally incapable of understanding the significance of questions put to him or his replies, then that person shall be treated as a mentally disordered or mentally handicapped person for the purposes of this code.

1.4　If anyone appears to be under the age of 17 then he shall be treated as a juvenile for the purposes of this code in the absence of clear evidence to show that he is older.

1.5　If a person appears to be blind or seriously visually handicapped, deaf, unable to read, unable to speak or has difficulty orally because of a speech impediment, he shall be treated as such for the purposes of this code in the absence of clear evidence to the contrary.

1.6　In this code the term 'appropriate adult' has the same meaning as in paragraph 1.7 of Code C, and the term 'solicitor' has the same meaning as in paragraph 6.12 of Code C.

1.7　Any reference to a custody officer in this code includes an officer who is performing the functions of a custody officer.

1.8　Where a record is made under this code of any action requiring the authority of an officer of a specified rank, his name (except in the case of enquiries linked to the investigation of terrorism, in which case the officer's warrant or other identification number shall be given) and rank must be included in the record.

1.9　All records must be timed and signed by the maker. Warrant or other identification numbers shall be used rather than names in the case of detention under the Prevention of Terrorism (Temporary Provisions) Act 1989.

1.10　In the case of a detained person records are to be made in his custody record unless otherwise specified.

1.11　In the case of any procedure requiring a person's consent, the consent of a person who is mentally disordered or mentally handicapped is only valid if given in the presence of the appropriate adult; and in the case of a juvenile the consent of his parent of guardian is required as well as his own (unless he is under 14, in which case the consent of his parent or guardian is sufficient in its own right). [See *Note 1E*]

1.12　In the case of a person who is blind or seriously visually handicapped or unable to read, the custody officer shall ensure that his solicitor, relative, the appropriate adult or some other person likely to take an interest in him (and not involved in the investigation) is available to help in checking any documentation. Where this code requires written consent or signification, then the person who is assisting may be asked to sign instead if the detained person so wishes. [See *Note 1F*]

1.13　In the case of any procedure requiring information to be given to or sought from a suspect, it must be given or sought in the presence of the appropriate adult if the suspect is mentally disordered or mentally handicapped or a juvenile. If the appropriate adult is not present when the information is first given or sought, the procedure must be repeated in his presence when he arrives. If the suspect appears to be deaf or there is doubt about his hearing or speaking ability or ability to understand English, and the officer cannot establish effective communication, the information must be given or sought through an interpreter.

1.14　Any procedure in this code involving the participation of a person (whether as a suspect or a witness) who is mentally disordered, mentally handicapped or a juvenile must take place in the presence of the appropriate adult; but the adult must not be allowed to prompt any identification of a suspect by a witness.

1.15　Subject to paragraph 1.16 below, nothing in this code affects any procedure under:

(i)　Sections 4 to 11 of the Road Traffic Act 1988 or sections 15 and 16 of the Road Traffic Offenders Act 1988; or

    (ii) paragraph 18 of Schedule 2 to the Immigration Act 1971; or

    (iii) the Prevention of Terrorism (Temporary Provisions) Act 1989, section 15(9), paragraph 8(5) of Schedule 2, and paragraph 7(5) of Schedule 5.

  1.16 Notwithstanding paragraph 1.15, the provisions of section 3 below on the taking of fingerprints, and of section 5 below on the taking of body samples, do apply to people detained under section 14 of, or paragraph 6 of Schedule 5 to, the Prevention of Terrorism (Temporary Provisions) Act 1989. (In the case of fingerprints, section 61 of PACE is modified by section 15(10) of, and paragraph 7(6) of Schedule 5 to, the 1989 Act.) In the case of samples, sections 62 and 63 of PACE are modified by section 15(11) of and paragraph 7(6A) of Schedule 5 to the 1989 Act. The effect of both of these modifications is to allow fingerprints and samples to be taken in terrorist cases to help determine whether a person is or has been involved in terrorism, as well as where there are reasonable grounds for suspecting that person's involvement in a particular offence. There is, however, no statutory requirement (and, therefore, no requirement under paragraph 3.4 below) to destroy fingerprints or body samples taken in terrorist cases, no requirement to tell the people from whom these were taken that they will be destroyed, and no statutory requirement to offer such people an opportunity to witness the destruction of their fingerprints.

  1.17 In this code, references to photographs, negatives and copies include reference to images stored or reproduced through any medium.

  1.18 This code does not apply to those groups of people listed in paragraph 1.12 of Code C.

Notes for guidance

1A A person, including a parent or guardian, should not be the appropriate adult if he is suspected of involvement in the offence, is the victim, is a witness, is involved in the investigation or has received admissions prior to attending to act as the appropriate adult. If the parent of a juvenile is estranged from the juvenile, he should not be asked to act as the appropriate adult if the juvenile expressly and specifically objects to his presence.

1B If a juvenile admits an offence to or in the presence of, a social worker other than during the time that the social worker is acting as the appropriate adult for that juvenile, another social worker should be the appropriate adult in the interest of fairness.

1C In the case of people who are mentally disordered or mentally handicapped, it may in certain circumstances be more satisfactory for all concerned if the appropriate adult is someone who has experience or training in their care rather than a relative lacking such qualifications. But if the person himself prefers a relative to a better-qualified stranger, or objects to a particular person as the appropriate adult, his wishes should if practicable be respected.

1D A solicitor or lay visitor who is present at the station in that capacity may not act as the appropriate adult.

1E For the purposes of paragraph 1.11 above, the consent required to be given by a parent or guardian may be given, in the case of a juvenile in the care of a local authority or voluntary organisation, by that authority or organisation.

1F People who are blind, seriously visually handicapped or unable to read may be unwilling to sign police documents. The alternative of their representative signing on their behalf seeks to protect the interests of both police and suspects.

1G Further guidance about fingerprints and body samples is given in Home Office circulars.

1H The generic term 'mental disorder' is used throughout this code. 'Mental disorder' is defined in section 1(2) of the Mental Health Act 1983 as 'mental illness, arrested or incomplete development of mind, psychopathic disorder and any other disorder or disability of mind'. It should be noted that 'mental disorder' is different from 'mental handicap' although the two are dealt with similarly throughout this code. Where the custody officer has any doubt as to the mental state or capacity of a person detained an appropriate adult should be called.

2 Identification by witnesses

2.0   A record shall be made of the description of the suspect as first given by a potential witness. This must be done before the witness takes part in the forms of identification listed in paragraph 2.1 or *Annex D* of this code. The record may be made or kept in any form provided that details of the description as first given by the witness can accurately be produced from it in a written form which can be provided to the suspect or his solicitor in accordance with this code. A copy shall be provided to the suspect or his solicitor before any procedures under paragraph 2.1 of this code are carried out. [See *Note 2D*]

(a) Cases where the suspect is known

2.1   In each case which involves disputed identification evidence, and where the identity of the suspect is known to the police and he is available (See *Note 2E*), the methods of identification by witnesses which may be used are:
   (i) a parade;
   (ii) a group identification;
   (iii) a video film;
   (iv) a confrontation.
2.2   The arrangements for, and conduct of, these types of identification shall be the responsibility of an officer in uniform not below the rank of inspector who is not involved with the investigation ('the identification officer'). No officer involved with the investigation of the case against the suspect may take any part in these procedures.

Identification parade

2.3   Whenever a suspect disputes an identification, an identification parade shall be held if the suspect consents unless paragraphs 2.4 or 2.7 or 2.10 apply. A parade may also be held if the officer in charge of the investigation considers that it would be useful, and the suspect consents.
2.4   A parade need not be held if the identification officer considers that, whether by reason of the unusual appearance of the suspect or for some other reason, it would not be practicable to assemble sufficient people who resemble him to make a parade fair.
2.5   Any parade must be carried out in accordance with *Annex A*. A video recording or colour photograph shall be taken of the parade.
2.6   If a suspect refuses or, having agreed, fails to attend an identification parade or the holding of a parade is impracticable, arrangements must if practicable be made to allow the witnesses an opportunity of seeing him in a group identification, a video identification, or a confrontation (see below).

Group identification

2.7   A group identification takes place where the suspect is viewed by a witness amongst an informal group of people. The procedure may take place with the consent and co-operation of a suspect or covertly where a suspect has refused to co-operate with an identification parade or a group identification or has failed to attend. A group identification may also be arranged if the officer in charge of the investigation considers, whether because of fear on the part of the witness or for some other reason, that it is, in the circumstances, more satisfactory than a parade.

2.8 The suspect should be asked for his consent to a group identification and advised in accordance with paragraphs 2.15 and 2.16 of this code. However, where consent is refused the identification officer has the discretion to proceed with a group identification if it is practicable to do so.

2.9 A group identification shall be carried out in accordance with *Annex E*. A video recording or colour photograph shall be taken of the group identification in accordance with *Annex E*.

Video film identification

2.10 The identification officer may show a witness a video film of a suspect if the investigating officer considers, whether because of the refusal of the suspect to take part in an identification parade or group identification or other reasons, that this would in the circumstances be the most satisfactory course of action.

2.11 The suspect should be asked for his consent to a video identification and advised in accordance with paragraphs 2.15 and 2.16. However, where such consent is refused the identification officer has the discretion to proceed with a video identification if it is practical to do so.

2.12 A video identification must be carried out in accordance with *Annex B*.

Confrontation

2.13 If neither a parade, a group identification nor a video identification procedure is arranged, the suspect may be confronted by the witness. Such a confrontation does not require the suspect's consent, but may not take place unless none of the other procedures are practicable.

2.14 A confrontation must be carried out in accordance with *Annex C*.

Notice to suspect

2.15 Before a parade takes place or a group identification or video identification is arranged, the identification officer shall explain to the suspect:
    (i) the purposes of the parade or group identification or video identification;
    (ii) that he is entitled to free legal advice (see paragraph 6.5 of Code C);
    (iii) the procedures for holding it (including his right to have a solicitor or friend present);
    (iv) where appropriate the special arrangements for juveniles;
    (v) where appropriate the special arrangements for mentally disordered or mentally handicapped people;
    (vi) that he does not have to take part in a parade, or co-operate in a group identification, or with the making of a video film and, if it is proposed to hold a group identification or video identification, his entitlement to a parade if this can practicably be arranged;
    (vii) if he does not consent to take part in a parade or co-operate in a group identification or with the making of a video film, his refusal may be given in evidence in any subsequent trial and police may proceed covertly without his consent or make other arrangements to test whether a witness identifies him;
    (vii)a that if he should significantly alter his appearance between the taking of any photograph at the time of his arrest or after charge and any attempt to hold an identification procedure, this may be given in evidence if the case comes to trial; and the officer may then consider other forms of identification;

(vii)b that a video or photograph may be taken of him when he attends for any identification procedure;

(viii) whether the witness had been shown photographs, photofit, identikit or similar pictures by the police during the investigation before the identity of the suspect became known; [See *Note 2B*]

(ix) that if he changes his appearance before a parade it may not be practicable to arrange one on the day in question or subsequently and, because of his change of appearance, the identification officer may then consider alternative methods of identification;

(x) that he or his solicitor will be provided with details of the description of the suspect as first given by any witnesses who are to attend the parade, group identification, video identification or confrontation.

2.16   This information must also be contained in a written notice which must be handed to the suspect. The identification officer shall give the suspect a reasonable opportunity to read the notice, after which he shall be asked to sign a second copy of the notice to indicate whether or not he is willing to take part in the parade or group identification or co-operate with the making of a video film. The signed copy shall be retained by the identification officer.

(b) Cases where the identity of the suspect is not known

2.17   A police officer may take a witness to a particular neighbourhood or place to see whether he can identify the person whom he said he saw on the relevant occasion. Before doing so, where practicable a record shall be made of any description given by the witness of the suspect. Care should be taken not to direct the witness's attention to any individual.

2.18   A witness must not be shown photographs, photofit, identikit or similar pictures if the identity of the suspect is known to the police and he is available to stand on an identification parade. If the identity of the suspect is not known, the showing of such pictures to a witness must be done in accordance with *Annex D*. [See paragraph 2.15(viii) and *Note 2E*]

(c) Documentation

2.19   The identification officer shall make a record of the parade, group identification or video identification on the forms provided.

2.20   If the identification officer considers that it is not practicable to hold a parade, he shall tell the suspect why and record the reason.

2.21   A record shall be made of a person's refusal to co-operate in a parade, group identification or video identification.

(d) Showing films and photographs of incidents

2.21A   Nothing in this code inhibits an investigating officer from showing a video film or photographs of an incident to the public at large through the national, or local media, or to police officers, for the purposes of recognition and tracing suspects. However when such material is shown to potential witnesses (including police officers [see *Note 2A*] for the purpose of obtaining identification evidence, it shall be shown on an individual basis so as to avoid any possibility of collusion, and the showing shall, as far as possible, follow the principles for Video Film Identification (see paragraph 2.10) or Identification by Photographs (see paragraph 2.18) as appropriate).

2.21B   Where such a broadcast or publication is made a copy of the material released by the police to the media for the purposes of recognising or tracing the suspect shall be kept and the suspect or his solicitor should be allowed to view such material before any procedures under paragraph 2.1 of this Code are carried out [see *Notes 2D* and *2E*] provided it is practicable to do so and would not unreasonably delay the investigation. Each witness who is involved in the procedure shall be asked by the investigating officer after they have taken part whether they have seen any broadcast or published films or photographs relating to the offence and their replies shall be recorded.

Notes for guidance

2A   *Except for the provisions of Annex D paragraph 1, a police officer who is a witness for the purposes of this part of the code is subject to the same principles and procedures as a civilian witness.*

2B   *Where a witness attending an identification parade has previously been shown photographs or photofit, identikit or similar pictures, it is the responsibility of the officer in charge of the investigation to make the identification officer aware that this is the case.*

2C   *[Not used]*

2D   *Where it is proposed to show photographs to a witness in accordance with Annex D, it is the responsibility of the officer in charge of the investigation to confirm to the officer responsible for supervising and directing the showing that the first description of the suspect given by that witness has been recorded. If this description has not been recorded, the procedure under Annex D must be postponed. (See Annex D paragraph 1A)*

2E   *References in this section to a suspect being 'known' means there is sufficient information known to the police to justify the arrest of a particular person for suspected involvement in the offence. A suspect being 'available' means that he is immediately available to take part in the procedure or he will become available within a reasonably short time.*

3 Identification by fingerprints

(a) Action

3.1   A person's fingerprints may be taken only with his consent or if paragraph 3.2 applies. If he is at a police station consent must be in writing. In either case the person must be informed of the reason before they are taken and that they will be destroyed as soon as practicable if paragraph 3.4 applies. He must be told that he may witness their destruction if he asks to do so within five days of being cleared or informed that he will not be prosecuted.

3.2   Powers to take fingerprints without consent from any person over the age of 10 years are provided by sections 27 and 61 of the Police and Criminal Evidence Act 1984. These provide that fingerprints may be taken without consent:

    (a)   from a person detained at a police station if an officer of at least the rank of superintendent has reasonable grounds for suspecting that the fingerprints will tend to confirm or disprove his involvement in a criminal offence and the officer authorises the fingerprints to be taken;

    (b)   from a person detained at a police station who has been charged with a recordable offence or informed that he will be reported for such an offence and he has not previously had his fingerprints taken in relation to that offence;

    (c)   from a person convicted of a recordable offence. Section 27 of the Police and Criminal Evidence Act 1984 provides power to require such a person to attend a police station for the purposes of having his fingerprints taken if he has not been in police detention for the offence nor had his fingerprints taken in the course of the investigation of the offence or since conviction.

Reasonable force may be used if necessary to take a person's fingerprints without his consent.

3.2A   A person whose fingerprints are to be taken with or without consent shall be informed beforehand that his prints may be subject of a speculative search against other fingerprints. [See *Note 3B*]

3.3   [Not used]

3.4   The fingerprints of a person and all copies of them taken in that case must be destroyed as soon as practicable if:

(a) he is prosecuted for the offence concerned and cleared; or

(b) he is not prosecuted (unless he admits the offence and is cautioned for it). An opportunity of witnessing the destruction must be given to him if he wishes and if, in accordance with paragraph 3.1, he applies within five days of being cleared or informed that he will not be prosecuted.

3.5   When fingerprints are destroyed, access to relevant computer data shall be made impossible as soon as it is practicable to do so.

3.6   References to fingerprints include palm prints.

(b) Documentation

3.7   A record must be made as soon as possible of the reason for taking a person's fingerprints without consent and of their destruction. If force is used a record shall be made of the circumstances and those present.

3.8   A record shall be made when a person has been informed under the terms of paragraph 3.2A that his fingerprints may be subject of a speculative search.

Notes for guidance

3A *References to recordable offences in this code relate to those offences for which convictions may be recorded in national police records. (See section 27(4) of the Police and Criminal Evidence Act 1984.) The recordable offences to which this code applies at the time when the code was prepared, are any offences which carry a sentence of imprisonment on conviction (irrespective of the period, or the age of the offender or actual sentence passed) and non-imprisonable offences under section 1 of the Street Offences Act 1959 (loitering or soliciting for purposes of prostitution), section 43 of the Telecommunications Act 1984 (improper use of public telecommunications system), section 25 of the Road Traffic Act 1988 (tampering with motor vehicles), section 1 of the Malicious Communications Act 1988 (sending letters etc with intent to cause distress or anxiety) and section 139(1) of the Criminal Justice Act 1988 (having article with a blade or point in a public place).*

3B *A speculative search means that a check may be made against other fingerprints contained in records held by or on behalf of the police or held in connection with or as a result of an investigation of an offence.*

4 Photographs

(a) Action

4.1   The photograph of a person who has been arrested may be taken at a police station only with his written consent or if paragraph 4.2 applies. In either case he must be informed of the reason for taking it and that the photograph will be destroyed in paragraph 4.4 applies. He must be told that if he should significantly alter his appearance between the taking of the photograph and any attempt to hold an identification procedure this may be given in evidence if the case comes to trial. He must be told that he may witness the destruction of the photograph or be provided with a certificate confirming its destruction if he applies within five days of being cleared or informed that he will not be prosecuted.

4.2   The photograph of a person who has been arrested may be taken without consent if:

(i) he is arrested at the same time as other people, or at a time when it is likely that other people will be arrested, and a photograph is necessary to establish who was arrested, at what time and at what place; or

(ii) he has been charged with, or reported for a recordable offence and has not yet been released or brought before a court [see *Note 3A*]; or

(iii) he is convicted of such an offence and his photograph is not already on record as a result of (i) or (ii). There is no power of arrest to take a photograph in pursuance of this provision which applies only where the person is in custody as a result of the exercise of another power (*e.g.* arrest for fingerprinting under section 27 of the Police and Criminal Evidence Act 1984); or

(iv) an officer of at least the rank of superintendent authorises it, having reasonable grounds for suspecting the involvement of the person in a criminal offence and where there is identification evidence in relation to that offence.

4.3   Force may not be used to take a photograph.

4.4   Where a person's photograph has been taken in accordance with this section, the photograph, negatives and all copies taken in that particular case must be destroyed if:

(a) he is prosecuted for the offence and cleared unless he has a previous conviction for a recordable offence; or

(b) he has been charged but not prosecuted (unless he admits the offence and is cautioned for it or he has a previous conviction for a recordable offence).

An opportunity of witnessing the destruction or a certificate confirming the destruction must be given to him if he so requests, provided that, in accordance with paragraph 4.1, he applies within five days of being cleared or informed that he will not be prosecuted. [See *Note 4B*]

(b) Documentation

4.5   A record must be made as soon as possible of the reason for taking a person's photograph under this section without consent and of the destruction of any photographs.

Notes for guidance

4A   The admissibility and value of identification evidence may be compromised if a potential witness in an identification procedure views any photographs of the suspect otherwise than in accordance with the provisions of this code.

4B   This paragraph is not intended to require the destruction of copies of a police gazette in cases where, for example, a remand prisoner has escaped from custody, or a person in custody is suspected of having committed offences in other force areas, and a photograph of the person concerned is circulated in a police gazette for information.

5 Identification by body samples and impressions

(a) Action
Intimate samples

5.1   Intimate samples may be taken from a person in police detention only:

(i) if an officer of the rank of superintendent or above has reasonable grounds to believe that such an impression or sample will tend to confirm or disprove the suspect's involvement in a recordable offence and gives authorisation for a sample to be taken; and

(ii) with the suspect's written consent.

5.1A   Where two or more non-intimate samples have been taken from a person in the course of an investigation of an offence and the samples have proved unsuitable or insufficient for a particular form of analysis and that person is not in police detention, an intimate sample may be taken from him if a police officer of at least the rank of superintendent authorises it to be taken, and the person concerned gives his written consent. [See *Note 5B and Note 5E*]

5.2   Before a person is asked to provide an intimate sample he must be warned that if he refuses without good cause, his refusal may harm his case if it comes to trial. [See *Note 5A*] If he is in police detention and not legally represented, he must also be reminded of his entitlement to have free legal advice (see paragraph 6.5 of Code C) and the reminder must be noted in the custody record. If paragraph 5.1A above applies and the person is attending a police station voluntarily, the officer shall explain the entitlement to free legal advice as provided for in accordance with paragraph 3.15 of Code C.

5.3   Except for samples of urine, intimate samples or dental impressions may be taken only by a registered medical or dental practitioner as appropriate.

Non-intimate samples

5.4   A non-intimate sample may be taken from a detained person only with his written consent or if paragraph 5.5 applies.

5.5   A non-intimate sample may be taken from a person without consent in accordance with the provisions of section 63 of the Police and Criminal Evidence Act 1984, as amended by section 55 of the Criminal Justice and Public Order Act 1994. The principal circumstances provided for are as follows:

(i)   if an officer of the rank of superintendent or above has reasonable grounds to believe that the sample will tend to confirm or disprove the person's involvement in a recordable offence and gives authorisation for a sample to be taken; or

(ii) where the person has been charged with a recordable offence or informed that he will be reported for such an offence; and he has not had a non-intimate sample taken from him in the course of the investigation or if he has had a sample taken from him, it has proved unsuitable or insufficient for the same form of analysis [See *Note 5B*]; or

(iii) if the person has been convicted of a recordable offence after the date on which this code comes into effect. Section 63A of the Police and Criminal Evidence Act 1984, as amended by section 56 of the Criminal Justice and Public Order Act 1994, describes the circumstances in which a constable may require a person convicted of a recordable offence to attend a police station in order that a non-intimate sample may be taken.

5.6   Where paragraph 5.5 applies, reasonable force may be used if necessary to take non-intimate samples.

(b) Destruction

5.7   [Not used]

5.8   Except in accordance with paragraph 5.8A below, where a sample or impression has been taken in accordance with this section it must be destroyed as soon as practicable if:

(a)   the suspect is prosecuted for the offence concerned and cleared; or

(b)   he is not prosecuted (unless he admits the offence and is cautioned for it).

5.8A   In accordance with section 64 of the Police and Criminal Evidence Act 1984 as amended by section 57 of the Criminal Justice and Public Order Act 1994 samples need not be destroyed if they were taken for the purpose of an investigation of an offence for which someone has been convicted, and from whom a sample was also taken. [See *Note 5F*]

(c) Documentation

5.9   A record must be made as soon as practicable of the reasons for taking a sample or impression and of its destruction. If force is used a record shall be made of the circumstances and those present. If written consent is given to the taking of a sample or impression, the fact must be recorded in writing.

5.10   A record must be made of the giving of a warning required by paragraph 5.2 above. A record shall be made of the fact that a person has been informed under the terms of paragraph 5.11A below that samples may be subject of a speculative search.

(d) General

5.11   The terms intimate and non-intimate samples are defined in section 65 of the Police and Criminal Evidence Act 1984, as amended by section 58 of the Criminal Justice and Public Order Act 1994, as follows:

    (a) 'intimate sample' means a dental impression or a sample of blood, semen or any other tissue fluid, urine, or pubic hair, or a swab taken from a person's body orifice other than the mouth;

    (b) 'non-intimate sample' means:

        (i) a sample of hair (other than pubic hair) which includes hair plucked with the root [See *Note 5C*];

        (ii) a sample taken from a nail or from under a nail;

        (iii) a swab taken from any part of a person's body including the mouth but not any other body orifice;

        (iv) saliva;

        (v) a footprint or similar impression of any part of a person's body other than a part of his hand.

5.11A   A person from whom an intimate or non-intimate sample is to be taken shall be informed beforehand that any sample taken may be the subject of a speculative search. [See *Note 5D*]

5.11B   The suspect must be informed, before an intimate or non-intimate sample is taken, of the grounds on which the relevant authority has been given, including where appropriate the nature of the suspected offence.

5.12   Where clothing needs to be removed in circumstances likely to cause embarrassment to the person, no person of the opposite sex who is not a medical practitioner or nurse shall be present, (unless in the case of a juvenile or a mentally disordered or mentally handicapped person, that person specifically requests the presence of an appropriate adult of the opposite sex who is readily available) nor shall anyone whose presence is unnecessary. However, in the case of a juvenile this is subject to the overriding proviso that such a removal of clothing may take place in the absence of the appropriate adult only if the person signifies in the presence of the appropriate adult that he prefers his absence and the appropriate adult agrees.

Notes for guidance

5A   In warning a person who is asked to provide an intimate sample in accordance with paragraph 5.2, the following form of words may be used:

    'You do not have to [provide this sample] [allow this swab or impression to be taken], but I must warn you that if you refuse without good cause, your refusal may harm your case if it comes to trial.'

5B   An insufficient sample is one which is not sufficient either in quantity or quality for the purpose of enabling information to be provided for the purpose of a particular form of analysis such as DNA analysis. An unsuitable sample is one which, by its nature, is not suitable for a particular form of analysis.

5C Where hair samples are taken for the purpose of DNA analysis (rather than for other purposes such as making a visual match) the suspect should be permitted a reasonable choice as to what part of the body he wishes the hairs to be taken from. When hairs are plucked they should be plucked individually unless the suspect prefers otherwise and no more should be plucked than the person taking them reasonably considers necessary for a sufficient sample.

5D A speculative search means that a check may be made against other samples and information derived from other samples contained in records or held by or on behalf of the police or held in connection with or as a result of an investigation of an offence.

5E Nothing in paragraph 5.1A prevents intimate samples being taken for elimination purposes with the consent of the person concerned but the provisions of paragraph 1.11, relating to the role of the appropriate adult, should be applied.

5F The provisions for the retention of samples in 5.8A allow for all samples in a case to be available for any subsequent miscarriage of justice investigation. But such samples – and the information derived from them – may not be used in the investigation of any offence or in evidence against the person who would otherwise be entitled to their destruction.

ANNEX A

Identification Parades

(a) General

1. A suspect must be given a reasonable opportunity to have a solicitor or friend present, and the identification officer shall ask him to indicate on a second copy of the notice whether or not he so wishes.

2. A parade may take place either in a normal room or in one equipped with a screen permitting witnesses to see members of the parade without being seen. The procedures for the composition and conduct of the parade are the same in both cases, subject to paragraph 7 below (except that a parade involving a screen may take place only when the suspect's solicitor, friends or appropriate adult is present or the parade is recorded on video).

2A Before the parade takes place the suspect or his solicitor shall be provided with details of the first description of the suspect by any witnesses who are to attend the parade. The suspect or his solicitor should also be allowed to view any material released to the media by the police for the purpose of recognising or tracing the suspect, provided it is practicable to do so and would not unreasonably delay the investigation.

(b) Parades involving prison inmates

3. If an inmate is required for identification, and there are no security problems about his leaving the establishment, he may be asked to participate in a parade or video identification.

4. A parade may be held in a Prison Department establishment, but shall be conducted as far as practicable under normal parade rules. Members of the public shall make up the parade unless there are serious security or control objections to their admission to the establishment. In such cases, or if a group or video identification is arranged within the establishment, other inmates may participate. If

an inmate is the suspect, he shall not be required to wear prison uniform for the parade unless the other people taking part are other inmates in uniform or are members of the public who are prepared to wear prison uniform for the occasion.

(c) Conduct of the parade

5. Immediately before the parade, the identification officer must remind the suspect of the procedures governing its conduct and caution him in the terms of paragraph 10.4 of Code C.

6. All unauthorised people must be excluded from the place where the parade is held.

7. Once the parade has been formed, everything afterwards in respect of it shall take place in the presence and hearing of the suspect and of any interpreter, solicitor, friend or appropriate adult who is present (unless the parade involves a screen, in which case everything said to or by any witness at the place where the parade is held must be said in the hearing and presence of the suspect's solicitor, friend or appropriate adult or be recorded on video).

8. The parade shall consist of at least eight people (in addition to the suspect) who so far as possible resemble the suspect in age, height, general appearance and position in life. One suspect only shall be included in a parade unless there are two suspects of roughly similar appearance in which case they may be paraded together with at least 12 other people. In no circumstances shall more than two suspects be included on one parade and where there are separate parades they shall be made up of different people.

9. Where all members of a similar group are possible suspects, separate parades shall be held for each member of the group unless there are two suspects of similar appearance when they may appear on the same parade with at least 12 other members of the group who are not suspects. Where police officers in uniform form an identification parade, any numerals or other identifying badges shall be concealed.

10. When the suspect is brought to the place where the parade is to be held, he shall be asked by the identification officer whether he has any objection to the arrangements for the parade or to any of the other participants in it. The suspect may obtain advice from his solicitor or friend, if present, before the parade proceeds. Where practicable, steps shall be taken to remove the grounds for objection. Where it is not practicable to do so, the officer shall explain to the suspect why his objections cannot be met.

11. The suspect may select his own position in the line. Where there is more than one witness, the identification officer must tell the suspect, after each witness has left the room, that he can if he wishes change position in the line. Each position in the line must be clearly numbered, whether by means of a numeral laid on the floor in front of each parade member or by other means.

12. The identification officer is responsible for ensuring that, before they attend the parade, witnesses are not able to:
    (i) communicate with each other about the case or overhear a witness who has already seen the parade;
    (ii) see any member of the parade;
    (iii) on that occasion see or be reminded of any photograph or description of the suspect or be given any other indication of his identity; or
    (iv) on that occasion, see the suspect either before or after the parade.

13. The officer conducting a witness to a parade must not discuss with him the composition of the parade, and in particular he must not disclose whether a previous witness has made any identification.

14. Witnesses shall be brought in one at a time. Immediately before the witness inspects the parade, the identification officer shall tell him that the person he saw may or may not be on the parade and if he cannot make a positive identification he should say so but that he should not make a decision before looking at each member of the

parade at least twice. The officer shall then ask him to look at each member of the parade at least twice, taking as much care and time as he wishes. When the officer is satisfied that the witness has properly looked at each member of the parade, he shall ask him whether the person he himself saw on an earlier relevant occasion is on the parade.

15.   The witness should make an identification by indicating the number of the person concerned.

16.   If the witness makes an identification after the parade has ended the suspect and, if present, his solicitor, interpreter or friend shall be informed. Where this occurs, consideration should be given to allowing the witness a second opportunity to identify the suspect.

17.   If a witness wishes to hear any parade member speak, adopt any specified posture or see him move, the identification officer shall first ask whether he can identify any persons on the parade on the basis of appearance only. When the request is to hear members of the parade speak, the witness shall be reminded that the participants in the parade have been chosen on the basis of physical appearance only. Members of the parade may then be asked to comply with the witness's request to hear them speak, to see them move or to adopt any specified posture.

17A.   Where video films or photographs have been released to the media by the police for the purpose of recognising or tracing the suspect, the investigating officer shall ask each witness after the parade whether he has seen any broadcast or published films or photographs relating to the offence and shall record his reply.

18.   When the last witness has left, the identification officer shall ask the suspect whether he wishes to make any comments on the conduct of the parade.

(d) Documentation

19.   A colour photograph or a video film of the parade shall be taken. A copy of the photograph or video film shall be supplied on request to the suspect or his solicitor within a reasonable time.

20.   The photograph or video film taken in accordance with paragraph 19 and held by the police shall be destroyed or wiped clean at the conclusion of the proceedings unless the person concerned is convicted or admits the offence and is cautioned for it.

21.   If the identification officer asks any person to leave a parade because he is interfering with its conduct the circumstances shall be recorded.

22.   A record must be made of all those present at a parade whose names are known to the police.

23.   If prison inmates make up a parade the circumstances must be recorded.

24.   A record of the conduct of any parade must be made on the forms provided.

ANNEX B

Video Identification

(a) General

1.   Where a video parade is to be arranged the following procedures must be followed.

2.   Arranging, supervising and directing the making and showing of a video film to be used in a video identification must be the responsibility of an identification officer or identification officers who have no direct involvement with the relevant case.

3.   The film must include the suspect and at least eight other people who so far as

possible resemble the suspect in age, height, general appearance and position in life. Only one suspect shall appear on any films unless there are two suspects of roughly similar appearance in which case they may be shown together with at least 12 other people.

4. The suspect and other people shall as far as possible be filmed in the same positions or carrying out the same activity and under identical conditions.

5. Provisions must be made for each person filmed to be identified by number.

6. If police officers are filmed, any numerals or other identifying badges must be concealed. If a prison inmate is filmed either as a suspect or not, then either all or none of the people filmed should be in prison uniform.

7. The suspect and his solicitor, friend, or appropriate adult must be given a reasonable opportunity to see the complete film before it is shown to witnesses. If he has a reasonable objection to the video film or any of its participants, steps shall, if practicable be taken to remove the grounds for objection. If this is not practicable the identification officer shall explain to the suspect and/or his representative why his objections cannot be met and record both the objection and the reason on the forms provided.

8. The suspect's solicitor, or where one is not instructed the suspect himself, where practicable shall be given reasonable notification of the time and place that it is intended to conduct the video identification in order that a representative may attend on behalf of the suspect. The suspect himself may not be present when the film is shown to the witness(es). In the absence of a person representing the suspect the viewing itself shall be recorded on video. No unauthorised people may be present.

8A. Before the video identification takes place the suspect or his solicitor shall be provided with details of the first description of the suspect by any witnesses who are to attend the parade. The suspect or his solicitor should also be allowed to view any material released to the media by the police for the purpose of recognising or tracing the suspect, provided it is practicable to do so and would not unreasonably delay the investigation.

(b) Conducting the video identification

9. The identification officer is responsible for ensuring that, before they see the film, witnesses are not able to communicate with each other about the case or overhear a witness who has seen the film. He must not discuss with the witness the composition of the film and must not disclose whether a previous witness has made any identification.

10. Only one witness may see the film at a time. Immediately before the video identification takes place the identification officer shall tell the witness that the person he saw may or may not be on the video film. The witness shall be advised that at any point he may ask to see a particular part of the tape again or to have a particular picture frozen for him to study. Furthermore, it should be pointed out that there is no limit on how many times he can view the whole tape or any part of it. However, he should be asked to refrain from making a positive identification or saying that he cannot make a positive identification until he has seen the entire film at least twice.

11. Once the witness has seen the whole film at least twice and has indicated that he does not want to view it or any part of it again, the identification officer shall ask the witness to say whether the individual he saw in person on an earlier occasion has been shown on the film and, if so, to identify him by number. The identification officer will then show the film of the person identified again to confirm the identification with the witness.

12. The identification officer must take care not to direct the witness's attention to any one individual on the video film, or give any other indication of the suspect's identity. Where a witness has previously made an identification by photographs, or a photofit, identikit or similar picture has been made, the witness must not be reminded

of such a photograph or picture once a suspect is available for identification by other means in accordance with this code. Neither must he be reminded of any description of the suspect.

12A. Where video films or photographs have been released to the media by the police for the purpose of recognising or tracing the suspect, the investigating officer shall ask each witness after the parade whether he has seen any broadcast or published films or photographs relating to the offence and shall record his reply.

(c) Tape security and destruction

13. It shall be the responsibility of the identification officer to ensure that all relevant tapes are kept securely and their movements accounted for. In particular, no officer involved in the investigation against the suspect shall be permitted to view the video film prior to it being shown to any witness.

14. Where a video film has been made in accordance with this section all copies of it held by the police must be destroyed if the suspect:

(a) is prosecuted for the offence and cleared; or

(b) is not prosecuted (unless he admits the offence and is cautioned for it).

An opportunity of witnessing the destruction must be given to him if he so requests within five days of being cleared or informed that he will not be prosecuted.

(d) Documentation

15. A record must be made of all those participating in or seeing the video whose names are known to the police.

16. A record of the conduct of the video identification must be made on the forms provided.

ANNEX C

Confrontation by a Witness

1. The identification officer is responsible for the conduct of any confrontation of a suspect by a witness.

2. Before the confrontation takes place, the identification officer must tell the witness that the person he saw may or may not be the person he is to confront and that if he cannot make a positive identification he should say so.

2A. Before the confrontation takes place, the suspect or his solicitor shall be provided with details of the first description of the suspect given by any witness who is to attend the confrontation. The suspect or his solicitor should also be allowed to view any material released by the police to the media for the purposes of recognising or tracing the suspect provided that it is practicable to do so and would not unreasonably delay the investigation.

3. The suspect shall be confronted independently by each witness, who shall be asked 'Is this the person?' Confrontation must take place in the presence of the suspect's solicitor, interpreter or friend, unless this would cause unreasonable delay.

4. The confrontation should normally take place in the police station, either in a normal room or in one equipped with a screen permitting a witness to see the suspect without being seen. In both cases the procedures are the same except that a room equipped with a screen may be used only when the suspect's solicitor, friend of appropriate adult is present or the confrontation is recorded on video.

5. Where video films or photographs have been released to the media by the police for the purposes of recognising or tracing the suspect, the investigating officer shall ask each witness after the procedure whether he has seen any broadcast or published films or photographs relating to the offence and shall record his reply.

ANNEX D

Showing of Photographs

(a) Action

1.   An officer of the rank of sergeant or above shall be responsible for supervising and directing the showing of photographs. The actual showing may be done by a constable or a civilian police employee.

1A.   The officer must confirm that the first description of the suspect given by the witness has been recorded before the witness is shown the photographs. If he is unable to confirm that the description has been recorded, he shall postpone the showing.

2.   Only one witness shall be shown photographs at any one time. He shall be given as much privacy as practicable and shall not be allowed to communicate with any other witness in the case.

3.   The witness shall be shown not less than 12 photographs at a time, which shall, as far as possible, all be of a similar type.

4.   When the witness is shown the photographs, he shall be told that the photograph of the person he saw may or may not be amongst them. He shall not be prompted or guided in any way but shall be left to make any selection without help.

5.   If a witness makes a positive identification from photographs, then, unless the person identified is otherwise eliminated from enquiries, other witnesses shall not be shown photographs. But both they and the witness who has made the identification shall be asked to attend an identification parade or group or video identification if practicable unless there is no dispute about the identification of the suspect.

6.   Where the use of a photofit, identikit or similar picture has led to there being a suspect available who can be asked to appear on a parade, or participate in a group or video identification, the picture shall not be shown to other potential witnesses.

7.   Where a witness attending an identification parade has previously been shown photographs or photofit, identikit or similar pictures (and it is the responsibility of the officer in charge of the investigation to make the identification officer aware that this is the case) then the suspect and his solicitor must be informed of this fact before the identity parade takes place.

8.   None of the photographs used shall be destroyed, whether or not an identification is made, since they may be required for production in court. The photographs shall be numbered and a separate photograph taken of the frame or part of the album from which the witness made an identification as an aid to reconstituting it.

(b) Documentation

9.   Whether or not an identification is made, a record shall be kept of the showing of photographs and of any comment made by the witness.

ANNEX E

Group Identification

(a) General

1.   The purpose of the provisions of this Annex is to ensure that as far as possible, group identifications follow the principles and procedures for identification parades so that the conditions are fair to the suspect in the way they test the witness's ability to make an identification.

2.   Group identifications may take place either with the suspect's consent and co-operation or covertly without his consent.

3.   The location of the group identification is a matter for the identification officer, although he may take into account any representations made by the suspect, appropriate adult, his solicitor or friend. The place where the group identification is held should be one where other people are either passing by, or waiting around informally, in groups such that the suspect is able to join them and be capable of being seen by the witness at the same time as others in the group. Examples include people leaving an escalator, pedestrians walking through a shopping centre, passengers on railway and bus stations waiting in queues or groups or where people are standing or sitting in groups in other public places.

4.   If the group identification is to held covertly, the choice of locations will be limited by the places where the suspect can be found and the number of other people present at that time. In these cases, suitable locations might be along regular routes travelled by the suspect, including buses or trains, or public places he frequents.

5.   Although the number, age, sex, race and general description and style of clothing of other people present at the location cannot be controlled by the identification officer, in selecting the location he must consider the general appearance and numbers of people likely to be present. In particular, he must reasonably expect that over the period the witness observes the group, he will be able to see, from time to time, a number of others (in addition to the suspect) whose appearance is broadly similar to that of the suspect.

6.   A group identification need not be held if the identification officer believes that because of the unusual appearance of the suspect, none of the locations which it would be practicable to use satisfy the requirements of paragraph 5 necessary to make the identification fair.

7.   Immediately after a group identification procedure has taken place (with or without the suspect's consent), a colour photograph or a video should be taken of the general scene, where this is practicable, so as to give a general impression of the scene and the number of people present. Alternatively, if it is practicable, the group identification may be video recorded.

8.   If it is not practicable to take the photograph or video film in accordance with paragraph 7, a photograph or film of the scene should be taken later at a time determined by the identification officer, if he considers that it is practicable to do so.

9.   An identification carried out in accordance with this code remains a group identification notwithstanding that at the time of being seen by the witness the suspect was on his own rather than in a group.

10.   The identification officer need not be in uniform when conducting a group identification.

11.   Before the group identification takes place the suspect or his solicitor should be provided with details of the first description of the suspect by any witnesses who are to attend the identification. The suspect or his solicitor should also be allowed to view any material released by the police to the media for the purposes of recognising or tracing the suspect provided that it is practicable to do so and would not unreasonably delay the investigation.

12.   Where video films or photographs have been released to the media by the police for the purposes of recognising or tracing the suspect, the investigating officer shall ask each witness after the procedure whether he has seen any broadcast or published films or photographs relating to the offence and shall record his reply.

(b) Identification with the consent of the suspect

13.   A suspect must be given a reasonable opportunity to have a solicitor or friend present. The identification officer shall ask him to indicate on a second copy of the notice whether or not he so wishes.

14.   The witness, identification officer and suspect's solicitor, appropriate adult,

friend or any interpreter for the witness, if present may be concealed from the sight of the persons in the group which they are observing if the identification officer considers that this facilitates the conduct of the identification.

15.   The officer conducting a witness to a group identification must not discuss with the witness the forthcoming group identification and in particular he must not disclose whether a previous witness has made any identification.

16.   Anything said to or by the witness during the procedure regarding the identification should be said in the presence and hearing of the identification officer and, if present, the suspect's solicitor, appropriate adult, friend or any interpreter for the witness.

17.   The identification officer is responsible for ensuring that before they attend the group identification witnesses are not able to:

   (i)   communicate with each other about the case or overhear a witness who has already been given an opportunity to see the suspect in the group;

   (ii) on that occasion see the suspect; or

   (iii) on that occasion see or be reminded of any photographs or description of the suspect or be given any other indication of his identity.

18.   Witnesses shall be brought to the place where they are to observe the group one at a time. Immediately before the witness is asked to look at the group, the identification officer shall tell him that the person he saw may or may not be in the group and if he cannot make a positive identification he should say so. The witness shall then be asked to observe the group in which the suspect is to appear. The way in which the witness should do this will depend on whether the group is moving or stationary.

Moving group

19.   When the group in which the suspect is to appear is moving, for example, leaving an escalator, the provisions of paragraphs 20 to 23 below should be followed.

20.   If two or more suspects consent to a group identification, each should be the subject of separate identification procedures. These may however be conducted consecutively on the same occasion.

21.   The identification officer shall tell the witness to observe the group and ask him to point out any person he thinks he saw on the earlier relevant occasion. When the witness makes such an indication the officer shall, if it is practical, arrange for the witness to take a closer look at the person he has indicated and ask him whether he can make a positive identification. If this is not practicable, the officer shall ask the witness how sure he is that the person he has indicated is the relevant person.

22.   The witness should continue to observe the group for the period which the identification officer reasonably believes is necessary in the circumstances for the witness to be able to make comparisons between the suspect and other persons of broadly similar appearance to the suspect in accordance with paragraph 5.

23.   Once the identification officer has informed the witness in accordance with paragraph 21, the suspect should be allowed to take any position in the group he wishes.

Stationary groups

24.   When the group in which the suspect is to appear is stationary, for example, people waiting in a queue, the provisions of paragraphs 25 to 28 below should be followed.

25.   If two or more suspects consent to a group identification, each should be the subject of separate identification procedures unless they are of broadly similar

appearance when they may appear in the same group. Where separate group identifications are held, the groups must be made up of different persons.

26.   The suspect may take any position in the group he wishes. Where there is more than one witness, the identification officer must tell the suspect, out of the sight and hearing of any witness, that he can if he wishes change his position in the group.

27.   The identification officer shall ask the witness to pass along or amongst the group and to look at each person in the group at least twice, taking as much care and time as possible according to the circumstances, before making an identification. When he has done this, the officer shall ask him whether the person he saw on an earlier relevant occasion is in the group and to indicate any such person by whatever means the identification officer considers appropriate in the circumstances. If this is not practicable, the officer shall ask the witness to point out any person he thinks he saw on the earlier relevant occasion.

28.   When the witness makes an indication in accordance with paragraph 27, the officer shall, if it is practicable, arrange for the witness to take a closer look at the person he has indicated and ask him whether he can make a positive identification. If this is not practicable, the officer shall ask the witness how sure he is that the person he had indicated is the relevant person.

All cases

29.   If the suspect unreasonably delays joining the group, or having joined the group, deliberately conceals himself from the sight of the witness, the identification officer may treat this as a refusal to co-operate in a group identification.

30.   If the witness identifies a person other than the suspect, an officer should inform that person what has happened and ask if they are prepared to give their name and address. There is no obligation upon any member of the public to give these details. There shall be no duty to record any details of any other member of the public present in the group or at the place where the procedure is conducted.

31.   When the group identification has been completed, the identification officer shall ask the suspect whether he wishes to make any comments on the conduct of the procedure.

32.   If he has not been previously informed the identification officer shall tell the suspect of any identifications made by the witnesses.

(c) Identification without suspect's consent

33.   Group identifications held covertly without the suspect's consent should so far as practicable follow the rules for conduct of group identification by consent.

34.   A suspect has no right to have a solicitor, appropriate adult or friend present as the identification will, of necessity, take place without the knowledge of the suspect.

35.   Any number of suspects may be identified at the same time.

(d) Identifications in police stations

36.   Group identifications should only take place in police stations for reasons of safety, security, or because it is impracticable to hold them elsewhere.

37.   The group identification may take place either in a room equipped with a screen permitting witnesses to see members of the group without being seen, or anywhere else in the police station that the identification officer considers appropriate.

38.   Any of the additional safeguards applicable to identification parades should be followed if the identification officer considers it is practicable to do so in the circumstances.

(e) Identifications involving prison inmates

39.   A group identification involving a prison inmate may only be arranged in the prison or at a police station.

40.   Where a group identification takes place involving a prison inmate, whether in a prison or in a police station, the arrangements should follow those in paragraphs 36 to 38 of this Annex. If a group identification takes place within a prison other inmates may participate. If an inmate is the suspect he should not be required to wear prison uniform for the group identification unless the other persons taking part are wearing the same uniform.

(f) Documentation

41.   Where a photograph or video film is taken in accordance with paragraph 7 or 8, a copy of the photograph or video film shall be supplied on request to the suspect or his solicitor within a reasonable time.

42.   If the photograph or film includes the suspect, it and all copies held by the police shall be destroyed or wiped clean at the conclusion of the proceedings unless the person is convicted or admits the offence and is cautioned for it.

43.   A record of the conduct of any group identification must be made on the forms provided. This shall include anything said by the witness or the suspect about any identifications or the conduct of the procedure and any reasons why it was not practicable to comply with any of the provisions of this code governing the conduct of group identifications.

E. CODE OF PRACTICE ON TAPE RECORDING OF INTERVIEWS WITH SUSPECTS

1 General

1.1   This code of practice must be readily available for consultation by police officers, detained persons and members of the public at every police station to which an order made under section 60(1)(b) of the Police and Criminal Evidence Act 1984 applies.

1.2   The notes for guidance included are not provisions of this code. They form guidance to police officers and others about its application and interpretation.

1.3   Nothing in this code shall be taken as detracting in any way from the requirements of the Code of Practice for the Detention, Treatment and Questioning of Persons by Police Officers (Code C). [See *Note 1A*]

1.4   This code does not apply to those groups of people listed in paragraph 1.12 of Code C.

1.5   In this code the term 'appropriate adult' has the same meaning as in paragraph 1.7 of Code C; and the term 'solicitor' has the same meaning as in paragraph 6.12 of Code C.

Note for guidance

   1A As in Code C, references to custody officers include those carrying out the functions of a custody officer.

2 Recording and the sealing of master tapes

2.1   Tape recording of interviews shall be carried out openly to instil confidence in its reliability as an impartial and accurate record of the interview. [See *Note 2A*]

2.2   One tape, referred to in this code as the master tape, will be sealed before it leaves the presence of the suspect. A second tape will be used as a working copy. The master tape is either one of the two tapes used in a twin deck machine or the only tape used in a single deck machine. The working copy is either the second tape used in a twin deck machine or a copy of the master tape made by a single deck machine. [See *Notes 2B and 2C*]

Notes for guidance

2A   *Police officers will wish to arrange that, as far as possible, tape recording arrangements are unobtrusive. It must be clear to the suspect, however, that there is no opportunity to interfere with the tape recording equipment or the tapes.*

2B   *The purpose of sealing the master tape before it leaves the presence of the suspect is to establish his confidence that the integrity of the tape is preserved. Where a single deck machine is used the working copy of the master tape must be made in the presence of the suspect and without the master tape having left his sight. The working copy shall be used for making further copies where the need arises. The recorder will normally be capable of recording voices and have a time coding or other security device.*

2C   *Throughout this code any reference to 'tapes' shall be construed as 'tape', as appropriate, where a single deck machine is used.*

3 Interviews to be tape recorded

3.1   Subject to paragraph 3.2 below, tape recording shall be used at police stations for any interview:
  (a) with a person who has been cautioned in accordance with section 10 of Code C in respect of an indictable offence (including an offence triable either way) [see *Notes 3A and 3B*];
  (b) which takes place as a result of a police officer exceptionally putting further questions to a suspect about an offence described in sub-paragraph (a) above after he has been charged with, or informed he may be prosecuted for, that offence [see *Note 3C*]; or
  (c) in which a police officer wishes to bring to the notice of a person, after he has been charged with, or informed he may be prosecuted for an offence described in sub-paragraph (a) above, any written statement made by another person, or the content of an interview with another person [see *Note 3D*].

3.2   Tape recording is not required in respect of the following:
  (a) an interview with a person arrested under section 14(1)(a) or Schedule 5 paragraph 6 of the Prevention of Terrorism (Temporary Provisions) Act 1989 or an interview with a person being questioned in respect of an offence where there are reasonable grounds for suspecting that it is connected to terrorism or was committed in furtherance of the objectives of an organisation engaged in terrorism. This sub-paragraph applies only where the terrorism is connected with the affairs of Northern Ireland or is terrorism of any other description except terrorism connected solely with the affairs of the United Kingdom or any part of the United Kingdom other than Northern Ireland. 'Terrorism' has the meaning given by section 20(1) of the Prevention of Terrorism (Temporary Provisions) Act 1989 [see *Notes 3E, 3F, 3G and 3H*];

(b) an interview with a person suspected on reasonable grounds of an offence under section 1 of the Official Secrets Act 1911 [see *Note 3H*].

3.3   The custody officer may authorise the interviewing officer not to tape record the interview:

(a) where it is not reasonably practicable to do so because of failure of the equipment or the non-availability of a suitable interview room or recorder and the authorising officer considers on reasonable grounds that the interview should not be delayed until the failure has been rectified or a suitable room or recorder becomes available [see *Note 3J*]; or

(b) where it is clear from the outset that no prosecution will ensue.

In such cases the interview shall be recorded in writing and in accordance with section 11 of Code C. In all cases the custody officer shall make a note in specific terms of the reasons for not tape recording. [See *Note 3K*].

3.4   Where an interview takes place with a person voluntarily attending the police station and the police officer has grounds to believe that person has become a suspect (*i.e.* the point at which he should be cautioned in accordance with paragraph 10.1 of Code C) the continuation of the interview shall be tape recorded, unless the custody officer gives authority in accordance with the provisions of paragraph 3.3 above for the continuation of the interview not to be recorded.

3.5   The whole of each interview shall be tape recorded, including the taking and reading back of any statement.

Notes for guidance

3A   *Nothing in this code is intended to preclude tape recording at police discretion of interviews at police stations with people cautioned in respect of offences not covered by paragraph 3.1, or responses made by interviewees after they have been charged with, or informed they may be prosecuted for, an offence, provided that this code is complied with.*

3B   *Attention is drawn to the restrictions in paragraph 12.3 of Code C on the questioning of people unfit through drink or drugs to the extent that they are unable to appreciate the significance of questions put to them or of their answers.*

3C   *Circumstances in which a suspect may be questioned about an offence after being charged with it are set out in paragraph 16.5 of Code C.*

3D   *Procedures to be followed when a person's attention is drawn after charge to a statement made by another person are set out in paragraph 16.4 of Code C. One method of bringing the content of an interview with another person to the notice of a suspect may be to play him a tape recording of that interview.*

3E   *Section 14(1)(a) of the Prevention of Terrorism (Temporary Provisions) Act 1989, permits the arrest without warrant of a person reasonably suspected to be guilty of an offence under section 2, 8, 9, 10 or 11 of the Act.*

3F   *Section 20(1) of the Prevention of Terrorism (Temporary Provisions) Act 1989 says 'terrorism means the use of violence for political ends, and includes any use of violence for the purpose of putting the public or any section of the public in fear'.*

3G   *It should be noted that the provisions of paragraph 3.2 apply only to those suspected of offences connected with terrorism connected with Northern Ireland, or with terrorism of any other description other than terrorism connected solely with the affairs of the United Kingdom or any part of the United Kingdom other than Northern Ireland, or offences committed in furtherance of such terrorism. Any interviews with those suspected of offences connected with terrorism of any other description or in furtherance of the objectives of an organisation engaged in such terrorism should be carried out in compliance with the rest of this code.*

3H   *When it only becomes clear during the course of an interview which is being tape recorded that the interviewee may have committed an offence to which paragraph 3.2 applies the interviewing officer should turn off the tape recorder.*

3J   Where practicable, priority should be given to tape recording interviews with people who are suspected of more serious offences.

3K   A decision not to tape record an interview for any reason may be the subject of comment in court. The authorising officer should therefore be prepared to justify his decision in each case.

4 The interview

(a) Commencement of interviews

4.1   When the suspect is brought into the interview room the police officer shall without delay, but in the sight of the suspect, load the tape recorder with clean tapes and set it to record. The tapes must be unwrapped or otherwise opened in the presence of the suspect. [See *Note 4A*]

4.2   The police officer shall then tell the suspect formally about the tape recording. He shall say:
   (a)   that the interview is being tape recorded;
   (b)   his name and rank and the name and rank of any other police officer present except in the case of enquiries linked to the investigation of terrorism where warrant or other identification numbers shall be stated rather than names;
   (c)   the name of the suspect and any other party present (*e.g.* a solicitor);
   (d)   the date, time of commencement and place of the interview; and
   (e)   that the suspect will be given a notice about what will happen to the tapes.
[See *Note 4B*]

4.3   The police officer shall then caution the suspect in the following terms:
'You do not have to say anything. But it may harm your defence if you do not mention when questioned something which you later rely on in court. Anything you do say may be given in evidence.'
Minor deviations do not constitute a breach of this requirement provided that the sense of the caution is preserved. [See *Note 4C*]

4.3A   The police officer shall remind the suspect of his right to free and independent legal advice and that he can speak to a solicitor on the telephone in accordance with paragraph 6.5 of Code C.

4.3B   The police officer shall then put to the suspect any significant statement or silence (*i.e.* failure or refusal to answer a question or to answer it satisfactorily) which occurred before the start of the tape-recorded interview, and shall ask him whether he confirms or denies that earlier statement or silence or whether he wishes to add anything. A 'significant' statement or silence means one which appears capable of being used in evidence against the suspect, in particular a direct admission of guilt, or failure or refusal to answer a question or to answer it satisfactorily, which might give rise to an inference under Part III of the Criminal Justice and Public Order Act 1994.

Special warnings under Sections 36 and 37 of the Criminal Justice and Public Order Act 1994

4.3C   When a suspect who is interviewed after arrest fails or refuses to answer certain questions, or to answer them satisfactorily, after due warning, a court or jury may draw a proper inference from this silence under sections 36 and 37 of the Criminal Justice and Public Order Act 1994. This applies when:
   (a)   a suspect is arrested by a constable and there is found on his person, or in or on his clothing or footwear, or otherwise in his possession, or in the place where he was arrested, any objects, marks or substances, or marks on such objects, and the person fails or refuses to account for the objects, marks or substances found; or
   (b)   an arrested person was found by a constable at a place at or about the time of the offence for which he was arrested, is alleged to have been committed, and the person fails or refuses to account for his presence at that place.

4.3D   For an inference to be drawn from a suspect's failure or refusal to answer a question about one of these matters or to answer it satisfactorily, the interviewing officer must first tell him in ordinary language:

(a) what offence he is investigating;
(b) what fact he is asking the suspect to account for;
(c) that he believes this fact may be due to the suspect's taking part in the commission of the offence in question;
(d) that a court may draw a proper inference from his silence if he fails or refuses to account for the fact about which he is being questioned;
(e) that a record is being made of the interview and may be given in evidence if he is brought to trial.

4.3E   Where, despite the fact that a person has been cautioned, failure to co-operate may have an effect on his immediate treatment, he should be informed of any relevant consequences and that they are not affected by the caution. Examples are when his refusal to provide his name and address when charged may tender him liable to detention, or when his refusal to provide particulars and information in accordance with a statutory requirement, for example, under the Road Traffic Act 1988, may amount to an offence or may make him liable to arrest.

(b) Interviews with the deaf

4.4   If the suspect is deaf or there is doubt about his hearing ability, the police officer shall take a contemporaneous note of the interview in accordance with the requirements of Code C, as well as tape record it in accordance with the provisions of this code. [See *Notes 4E and 4F*]

(c) Objections and complaints by the suspect

4.5   If the suspect raises objections to the interview being tape recorded either at the outset or during the interview or during a break in the interview, the police officer shall explain the fact that the interview is being tape recorded and that the provisions of this code require that the suspect's objections shall be recorded on tape. When any objections have been recorded on tape or the suspect has refused to have his objections recorded, the police officer may turn off the recorder. In this eventuality he shall say that he is turning off the recorder and give his reasons for doing so and then turn it off. The police officer shall then make a written record of the interview in accordance with section 11 of Code C. If, however, the police officer reasonably considers that he may proceed to put questions to the suspect with the tape recorder still on, he may do so. [See *Note 4G*]

4.6   If in the course of an interview a complaint is made by the person being questioned, or on his behalf, concerning the provisions of this code or of Code C, then the officer shall act in accordance with paragraph 12.8 of Code C. [See *Notes 4H and 4J*]

4.7   If the suspect indicates that he wishes to tell the police officer about matters not directly connected with the offence of which he is suspected and that he is unwilling for these matters to be recorded on tape, he shall be given the opportunity to tell the police officer about these matters after the conclusion of the formal interview.

(d) Changing tapes

4.8   When the recorder indicates that the tapes have only a short time left to run, the police officer shall tell the suspect that the tapes are coming to an end and round off that part of the interview. If the police officer wishes to continue the interview but does not already have a second set of tapes, he shall obtain a set. The suspect shall not be left unattended in the interview room. The police officer will remove the tapes from the tape recorder and insert the new tapes which shall be unwrapped or otherwise opened in the suspect's presence. The tape recorder shall then be set to record on the new tapes. Care must be taken, particularly when a number of sets of tapes have been used, to ensure that there is no confusion between the tapes. This may be done by marking the tapes with an identification number immediately they are removed from the tape recorder.

(e) Taking a break during interview

4.9   When a break is to be taken during the course of an interview and the interview room is to be vacated by the suspect, the fact that a break is to be taken, the reason for it and the time shall be recorded on tape. The tapes shall then be removed from the tape recorder and the procedures for the conclusion of an interview set out in paragraph 4.14 below followed.

4.10   When a break is to be a short one and both the suspect and a police officer are to remain in the interview room the fact that a break is to be taken, the reasons for it and the time shall be recorded on tape. The tape recorder may be turned off; there is, however, no need to remove the tapes and when the interview is recommenced the tape recording shall be continued on the same tapes. The time at which the interview recommences shall be recorded on tape.

4.11   When there is a break in questioning under caution the interviewing officer must ensure that the person being questioned is aware that he remains under caution and of his right to legal advice. If there is any doubt the caution must be given again in full when the interview resumes. [See *Notes 4K and 4L*]

(f) Failure of recording equipment

4.12   If there is a failure of equipment which can be rectified quickly, for example by inserting new tapes, the appropriate procedures set out in paragraph 4.8 shall be followed, and when the recording is resumed the officer shall explain what has happened and record the time the interview recommences. If, however, it will not be possible to continue recording on that particular tape recorder and no replacement recorder or recorder in another interview room is readily available, the interview may continue without being tape recorded. In such circumstances the procedures in paragraphs 3.3 above for seeking the authority of the custody officer will be followed. [See *Note 4M*]

(g) Removing tapes from the recorder

4.13   Where tapes are removed from the recorder in the course of an interview, they shall be retained and the procedures set out in paragraph 4.15 below followed.

(h) Conclusion of interview

4.14   At the conclusion of the interview, the suspect shall be offered the opportunity to clarify anything he has said and to add anything he may wish.

4.15   At the conclusion of the interview, including the taking and reading back of any written statement, the time shall be recorded and the tape recorder switched off. The master tape shall be sealed with a master tape label and treated as an exhibit in accordance with the force standing orders. The police officer shall sign the label and ask the suspect and any third party present to sign it also. If the suspect or third party refuses to sign the label, an officer of at least the rank of inspector, or if one is not available the custody officer, shall be called into the interview room and asked to sign it. In the case of enquiries linked to the investigation of terrorism, an officer who signs the label shall use his warrant or other identification number.

4.16   The suspect shall be handed a notice which explains the use which will be made of the tape recording and the arrangements for access to it and that a copy of the tape shall be supplied as soon as practicable if the person is charged or informed that he will be prosecuted.

Notes for guidance

4A *The police officer should attempt to estimate the likely length of the interview and ensure that the appropriate number of clean tapes and labels with which to seal the master copies are available in the interview room.*

4B *It will be helpful for the purpose of voice identification if the officer asks the suspect and any other people present to identify themselves.*

4C *If it appears that a person does not understand what the caution means, the officer who has given it should go on to explain it in his own words.*

4D *[Not used]*

4E *This provision is intended to give the deaf equivalent rights of first hand access to the full interview record as other suspects.*

4F *The provisions of paragraphs 13.2, 13.5 and 13.9 of Code C on interpreters for the deaf or for interviews with suspects who have difficulty in understanding English continue to apply. In a tape recorded interview there is no requirement on the interviewing officer to ensure that the interpreter makes a separate note of interview as prescribed in section 13 of Code C.*

4G *The officer should bear in mind that a decision to continue recording against the wishes of the suspect may be the subject of comment in court.*

4H *Where the custody officer is called immediately to deal with the complaint, wherever possible the tape recorder should be left to run until the custody officer has entered the interview room and spoken to the person being interviewed. Continuation or termination of the interview should be at the discretion of the interviewing officer pending action by an inspector under paragraph 9.1 of Code C.*

4I *[Not used]*

4J *Where the complaint is about a matter not connected with this code of practice or Code C, the decision to continue with the interview is at the discretion of the interviewing officer. Where the interviewing officer decides to continue with the interview the person being interviewed shall be told that the complaint will be brought to the attention of the custody officer at the conclusion of the interview. When the interview is concluded the interviewing officer must, as soon as practicable, inform the custody officer of the existence and nature of the complaint made.*

4K *In considering whether to caution again after a break, the officer should bear in mind that he may have to satisfy a court that the person understood that he was still under caution when the interview resumed.*

4L *The officer should bear in mind that it may be necessary to show to the court that nothing occurred during a break in an interview or between interviews which influenced the suspect's recorded evidence. The officer should consider, therefore, after a break in an interview or at the beginning of a subsequent interview summarising on tape the reason for the break and confirming this with the suspect.*

4M *If one of the tapes breaks during the interview it should be sealed as a master tape in the presence of the suspect and the interview resumed where it left off. The unbroken tape should be copied and the original sealed as a master tape in the suspect's presence, if necessary after the interview. If equipment for copying the unbroken tape is not readily available, both tapes should be sealed in the suspect's presence and the interview begun again. If the tape breaks when a single deck machine is being used and the machine is one where a broken tape cannot be copied on available equipment, the tape should be sealed as a master tape in the suspect's presence and the interview begun again.*

5 After the interview

5.1   The police officer shall make a note in his notebook of the fact that the interview has taken place and has been recorded on tape, its time, duration and date and the identification number of the master tape.

5.2   Where no proceedings follow in respect of the person whose interview was recorded the tapes must nevertheless be kept securely in accordance with paragraph 6.1 and *Note 6A*.

Note for guidance

5A *Any written record of a tape recorded interview shall be made in accordance with national guidelines approved by the Secretary of State.*

6 Tape security

6.1   The officer in charge of each police station at which interviews with suspects are recorded shall make arrangements for master tapes to be kept securely and their movements accounted for on the same basis as other material which may be used for evidential purposes, in accordance with force standing orders. [See *Note 6A*]

6.2   A police officer has no authority to break the seal on a master tape which is required for criminal proceedings. If it is necessary to gain access to the master tape, the police officer shall arrange for its seal to be broken in the presence of a representative of the Crown Prosecution Service. The defendant or his legal adviser shall be informed and given a reasonable opportunity to be present. If the defendant or his legal representative is present he shall be invited to reseal and sign the master tape. If either refuses or neither is present this shall be done by the representative of the Crown Prosecution Service. [See *Notes 6B and 6C*]

6.3   Where no criminal proceedings result it is the responsibility of the chief officer of police to establish arrangements for the breaking of the seal on the master tape, where this becomes necessary.

Notes for guidance

6A *This section is concerned with the security of the master tape which will have been sealed at the conclusion of the interview. Care should, however, be taken of working copies of tapes since their loss or destruction may lead unnecessarily to the need to have access to master tapes.*

6B *If the tape has been delivered to the crown court for their keeping after committal for trial the crown prosecutor will apply to the chief clerk of the crown court centre for the release of the tape for unsealing by the crown prosecutor.*

6C *Reference to the Crown Prosecution Service or to the crown prosecutor in this part of the code shall be taken to include any other body or person with a statutory responsibility for prosecution for whom the police conduct any tape recorded interviews.*

APPENDICES

APPENDICES

APPENDIX 1

The Police and Criminal Evidence Act 1984
(Application to Armed Forces) Order 1985
(S.I. 1985 No. 1882)

The Secretary of State, in exercise of the powers conferred upon him by section 113(1) of the Police and Criminal Evidence Act 1984**(a)**, and of all other powers enabling him in that behalf, hereby makes the following Order:—

Citation and commencement

1. This Order may be cited as the Police and Criminal Evidence Act 1984 (Application to Armed Forces) Order 1985 and shall come into operation on 1st January 1986.

Interpretation

2. In this Order, unless the context otherwise requires—

"the Act" means the Police and Criminal Evidence Act 1984;

"legal adviser" means every person who is qualified as a barrister-at-law or solicitor according to the law of England or Northern Ireland or who is qualified as an advocate or as a solicitor according to the law of Scotland, or any person having in any Commonwealth country or territory outside the United Kingdom rights and duties similar to those of a barrister-at-law or a solicitor in England and is subject to punishment or disability for a breach of professional rules;

"serious service offence" means an offence under any of the service discipline Acts which cannot be dealt with summarily or which appears to a service policeman to be serious;

"service discipline Acts" means the Army Act 1955**(b)**, the Air Force Act 1955**(c)** or the Naval Discipline Act 1957**(d)**;

"service policeman" means a member of the Corps of Royal Military Police or Women's Royal Army Corps Provost, a Provost Officer of the Royal Air Force or a member of the Royal Air Force Police, or a member of the Royal Naval Special Investigation Branch or a member of the Royal Marines Police.

Application of the Act

3. The following provisions of the Act shall apply to the investigation of offences under any of the service discipline Acts conducted by service policemen or to persons held in arrest thereunder, subject to the modifications specified below.

Access to legal advice

4. Section 58 of the Act (which provides for persons arrested and held in custody in a police station of other premises to be entitled to consult a solicitor) shall have effect as if—

(a) for subsection (1) there were substituted the following subsection—

"(1) A person arrested under any of the service discipline Acts and being

(a) 1984 c.60.
(b) 1955 c.18.
(c) 1955 c.19.
(d) 1957 c.53.

interviewed in connection with a serious service offence shall be entitled, if he so requests, to consult a legal adviser privately at any time.";

(b) for subsection (2) there were substituted the following subsection—

"(2) A request under subsection (1) above and the time at which it was made shall be recorded in writing by a service policeman.";

(c) subsections (3), (5) to (7) and (12) to (18) were omitted;

(d) in subsection (4) for the word "solicitor" there were substituted the words "legal adviser" and for the words "is practicable" there were substituted the words "it appears to the interviewing service policeman to be practicable";

(e) in subsection (8) for the words "An officer may only authorise delay" there were substituted the words "A service policeman may authorise delay but he may only do so" and for the words "serious arrestable offence" there were substituted the words "any serious service offence";

(f) in subsection (9) for the word "detained" there were substituted the word "arrested" and for the words "noted on his custody record" there were substituted the words "recorded in writing by the service policeman."

Legal Aid

5. Section 59 of the Act (which amends section 1 of the Legal Aid Act 1982**(a)** so as to extend its provisions concerning advice and representation by duty solicitors at magistrates' courts to persons attending at a police station voluntarily or who are entitled to consult a solicitor under section 58(1) of the Act) shall have effect as if—

(a) in paragraph (*a*) for the word "and" contained at the end of the words inserted by that paragraph as an additional paragraph (*aa*) following section 1(1)(*a*) of the Legal Aid Act 1982, there were substituted the following words—

or

(iii) being interviewed in connection with a serious service offence; and";

(b) in paragraph (*c*) at end of subsection (1A) to be inserted after section 1 of the Legal Aid Act 1982 there were added the words "(including persons arrested and held in custody under the Army Act 1955, the Air Force Act 1955, or the Naval Discipline Act 1957)."

Finger printing

6. Section 61 of the Act (which provides that no finger prints may be taken from a person without the appropriate consent except under the procedures set out in that section) shall have effect as if—

(a) in subsection (2) the words "if it is given at a time when he is at a police station" were omitted;

(b) for subsections (3) and (4) there were substituted the following subsection—

"(3) The fingerprints of a person arrested under any of the service discipline Acts may be taken without the appropriate consent—

(a) if he has been charged with or reported for an offence under any of those Acts and his case has not then been disposed of; or

(a) 1982 c.44.

(b) if, before he has been charged with or reported for such an offence a service policeman has reasonable grounds to believe that his fingerprints will tend to confirm or disprove his involvement in such an offence; or

(c) he has been convicted or found guilty of such an offence and his fingerprints are not already on record under paragraphs (*a*) or (*b*) above.";

(c) subsections (5) and (6) were omitted;

(d) in subsection (7) the words "or (6)" were omitted;

(e) in subsection (8) the words "If he is detained at a police station" and "on his custody record" were omitted;

(f) subsection (9) were omitted.

Intimate samples

7. Section 62 of the Act (which provides that no intimate sample may be taken from a person except under the procedures set out in that section) shall have effect as if—

(a) in subsection (1) for the words "in police detention" there were substituted the words "arrested under any of the service discipline Acts" and for the words "police officer of at least the rank of superintendent" there were substituted the words "service policeman";

(b) in subsection (2) for the words "An officer" there were substituted the words "A service policeman" and for the words "serious arrestable offence" there were substituted the words "any serious service offence";

(c) in subsection (3) for the words "An officer" there were substituted the words "A service policeman";

(d) in subsection (5) for the words "an officer" there were substituted the words "a service policeman";

(e) subsection (8) were omitted;

(f) in subsection (9) after the words "registered medical practitioner" there were inserted the words "or by or on behalf of a service medical authority";

(g) in subsection (10) for the word "charged," at the end of paragraph (b) there were substituted the words—

"charged, or
(*c*) the court or officer exercising jurisdiction under any of the service discipline Acts."

Other samples

8. Section 63 of the Act (which provides that non-intimate samples may not be taken from a person without the appropriate consent except under the procedures set out in that section) shall have effect as if—

(a) for subsections (3) and (4) there were substituted the following subsection—

"(3) A non-intimate sample may be taken from a person without the appropriate consent if he is in arrest under any of the service discipline Acts and its taking is authorised by a service policeman having reasonable grounds for believing that the sample will tend to confirm or disprove his involvement in any serious service offence.";

(b) subsection (5) were omitted;

(c) in subsection (6) for the words "an officer" there were substituted the words "a service policeman";

(d) subsection (9) were omitted.

Destruction of fingerprints and samples

9. Section 64 of the Act (which provides for the destruction of fingerprints and samples) shall have effect as if—

(a) in subsections (1) and (3) for the words "the investigation of an offence" there were substituted the words "investigations under any of the service discipline Acts of an offence";

(b) in subsection (2) there were substituted for paragraph (b) the following paragraph—

"(b) it is decided that no disciplinary proceedings under any of the service discipline Acts or any other proceedings are to be taken against him in respect of that offence";

(c) subsection (7) were omitted.

Definitions

10. Sections 65 and 118 of the Act (which provide for the definition of expressions) shall have effect to the extent necessary for defining such of those expressions as are contained in the sections of the Act which are applied under the foregoing Articles of this Order.

Use of force

11. Section 117 of the Act (which confers power on a constable to use reasonable force for the purpose of exercising any power conferred on him under the Act) shall have effect as if for the expressions "constable," "police officer," or "officer," wherever they appear, there were substituted the expression "service policeman."

12.—(1) This Order, except Article 5, shall extend to any place to which the service discipline Acts extend.
(2) Article 5 shall extend to England and Wales only.

APPENDIX 2

The Police and Criminal Evidence Act 1984
(Application to Customs and Excise) Order 1985
(S.I. 1985 No. 1800)

The Treasury, in exercise of the powers conferred on them by section 114(2) of the Police and Criminal Evidence Act 1984**(a)**, hereby make the following Order:

1. This Order may be cited as the Police and Criminal Evidence Act 1984 (Application to Customs and Excise) Order 1985 and shall come into operation on 1st January 1986.

2.—(1) In this Order, unless the context otherwise requires—

"the Act" means the Police and Criminal Evidence Act 1984;

"assigned matter" has the meaning given to it by section 1 of the Customs and Excise Management Act 1979**(b)**;

"the customs and excise Acts" has the meaning given to it by section 1 of the Customs and Excise Management Act 1979;

"customs office" means a place for the time being occupied by Her Majesty's Customs and Excise;

"officer" means a person commissioned by the Commissioners of Customs and Excise under section 6(3) of the Customs and Excise Management Act 1979.

(2) A person is in customs detention for the purpose of this Order if—

    (a) he has been taken to a customs office after being arrested for an offence; or

    (b) he is arrested at a customs office after attending voluntarily at the office or accompanying an officer to it,

and is detained there or is detained elsewhere in the charge of an officer, and nothing shall prevent a detained person from being transferred between customs detention and police detention.

3.—(1) Subject to the modifications in paragraphs (2) and (3) of this article, in articles 4 to 11 below and in Schedule 2 to this Order, the provisions of the Act contained in Schedule 1 to this Order which relate to investigations of offences conducted by police officers or to persons detained by the police shall apply to investigations conducted by officers of Customs and Excise of offences which relate to assigned matters, and to persons detained by such officers.

(2) The Act shall have effect as if the words and phrases in Column 1 of Part 1 of Schedule 2 to this Order were replaced by the substitute words and phrases in Column 2 of that Part.

(3) Where in the Act any act or thing is to be done by a constable of a specified rank, that act or thing shall be done by an officer of at least the grade specified in Column 2 of Part 2 of Schedule 2 to this Order, and the Act shall be interpreted as if the substituted grade were specified in the Act.

4. Nothing in the application of the Act to Customs and Excise shall be construed as conferring upon an officer any power—

    (a) to charge a person with any offence;

(a) 1984 c.60.
(b) 1979 c.2.

(b) to release a person on bail;

(c) to detain a person for an offence after he has been charged with that offence.

5.—(1) Where in the Act a constable is given power to seize and retain any thing found upon a lawful search of person or premises, an officer shall have the same power notwithstanding that the thing found is not evidence of an offence in relation to an assigned matter.

(2) Nothing in the application of the Act to Customs and Excise shall be construed to prevent any thing lawfully seized by a person under any enactment from being accepted and retained by an officer.

(3) Section 21 of the Act (access and copying) shall not apply to any thing seized as liable to forfeiture under the customs and excise Acts.

6. In its application by virtue of article 3 above the Act shall have effect as if the following section were inserted after section 14—

"14A. Material in the possession of a person who acquired or created it in the course of any trade, business, profession or other occupation or for the purpose of any paid or unpaid office and which relates to an assigned matter, as defined in section 1 of the Customs and Excise Management Act 1979, is neither excluded material nor special procedure material for the purposes of any enactment such as is mentioned in section 9(2) above."

7. Section 18(1) of the Act shall be modified as follows—

"18.—(1) Subject to the following provisions of this section, an officer of Customs and Excise may enter and search any premises occupied or controlled by a person who is under arrest for any arrestable offence which relates to an assigned matter, as defined in section 1 of the Customs and Excise Management Act 1979, if he has reasonable grounds for suspecting that there is on the premises evidence, other than items subject to legal privilege, that relates—

(a) to that offence; or

(b) to some other arrestable offence which is connected with or similar to that offence."

8.—(1) The Commissioners of Customs and Excise shall keep on an annual basis the written records mentioned in subsection (1) of section 50 of the Act.

(2) The Annual Report of the Commissioners of Her Majesty's Customs and Excise shall contain information about the matters mentioned in subsection (1) of section 50 of the Act in respect of the period to which it relates.

9.—(1) Section 55 of the Act shall have effect as if it related only to things such as are mentioned in subsection (1)(a) of that section.

(2) The Annual Report of the Commissioners of Her Majesty's Customs and Excise shall contain the information mentioned in subsection (15) of section 55 of the Act about searches made under that section.

10. Section 77(3) of the Act shall be modified to the extent that the definition of "independent person" shall, in addition to the persons mentioned therein, also include an officer or any other person acting under the authority of the Commissioners of Customs and Excise.

11. Where any provision of the Act as applied to Customs and Excise—

(a) confers a power on an officer, and

(b) does not provide that the power may only be exercised with the consent of some person other than an officer,

the officer may use reasonable force, if necessary, in the exercise of power.

SCHEDULES

(Article 3)   SCHEDULE 1

PROVISIONS OF THE ACT APPLIED TO CUSTOMS AND EXCISE

Section   8
Section   9 and Schedule 1
Section   15
Section   16
Section   17(1)(b), (2), (4)
Section   18 subject to the modification in article 7 hereof
Section   19
Section   20
Section   21 subject to the modifications in article 5 hereof
Section   22(1) to (4)
Section   28
Section   29
Section   30(1) to (4)(a) and (5) to (11)
Section   31
Section   32(1) to (9) subject to the modifications in article 5 hereof
Section   34(1) to (5)
Section   35
Section   36
Section   37
Section   39
Section   40
Section   41
Section   42
Section   43
Section   44
Section   50 subject to the modification in article 8 hereof
Section   51(d)
Section   52
Section   54
Section   55 subject to the modifications in articles 5 and 9 hereof
Section   56(1) to (9)
Section   57(1) to (9)
Section   58(1) to (11)
Section   62
Section   63
Section   64(1) to (6)

Appendix 2

(*Article 3*)   SCHEDULE 2

Part 1

Substitution of equivalent words and phrases in the Act

Where in the Act a word or phrase specified in Column 1 below is used, in the application of the Act to Customs and Excise, there shall be substituted the equivalent word or phrase in Column 2 below—

Column 1	Column 2
WORDS AND PHRASES USED IN THE ACT	SUBSTITUTED WORDS AND PHRASES
area	collection
chief officer	collector
constable	officer
designated police station	designated customs office
officer of a force maintained by a police authority	officer
police area	collection
police detention (except in section 118 and in section 39(1)(a) the second time the words occur)	customs detention
police force	HM Commissioners of Customs and Excise
police officer	officer
police station	customs office
rank	grade
station	customs office
the police	HM Customs and Excise

Part 2

Equivalent grades of officers

Where in the Act an act or thing is to be done by a constable of the rank specified in Column 1 below, that same act or thing shall, in the application of the Act to Customs and Excise, be done by an officer of at least the grade specified in Column 2 below—

Column 1	Column 2
RANK OF CONSTABLE	GRADE OF OFFICER
sergeant	executive officer
inspector	higher executive officer
superintendent	senior executive officer

APPENDIX 3

Table of Derivations of England and Wales Code Provisions

The following Table, for convenience, sets out the derivation in the original Codes of provisions in the 1991 revised Codes where these have different numbers. Those not listed are those where the numbering is the same as before and those which are wholly or mainly new. Those provisions new in the 1995 revision of the codes are marked in the text of the Codes by a vertical line on the side of the page.

1990 Codes	1985 Codes	1990 Codes	1985 Codes
	Code A	6.12	6.9
		6.14	6.10
1.6	Annex B	6.16	6.11
1.7	Annex B	6.17	6.12
1B	1.6	7.2	7.3
		7.3	7.5
	Code B	7.4	7.6
		7.5	7.7
4.4	4.3	10.6	13.1
5.9	5.8	10.7	10.6
5.10	5.9	11.3	11.1
5.11	5.10	11.4	11.2
5.12	5.11	11.5	11.3
5.13	5.12	11.7	11.4
5.14	5.13	11.8	11.5
		11.9	11.6
	Code C	11.11	12.15
		11.12	11.7
1C	13A	11.15	13.3
1E	1C	11.16	13C
2.5	2A	11B	13B
2.6	2.5	11C	13D
2.7	2.6	12A	12B
3.4	3.3	12B	12C
3.6	3.5	13.2	14.1
3.8	3.10	13.3	14.2
3.9	3.6	13.4	14.3
3.11	3.6	13.5	14.4
3.12	3.8	13.7	14.5
3.13	13.2	13.8	14.6
3.15	3.9	13.9	14.7
3.17	3.10	13.10	14.8
3.18	3.11	13.11	14.9
3C	3A	13A	14A
3F	3F	14.1	15.1
5.6	5.6/7	14.2	15.2
5.7	5.8	14A	15A
5.8	5.9	15.1	16.1
6.6	6.3	15.2	16.2
6.7	6.4	15.4	16.3
6.8	6.5	15.5	16.4
6.9	6.6	15.6	16.5
6.10	6.7	15B	16A
6.11	6.8	15C	16B

Appendix 3

1990 Codes	1985 Codes	1990 Codes	1985 Codes
16.1	17.1		*Code D*
16.2	17.2		
16.3	17.3	1.7	1.6
16.4	17.4	1.8	1.7
16.5	17.5	1.9	1.8
16.6	17.6	1.10	1.9
16.7	17.7	1.11	1.10
16.8	17.8	1.13	1.11
16.9	17.9	1.14	1.12
16B	17A	1.15	1.13
		1.17	1.14
	Annex A	1E	1A
		2.3	2.1
3	2	2.4	2.3
4	3	2.5	2.9
5	4	2.6	2.4
6	5	2.7	2.4
7	6	2.13	2.5
8	7	2.14	2.10
9	8	2.15	2.7
10	9	2.16	2.8
		2.17	2.11
	Annex B	2.18	2.6
		2.19	2.13
3	2	2.20	2.14
4	3	2.21	2.15
5	4	3.6	3.5
6	5	3.7	3.6
8	6	5.6	5.7
9	7	5.7	5.6
			Annex A
	Annex E	19	20
4	6	20	21
5	4	21	22
8	5	22	23
9	13C	23	24
10	7	24	25
11	8		
12	9	Annex C	Annex B
E1	E4		
E3	E1	3	2
E4	E3	4	3

APPENDIX 4

Proposal for a Draft Order in Council—Police (Amendment) (Northern Ireland) Order 1995—Explanatory Document Accompanying the Draft Order issued for Consultation by the Northern Ireland Office in April 1995

PART I

BACKGROUND AND SCOPE

1. Introduction

The proposed draft Order makes changes to police powers, police discipline and police complaints procedures. These reforms represent a balanced package of measures which will allow the RUC to take full advantage of developments in the investigation and detection of crime, while enhancing police accountability by modernising and streamlining discipline and complaints procedures. Changes to police powers to take body samples will help the RUC maintain its high levels of success in clearing up crime. Reform of disciplinary procedures will provide increased flexibility for dealing with performance which does not meet expected levels. The changes will allow police managers more scope to manage individuals and to maintain and improve standards, while ensuring that procedures are fair and seen to be so. Many of the provisions of the draft Order follow consultation and the majority are analogous to changes which the Government has implemented in England and Wales.

...

The major changes made by the draft Order to police powers are:

- a person who is brought to a police station from a custodial establishment and is arrested will be in police detention for the purposes of the Police and Criminal Evidence (Northern Ireland) Order 1989.
- police will be allowed to search a person's mouth upon arrest;
- arrested persons may be detained in police custody if it is considered necessary to prevent them committing another offence;
- persons granted police bail who fail to attend a police station as instructed in the bail conditions will be liable to arrest;
- fingerprints and/or other samples or information derived from them will be liable to speculative search against records held by or on behalf of the police, and
- an enhanced power for the police to enter premises to arrest without warrant those who are unlawfully at large. Presently the power is only available where an officer is in active pursuit of someone unlawfully at large—a very restricted circumstance. The Government believes it is right that those who fail to return to custody should be apprehended as quickly and effectively as possible.

2.2 Police Discipline: at present, the only formal way of dealing with a failure to meet police standards lies in the disciplinary regulations which are made under sections 25 and 26 of the Police Act (NI) 1970. These regulations have led to procedures which are complex, legalistic and inflexible. The current system is quasi-criminal in nature and links failure to meet standards with commission of one of a rigidly defined list of disciplinary offences. Following the publication of consultation papers by the Home Secretary and the Secretary of State for Scotland, the Secretary of State issued a consultation paper on the reform of police discipline procedures in August 1993. The responses to the consultation paper were broadly favourable, and interested parties were again consulted after the Police and Magistrates' Courts Act 1994 introduced changes to police discipline in England and Wales.

The reforms made by the Order enable more flexible arrangements to be introduced: these will draw upon modern personnel management practices prevalent elsewhere in the public service, while recognising the special circumstances faced by the police. Specifically, there will be a new mechanism for dealing with poor performance or failure to meet acceptable standards by police officers, as well as simplified procedures for dealing with instances of misconduct. The main changes are:

- a more flexible definition of when it is appropriate to institute disciplinary proceedings, to replace the current rigidly defined list of offences, breach of which constitutes an offence against discipline;
- a new procedure to deal with poor performance or failure to meet acceptable standards, which will complement misconduct procedures;
- a new independent police appeals tribunal to replace the right of appeal to the Secretary of State; and
- the abolition of the restriction on related disciplinary proceedings being brought against an officer who has been convicted or acquitted of a criminal offence—the so-called "double jeopardy" rule. This will mean that management will be free to take appropriate action in respect of an officer who has not met police standards (even though he or she may have been acquitted of a criminal offence).

2.3 Police Complaints: the draft Order revokes and re-enacts the provisions of the Police (NI) Order 1987 which relate to complaints against the police. Some of the amendments made by the draft Order are for technical reasons, to allow matters of detail to be dealt with in regulations. The draft Order also gives effect to the Government's decisions on the recommendations of the Independent Commission for Police Complaints. The Commission is required to carry out a review of the complaints system every three years, and to report to the Secretary of State. The main changes which the Order makes are:

- complaints will be referred to the Commission at an earlier stage, when the complaint has been recorded by the appropriate authority: the effect of this is that complaints which are subsequently withdrawn will still have been referred to the Commission,
- the Commission will have discretion to discontinue the supervision of cases in certain circumstances: this will, for example, enable the Commission to relinquish the supervision of an investigation alleging serious injury (which it *must* supervise) if the injury turns out to be less serious than was initially alleged;
- the Commission will in future be required to give to the Chief Constable its reasons for preferring disciplinary charges at the earlier *recommendation* stage, when, in practice, consultations take place with the Chief Constable (rather than at the later direction stage);
- the Commission will have a new power to draw to the attention of the Secretary of State any matter, which is not the subject of a complaint, if it appears to the Commission that it is in the public interest that the investigation should be supervised: this will enable the Commission to make its concerns in non-complaint matters known to the Secretary of State;
- there will be a duty upon the Chief Constable, and where appropriate the Police Authority, to notify the Commission where death has been or may have been caused to a person by an officer (when the matter is not the subject of a complaint); and

- there will be a duty for the Chief Constable to inform the Commission of what action he has taken in response to a recommendation or direction to bring disciplinary proceedings: this is a reversal of the current position.

3. Parity with England and Wales

3.1 The draft Order makes changes, similar to those made in England and Wales by Part IV of the Criminal Justice and Public Order Act 1994, to the powers of the police in Northern Ireland to take and analyse body samples. These provisions in part reflect the recommendations of the Royal Commission on Criminal Justice and, although the Commission's remit did not extend to Northern Ireland, the Government believes that the RUC should also be able to make the fullest use of developments in the investigation and detection of crime as soon as possible. Other changes regarding police bail and the power to detain after charge mirror changes made by the Criminal Justice and Public Order Act 1994 in England and Wales.

3.2 The changes to discipline procedures for the RUC are analogous to those introduced for England and Wales by the Police and Magistrates' Courts Act 1994. The Government, while recognising the special circumstances of the RUC, appreciates the value of maintaining a broadly similar approach to police conditions of service throughout the UK. The changes to disciplinary arrangements also reflect the move across public services both in GB and Northern Ireland towards placing an increased emphasis on management.

PART II

THE PROVISIONS OF THE DRAFT ORDER

Title and Commencement

Article 1 sets out the title and provides that the Order shall come into operation on such day or days as the Secretary of State may by order appoint. Such an order may make transitional provisions and savings.

Interpretation

Article 2 deals with the interpretation of expressions which are used in the Order.

Police Powers (Part II)

Article 3 amends article 2(3) of the Police and Criminal Evidence (Northern Ireland) Order 1989 to include in the definition of police detention for the purposes of the Order persons who are produced to a police station from a custodial establishment are arrested for an offence. This article also amends article 31 of the Police and Criminal Evidence (Northern Ireland) Order 1989 to ensure that as soon as it appears to a constable that a person so produced is liable to arrest for an offence the arrest will not be delayed. Article 35 of the Police and Criminal Evidence (Northern Ireland) Order 1989 has been amended to ensure that persons produced from a custodial establishment are released back into the lawful custody of the prison authorities.

Article 4 amends article 19(1) of the Police and Criminal Evidence (Northern Ireland) Order 1989 to allow the police to enter and search premises without a warrant for the purposes of arresting a person who is unlawfully at large from a prison or other listed institution. The power will also be available to the police in Northern Ireland even if someone is unlawfully at large from a custodial institution elsewhere in the UK.

Article 5 provides that where a person is searched at a place other than a police station this search may include a search of the mouth. The definition of "intimate search" in Article 53 of Police and Criminal Evidence (Northern Ireland) Order 1989 has been amended to exclude searches of the mouth.

Article 6 provides for a Custody Officer to detain a person, after charge, if that person has been arrested for an imprisonable offence and the Custody Officer has reasonable grounds for believing that the detention is necessary to prevent the person committing an offence. The article also provides, a meaning of "imprisonable offence" for the purposes of the Order.

Article 7 provides for the arrest, without warrant, of any person who, having been released on police bail subject to a duty to attend at a police station fails to do so at the place and time appointed. It further provides for a person so arrested to be treated as having been arrested for an offence and that offence shall be deemed to be the offence in connection with which he was granted bail.

Article 8 contains amendments to the definitions of intimate and non-intimate samples and other relevant definitions.

Article 9 provides for a person, from whom fingerprints are to be taken, to be informed before the fingerprints are taken that they may be the subject of a speculative search (see article 12). It further provides that a record shall be made as soon as it is practicable after the fingerprints have been taken of the fact that the person has been so informed.

Article 10 provides for the taking of an intimate sample from a person who is not in police detention if two or more non-intimate samples, suitable for the same means of analysis, (*i.e.* DNA testing) have already been taken but have proved insufficient under analysis. An intimate sample can only be taken if a police officer of at least the rank of superintendent authorises it to be taken and if the consent of the person is given. This article also provides that dental impressions (which are defined for the purposes of the Order as an intimate sample) may only be taken by a registered dentist.

The article also extends application of sample taking powers to recordable offences and provides that before the sample is taken the person is to be informed that it may be the subject of a speculative search (see article 12) and that fact recorded as soon as practicable after the sample has been taken. Paragraph (8) of Article 10 adapts the new provisions for the purposes of an arrest on suspicion of involvement in terrorism. It replaces Article 87(5) of the Police and Criminal Evidence (NI) Order 1989 which currently governs this.

Article 11 provides the police with powers to take a non-intimate sample, without consent, from a person whether or not he is in police detention providing that person has been convicted of, or charged with, or informed that he will be reported for, a recordable offence and either:

(a) he has not had a non-intimate sample taken from him during the course of police investigations; or,

(b) a sample previously taken was not suitable or not sufficient for analysis. It also provides that where a sample is to be taken in these circumstances the person shall be told the reason for the taking of a sample and that it may be the subject of a speculative search, these facts to be recorded as soon as practicable after the sample has been taken.

This provision does not apply to persons convicted before the date on which it comes into operation.

Paragraph (7) of Article 11 adapts the new provisions for the purposes of an arrest on suspicion of involvement in terrorism. It replaces Article 87(5) of the Police and Criminal Evidence (NI) Order 1989 which currently governs this.

Article 12 contains supplementary provisions relating to the taking of fingerprints and samples. It provides for a speculative search in the form of checking of fingerprints or samples against other fingerprints or samples or information derived from other samples contained in records held by or on behalf of the police in connection with or as the result of an investigation of an offence. It also specifies how samples of hair may be taken and that samples may be taken in prisons or other institutions to which the Prison Act (Northern Ireland) 1953 applies.

It further provides that persons who are not in police detention or other police custody may, in specified circumstances, be required to attend at a police station for samples to be taken and that they may be arrested, without warrant, if they fail to comply with such a requirement. It also imposes time limits within which such requirements may be made.

Article 13 provides for the retention of samples in circumstances when they would otherwise normally be required to be destroyed. It specifies that where samples have been taken from a number of persons for the purpose of an investigation into the same offence and a person from whom one was taken is convicted, the remaining samples need not be destroyed. However any information derived from a sample which would otherwise have been destroyed shall not be used either in evidence against the person so entitled or for the purposes of any investigation of an offence.

Police Conduct and Discipline (Part III)

Article 14 widens the power of the Secretary of State to make regulations, under Section 25 of the Police Act (NI) 1970, which will establish new procedures for dealing with unsatisfactory performance and instances of misconduct by members of the RUC. It provides for appeals for officers who are dismissed, required to resign or reduced in rank by these proceedings. This will be to a new independent appeals tribunal, which will replace the current right of appeal to the Secretary of State.

Article 15 makes the same provision in respect of members of the RUC Reserve.

Police Complaints (Part IV)

Article 16 provides definitions of the terms used in this Part of the draft Order.

Article 17 reproduces article 4 of the 1987 Order without amendment. It requires the Chief Constable, when a complaint is made, to obtain or preserve evidence relating to the conduct which is the subject of the complaint. If the complaint relates to the conduct of a senior officer (*i.e.* above the rank of superintendent), the Chief Constable must send the details to the Police Authority for Northern Ireland.

Article 18 prescribes the procedure for the investigation of complaints against officers other than senior officers. A change is made here which will require the Chief Constable to refer a complaint to the Independent Commission for Police Complaints at an earlier stage, as soon as he has recorded it. The Chief Constable must then consider whether the complaint is suitable for informal resolution; if it is not, an officer must be appointed by the Chief Constable to investigate the complaint formally.

Article 19 prescribes the procedure for the investigation of complaints against senior officers. The Police Authority must record the complaint and will have to refer it to the Commission at this earlier stage. The Police Authority may deal with the complaint according to its discretion if it is satisfied that the conduct complained of (even if proved) would not justify criminal or disciplinary proceedings. Otherwise, the Authority must appoint an officer to investigate the complaint.

Article 20 restates the circumstances in which *non-complaint* matters can be drawn to the attention of the Commission. Two new powers are added: firstly, a matter must be referred to the Commission if it indicates that the conduct of an officer may have resulted in the death of another person. Secondly, the Commission will have a new power to draw a matter to the attention of the Secretary of State if it wishes: the Secretary of State may then refer the matter to the Commission if it appears to him that it is desirable in the public interest that the Commission should supervise the investigation.

Article 21 restates the present conditions in which the Commission may, or must, supervise the investigation. In addition, in response to a recommendation by the Commission, it will have a new power to withdraw from the supervision of the investigation, for example, when the "serious injury" turns out to be less serious than was initially alleged.

Article 22 reproduces Article 10 of the 1987 Order without significant change. The Police Authority, in the case of senior officers, is required to send the Director of Public Prosecutions the investigation report, unless it is satisfied that no criminal offence has been committed. For other officers, the Chief Constable has discretion: he may decide not to send the report to the DPP if he does not think that the conduct is serious enough for the officer to be charged with it. However, he must tell the Commission (except in certain circumstances) whether or not he will discipline the officer for this conduct.

Article 23 reproduces Article 12 of the 1987 Order without substantive amendment. It gives the Commission a duty, if it disagrees with the Chief Constable and believes that the investigation report *should* be sent to the DPP, to direct him to do so.

Article 24 enables the Commission, if it believes that disciplinary proceedings should be brought, to recommend, and if necessary to direct, the Chief Constable to do so. The Commission will be required to give the Chief Constable its reasons at the earlier recommendation stage. A special disciplinary tribunal is held when such a direction is given (and may also be held when the Commission directs that one should be held). In response to one of the recommendations of the Commission, this tribunal will consist of the Chief Constable as chairman and two independent members, drawn from a panel appointed for this purpose. Provision for this tribunal will be made by regulations under Sections 25 and 26 of the 1970 Act.

Article 25 reproduces Article 15 of the 1987 Order without amendment. It places a duty on the Police Authority to keep itself informed as to the working of this Part of the draft Order.

Article 26 reproduces Article 16 of the 1987 Order without substantive amendment. It enables the Commission, with the approval of the Secretary of State, to agree to arrangements for the handling of complaints against constabularies maintained by bodies other than the Police Authority. It provides that these other constabularies whose complaints procedures are based on the 1987 Order can continue their present complaints system after the draft Order introduces new procedures for the RUC.

Article 27 reproduces Article 17 of the 1987 Order without amendment. It provides for the Commission to make annual and triennial reports to the Secretary of State, and special reports requested by the Secretary of State, or on its own initiative.

Article 28 reproduces Article 18 of the 1987 Order without amendment. It places restrictions on the disclosure of information received by the Commission in the performance of its functions.

Article 29 empowers the Secretary of State to make regulations as to the procedure to be followed under this Part of the draft Order. It requires the Secretary of State to make provision by regulation for certain matters, after consultation with the Police Authority and police staff associations.

Article 30 removes the current restriction on related disciplinary proceedings following criminal proceedings—the so-called "double jeopardy rule". This change means that in future police managers will be free to take appropriate action in relation to an officer who has not met the acceptable standard of behaviour for a police officer, although he may not have committed a crime. It will still be the case that no statement made by any person for the purpose of informal resolution can be admitted in any subsequent criminal, civil or disciplinary proceedings.

Article 31 places on a statutory basis the issuing of guidance by the Secretary of State to the police, the Police Authority and the Commission concerning the discharge of their functions in relation to complaints and discipline.

Miscellaneous and Supplementary (Part V)

Article 32 provides for the amendments and repeals set out in schedules 1 and 2 to the draft Order to be made.

Schedule 1 outlines amendments made by the draft Order.

Schedule 2 outlines repeals made by the draft Order.

APPENDIX 5

National DNA Database
Home Office Circular No. 16/95

The DNA database

21. The DNA database will be a national database and will comprise details of individuals suspected, cautioned and convicted of a recordable offence. Together with the DNA profile, these details will include:

    (i) the sample identification number;

    (ii) the Phoenix Arrest/Summons Report number (which provides a link to the PNC Phoenix Criminal Record);

    (iii) the subject's full name, sex, date of birth, ethnic appearance;

    (iv) the force/station code; and

    (v) the name of the officer taking the sample.

The database will also hold DNA profiles derived from crime stains.

22. The DNA database will be a single, consolidated, central database; it will not be partitioned by force, region or on any other such basis. This does not, however, preclude local searches being carried out. It is anticipated that, in time, the database will hold up to approximately 5 million records.

23. The DNA database is an *intelligence* database only. It is not intended that the results of any analysis carried out solely for the database or that the fact that a match was found during a speculative search will be used for prosecuting purposes. Casework and statements to be used for such purposes will be handled separately in the same manner as at present.

24. Where a person is suspected of a particular crime and where a crime stain relating to that crime exists, *CJ samples should not be taken*. Instead, samples should be taken and the analysis carried out in the same way as for casework. (This is essential since it may not be possible to obtain a further sample for prosecuting purposes.) The results of the analysis will still be added to the database and will be used to check whether the suspect has been involved in any unsolved crimes that have a record on the database.

25. Where no crime stain exists, the body sample will be taken and the analysis carried out as described in the rest of this circular. If a match is found as a result of a speculative search on the database, a further sample will be obtained and analyzed to normal case-working standards. This further sample *can* be taken under PACE because it will be taken as part of the investigation of a different offence (that relating to the unsolved crime stain).

26. Initially, DNA profiles for the database will be obtained from the sample using a technique known as polymerase chain reaction (PCR) to analyze short tandem repeats (STR).

27. The results of the profiling processes will be stored electronically as a digital record in compliance with the Data Protection Act 1984. These records will provide a high level of discrimination between profiled offenders. They will also provide information for investigating officers, such as potential links between individuals and crime scenes, which will directly contribute to investigations.

28. Unlike the practice with fingerprints, if a convicted person's DNA profile is already on the DNA database, another DNA sample need not be taken for the database if that person is subsequently suspected of involvement in another crime. However, a further sample does need to be taken if a prosecution is to follow and DNA evidence will be used, for the reasons set out in paras. 23 to 25 above.

Service providers

29. The DNA database service can be considered as two distinct parts:

(i) The DNA database, which stores the data derived from DNA profiles and is where the searches are carried out; and
(ii) profiling services, which take individual samples and analyze them to produce the DNA profiles.

30. The DNA database will be managed and run by a single custodian, chosen by agreement amongst chief officers and endorsed by the Home Office. This custodian will make available and run the computer system on which the database will be held. The initial custodian will be the Forensic Science Service.

31. The Forensic Science Service as custodian of the DNA database will provide and run a system for the database which:

(i) has a capacity which has been agreed with chief officers;
(ii) conforms to the requirements of the National Strategy for Police Information Systems (ACPO IS/IT Strategy); and
(iii) conforms with the requirements of the Data Protection Act 1984.

32. In addition, the custodian will be expected to have BSI registration and NAMAS accreditation. This may not be possible in time for the start of the DNA database service, but the Forensic Science Service, as initial custodian, is seeking these certifications at the earliest possible opportunity.

33. If research leads to new methods of DNA profiling, it is essential that any investment in DNA profiles already stored on the DNA database is not lost. The custodian must therefore ensure that the DNA database system is capable of being adapted to new methods of DNA profiling. (New profiles will have to be derived by reanalyzing stored samples.) Any such change will be the subject of a separate agreement between the custodian and individual police forces.

34. The Forensic Science Service, in addition to being the custodian of the database, has expertise in molecular biology. It is possible that future custodians might not have this expertise and will only provide and run the database system. A change in custodian may therefore require the duties initially undertaken by the Forensic Science Service as molecular biologists and those undertaken as custodian to be split and suitable arrangements made for their separate provision. A change in custodian will require agreement among chief officers and endorsement by the Home Office.

35. Profiling may be carried out by the Forensic Science Service or by other organizations; this will be for individual police forces to decide. Whilst individual police forces are free to choose who provides their profiling services, it is essential that quality standards and compatibility with the central DNA database services are maintained. The Forensic Science Service as custodian of the database is responsible for ensuring compliance with set standards. These standards will be agreed with chief officers and are subject to continuing Home Office endorsement.

36. Any organization providing profiling services will use a standard protocol for DNA profiling to analyze specified regions of DNA as agreed by chief officers and the Forensic Science Service and endorsed by the Home Office.

37. Any profiling service must satisfy the Forensic Science Service as database custodian that they are competent and licensed to use the profiling technique agreed by chief officers and the Forensic Science Service and endorsed by the Home Office. In future, profiling services should have BSI registration and NAMAS accreditation.

38. Any profiling service should adopt procedures and carry out an internal quality programme to the specification set by the Forensic Science Service as custodian of the database and endorsed by the Home Office. The Forensic Science Service will submit samples to all profiling services for repeat analysis at an agreed percentage of the total number of samples analyzed. These samples will be re-coded so that they are

identified as test samples, but in a way that does not allow the profiling organization to know their previous identity. The results of the two analyses will then be compared. In the event of the failure of any quality assurance trial, the Forensic Science Service will not accept any further samples or the data derived from samples from that profiling service without re-inspection and revalidation. The Forensic Science Service will provide a written explanation to the DNA profiling service provider, to chief officers and to the Home Office.

Profiling of CJ samples and analysis of crime stains

39. Material for DNA profiling will come from either:

    (i) CJ samples (from charged, reported or convicted persons);
    (ii) casework samples (from suspects);
    (iii) crime stains (via normal caseworking routes); or
    (iv) samples for elimination purposes (*i.e.* from victims, witnesses, etc.).

The profiles derived from samples taken for elimination purposes will not be used in speculative searches and will not be placed on the DNA intelligence database.

40. The new PACE provisions allows CJ samples to be taken in all recordable offences. Chief officers have agreed that all offenders committing recordable offences will be profiled but that, in the first instance, the police should obtain samples from offenders in the categories:

    (i) offences against the person;
    (ii) sexual offences; and
    (iii) burglaries.

This does not, however, preclude forces from obtaining CJ samples for other recordable offences for inclusion on the database nor does it compel forces to take samples in all the above categories or in all cases in selected categories. *All forces should have a clearly stated policy for sampling.* This policy should be notified to the Forensic Science Service (as database custodian) and any other organizations used for profiling services to ensure that sufficient infrastructure capacity is made available.

41. The demand on the database service may vary. For example, in time, sample numbers may fall due to recidivism. However, if other offender categories are included, this will negate the effect.

42. As with all forensic casework, the procedures for taking samples by the police, transferring them to the laboratory, all the internal handling processes used to profile them and the database handling procedures will conform to the rules of evidence. All procedures should be capable of withstanding such examination, ensuring that evidence relating a named person to a crime stain is capable of total support. However, it is not intended (as stated in para. 23) that the database will be used for prosecution evidence. DNA evidence will come via normal caseworking routes.

43. Training will be available from the Forensic Science Service to enable trainees to train others in the collection and submission of samples.

Sampling procedures

44. CJ samples will normally be collected in the form of two swabs taken from the mouth in accordance with PACE regulations. This is the preferred option. As an alternative, they will be taken by plucking not fewer than 10 body hairs (not pubic hair) with the roots.

45. Samples from victims, where required for elimination purposes, will be collected by normal caseworking methods. In future, all mass screenings analyzed by the Forensic Science Service will be analyzed at the DNA Database Unit at Birmingham. Mouth swabs and hair kits will be provided for this purpose.

46. The prescribed buccal comb swabs will be supplied as part of a sample collection kit by the Forensic Science Service or other approved profiling organizations and must be handled and used in accordance with the instructions laid down in the kit. A sample consisting of two swabs per individual will be required. Normally, only one swab will be analyzed to produce the DNA profile. However, analysis of the first swab will occasionally be unsuccessful and the second swab will then be used to complete the analysis. Otherwise, it will be stored by the Forensic Science Service (or a sub-contractor chosen by the Forensic Science Service) until informed by the police that it is to be destroyed. Swabs will be destroyed when the corresponding record is removed from the database. Swabs will be stored in such a way as to ensure that they can, if required, be retained for the lifetime of the offender.

47. Exceptionally, where a CJ sample forms part of the evidence, the stored sample should be accessible by the defence.

48. Mouth swabs must not be taken within 20 minutes of the subject consuming food or drink.

49. Samples should be sealed, packaged and labelled in the presence of the donor and sent to the profiler by one of the approved delivery arrangements. The following details should be provided on a form DNA-1:

    (i) the subject's name, date of birth, sex and ethnic appearance;
    (ii) the sample type—mouth swab or hairs;
    (iii) the date that the sample was taken;
    (iv) the name, rank and number of the officer taking the sample;
    (v) the sample identification number;
    (vi) the force/station code; and
    (vii) the Phoenix arrest/summons report number.

Where delivery is not possible within 48 hours, samples should be stored at $-20°C$ (with the necessary identification information).

Profiling

50. The profiling agency will reject samples that do not arrive in a satisfactory condition, where they arrive without proper identification or where continuity is in doubt.

51. The results of the profiling process will be sent for entry onto the database in a format agreed with the Forensic Science Service, compatible with the computer system and capable of quality assessing before addition to the database itself.

Addition to the database

52. Profiles derived from CJ samples, case work samples and crime stains will be checked against the searchable profiles already held on the database. Profiles from victims and witnesses will only be used for elimination purposes and will not be entered onto the database.

53. Sample test results and reports will be confidential and will be available in a standard hard copy form agreed between the Forensic Science Service and chief officers. In the first instance, this will be by facsimile message.

54. Samples which give a clear unambiguous result and which are supported by the appropriate controls will be reported. Partial identifications may, on some occasions, be reported for further investigation.

55. Reports from CJ samples will fall into three groups:

    (i) no matches found;
    (ii) a match found with a profile obtained from a person analyzed previously indicating either a duplicate record or an alias;
    (iii) a match with an unsolved crime stain profile indicating a possible link between that individual and the crime.

56. Likewise, reports from scene of crime stains will fall into three groups:

    (i) no matches found;
    (ii) a match found with a profile obtained from a person analyzed previously indicating a possible link between that individual and the crime;
    (iii) a match with another unsolved crime stain profile potentially linking the two unsolved crimes.

57. Normally, only one profile will be retained on the database per subject. Where a profile is accepted as matching another profile already on the database and it is shown to be from the same person, the new profile will be retained on the database but flagged as a duplicate/alias.

58. It is intended that the Forensic Science Service will have direct access to relevant areas of the Phoenix database of criminal records and a user requirement is being produced by chief officers. Phoenix is expected to go into service in the course of 1995, but will not initially have the necessary links for the DNA database. Once these links have been implemented, and provided that the identity of an offender can be verified, the Forensic Science Service will enter a marker on the offender's Phoenix record to denote that a sample has been profiled for DNA purposes, and will remove the marker when the sample is destroyed. Such a procedure will prevent the unnecessary re-sampling of recidivists.

Actions following matches on the database

59. There will be a nominated point in each force for receiving information from the database. Any identifications found on the database will be sent to the nominated point. Where an identification is relevant to more than one force (for example, if it relates to offences in different force areas) the information will be sent to the nominated point in each force. For casework samples, the information will be passed in the normal way to the investigating officer submitting the case sample. Any identifications made on the database relating to other offences will be sent to the nominated point in each relevant force.

Data Protection Act

60. All results and administrative details will be stored electronically and the operation of the database will be subject to the Data Protection Act 1984.

61. The DNA database has been registered under the terms of the Data Protection Act by the Forensic Science Service and all access to the DNA database will be via the Forensic Science Service for so long as it remains the database custodian. However, all police forces and other agencies with a statutory investigative role and who use the database will register their individual use of the data and the purpose for that use with the Data Protection Registrar.

62. The Forensic Science Service as database custodian will nominate a database system administrator who will maintain a list of those authorized users registered with the Data Protection Registrar and also of those persons with direct access to the database (*i.e.*, the operators).

63. Data will be held on a password protected system and the security will be layered so that Data Protection Act requirements will be met. Access will be to authorized operators only. According to the status of the accessor, this will allow:

    (i) the addition of individuals' profiles and the associated unique identifiers;
    (ii) the addition of case stain profiles and the associated unique identifiers;
    (iii) interrogation of the database.

64. Under the Data Protection Act, individuals whose profiles appear on the

database will have a right to a copy of any personal data relating to them. Standardized access procedures will need to be established by chief officers and the Forensic Science Service and endorsed by the Home Office.

65. Further disclosure may also be necessary since, under the Data Protection Act 1984, personal data is exempt from the non-disclosure provisions in any case in which the disclosure is:

(i) required by or under any enactment, by any rule of law or by the order of a court; or

(ii) made for the purpose of obtaining legal advice or for the purposes of, or in the course of, legal proceedings in which the person making the disclosure is a party or a witness.

Destruction of samples, profiles and data records

66. Records on the DNA database should be retained for the same period as the offender's criminal record on Phoenix. Samples that can be kept under s.64 of PACE (either those from the offender or those linked to an offender as described in para. 15) should be destroyed when the associated database record is weeded.

67. Weeding will be triggered by information regarding case results or the death of an individual being notified to the Forensic Science Service by the link with the Phoenix PNC System mentioned in para. 58.

68. Weeding of records from those convicted of a crime or cautioned will entail the record being removed from the database. Such amendments of the database records will be carried out solely by nominated, authorized operators and audits will be undertaken routinely. These audits will include all back-ups of the database.

69. In cases where a crime is solved, the database record relating to that crime stain will be retained until the offender has been convicted. It will then be removed.

Inquiries

70. Inquiries about force procedures should be directed to the in-force contact for the DNA database. Force contacts have access to a DNA database inquiry service provided by the FSS.

71. Any *inquiries about this circular* should be addressed to F3 Division (0171 273 4387).

APPENDIX 6

Right to Silence Provisions in Criminal Justice and Public Order Act 1994*

Inferences from accused's silence

34.—(1) Where, in any proceedings against a person for an offence, evidence is given that the accused—

    (a) at any time before he was charged with the offence, on being questioned under caution by a constable trying to discover whether or by whom the offence had been committed, failed to mention any fact relied on in his defence in those proceedings; or

    (b) on being charged with the offence or officially informed that he might be prosecuted for it, failed to mention any such fact,

being a fact which in the circumstances existing at the time the accused could reasonably have been expected to mention when so questioned, charged or informed, as the case may be, subsection (2) below applies.

(2) Where this subsection applies—

    (a) a magistrates' court, in deciding whether to grant an application for dismissal made by the accused under section 6 of the Magistrates' Courts Act 1980 (application for dismissal of charge in course of proceedings with a view to transfer for trial);

    (b) a judge, in deciding whether to grant an application made by the accused under—

        (i) section 6 of the Criminal Justice Act 1987 (application for dismissal of charge of serious fraud in respect of which notice of transfer has been given under section 4 of that Act); or

        (ii) paragraph 5 of Schedule 6 to the Criminal Justice Act 1991 (application for dismissal of charge of violent or sexual offence involving child in respect of which notice of transfer has been given under section 53 of that Act);

    (c) the court, in determining whether there is a case to answer; and

    (d) the court or jury, in determining whether the accused is guilty of the offence charged,

may draw such inferences from the failure as appear proper.

(3) Subject to any directions by the court, evidence tending to establish the failure may be given before or after evidence tending to establish the fact which the accused is alleged to have failed to mention.

(4) This section applies in relation to questioning by persons (other than constables) charged with the duty of investigating offences or charging offenders as it applies in relation to questioning by constables; and in subsection (1) above "officially informed" means informed by a constable or any such person.

(5) This section does not—

    (a) prejudice the admissibility in evidence of the silence or other reaction of the accused in the face of anything said in his presence relating to the conduct in respect of which he is charged, in so far as evidence thereof would be admissible apart from this section; or

* These sections all come into force on April 10, 1995.

    (b) preclude the drawing of any inference from any such silence or other reaction of the accused which could properly be drawn apart from this section.

(6) This section does not apply in relation to a failure to mention a fact if the failure occurred before the commencement of this section.

(7) In relation to any time before the commencement of section 44 of this Act, this section shall have effect as if the reference in subsection (2)(a) to the grant of an application for dismissal was a reference to the committal of the accused for trial.

35.—(1) At the trial of any person who has attained the age of fourteen years for an offence, subsections (2) and (3) below apply unless—

    (a) the accused's guilt is not in issue; or
    (b) it appears to the court that the physical or mental condition of the accused makes it undesirable for him to give evidence;

but subsection (2) below does not apply if, at the conclusion of the evidence for the prosecution, his legal representative informs the court that the accused will give evidence or, where he is unrepresented, the court ascertains from him that he will give evidence.

(2) Where this subsection applies, the court shall, at the conclusion of the evidence for the prosecution, satisfy itself (in the case of proceedings on indictment, in the presence of the jury) that the accused is aware that the stage has been reached at which evidence can be given for the defence and that he can, if he wishes, give evidence and that, if he chooses not to give evidence, or having been sworn, without good cause refuses to answer any question, it will be permissible for the court or jury to draw such inferences as appear proper from his failure to give evidence or his refusal, without good cause, to answer any question.

(3) Where this subsection applies, the court or jury, in determining whether the accused is guilty of the offence charged, may draw such inferences as appear proper from the failure of the accused to give evidence or his refusal, without good cause, to answer any question.

(4) This section does not render the accused compellable to give evidence on his own behalf, and he shall accordingly not be guilty of contempt of court by reason of a failure to do so.

(5) For the purposes of this section a person who, having been sworn, refuses to answer any question shall be taken to do so without good cause unless—

    (a) he is entitled to refuse to answer the question by virtue of any enactment, whenever passed or made, or on the ground of privilege; or
    (b) the court in the exercise of its general discretion excuses him from answering it.

(6) Where the age of any person is material for the purposes of subsection (1) above, his age shall for those purposes be taken to be that which appears to the court to be his age.

(7) This section applies—

    (a) in relation to proceedings on indictment for an offence, only if the person charged with the offence is arraigned on or after the commencement of this section;
    (b) in relation to proceedings in a magistrates' court, only if the time when the court begins to receive evidence in the proceedings falls after the commencement of this section.

36.—(1) Where—

    (a) a person is arrested by a constable, and there is—

(i) on his person; or
(ii) in or on his clothing or footwear; or
(iii) otherwise in his possession; or
(iv) in any place in which he is at the time of his arrest,
any object, substance or mark, or there is any mark on any such object; and
(b) that or another constable investigating the case reasonably believes that the presence of the object, substance or mark may be attributable to the participation of the person arrested in the commission of an offence specified by the constable; and
(c) the constable informs the person arrested that he so believes, and requests him to account for the presence of the object, substance or mark; and
(d) the person fails or refuses to do so,

then if, in any proceedings against the person for the offence so specified, evidence of those matters is given, subsection (2) below applies.
(2) Where this subsection applies—

(a) a magistrates' court, in deciding whether to grant an application for dismissal made by the accused under section 6 of the Magistrates' Courts Act 1980 (application for dismissal of charge in course of proceedings with a view to transfer for trial);
(b) a judge, in deciding whether to grant an application made by the accused under—
(i) section 6 of the Criminal Justice Act 1987 (application for dismissal of charge of serious fraud in respect of which notice of transfer has been given under section 4 of that Act); or
(ii) paragraph 5 of Schedule 6 to the Criminal Justice Act 1991 (application for dismissal of charge of violent or sexual offence involving child in respect of which notice of transfer has been given under section 53 of that Act);
(c) the court, in determining whether there is a case to answer; and
(d) the court or jury, in determining whether the accused is guilty of the offence charged,

may draw such inferences from the failure or refusal as appear proper.
(3) Subsections (1) and (2) above apply to the condition of clothing or footwear as they apply to a substance or mark thereon.
(4) Subsections (1) and (2) above do not apply unless the accused was told in ordinary language by the constable when making the request mentioned in subsection (1)(c) above what the effect of this section would be if he failed or refused to comply with the request.
(5) This section applies in relation to officers of customs and excise as it applies in relation to constables.
(6) This section does not preclude the drawing of any inference from a failure or refusal of the accused to account for the presence of an object, substance or mark or from the condition of clothing or footwear which could properly be drawn apart from this section.
(7) This section does not apply in relation to a failure or refusal which occurred before the commencement of this section.
(8) In relation to any time before the commencement of section 44 of this Act, this section shall have effect as if the reference in subsection (2)(a) to the grant of an application for dismissal was a reference to the committal of the accused for trial.

37.—(1) Where—

(a) a person arrested by a constable was found by him at a place at or about the time the offence for which he was arrested is alleged to have been committed; and

(b) that or another constable investigating the offence reasonably believes that the presence of the person at that place and at that time may be attributable to his participation in the commission of the offence; and

(c) the constable informs the person that he so believes, and requests him to account for that presence; and

(d) the person fails or refuses to do so,

then if, in any proceedings against the person for the offence, evidence of those matters is given, subsection (2) below applies.

(2) Where this subsection applies—

(a) a magistrates' court, in deciding whether to grant an application for dismissal made by the accused under section 6 of the Magistrates' Courts Act 1980 (application for dismissal of charge in course of proceedings with a view to transfer for trial);

(b) a judge, in deciding whether to grant an application made by the accused under—

  (i) section 6 of the Criminal Justice Act 1987 (application for dismissal of charge of serious fraud in respect of which notice of transfer has been given under section 4 of that Act);

  (ii) paragraph 5 of Schedule 6 to the Criminal Justice Act 1991 (application for dismissal of charge of violent or sexual offence involving child in respect of which notice of transfer has been given under section 53 of that Act);

(c) the court, in determining whether there is a case to answer; and

(d) the court or jury, in determining whether the accused is guilty of the offence charged,

may draw such inferences from the failure or refusal as appear proper.

(3) Subsections (1) and (2) do not apply unless the accused was told in ordinary language by the constable when making the request mentioned in subsection (1)(c) above what the effect of this section would be if he failed or refused to comply with the request.

(4) This section applies in relation to officers of customs and excise as it applies in relation to constables.

(5) This section does not preclude the drawing of any inference from a failure or refusal of the accused to account for his presence at a place which could properly be drawn apart from this section.

(6) This section does not apply in relation to a failure or refusal which occurred before the commencement of this section.

(7) In relation to any time before the commencement of section 44 of this Act, this section shall have effect as if the reference in subsection (2)(a) to the grant of an application for dismissal was a reference to the committal of the accused for trial.

38.—(1) In sections 34, 35, 36 and 37 of this Act—

"legal representative" means an authorised advocate or authorised litigator, as defined by section 119(1) of the Courts and Legal Services Act 1990; and

"place" includes any building or part of a building, any vehicle, vessel, aircraft or hovercraft and any other place whatsoever.

(2) In sections 34(2), 35(3), 36(2) and 37(2), references to an offence charged include references to any other offence of which the accused could lawfully be convicted on that charge.

(3) A person shall not have the proceedings against him transferred to the Crown Court for trial, have a case to answer or be convicted of an offence solely on an inference drawn from such a failure or refusal as is mentioned in section 34(2), 35(3), 36(2) or 37(2).

(4) A judge shall not refuse to grant such an application as is mentioned in section

34(2)(b), 36(2)(b) and 37(2)(b) solely on an inference drawn from such a failure as is mentioned in section 34(2), 36(2) or 37(2).

(5) Nothing in sections 34, 35, 36 or 37 prejudices the operation of a provision of any enactment which provides (in whatever words) that any answer or evidence given by a person in specified circumstances shall not be admissible in, evidence against him or some other person in any proceedings or class of proceedings (however described, and whether civil or criminal).

In this subsection, the reference to giving evidence is a reference to giving evidence in any manner, whether by furnishing information, making discovery, producing documents or otherwise.

(6) Nothing in sections 34, 35, 36 or 37 prejudices any power of a court, in any proceedings, to exclude evidence (whether by preventing questions being put or otherwise) at its discretion.

39.—(1) The Secretary of State may by order direct that any provision of sections 34 to 38 of this Act shall apply, subject to such modifications as he may specify, to any proceedings to which this section applies.

(2) This section applies—

- (a) to proceedings whereby a charge is dealt with summarily under Part II of the Army Act 1955;
- (b) to proceedings whereby a charge is dealt with summarily under Part II of the Air Force Act 1955;
- (c) to proceedings whereby a charge is summarily tried under Part II of the Naval Discipline Act 1957;
- (d) to proceedings before a court martial constituted under the Army Act 1955;
- (e) to proceedings before a court martial constituted under the Air Force Act 1955;
- (f) to proceedings before a court martial constituted under the Naval Discipline Act 1957;
- (g) to proceedings before a disciplinary court constituted under section 50 of the Naval Discipline Act 1957;
- (h) to proceedings before the Courts-Martial Appeal Court;
- (i) to proceedings before a Standing Civilian Court;

and it applies wherever the proceedings take place.

(3) An order under this section shall be made by statutory instrument and shall be subject to annulment in pursuance of a resolution of either House of Parliament.

BIBLIOGRAPHY[1]

ALLEN, C.J.W. (1990) "Discretion and security: excluding evidence under s.78(1) of the Police and Criminal Evidence Act 1984", 49 *Cambridge Law Journal*, p. 80.

BALDWIN, J. and BEDWARD, J. (1991) "Summarising tape recordings of police interviews" *Criminal Law Review*, pp. 671–79.

BALDWIN, J. (1992a) *Preparing the record of taped interviews* (Royal Commission on Criminal Justice, Research Study No. 2).

BALDWIN, J. (1992b) *The role of legal representatives at the police station* (Royal Commission on Criminal Justice, Research Study No. 3).

BALDWIN, J. and MOLONEY, T. (1992c) *Supervision of criminal investigations* (Royal Commission on Criminal Justice, Research Study No. 4).

BIRCH, D.J. (1989) "The PACE hots up: confessions and confusions under the 1984 Act" *Criminal Law Review*, pp. 95–116.

BOTTOMLEY, A.K., COLEMAN, C.A., DIXON, D., GILL, M. and WALL, D. (1991a) *The Impact of PACE: Policing in a Northern Force* (Hull University, Centre for Criminological Research).

BOTTOMLEY, A.K., COLEMAN, C.A., DIXON, D., GILL, M. and WALL, D. (1991b) "The Detention of Suspects in Police Custody" (*British Journal of Criminology*, vol. 31, pp. 347–64).

BROWN, D. (1987) *The Police Complaints Procedure: A Survey of Complainants' Views* (Home Office Research Study No. 93, HMSO).

BROWN, D. (1989) *Detention at the Police Station under the Police and Criminal Evidence Act 1984* (Home Office Research Study No. 104, HMSO).

BROWN, D. (1991) *Investigating Burglary: the effects of PACE* (Home Office Research Study No. 123, HMSO).

BROWN, D., ELLIS, T. and LARCOMBE, K. (1992) *Changing the Code: Police Detention under the Revised PACE Codes of Practice.* (Home Office Research Study No. 129, HMSO). (For a summary, see *Research Findings No. 5*, Home Office Research and Statistics Department, March 1993.)

BROWN, D. (1993) *Detention under the Prevention of Terrorism Provisions Act 1989: Legal Advice and Outside Contact* (Home Office Research and Planning Unit Paper No. 75).

CLARE, I. and GUDJONNSON, G. (1993) *Devising and piloting an experimental version of the 'notice to detained persons'* (Royal Commission on Criminal Justice, Research Study No. 7).

COLEMAN, C.A., DIXON, D. and BOTTOMLEY, A.K. (1993) "Police Investigative Procedures: Researching the Impact of PACE" in C. Walker and K. Starmer (eds.) in *Justice in Error* (Blackstone Press) pp. 17–36.

CORBETT, C. (1991) "Complaints against the police: the new procedure of informal resolution" (*Policing and Society*, vol. 2(1)).

DIXON, D., BOTTOMLEY, A.K., COLEMAN, C.A., GILL, M. and WALL, D. (1989a) "Safeguarding the rights of suspects in police custody" (*Policing and Society*, vol. 1, pp. 115–40).

DIXON, D., BOTTOMLEY, A.K., COLEMAN, C.A., GILL, M. and WALL, D. (1989b) "Reality and rules in the construction and regulation of police suspicion" (*International Journal of the Sociology of Law*, vol. 17, pp. 185–206).

---

[1] This bibliography draws heavily with his permission on one prepared by David Brown in his study *Research on PACE: A Review of the Literature* (forthcoming, HMSO).

547

DIXON, D., COLEMAN, C.A. and BOTTOMLEY, A.K. (1990) "Consent and the legal regulation of policing" (*Journal of Law and Society*, vol. 17, pp. 345–62).

DIXON, D. (1990) "Juvenile suspects and the Police and Criminal Evidence Act" in D.A.C. Freestone (ed.) *Children and the Law* (Hull University Press) pp. 107–29.

EVANS, R. (1993) *The conduct of police interviews with juveniles* (Royal Commission on Criminal Justice, Research Study No. 8).

GELOWITZ, M. (1990) "Section 78 of the Police and Criminal Evidence Act 1984" (*Law Quarterly Review*, vol. 106, p. 327).

GEMMILL, R. and MORGAN-GILES, R.F. (1980) *Arrest, Charge and Summons: Current Practice and Resource Implications* (Royal Commission on Criminal Procedure Research Study No. 9).

GREER, S. (1990) "The right to silence: a review of the current debate" (*Modern Law Review*, vol. 53, pp. 709–21).

GUDJONSSON, G. (1992) *The Psychology of Interrogations, Confessions and Testimony* (John Wiley).

IRVING, B.L. (1980) *Police Interrogation* (Royal Commission on Criminal Procedure Research Study No. 1, HMSO).

IRVING, B.L. and McKENZIE, I. (1989) *Police Interrogation: the effects of the Police and Criminal Evidence Act 1984* (Police Foundation).

LENG, R. (1993) *The right to silence in police interrogation: a study of some of the issues underlying the debate* (Royal Commission on Criminal Justice, Research Study No. 10).

LIDSTONE, K. (1989) "The Police and Criminal Evidence (Northern Ireland) Order 1989: Powers of Entry, Search and Seizure" (*Northern Ireland Legal Quarterly*, pp. 333–62).

McCONVILLE, M., SANDERS, A. and LENG, R. (1991) *The Case for the Prosecution* (Routledge).

McCONVILLE, M. and HODGSON, J. (1993) *Custodial legal advice and the right to silence* (Royal Commission on Criminal Justice, Research Study No. 16).

McCONVILLE, M., HODGSON, J., BRIDGES, L. and PAVLOVIC, A. (1994) *Standing Accused* (Clarendon, Oxford).

McKENZIE, I., MORGAN, R. and REINER, R. (1990) "Helping the police with their enquiries: the necessity principle and voluntary attendance at the police station" (*Criminal Law Review*, pp. 22–33).

MAGUIRE, M. (1988) "Effects of the PACE provisions on detention and questioning: some preliminary findings" (*British Journal of Criminology*, vol. 28(1) pp. 19–43).

MAGUIRE, M. and CORBETT, C. (1989) "Patterns and profiles of complaints against the police" in Morgan, R. and Smith, D.J. (eds.) *Coming to Terms with Policing* (Routledge).

MAGUIRE, M. and CORBETT, C. (1991) *A Study of the Police Complaints System* (HMSO).

MAGUIRE, M. and NORRIS, C. (1993) *The conduct and supervision of criminal investigations* (Royal Commission on Criminal Justice, Research Study No. 5).

MORGAN, R. and MAGGS, C. (1985) *Setting the PACE: Police Community Consultation Arrangements in England and Wales* (University of Bath: Bath Social Policy Paper No. 4).

MORGAN, R. (1987) "The local determinants of policing policy", in Willmott, P. (ed). *Policing and the Community* (Policy Studies Institute Discussion Paper No. 16).

MORGAN, R. (1989) "Policing by consent: legitimating the doctrine" in R. Morgan and D.J. Smith (eds.) *Coming to Terms with Policing* (Routledge) pp. 217–34.

MORGAN, R. (1992) "Talking about Policing" in D. Downes (ed.) *Unravelling Criminal Justice* (Macmillan) pp. 165–83.

MORGAN, R., REINER, R. and McKENZIE, I.K. (1991) *Police Powers and Police: a study of the work of custody officers.* (Final report to the ESRC. Unpublished.)

MOSTON, S., STEPHENSON, G. and WILLIAMSON, T. (1992) "The incidence, antecedents and consequences of suspects' use of the right of silence" (*Criminal Behaviour and Mental Health*, vol. 3, pp. 30–47).

MOSTON, S. and STEPHENSON, G. (1993) *The questioning and interviewing of suspects outside the police station* (Royal Commission on Criminal Justice Research Study No. 22).

PAINTER, K., LEA, J., WOODHOUSE, T. and YOUNG, J. (1989) *Hammersmith and Fulham crime and police survey, 1988* (Centre for Criminology Middlesex Polytechnic).

ROYAL COMMISSION ON CRIMINAL PROCEDURE (1981) Report (Cmnd 8092 HMSO).

ROYAL COMMISSION ON CRIMINAL PROCEDURE (1981a) *The Investigation and Prosecution of Criminal Offences in England and Wales: the Law and Procedure* (Cmnd. 8092–1 HMSO).

ROYAL COMMISSION ON CRIMINAL JUSTICE (1993) Report Cm. 2263.

SANDERS, A., BRIDGES, L., MULVANEY, A. and CROZIER, G. (1989) *Advice and Assistance at Police Stations and the 24-hour Duty Solicitor Scheme* (Lord Chancellor's Department).

SCARMAN (1981) *The Brixton Disorders 10–12 April 1981*. Report of an Inquiry by the Rt. Hon. Lord Scarman. (Cmnd. 8427, HMSO).

SMITH, D., and GRAY, J. (1985) *Police and People in London: The PSI Report* (Aldershot, Gower).

SOFTLEY, P. with BROWN, D., FORDE, B., MAIR, G. and MOXON, D. (1980) *Police Interrogation: an observational study in four police stations* (Home Office Research Study No. 61, HMSO).

TULLY, B., and CAHILL, D. (1984) *Police Interviewing of the Mentally Handicapped: an Experimental Study* (Police Foundation).

WILLIS, C.F. (1983) *The Use, Effectiveness and Impact of Police Stop and Search Powers* (Research and Planning Unit Paper 15, Home Office).

WILLIS, C.F., MACLEOD, J., and NAISH, P. (1988) *The tape-recordings of Police Interviews with Suspects: a second interim report* (Home Office Research Study No. 97, HMSO).

ZUCKERMAN, A.A.S. (1989) "Trial by unfair means—the Report of the Working Group on the Right of Silence" (*Criminal Law Review*, p. 855).

INDEX

Note—Roman type is used to indicate pages in the Commentary and Appendices, **bold** type to indicate sections of the Police and Criminal Evidence Act and *italic* type to indicate paragraphs in the Codes of Practice (A to E). The abbreviation *N.* stands for Notes for guidance. The abbreviation A,B,C,D,E, stands for Code A, Code B etc. (*B6.9, N.B6A* means therefore Code B, para. 6.9 and note for guidance 6A of Code B).

Access to detainee, 119–123; **s.56**; *C5*
  items seized, owners', 54; **s.21**; *B6.9,*
    N.B6A
Acquittals, evidence of, 214; **s.73**
Acting custody officer, 86; **s.36(4)**, **(7)**
Advance notice, evidence of, 249–50;
  s.81
Alcohol at sporting events, 72
"Appropriate adult", 186–189
  cautions, *C10.6*
  charging, *C16.1–3*
  custody records, *C2.4–5*
  deaf persons, *C13.6*
  definition, *C1.7*
  disqualification, *N.C1C, N.D1A, N.D1D*
  extensions of detention, *C15.1*
  interviews, *C11.11, 11.14–16, D1.13*
  intimate searches, *C Annex A*
  legal advice, *N.C1EE, 3.13, N.C3G*
  mentally handicapped persons, *C1.7(b),*
    N.C1E, C3.9, C Annex E
  notification of arrest, *C3.9, 1–8, C Annex*
    B
  social workers, *C1.7(a), N.C1D, N.D1A–B*
  solicitors as, *N.C1F, N.D1D*
  strip searches, *C Annex A*
"Appropriate authority"
  definition, **s.84(4)**
  role of, 263–266; **ss.86**, **87(1)**
"Appropriate consent", definition, **s.65**
"Appropriate criminal intent",
  definition, **s.55(17)**
"Appropriate person", definition, **s.2(5)**
"Appropriate statement", definition,
  s.89(10)
Approved social worker, *C3.10*
Armed forces, application to, 294–295; **s.113**;
  Appendix 1,
Arrest, 65–83
  arrestable offences, 66–70, 82–83; **s.24**,
    see also "serious arrestable
    offence"
  bail, of someone after, 104–105; **s.47**
  cautions, *C10.1–7*
  "citizen's", 66–67; **s.24(4)**, **(5)**
  cross-border, 70–71, 73

Arrest—*cont.*
  delay in notifying fact of, 119–123;
    s.56(2)–(7), **(9)–(11)**; *C Annex B*
  entry on premises after, 50–52, 79–80;
    ss.18, **32**
  entry on premises for, 49–50; **s.17**
  fingerprinting, for, 73; **s.27**
  further offences, for, 78; **ss.31**, **41(9)**,
    43(19)
  "general arrest conditions", 71–72; **s.25(3)**
  grounds for, 66–70, 82–83; **ss.24**, **25**
  information to be given on, 74–75; **s.28**
  informing someone of, 119–123; **ss.56**, **57**,
    C3.1, C3.9, C5.1–8, C7
  not at police station, 77–78; **s.30**
  Questions and Answers on, 82–83
  reasonable cause, for, 67–70
  search upon, 79–80; **s.32**
  statistics, 81
  statutory powers repealed, 72–73; **s.26**
  summary, 66–70; **s.24**
  without warrant, 66–70, 72, 73–74; **ss.24**,
    26, **27**
Arrestable offences, 66–70, 299; **ss.24**, **118**
"Arrested juvenile", definition, **s.37(15)** *see*
  also Juveniles

Bail,
  after arrest, 89–92, 104–105, **ss.38**, **47**
  after charge, 89–92; **s.38**
  arrest for failure to comply with
    conditions of bail, 104–105
  conditions on police bail, 89, 90, 104;
    s.471A
  juveniles, 91–92
  no bail in some cases, 89
Blind suspects, interviews, 163; *C1.6, C3.14,*
  N.C3F, D1.12, N.D1F
Body orifices, search of, 115–118; **s.55**; *D.5*
  samples, intimate, 149–152; **s.62**, **65**; *D5*
  non-intimate, 152–153; **ss.63**, **65**; *D5*

Caution, 161–64, 179–180, 308; *C10.1–7*
  breaks in questioning, *C10.5, N.C10A*

551